THE
MIND
of the
SPIRIT

THE MIND of the SPIRIT

Paul's Approach to Transformed Thinking

CRAIG S. KEENER

Baker Academic

a division of Baker Publishing Group
Grand Rapids, Michigan

Published by Baker Academic
a division of Baker Publishing Group
P.O. Box 6287, Grand Rapids, MI 49516-6287
www.bakeracademic.com

Printed in the United States of America

Library of Congress Cataloging-in-Publication Data
Names: Keener, Craig S., 1960– author.
Title: The mind of the spirit : Paul's approach to transformed thinking / Craig S. Keener.
Description: Grand Rapids, MI : Baker Academic, 2016. | Includes bibliographical references and index.
Identifiers: LCCN 2015045921 | ISBN 9780801097768 (cloth)
Subjects: LCSH: Bible. Epistles of Paul—Theology. | Thought and thinking—Biblical teaching.
Classification: LCC BS2655.T57 K44 2016 | DDC 227/.06—dc23
LC record available at http://lccn.loc.gov/2015045921

Unless noted otherwise, all translations of Scripture are those of the author.

Scripture quotations labeled NEB are from *The New English Bible*. Copyright © 1961, 1970, 1989 by The Delegates of Oxford University Press and The Syndics of the Cambridge University Press. Reprinted by permission.

Scripture quotations labeled NRSV are from the New Revised Standard Version of the Bible, copyright © 1989, by the Division of Christian Education of the National Council of the Churches of Christ in the United States of America. Used by permission. All rights reserved.

Chapter 4, "The Mind of the Spirit (Rom. 8:5–7)," is mostly new work, but, with the permission of Brill, incorporates a revision of Craig S. Keener, "'Fleshly' versus Spirit Perspectives in Romans 8:5–8," in *Paul: Jew, Greek and Roman*, ed. Stanley Porter, PAST 5 (Leiden: Brill, 2008), 211–29.

Chapter 8, "The Heavenly Mind (Col. 3:1–2)," is adapted, with the permission of Sheffield Phoenix Press, from Craig S. Keener, "Heavenly Mindedness and Earthly Good: Contemplating Matters Above in Colossians 3.1–2," *JGRCJ* 6 (2009): 175–90.

In keeping with biblical principles of creation stewardship, Baker Publishing Group advocates the responsible use of our natural resources. As a member of the Green Press Initiative, our company uses recycled paper when possible. The text paper of this book is composed in part of post-consumer waste.

16   17   18   19   20   21   22   7   6   5   4   3   2   1

For our beloved children, David and Keren

Contents

Acknowledgments

I am grateful to Professor Virginia (Toddy) Holeman from the School of Counseling at Asbury Theological Seminary for her insights on the relevant portions of this manuscript. I am grateful to my editors at Baker Academic, Jim Kinney, James Ernest (formerly at Baker), Tim West, and Amy Donaldson. I am also grateful to the Assemblies of God Theological Seminary for welcoming me as the Horton lecturer and providing dialogue on the subject of this book on February 3–5, 2015, and to New Theological College, Dehradun, India, to Urshan Graduate School of Theology, and to Southern Adventist University for interacting with my lectures on this topic in January and March 2016.

Introduction

Pauline scholars have rightly explored at great length Paul's soteriology, Christology, and pneumatology and his views of Israel and Scripture. Yet even among the fewer discussions of Pauline anthropology, very rarely have scholars devoted extensive attention to his view of the mind,[1] especially in a way that explains how he may have shaped his language to communicate to his contemporaries.

More recent insights into this subject by scholars conversant in ancient philosophy, such as Stanley Stowers and Troels Engberg-Pedersen, have not always been incorporated into exegetical or theological discussions to the extent that their contributions merit.[2] I hope that subsequent interpreters will take more account of their contributions (and mine), although further research will undoubtedly draw on a wider range of sources and provide further nuance to our earlier discussions on these topics.

Previous interpreters have rightly emphasized the importance of believers' righteousness in Romans, usually in terms of one's status or relationship with God and/or in terms of moral righteousness or transformation. What interpreters have often missed, however, is how Paul uses cognition to connect these key elements. How does one move from righteous identity to righteous

1. There are exceptions, such as recently Wright, *Faithfulness*, 1121–26, as well as my own attempts in Keener, "Perspectives"; Keener, "Heavenly Mindedness"; Keener, "Minds."

2. In citing them, I am not implying agreement on every point but noting that their familiarity with ancient philosophy has allowed them to recognize and approach some issues in Paul from a vantage point too often neglected by scholars. Despite his helpful insights, some scholars have reasonably questioned Engberg-Pedersen's disproportionate dependence on Cic. *Fin.* 3 for reconstructing Stoicism in *Paul and Stoics* (see Wright, *Faithfulness*, 1391, 1395). I deliberately draw on a wider range of sources for Stoicism here, highlighting not only Arius Didymus's *Epitome* in particular but also various Stoic writers.

living? Paul emphasizes the importance of a right understanding corresponding to the divine perspective—an understanding that may complement, or even more likely that functions as another aspect of, what Paul calls faith.

What This Book Addresses

Chapter 1 of this book addresses Paul's depiction of the corrupted pagan mind in Romans 1:18–32. In this passage the supposedly wise pagan mind became subject to passions, what philosophers viewed as the antithesis of self-controlled reason, after rejecting the knowledge of God. Chapter 2 explores the new way of thinking in Christ in Romans 6:1–11: having been righted with God in God's sight through faith, believers are now invited to share God's perspective on their union with Christ's death (6:11). Chapter 3 is my longest chapter, due to the major issues in Romans 7:15–25 that must be surveyed before any further exegesis may be developed. Here I revisit the fallen mind, but in this case no longer the law-uninformed pagan mind of 1:18–32. The religious mind informed by God's righteous requirements is all the more frustrated by passions, because it knows right from wrong yet is unable to silence passion.

Chapter 4 addresses the way of thinking empowered by God's Spirit in Romans 8:5–7. Here, those already put right with God are now depicted as motivated and empowered to serve God by the internal life of God's Spirit. Romans 12:1–3, surveyed in chapter 5, describes the renewing of the mind according to the standards of the coming age instead of the present one. Such a mind leads one to devote one's individual body to the service of the larger body of Christ. Chapter 6 considers the mind of Christ in 1 Corinthians 2:16 and its context: the indwelling of God's Spirit shares with the spiritually mature—those attentive to the Spirit's explication of the message of Christ—a measure of God's own wisdom. Here too the Spirit offers a foretaste of eschatological reality as well as experience of God. At the end of this chapter, I briefly consider also a passage from 2 Corinthians (3:18) that sheds some light on how the Spirit enlightens our minds in Christ.

Because Paul's Roman and Corinthian correspondence sufficiently establish his interest in cognition and the divine, I sample the theme only more briefly elsewhere. Chapter 7 more briefly surveys some of this cognitive theme in Philippians: those who entrust their worries to God can experience peace (4:6–8); a Christlike way of thinking involves serving one another (2:5); and the new mind should look to heavenly rather than earthly matters (3:19–20). Finally, chapter 8 develops the theme of the heavenly mind in Colossians 3:1–2: a focus on the enthroned Christ that transforms how believers live on earth.

What This Book Is Not Addressing

In treating passages, I omit many exegetical details and surveys of views where they are not relevant to the matter in question; the reader interested in my perspectives on such topics often may find them treated, albeit briefly, in my short commentary on Romans,[3] which I hope to revisit in the future with a larger work. The study of cognition in Paul does not depend on any specific major debated approach to other aspects of Pauline theology, with the exception of the chapter on Romans 7.

Although Paul uses a range of words treating the concepts of thinking, understanding, and the mind, my focus here is not lexical study, which can easily be addressed today with a variety of readily available tools.[4] Addressing the wider ancient usage of all the terms on which Paul draws is a useful exercise, but it is not the point of the present study. Although I work from the Greek text, I render words in English where possible to keep the book less cumbersome for a wider range of readers. The reader should keep in mind that Paul uses various terms in the same semantic domain even though these terms are not always consistently differentiated in English translations.[5]

I do not propose to treat every possibly relevant passage or every detail of the passages that I address; instead, I propose a fuller treatment of particular sample passages and of how discussions of the mind among Paul's contemporaries may inform the ways that his first audiences would have understood him. In my major exception to this rule, I address Romans 7 in greater detail because it remains a point of some controversy. I will not elaborate in later chapters points already established (or at least argued) in earlier ones, with the consequence that the book's final two chapters will be relatively brief. My translations opening each chapter are meant only to introduce some of the issues of some key texts in question; clearly, no translation can convey all the possible nuances implied by Paul's literary context or intellectual milieu.

Although I am interested in Paul's theology on the matter in question, I am not staking out positions on many of the contested issues of Pauline

---

3. Keener, *Romans*.

4. At the scholarly high end one may consult *TLG*; nonspecialists (as well as scholars for less-detailed work) may consult Accordance, Logos, and BibleWorks.

5. I base my own work in Paul on the Greek text but am writing in English. Those concerned about the particular terms used should consult the Greek text but also keep in mind that the wider semantic domain will be more crucial for our general purposes here than extensive lexical investigation of specific terms. This can be undertaken by concordance searches rather than the more conceptual work I have done by working through the wider range of ancient sources.

theology today. For example, the book's primary contributions should not be affected by whether the reader supports the "new perspective" (really, perspectives)[6] on Pauline soteriology or more traditional versions.[7] I am trying to exegete texts fairly, which might make my approach eclectic on some points,[8] but I have not sacrificed the space to qualify much of my language to repeatedly declare neutrality on contemporary debates. Admittedly, there are undoubtedly controversies on minor matters with which I am not yet familiar.

Too often scholars settle on a particular background for Paul's language (e.g., Cynic or targumic) without having read more widely in ancient sources. Sometimes too they concisely classify other scholars' works based on their focus (such as proposed rabbinic, Hellenistic Jewish, or Stoic backgrounds for Paul). By contrast, because our best sources suggest that Paul was a Judean with a Diaspora background and mission, the most helpful approach may be more eclectic, drawing on various sources where they each contribute most to particular points.

Given this book's focus on cognitive themes in Paul, part of my attention to Paul's context must address ancient philosophy, which shared this cognitive focus. In examining at many points a popular philosophic context for Paul, I am not claiming that Paul had a philosophic education; certainly, he did not study in a philosophic school. Nevertheless, Paul was interested in reaching urban Greek speakers in Roman Asia, Macedonia, Achaia, and Rome. The most influential people in his congregations were normally educated, which in these regions meant some exposure to philosophy (e.g., anecdotes about and sayings of philosophers), although a majority of those who received an advanced education opted to focus on rhetoric. Others, who often may have had little education (cf. 1 Cor. 1:26), nevertheless were exposed to some popular philosophy from speakers in markets and public competitions, as well as (for those who were citizens of their cities) allusions in speeches in public assemblies. Egyptian papyri take us closer to everyday village life, but common teachings of popular philosophy (if not always the technical details of various schools of philosophic thought) tell us something about the intellectual milieu for many people in the cities.

6. As is often noted by proponents, e.g., Wright, *Justification*, 28; Wright, *Faithfulness*, 1458. Likewise, critics also recognize multiple "new perspectives"; see, e.g., Waters, *Justification*, 154.

7. Sometimes differences can also be exaggerated. Thus, for example, Dunn (*Perspective*, 18–23, 28–30) notes that his focus on culturally specific issues highlighted in Romans is not meant to deny wider principles that such issues may reflect.

8. If a reader feels that I lean too far toward either the old or the new perspective for their taste, the reader can, with minimal adjustments, make my exegetical observations work within her or his own system.

For better or for worse, our best access to this thought today comes from the works that have survived. I highlight Stoicism somewhat more than other schools because it was the dominant philosophic system in this period in this region; because it influenced nonphilosophic intellectual discourse through elite education; and because it influenced popular urban thinking through the control of the educated over most public discourse.[9] (Middle Platonism may have already held a stronger grip among Alexandrian intellectuals; its eclectic approach and other factors made it dominant more widely after Paul.)

Roman background is relevant not only in Rome but also in Corinth and Philippi, both heavily romanized colonies. In both locations, however, the message about Jesus probably circulated first among Greek-speaking Jews, making Greek and Jewish contexts (not least Hellenistic Jewish contexts) no less relevant. I draw here on as wide a range of potentially relevant background as possible, while acknowledging (with other historians of antiquity) that it usually is not possible to provide parallels for the exact city and decade that Paul was addressing.

I provide here exegetical samples for Paul's approach to the renewed mind and do not claim to treat all undisputed Pauline texts. I have given even less attention here to the theme in disputed Pauline literature. I personally do accept the Pauline authorship of Ephesians, but insights there would not alter significantly the results of this study. I treat Colossians here as Pauline, but those who demur will at least find my brief treatment of Colossians 3:1–2 relevant to early developments of Pauline thought, developments that cohere naturally, in a Diaspora context, with the undisputed Pauline works.

I respect Luke's depiction of Paul more highly than do some other Acts scholars; my respect stems not from ignorance of critical scholarship (as critics sometimes suppose must be true of all who do not share their convictions) but from detailed research.[10] The present work has little occasion to draw on Acts, but suffice it to say that Luke's general portrayal of Paul as a skilled, literate, and brilliant thinker is consistent with what we find in Paul's own letters. Luke's Paul, like the letters' Paul, apparently experienced no conflict as a believer between life in the Spirit and an intellect directed by faith.[11]

---

9. Cf. here, e.g., Brookins, "Wise Corinthians."

10. See Keener, *Acts*, 4 vols. (esp. the samples in vol. 1, chap. 7). I believe that my work on Acts stands in the mainstream of Acts scholarship but hope that even those who are more skeptical will recognize the level of research in the commentary, which cites tens of thousands of primary references from antiquity.

11. For fuller discussion of this point, see Keener, "Teaching Ministry." For the Lukan Paul's rhetorical sophistication, see Keener, "Rhetorical Techniques"; for his claim of a sober mind, see Keener, "Madness." For Luke's portrayal of Paul's education before he became a follower of

Implications for Theological Reflection in Today's Church

Modern thinkers have much to learn from ancient ones, sometimes even the seeds of modern thought. For Christians, Paul's works are seminal and offer many insights for subsequent issues in the church. Some divisions that many modern readers assume are biblical in fact stem from postbiblical discussions.

The Reformation, in which scholars figured prominently, emphasized disciplined study of the biblical text. Not everyone had access to scholarly training and resources, however, and many other people of faith (including many Anabaptists, later Pietists, participants in North American frontier revivals, early African-American religion, early Pentecostalism, etc.) particularly highlighted dependence on the Spirit. Some circles have succeeded better than others at bringing together these sorts of emphases—for example, some of the early church fathers, many medieval monasteries, Jonathan Edwards, and John Wesley.

Nevertheless, at least among modern Protestants there sometimes remain serious divisions among those who emphasize the academic heritage of the Reformation and those who emphasize the heritage of some subsequent revival movements. (Among Catholics, different monastic orders have also tended to value different emphases, although such differences are undoubtedly less pronounced today than in the past.)

In principle, most of us would affirm the value of both exploring the biblical text cognitively and embracing the Spirit experientially; the biblical text invites such experience, and without the objective constraints of Scripture, experience can quickly lose its Christocentric mooring. But each Christian tradition has its own predilections, each has focused on some different yet genuine biblical emphases, and each therefore has something valuable to learn from the other. We need both Word and Spirit; for Paul, certainly, the two are inextricably bound together. This book will argue that, against some circles, the Spirit does in fact often work through the mind and not only apart from it.

Sometimes the dichotomy is less about the human mind versus God's Spirit and more about the differences between the human mind and the human spirit. Yet, as whole persons, we need to cultivate both the cognitive and affective aspects of our humanity to fully honor the Lord (cf., for example, Paul's interest in both aspects in 1 Cor. 14:15). Some of us naturally gravitate

---

Christ, see the discussion in Keener, *Acts*, 3:3205–15. For the consistent but different depictions of Paul in both sources, see, e.g., Porter, *Paul in Acts*; for concrete analogies in other biographies about and letters by a single figure, see Hillard, Nobbs, and Winter, "Corpus."

toward churches that emphasize rational exposition, and others of us toward churches that engage the emotions with rousing preaching, celebratory worship, or, in some more sacramental circles, the touch and sometimes smell of worship.[12] Many of us undoubtedly feel torn and wish that more of our churches engaged both the mind and the spirit. Some may have already found churches that do both to their satisfaction.

Unfortunately, circles persist that value only one or the other approach to God, often despising the other as either irrational or unspiritual. Citing the Spirit bearing witness with our spirit (Rom. 8:16), some circles highlight our spirit as an organ of God's Spirit in a way that they deem impossible for the mind.[13] Some other circles almost substitute rational exegetical or theological skill for any other means of hearing God's voice. Each of these two extremes often views the other approach to God with suspicion. Many of the rest of us simply feel more comfortable one way or the other without needing to denigrate those whose predilections differ. As a charismatic scholar, I feel comfortable embracing God's transformation of both mind and spirit, although my own gifts and calling have often inclined my focus more toward the former. This book focuses more on affirming the value of the cognitive side, but biblically God works with both.

Another area in which Paul's discussion of cognition raises questions concerns how to explain it in language more widely intelligible today. Paul communicated in the common language of his day, language that does not easily align with today's psychological terminologies. For that matter, both the psychologizing philosophers of Paul's day and the range of philosophic and psychological schools today often vary in their understanding and terminology from one school to another.

12. Personality types sometimes make us better fitted for some environments than others; some individuals are more constitutionally (and sometimes environmentally) suited for analysis, for example, and some flourish most in a highly relational setting. As long as we appreciate other gifts and are willing to grow in our own weaker areas, our differences on these points may be complementary rather than contradictory. By way of illustration, I scored as an INFJ on the Myers-Briggs personality test, but (apart from being an extreme introvert) on some points just barely. I cannot easily play some aspects of my personality off against others; that concern presumably plays a role in how I approach this subject. As students of hermeneutics have long emphasized (e.g., Bultmann, "Exegesis"; Thiselton, "New Hermeneutic," 86), our past experiences influence our perceptions.

13. As discussed in chap. 4, however, the same context also addresses the "mind of the Spirit" (Rom. 8:5–7). Paul calls praying in tongues prayer with one's "spirit" (1 Cor. 14:2, 14), a valuable gift from God; but the same context seems to identify the gift of interpreting prayer in tongues as praying with the understanding (14:13–15). Paul already identified both tongues and interpretation as gifts inspired by the Spirit (12:7, 10); prayer with the understanding in this way, then, is also prayer inspired by God's Spirit. Elsewhere in early Christianity, worship "in Spirit and in truth" probably refers not to the human spirit but to God's Spirit (so, e.g., Scott, *Spirit*, 196; Keener, *John*, 615–19; *pace*, e.g., Morris, *John*, 270; Collins, "Spirit").

I hope that clarifying some of Paul's psychology in this book will provide Christian psychologists and counselors better ways to articulate his principles in their own language. I hope also that through translating these principles we may learn to understand and apply Paul's wisdom in new contexts. That objective, however, must be followed through in subsequent research cooperating between these disciplines; it is simply too far-reaching and too interdisciplinary to be achieved adequately in this book alone.

Abbreviations

Ancient Sources

Note: Works are normally listed under their traditional authors for the sake of locating them, not to take a position regarding authorship claims.

General

Bk.	Book	MS(S)	manuscript(s)
chap(s).	chapter(s)	MT	Masoretic Text
col(s).	column(s)	NT	New Testament
DSS	Dead Sea Scrolls	*Or.*	*Orations*
Ep.	*Epistles*	OT	Old Testament
ext.	external	pref.	preface
frg(s).	fragment(s)	Q	Quelle (hypothetical common source for Matthew and Luke)
intro.	introduction		
inv.	inventory number	rec.	recension
LCL	Loeb Classical Library	Sup.	Supplement(s)
LXX	Septuagint	v./vv.	verse/verses

Old Testament

Gen.	Genesis	Judg.	Judges	Neh.	Nehemiah
Exod.	Exodus	Ruth	Ruth	Esther	Esther
Lev.	Leviticus	1–2 Sam.	1–2 Samuel	Job	Job
Num.	Numbers	1–2 Kings	1–2 Kings	Ps(s).	Psalm(s)
Deut.	Deuteronomy	1–2 Chron.	1–2 Chronicles	Prov.	Proverbs
Josh.	Joshua	Ezra	Ezra	Eccles.	Ecclesiastes

Song	Song of Songs/Song of Solomon	Hosea	Hosea	Hab.	Habakkuk
		Joel	Joel	Zeph.	Zephaniah
Isa.	Isaiah	Amos	Amos	Hag.	Haggai
Jer.	Jeremiah	Obad.	Obadiah	Zech.	Zechariah
Lam.	Lamentations	Jon.	Jonah	Mal.	Malachi
Ezek.	Ezekiel	Mic.	Micah		
Dan.	Daniel	Nah.	Nahum		

New Testament

Matt.	Matthew	Eph.	Ephesians	Heb.	Hebrews
Mark	Mark	Phil.	Philippians	James	James
Luke	Luke	Col.	Colossians	1–2 Pet.	1–2 Peter
John	John	1–2 Thess.	1–2 Thessalonians	1–3 John	1–3 John
Acts	Acts			Jude	Jude
Rom.	Romans	1–2 Tim.	1–2 Timothy	Rev.	Revelation
1–2 Cor.	1–2 Corinthians	Titus	Titus		
Gal.	Galatians	Philem.	Philemon		

Old Testament Apocrypha

Bar.	Baruch	Sir.	Sirach/Ecclesiasticus
1–2 Esd.	1–2 Esdras	Sus.	Susanna
Jdt.	Judith	Tob.	Tobit
1–4 Macc.	1–4 Maccabees	Wis.	Wisdom of Solomon
Pr. Man.	Prayer of Manasseh		

Old Testament Pseudepigrapha

APOT	The Apocrypha and Pseudepigrapha of the Old Testament. Edited by R. H. Charles. 2 vols. Oxford: Clarendon, 1913.	Apoc. Elij.	Apocalypse of Elijah
		Apoc. Ezek.	Apocryphon of Ezekiel
		Apoc. Mos.	Apocalypse of Moses
		Apoc. Zeph.	Apocalypse of Zephaniah
		Asc. Isa.	Ascension of Isaiah
OTP	The Old Testament Pseudepigrapha. Edited by James H. Charlesworth. 2 vols. Garden City, NY: Doubleday, 1983–85.	2–4 Bar.	2–4 Baruch
		1–3 En.	1–3 Enoch (2 En. has recensions A and J)
		4 Ezra	4 Ezra
		Jos. Asen.	Joseph and Aseneth[1]
Ahiq.	Ahiqar	Jub.	Jubilees
Apoc. Ab.	Apocalypse of Abraham	L.A.B.	Pseudo-Philo Biblical Antiquities

1. The citations give double enumerations where the OTP translation (listed first) and the standard Greek text differ.

L.A.E.	*Life of Adam and Eve*	*Gad*	*Gad*
Let. Aris.	*Letter of Aristeas*	*Iss.*	*Issachar*
Odes Sol.	*Odes of Solomon*	*Job*	*Job*[2]
Pr. Jos.	*Prayer of Joseph*	*Jos.*	*Joseph*
Ps.-Phoc.	Pseudo-Phocylides	*Jud.*	*Judah*
Pss. Sol.	*Psalms of Solomon*	*Levi*	*Levi*
Sib. Or.	*Sibylline Oracles*	*Mos.*	*Moses*
T.	*Testament of*	*Naph.*	*Naphtali*
Ab.	*Abraham* (recensions A and B)	*Reub.*	*Reuben*
Adam	*Adam*	*Sim.*	*Simeon*
Ash.	*Asher*	*Sol.*	*Solomon*
Benj.	*Benjamin*	*Zeb.*	*Zebulun*
Dan	*Dan*		

Dead Sea Scrolls and Related Texts

1QH/1QH[a]	Hodayot or *Thanksgiving Hymns*
1QM	*Milḥamah* or *War Scroll*
1QpHab	*Pesher Habakkuk*
1QS	*Serek Hayaḥad* or *Rule of the Community* or *Manual of Discipline*
1QSa	*Rule of the Congregation* (Appendix A to 1QS)
1QSb	*Rule of the Blessings* (Appendix B to 1QS)
11QPs[a]	*Psalms Scroll*[a]
11QT	*Temple Scroll*
CD	Cairo Genizah copy of the *Damascus Document*

Josephus and Philo

Jos.   Josephus

Ag. Ap.	*Against Apion*
Ant.	*Antiquities of the Jews*
Life	*Life*
War	*Jewish War*

Philo

Abr.	*On Abraham*
Agr.	*On Husbandry/ Agriculture*
Alleg. Interp.	*Allegorical Interpretation (1–3)*
Cher.	*On the Cherubim*
Conf.	*On the Confusion of Languages*
Contempl.	*On the Contemplative Life*
Creation	*On the Creation*
Decal.	*The Decalogue*
Dreams	*On Dreams, That They Are God-Sent (1–2)*
Drunkenness	*On Drunkenness*
Embassy	*Embassy to Gaius*
Eternity	*On the Eternity of the World*
Flacc.	*Flaccus*
Flight	*On Flight and Finding*
Giants	*On the Giants*
Good Person	*Every Good Person Is Free*

2. Where editions diverge, I cite the enumeration in both Spittler (in *OTP*) and Kraft.

Heir	Who Is the Heir of Divine Things	*Rewards*	On Rewards and Punishments
Hypoth.	Hypothetica	*Sacr.*	On the Birth of Abel
Jos.	Joseph		and the Sacrifices Of-
Migr.	The Migration of Abraham		fered by Him and His Brother Cain
Mos.	Life of Moses (1–2)	*Sober*	On the Prayers and
Names	On the Change of Names		Curses Uttered by Noah
Plant.	Concerning Noah's Work as a Planter		When He Became Sober
		Spec. Laws	Special Laws (1–4)
Posterity	On the Posterity of Cain and His Exile	*Studies*	On Mating with the Preliminary Studies
Prelim. St.	Preliminary Studies	*Unchangeable*	Unchangeableness of God
QE	Questions and Answers on Exodus (1–2)	*Virt.*	On Virtues
QG	Questions and Answers on Genesis (1–4)	*Worse*	That the Worse Is Wont to Attack the Better

Targumic Texts

Tg.	Targum (+ biblical book)	*Tg. Onq.*	Targum Onqelos
Tg. Jer.	Targum Jeremiah	*Tg. Ps.-Jon.*	Targum Pseudo-Jonathan
Tg. Jon.	Targum Jonathan	*Tg. Qoh.*	Targum Qoheleth
Tg. Neof.	Targum Neofiti		

Mishnah, Talmud, and Related Literature

Soncino	The Babylonian Talmud. Edited by Isidore Epstein. 35 vols. London: Soncino, 1935–52.	*Ber.*	Berakot
		Demai	Demai
		Ed.	'Eduyyot
		Erub.	'Erubin
b.	Babylonian Talmud	*Git.*	Gittin
bar.	baraita (with rabbinic text)	*Hag.*	Hagigah
m.	Mishnah	*Hal.*	Hallah
t.	Tosefta	*Hor.*	Horayot
y.	Jerusalem (Yerushalmi, Palestinian) Talmud	*Hul.*	Hullin
		Ketub.	Ketubbot
		Kip.	Kippurim
Ab.	'Abot	*Maas.*	Ma'aśerot
Abod. Zar.	'Abodah Zarah	*Meg.*	Megillah
B. Bat.	Baba Batra	*Moed Qat.*	Mo'ed Qatan
B. Metsia	Baba Meṣi'a	*Ned.*	Nedarim
B. Qam.	Baba Qamma	*Nid.*	Niddah
Bek.	Bekorot	*Peah*	Pe'ah

Pesaḥ.	*Pesaḥim*	*Taan.*	*Ta'anit*
Qid.	*Qiddušin*	*Tamid*	*Tamid*
Rosh Hash.	*Roš Haššanah*	*Tem.*	*Temurah*
Sanh.	*Sanhedrin*	*Ter.*	*Terumot*
Shab.	*Šabbat*	*Yebam.*	*Yebamot*
Sot.	*Soṭah*	*Yoma*	*Yoma*
Suk.	*Sukkah*		

Other Rabbinic Works

Abot R. Nat.	*'Abot de Rabbi Nathan* (recensions A and B)	*Pesiq. Rab.*	*Pesiqta Rabbati*
		Pesiq. Rab Kah.	*Pesiqta de Rab Kahana*
Der. Er. Rab.	*Derek Ereṣ Rabbah*	*Ruth Rab.*	*Ruth Rabbah*
Deut. Rab.	*Deuteronomy Rabbah*	*Sipra*	
Eccl. Rab.	*Ecclesiastes (Qoheleth) Rabbah*	*A.M.*	*'Aḥarê Mot*
		Behuq.	*Behuqotai*
Exod. Rab.	*Exodus Rabbah*	*par.*	*parashah*
Gen. Rab.	*Genesis Rabbah*	*pq.*	*pereq*
Lam. Rab.	*Lamentations Rabbah*	*Qed.*	*Qedošim*
Lev. Rab.	*Leviticus Rabbah*	*Sh. M. d.*	*Shemini Mekhilta deMiluim*
Mek.	*Mekilta* (ed. Lauterbach)		
Baḥ.	*Bahodesh*	*VDDeho.*	*Vayyiqra Dibura Dehobah*
Pisha	*Pisha*	*VDDen.*	*Vayyiqra Dibura Denedabah*
Shir.	*Shirata*		
Midr. Pss.	*Midrash on Psalms (Tehillim)*	*Sipre Deut.*	*Sipre on Deuteronomy*
		Sipre Num.	*Sipre on Numbers*
Num. Rab.	*Numbers Rabbah*	*Song Rab.*	*Song of Solomon Rabbah*

Apostolic Fathers

Barn.	*Epistle of Barnabas*	*Pol.*	*Epistle to Polycarp*
1–2 Clem.	*1–2 Clement*	*Smyrn.*	*Epistle to the Smyrnaeans*
Did.	*Didache*	*Trall.*	*Epistle to the Trallians*
Diogn.	*Epistle to Diognetus*	*Mart. Pol.*	*Martyrdom of Polycarp*
Herm.	*Shepherd of Hermas*	*Poly. Phil.*	Polycarp *Letter to the Philippians*
Ign.	Ignatius of Antioch		
Magn.	*Epistle to the Magnesians*		
Phld.	*Epistle to the Philadelphians*		

Patristic and Other Early Christian Sources

Acts John	*Acts of John*
Ambrose	
Exc.	*De excessu fratris sui Satyri* / *On the Death of His Brother Satyrus*

Ambrosiaster
   Comm.   *Commentary on Paul's Epistles*
Athanas.   **Athanasius**
   Inc.   *On the Incarnation*
Athenag.   **Athenagoras**
   Plea   *A Plea for Christians*
Aug.   **Augustine**
   Ag. Jul.   *Against Julian*
   Ag. Pelag. *Against Two Letters of the Pelagians*
   City   *City of God*
   Contin.   *Continence*
   Div. Q.   *Diverse Questions*
   Ep.   *Epistles*
   Guilt   *On Guilt and Remission of Sins*
   Marr.   *On Marriage and Concupiscence*
   Nat. Grace *On Nature and Grace*
   Prop. Rom. *Propositions from the Epistle to the Romans*
   Retract.   *Retractations*
   Simp.   *To Simplician on Various Questions*
   Spir. Lett. *On the Spirit and the Letter*
Basil   **Basil of Caesarea (the Great)**
   Baptism   *Concerning Baptism*
   Rules   *The Long Rules*
Caesarius   **Caesarius of Arles**
   Serm.   *Sermons*
Chrys.   **John Chrysostom**
   Hom. Cor. *Homilies on the First and Second Epistles of Paul to the Corinthians*
   Hom. Gen. *Homilies on Genesis*
   Hom. Rom. *Homilies on Romans*
Clem. Alex. **Clement of Alexandria**
   Instr.   *Instructor*
   Strom.   *Stromata*
Cyril Alex.   **Cyril of Alexandria**
   Rom.   *Explanation of the Letter to the Romans*
Euseb.   **Eusebius**
   H.E.   *Historia ecclesiastica / Ecclesiastical History*
   P.E.   *Praeparatio evangelica / Preparation for the Gospel*
Hippol.   **Hippolytus**
   Ref.   *Refutation of Heresies*
Iren.   **Irenaeus**
   Her.   *Against Heresies*
Jerome
   Hom. Ps.   *Homilies on the Psalms*
   Ruf.   *Against Rufinus*
Justin   **Justin Martyr**
   1 Apol.   *1 Apology*
   Dial.   *Dialogue with Trypho*

Mac. Magn.	**Macarius Magnes**
Apocrit.	*Apocriticus*
Origen	
Cels.	*Against Celsus*
Comm. Rom.	*Commentary on Romans*
Princ.	*On First Principles*
Pelagius	
Comm. Rom.	*Commentary on Romans*
Photius	
Bibl.	*Bibliotheca*
Ps.-Clem.	**Pseudo-Clementines**
Ps.-Const.	**Pseudo-Constantius**
Rom.	*The Holy Letter of St. Paul to the Romans*
Sent. Sext.	**Sentences of Sextus**
Tatian	
Or. Gks.	*Oration to the Greeks*
Tert.	**Tertullian**
Apol.	*Apologeticus / Apology*
Carn. Chr.	*De carne Christi / The Flesh of Christ*
Spec.	*De spectaculis / The Shows*
Theodoret	**Theodoret of Cyrrhus**
Comm. 1 Cor.	*Commentary on 1 Corinthians*
Comm. 2 Cor.	*Commentary on 2 Corinthians*
Interp. Rom.	*Interpretation of Romans*
Theoph.	**Theophilus of Antioch**
To Autolycus	

Other Greek and Latin Works and Authors

Ach. Tat.	**Achilles Tatius**
Leucippe and Clitophon	
Ael. Arist.	**Aelius Aristides**
Def. Or.	*Defense of Oratory*
Leuct. Or.	*Leuctrian Orations*
Aelian	**Claudius Aelianus**
Nat. An.	*Nature of Animals*
Var. hist.	*Varia historia*
Aeschines	
Embassy	*False Embassy*
Tim.	*Timarchus*
Aeschylus	
Ag.	*Agamemnon*
Lib.	*Libation-Bearers (Choephori)*
Prom.	*Prometheus Bound*
Suppl.	*Suppliant Women*
Alciph.	**Alciphron**
Farm.	*Farmers*
Paras.	*Parasites*

Anacharsis	**[Pseudo]-Anacharsis**
Ep.	*Epistles*
Aphth.	**Aphthonius**
Progymn.	*Progymnasmata*
Apollod.	**Apollodorus**
Bibl.	*Bibliotheca / Library*
Epitome	*Epitome of the Library*
Appian	
C.W.	*Civil Wars*
R.H.	*Roman History*
Ap. Rhod.	**Apollonius of Rhodes**
Argonautica	
Apul.	**Apuleius**
Apol.	*Apology*
De deo Socr.	*De deo Socratis / God of Socrates*
Flor.	*Florida*
Metam.	*Metamorphoses*

Arist.	**Aristotle**		*Cat.*	*In Catilinam*
E.E.	*Eudemian Ethics*		*De or.*	*De oratore*
Heav.	*On the Heavens*		*Div.*	*De divinatione*
N.E.	*Nicomachean Ethics*		*Fam.*	*Epistulae ad familiares /*
Poet.	*Poetics*			*Letters to Friends*
Pol.	*Politics*		*Fin.*	*De finibus*
Rhet.	*Art of Rhetoric*		*Flacc.*	*Pro Flacco*
Soul	*On the Soul*		*Font.*	*Pro Fonteio*
V.V.	*Virtues and Vices*		*Inv.*	*De inventione*
Aristob.	**Aristobulus**		*Leg.*	*De legibus*
Fragments (in Eusebius *H.E.*)			*Marcell.*	*Pro Marcello*
Aristoph.	**Aristophanes**		*Mil.*	*Pro Milone*
Acharn.	*Acharnians*		*Mur.*	*Pro Murena*
Arius Did.	**Arius Didymus**		*Nat. d.*	*De natura deorum*
Epitome of Stoic Ethics			*Off.*	*De officiis*
Arrian			*Opt. gen.*	*De optimo genere*
Alex.	*Anabasis of Alexander*			*oratorum*
Ind.	*Indica*		*Or. Brut.*	*Orator ad M. Brutum*
Artem.	**Artemidorus Daldianus**		*Parad.*	*Paradoxa Stoicorum*
Oneir.	*Oneirocritica*		*Phil.*	*Orationes philippicae*
Athen.	**Athenaeus**		*Pis.*	*In Pisonem*
Deipn.	*Deipnosophists*		*Prov. cons.*	*De provinciis consularibus*
Aul. Gel.	**Aulus Gellius**		*Quinct.*	*Pro Quinctio*
Attic Nights			*Quint. fratr.*	*Epistulae ad Quintum*
Aur. Vict.	**Aurelius Victor**			*fratrum*
Epit. Caes.	*Epitome de Caesaribus*		*Rab. Perd.*	*Pro Rabirio Perduellionis*
Babr.	**Babrius**			*Reo*
Fables			*Resp.*	*De re publica*
Caesar	**Julius Caesar**		*Scaur.*	*Pro Scauro*
C.W.	*Civil War*		*Senect.*	*De senectute*
Gall. W.	*Gallic War*		*Sest.*	*Pro Sestio*
Callim.	**Callimachus**		*Sull.*	*Pro Sulla*
Epig.	*Epigrammata*		*Top.*	*Topica*
Poems	*Minor Poems*		*Tull.*	*Pro Tullio*
Cato	**Dionysius Cato**		*Tusc.*	*Tusculan Disputations*
Coll. Dist.	*Collection of Distichs*		*Vat.*	*In Vatinium*
Catullus			*Verr.*	*In Verrem*
Carmina			**Corn. Nep.**	**Cornelius Nepos**
Char.	**Chariton**		*Generals*	
Chaer.	*Chaereas and Callirhoe*		**Crates**	**Pseudo-Crates**
Cic.	**Cicero**		*Ep.*	*Epistles*
Ag. Caec.	*Against Caecilius*		**Demet.**	**Demetrius Phalereus**
Amic.	*De amicitia*		*Style*	*On Style / De elocutione*
Att.	*Letters to Atticus*		**Demosth.**	**Demosthenes**
Brut.	*Brutus, or De claris*		*Aphob. 1–3*	*Against Aphobus*
	oratoribus		*Con.*	*Against Conon*
Cael.	*Pro Caelio*		*Embassy*	*On the False Embassy*

Ep.	*Epistulae / Letters*	*Ad M. Caes.*	*Ad Marcum Caesarem*
Meidias	*Against Meidias*	*Ad verum imp.*	*Ad verum imperatorem*
Dio Cass.	**Dio Cassius**	*Eloq.*	*Eloquence*
Roman History		*Ep. graec.*	*Epistulae graecae*
Dio Chrys.	**Dio Chrysostom**	*Nep. am.*	*De nepote amisso*
Or.	*Orations*	**Gaius**	
Diod. Sic.	**Diodorus Siculus**	*Inst.*	*Institutes*
Library of History		**Galen**	
Diogenes	**[Pseudo-]Diogenes**	*Grief*	*On the Avoidance of*
Ep.	*Epistle*		*Grief*
Diog. Laert.	**Diogenes Laertius**	*Hippoc. et Plat.*	*Hippocrates and Plato*
Lives of Eminent Philosophers		**Gorg.**	**Gorgias**
Dion. Hal.	**Dionysius of**	*Hel.*	*Encomium of Helen*
	Halicarnassus	**Gr. Anth.**	**Greek Anthology**
2 Amm.	*2 Epistle to Ammaeus*	**Hdn.**	**Herodian**
Ant. rom.	*Antiquitates romanae /*	*History*	
	Roman Antiquities	**Hdt.**	**Herodotus**
Demosth.	*Demosthenes*	*Histories*	
Epict.	**Epictetus**	**Heliod.**	**Heliodorus**
Diatr.	*Diatribai / Discourses*	*Eth.*	*Ethiopian Story*
Encheir.	*Encheiridion / Handbook*	**Heracl.**	**Heraclitus**
Epicurus		*Hom. Prob.*	*Homeric Problems*
Let. Men.	*Letter to Menoeceus*	**Hermog.**	**Hermogenes**
Eunapius		*Inv.*	*Invention*
Lives	*Lives of the Philoso-*	*Method*	*Method in Forceful*
	phers and Sophists		*Speaking*
Eurip.	**Euripides**	*Progymn.*	*Progymnasmata*
Aeol.	*Aeolus*	**Hesiod**	
Andr.	*Andromache*	*Melamp.*	*Melampodia*
Bacch.	*Bacchanals*	*W.D.*	*Works and Days*
Chrys.	*Chrysippus*	**Hierocles**	**Hierocles (the Stoic)**
El.	*Electra*	*Ethics*	*Elements of Ethics*
Hec.	*Hecuba*	*Gods*	*On Duties: How to*
Hipp.	*Hippolytus*		*Conduct Oneself*
Med.	*Medea*		*toward the Gods*
Oed.	*Oedipus*	*Love*	*On Duties: On Fraternal*
Oenom.	*Oenomaus*		*Love*
Orest.	*Orestes*	*Marr.*	*On Duties: On*
Phoen.	*Phoenician Maidens*		*Marriage*
Firm. Mat.	**Firmicus Maternus**	**Hom.**	**Homer**
Err. prof. rel.	*De errore profanarum*	*Il.*	*Iliad*
	religionum	*Od.*	*Odyssey*
Fronto	**Marcus Cornelius Fronto**	**Hom. Hymns**	**Homeric Hymns**
Ad Ant. imp.	*Ad Antoninum*	**Hor.**	**Horace**
	imperatorem	*Ep.*	*Epistles*
Ad Ant. Pium	*Ad Antoninum Pium*	*Sat.*	*Satires*

Iambl.	**Iamblichus of Chalcis**		*Cock*	*The Dream, or The*
Myst.	*Mysteries*			*Cock*
Pyth. Life	*On the Pythagorean Life /*		*Cynic*	*The Cynic*
	Life of Pythagoras		*Dance*	*The Dance*
Soul	*On the Soul*		*Dem.*	*Demonax*
Iambl. (nov.)	**Iamblichus (novelist)**		*Dial. C.*	*Dialogues of Courtesans*
Bab. St.	*Babylonian Story*		*Dial. D.*	*Dialogues of the Dead*
Isaeus			*Dial. G.*	*Dialogues of the Gods*
Menec.	*Estate of Menecles*		*Dial. S-G.*	*Dialogues of Sea-Gods*
Isoc.	**Isocrates**		*Eunuch*	*The Eunuch*
Ad Nic.	*Ad Nicoclem / To Nicocles*		*Fisherman*	*The Dead Come to Life,*
	(Or. 2)			*or The Fisherman*
Antid.	*Antidosis (Or. 15)*		*Fly*	*The Fly*
Demon.	*To Demonicus (Or. 1)*		*Hall*	*The Hall*
Nic.	*Nicocles / Cyprians (Or. 3)*		*Hermot.*	*Hermotimus, or Sects*
Paneg.	*Panegyricus (Or. 4)*		*Icar.*	*Icaromenippus, or The*
Juv.	**Juvenal**			*Sky-Man*
Sat.	*Satires*		*Indictment*	*Double Indictment*
Libanius			*Lover of Lies*	*The Lover of Lies*
Anec.	*Anecdote*		*Lucius*	*Lucius, or The Ass*
Comp.	*Comparison*		*Nigr.*	*Nigrinus*
Declam.	*Declamations*		*Oct.*	*Octogenarians*
Descr.	*Description*		*Parl. G.*	*Parliament of the Gods*
Encom.	*Encomium*		*Patriot*	*The Patriot*
Invect.	*Invective*		*Peregr.*	*The Passing of*
Narr.	*Narration*			*Peregrinus*
Speech Char.	*Speech in Character*		*Phil. Sale*	*Philosophies for Sale*
Topics	*Common Topics*		*Portr.*	*Essays in Portraiture*
Livy			*Portr. D.*	*Essays in Portraiture*
Ab urbe condita				*Defended*
Longin.	**Longinus**		*Posts*	*Salaried Posts in Great*
Subl.	*On the Sublime*			*Houses*
Longus			*Prof. P.S.*	*A Professor of Public*
Daphnis and Chloe				*Speaking*
Lucan			*Prom.*	*Prometheus*
C.W.	*Civil War*		*Runaways*	*The Runaways*
Lucian			*Sacr.*	*Sacrifices*
Affairs	*Affairs of the Heart*		*Tim.*	*Timon, or The*
Alex.	*Alexander the False*			*Misanthrope*
	Prophet		*Tox.*	*Toxaris, or Friendship*
Astr.	*Astrology*		*True Story*	*A True Story*
Book-Coll.	*The Ignorant*		*Z. Cat.*	*Zeus Catechized*
	Book-Collector		*Z. Rants*	*Zeus Rants*
Carousal	*The Carousal (Sympo-*		**Lucret.**	**Lucretius**
	sium), or The Lapiths		*Nat.*	*De rerum natura*
Charid.	*Charidemus*		**Lycophron**	**Lycophron of Chalcis**
Charon	*Charon, or The Inspectors*		*Alex.*	*Alexandra*

Lysias
  Or.   *Orationes*
Macrob.   **Macrobius**
  Comm.   *Commentary on the Dream of Scipio*
Marc. Aur.   **Marcus Aurelius**
  Meditations
Mart.   **Martial**
  Epig.   *Epigrams*
Max. Tyre   **Maximus of Tyre**
  Or.   *Orationes*
Men. Rhet.   **Menander Rhetor (of Laodicea)**
  Treatises
Musaeus
  Hero   *Hero and Leander*
Mus. Ruf.   **Musonius Rufus**
Nicolaus   **Nicolaus the Sophist**
  Progymn.   *Progymnasmata*
Olympiodorus
  In Gorg.   *In Platonis Gorgiam Commentaria*
Orph. H.   **Orphic Hymns**
Ovid
  Am.   *Amores*
  Fast.   *Fasti*
  Her.   *Heroides*
  Metam.   *Metamorphoses*
Parth.   **Parthenius**
  L.R.   *Love Romance*
Paus.   **Pausanias**
  Description of Greece
Perv. Ven.   **Pervigilium Veneris**
Petron.   **Petronius**
  Sat.   *Satyricon*
Phaedrus
  Fables
Philod.   **Philodemus**
  Crit.   *On Frank Criticism*
  Death   *On Death*
  Prop.   *On Property Management*
Philost.   **Flavius Philostratus (the Athenian)**
  Ep.   *Epistulae / Love Letters*
  Ep. Apoll.   *Epistles of Apollonius*
  Hrk.   *Heroikos*

Vit. Apoll.   *Vita Apollonii / Life of Apollonius*
Vit. soph.   *Vitae sophistarum / Lives of the Sophists*
Pindar
  Ol.   *Olympian Odes*
  Paean.   *Paeanes / Hymns*
  Pyth.   *Pythian Odes*
  Thren.   *Threnoi / Dirges*
Plato
  Alcib.   *Alcibiades (1–2)*
  Charm.   *Charmides*
  Cratyl.   *Cratylus*
  Ep.   *Epistles*
  Gorg.   *Gorgias*
  Hipp. maj.   *Hippias major*
  Lov.   *The Lovers*
  Phaedr.   *Phaedrus*
  Pol.   *Politicus / Statesman*
  Prot.   *Protagoras*
  Rep.   *Republic*
  Theaet.   *Theaetetus*
  Tim.   *Timaeus*
Pliny   **Pliny the Younger**
  Ep.   *Epistles*
Pliny E.   **Pliny the Elder**
  N.H.   *Natural History*
Plot.   **Plotinus**
  Enn.   *Enneads*
Plut.   **Plutarch**
  Aff. Soul   *Whether the Affections of the Soul Are Worse Than Those of the Body*
  Alex.   *Alexander*
  Apoll.   *Letter of Consolation to Apollonius*
  Borr.   *On Borrowing (That We Ought Not to Borrow)*
  Bride   *Advice to Bride and Groom*
  Busybody   *On Being a Busybody*
  Caes.   *Caesar*
  Cic.   *Cicero*
  Cim.   *Cimon*
  Comm. Conc.   *Against the Stoics on Common Conceptions*
  Contr. A.   *On the Control of Anger*

Coriol.	Coriolanus	Stoic Cont.	Stoic Self-Contradictions
Demosth.	Demosthenes	Superst.	Superstition
Dial. L.	Dialogue on Love	Table	Table Talk
Dinner	Dinner of Seven Wise Men	Ten Or.	Ten Orators
Div. V.	Delays of Divine	Themist.	Themistocles
	Vengeance	Uned. R.	To an Uneducated Ruler
E Delph.	E at Delphi	Virt.	Virtue and Vice
Educ.	On the Education of	**Polyb.**	**Polybius**
	Children		History of the Roman Republic
Exile	On Exile	**Porph.**	**Porphyry**
Face M.	Face on the Moon	Abst.	De abstinentia
Flatt.	How to Tell a Flatterer	Marc.	To Marcella
	from a Friend	Plot.	Life of Plotinus
Garr.	On Garrulousness	**Proclus**	**Proclus the Successor**
Gen. of Soul	Generation of the Soul in	Poet.	On Poetics
	the "Timaeus"	**Ps.-Callisth.**	**Pseudo-Callisthenes**
Isis	Isis and Osiris	Alex.	Alexander Romance
L. Wealth	Love of Wealth	**Ps.-Ocellus**	**Pseudo-Ocellus Lucanus**
Lect.	On Lectures	Nat. Univ.	On the Nature of the
Lyc.	Lycurgus		Universe
M. Cato	Marcus Cato	**Ps.-Simpl.**	**Pseudo-Simplicius**
Mal. Hdt.	Malice of Herodotus	De an.	In de anima
Mor.	Moralia	**Publ. Syr.**	**Publilius Syrus**
Nic.	Nicias	Sentences	
Old Men	Old Men in Public Affairs	**Pyth. Sent.**	**Pythagorean Sentences**
Or. Delphi	Oracles at Delphi No	**Quint.**	**Quintilian**
	Longer Given in Verse	Decl.	Declamations
Par. St.	Greek and Roman Parallel	Inst.	Institutes of Oratory
	Stories	**Quint. Curt.**	**Quintus Curtius Rufus**
Plac.	De placita		History of Alexander
	philosophorum	**Res gest.**	**Res gestae divi Augusti**
Plat. Q.	Platonic Questions	**Rhet. Alex.**	**Rhetorica ad Alexandrum**
Pleas. L.	Epicurus Actually Makes	**Rhet. Her.**	**Rhetorica ad Herennium**
	a Pleasant Life Impossible	**Sall.**	**Sallust**
Poetry	How the Young Man	Catil.	War with Catiline
	Should Study Poetry	Ep. Caes.	Epistulae ad Caesarem /
Pomp.	Pompey		Letters to Caesar
Profit by	How to Profit by One's	Jug.	War with Jugurtha
Enemies	Enemies	Pomp.	Letter of Gnaeus Pompeius
Progr. Virt.	How One May Become	Sp. Caes.	Speech to Caesar
	Aware of One's Progress	**Sen. E.**	**Seneca the Elder**
	in Virtue	Controv.	Controversiae
R. Col.	Reply to Colotes	Suas.	Suasoriae
Rom. Q.	Roman Questions	**Sen. Y.**	**Seneca the Younger**
S. Kings	Sayings of Kings and	Ben.	On Benefits
	Commanders	Clem.	De clementia
S. Rom.	Sayings of Romans	Dial.	Dialogues

Ep. Lucil.	*Epistles to Lucilius*		*Hist.*	*History*
Herc. fur.	*Hercules furens*	**Terence**		
Hippol.	*Hippolytus*		*Andr.*	*Lady of Andros*
Ira	*De ira*		*Moth.*	*The Mother-in-Law*
Med.	*Medea*		*Phorm.*	*Phormio*
Nat. Q.	*Natural Questions*	**Theon**		**Aelius Theon**
Troj.	*Trojan Women*		*Progymn.*	*Progymnasmata* (citing the
Vit. beat.	*De vita beata*			Butts edition except where
Sext. Emp.	**Sextus Empiricus**			otherwise noted)
Eth.	*Against the Ethicists*	**Theophr.**		**Theophrastus**
Pyr.	*Outlines of Pyrrhonism*		*Char.*	*On Characters*
Sil. It.	**Silius Italicus**	**Thucyd.**		**Thucydides**
Punica				*History of the Peloponnesian War*
Socratics		**Tibullus**		
Ep.	*Epistles*		*Elegies*	
Soph.	**Sophocles**	**Val. Flacc.**		**Valerius Flaccus**
Antig.	*Antigone*		*Argonautica*	
Oed. tyr.	*Oedipus the King*	**Val. Max.**		**Valerius Maximus**
Wom. Tr.	*Women of Trachis*		*Memorable Deeds and Sayings*	
Soranus		**Varro**		
Gynec.	*Gynecology*		*L.L.*	*On the Latin Language*
Statius		**Vell. Paterc.**		**Velleius Paterculus**
Silv.	*Silvae*		*Compendium of Roman History*	
Stob.	**Stobaeus**	**Virg.**		**Virgil**
Anth.	*Anthology*		*Aen.*	*Aeneid*
Strabo			*Ecl.*	*Eclogues*
Geography		**Vitruv.**		**Vitruvius**
Suet.	**Suetonius**		*Arch.*	*On Architecture*
Aug.	*Augustus*	**Xen.**		**Xenophon**
Calig.	*Caligula*		*Apol.*	*Apologia Socratis*
Claud.	*Claudius*		*Cyr.*	*Cyropaedia*
Tib.	*Tiberius*		*Hell.*	*Hellenica*
Symm.	**Quintus Aurelius Symmachus**		*Lac.*	*Constitution of*
Ep.	*Epistles*			*Lacedemonians*
Tac.	**Tacitus**		*Mem.*	*Memorabilia*
Ann.	*Annals*		*Oec.*	*Oeconomicus*
Dial.	*Dialogus de oratoribus*	**Xen. Eph.**		**Xenophon of Ephesus**
Germ.	*Germania*		*Anthia*	*Anthia and Habrocomes*

Other Ancient and Medieval Sources

ANET	*Ancient Near Eastern Texts Relating to the Old Testament.* Edited by James B. Pritchard. 2nd ed. Princeton: Princeton University Press, 1955.
BGU	*Aegyptische Urkunden aus den Königlichen Staatlichen Museen zu Berlin, Griechische Urkunden.* 15 vols. Berlin: Weidmann, 1895–1937.
Book of Dead	*Book of the Dead* (Egyptian)

CER	Origen. *Commentarii in Epistulam ad Romanos*. Edited by T. Heither. 5 vols. New York: Herder, 1990–95.
Confuc. *Anal.*	Confucius *Analects*[3]
CSEL	Corpus Scriptorum Ecclesiasticorum Latinorum
Cyn. Ep.	*The Cynic Epistles: A Study Edition*. Edited by Abraham J. Malherbe. SBLSBS 12. Missoula, MT: Scholars Press, 1977.
ENPK	*Ein neuer Paulustext und Kommentar*. Edited by H. J. Frede. 2 vols. Freiburg im Breisgau: Herder, 1973–74.
GBP	*The Greek Bucolic Poets*. Translated by J. M. Edmonds. LCL. Cambridge, MA: Harvard University Press; London: Heinemann, 1912.
Gnom. Vat.	*Gnomologium Vaticanum*
Incant. Text	Incantation text from *Corpus of the Aramaic Incantation Bowls*. By Charles D. Isbell. SBLDS 17. Missoula, MT: Scholars Press, 1975.
PCR	*Pelagius's Commentary on Romans*. Edited by M. De Bruyn. Oxford: Oxford University Press, 1993.
PG	Patrologia Graeca [= Patrologiae Cursus Completus: Series Graeca]. Edited by J.-P. Migne. 162 vols. Paris, 1857–86.
PGK	*Pauluskommentare aus der griechischen Kirche*. Edited by K. Staab. NTAbh 15. Münster: Aschendorff, 1933.
PL	Patrologia Latina [= Patrologiae Cursus Completus: Series Latina]. Edited by J.-P. Migne. 217 vols. Paris, 1844–64.

Papyri, Inscriptions, and Fragment Collections

CIG	*Corpus Inscriptionum Graecarum*. Edited by August Boeckh. 4 vols. Berlin, 1828–77.
CIJ	*Corpus Inscriptionum Judaicarum*. Edited by Jean-Baptiste Frey. 2 vols. Rome: Pontifical Biblical Institute, 1936–52.
CIL	*Corpus Inscriptionum Latinarum*. Berlin, 1862–.
Nauck	*Tragicorum graecorum fragmenta*. Edited by A. Nauck. 2nd ed. Leipzig: Teubner, 1889.
OGIS	*Orientis Graeci Inscriptiones Selectae*. Edited by W. Dittenberger. 2 vols. Leipzig: Hirzel, 1903–5.
P.Duk.	Duke University papyrus collection
P.Fay.	*Fayum Towns and Their Papyri*. Edited by B. P. Grenfell, A. S. Hunt, and D. G. Hogarth. London, 1900.
P.Flor.	*Papyri greco-egizii, Papiri Fiorentini*. Edited by G. Vitelli and D. Comparetti. Milan, 1906–15.
P.Gen.	*Les Papyrus de Genève* I. Edited by J. Nicole. Geneva, 1896–1900.
P.Lille	*Papyrus Grecs de Lille* I. Parts i, ii, iii. Edited by P. Jouguet. Paris, 1907–23.
P.Mich.	Michigan Papyri. 19 vols. in 20. Ann Arbor, MI, 1931–99.
P.Oxy.	*The Oxyrhynchus Papyri*. London: British Exploration Fund; Egypt Exploration Society, 1898–.

3. Chai's enumeration is followed parenthetically by the original enumeration.

P.Stras.   *Griechische Papyrus der Kaiserlichen Universitäts- und Landes-bibliothek
                zu Strassburg.* Edited by F. Priesigke. Leipzig, 1912–.
PDM   *Papyri Demoticae Magicae.* Demotic texts in the *PGM* corpus as collated
                in *The Greek Magical Papyri in Translation, Including the Demotic Spells.*
                Edited by Hans Dieter Betz. Chicago: University of Chicago Press, 1996.
PDM Suppl.   *PDM Supplement*
PGM   *Papyri Graecae Magicae: Die griechischen Zauberpapyri.* Edited by
                K. Preisendanz. 2 vols. Leipzig and Berlin: Teubner, 1928–31.
Priene   *Die Inschriften von Priene.* Edited by H. von Gaertringen. Berlin, 1906.
SP   *Select Papyri.* Edited by A. S. Hunt, C. C. Edgar, and D. L. Page. 5 vols.
                LCL. Cambridge, MA: Harvard University Press, 1932–41.
SVF   *Stoicorum Veterum Fragmenta.* Edited by H. von Arnim. 4 vols. Leipzig:
                Teubner, 1903–24.

Modern Sources

General

BCE	Before the Common Era	n(n).	note(s)
ca.	circa	n.d.	no date
CE	Common Era	n.s.	new series
cf.	*confer*, compare	p(p).	page(s)
ed(s).	edition(s), editor(s), edited by	R.	Rabbi
e.g.	*exempli gratia*, for example	rev.	revised
esp.	especially	ser.	series
ET	English translation	trans.	translator(s), translated by
ff.	and following	vs.	versus
i.e.	*id est*, that is		

Bible Translations

ASV	American Standard Version	NEB	New English Bible
CEB	Common English Bible	NET	New English Translation (NET
ESV	English Standard Version		Bible)
GNT	Good News Translation	NIV	New International Version
KJV	King James Version	NKJV	New King James Version
Message	The Message	NLT	New Living Translation
NAB	New American Bible	NRSV	New Revised Standard Version
NASB	New American Standard Bible	RSV	Revised Standard Version
NCV	New Century Version		

Journals, Series, and Other Reference Works

AB	Anchor Bible
ABD	*Anchor Bible Dictionary*. Edited by David N. Freedman. 6 vols. New York: Doubleday, 1992.
ABR	*Australian Biblical Review*
ABRL	Anchor Bible Reference Library
ACCS	Ancient Christian Commentary on Scripture
AJA	*American Journal of Archaeology*
AJAH	*American Journal of Ancient History*
AJP	*American Journal of Philology*
ALGHJ	Arbeiten zur Literatur und Geschichte des hellenistichen Judentums
ALUOS	*Annual of Leeds University Oriental Society*
AnBib	Analecta Biblica
ANRW	*Aufstieg und Niedergang der römischen Welt: Geschichte und Kultur Roms im Spiegel der neueren Forschung*. Part 2, *Principat*. Edited by H. Temporini and W. Haase. Berlin: de Gruyter, 1972–.
ANTC	Abingdon New Testament Commentaries
AramSt	*Aramaic Studies*
ArBib	Aramaic Bible
Arch	*Archaeology*
ASDE	*Annali di storia dell' esegesi*
AshTJ	*Ashland Theological Journal*
AsTJ	*Asbury Theological Journal*
AT	*Annales Theologici*
AugCNT	Augsburg Commentary on the New Testament
AUSS	*Andrews University Seminary Studies*
BA	*Biblical Archaeologist*
BASOR	*Bulletin of the American Schools of Oriental Research*
BBR	*Bulletin for Biblical Research*
BCompAW	Blackwell Companions to the Ancient World
BCompRel	Blackwell Companions to Religion
BDAG	Danker, F. W., W. Bauer, W. F. Arndt, and F. W. Gingrich. *Greek-English Lexicon of the New Testament and Other Early Christian Literature*. 3rd rev. ed. Chicago: University of Chicago Press, 2000.
BECNT	Baker Exegetical Commentary on the New Testament
BegChr	*The Beginnings of Christianity*. Part 1: *The Acts of the Apostles*. Edited by F. J. Foakes-Jackson and Kirsopp Lake. 5 vols. London: Macmillan, 1922. Reprint, Grand Rapids: Baker, 1977.
BeO	*Bibbia e Oriente*
BHT	Beiträge zur historischen Theologie
Bib	*Biblica*
BiBh	*Bible Bhashyam*
BibInt	*Biblical Interpretation*
BibLeb	*Bibel und Leben*
BibT	*The Bible Today*
Bijdr	*Bijdragen*

BJRL	*Bulletin of the John Rylands University Library of Manchester*
BJS	Brown Judaic Studies
BK	*Bibel und Kirche*
BLE	*Bulletin de Littérature Ecclésiastique*
BollS	Bollingen Series
BrillPauly	*Brill's New Pauly: Encyclopaedia of the Ancient World*. Edited by Hubert Cancik. Leiden: Brill, 2002–11.
BSac	*Bibliotheca Sacra*
BTCB	Brazos Theological Commentary on the Bible
BTr	*Bible Translator*
BZ	*Biblische Zeitschrift*
BZNW	Beihefte zur Zeitschrift für die neutestamentliche Wissenschaft
CBET	Contributions to Biblical Exegesis and Theology
CBQ	*Catholic Biblical Quarterly*
CBull	*Classical Bulletin*
CC	Continental Commentaries
CH	*Church History*
CHSP	*Center for Hermeneutical Studies Protocol*
CJ	*Classical Journal*
Coll	*Collationes*
ConBNT	Coniectanea Biblica: New Testament Series
CP	*Classical Philology*
CQ	*Classical Quarterly*
CRINT	Compendia Rerum Iudaicarum ad Novum Testamentum
CT	*Christianity Today*
CTM	*Concordia Theological Monthly*
CurTM	*Currents in Theology and Mission*
CW	*Classical World*
DBM	*Deltion Biblikon Meleton*
DBSJ	*Detroit Baptist Seminary Journal*
DCDBCN	The Development of Christian Doctrine before the Council of Nicaea
DNTB	*Dictionary of New Testament Background*. Edited by Craig A. Evans and Stanley E. Porter. Downers Grove, IL: InterVarsity, 2000.
DSD	*Dead Sea Discoveries*
EHPR	Études d'Histoire et de Philosophie Religieuses
EHRel	Études d'Histoire des Religions
Enc	*Encounter*
EPROER	Études préliminaires aux religions orientales dans l'empire romain
EspV	*Esprit et Vie*
EstBib	*Estudios bíblicos*
EthRacSt	*Ethnic and Racial Studies*
ETL	*Ephemerides Theologicae Lovanienses*
ETR	*Études Théologiques et Religieuses*
EvQ	*Evangelical Quarterly*
ExpT	*Expository Times*
FAT	Forschungen zum Alten Testament
FilNeot	*Filología Neotestamentaria*

FoiVie	*Foi et Vie*
FreiRund	*Freiburger Rundbrief*
FZPhTh	*Freiburger Zeitschrift für Philosophie und Theologie*
GR	*Greece and Rome*
GRBS	*Greek, Roman, and Byzantine Studies*
Greg	*Gregorianum*
Hen	*Henoch*
Hermeneia	Hermeneia: A Critical and Historical Commentary on the Bible
Historia	*Historia: Zeitschrift für alte Geschichte*
HNTC	Harper's New Testament Commentaries
Hok	*Hokhma*
HR	*History of Religions*
HSCP	*Harvard Studies in Classical Philology*
HTR	*Harvard Theological Review*
HTS	Harvard Theological Studies
HUCA	*Hebrew Union College Annual*
HvTS	*Hervormde teologiese studies*
IBC	Interpretation: A Bible Commentary for Teaching and Preaching
IBS	*Irish Biblical Studies*
ICC	International Critical Commentary
ICS	*Illinois Classical Studies*
Identity	*Identity: An International Journal of Theory and Research*
Int	*Interpretation*
IsNumR	*Israel Numismatic Research*
ITS	*Indian Theological Studies*
IVPNTC	InterVarsity Press New Testament Commentary
JBL	*Journal of Biblical Literature*
JBLMS	Journal of Biblical Literature Monograph Series
JBQ	*Jewish Bible Quarterly*
JDharm	*Journal of Dharma*
Jeev	*Jeevadhara*
JETS	*Journal of the Evangelical Theological Society*
JGRCJ	*Journal of Greco-Roman Christianity and Judaism*
JHI	*Journal of the History of Ideas*
JHistPhil	*Journal of the History of Philosophy*
JHistSex	*Journal of the History of Sexuality*
JHS	*Journal of Hellenic Studies*
Jian Dao DS	Jian Dao Dissertation Series
JJS	*Journal of Jewish Studies*
JJTP	*Journal of Jewish Thought and Philosophy*
JNES	*Journal of Near Eastern Studies*
JPFC	*The Jewish People in the First Century: Historical Geography; Political History; Social, Cultural, and Religious Life and Institutions.* Edited by S. Safrai and M. Stern with D. Flusser and W. C. van Unnik. 2 vols. CRINT 1. Vol. 1: Assen: Van Gorcum, 1974; vol. 2: Philadelphia: Fortress, 1976.
JPT	*Journal of Pentecostal Theology*
JQR	*Jewish Quarterly Review*

JRelHealth	*Journal of Religion and Health*
JRS	*Journal of Roman Studies*
JSJ	*Journal for the Study of Judaism in the Persian, Hellenistic, and Roman Periods*
JSNT	*Journal for the Study of the New Testament*
JSNTSup	Journal for the Study of the New Testament Supplement Series
JSOT	*Journal for the Study of the Old Testament*
JSOTSup	Journal for the Study of the Old Testament Supplement
JSP	*Journal for the Study of the Pseudepigrapha*
JSQ	*Jewish Studies Quarterly*
JSS	*Journal of Semitic Studies*
JS/TS	*Journal for Semitics / Tydskrif vir Semitistiek*
JTI	*Journal of Theological Interpretation*
JTS	*Journal of Theological Studies*
KD	*Kerygma und Dogma*
KK	*Katorikku Kenkyu*
LCL	Loeb Classical Library
LEC	Library of Early Christianity
LNTS	Library of New Testament Studies
LPSt	Library of Pauline Studies
LTJ	*Lutheran Theological Journal*
Mnemosyne	*Mnemosyne: A Journal of Classical Studies*
MNTC	Moffatt New Testament Commentary
MScRel	*Mélanges de Science Religieuse*
NCamBC	New Cambridge Bible Commentary
NCBC	New Century Bible Commentary
NCCS	New Covenant Commentary Series
Neot	*Neotestamentica*
NFTL	New Foundations Theological Library
NIBCNT	New International Biblical Commentary on the New Testament
NICNT	New International Commentary on the New Testament
NovT	*Novum Testamentum*
NovTSup	Supplements to Novum Testamentum
NTA	*New Testament Abstracts*
NTAbh	Neutestamentliche Abhandlungen
NTL	New Testament Library
NTS	*New Testament Studies*
NTT	*Norsk Teologisk Tidsskrift*
Numen	*Numen: International Review for the History of Religions*
OCD³	*Oxford Classical Dictionary*. Edited by Simon Hornblower and Antony Spawforth. 3rd rev. ed. Oxford: Oxford University Press, 2003.
OrChrAn	Orientalia Christiana Analecta
OTP	*The Old Testament Pseudepigrapha*. Edited by James H. Charlesworth. 2 vols. New York: Doubleday, 1983–85.
PAST	Pauline Studies (Brill)
PastRev	*Pastoral Review*
PCNT	Paideia Commentaries on the New Testament
PhA	Philosophia Antiqua

Phil	Philologus
PHR	Problèmes d'Histoire des Religions
PIBA	Proceedings of the Irish Biblical Association
PillNTC	Pillar New Testament Commentary
PJBR	Polish Journal of Biblical Research
ProcC	Proclamation Commentaries
PRSt	Perspectives in Religious Studies
PrTMS	Princeton Theological Monograph Series
PTMS	Pittsburgh Theological Monograph Series
QC	Qumran Chronicle
R&T	Religion and Theology
RB	Revue biblique
RBL	Review of Biblical Literature
RechBib	Recherches bibliques
RelS	Religious Studies
RelSRev	Religious Studies Review
ResQ	Restoration Quarterly
RevExp	Review and Expositor
RevistB	Revista bíblica
RevQ	Revue de Qumran
RHPR	Revue d'Histoire et de Philosophie Religieuses
RHR	Revue de l'histoire des religions
RivB	Rivista biblica italiana
RMPhil	Rheinisches Museum für Philologie
RocT	Roczniki Teologiczne
RSR	Recherches de science religieuse
RTR	Reformed Theological Review
Salm	Salmanticensis
SAOC	Studies in Ancient Oriental Civilizations
SBLDS	Society of Biblical Literature Dissertation Series
SBLECL	Society of Biblical Literature Early Christianity and Its Literature
SBLRBS	Society of Biblical Literature Resources for Biblical Study
SBLSBS	Society of Biblical Literature Sources for Biblical Study
SBLSCS	Society of Biblical Literature Septuagint and Cognate Studies
SBLSymS	Society of Biblical Literature Symposium Series
SBLTT	Society of Biblical Literature Texts and Translations
SBLWGRW	Society of Biblical Literature Writings from the Greco-Roman World
SBT	Studies in Biblical Theology
ScC	La Scuola Cattolica
SCHNT	Studia ad Corpus Hellenisticum Novi Testamenti
ScrTh	Scripta Theologica
SEÅ	Svensk Exegetisk Årsbok
SGRR	Studies in Greek and Roman Religion
SHBC	Smyth & Helwys Bible Commentary
SHR	Studies in the History of Religions (supplements to Numen)
SJT	Scottish Journal of Theology
SJTOP	Scottish Journal of Theology Occasional Papers

SNTSMS	Society for New Testament Studies Monograph Series
SP	Sacra Pagina
SPhilA	*Studia Philonica Annual (Studia Philonica)*
SPhilMon	Studia Philonica Monographs
SR	*Studies in Religion*
StBibLit	Studies in Biblical Literature (Lang)
StBibSlov	*Studia Biblica Slovaca*
STJ	*Stulos Theological Journal*
StSpir	*Studies in Spirituality*
StZ	*Stimmen der Zeit*
SUSIA	Skrifter Utgivna av Svenska Institutet I Athen
SVTQ	*St. Vladimir's Theological Quarterly*
SWJT	*Southwestern Journal of Theology*
TBei	*Theologische Beiträge*
TDNT	*Theological Dictionary of the New Testament*. Edited by Gerhard Kittel and Gerhard Friedrich. Translated by Geoffrey W. Bromiley. 10 vols. Grand Rapids: Eerdmans, 1964–76.
ThQ	*Theologische Quartalschrift*
TJ	*Trinity Journal*
TLG	*Thesaurus Linguae Graecae: Canon of Greek Authors and Works*. Edited by Luci Berkowitz and Karl A. Squitier. 3rd ed. New York: Oxford University Press, 1990.
TLZ	*Theologische Literaturzeitung*
TNTC	Tyndale New Testament Commentaries
TS	*Theological Studies*
TSHP	Texts and Studies in the History of Philosophy
TSJTSA	Texts and Studies of the Jewish Theological Seminary of America
TTKi	*Tidsskrift for Teologi og Kirke*
TTZ	*Trierer Theologische Zeitschrift*
TynBul	*Tyndale Bulletin*
TZ	*Theologische Zeitschrift*
VC	*Vigiliae Christianae*
VE	*Vox Evangelica*
VerbEc	*Verbum et Ecclesia*
VH	*Vivens Homo*
WBC	Word Biblical Commentary
WUNT	Wissenschaftliche Untersuchungen zum Neuen Testament
YCS	Yale Classical Studies
ZAW	*Zeitschrift für die alttestamentliche Wissenschaft*
ZKG	*Zeitschrift für Kirchengeschichte*
ZKT	*Zeitschrift für katholische Theologie*
ZNT	*Zeitschrift für Neues Testament*
ZNW	*Zeitschrift für die neutestamentliche Wissenschaft und die Kunde der älteren Kirche*
ZRGG	*Zeitschrift für Religions- und Geistesgeschichte*
ZTK	*Zeitschrift für Theologie und Kirche*

1

⊚ ⊚ ⊘ ⊚

The Corrupted Mind
(Rom. 1:18–32)

> Just as they did not judge it fitting to have God in their cognitive
> purview, God delivered them over to a mind that was unfit, so they
> would do things that should not be done.
>
> —Romans 1:28

In the first chapter of Romans, Paul addresses the corrupted mind of the Gentile world; he will address the more knowledgeable Jewish mind in Romans 7:7–25. Ancient thinkers regularly opposed reason to the passions: the wise would overcome passions through truth. In Romans 1:18–32 Paul paints a more complicated picture of reason and passions, one that fits Jewish condemnations of paganism.[1]

In this passage Paul argues that humanity irrationally distorted God's image through idolatry and that God in turn expressed his wrath against this idolatry by handing them over to their own irrational desires. Unreasonable thinking

---

1. I use "pagan" not to designate a set of religious views but to communicate the essential perspective that most early Jews and Christians held concerning most non-Jews, especially polytheists.

led to humanity's subjection to passion. People's unfit ways of thinking are
the consequence of their rejection of God's truth.[2]

The Pagan World's Corrupted Mind

To establish that all humanity needs Christ, Paul first establishes what was
probably not actually in dispute among believers in Jesus: that the Gentile
world (i.e., unconverted non-Jews) did not know God (cf. Gal. 4:8; 1 Thess.
4:5). This premise will prepare for Paul's argument that the possession of
the Torah, a revelation far superior to what the Gentiles possessed, does not
guarantee that Paul's own Jewish people know God adequately either (cf. Rom.
2:1–29). Indeed, it merely makes them more culpable, so that all humanity
stands under sin (Rom. 3:9–20).

Summary of Paul's Likely Argument

Paul's argument in Romans 1:18–32, in summary, appears to run as follows:
God judges humanity for their wicked action of suppressing and perverting
the truth about him through idolatry (1:18, 23). Humanity is culpable for
their false images of God because in creation—especially in humans, created
in God's image—God has revealed what he is like (1:19–20). God therefore
judges humanity by handing them over to their own corrupted thinking (1:24,
26, 28). This wrong thinking probably includes distorting the image of God in
themselves (1:24–27). As they have dishonored God (1:21), God has allowed
them to dishonor each other (1:24) with what Paul calls "dishonorable" and
"shameful" passions (1:26–27). In the end they have committed all kinds of
sins, even though they ultimately know better (1:28–32).

Although worded in various ways, the language of reason, knowledge,
and truth pervades this passage, explaining that pagans' current irrationally
immoral "mind" or "way of thinking" (1:28) stems from humanity's own
sinful choices. Such language includes the following elements: Humanity originally had enough knowledge about God to honor him (1:19–21); by finding
imaginative ways around that truth, they willfully distorted it (1:21, 25). Their
reasoning became void and empty, like the idols they made; their hearts, now
lacking understanding, were darkened (1:21). They became foolish—even
while claiming to be wise (1:21–22; cf. 1:14). They no longer approved true
knowledge about God, so God gave them disapproved minds so they would
do what was improper (1:28). Just as humanity initially knew enough that

2. Cf. also minds alienated from God in Eph. 2:3; 4:18; Col. 1:21.

they should have honored God, they also knew enough to understand that their wicked treatment of God and others—who, like themselves, were all created in God's image—merited judgment (1:32). Nevertheless, they chose to justify rather than to reject such behavior (1:32).[3] Thus they rejected truth, and God punished them by allowing them to become incapable of discerning truth, not only theologically but morally as well.[4]

Paul's depiction of the culpable Gentile world under sin fits one line of Jewish thought about Gentiles[5] and prepares for his larger argument about all of humanity being under sin (2:1–3:31).[6] Gentiles lack the fuller moral truth of God's Torah; Paul will argue in chapter 7 that even that knowledge cannot transform fully. My focus in this chapter, however, is more specifically on Paul's depiction of Gentile thinking ruled by, and sometimes justifying, passion.

An Early Jewish Analogy

The intellectual elements of Paul's argument should have been intelligible to a Diaspora Jewish audience and therefore probably to an early Christian audience, whether Jewish, Gentile, or mixed, many of whose inherited beliefs had been formed in a Diaspora Jewish milieu. Most scholars acknowledge that Paul develops existing Hellenistic Jewish arguments in this section.[7]

Paul's argument follows most closely the popular Wisdom of Solomon.[8] Wisdom declares that truth about God is evident in creation (Wis. 13:1–9); people, however, have failed to infer that truth from the good things that are visible (13:1). Thus, they ended up reducing God's rightful glory by worshiping images of humans or beasts (13:13–14), images of created things (13:10–14:1;

---

3. As Keck (*Romans*, 73) notes, not only does theology affect morality, but morality affects theology and how people think, "largely because we rationalize our behavior."

4. The distortion presumably increases with greater proximity to direct discussion of divine matters, and the level of distortion might be greater in some cultures than others. Paul, however, is offering a graphic depiction of human responsibility that will ultimately encompass even Israel (Rom. 2:1–3:20), not intending a nuanced and systematic anthropology.

5. For the range of ancient Jewish views about Gentiles, see especially Donaldson, *Paul and Gentiles*.

6. Paul's starting place may seem unpleasant, but some other ancient thinkers also recognized that knowledge of one's faults must precede transformation (e.g., Sen. Y. *Ep. Lucil.* 28.9–10).

7. E.g., Jeremias, "Zu Rm 1 22–32"; Schulz, "Anklage," 173.

8. Sanday and Headlam, *Romans*, 52; Stuhlmacher, *Romans*, 35; deSilva, "Wisdom," 1274; Dunn, *Theology*, 91; see esp. schematically Talbert, *Romans*, 63; cf. Lucas, "Unearthing"; arguing for deliberate allusion but by way of contrast, Linebaugh, "Announcing." Although some now date the work later, the traditional first-century BCE date (e.g., Rost, *Judaism*, 59) better explains the many allusions to it in Paul (e.g., Keener, *Corinthians*, 38, 170, 174).

14:8, 11).[9] Once introduced, idolatry grew increasingly worse (14:15–16), and it has led to other vices (14:22–24). These moral consequences include sexual sin (14:12, 24) and have climaxed in a number of vices (14:25–26).

Like Paul, the author of Wisdom of Solomon notes the intellectual element in humanity's folly. Idols deceived the ignorant (Wis. 14:18), and idolatry led people astray from the knowledge of God (14:22).[10] Such images, or idols, revealed that people harbored wrong thinking about God (14:30). Paul, however, condemns Gentiles even more harshly than Wisdom of Solomon does, by emphasizing that Gentiles knew the truth and were not simply ignorant (Rom. 1:20–21, 32).[11] Paul's argument may presuppose an element of corporate guilt in that some earlier Gentiles made truth less accessible to later generations; while Paul might expect his ideal audience to share his knowledge of this element of the biblical narrative, however, he does not address such explanations. He is establishing a premise for his following argument in Romans 2, not writing a complete essay on salvation history.

God's Wrath against Idolaters

In Romans 1:18–23 God is angry (1:18) with those who suppress the obvious truth about him and substitute false and inferior conceptions of deity in place of the truth (1:19–23).[12] Paul views this deliberate ignorance in both moral and intellectual terms.

Although it becomes most explicit in 1:23, Paul is probably challenging idolatry throughout 1:18–23. In principle, Paul's language of "ungodliness" or "impiety" (ἀσέβεια, 1:18) could refer to any action hostile toward a deity,[13] and some thinkers viewed ignorance—especially about the right way to serve

---

9. See Poniży, "Recognition"; here and elsewhere, cf. Dafni, "Theologie." But this work may not be representative of Diaspora Judaism here; see Collins, "Natural Theology."

10. For idolatry as foolish, see also *Jub.* 36:5; Wis. 11:15; 14:11; condemning the "wisdom" of idolatry, see *Let. Aris.* 137.

11. Hooker, "Adam," 299; Talbert, *Romans*, 62–63; Bryan, *Preface*, 78; Keck, *Romans*, 62; Matera, *Romans*, 44, 49; viewing this difference as a source of later patristic intolerance, cf. Gaca, "Declaration," 3–6.

12. The meaning of Paul's euphemistic circumlocution "from heaven" was likely obvious enough to ancient hearers; see, e.g., Dan. 4:26; *1 En.* 6:2; 1 Macc. 3:18–19, 50, 60; 3 Macc. 4:21; Luke 15:18; *m. Ab.* 1:3; *Sipra Behuq. pq.* 6.267.2.1. On periphrasis, see, e.g., *Rhet. Her.* 4.32.43; Hermog. *Method* 8 (esp. 8.421–23); Rowe, "Style," 127; Anderson, *Glossary*, 102. For euphemism, cf. Hermog. *Inv.* 4.11.200–201; *Pesiq. Rab Kah.* 4:2; Anderson, *Glossary*, 60; Tal, "Euphemisms." For avoiding anthropomorphisms already in the LXX, see Gard, *Method*, esp. 32–46. For divine wrath from heaven, see, e.g., *1 En.* 83:9; 91:7; *Sib. Or.* 1.165.

13. E.g., Dio Chrys. *Or.* 32.80; Arius Did. 2.7.11k, p. 84.4–6, 11–12, 21–22.

the gods—as impiety.[14] Paul is not thinking in merely general terms, however. The climactic sin in this paragraph is idolatry (1:23).[15] In this context the truth that people have suppressed unjustly (1:18) is the truth about God (1:19–21), and they especially suppressed this truth by worshiping created things rather than the creator (1:23, 25).[16]

Some Greek philosophers rejected the notion of divine wrath,[17] but other Gentiles thought differently.[18] Jewish sources certainly acknowledge God's wrath,[19] including in response to idolatry.[20] In the context of Romans 1:24–32, God expresses this wrath in the present (1:18) by handing humanity over to their own moral insanity (see discussion below).

Information about God in Creation

Paul treats faith as accepting divine truth, and the rebellion of sin as the result of deliberately rejecting divine truth (Rom. 1:16–18). Thus, as God's righteousness is revealed for salvation in the good news about Jesus (1:16–17), it apparently is also revealed in just wrath against those who suppress the truth (1:18).[21] This observation contrasts not only salvation with wrath but also faith (1:16–17) with suppression of the truth (1:18), suggesting that what Paul means by "faith" is, in contrast to some applications of the English term in recent centuries, simply embracing the divine truth.[22]

14. Esp. Stoics, e.g., Arius Did. 2.7.5b12, p. 26.12–15; 2.7.11k, p. 84.24, 29; though cf. 2.7.5b, p. 12.2–12; cf. Diog. Laert. 2.93; Marc. Aur. 9.1.2. Others besides Stoics associated ignorance with evil, e.g., Porph. *Marc.* 13.225.

15. Diaspora Jews could associate impiety with idolatry (e.g., *Sib. Or.* 3.36; cf. connection with homosexual acts in *Sib. Or.* 3.184–86 and with judgment in 3.568).

16. Note the interpretations (in Bray, *Romans*, 34–35) of Origen *Comm. Rom.* on 1:18 (*CER* 1:134, 140); Ambrosiaster *Comm.* (CSEL 81:39); Apollinaris of Laodicea, catena on Rom. 1:18 (*PGK* 15:59). For idolatry as turning from truth, see, e.g., *T. Mos.* 5:2–4 (Israel); cf. even the later Neoplatonist concern with some images distorting divine truth (Iambl. *Letter* 18.1–3, in Stob. *Anth.* 3.11.35).

17. See, e.g., Epict. *Diatr.* 2.19.26 (though contrast 2.8.14); Max. Tyre *Or.* 9.2; Porph. *Marc.* 18.302–4; more moderately, Iambl. *Myst.* 1.13.

18. See, e.g., Val. Max. 1.1.16–21; 1.1.ext.1–1.1.ext.9; Philost. *Hrk.* 53.17; especially in the ancient Near East, see Kratz and Spieckermann, *Wrath.*

19. E.g., 1 Esd. 8:21; 1 Macc. 3:8; Jdt. 9:9; Bar. 2:13, 20; *Jub.* 15:34; CD 8.3; *Sib. Or.* 1.179.

20. E.g., *Sib. Or.* 3.763, 766; 5.75–76 (in view of 5.77–85); *Sipre Deut.* 96.2.1.

21. See, e.g., Reicke, "Natürliche Theologie"; Stagg, "Plight." This need not mean (*pace* Cranfield, "Romans 1.18," 335) that the wrath of Rom. 1:18 is also revealed in the gospel. Technically, 1:18 says only that "wrath" is revealed, but a contextual contrast with God's righteousness as salvation (1:16–17) is rendered more likely because Paul contrasts wrath and salvation elsewhere (Rom. 5:9; 1 Thess. 5:9; cf. Rom. 9:22–24).

22. Contrast Rom. 1:25; 2:8. For Paul, Jewish people, conversely, have some truth in the law (Rom. 2:20), though not the fullness available in Christ; cf. Eph. 1:13; 2 Thess. 2:12–13. Here Paul would envision faith not as a "leap in the dark" (to borrow Kierkegaard's oft-cited

Excursus: Knowledge of God in Ancient Mediterranean Thought

Greek thought highly valued the knowledge of deity.[23] Although this interest was not limited to philosophers, it particularly predominates there.[24] For example, a Cynic writer believes that the true knowledge of God includes right understanding of God's character, as revealed by creation rather than mortals' rituals.[25] The Stoic Seneca contends that knowing what God is like would deliver mortals from superstition.[26] A later Neoplatonist emphasizes correct understanding about God that leads to correctly approaching him and to one's mind being conformed to his character.[27] To a Pythagorean writer, knowledge of God leads to quietness,[28] which perhaps reflects the understanding of one's proper station that correct self-knowledge was thought to produce. Yet most philosophers held that knowledge of God was quite rare.[29] Many writers echoed Plato's view concerning knowledge of God: "To discover the Maker and Father of this universe is a task, and after discovering him it is impossible to tell of him" to others.[30]

---

but perhaps differently intended phrase, presupposing a Kantian dichotomy of subjective faith and objective reason) but as a deliberate response to the convincing and persuasive light of truth. He never would have associated it with our popular conception of "make-believe," in which one tries to convince oneself and so, by strong wishing, to exercise power over internal or (magically) external reality.

23. I condense the following discussion from Keener, *John*, 237–38, 240–43. Translators typically use "God" for the universal or ultimate deity in these passages, without implying any assimilation to the Judean God.

24. For one mystery cult's interest in the knowledge of God, as interpreted by an educated Greek for an intellectual audience, see Plut. *Isis* 2, *Mor.* 352A. For revelatory knowledge of the divine in the mysteries, cf. also Goodenough, *Church*, 7. Reitzenstein (*Mystery-Religions*, 364–425) emphasizes the mysteries but relies much too heavily on later sources, many of which may betray Christian influence. Paul's desire to transmit λόγος and acquire "knowledge" places him closer to philosophical schools than to the mysteries (cf. also Malherbe, *Social Aspects*, 47–48, on Edwin Judge's approach).

25. Heracl. *Ep.* 4, to Hermodorus; cf. Epict. *Diatr.* 1.6.24.

26. Sen. Y. *Ep. Lucil.* 95.48. For Seneca, to know God (*deum nosse*) meant to know the mind of the universe (*Nat. Q.* 1.pref.13). For Musonius Rufus, cutting off the dead part of the soul enabled one to know God (Mus. Ruf. 53, p. 144.24–25).

27. Porph. *Marc.* 11.194–95; 13.229; 17.282; 20.331; 21.347–48; 22.355, 359; 24.379–81; cf. 11.204.

28. *Pyth. Sent.* 16 (Malherbe, *Moral Exhortation*, 110). Apollonius of Tyana reportedly knew the gods personally rather than by mere opinion (Philost. *Vit. Apoll.* 1.1).

29. Sen. Y. *Ep. Lucil.* 31.10.

30. Plato *Tim.* 28C, as quoted and interpreted in Nock, "Gnosticism," 267; see also Dodd, "Prologue," 16.

The Alexandrian Jewish philosopher Philo insists on proper knowledge about God;[31] he even replaces manna with heavenly knowledge[32] and indicates that the Logos dwells in knowledge.[33] Those with true knowledge of God are aptly entitled God's children.[34] Nature attests God's reality, but God himself remains essentially unknowable by natural means.[35] Wisdom also leads to the knowledge of God,[36] but even philosophic reflection on what is proper does not necessarily lead beyond human thoughts; the mind must value God above all else, do everything it does on account of God, and ascend into knowledge of God.[37] Philo combines revelation with intuition;[38] as important as reason is, the highest mysteries are available only through direct experience with God.[39]

Judean sources also valued divine knowledge. In Scripture, knowing God often has an ethical component (e.g., Jer. 22:16).[40] "Knowledge of God" in the Hebrew Bible usually indicates a right relationship with him, one predicated on proper knowledge about him and expressed in genuine piety.[41] Knowing God also can express intimacy with God[42] and can indicate the covenant relationship (cf. Hosea 2:20).[43] In Scripture God often acts in a self-revealing way so that people "might know that I am YHWH."[44]

The Dead Sea Scrolls heavily emphasize knowledge of God.[45] Thus, the author of one Qumran document extols God as the source of knowledge who enlightens the writer to understand God's mysteries.[46] For the Qumran

31. Philo *Mos.* 1.212; *Drunkenness* 43, 45; cf. *Posterity* 12; *Dreams* 1.231.

32. See Borgen, *Bread*, 127–28.

33. Philo *Flight* 76.

34. Philo *Conf.* 145.

35. For a discussion of Philo's view of divine ineffability, see Wolfson, *Philo*, 2:94–164, esp. 110–38; Mondin, "Esistenza."

36. Philo *Unchangeable* 143.

37. Philo *Alleg. Interp.* 3.126.

38. Wolfson, *Philo*, 1:36, citing Philo *Sacr.* 78, 79. Wolfson thinks Philonic knowledge is essentially intellectual, although it includes philosophical frenzy (*Philo*, 2:3–10). Dodd emphasizes the mystical element (*Interpretation*, 62).

39. Hagner, "Vision," 87, provides references.

40. This dimension continued in early Judaism; cf. Shapiro, "Wisdom." Cf. moral dimensions of knowledge, sometimes connected with justice, in the Dead Sea Scrolls (1QM 13.3; Wilcox, "Dualism," 89, cites 1QS 3.1; 1QH 19.8 [Sukenik 11.8]; cf. 1QS 8.9; 9.17).

41. Dentan, *Knowledge*, 35.

42. Cf. the sense of knowing in Gen. 4:1; Pss. 1:6; 55:13; 88:18; Dentan, *Knowledge*, 37–38.

43. Cf. Huffmon, "Background," 37; cf. obedience in Hosea 4:1; 5:4; 8:2.

44. E.g., Exod. 6:7; 7:5, 17; 10:2; 14:4, 18; 16:12; 1 Kings 20:13; 20:28; and more than fifty times in Ezekiel.

45. See, e.g., Fritsch, *Community*, 73–74; Allegro, *Scrolls*, 132–33; Price, "Light from Qumran," 26; Flusser, *Judaism*, 57–59; Lohse, *Colossians*, 25.

46. 1QS 10.12; 11.3.

sect, knowledge was a gift from the Spirit.[47] Knowledge was salvific, and its focus was on understanding the Torah, which God had given to the Teacher of Righteousness and those who followed him.[48] In the Scrolls,[49] as in the Old Testament,[50] knowledge will be complete in the eschatological time.

For pre-Christian sages, knowledge of God included the recognition that he alone is the true God.[51] The wicked were those who did not know him[52] or his law[53] and might mock the righteous for claiming to have the knowledge of God.[54] In the late second century Rabbi Meir interpreted "know the Lord" in Hosea 2:22 (2:20 ET) as referring to those sharing the qualities listed in Hosea 2:21–22 (2:19–20 ET) knowing God's will.[55] The rabbis, who emphasized knowledge specifically of the law,[56] taught that one would know God through learning[57] and obeying[58] his law; some rabbis believed that one would come to know God truly even through studying haggadah.[59] In Jewish thought only Israel possessed the law, and therefore only Israel knew God.[60]

Because many Gentile thinkers highly valued the knowledge of God, they would have agreed that suppressing the truth about God is a serious act of impiety. Some ancient thinkers insisted that nature gave human minds a longing for truth;[61] thus, knowingly suppressing it by denying the existence of the gods is not merely ignorance but evil.[62] For some, as for Paul here, belief in a deity could be a basic element of reason, "one of those norms of which

47. Lohse, *Colossians*, 25–26, citing 1QS 4.4; 1QSb 5.25; 1QH^a 20.11–12; 6.25 (Sukenik 12.11–12; 14.25). Painter, "Gnosticism," 2, cites 1QS 3.6–7; 4.6.

48. Garnet, "Light," 20, citing 1QH 4.5–6, 23–24, 27–28; 5.20–39; 8.4–26; 9.29–36.

49. 1QS 4.22; 1QM 11.15; 1Q27 1.7.

50. E.g., Isa. 11:9; 52:6; Jer. 24:7; 31:34 (toned down in *Tg. Jer.* on 31:34); Ezek. 34:30; 36:23–28; 37:6, 12–14, 27–28; Hosea 2:19–20; Joel 3:17; Hab. 2:14; cf. 1 Cor. 13:8–12.

51. Sir. 36:5 (alternative location 33:5).

52. Wis. 2:22; 12:27; 13:1; 14:22; 16:16; Sir. 36:5.

53. *2 Bar.* 48:40.

54. Wis. 2:13.

55. *Abot R. Nat.* 37 A.

56. E.g., *b. Ber.* 33a; *Sanh.* 92a; earlier, Bar. 3:36; 4:1. See also Wewers, "Wissen," 143–48; Bultmann, "Γινώσκω," 701.

57. *Sipre Deut.* 41.3.2.

58. *Sipre Deut.* 33.1.1.

59. *Sipre Deut.* 49.2.2.

60. E.g., *4 Ezra* 3:32; *2 Bar.* 14:5; 48:40.

61. Cic. *Tusc.* 1.19.44.

62. Cic. *Nat. d.* 2.16.44 (reporting the Stoic view).

reason consists."[63] Some Gentiles believed that the earliest people had true knowledge that became enshrined in religion.[64] Many Gentiles also believed that humanity had declined morally from the earlier era.[65]

One basic conviction about deity that was widely shared was that the existence of deity was self-evident. As in Paul's perspective, exemplified in Romans 1, most ancient thinkers believed that they recognized divine design in nature.[66] Epicureans, who denied divine design in nature, were deemed idiosyncratic.[67] Socrates, for example, thought that nature revealed divine benevolence and thus invited praise.[68] Stoics also inferred God's existence from order in nature.[69] They could thus claim that Zeus was manifest in his works in creation.[70] The Jewish philosopher Philo also believed that creation provided understanding about its designer.[71] Some other Jews conversant with Greek thought affirmed that Moses declared that God was revealed by his works.[72]

---

63. Stowers, "Self-Mastery," 543. Though some atheists existed (see Winiarczyk, "Altertum"), they were a clear minority (Sext. Emp. *Pyr.* 3.218). Sextus Empiricus suspended judgment about the existence of the gods (*Pyr.* 3.218–38). For a survey including ancient rationalism and atheism, see Meijer, "Philosophers." For their arguments, see Ps.-Plut. *Plac.* 1.7.1–10, especially in Runia, "Atheists." On Prodicus's atheism, see Henrichs, "Notes" (though even Prodicus did not reject all deities, only the Olympians; Henrichs, "Atheism").

64. See Van Nuffelen, "*Divine Antiquities.*"

65. See Max. Tyre *Or.* 36.1–2 (in Malherbe, *Moral Exhortation*, 73); Stowers, *Rereading*, 85, 98–99, 122 (citing, e.g., Sen. Y. *Ep. Lucil.* 90; Anacharsis *Ep.* 9). For the decline from the primeval golden age, see, e.g., Hesiod *W.D.* 110–201 (though not all were inferior to their predecessors; Ovid *Metam.* 1.89–312 (with further impiety growing from the first impieties; *Metam.* 15.111–13); Babr. prologue 1–4. Moral decline also recapitulated itself in the Roman state (Sall. *Catil.* 6.6–13.5).

66. Cic. *Nat. d.* 2.32.81–82; 2.54.133–58.146 (though this Stoic argument also identifies God with the cosmos; cf. Gelinas, "Argument"); Dio Chrys. *Or.* 12.33–34; Plut. *Isis* 76, *Mor.* 382A. Though some readers today know of divine design as a traditional argument in monotheistic religions (sometimes deployed for or against evolution), it was actually common among polytheistic thinkers in antiquity.

67. Dio Chrys. *Or.* 12.36–37.

68. Xen. *Mem.* 4.3.12–13. For divine benevolence, see also Sen. Y. *Ep. Lucil.* 95.50; Epict. *Diatr.* 2.14.11.

69. Epict. *Diatr.* 1.6.7–8; cf. Sen. Y. *Nat. Q.* 1.pref.14–15. Paul uses further language amenable to Stoics in Rom. 1:26, 28; cf. other passages noted in Glover, *Paul*, 20–21. For Stoics deploying creation discourse for moral instruction (as Paul does), cf. Sisson, "Discourse."

70. Epict. *Diatr.* 1.6.23–24.

71. Di Mattei, "Physiologia." For Philo's proofs of God's existence, see Wolfson, *Philo*, 2:73–93.

72. *Let. Aris.* 131–32; Jos. *Ag. Ap.* 2.190; perhaps *T. Naph.* 3:3. This revelation of his power does not reveal his essence (Jos. *Ag. Ap.* 2.167). Gentiles failed to infer the craftsman from his works (Wis. 13:1). The OT writers already saw God's order in creation, sometimes even in language comparable to laws; cf. Pss. 19:1–6 (in the context of 19:7–11); 33:6, 9 (in the context of 33:4); 119:90–91; 147:15–19; in Egypt and Mesopotamia, cf. Walton, *Thought*, 192–93.

Later rabbis even developed the tradition that Abraham reasoned back to a first cause.[73]

Ancient thinkers would also understand Paul's language about some knowledge of God being obvious within humans (Rom. 1:19).[74] Many regarded knowledge about God as innate within people.[75] Early humans could not remain ignorant, some thinkers opined, because Zeus had given them "intelligence and the capacity for reason," and nature's splendors testified about him.[76] That all peoples had some conception of deities, they reasoned, showed that this truth was innate or implanted in everyone.[77] Similarly, divine design is evident within the human body[78] and especially in human reason.[79]

Some thinkers connected human reason with the divine Reason that designed the universe.[80] Like many other Middle Platonists,[81] Philo believed that God used the world of intellect as a pattern for the material world.[82] He argues that God formed the universe through his *logos*, or reason.[83] In Philo *logos* is not only divine Reason structuring matter but, as in some other Middle Platonic thought, a pattern that is God's image.[84] Philo connects the creative *logos* with the wisdom of Reason by which God draws the ideal wise

73. Davies, *Paul*, 28–29; cf. comment below (p. 15).

74. Paul could mean that it was simply obvious *to* them (cf. Jer. 40:6 LXX [33:6 ET]; perhaps Gal. 1:16), but analogous language in Rom. 8:17–19 probably suggests that Paul refers to something within them (cf. Rom. 1:24; 2:15; 11:17; 2 Cor. 6:16). Among ancient commentators, see (in Bray, *Romans*, 38) Chrys. *Hom. Rom.* 3; Ps.-Const. *Rom.* (*ENPK* 24); Pelagius *Comm. Rom.* on 1:19.

75. E.g., Dio Chrys. *Or.* 12.27; Iambl. *Myst.* 1.3. In Stoicism, cf. Jackson-McCabe, "Preconceptions."

76. Dio Chrys. *Or.* 12.28 (trans. Cohoon, LCL, 1:33).

77. Cic. *Tusc.* 1.13.30; Sen. Y. *Ep. Lucil.* 117.6; cf. Max. Tyre *Or.* 11.5; Artem. *Oneir.* 1.8.

78. Cic. *Fin.* 5.12.35–36; cf. Sen. Y. *Ben.* 6.23.6–7; *Let. Aris.* 156–57.

79. Cic. *Nat. d.* 2.59.147–61.153; Epict. *Diatr.* 1.6.10; 1.6.25.

80. Philo uses ἀρχιτέκτονος, "master builder," for God in *Creation* 24; *Names* 30. Some Middle Platonists blended Plato's creator with the Stoic logos (Dillon, "Plato," 806).

81. Plato thought that God had built the universe according to the ideal pattern shaped by reason (Plato *Tim.* 29A–30), and some Middle Platonists came to take this literally, attributing matter's origin to Soul (Plut. *Epitome of Gen. of Soul* 2, *Mor.* 1030E; *Table* 8.2.4, *Mor.* 720AB; later, cf. Plot. *Enn.* 3.2).

82. Philo *Creation* 16; *Conf.* 171.

83. Philo *Creation* 20, 26, 31; *Migr.* 6. I borrow and condense material here from Keener, *John*, 376–79.

84. Philo *Creation* 17–19, 25, 31. For the Logos as God's image, see also Philo *Conf.* 97; *Flight* 101; Wisdom as God's image, *Alleg. Interp.* 1.43. Thus, God made the world as a copy of his divine image, the *logos* being his archetypal seal imprinted on them (Philo *Creation* 16, 26, 36). For God using a pattern in creation, cf. also *Jub.* 2:2; 1QS 11.11; *m. Sanh.* 4:5; *Gen. Rab.* 1:1.

person to himself.[85] The human mind is allied to this divine Reason, or *logos*, because it is a copy of it.[86]

Some early Christian thinkers also developed this conventional notion that truth about God could be inferred from creation,[87] although they differed as to the extent to which this potential proved effective.[88] Contrary to what is argued by some of Paul's interpreters, Paul apparently does believe that people can infer some truth about God from nature, although in a limited way.[89] What this belief means is debated; some distinguish between natural theology and general revelation, or between knowledge about God that humans can infer from nature on their own and God revealing himself to them in nature.[90] In any case, Paul is not trying to demonstrate God's existence but is insisting that Gentiles already know of him.[91] The revelation was sufficient to bring just condemnation, but not salvation, which is revealed only in the good news about Jesus (Rom. 1:16–17).[92]

Corrupted Minds Resist Rational Evidence from Creation

Paul complains that God had revealed rationally perceptible truth in creation, but people created alternative and inferior frameworks of thought

---

85. Philo *Sacr.* 8; each individual's mind fits the image of the universal mind in *Creation* 69. Cf. *logos* as the shared element of human reason and the reason that structured the cosmos in Thorsteinsson, "Stoicism," 23; Long, *Philosophy*, 108. For Stoics, the human mind was an example of universal reason (Cic. *Nat d.* 2.6.18–2.8.20; cf. 2.8.21–2.13.32; cf. also Murray, *Stages*, 167, citing Chrysippus frg. 913 [*SVF*]). The connection goes back to Heraclitus (see Long, *Philosophy*, 131, 145), who identified thought (γνώμη) as what guides the cosmos (Diog. Laert. 9.1.1). (Some have doubted Heraclitus's *logos* doctrine [Glasson, "Doctrine"], but the evidence, while scant [Glasson, "Doctrine," 232], remains [Lee, *Thought*, 79; Miller, "Logos," 174–75].) Zeno reportedly identified the all-pervasive *logos* with both the universal law of nature and Zeus (Diog. Laert. 7.1.88). For Stoics, reason (λόγος) was the active principle that acted on matter (Diog. Laert. 7.1.134); Anaxagoras described mind (νοῦς, Diog. Laert. 2.8) in this way. Later Platonism also absorbed many of these concepts (Dillon, *Middle Platonists*, 80, 83).

86. Philo *Creation* 146.

87. E.g., Theoph. 1.5–6; and (in Bray, *Romans*, 37–38) Origen *Comm. Rom.* on 1:19 (*CER* 1:136–42), and on 1:20 (esp. regarding philosophers; *CER* 1:142); Ambrosiaster *Comm.* (CSEL 81:39, 41); Apollinaris of Laodicea, catena on Rom. 1:19 (*PGK* 15:59).

88. Most believed that it secured humanity's just condemnation (Bray, *Romans*, 34; Reasoner, *Full Circle*, 12); only rarely did it lead some to divine knowledge (Reasoner, *Full Circle*, 12–13). But cf. Theodoret *Comm. 1 Cor.* 171 (in Bray, *Corinthians*, 14–15).

89. See observations in Moo, *Romans*, 123.

90. Ott, "Dogmatisches Problem," 50; Coffey, "Knowledge," 676; Johnson, "Knowledge," 73; Talbert, *Romans*, 62–63 (following Reicke, "Natürliche Theologie"; Brunner, *Romans*, 17); Efferin, "Study." For natural revelation as needing or inseparable from special revelation in Christ, cf. Dennison, "Revelation"; historic views in Vandermarck, "Knowledge."

91. O'Rourke, "Revelation," 306; Hooker, "Adam," 299.

92. Cf. Oden, "Excuse"; Young, "Knowledge"; Cobb and Lull, *Romans*, 41; Calvin in Reasoner, *Full Circle*, 16–17.

to evade God's truth. Because they refused the truth they had, they became incapable of discerning truth. In Romans 1:20–21 Paul argues that God's revelation, including his "invisible characteristics" (ἀόρατα), is "seen" (καθορᾶται, 1:20) and that the resistant heart has been "darkened" (ἐσκοτίσθη, 1:21), playing on the widespread ancient use of vision as an analogy for knowing.[93] Many thinkers emphasized the vision of the mind, often of the divine,[94] especially in the Platonic tradition.[95] This emphasis is frequent in Philo, a Jewish eclectic Middle Platonist thinker;[96] for example, he condemns blindness of soul[97] and emphasizes that, given the transcendence of God,[98] divine inspiration in the soul is the best way to envision him.[99]

Humanity refused to act on true knowledge about the creator by honoring him or being grateful (Rom. 1:21). Paul probably viewed this expression of resisting true knowledge as not merely negligent but also defiant. Ingratitude was considered an abominable offense;[100] Seneca deemed it a more fundamental vice than adultery, murder, or tyranny, allowing that these other vices might spring from it.[101] Ingratitude toward deities, however, was easily recognizable as the worst expression of ingratitude.[102] Failure to act in accordance with truth about God ultimately deprived mortals of truth.

Paul emphasizes the corruption of Gentile minds in Romans 1:21–22 and 28, often echoing biblical phraseology. Thus in 1:21, for example, "they became

93. E.g., Max. Tyre *Or.* 6.1. See the discussion later in the book (pp. 207–9; probably 2 Cor. 3:17); much more fully, Keener, *John,* 247–50; and esp. Keener, *Acts,* 4:3524–26.

94. E.g., Cic. *Tusc.* 1.19.44; Marc. Aur. 11.1.1 (cf. 10.26).

95. E.g., Plato *Phaedo* 65E; 66A; 83A; Max. Tyre *Or.* 9.6; 10.3; 11.9, 11; 38.3; Iambl. *Pyth. Life* 6.31; 16.70; 32.228; Plot. *Enn.* 1.6.9; Porph. *Marc.* 16.274; cf. Kirk, *Vision,* 16–18.

96. Cf. Philo *Flight* 19; *Spec. Laws* 1.37; 3.4, 6; *Unchangeable* 181; *Sacr.* 36, 69, 78; *Posterity* 8, 118; *Worse* 22; *Plant.* 22; *Drunkenness* 44; *Sober* 3; *Conf.* 92; *Migr.* 39, 48, 165, 191; *Heir* 89; *Prelim. St.* 135; *Names* 3, 203; *Abr.* 58, 70; *Dreams* 1.117; 2.160; *Mos.* 1.185, 289; *Rewards* 37.

97. Philo *Worse* 22; *Dreams* 1.164; Isaacs, *Spirit,* 50; Dillon, "Transcendence in Philo"; Hagner, "Vision," 89–90. The image was long standard even in drama; see, e.g., Soph. *Oed. tyr.* 371, 375, 402–3, 419, 454, 747, 1266–79.

98. Cf., e.g., Philo *Abr.* 80; *Spec. Laws* 1.37; for limitations, cf., e.g., *Rewards* 36, 39–40.

99. Philo *Sacr.* 78; *Conf.* 92; *Names* 3–6; *QG* 4.138. For "Israel" as "the one who sees God," see *Conf.* 92, 146; *Dreams* 1.171; *Abr.* 57.

100. See, e.g., Xen. *Mem.* 2.2.2–3; *Cyr.* 1.2.6–7; *Rhet. Alex.* 36, 1442a.13–14; Polyb. 6.6.6; Val. Max. 2.6.6; 2.6.7a; 5.3; Vell. Paterc. 2.57.1; 2.62.5; 2.69.1; Sen. Y. *Ep. Lucil.* 81.1, 28; Pliny *Ep.* 8.18.3; Suet. *Claud.* 25.1; Arius Did. 2.7.11k, pp. 80–81.21–25; Lucian *Fisherman* 5; *Tim.* 35; Jos. *Ant.* 19.361; 2 Tim. 3:2; see, further, the commentary in Keener, *Acts,* 3:3314–15.

101. Sen. Y. *Ben.* 1.10.4. Likewise, Cicero charged that ingratitude "includes all sins" (Cic. *Att.* 8.4 [trans. Winstedt, LCL, 2:117]). For Roman gratitude in terms of repaying benefaction, see Harrison, *Grace,* 40–43.

102. Porph. *Marc.* 23.372.

worthless" (ἐματαιώθησαν, from ματαιόω) in their "reasonings" (διαλογισμοῖς) echoes the language of Psalm 93:11 (LXX; 94:11 ET), where merely human reasonings are worthless (διαλογισμοὺς . . . μάταιοι).[103] Paul may choose this wording for another reason, since "worthless" was also a common Jewish designation for, or was often associated with, idols.[104]

That sinners' hearts, lacking understanding, were darkened probably also echoes biblical language[105] and would have been widely intelligible. Ignorance could be viewed as darkness,[106] the realm that impaired vision. Similarly, Stoics viewed the ignorant masses as "blind,"[107] and many depicted ignorance as blindness,[108] particularly in moral or divine matters.[109] Gentile thinkers recognized that vices blinded people.[110] Jewish authors agreed that sin blinded people;[111] they also recognized that, as here, God could punish deliberate ignorance with further spiritual blindness.[112]

In the very process of boasting of their self-made wisdom, mortals became more foolish (Rom. 1:22). That professed wisdom could be folly was recognized by all who criticized some other, often rival, philosophic schools.[113] That a Jewish writer would view idolatrous Gentiles as ignorant is even less surprising.[114]

103. With Byrne, *Romans*, 74. Paul cites the verse more explicitly in 1 Cor. 3:20.

104. E.g., *Let. Aris.* 136, 139; Wis. 15:8; *Sib. Or.* 3.29, 547–48, 555; Acts 14:15; probably Wis. 13:1; Lev. 17:7; Jer. 2:5. The LXX sometimes translates "idols" with such language (e.g., 1 Kings 16:13, 26; 2 Kings 17:15; 2 Chron. 11:15; Pss. 30:7 [31:6 ET]; 39:5 [40:4 ET]; Jon. 2:9 [2:8 ET]; Isa. 44:9; Jer. 8:19; 10:3, 14–15; 51:18; Ezek. 8:10). It is associated with pagan background in Eph. 4:17; 1 Pet. 1:18.

105. Lack of understanding in the heart may echo Ps. 75:5–6 LXX (76:4–5 ET; Jewett, *Romans*, 158). Jewish sources often used darkness and light figuratively for evil and good, respectively (e.g., 1QS 3.3; 1Q27 1.5–6; 4Q183 2.4–8; *T. Job* 43:6/4; *Sib. Or.* frg. 1.26–27), or with reference to enlightenment in wisdom (Sir. 34:17 [32:20 ET]); this dualism is especially prominent in the DSS (e.g., 1QS 3.19–22; 1QM 13.5–6, 14–15; cf. Charlesworth, "Comparison").

106. Darkness is portrayed as ignorance in Max. Tyre *Or.* 10.6; 29.5. In Val. Max. 7.2.ext.1a, Socrates opines that mortal minds, unlike those of the gods, can be in darkness. Idolatry darkens minds in *T. Sol.* 26:7.

107. Sen. Y. *Ep. Lucil.* 50.3; Epict. *Diatr.* 1.18.4, 6; 2.20.37; 2.24.19; Marc. Aur. 4.29.

108. E.g., Lucian *Phil. Sale* 27; Iambl. *Pyth. Life* 6.31. The image extended beyond philosophic use (e.g., Catullus 64.207–9; Aeschylus *Prom.* 447–48; Val. Max. 7.3.6; Dio Chrys. *Or.* 32.26).

109. E.g., Epict. *Diatr.* 1.18.4, 6; 2.20.37; 2.24.19; Porph. *Marc.* 18.307.

110. Cic. *Tusc.* 1.30.72; Sen. Y. *Ep. Lucil.* 50.3. Cf. sources in Renehan, "Quotations," 20.

111. See, e.g., Isa. 42:18–20; Jer. 5:21; Ezek. 12:2; Wis. 2:21; Jos. *War* 5.343; *T. Jos.* 7:5; cf. *1 En.* 89:33, 41, 54; 90:7; 93:8; 99:8.

112. Isa. 6:9–10; 29:9–10; cf. Deut. 29:4; 2 Thess. 2:10–12.

113. Cf., e.g., Lucian *Phil. Sale* 27.

114. See, e.g., *Jub.* 6:35; 22:18; *t. Shab.* 8:5; Eph. 4:17–18.

The Folly of Idolatry

Paul, like most other Jewish critics of idolatry, expects his audience to understand that idolatry is foolish.[115] This is not to say that most unconverted Gentiles would have agreed. Polytheism was the dominant worldview of antiquity and exerted considerable social pressure, not unlike the force of popular worldviews today.[116] Even many Gentiles, however, would have scorned some of the image veneration described here in Romans 1.

Egyptians were known for worshiping animal images.[117] Greeks and Romans, however, usually despised Egyptian use of animal images,[118] though even Greeks and Romans themselves traditionally thought there were spirits in nature—for example, in trees.[119] Hellenistic and Greco-Roman culture propagated the use of human images for deities,[120] which they viewed as much superior, since people were more like the gods.[121] It is on such human images, however, that Paul will begin his list of idols in Romans 1:23.

Paul already has in mind his explicit argument, in the next section, that all people are sinners. Jewish practices were well known in Rome,[122] and everyone

---

115. The cognitive defect of such behavior appears widely; among second-century Christians, see, e.g., *Diogn.* 2.1.

116. See discussion in Albright, *Biblical Period*, 61; Albright, *Yahweh*, 264, albeit focused on an earlier era; see examples in Pliny E. *N.H.* 28.4.18.

117. E.g., Apollod. *Bibl.* 1.6.3; Pliny E. *N.H.* 8.71.184–86; Libanius *Encom.* 8.14; Lewis, *Life*, 94; Brenk, "Image," 225, 230–31; cf. the animal necropolis in Dhennin, "Necropolis."

118. Pliny E. *N.H.* 2.5.16; Tac. *Hist.* 5.5; Plut. *Isis* 71, *Mor.* 379DE; Lucian *Astr.* 7; *Parl. G.* 10–11; *Sacr.* 14; *Portr.* 11; Philost. *Vit. Apoll.* 6.18–19; Max. Tyre *Or.* 2.5; less judgmental, Sext. Emp. *Pyr.* 3.219. Cf. also Jews, e.g., *Let. Aris.* 138; Wis. 11:15; Philo *Posterity* 165; Jos. *Ag. Ap.* 1.224–25; 2.81, 128, 139; Strabo 16.2.35; but contrast, distinctively, Artapanus (Collins, "Artapanus," 893). Cf. Ambrosiaster *Comm.* 1.23 (Burns, *Romans*, 31).

119. See, e.g., Gödde, "Hamadryads." Cf. Stoics linking various deities with various aspects of the universe in Diog. Laert. 7.1.147. Some mocked myths in which deities became animals (cf., e.g., Varro *L.L.* 5.5.31; *Thebaid* frg. 11; Apollod. *Bibl.* 3.1.1), as in Lucian *Dial. S-G.* 325–26 (15, *West Wind and South Wind* 2); *Dial. G.* 206 (6/2, *Eros and Zeus* 1); 269–71 (2/22, *Pan and Hermes* 1–2); Ps.-Lucian *Patriot* 4; or when deities mated with them (*Cypria* frg. 11; Apollod. *Bibl.* 3.10.7; 3.12.6; Lucian *Dial. S-G.* 305–6 (11/7, *South Wind and West Wind* 1). Earlier, cf. Canaanite myth (Albright, *Yahweh*, 128; Gordon, *Near East*, 99)—although the alleged ritual reenactment is less clear.

120. Rives, *Religion*, 146. Cf. also emperor worship (Keener, *Acts*, 2:1782–86 [esp. 1784–86], 1963–64), though this was less an issue in Rome itself (the destination of Paul's letter) than in many cities in Roman Asia.

121. E.g., Max. Tyre *Or.* 2.3.

122. See Tobin, *Rhetoric*, 25–28; Judge, *First Christians*, 427–30; Gager, *Anti-Semitism*, 57. More generally on Roman Jews, see, e.g., Leon, *Jews of Rome*; Kraabel, "Jews in Rome"; Penna, "Juifs à Rome"; and esp. Barclay, *Jews in Diaspora*, 282–319; essays in Donfried and Richardson, *Judaism*.

knew that Jews abhorred deity images (Rom. 2:22).[123] Jewish tradition deemed idolatry the worst of all sins[124] and emphasized that it invited judgment.[125] Jewish people told stories of Abraham rejecting idolatry,[126] sometimes (as already noted) by reasoning back to a first cause.

Nevertheless, Paul's language here implicitly prepares for his denunciation of Jewish sins in Romans 2; Israel had never forgotten its own past idolatry.[127] When Paul speaks of "exchanging" God's "glory" for an animal image, his wording clearly evokes Israel's sin with the golden calf in Psalm 106:20 (105:20 LXX).[128] Changing their glory—accepting other deities—may also recall Jeremiah 2:11.[129] Paul's listing of classes of animals in Romans 1:23 could recall the warning to Israel in Deuteronomy 4:16–18, which specifically denounces idolatry,[130] though the ultimate source of Deuteronomy's list could be Genesis 1:20–25.[131]

Paul emphasizes the intellectual emptiness of the same action ("changing" God's glory, from ἀλλάσσω, Rom. 1:23) when he describes it as exchanging (from μεταλλάσσω) truth about God for a lie (i.e., idolatry) in Romans 1:25, behavior that in turn leads to the moral consequence of exchanging (from μεταλλάσσω) what accords with nature for what does not (1:26).[132]

123. E.g., Tac. *Hist.* 5.9; *Sib. Or.* 5.285; cf. Satlow, "Philosophers." Originally, Exodus prohibited deity images, not all images (see Tatum, "Second Commandment"; Schubert, "Wurzel"), though some of the Holy Land remained aniconic in this period (e.g., Meyers, "Judaism," 74; but see, later, Avi-Yonah, "Archaeological Sources," 53). Birds and other creatures appear in Roman Jewish funerary inscriptions (Leon, *Jews of Rome*, 196–97, 228).

124. E.g., *Mek. Pisha* 5.40–41; *Sipre Deut.* 54.3.2; *b. Qid.* 40a; cf. *Sipra VDDeho. par.* 1.34.1.3; sources in Safrai, "Religion," 829. Most agreed that the prohibition applied also to Gentiles (*Sipre Num.* 112.2.2).

125. E.g., *Sib. Or.* 3.34; *t. Bek.* 3:12; *Peah* 1:2; *Abot R. Nat.* 40 A.

126. *Jub.* 11:12, 16–17; 12:1–8; 21:3; *Apoc. Ab.* chaps. 1–8; *b. Abod. Zar.* 3a; *Gen. Rab.* 38:13; *Pesiq. Rab.* 33:3; later, cf. Qur'an 21.58–69; 26.70–76. Cf. Job in *T. Job* chaps. 2–5.

127. See, e.g., *T. Mos.* 2:8–9; *L.A.B.* 12:1–10; *Sipre Deut.* 1.9.1–2; *Abot R. Nat.* 34 A; *Tg. Neof.* 1 on Exod. 32.

128. With Schlatter, *Romans*, 41; Hyldahl, "Reminiscence," 285; Moo, *Romans*, 108–9; Fitzmyer, *Romans*, 283; Hays, *Conversion*, 152; Schreiner, *Romans*, 89; Byrne, *Romans*, 75; Dunn, *Theology*, 93; Dunn, "Adam," 128; Matera, *Romans*, 50. For both Adam and Ps. 106, see Hooker, "Adam," 300; Allen, "Romans I–VIII," 15.

129. Hyldahl, "Reminiscence," 285; Moo, *Romans*, 108; Hays, *Conversion*, 152; Byrne, *Romans*, 75; Dunn, *Theology*, 93.

130. Hyldahl, "Reminiscence," 285; Byrne, *Romans*, 75; Fitzmyer, *Romans*, 283.

131. Hyldahl, "Reminiscence," 286–88; Hooker, "Adam," 300; Byrne, *Romans*, 75. Summaries of creatures do appear elsewhere, of course (e.g., Gen. 8:17; Lev. 20:25; 1 Kings 4:33; Ezek. 38:20; Hosea 2:18; Cic. *Amic.* 21.81).

132. The clustering of these verbs in Rom. 1:23–26 seems deliberate. They appear elsewhere in Pauline literature only in 1 Cor. 15:51–52 (twice) and in Gal. 4:20.

Paul need not elaborate the connection between idolatry (1:23) and immorality (1:24–27) for the topics' conjunction to evoke themes that had often provoked Jewish polemic. Gentile myths abounded with accounts of their deities' immoral behavior.[133] Even Gentile intellectuals found these stories of divine immorality to be problematic and sometimes criticized[134] or ridiculed[135] Greek myth, though Jews and Christians ridiculed the stories far more.[136] Gentile thinkers sometimes tried to reinterpret tales of divine immorality[137]—an approach that some Jews and Christians viewed as a flimsy apologetic.[138] Josephus charged that Gentiles created stories of divine immorality to justify their own irrational desires.[139] Indeed, mortals could occasionally appeal even directly to the gods' example for their behavior.[140] If gods could not resist lust, some reasoned, how could mortals?[141] "When myths are not discredited," one pagan intellectual warned, "they may be the counsellors of evil deeds."[142]

133. E.g., Aeschylus *Suppl.* 299–301; *Aetna* frg.; Eurip. *Bacch.* 94–98; *Antiope* 69–71; *Cypria* frg. 10; *Andromeda* frg. 136 (Stob. *Anth.* 4.20.42); Ap. Rhod. 1.1226–39; Apollod. *Bibl.* 1.4.1, 3; 1.5.1; 1.9.3; 2.4.1, 3, 8; 3.2.1; 3.4.3–4; 3.5.5; 3.7.6; 3.8.2; 3.10.1, 3; 3.12.2–6; 3.15.2, 4; *Epitome* 1.9, 22; Callim. *Hymn* 4 (to Delos), 55–58; Hom. *Hymn* 3, to Pythian Apollo 343–44; Parth. *L.R.* 15.3; Ovid *Metam.* 2.434–37, 477–88, 603–13, 685–707, 714–47; 3.1–2, 260–72; 4.234–44, 368–79, 416–530, 543–62; 5.391–437; 14.765–77; Sen. Y. *Herc. fur.* 1–29; Sil. It. 5.15–21; Appian *R.H.* 12.15.101; Lucian *Charid.* 7; *Dial. G.* 239–40 (16/14, *Hermes and Apollo* 1–2). For accounts of their sexual behavior, see, e.g., *Dial. G.* 219 (9/6, *Hera and Zeus* ¶5); 229 (14/10, *Hermes and Helios* 1); 231 (19/11, *Aphrodite and Selene* 1); 233–34 (20/12, *Aphrodite and Eros* 1). For accounts of envy, see *Dial. G.* 228 (12/9, *Poseidon and Hermes* 2); 241 (17/15, *Hermes and Apollo* 1); *Dial. S-G.* 315 (9/10, *Iris and Poseidon* ¶1); Apul. *Metam.* 6.22; Philost. *Ep.* 30 (58); Libanius *Narr.* 2; 4.1–2; 12; 17; 27.3–4; 39; 41.

134. Pindar *Ol.* 1.52–53; Val. Max. 4.7.4; Pliny E. *N.H.* 2.5.17; Dio Chrys. 11.23; [Favorinus] *Or.* 37.32; Philost. *Vit. Apoll.* 5.14; Iambl. *Pyth. Life* 32.218; Hermog. *Progymn.* 5, "On Refutation and Confirmation," 11; Proclus *Poet.* 5, K44.7–16; K45.18–21; 6.1, K72.20–26; Libanius *Invect.* 7.2.

135. E.g., Pliny E. *N.H.* 2.5.17; Dio Chrys. *Or.* 11.154; Lucian Z. *Cat.* 2–6; Z. *Rants* 40, 44; *Prom.* 17; *Astr.* 7; *Sacr.* 5–7; *Amber* 3–6; *Parl. G.* 7–8; *Icar.* 9, 28; *Indictment* 2; *Lover of Lies* 2–5; *Dial. G.* 225 (13/8, *Hephaistos and Zeus* 1); 244 (18/16, *Hera and Leto* 1); 250 (23/19, *Aphrodite and Eros* 1); 278–80 (24/25, *Zeus and Helios* 1–2); 281, 286 (25/26, *Apollo and Hermes*). See, further, the discussion in Keener, "Exhortation"; Keener, *Acts*, 2:2159–62.

136. *Let. Aris.* 134–38; Wis. 13:10–14:7; *Sib. Or.* 3.8–35; 4.4–23; Athenag. *Plea* 20–21; Theoph. 1.9; Tatian *Or. Gks.* 33–34; Tert. *Apol.* 5.2; Pearson, "Idolatry, Jewish Conception of."

137. E.g., Cic. *Nat. d.* 2.28.70 (Stoics); Max. Tyre *Or.* 35.1; Heracl. *Hom. Prob.* 26.1, 7; 30.1; 31.1; 52.1–53.1; 68.8; 69.8–16; Proclus *Poet.* 6.1, K82.2–5; K90.8–14; K131.5–9; K147.21–25; Libanius *Encom.* 1.10.

138. Jos. *Ag. Ap.* 2.255; cf. Athenag. *Plea* 22. For criticism of mythical deities' immorality, see, e.g., Jos. *Ag. Ap.* 2.241, 244–46; for their immoral example, *Ps.-Clem.* 15.1–19.3.

139. Jos. *Ag. Ap.* 2.275.

140. E.g., Soph. *Wom. Tr.* 441–48; Gorg. *Hel.* 19; Ach. Tat. 1.5.5–7; Libanius *Thesis* 1.3 (ignoring Zeus's alleged promiscuity); cf. Menander *Heros* frg. 2.1–3 (in Stob. *Anth.* 5.20a.21). For peoples' misbehavior attributed to the gods' examples, see Pindar frg. 199 (in Strabo 17.1.19); Diod. Sic. 1.27.1.

141. Gorg. *Hel.* 19. Sext. Emp. *Pyr.* 1.159 suggests the inconsistency.

142. Philost. *Vit. soph.* 2.1.554 (trans. Wright, LCL, 155).

Paul is using polemical generalization here, not trying to offer a nuanced description of image veneration.[143] Many Gentile intellectuals protested treating images as if they were the deities themselves,[144] although they often affirmed the value of these images in pointing beyond themselves to the divine.[145] Still, even Gentiles who criticized abuses in polytheism or worship of images sometimes warned against being too critical of image veneration, as they thought Jews and Christians were.[146]

The Madness of Sin as Its Own Punishment

After charging Gentiles with moral and intellectual rebellion in their worship of idols, Paul revisits his mention in Romans 1:18 of heavenly wrath. Although God's wrath would be expressed more explicitly in the future (2:5, 8–9), God expresses his wrath in the present (1:18) by handing humanity over to their own moral madness. Both ancient[147] and modern[148] interpreters of Romans have often recognized this connection here. Humanity sought autonomy from God (1:21–23), and God punished them accordingly by permitting them to become increasingly debased.

Handed Over to Irrational Desires

Three times Paul repeats his refrain that "God gave [humans] over" (παραδίδωμι) to sins (Rom. 1:24, 26, 28),[149] an idea that his audience probably

143. Note here, e.g., Nock, "Vocabulary," 139; Grant, *Gods*, 20, 66–67. Sandnes, "Idolatry and Virtue," suggests that Paul was sometimes more nuanced.

144. Dio Chrys. *Or.* 12.52, 54; Lucian *Sacr.* 11; *Portr. D.* 23; more fully, Grant, *Gods*, 20. For later Platonists, images *reflected* deity; Max. Tyre *Or.* 2.2; Ritner, *Mechanics*, 247. For images as bodies for the gods, cf. the Memphite Theology in *ANET* 5. The idea that the gods animated statues may be rare (Halusza, "Sacred") or late (Johnston, "Animating Statues").

145. Dio Chrys. *Or.* 12.60, 74–75; Max. Tyre *Or.* 2.5 (cf. 11.12); Iambl. *Myst.* 7.1.

146. Mac. Magn. *Apocrit.* 4.20–23; Cook, *Interpretation*, 94–97.

147. See (in Bray, *Romans*, 44, 47) Chrys. *Hom. Rom.* 3; Ambrosiaster *Comm.* (CSEL 81:47, 49); Ps.-Const. *Rom.* (ENPK 25–26); Aug. *Prop. Rom.* 5; Oecumenius, catena on Rom. 1:26 (*PGK* 15:423). This present judgment contrasts with the more direct future wrath (Rom. 2:5; 5:9; 9:22; cf. 3:5). Early interpreters (in Bray, *Romans*, 35–36) saw God's present wrath as corrective, to turn people from the greater wrath to come (Theodore of Mopsuestia, catena on Rom. 1:18 [*PGK* 15:115]; Chrys. *Hom. Rom.* 3).

148. See, e.g., Barth, "Speaking," 290–91; Coffey, "Knowledge," 675; Hooker, *Preface*, 37; Fitzmyer, *Romans*, 271; Jewett, *Romans*, 163, 165; cf. 1 Sam. 2:25.

149. The repetition is *anaphora* (Keck, "Pathos," 85; Longenecker, *Introducing Romans*, 201) and hammers home the point. Cf. also repeated refrains in, e.g., Judg. 17:6; 19:1; 21:25; Pss. 42:5, 11; 43:5; Catullus 61.4–5, 39–40, 49–50, 59–60; 64.327, 333, 337, 342, 347, 352, 356, 361, 365, 371, 375, 381; *Perv. Ven.* 1, 8, 27, 36, 48, 57–58, 68, 75, 80, 93. All three occasions here

would have understood. Jewish people recognized that God could punish sin by handing people over to the power of the sin[150] or by blinding their minds.[151] When God's people abandoned him, he often abandoned them to their folly or to the course of human activity without his help.[152]

Ancient hearers who were not Jewish could also understand the concept of false beliefs reaping their own consequences.[153] Plato opined that the greatest punishment for evildoers was their becoming more evil.[154] Cretans allegedly cursed their enemies by praying that they would "delight in their evil courses," so the enemies would choose for themselves what "borders on destruction."[155] A second-century orator warns that someone seduced by pleasure is finally "swept away into ignorance and then into hedonism."[156]

Jewish tradition often spoke of God punishing people in ways fitting their sins;[157] Paul depicts the punishment here as fitting the crime. Having by idolatry failed to honor God (Rom. 1:21), human beings now by immorality have dishonored their own bodies (1:24).[158] Likewise, in 1:26

probably represent the same divine act (with Origen *Comm. Rom.* on 1:26 [*CER* 1:156, 158; Bray, *Romans*, 46]). Jeremias ("Zu Rm 1 22–32," 119–20) suggests that this is a traditional *Stichwort* (keyword). For various interpretations, cf. Bouwman, "Noch einmal," 411–12.

150. *Jub.* 21:22.

151. Jos. *War* 5.343. For sin leading to more sin, see also Bonsirven, *Judaism*, 14; for idolatry as the final result of the evil impulse, see Davies, *Paul*, 30. If one went astray from Wisdom, Ben Sira warned, she would "hand one over" (παραδώσει) to one's fall (Sir. 4:19). Both YHWH (1 Sam. 2:25; 2 Sam. 17:14) and Greek deities (Hom. *Il.* 16.688; 18.311; *Od.* 18.155–56; Sen. Y. *Troj.* 34–35) could render people senseless to lead them to destruction. God made the wicked go astray (esp. in the Dead Sea Scrolls; e.g., CD 2.13; 4Q266 frg. 11.9–10); the prototypical biblical example is Pharaoh, who hardened his heart (Exod. 8:15, 32; 9:34; 1 Sam. 6:6), yet God also hardened his heart (Exod. 4:21; 7:3; 9:12; 10:1, 20, 27; 11:10; 14:4, 8; Rom. 9:17–18).

152. See, e.g., how he abandoned them to their enemies in Neh. 9:28; Ps. 106:41; cf. similarly, among later Gentiles, Iambl. *Myst.* 1.13. God also gave Israel over to their ways in the wilderness (Ps. 81:12, though the LXX and MT could be rendered simply "sent"; Acts 7:42).

153. Epict. *Diatr.* 1.12.21–22; 3.11.1–3; Porph. *Marc.* 22.348–60, esp. 358–59.

154. Plato *Laws* 5.728B.

155. Val. Max. 7.2.ext.18 (trans. Bailey, LCL, 2:127).

156. Max. Tyre *Or.* 25.5 (trans. Trapp, 211).

157. Sir. 27:25–27; 2 Macc. 4:38; 9:5–6; 13:7–8; *L.A.B.* 44:9–10; 1QpHab 11.5, 7, 15; 12.5–6; 4Q181 frg. 1.1–2; *Jub.* 4:32; 35:10–11; 37:5, 11; Wis. 11:15–16; *m. Ab.* 2:6/7; *Sipre Deut.* 238.3.1; Rev. 16:6; see, further, the discussion in Keener, *Acts*, 2:1052.

158. For sexual dimensions of dishonor, see, e.g., Eurip. *El.* 44–45; Lysias *Or.* 3.6, §97; 3.23, §98; Diod. Sic. 10.31.1; 12.15.2; 12.21.2; 33.15.2; Dion. Hal. *Ant. rom.* 1.78.5; Mus. Ruf. 12, p. 86.11–16, 30–32; Arrian *Ind.* 17.3; Dio Chrys. *Or.* 40.27; 71.6; Apul. *Apol.* 74; Libanius *Speech Char.* 18.2; Nicolaus *Progymn.* 7, "On Commonplace," 45. For dishonor and unrestrained passions, cf. Arist. *N.E.* 7.6.1, 1149a. For homosexual intercourse or when men were viewed as effeminate, cf. Diod. Sic. 5.32.7; Lucian *Lucius* 38; a speaker in Ps.-Lucian *Affairs* 23; Jos. *Ant.* 19.30–31. Marriage to a hermaphrodite appears in Diod. Sic. 32.10.9.

they indulged in "dishonorable" passion,[159] and in 1:27 they committed "disgraceful acts."

Exploitation of the body for sin did not reflect any inherent deficiency in the original creation but distorted the body's purpose and design. Rather, the mind that lacked the Spirit became warped without its role in the larger purpose. Too "futile" to recognize God in creation, ungrateful minds distorted creation by idolatry (Rom. 1:19–23), and hence ultimately their own sacred sexuality based on God's image as male and female (1:24–27; 5:1–2). Thus creation was subjected to "futility"[160] until the glorification of God's children, when the original divine image will be restored (8:20–23, 29).[161] For Paul, however, believers with the first fruits of the Spirit are not bound by the same "futility" of the fleshly mind that is blinded by the world's idolatry.

Thoughts Corrupted by Passions

Most ancient thinkers believed that passions corrupted rational thinking and that reason should control passions; Jewish apologists, however, often chided Gentiles for being ruled by passion and sometimes offered Jewish law as a way to achieve genuine mastery over passion.[162] In Romans 1:24–27, in keeping with Jewish polemic against idolatry,[163] humanity's corrupted thinking subjects people to irrational passions (1:24, 26).

In ordinary conversation people might use the language of "passions" or "desires" positively.[164] Nevertheless, many intellectuals considered desire a

159. Stoics warned against passion (πάθος) as disobedient to reason and contrary to nature (παρὰ φύσιν; Arius Did. 2.7.10, p. 56.1–4) and potentially overwhelming (56.25); one of the fundamental passions was pleasure (56.9–10). Some deemed uncontrollable passion effeminate (Max. Tyre Or. 19.4; cf. Gemünden, "Femme").

160. Rom. 8:20 offers the only use of a ματαιο- cognate in Romans outside 1:21. One might therefore suppose that Adam subjects creation to futility by his embrace of the spirit of idolatry (cf. Gen. 3:5–6), but elsewhere Pauline literature uses ὑποτάσσω in the active with respect to God subjecting all things to Christ (1 Cor. 15:27–28; Eph. 1:22) or Christ subjecting all things to himself (Phil. 3:21). While none of these references speak of subjecting creation to "futility," and Christ is for Paul the second Adam, Pauline usage may still favor God being the one subjecting creation here.

161. For "image" and "glory" in Paul, see 1 Cor. 11:7; 2 Cor. 3:18; 4:4. This is a reversal of distorting God to resemble the "image" of creation (Rom. 1:23). Slavery to "corruption" in Rom. 8:21 echoes the "corruptible" creation worshiped in 1:23 (liberated in the future, in 8:21–23; cf. imperishable resurrection bodies in 1 Cor. 15:42, 50, 53–54).

162. Stowers, "Self-Mastery," 531–34; for Paul, however, "only identification with Christ . . . can bring about sinlessness and self-mastery" (536; cf. Stowers, Rereading, 82).

163. For discussion of such polemic, see Keener, "Exhortation"; Keener, Acts, 2:2159–62.

164. E.g., Ael. Arist. Def. Or. 432, §§146D–147D; Phil. 1:23; 1 Thess. 2:17. Cf. desire for wisdom in Wis. 6:13–20, esp. 6:13, 20.

fundamental evil; thus one philosophically informed second-century orator opines, "The greatest human evil is desire."[165] Many therefore warned against passions and desires;[166] such cravings were insatiable, they felt.[167] Many thinkers spoke of slavery to passions and sought freedom from their tyranny.[168] Overcoming desire was thus praiseworthy,[169] and some philosophers were said to have worked to rid the world of passion.[170] The ideal Stoic sage was supposed to lack passions, at least in the form of negative emotions;[171] Stoics valued this objective because passion was a kind of impulse not subject to reason.[172] Later Platonists warned that passions defiled the soul.[173] Even Epicureans affirmed that controlling the passions leads to happiness.[174]

Stoics counted pleasure (ἡδονή) a fundamental form of passion.[175] Although ordinary people often must have viewed pleasure positively,[176] Stoics treated it as negative or at least not to be valued.[177] Many other thinkers

165. Max. Tyre Or. 24.4 (trans. Trapp, 203); cf. Apoc. Mos. 19:3. For the sake of brevity, I am treating together ἐπιθυμία, which Paul often uses (even in Romans: 1:24; 6:12; 7:7–8; 13:14), and πάθος, which appears in Pauline literature rarely (only Rom. 1:26; Col. 3:5; 1 Thess. 4:5).
166. E.g., Epict. Diatr. 2.1.10; Iambl. Pyth. Life 31.187; Porph. Marc. 27.438.
167. Galen Grief 42–44, 80; Iambl. Pyth. Life 31.206; Porph. Marc. 29.457–60; cf. Dion. Hal. Ant. rom. 9.52.6; Max. Tyre Or. 36.4. Passions spawned all crimes (Cic. Senect. 12.40) and illnesses of the soul (Porph. Marc. 9.157–58). Vice proliferates passion (Lucian Nigr. 16), and one can become psychologically ill through addiction to pleasures (Arius Did. 2.7.10e, p. 62.20–23).
168. Xen. Oec. 1.22; Mus. Ruf. 3, p. 40.19; Pliny Ep. 8.22.1; Plut. Bride 33, Mor. 142E; Arius Did. 2.7.10a, p. 58.15; Iambl. Letter 3, frg. 3.4–6 (Stob. Anth. 3.5.46); Porph. Marc. 34.522–25; 4 Macc. 13:2; T. Jos. 7:8; T. Ash. 3:2. Slavery to pleasure appears in Max. Tyre Or. 25.5–6; 33.3; 36.4.
169. Xen. Hell. 4.8.22; Polyb. 31.25.8; Publ. Syr. 40, 181; Dio Chrys. Or. 8.20; 9.12; T. Reub. 4:9; Jos. Ant. 4.328–29. Alexander as an example of overcoming desire (as in Arrian Alex. 7.28.2) was not plausible outside eulogy (Sen. Y. Ep. Lucil. 113.29–31; Plut. Flatt. 25, Mor. 65F; Dio Chrys. Or. 4.4, 60; cf. b. Tamid 32a).
170. Apul. Flor. 14.3–4, on Crates the Cynic.
171. Engberg-Pedersen, "Vices," 612–13. For a Stoic list of negative expressions of desire, see Arius Did. 2.7.10b, pp. 58.32–60.1. Controlling emotion naturally appealed to Roman traditions of discipline (see, e.g., Val. Max. 4.1.pref.; 4.1.13).
172. Arius Did. 2.7.10, p. 56.1–4; 2.7.10a, p. 56.24–25; 2.7.10b, p. 58.17–18. As a type of passion, pleasure also disobeyed reason (2.7.10b, p. 58.29).
173. Porph. Marc. 13.236–37.
174. Cic. Fin. 1.18.57–58.
175. Arius Did. 2.7.10, p. 56.6–7; see also Engberg-Pedersen, Paul and Stoics, 311n32.
176. E.g., Ach. Tat. 2.8.3. On positive Epicurean views of pleasure, see, e.g., Cic. Fin. 1.9.29; Plut. R. Col. 27, Mor. 1122D; Athen. Deipn. 12.546e; Long, Philosophy, 61–69; Klauck, Context, 395–98. Epicurus's own views appear more moderate; see Cic. Tusc. 3.21.50; Diog. Laert. 10.145–20. For intellectual pleasures in Plato, see Lodge, Ethics, 27–31.
177. Negatively, e.g., Cic. Fin. 2.12.35–2.13.43; Sen. Y. Ep. Lucil. 59.1; Dial. 7.11.1; Arius Did. 2.7.10, p. 56.13–18; 2.7.10b, p. 60.1–2. Earlier Stoic tradition apparently viewed it among indifferents; see Arius Did. 2.7.5a, p. 10.12–13; as not a good, Mus. Ruf. 1, p. 32.22; at least when associated with what is dishonorable, Mus. Ruf. 12, p. 86.27–29; frg. 51, p. 144.8–9; see Brennan, "Theory," 61–62n31.

also viewed it as negative, especially when embraced in excess.[178] Epicureans demurred, valuing pleasure, but this was partly because Epicurus defined it differently from others; Stoics and others often criticized Epicurean views of pleasure.[179]

A major emphasis in ancient philosophy was how to overcome one's passions.[180] Aristotle's followers, the Peripatetics, merely wanted to moderate passions, but many others, including Stoics, wanted to eradicate them.[181] Philosophers in the Platonist tradition felt that thinking about virtue or the divine, which was pure intellect, would free one from passions.[182] Thus, one later Platonist emphasized that philosophy should cast passion from the soul, as medicine drives sickness from the body.[183]

Despite differences among particular schools, most intellectuals agreed that one must use reason, guided by virtue, to control the passions.[184] Passions could challenge and overpower reason if the latter were not sufficiently strong.[185] Stoics and Platonists alike agreed that one must distinguish real happiness

178. E.g., Xen. *Mem.* 1.2.23–24; 4.5.3; *Hell.* 4.8.22; Cic. *Senect.* 12.40; Dio Chrys. *Or.* 1.13; 3.34; 8.20; Pliny *Ep.* 5.5.4; Plut. *Bride* 33, *Mor.* 142E; Max. Tyre *Or.* 7.7; 14.1–2; 25.5–6; 33.3–8; 38.6; Men. Rhet. 2.10, 416.19; Proclus *Poet.* 6.1, K121.14–15; Iambl. *Pyth. Life* 31.204–6; Libanius *Comp.* 1.7–8; 5.7; *Speech Char.* 16.2; Porph. *Marc.* 6.103–8; 7.125–26, 131–34; 33.508–9; 35.535–36.

179. For Stoic criticisms, see Cic. *Fin.* 2, esp. 2.4.11–2.6.18; Arius Did. 2.7.10a, p. 58.8–11; for others' criticisms, see, e.g., Cic. *Pis.* 28.68–69; Aul. Gel. 9.5; Max. Tyre *Or.* 30–33, esp. 30.3–5; 31; 33; Galen *Grief* 62, 68. See also Keener, *Acts,* 3:2584–93 (on Epicureans) and 2593–95 (on Stoicism; cf. Keener, "Epicureans"). Cf. Seneca's attack on the Epicurean goal of pleasure in Dyson, "Pleasure" (on Sen. Y. *Vit. beat.* 11.1).

180. See, e.g., Xen. *Mem.* 1.2.24; Val. Max. 3.3.ext.1; Mus. Ruf. 6, p. 52.15–17; 7, p. 56.27; 12, pp. 86.39–88.1; Max. Tyre *Or.* 1.9; 7.7; 25.6; Iambl. *Letter* 3, frg. 3 (Stob. *Anth.* 3.5.46); Porph. *Marc.* 31.479–81; *Let. Aris.* 256; 4 Macc. 13:1; Malherbe, "Beasts." Many sources use figurative war imagery, discussed later in this book in connection with Rom. 7:23 (pp. 109–11, esp. 110). Control of oneself was the greatest conquest (Sen. Y. *Nat. Q.* 1.pref.5; 3.pref.10; *Ep. Lucil.* 113.29–31; Publ. Syr. 137; Prov. 16:32; cf. Xen. *Mem.* 1.5.1).

181. Tobin, *Rhetoric,* 229; Dillon, "Philosophy," 796. In 4 Macc. 3:2–5 reason expressly controls and fights passions rather than eradicates them.

182. E.g., Philo *Sacr.* 45; cf. discussions—later in this book, chaps. 6 and 7—of 2 Cor. 3:18; Phil. 4:8.

183. Porph. *Marc.* 31.483.

184. Cic. *Inv.* 2.54.164; *Off.* 2.5.18; *Leg.* 1.23.60; Sall. *Catil.* 51.3; Plut. *Lect.* 1, *Mor.* 37E; Max. Tyre *Or.* 33.3; Porph. *Marc.* 6.99; 29.453–60; 31.478–83; 34.521–22; cf. in other cultures, e.g., traditional Morocco (Eickelman, *Middle East,* 205). For reason ruling the senses, see Sen. Y. *Ep. Lucil.* 66.32.

185. Dion. Hal. *Ant. rom.* 5.8.6; Cic. *Senect.* 12.40; Char. *Chaer.* 2.4.4; Arius Did. 2.7.10a, p. 58.5–6, 12–16; Marc. Aur. 3.6.2; Porph. *Marc.* 9.154–55; for passions as a distraction from attention to God, see Max. Tyre *Or.* 11.10. One or the other would be in control, with passion being more feminine (Max. Tyre *Or.* 33.2, from an androcentric perspective; cf. Philo *Unchangeable* 111). Greek thinkers associated passion both with females and with barbarians; see McCoskey, *Race,* 56 (for barbarians as like beasts, e.g., Libanius *Invect.* 2.1; *Topics* 2.6).

from transient pleasures and that one learns this discernment by "repeated, deliberate choice, a lifelong struggle for rational mastery."[186] Thus, one rhetorical historian concludes that philosophy "drives away every unseemly and useless emotion," making reason "more powerful than fear and pain."[187]

For Stoics, the process was purely cognitive: genuinely understanding what was true would eradicate the emotions that were tied to false assumptions about what really mattered.[188] Although the Stoic approach offered some positive insights that can be used even today in cognitive psychology,[189] in practice it also severely underestimated (for all the Stoic emphasis on living according to nature!) the physiological connections between natural bodily instincts and emotion, as well as connections between emotion and reason.[190] Modern research has shown that powerful stimuli can alert the brain's amygdala, generating emergency physical responses, before the signals are even processed by the cortex. Only at that point can stimuli be rationally evaluated and, when needed, deescalated rationally.[191]

Stoics were nevertheless sensitive to experiences they inevitably encountered when seeking to subject emotion to reason. Recognizing that humans experience physical reactions that precede cognitive judgments, Seneca counted these reactions "first movements," a sort of pre-emotion that could be nipped in the bud by rational decisions once one had the opportunity to consider them.[192] Because Origen misconstrued "first movements" themselves as cognitive, Christians later imagined "many intermediate degrees of sin," provoking

186. Meeks, *Moral World*, 47.
187. Val. Max. 3.3.ext.1 (trans. Bailey, LCL, 1:275).
188. See Sorabji, *Emotion*, 2–4; Stowers, "Self-Mastery," 540; Epict. *Diatr.* 1.28.6. Cf., however, Arius Did. 2.7.10a, p. 58.11–16, where passions overpower teaching.
189. As with the limitations of Stoicism (Sorabji, *Emotion*, 153–54), cognitive therapy when used by itself is more useful for some disorders than others (e.g., for reducing phobias but not helpful for anorexia; 155).
190. For the connections between emotion and reason in modern psychology, see discussion in Elliott, *Feelings*.
191. Sorabji, *Emotion*, 6, 144–55 (esp. 145–50). Galen viewed emotion as flowing from bodily states (see esp. 253–62). The Stoic emphasis on indifference is not natural or desirable for modern therapy (169–80).
192. Sorabji, *Emotion*, 2–5. Seneca would have included among such first movements the involuntary stimulation of male organs, more rapid respiration when provoked, loss of color when startled, and the like (11). Such "first movements" become problematic only if, once wrong judgments are identified, one chooses them, allowing emotion to become worse (see more fully 55–65). Thus if one assents to the movement rather than preferring reason, it becomes full-fledged emotion (73); but it is not a matter of choice so long as it remains involuntary, like anything that befalls the body (73–74, citing Sen. Y. *Ira* 2.2.1–2.4.2). Earlier, Posidonius, who felt that judgments were not always necessary for emotion to occur (Sorabji, *Emotion*, 121–32; cf. others in 133, 142), accepted something like first movements but did not deny that they involved some emotion (118–19). Because first movements did not involve reason, Aquinas (lecture 1 on

new questions, such as "Did you let it linger? Did you enjoy it?"[193] Although such exercises stimulated and developed self-discipline, they probably also often bred the very sort of fixation on sin that Romans 7 parodies.

Although details varied among ancient thinkers, most viewed reason and passion as mutually opposed. In Romans 1, however, those who fancied themselves wise (1:22) have become slaves of passion (1:24–27; cf. 6:12, 16; 16:18). In 1:27 Paul not only speaks of intense desire (ὄρεξις) but uses the image of "burning" (ἐξεκαύθησαν, from ἐκκαίω), an image (not always the same term) to which he appeals more explicitly in depicting intense emotion (2 Cor. 11:29),[194] including, as often elsewhere, consuming sexual passion (1 Cor. 7:9).[195]

Changing God's Image (Rom. 1:23–27)

Having exchanged God's image or glory for other images, humanity eventually corrupted God's image in themselves. Whereas people once knew the true creator, in whose image they were created, now they worshiped even animals, debasing God's image.[196] Some ancient listeners would hear irony here. Passions were thought to make people irrational, like beasts,[197] and thinkers often compared to beasts those ruled by passions rather than by intellect or virtue.[198]

Rom. 8:1) denied that they incurred condemnation (Levy, Krey, and Ryan, *Romans*, 175); cf., similarly, William of St. Thierry on Rom. 2:14–16 (ibid., 90, 91n11).

193. Sorabji, *Emotion*, 8–9 (quotations from 9); more fully, 343–56 (on Origen, esp. 346–51). This led further to the seven cardinal sins (357–71) and Augustine's philosophic and linguistic misunderstanding of Stoics regarding emotion, through which sin was thought to pervade every layer of one's being (372–84). Though respecting Augustine, Sorabji prefers Pelagius's approach to lust (417); monasticism's legacy in parts of Europe may have contributed to Freud's interest in repressed passions. On prepassion, see also Graver, "Origins."

194. For nonsexual cravings or feelings similarly described, see, e.g., Corn. Nep. 6 (Lysander), 3.1; Cic. *Tusc.* 1.19.44; Virg. *Aen.* 7.456; Plut. *Coriol.* 21.1–2; Fronto *Ad M. Caes.* 3.13.3; *Ep. graec.* 6; Men. Rhet. 2.3, 384.29–30; Sir. 28:10–12; 4 Macc. 16:3; Jos. *Life* 263; Luke 24:32.

195. E.g., Musaeus *Hero* 40–41; Xen. *Cyr.* 5.1.16; Menander *Fabula Incerta* 8.21; Catullus 45.16; 61.169–71; 64.19; Virg. *Aen.* 1.660, 673; 4.2, 23, 54, 66, 68; *Ecl.* 8.83; Ovid *Fast.* 3.545–46; *Her.* 4.17–20; 7.23; 15.9; *Am.* 1.1.25–26; 1.2.9, 46; Val. Max. 4.6.2 (conjugal); Plut. *Table* 1.2.6, *Mor.* 619A; *Dial. L.* 16, *Mor.* 759B; Lucian *Lucius* 5; Philost. *Ep.* 13 (59); Athen. *Deipn.* 1.10d; Sir. 9:8; 23:16; *T. Jos.* 2:2. In erotic spells, cf. LiDonnici, "Burning"; further in Keener, "Marriage," 686–87. See esp. the romances, e.g., Longus 3.10; Char. *Chaer.* 1.1.8, 15; 2.3.8; 2.4.7; 4.7.6; 5.9.9; 6.3.3; 6.4.5; 6.7.1; Ach. Tat. 1.5.5–6; 1.11.3; 1.17.1; 2.3.3; 4.6.1; 4.7.4; 5.15.5; 5.25.6; 6.18.2; Apul. *Metam.* 2.5, 7; 5.23; Xen. Eph. *Anthia* 1.3, 5, 9, 14; 2.3; 3.6.

196. For northern Mediterranean disdain for Egyptian animal images, see comment above, p. 14.

197. Iambl. *Letter* 3, frg. 3.4–6 (Stob. *Anth.* 3.5.46; cf. *Letter* 13, frg. 1.18, in Stob. *Anth.* 2.2.6).

198. Philosophers sometimes depicted the passions as beasts (Malherbe, *Philosophers*, 82–89; cf. the body in Max. Tyre *Or.* 7.5), but even more often intellectuals used this imagery for those who were ruled by passions (e.g., Xen. *Hiero* 7.3; *Mem.* 1.2.30; *Rhet. Alex.* pref. 1420ab.4–5; Polyb. 1.80.10; Cic. *Mil.* 12.32; 31.85; *Pis.* 1.1; Sen. Y. *Ep. Lucil.* 103.2; Mus. Ruf. 10, p. 78.27–28;

The beginning of Paul's list of false images in Romans 1:23, however, is that of people themselves. Instead of recognizing that they should bear the image of the true God, they debased God's image into something they made, exchanging the creator's image with which they had been entrusted for images of creation. In so doing, they obscured God's image in themselves, an image renewed in Christ (8:29). Because Paul does not repeat "image" in 1:24–27, the inference of God's image here is the least textually certain of the major proposals I offer in this chapter, yet the clues seem sufficient to make it more probable than not.

Many have argued that the progressive fall of humanity in Romans 1:21–23 echoes the fall of Adam, offering a prelude to 5:12–21.[199] Certainly, as a Jew Paul does presuppose Adam's sin, a premise that becomes explicit in 5:12–21.[200] Further, if there is reason to see an allusion to Adam (see discussion below), the list of false images beginning with images of humans could evoke the sin of the primeval humans in Genesis 3: rejecting the obvious truth about their creator, they accepted the lies that they would not die and that their knowledge would make them like God (Gen. 3:4–5).[201]

As others point out, however, many of the allusions to Adam's fall proposed for Romans 1:21–23 are too general to prove compelling by themselves.[202] Thus, for example, in the Wisdom of Solomon, idolatry introduced

---

14, p. 92.21; 18B, p. 116.14; Epict. *Diatr.* 1.3.7, 9; 2.9.3, 5; 4.1.127; 4.5.21; Dio Chrys. *Or.* 8.14, 21; 32.26; 77/78.29; Plut. *Demosth.* 26.4; *Bride* 7, *Mor.* 139B; *R. Col.* 2, *Mor.* 1108D; Diogenes *Ep.* 28; Max. Tyre *Or.* 15.2; 33.7–8; Marc. Aur. 3.16; Philod. *Death* 35.14–15; *Crit.* frg. 52.2–3; Philost. *Vit. Apoll.* 7.30; Libanius *Anec.* 2.1). Animals' souls, unlike those of humans, were usually deemed devoid of reason (e.g., Polyb. 6.6.4; Cic. *Fin.* 2.14.45; *Tusc.* 1.33.80; *Off.* 1.4.11; Diog. Laert. 7.1.85–86).

199. Hooker, "Adam"; Barrett, *Adam*, 17–19; Dunn, *Romans*, 1:53; Dunn, *Theology*, 91–92; Dunn, "Adam," 127–28. For parallels to Adam and Eve in the *Life of Adam and Eve*, see Levison, "*Adam and Eve*." One significant connection may be the futility in Rom. 8:20 (see Hooker, "Adam," 303).

200. Phrases such as "from creation" or "from the beginning" could imply this period (see, e.g., Mark 10:6; *L.A.B.* 1:1) or could be used more generally (e.g., *1 En.* 69:18; *T. Mos.* 12:4; *L.A.B.* 32:7; Incant. Text 20:11–12).

201. In Rom. 16:20 the crushing of Satan underfoot probably alludes to one line of ancient Jewish interpretation about Gen. 3:15 (but cf. Ps. 8:6 in 1 Cor. 15:27); thus, it is plausible that wisdom in what is good and innocence concerning evil in Rom. 16:19 adapts the image of the tree of knowing good and evil (experimenting with sin rather than depending on the Spirit of life, Rom. 8:2). If so, Adam allusions could be among the elements toward the letter's beginning and ending that frame the letter (cf. also wisdom vs. foolishness here, as in Rom. 1:22). Paul's terms for "good" and "evil" in 16:19 differ from those in LXX Gen. 2:9; 3:5, however (as, less significantly, his language in Rom. 16:20 differs from that in Gen. 3:15); if Paul intended an allusion in Rom. 16:19, he does not make this clear.

202. See Scroggs, *Adam*, 75–76n3; Fitzmyer, *Romans*, 274, 283; Keck, *Romans*, 63; Stowers, *Rereading*, 86, 90, 92.

other sins, including sexual immorality (Wis. 14:12, 22–27, esp. 27), without immediate reference to Adam (cf. 10:1–2). Josephus depicts humanity gradually abandoning the practice of honoring God and sinking into depravity only several generations after Adam (*Ant.* 1.72). Likewise, Jewish tradition spoke of Gentiles continuing to disobey even after God enlightened Gentiles further through Noah.[203] Paul's plurals and present-tense verbs here (e.g., in Rom. 1:18–19) might also militate against envisioning Adam's fall in this passage.[204]

Paul presumably presupposes biblical creation accounts even where he does not explicitly address them. This need not mean, however, that he is directly evoking them for his audience; such a conclusion must rest on clues in the text. Paul must treat humanity's failure here as theologically coherent with the backstory of humanity's fall that he later recounts in Romans 5:12–21, but just as Genesis can use different stories to recount a coherent theology of creation, so can Paul. This story will be coherent with Paul's story of Adam, but Paul is not emphasizing the particular story of Genesis 2–3 here as clearly as some interpreters have argued. The connection might not even occur to a first-time listener at this point in the letter, though of course Paul would hope that Romans would be heard more than once.[205]

But whereas there is at most limited reason to think that Paul emphasizes Genesis 2–3 here, there are some stronger possible echoes of Genesis 1.[206] Although in the Septuagint "image" (εἰκών) most often means "idol," in Paul it evokes either Wisdom or the first human.[207] In view of Paul's usage elsewhere (1 Cor. 11:7; 2 Cor. 3:18; cf. 4:4), God's "glory" here (Rom. 1:23) probably implies his image; later in Romans, those conformed to the image of the new Adam are "glorified" (8:29–30).[208]

---

203. See, e.g., *Jub.* 7:20; van der Horst, "Pseudo-Phocylides," 569; *Mek. Bah.* 5.90ff.; *Sipre Deut.* 343.4.1; *b. Sanh.* 56a, bar.; Schultz, "Views of Patriarchs," 48–49; further discussion in Keener, *Acts,* 3:2264–65.

204. See, e.g., O'Rourke, "Revelation."

205. Ancient writers recognized the value of rereading a document as often as necessary to catch the main themes and subtleties; for speeches, see, e.g., Quint. *Inst.* 10.1.20–21. Still, speeches were deliberately designed so as to invite hearers to follow the flow of thought (Theon *Progymn.* 2.149–53).

206. Herein I offer my belated public apology to Prof. Morna Hooker; as a PhD student in one of her classes, I wrote a paper arguing in part against her case for Adam allusions in Rom. 1.

207. Hooker, "Adam," 297–98, emphasizing Adam and conceding that by itself ὁμοίωμα (Rom. 1:23) reflects Ps. 105:20 LXX (106:20 ET). Cf. also humanity in Philo *Mos.* 2.65.

208. For God's image in humanity here, see also Hooker, "Adam," 305. "Likeness" (ὁμοίωμα) in Rom. 1:23 may also prepare for references to the likeness of the first (5:14; cf. 8:3; Phil. 2:7) or second (Rom. 6:5) Adam—though its primary echo is Ps. 105:20 LXX (106:20 ET), as just noted.

In the beginning of Paul's Bible, humans were formed in God's image, male and female (Gen. 1:26–27; 5:1–2). Here, however, humans degraded the divine to the image of themselves and even lower animals (Rom. 1:23, 25). In so doing, they distorted God's true image in their own creation as male and female (Rom. 1:24; Gen. 1:27; 5:1–2). The terms that Paul uses in Romans 1:26–27 for male and female (ἄρσην and θῆλυς) are not his usual ones; he employs these elsewhere only at Galatians 3:28. Of the passages where they occur together in the Septuagint, easily the most relevant and fundamental is the creation narrative (Gen. 1:27; 5:2; cf. Mark 10:6).[209]

When Paul speaks of the reversal of sexual gender roles in terms of "nature" (φύσις, 1:26–27), he employs a common argument esteemed among Stoics and also some Jewish thinkers.[210] At the same time, for Paul as a Jew, a claim about nature is also (as with other Jewish thinkers) an appeal to creation, to the way Paul believes that God originally designed nature. This interest in the beginning is explicit in the preceding context at 1:20: Paul talks about distortion of what was clear from creation.[211] When Paul thinks of "image" later in Romans, he has new creation in mind (Rom. 8:29); perhaps even the mention of sonship there might evoke the restoration of Genesis (Gen. 5:1–3). In any case, Paul presents as the consequence of failed reasoning behavior that Jewish audiences (whom he will address directly in Rom. 2) and presumably Christian converts deemed moral madness.

Unfit Minds (Rom. 1:28)

In Romans 1:28 the final mention of handing over continues Paul's concern with knowledge and truth. Just as humans did not think fitting, or approve of (using δοκιμάζω), continuing to hold true knowledge of God in their reasoning

---

209. In the context of Gen. 1:27, the complementarity of genders involves procreativity (1:28). That is, it relates not to ancient gender roles, known to vary somewhat among societies, but to distinct persons designed to complement each other.

210. Cf., e.g., Mus. Ruf. 12, pp. 84.2–86.1; Artem. *Oneir.* 1.80; Diog. Laert. 6.2.65; Jos. *Ag. Ap.* 2.273–75; Ps.-Phoc. 190–92; *T. Naph.* 3:4–5; van der Horst, "Hierocles," 158; Grant, *Paul*, 55, 124. For both Gentile and Jewish sources on nature as applied to gender reversal especially in sexual contexts, see, e.g., Talbert, *Romans*, 66, 75–76; Byrne, *Romans*, 76–77; Jewett, *Romans*, 175–76; discussion of the diverse sources in Greenberg, *Homosexuality*, 207. Paul is not thinking in terms of modern genetics, about which he neither knew nor could not have known, but presumably in terms of how the male genital organ fits as if by design inside that of the female.

211. In the next chapter humanity retains some moral sensibility by "nature" (φύσις, Rom. 2:14). For the nature of natural law in ancient thought, see discussion in Keener, *Acts*, 3:2265–68; also Inwood, "Rules," 96–97; Inwood, "Natural Law"; Watson, "Natural Law."

(cf. 1:21), God gave them up to an unfit, or disapproved, mind (ἀδόκιμον νοῦν) to do things that were unfitting.[212]

The adjective ἀδόκιμος can refer to something tested and found unfit or, by extension, to what is worthless and disqualified.[213] This failed mind contrasts with the renewed mind that Paul will mention later, which will test or evaluate (δοκιμάζω) matters to ascertain what is good and thus belongs to God's will (12:2).[214] In other words, those who did not rightly discern God became morally incapable of discerning right from wrong, whereas those whose minds are renewed in Christ experience this discernment.

Paul follows this general declaration with a rhetorically designed vice list, concluding in 1:32 that people "know" (from ἐπιγινώσκω) that such deeds are deathworthy yet practice them anyway.[215] Thus, Paul concludes his depiction of pagans in 1:18–32 by suggesting that they have sufficient innate or natural knowledge to be condemned by their own consciences (cf. 2:15). Rejection of divine truth leads to corrupted minds; the opposite of the corrupt mind is faith (1:16–17), that is, accepting divine truth.

Stoics believed that genuine rational understanding would eradicate passion.[216] Yet as Robert Jewett observes, "In contrast to the Greek outlook, the flaw in the human race does not lie in ignorance that can be excused or modulated through education but rather in a direct and multifaceted campaign to

212. As is often noted (e.g., Kennedy, *Epistles*, 26; Hunter, *Romans*, 34; Dunn, *Romans*, 1:66; Engberg-Pedersen, *Paul and Stoics*, 71; Engberg-Pedersen, "Vices," 624; Ramelli, *Hierocles*, lxxii–lxxiii, lxxviii), the term καθήκω appears in Stoic ethics (Mus. Ruf. frg. 31; Arius Did. 2.7.5b2, p. 14.4–5, 25–26; 2.7.6a, p. 38.11–12; 2.7.7b, p. 44.27; 2.7.11a, p. 62.33; 2.7.8, pp. 50.36–52.2; p. 52.6–7, 21–23; 2.7.11m, p. 90.30–31; p. 92.1–3; cf. Inwood, "Rules," 100–101; Sedley, "Debate," esp. 128); however, it is in no wise limited to them (Moulton and Milligan, *Vocabulary*, 312, citing, e.g., P.Lille 1.3.42; P.Fay. 91.20; 107.9; P.Oxy. 1.115.5; see also Jewett, *Romans*, 183). Nature provides a criterion for choosing among the καθήκοντα (Arius Did. 2.7.8a, p. 52.25–26).

213. See BDAG.

214. Cf. 1 Cor. 2:15, where the spiritual person evaluates everything from the right perspective but cannot be rightly evaluated by those without this eternal, Spirit perspective.

215. Vice lists were widespread in antiquity. See, e.g., Plato *Laws* 1.649D; Arist. *E.E.* 2.3.4, 1220b–1221a; Ps.-Arist. *V.V.* 1249a–1251b; *Rhet. Alex.* 36, 1442a.13–14; Cic. *Pis.* 27.66; *Cat.* 2.4.7; 2.5.10; 2.10.22, 25; *Cael.* 22.55; *Phil.* 3.11.28; 8.5.16; *Mur.* 6.14 (negated); Sen. Y. *Dial.* 9.2.10–12; Epict. *Diatr.* 2.8.23; Arius Did. 2.7.5b, p. 12.2–12; 2.7.10b, pp. 58.32–60.1; 2.7.10b, p. 60.1–7; 2.7.10e, p. 62.14–19; 2.7.11e, p. 68.17–20; Dio Chrys. *Or.* 1.13; 3.53; 4.126; 8.8; 32.28, 91; 33.23, 55; 34.19; Fronto *Nep. am.* 2.8; Diogenes *Ep.* 36; Diog. Laert. 2.93; 1QS 4.9–11; Wis. 14:25–26; Philo *Posterity* 52. See, further, the discussion in Charles, "Vice Lists."

216. Engberg-Pedersen, *Paul and Stoics*, 53. Cf. Epictetus (*Diatr.* 1.2.1–4), who opines that once someone knows that something is rational, one will suffer anything for it. Stoics valued "right reason" (λόγος ὀρθός; Epict. *Diatr.* 2.8.2; Marc. Aur. 9.9; Arius Did. 2.7.11i, p. 76.31; 2.7.11k, p. 80.28; 2.7.11m, p. 88.38–39; cf. Mus. Ruf. frg. 38, p. 136.1–3), an expression also found in *Let. Aris.* 161, 244 (Hadas, *Aristeas*, 195; elsewhere, e.g., Philost. *Hrk.* 19.3).

disparage God and replace him/her with a human face or institution."[217] Even if the philosophers were right that reason alone could defeat the passions, the pagan world had relinquished true reason and true knowledge of God, and God had surrendered them to the rule of their passions, clouding their intellects. That is why, Paul argues, they have neither worshiped the true God nor lived by basic standards of morality.[218]

Some scholars think that Paul goes on to address, separate from the pagan world in general in Romans 1:18–32, Gentile intellectuals, starting in 2:1–3,[219] before explicitly addressing a Jewish interlocutor in 2:17–29. A larger number of scholars, including myself, apply all of chapter 2 to a Jewish audience or at least to a hyperbolically depicted, hypothetical Jewish critic.[220] In any case, all agree that in 1:18–2:29 Paul addresses the sinfulness of both Jews and Gentiles (cf. also 1:16; 3:9, 19, 23, 29), both those with and those without biblical law. Because Paul's depiction of Gentiles in 1:18–32 fits a common early Jewish stereotype of pagans, it suits his purpose well enough in setting the stage for his challenge to Jewish hearers who depend on the law (explicit in 2:17–29; cf. already 2:9–10). For Paul, ultimately neither the pagan mind, which has abandoned natural revelation, nor the Jewish mind, which has not fully obeyed special revelation in the law, can truly overcome passion.[221]

Conclusion

The corrupted mind of Romans 1:18–32 is the pagan mind, corrupting the evidence for God with a false worldview and thus misconstruing the rest of reality, including humans' own identity and purpose. These Gentiles had only divine revelation in nature; but what of those who have more detailed revelation in the written Torah? Idolatry (1:19–23, esp. 1:23) and sexual immorality (1:24–27), especially in its homosexual forms (1:26–27), were viewed as distinctly Gentile sins. Yet Paul applies the same principles to sins more

217. Jewett, *Romans*, 181; cf. Schlatter, *Romans*, 47; Keck, *Romans*, 188.

218. Cf. Jewish discussions of the basic morality expected for Gentiles in Keener, *Acts*, 3:2263–69.

219. Owen, "Scope," 142–43 (Paul addresses only ordinary idolaters in Rom. 1, not philosophers); cf. a particular Gentile in Stowers, *Diatribe*, 112; Stowers, *Rereading*, 104; Stowers, "Self-Mastery," 535; any person that it fits, whether Jewish or Gentile, in Matera, *Romans*, 69.

220. E.g., Nygren, *Romans*, 113–16; Käsemann, *Romans*, 53; Moo, *Romans*, 126; Fitzmyer, *Romans*, 297; Schreiner, *Romans*, 102–3; Wischmeyer, "Römer 2.1–24"; Watson, *Gentiles*, 198; Keener, *Romans*, 42. The interlocutor's Jewish identity may remain ambiguous until Rom. 2:17 (Bryan, *Preface*, 92; cf. Tobin, *Rhetoric*, 111–12).

221. Cf. Stowers, "Self-Mastery," 536.

widely acknowledged as universal (1:28–32), preparing for Paul's challenge to those with the written Torah in 2:12–29.

Jewish teachers expected the Torah to enlighten reason to provide power to overcome passions. Yet whereas Paul will grant the value of reason and Torah in identifying sin, he will show that such sins merely become more transgressive once identified. The mind equipped with the law without the Spirit remains the mind of the flesh (Rom. 7:5–6, 22–25; 8:3–9)—the subject of chapter 3 of this book.

2

⊚ ⊚ ⊚ ⊚

The Mind of Faith
(Rom. 6:11)

In just the same way, because you are in Christ Jesus, count yourselves both dead with regard to sin and alive with regard to God.

—Romans 6:11

In Romans 6:1–10 Paul affirms the believer's new identity in Christ. This
identity reflects believers' death with Christ and their concomitant liberation from slavery to sin. Likewise, believers are defined by their destiny in
Christ. The climax of the first part of Romans 6, however, is Paul's exhortation to embrace the new reality by faith (6:11: ὑμεῖς λογίζεσθε ἑαυτούς,
"reckon yourselves"—a cognitive action). The letter's ideal hearers may have
understood this cognitive reckoning in light of discussions about cognition
then current, which are attested in some philosophic sources. Paul wants
his hearers to recognize their identification with Christ and so live out their
new identity.

For Stoics, corrected beliefs would allow one to reconstitute one's identity
based on reality. For Paul, correct understanding of the believer's union with
Christ and his death should have the same effect (Rom. 6:2–11). Although
Paul is aware that believers do not always live consistently with this reality, he

is deeply concerned about this incongruity (6:1–2; 8:12–13), which he regards as unnatural for those who truly understand the new reality into which their conversion has initiated them (6:3–4, 12–23). Paul will develop these ideas also in his exposition of the renewed mind in Romans 12:2–3.

Death with Christ (Rom. 6:1–10)

Paul grounds the "reckoning" of death to sin in a situation already achieved by Christ, effective through identification and/or union with Christ, and experienced through faith.

Producing Righteousness

Paul is interested in Romans not only in God's forensic decree that those who belong to Christ are righteous.[1] He is interested also in showing that Christ, in contrast with human conscience and even a purely moral approach to God's law, produces righteousness that can be effective in relationships (cf. 12:1–15:12). This righteousness contrasts with the behavior of both Gentiles and Jewish people;[2] all the world lies under sin and needs what Christ offers.

Thus, Romans 1:18–32 showed the failure of human wisdom to produce righteousness; by declaring autonomy from God, human wisdom became darkened and subject to the passions against which most philosophers protested. Romans 7:7–25 shows the failure of knowledge of the law to decisively defeat such passions; far more than the Gentile mind of Romans 1, the mind under the law knows God's standard, yet such knowledge has not brought freedom from wrong desire.

In Romans 6:1–10 Paul speaks of not only a change in status but a change in identity. Ancient analogies here appear very limited, but several will be explored; at the least, it seems relevant that some ancient thinkers believed that one's identity could be transformed. For Paul, as for some others, *implementing* the change in *practice* requires cognitive recognition of the change. For Paul, this cognitive recognition is best described as faith; although it may be a practical step beyond initial justifying faith, it is an inseparable corollary of that faith. Subsequent Christian thought has sometimes discarded the

---

1. Jewish people would understand God's decrees to be efficacious in any case; see, e.g., Gen. 1:3, 9, 11, 14–15. Paul also compares God's efficacious command of light to exist with the transformation of hearts through God's message (2 Cor. 4:6).

2. Cf. Engberg-Pedersen, *Paul and Stoics*, 218–19, contending that enabling righteousness is what Paul believes distinguishes Christ faith from Jewish and Gentile efforts.

corollary, but Paul would have regarded it as necessary to be consistent with (even though not a prerequisite for) genuine justifying faith.

The New Identity

We humans tend to identify ourselves in terms such as (naturally) our personal past, our family models, or our social embeddedness within external culture; parental models and others' views of us are among the influences that shape our identity formation.[3] Paul, however, argues that our strongest level of identification should be our identity as followers of Christ: embedded in a new community, a new relationship with God, and thinking as Christ would, being conformed to his image (cf. Rom. 6:5; 8:29). For Paul, this new identity is not merely a cognitive strategy but an affirmation of a new reality.

In some ancient settings baptism could signify initiation; in a Jewish context it could be used to initiate proselytes who became part of God's people.[4] (In the limited surviving ancient Jewish sources on the subject, conversion was also sometimes held to make one a new person.)[5] If some claimed superiority by virtue of their solidarity with Abraham (cf. Paul's response in Rom. 4:9–16), Paul responds both by showing universal human solidarity with the prototypical sinner (5:12–21) and by noting that all those baptized into Christ have become part of God's people (cf. also Gal. 3:27–29).[6]

3. Identity formation is an important area of discussion in social sciences (e.g., Côte and Schwartz, "Approaches"; Somers, "Constitution"; Danielson, Lorem, and Kroger, "Impact"; Bosma and Kunnen, "Determinants"; Apple, "Power"; Adams, "Habitus"; Thomas and Azmitia, "Class"; Hoof, "Field") that invites further exploration with regard to Pauline anthropology but that I do not address here. Self-concept is sometimes discussed in terms of ethnic, cultural, religious, and gender identity (cf., e.g., Portes and MacLeod, "Hispanic Identity Formation"; Kibria, "Construction"; Côte, "Perspectives"; Jensen, "Coming of Age"; Brega and Coleman, "Effects"; Yoder, "Barriers"), with obvious relevance here; group identity through affiliations and collective identity that can rank over individual identity are relevant areas of discussion in terms of interpersonal identity development.
4. See, e.g., *t. Abod. Zar.* 3:11; *b. Ber.* 47b; *Abod. Zar.* 57a; *Yebam.* 46ab; *y. Qid.* 3:12, §8; Epict. *Diatr.* 2.9.20 (perhaps also Juv. *Sat.* 14.104; *Sib. Or.* 4.165; Justin *Dial.* 29.1); Pusey, "Baptism"; Schiffman, "Crossroads," 128–31; Schiffman, *Jew*, 26; Goppelt, *Theology*, 1:37; Bruce, *History*, 156; Ladd, *Theology*, 41; Meeks, *Urban Christians*, 150; my discussion more fully in Keener, *Acts*, 1:977–82, esp. 979–82. It is highly unlikely that early Judaism borrowed the practice from Christians. I do not address here whether Paul applies this image figuratively or literally, though initiation was sometimes applied figuratively (e.g., Max. Tyre *Or.* 8.7).
5. White, *Initiation*, 66; Keener, *John*, 542–44. For deliverance from evil in conversion to the covenant, see CD 16.4–5. For moral transformation and newness, see, e.g., *L.A.B.* 20:2; 27:10; *Jos. Asen.* 8:9/8:10–11.
6. For Paul, identity "in Christ" does not eliminate ethnic identities but is more central (see Johnson Hodge, "Apostle").

Paul describes the new identity in terms of being dead with Christ (Rom. 6:3–8), being freed from sin (6:6), and being promised a new destiny with Christ (cf. 6:5; 8:11).[7]

Dead with Christ

People in antiquity sometimes spoke of death figuratively or by way of comparison with an abject state.[8] One might also be "dead" to a person—in other words, alienated from them.[9] More relevant are spiritual and intellectual uses of the image. Pythagoreans treated apostates as dead.[10] Others might describe someone who lives for pleasure as continually dying or dead.[11] A Stoic could recommend amputating the dead part of one's soul;[12] when a person became incapable of grasping truth, their soul had become dead.[13] In general, the mortal masses who lived in ignorance could be deemed virtually dead.[14] For Philo too, genuine life and death had to do with the condition of the soul;[15] Adam's death was in his soul, "becoming entombed in passions."[16] In traditional Jewish wisdom a fool was like one who was dead.[17] A convert might be thought to have been brought to life.[18] In later Jewish tradition the wicked were deemed dead.[19]

Such figurative uses make Paul's appeal to the image of death more intelligible, but for him the primary connection is with Christ's death and being united through baptism with him. All people are connected with the prototypical sinner, Adam, as his offspring. Yet Christ died to Adam's sin (Rom. 5:12–21), so those who have been baptized into Christ now share his death to their sinful past in Adam (6:1–10). Now they must recognize this result of their new identity in Christ.

7. Although there is some debate about whether the activation of some aspects of new life in Rom. 6 is present or future, it is clear in the larger context of Romans that the present experience of life in Christ (6:11; 8:10) foreshadows future resurrection (8:11) for those who persevere (8:12–13).

8. E.g., Dio Cass. 45.47.5; *Exod. Rab.* 5:4.

9. Klauck, *Context*, 225, citing a curse tablet in *CIL* 1.1012; 6.140.

10. Iambl. *Pyth. Life* 17.73–75; 34.246; Burkert, "Craft," 18.

11. Dead in Sen. Y. *Ep. Lucil.* 60.4; 1 Tim. 5:6; continually dying in Philost. *Vit. Apoll.* 1.9.

12. Mus. Ruf. frg. 53, p. 144.24–25.

13. Epict. *Diatr.* 1.5.4.

14. Lucret. *Nat.* 3.1046; Epict. *Diatr.* 1.13.5. For references specifically to mortality or one under the sentence of death, cf. Gen. 20:3; *b. Pesah.* 110a; Diog. Laert. 2.35; perhaps Macrob. *Comm.* 1.11.2 (in van der Horst, "Macrobius," 224).

15. Philo *Mos.* 1.279; cf. Zeller, "Life"; Conroy, "Death."

16. Philo *Alleg. Interp.* 1.106.

17. Sir. 22:11–12. Cf. perhaps the proverb in Aeschylus *Lib.* 926.

18. *Jos. Asen.* 8:9 (Greek 8:11); cf. perhaps Daube, *New Testament and Judaism*, 137, and the sources cited in Buchanan, *Consequences*, 201 (*m. Ed.* 5:2; *Pesah.* 8:8; *b. Pesah.* 92a).

19. E.g., *y. Ber.* 2:2, §9; *Gen. Rab.* 39:7; *Eccl. Rab.* 9:5, §1. "As dead in the world to come" appears in *Tg. Qoh.* on 9:5.

Excursus: Mystery Background
for Dying and Rising with Christ?

In a sense, whatever particular background is employed here, it may not heavily shape the meaning of the text; nevertheless, some backgrounds are more or less plausible than others. One analogy often cited in earlier literature was the dying and rising gods of the mysteries, but the value of this analogy has proved quite limited. Many have associated mystery cults with dying-and-rising deities.[20] The idea of dying-and-rising deities predates Paul in both Greek[21] and ancient Near Eastern sources.[22]

But Osiris was magically revivified, not transformed into an eschatological new creation; his corpse was awakened through the same potencies that exist in procreation, and he remained in the netherworld, still needing to be protected there by vigilant gods and to be replaced on earth by his heir.[23] Adonis's death was mourned annually,[24] but the claim of his rising is not documented prior to the middle of the second century CE.[25] Apart from one third-century Christian testimony, no claims for Attis's resuscitation appear before the sixth century CE.[26]

Dionysus's return from death[27] belongs to the same category as mortals being deified and deities suffering harm;[28] some also understood him as returning annually for his holy days in the spring.[29] Frazer's scheme of the "dying and rising god" has thus come under heavy criticism in recent times.[30]

At least in later sources, initiation into some mysteries sometimes was thought to cause initiates to transcend their mortality through union with

---

20. E.g., Bultmann, *Christianity*, 158–59; Klausner, *Jesus to Paul*, 106, citing a fourth-century Christian text.

21. E.g., Persephone in Apollod. *Bibl.* 1.5.3 (though she was taken to the underworld alive); cf. Burkert, *Religion*, 160; Casadio, "Failing God."

22. E.g., *ANET* 52–57. Greeks were familiar with the motif in Egyptian sources; see, e.g., the second-century writers Plut. *Isis* 35, *Mor.* 364F; Max. Tyre *Or.* 2.5.

23. Wagner, *Baptism*, 119.

24. E.g., Plut. *Nic.* 13.7.

25. Wagner, *Baptism*, 171–207, esp. 195. Some sources suggest seasonal revivification (Apollod. *Bibl.* 3.14.4), but as noted below, this differs greatly from early Jewish and Christian notions and origins of the resurrection.

26. Wagner, *Baptism*, 219, 229.

27. Cf. Otto, *Dionysus*, 79–80, 103–19.

28. E.g., Hom. *Il.* 5.339–42, 382–404, 855–59, 870; on the death of Pan in Plut. *Mor.* 419.17, see Borgeaud, "Death."

29. See fragments of dithyrambic poetry (ca. 1 BCE) in *SP* 3:390–93.

30. See the documentation in Gasparro, *Soteriology*, 30n16; Mettinger, "Dying God."

deities.[31] Yet this later-attested view might even have depended on early Christianity, which had become increasingly popular (sometimes at their expense) by that period.[32] Indeed, many alleged parallels derive from the later Christian sources. That the church fathers understood the mysteries as "imitation démoniaque du Christianisme"[33] may suggest that they, like many early modern students of these cults, read them through the grid of their own Christian background, and the ready-to-hand explanation of demonic imitation may have led them to heighten rather than play down the similarities between the two.

Many Christian writers have asserted, again perhaps through the grid of their own religious understanding, that the mysteries must have provided salvation through union with dying-and-rising gods.[34] While there may be some truth in the idea that a god not subject to death could grant immortality, Walter Burkert, noted scholar of mystery cults, cautions that "this multiplicity of images can hardly be reduced to a one-dimensional hypothesis, one ritual with one dogmatic meaning: death and rebirth of 'the' god and the initiand."[35] Although the mysteries are well documented from an early period, much of the evidence for this proposed aspect of the mysteries is late[36] and often specifically Christian.[37]

In the Eleusinian rites, the initiate (μύστης) received the promise of a happy afterlife, but this took place by being pledged to the goddess, rather than by being reborn or by dying and rising with the deity.[38] The cult of Cybele also does not support dying and rising with her, as Cybele scholar Giulia Sfameni Gasparro notes.[39] The main problem with the view articulated by many members of the old *Religionsgeschichte* school, eager to produce "parallels" to primitive Christianity, is that most of the people who turned to the mysteries already believed in some afterlife in the netherworld anyway; it was merely a happier afterlife in that world that various gods could guarantee.

31. Proclus *Poet.* 6.1, K75.6–11.
32. For many mystery "parallels" with Christianity deriving only from a later period, see Metzger, "Considerations," 10–11; Eliade, *Rites,* 115.
33. Benoit, "Mystères," 79–81.
34. E.g., Conzelmann, *Theology,* 11; cf. Case, *Origins,* 111; Bultmann, *Christianity,* 158–59; Ridderbos, *Paul: Outline,* 22–29.
35. Burkert, *Mystery Cults,* 100.
36. Wagner, *Baptism,* 266–67. See, e.g., Apul. *Metam.* 11, whom Dunand ("Mystères," 58) interprets thus. For Apuleius dying and rising there, see Apul. *Metam.* 11.18, 23.
37. E.g., Firm. Mat. *Err. prof. rel.* 22, in Grant, *Religions,* 146.
38. Wagner, *Baptism,* 87. Thus, Heracles sought initiation so he could capture Cerberus in Hades (Apollod. *Bibl.* 2.5.12).
39. Gasparro, *Soteriology,* 82.

Nineteenth- and early twentieth-century scholars who drew such connections[40] did not take adequate account of the vegetative, cyclical, and seasonal nature of most of the resuscitation rituals.[41] This differs starkly from the earliest Christian picture of Christ's *bodily* resurrection rooted in explicit Jewish eschatological hopes—a perspective on the resurrection that Paul affirms is guaranteed by hundreds of eyewitnesses, including himself, and argues, despite his Hellenistic audience, is a necessary understanding of resurrection for a true follower of Jesus (1 Cor. 15:1–11). One would not think that earlier Palestinian Christianity held a less rigorously Jewish perspective than Paul did.[42]

Because the eschatological resurrection was envisioned as a singular event, Jesus's resurrection in advance necessarily entailed that of those who would be raised afterward (1 Cor. 15:20, 23). That is, the solidarity with Christ's resurrection is already built into the earliest Jewish-Christian concept of his rising.

At best the mysteries offer one among many analogies that some ancient hearers may have considered; mysteries by definition were secretive,[43] and Paul would hardly have appealed primarily to an analogy that only past mystery initiates (of whom he himself was not one) could have understood. Thus, however hearers in later centuries may have heard Paul's teaching in this passage, Paul's first audience shared with him the Jewish conception of corporate, eschatological resurrection, of which Christ's followers held Jesus's resurrection to be the foretaste. Most scholars today reject any connection with the mysteries here.[44]

The solidarity with Christ fits the Jewish conception of solidarity with Adam that directly precedes this passage in Paul's text (Rom. 5:12–21), on

40. Bousset, *Kyrios Christos*, 57, 191; cf. also Reitzenstein, *Mystery-Religions*, 9–10, 13; Käsemann, *Romans*, 161.

41. For vegetative associations, see, e.g., Ovid *Metam.* 5.564–71; Gasparro, *Soteriology*, 29, 43–49; Ruck, "Mystery," 44–45; Guthrie, *Orpheus*, 55–56.

42. Cf. Metzger, "Considerations," 19–20; Ring, "Resurrection," 228.

43. See, e.g., Hor. *Ode* 3.2.25–29; Livy 39.13.1–8; Plut. *Educ.* 14, *Mor.* 10F; Paus. 2.3.4; Heracl. *Ep.* 8; Apul. *Metam.* 3.15; Diog. Laert. 7.7.186; Athenag. *Plea* 4; Tatian *Or. Gks.* 27; Tert. *Apol.* 7.6; Burkert, *Mystery Cults*, 7–8; Mylonas, *Eleusis*, 224–29. Punishments for profaning mysteries appear in Xen. *Hell.* 1.4.14; Demosth. *Meidias* 175; Thucyd. 6.53.1–2; Ovid *Metam.* 3.710–20; Ps.-Plut. *Ten Or.* 2, *Andocides*, *Mor.* 834CD.

44. Wagner, *Baptism*; Goppelt, *Theology*, 2:49; Dunn, "Demythologizing," 293; Dunn, *Romans*, 1:308–11; Cranfield, *Romans*, 1:301–3; Wedderburn, "Soteriology"; Fitzmyer, *Romans*, 431.

which his mention of the "old person" (6:6) depends.[45] Others have appealed to various other additional analogies, such as Jewish people's participation in their ancestral experience at Passover.[46]

Does Death to Sin Eradicate Passions?

Some philosophers spoke of using reason to eradicate emotion; others criticized this view.[47] Earlier Stoics wanted to achieve a state of ἀπάθεια ("impassivity"), with choices no longer influenced by emotion.[48] Seneca felt that Peripatetics' halfway measures (seeking moderation) were ineffectual, preferring the Stoic approach of rejecting emotions fully.[49] Middle Platonists rightly noted that emotion remained part of one's being,[50] though they also mistrusted emotion.[51] Aristotle was more positive toward emotions than were either Stoics or Platonists,[52] though he insisted that persuasion rest on reason more than on emotion.[53]

45. For connection of the "old person" here with Adam, see Cyril Alex. *Rom.* on 6:6 (PG 74:796; Bray, *Romans*, 159); Barth, *Romans*, 197; Tannehill, *Dying*, 24; Moo, *Romans*, 374; Fitzmyer, *Romans*, 436; Keck, *Romans*, 163; Vlachos, "Operation," 55–56; cf. the allusion in Eph. 4:22–24 and esp. Col. 3:9–10. In Jewish thought, Adam introduced sin and thus death (*4 Ezra* 3:7; 4:30; *2 Bar.* 17:2–3; 23:4; 48:42–45; 56:5–6; *L.A.E.* 44:3–4; *Sipre Deut.* 323.5.1; 339.1.2; cf. Gen. 2:17), even though individuals replicated Adam's sin for themselves (*4 Ezra* 3:21; *2 Bar.* 18:1–2; 54:15, 19).

46. Davies, *Paul*, 103–4; Haacker, *Theology*, 65 (citing Wedderburn, "Soteriology," 71, who cites *m. Pesah.* 10:5).

47. Stoics went further than Platonists in believing that the passions could be extirpated, a view that many others criticized (Knuuttila and Sihvola, "Analysis," 16–17). Platonists shared the ideal, but more realistically (cf., e.g., Emilsson, "Plotinus on Emotions," 359). Paul may resemble Stoics to some extent here (Tobin, *Rhetoric*, 229) but, perhaps more important, follows the Jewish notion of the eschatological destruction of sin (see discussion below, pp. 41–42).

48. Meeks (*Moral World*, 44–45) notes that Stoics had backed away from this position by the time of Plutarch.

49. Sen. Y. *Ep. Lucil.* 116.1 (allowing Lucilius to keep his emotions once Seneca has purged them of vice). Cf. also *Ep. Lucil.* 75.1–3; the favorable opinion of Fabianus's self-control appears in Sen. E. *Controv.* 2.pref.2. For Stoics opposing it in speeches, see Mus. Ruf. frg. 36, p. 134.14–16; Anderson, *Rhetorical Theory*, 61.

50. Meeks, *Moral World*, 45. Modern studies show that emotion and intellect cannot be separated as neatly as ancient thinkers often wished (see Elliott, *Feelings*).

51. Knuuttila and Sihvola ("Analysis," 16–17) note that Plato was negative toward emotions because he wanted "to achieve detachment from a changing reality" (e.g., *Tim.* 42AD), but, like the Stoics, he did not believe that it was possible to extirpate them.

52. Knuuttila and Sihvola, "Analysis," 16; Tobin, *Rhetoric*, 229. Plotinus, a Neoplatonist, advises "eliminating the affections to the extent this is possible" (Emilsson, "Plotinus on Emotions," 359).

53. Kraftchick ("Πάθη") argues that Aristotle urged use of rational arguments to generate pathos (48–50) but that Paul's letter to the Romans used pathos as an appeal to stir or sway audience emotion (52–53). Paul employs pathos in his letters, formally like Roman orators, but

Those who were not Stoics generally criticized the Stoic ideal of ἀπάθεια; even those who distrusted emotion thought a moderate degree of emotion more realistic.[54] Philo, an eclectic Middle Platonist, valued moderation in various matters,[55] but sometimes he does use the term ἀπάθεια positively,[56] even valuing the extirpation of passions rather than moderation.[57] He allows that the one progressing toward perfection may still be moderating passions, but the ideal, perfect person has already eradicated them.[58]

Paul is plainly not a Stoic who wants to eradicate passion, even by virtue of the new creation. Paul's surviving letters reveal that he does not oppose all desire[59] or unpleasant emotion (cf. 1 Cor. 7:5, 7; 2 Cor. 7:5; 11:28; 1 Thess. 3:1, 5). When he offers concrete examples of desires related to sin, he seems to limit the designation to those expressed in behaviors that Scripture already circumscribed as sinful.[60]

Freed from Slavery

At least in later sources, rabbis agreed that, immediately upon coming up from immersion, a proselyte was to be considered fully an Israelite, now

---

appeals to arguments like Aristotle (56). On *ēthos* and *pathos* in Paul's letters, see also Sumney, "Rationalities." On Aristotle's use of emotion, see Hall, "Delivery," 232; Walde, "Pathos," 599; Olbricht, "*Pathos* as Proof," 12–17. Others also complained about excessive use of rhetorical passion (Plut. *Cic.* 5.4).

54. Knuuttila and Sihvola, "Analysis," 17; cf. Meeks, *Moral World*, 44–45; Dillon, "Philosophy," 796. Although Plato also valued the mean or moderation (Lodge, *Ethics*, 392, 442–55), it was particularly associated with Aristotle (Arist. *N.E.* 2.7.1–9.9, 1107a–1109b; *E.E.* 2.3.1–5.11, 1220b–1222b). For others, see, e.g., Cic. *Fin.* 3.22.73; Hor. *Sat.* 1.1.106–7; 1.2; *Ep.* 1.18.9; Pliny E. *N.H.* 28.14.56; Plut. *Dinner* 20, *Mor.* 163D; 21, *Mor.* 164B; Diog. Laert. 1.93 (Cleobulus, ca. 600 BCE); *Let. Aris.* 111, 122, 223, 256; Ps.-Phoc. 36, 59–69b, 98. See also the Delphic inscription counseling avoidance of extremes, Plut. *E Delph.* 2, *Mor.* 385D; *Or. Delphi* 29, *Mor.* 408E.

55. Philo *Abr.* 257; *Jos.* 26; *Spec. Laws* 3.96; 4.102 (cf. 4.144); *Virt.* 195; *Migr.* 147; Wolfson, *Philo*, 2:277.

56. Philo *Alleg. Interp.* 2.100, 102; 3.129; *Plant.* 98.

57. Philo *Alleg. Interp.* 3.129, 131, 134; *Unchangeable* 67; *Agr.* 17.

58. Philo *Alleg. Interp.* 3.140, 144.

59. Sometimes Paul employs the verb ἐπιθυμέω and its cognates in a neutral manner (cf. Phil. 1:23; 1 Thess. 2:17), but this usage was not unusual. Assuming that the Spirit as well as the flesh exercises desires, the same verb can apply both positively and negatively in Gal. 5:17; it is positive in 1 Tim. 3:1.

60. See esp. Rom. 1:24; 7:7; 13:9, 13–14; 1 Cor. 10:6; Gal. 5:17, 24 (surrounding a vice list in 5:19–21); Col. 3:5 (as part of a vice list). Stoics applied Paul's term for "sin" more widely, for anything not according to reason (e.g., Arius Did. 2.7.8a, p. 52.21–22; 2.7.11a, p. 62.31–33; 2.7.11d, p. 66.28–32; 2.7.11e, p. 68.17–20; 2.7.11g, p. 72.12; 2.7.11i, p. 78.20; 2.7.11k, p. 84.4, 9–10; 2.7.11L, p. 85.35; Mus. Ruf. 2, p. 36.16–17; 8, p. 64.11; 16, p. 102.14–16; Epict. *Diatr.* 1.18; 4.12.19; Marc. Aur. 9.4; but cf. Mus. Ruf. frg. 44, p. 138.26–30). For Paul, however, the term applies "only to moral conduct" (Deming, *Celibacy*, 173). In ordinary Greek it could apply merely to "error" (*Rhet. Alex.* 4, 1427a.30–31, 38–39).

like a new person.[61] But this raised a problem for Jewish slaveholders whose Gentile slaves converted. Amoraim agreed that a slave who performed the immersion of conversion was thereby freed from their former holder; thus, to maintain a slave's status as a slave, the slave must be baptized with marks of servitude.[62] Although the conjunction of the images of baptism and slavery here might be suggestive, we cannot be certain to what extent such practices may already have obtained in Paul's day.

Some earlier scholars saw in sacral manumissions[63] a probable background for Paul's imagery of Christ buying followers out of slavery to become his slaves.[64] While this proposal was not implausible, the actual verbal connections are extremely meager,[65] and specifically sacral manumission was very limited in light of the many figurative uses of slavery language in antiquity.

The general figures for slavery are more helpful. Jewish tradition recognized that God's people could be his servants in a positive sense;[66] Philo claims that the one who serves God alone is the only one who is free.[67] The Torah brought freedom, whether freedom from worldly cares, from national bondage, or from slavery in the coming world.[68] Greek texts could similarly speak of divine truth "freeing" one from slavery to worldly concerns.[69] Greek thinkers quite often warned against being enslaved by false ideologies[70] or passions.[71] Some

61. E.g., *b. Yebam.* 47b.

62. *B. Yebam.* 45b–46a. Cf. discussions in Bamberger, *Proselytism*, 127; Buchanan, *Consequences*, 206; Falk, "Law," 509; Stern, "Aspects," 628; Schiffman, *Jew*, 36–37.

63. For these, see, e.g., inscriptions in Deissmann, *Light*, 319–23 (including among Diaspora Jews, 321–22).

64. See esp. Deissmann, *Light*, 323–27.

65. Bartchy, *Slavery*, 121–25.

66. See, e.g., Deut. 32:36; Urbach, *Sages*, 1:386 (citing *Sipre Shelah* 115). I draw here from Keener, *John*, 750–51.

67. Philo *Good Person* 20.

68. E.g., *m. Ab.* 6:2; *b. B. Metsia* 85b; *Qid.* 22b (attributed to ben Zakkai); *Gen. Rab.* 92:1; *Num. Rab.* 10:8; *Pesiq. Rab.* 15:2; see, further, Abrahams, *Studies* (2), 213; Odeberg, *Pharisaism*, 50.

69. Crates *Ep.* 8, to Diogenes; Epict. *Diatr.* 4.7.17; cf. similarly Epict. *Diatr.* 3.24.68; Iambl. *Pyth. Life* 7.33; 17.78. Eurip. *Hec.* 864–67 says all are enslaved by something (money, fate, or law).

70. E.g., Arrian *Alex.* 3.11.2; Sen. Y. *Ep. Lucil.* 8.7; 27.4; Plut. *Lect.* 1, *Mor.* 37E; *Superst.* 5, *Mor.* 167B. One is also a slave of goals one serves (Philost. *Hrk.* 53.2).

71. E.g., Aeschines *Tim.* 42; Xen. *Oec.* 1.22–23; *Hell.* 4.8.22; *Apol.* 16; *Mem.* 1.3.8, 11; 1.5.1, 5; 4.5.3, 5; Soph. *Antig.* 756; *Wom. Tr.* 488–89; Plato *Phaedr.* 238E; Isoc. *Demon.* 21; *Nic.* 39 (*Or.* 3.34); Arrian *Alex.* 4.9.1; Diod. Sic. 10.9.4; 32.10.9; Sall. *Catil.* 2.8; *Sp. Caes.* 8.2; Cic. *Amic.* 22.82; *Off.* 1.29.102; 1.38.136; 2.5.18; *Senect.* 14.47; *Prov. cons.* 1.2; Hor. *Sat.* 2.7.83–87; Tibullus 2.4.1–3; Appian *C.W.* 5.1.8–9; Mus. Ruf. 3, p. 40.19; Sen. Y. *Ben.* 3.28.4; *Ep. Lucil.* 14.1; 39.6; 47.17; 110.9–10; 116.1; *Nat. Q.* 1.16.1; Epict. *Diatr.* 3.24.70–71, 75; Plut. *Bride* 33, *Mor.* 142E; Max. Tyre *Or.* 36.6; Porph. *Marc.* 34.523–25; Ach. Tat. 1.7.2–3; 5.25.6; Longin. *Subl.* 44.6; Diog. Laert. 2.75; 6.2.66; Diogenes *Ep.* 12; Heracl. *Ep.* 9; Socratics *Ep.* 14; *Pyth.*

spoke of internal freedom that enabled them to ignore external troubles.[72] Occasionally, those writing from an aristocratic perspective might warn that excess political freedom might bring the masses into moral excess.[73] Jewish writers influenced by Hellenism repeated the demand that people avoid slavery to passions;[74] other Jewish thinkers also recognized that one should not be enslaved to sin or the evil impulse (the *yēṣer hārā'*).[75]

Defined by Destiny in Christ

Some have regarded Paul as essentially a Pharisee who believed that the messianic era had come.[76] Even if this characterization is too simplistic, it reminds us of a central tenet in Pauline and other early Christian thought: the promised Messiah and resurrection had already come, thus inaugurating at least the initial phase of the promised kingdom, which would be consummated at Jesus's return.[77]

Whereas a struggle to overcome internal evil might appear in Romans 7:7–25 (see comment on pp. 85–92) in a manner similar to many Jewish sources, a decisive deliverance from evil (cf. 6:1–11) appears in Jewish sources as eschatological.[78] Later rabbis were convinced that God would destroy the

---

Sent. 21, 23; Apul. *Metam.* 11.15; Sir. 47:19. Derrett ("Sources") also finds the idea in ancient Buddhist texts, though these are much further removed geographically.

72. E.g., Sen. Y. *Ben.* 3.20.1–2; Epict. *Diatr.* 1.11.37; 1.19.8; 3.24.68; 4.7.16–18; Aul. Gel. 2.18.9–10; Diog. Laert. 7.1.121–22; cf. Philo *Cher.* 107. Epictetus considered freedom to be pursuing only what one can control (see Pérez, "Freedom").

73. E.g., Phaedrus 1.2.1–3, 11–31.

74. E.g., 4 Macc. 3:2; 13:1–2; *T. Ash.* 3:2; 6:5; *T. Jos.* 7:8; *T. Jud.* 18:6; Jos. *Ant.* 1.74; 4.133; 15.88; *War* 1.243; Philo *Abr.* 241; *Alleg. Interp.* 2.49; *Creation* 165; *Good Person* 17; *Heir* 269; *Unchangeable* 111; cf. Decharneux, "Interdits"; *Let. Aris.* 211, 221–23; *T. Jud.* 15:2, 5; *T. Sim.* 3:4; Rom. 6:6; 16:18; Phil. 3:19.

75. Odeberg, *Gospel*, 297–301; Odeberg, *Pharisaism*, 50–52, 56; cf. *Gen. Rab.* 94:8; Wis. 1:4. Cf. freedom from the hostile angel in CD 16.4–6; from the Angel of Death in late material in *Exod. Rab.* 41:7; 51:8; *Num. Rab.* 16:24; *Song Rab.* 8:6, §1; from astrological powers in *t. Suk.* 2:6; *b. Ned.* 32a; *Shab.* 156a; *Suk.* 29a; *Gen. Rab.* 44:10; *Pesiq. Rab.* 20:2.

76. Davies, *Paul*, 216; cf. already Ramsay, *Other Studies*, 89–90.

77. Although Paul usually reserves "kingdom" language for the future, he depicts Jesus's current lordship in other ways (Rom. 8:34; 1 Cor. 15:24–25; Phil. 2:9; Col. 3:1). Scholars often remark on the early Christian principle of the already/not yet (Minear, *Kingdom*, 147; Aune, "Significance," 5:93–94; Ladd, *Theology*, 322; Ridderbos, *Paul and Jesus*, 67), including in Pauline thought (Kümmel, *Theology*, 149; Howell, "Dualism"; Dunn, *Theology*, 466–72); for a possible relation to the foreshadowing and future day of the Lord in biblical prophets, cf. Ladd, *Kingdom*, 36.

78. See, e.g., Abrahams, *Studies* (1), 42. It is particularly for his failure to embrace the eschatological worldview that depends on divine activity that Martyn ("De-apocalypticizing") criticizes Engberg-Pedersen; see also Wright, *Faithfulness*, 1386–1406, esp. (for this point) 1389, 1393.

evil impulse in the eschatological time;[79] indeed, some said that he would publicly slay it in front of all humanity.[80] At least some later rabbis derived this idea from biblical promises that God would transform his people's hearts (Ezek. 36:26–27).[81]

The general concept did not originate with later rabbis. Already before Paul's era, Qumran's *Manual of Discipline* expected God to circumcise away Israel's *yēṣer* in the end time.[82] One or two generations after Paul, an apocalyptic writer declares that the first joy of the righteous in the coming age will be "their victory in the long fight against their inborn impulses to evil, which have failed to lead them astray from life into death."[83] Jewish tradition had long anticipated eschatological deliverance from sin[84] and from Satan.[85] Indeed, as the rabbis suggested, the idea appears already in the biblical prophets (Jer. 3:17; 31:32–34).

For Paul, the expected messianic time had come, and sin and the evil impulse had already been proleptically defeated.[86] The matter was not yet complete, but believers already had more than their own efforts to depend on; in the words of another early Christian writer, they had tasted "the powers of the

---

79. *Pesiq. Rab Kah.* Sup. 3:2; *Gen. Rab.* 89:1; *Exod. Rab.* 46:4; *Deut. Rab.* 2:30; *Eccl. Rab.* 2:1, §1; 12:1, §1 (according to the likeliest sense); one rabbi in *y. Suk.* 5:2, §2. Schechter (*Aspects*, 257, 289–92) also cites *Gen. Rab.* 48:11; *Exod. Rab.* 46:4; *Num. Rab.* 15:16; and other texts. Montefiore and Loewe (*Anthology*, 122–23) also cite *Num. Rab.* 17:6. Bonsirven (*Judaism*, 246) adds *Gen. Rab.* 26:6; *Song Rab.* 6:14. The evil impulse ceases at death for the righteous in *Gen. Rab.* 9:5; even for the wicked in *L.A.B.* 33:3. But in *b. Suk.* 52b, in the judgment the evil impulse will testify against those it has seduced.

80. *B. Suk.* 52a; cf. *Exod. Rab.* 30:17; Moore, *Judaism*, 493.

81. *Pesiq. Rab Kah.* 24:17; *b. Suk.* 52a; *Exod. Rab.* 41:7; *Deut. Rab.* 6:14; *Song Rab.* 1:2; 6:11, §1. Other, earlier texts echo Ezekiel's promise; see, e.g., 1QS 4.21; probably 4Q393 frgs. 1–2, col. 2.5 (cf. Ps. 51:10; Ezek. 11:19; 18:31).

82. 1QS 5.5 (according to the most likely way to translate the text); the idea here probably develops Deut. 30:6. The inclination appears in the context of straying after one's own heart and eyes. Turning to God's covenant also delivered one from sin, as long as one persevered (CD 16.4–6).

83. 2 Esd. 7:92 (NEB); cf. 7:114. See Wells, "Power," esp. 101–3.

84. 1QS 3.18–19, 23; 4.18–26 (esp. 4.19, 23); *Jub.* 50:5; *1 En.* 5:8–9; 10:16 (prefigured in the flood); 91:8–9, 16–17; 92:3–5; 107:1; 108:3; *Pss. Sol.* 17:32; *T. Mos.* 10:1; *Sib. Or.* 5.430 (if not a Christian interpolation); *y. Abod. Zar.* 4:7, §2; *Deut. Rab.* 3:11. For the annulling of sin offerings in some later rabbinic sources, cf. Davies, *Torah*, 54–55.

85. 4Q88 10.9–10; *T. Mos.* 10:1; *T. Zeb.* 9:8 MSS; cf. *Jub.* 50:5; Matt. 25:41; Rev. 20:10. Early Jewish sources often associated Satan with evil desires (*T. Ash.* 3:2; *Apoc. Mos.* 19:3; cf. Baudry, "Péché dans les écrits") or the spirit (of the two spirits) that incites sin (*Jub.* 1:20–21; 1QS 3.18–22 [with CD 5.18]); as probably in 1QH[a] 15.6, some later rabbis associated Satan with the evil impulse (Schechter, *Aspects*, 244–45; Best, *Temptation*, 48; cf. *b. B. Bat.* 16a; *Exod. Rab.* 30:17).

86. Davies, *Paul*, 23; Ellison, *Mystery*, 62.

coming age" (Heb. 6:5).[87] For Paul, Christ gave himself for our sins to deliver us from this present evil age (Gal. 1:4). This observation has implications for how believers should think. The gospel is a wisdom that transcends that of this age (1 Cor. 1:20; 2:7–10; 3:18), when people are blinded (2 Cor. 4:4).

Most relevant for this letter, believers should not be conformed to this age but rather be transformed by the renewing of their minds (Rom. 12:2). The new way of thinking reckons with the new situation: believers already belong to the future age (cf. 2 Cor. 1:22; 5:5) and should think and live accordingly.

Jewish tradition employed the phrase "new creation" in multiple ways,[88] but the dominant one in this period reflected the promise of a new heavens and new earth in Isaiah 65:17–18.[89] For Paul, being in Christ means that the new creation has already begun, and promised new things have come (2 Cor. 5:17).[90] The present, partial experience of this new reality should shape believers' thinking, toward Christ and everything else (2 Cor. 5:16).[91] Worldly evaluations of anyone (5:16a, 17a) are thus illegitimate,[92] and this includes the critical evaluations of Paul (5:11–16a; cf. 3:1; see also 1 Cor. 2:15; 3:4–5; 4:3; 9:3).

87. Although some translations render αἰών as "world" in some of these passages, "age" remains a more suitable English equivalent in the texts cited here.

88. For conversion as new creation in some sources, cf. *Jub.* 1:20–21; 5:12 (on which cf. Charles, *Jubilees*, lxxxiv); *Sipre Deut.* 32.2.1; *Abot R. Nat.* 12 A; 26, §54 B; *b. Sanh.* 99b; *Song Rab.* 1:3, §3; Davies, *Paul*, 119; Hunter, *Gospel according to Paul*, 24n1; Buchanan, *Consequences*, 210; more fully, Chilton, "Galatians 6:15"; Hubbard, *New Creation*, 54–76, esp. 73–74. For Rosh Hashanah, see, e.g., *Lev. Rab.* 29:12; Moore, *Judaism*, 1:533; cf. Moses in *Exod. Rab.* 3:15 (based on a wordplay); the Messiah in *Midr. Pss.* 2, §9 (on Ps. 2:7).

89. *1 En.* 72:1; *Jub.* 1:29; 4:26; cf. 1QS 4.25 (on which see also Ringgren, *Faith*, 165). See further Stephens, "Destroying"; Stephens, *Annihilation*; for OT usage, see Hubbard, *New Creation*, 11–25; in *Jubilees*, Hubbard, *New Creation*, 26–53. Later, cf. Qur'an 56.35.

90. See Strachan, *Corinthians*, 113–14; Héring, *Second Epistle*, 43; Bultmann, *Corinthians*, 157; Bornkamm, *Experience*, 22; Furnish, *Corinthians*, 314–15; Beale, "Background"; Dunn, *Theology*, 180; Barnett, *Corinthians*, 46, 225; Wright, *Faithfulness*, 478. For an individual's renewal as part of a wider new creation, cf. 1QHᵃ 19.16–17; Jackson, *Creation*.

91. For discussion of the connection between 2 Cor. 5:16 and 5:17 (and taking κατὰ σάρκα with οἴδαμεν and ἐγνώκαμεν, not Χριστόν), see further, e.g., Davies, *Paul*, 195; Martyn, "Epistemology," 286; Ladd, *Theology*, 373; Betz, "Christuserkenntnis"; Stanton, *Jesus of Nazareth*, 89–90; Witherington, *Corinthians*, 347; Scott, *Corinthians*, 134; Lambrecht, *Corinthians*, 95–96. "From now on" in 5:16 points in this direction (Martin, *Corinthians*, 151). Paul's opponents evaluate according to the flesh (2 Cor. 10:10; cf. 11:18), unlike Paul (10:2–4). In the Corinthian correspondence Paul repeatedly contrasts "this age," "this world," or "according to the flesh" with God's perspective (Litfin, *Theology*, 175–76).

92. See Furnish, *Corinthians*, 330; cf. Robinson, *Ephesians*, 52; Héring, *Second Epistle*, 42; Bruce, *Message*, 27. Ancients could understand a changed perspective: after Isaeus had left his life of promiscuity, someone asked him whether a particular woman was beautiful; he retorted, "I have ceased to suffer from eye trouble" (Philost. *Vit. soph.* 1.20.513, trans. Wright, LCL, 69).

Reckoning the New Reality by Faith

After establishing believers' new identity and status in God's sight (which is what counts, Rom. 6:1–10), Paul encourages believers to embrace God's perspective on them. They must share God's verdict that their life in Christ is new, and they can learn to live new life based on that belief. Paul has been preparing for this cognitive emphasis throughout the preceding discussion (recall ἀγνοεῖτε in 6:3, γινώσκοντες in 6:6, εἰδότες in 6:9).

Faith and Reckoning

As noted above, faith, for Paul, is embracing God's truth as opposed to suppressing that truth with false ideologies. Faith is the sound and right response to God's reliability.[93] For Paul, faith is a choice or a conviction, not a subjective emotional state. It is not, as it has come to mean in some circles today, wishing so powerfully ("make-believe") that one's imagination or will exerts a force in the external world. It is not a desperate and subjective leap into the dark. It is not even a rational determination that arises from excluding all the alternatives, as in some modern epistemology, although either this or an act of will might lead toward faith. Faith is more a sense that recognizes the accurate, divine perspective on reality and acts accordingly.[94]

In the sections between Romans 1:18–32 and 6:1–11, Paul has heavily emphasized believing (πιστεύω); after the thesis statement in 1:16,[95] it appears in another key statement in 3:22 and then six times in Paul's exposition of the text about Abraham's faith in 4:3, 5, 11, 17, 18, 24. If[96] we add uses of the cognate noun in 1:17; 3:22, 25–31; 4:5, 9, 11, 12, 13, 14, 16, 19, 20; 5:1, 2,[97] it becomes clear that this is a major motif of the preceding context for our present passage. Modern interpreters, thinking of the English terms "believe" and "faith" in subjective terms,[98] risk approaching Pauline faith's direction

93. That is, because God is πιστός, πίστις in him is genuinely rational (cf. Heb. 11:11).

94. Cf. the virtue of wisdom as the ability to perceive what is true and real (Cic. Off. 2.5.18).

95. Scholars often accept Rom. 1:16–17 as a thesis statement introducing the argument of either Romans or its first section. Ancient arguments sometimes had thesis statements, though not always (see comment in Keener, Acts, 1:708–9).

96. Although it would be difficult to separate Abraham's faith from his believing in Rom. 4:3–24, scholars currently debate whose πίστις appears in some of the passages, especially with references to "the faith[fulness] of Jesus" (3:22, 26). Aside from the disputed cases, however, enough emphasis on trust or faith(fulness) of Jesus's followers remains in the section to make the point here. (Also in any case, believers' faith rests on God's/Jesus's reliability/faithfulness.)

97. There is a variant in 5:2, though the majority of early texts do contain πίστις in some form.

98. Kant's relegation of faith to the subjective realm (though Kant himself still regarded the subjective realm as real) created the impasse that Kierkegaard sought to surmount with a leap into the dark. This modern conception that often informs our contemporary usage is not,

backward. Pauline faith is not meant to invite focus on the subject's ability to believe, thus initiating a never-ending cycle of self-questioning, but rather focuses on the object's trustworthiness. Because God and Christ are faithful, people can depend on them.[99]

In Romans 4:3–25 (and possibly also 5:1–11) Paul offers an extended midrash on Genesis 15:6: "And Abraham trusted God, and it was reckoned to his account as righteousness." Although Paul by no means limits his use of λογίζομαι ("reckon") to accounting language (cf., e.g., probably Rom. 8:18, 36; 14:14), it is no accident that his greatest cluster of the term appears in his exposition of this verse from Genesis (Rom. 4:3, 4, 5, 6, 8, 9, 10, 11, 22, 23, 24—eleven times). In Romans 4 God has reckoned righteousness to Abraham's account, and thus to the account of those who, like their spiritual father Abraham, believe.

Now, in his next use of the term, climaxing a discussion of new life in Christ accomplished by God (Rom. 6:1–10), Paul urges believers to "reckon" themselves the way that God has reckoned them (6:11).[100] That is, having already been made right by trusting God, they now ought to trust the reality that God has accomplished—that God has made them right in Christ. This includes the reality that they have a new identity in Christ as those who have died to sin. This reckoning follows God's reckoning; it does not give the person a new identity, but it does recognize the new identity that God has given.

Origen recognized both the reality of temptation and the higher dimension of reality of what was true in his identification with Christ: "Whoever thinks or considers that he is dead will not sin. For example, if lust for a woman gets hold of me or if greed for silver, gold or riches stirs me and I say in my heart that I have died with Christ . . . the lust is immediately quenched and sin disappears."[101]

---

however, the biblical sense of the term translated "faith." But even some Puritans apparently focused on the reliability of their faith. Analysis of subjective faith seems more prevalent in heavily Protestant societies that emphasize faith for soteriology and the necessity of election and/or conversion; such analysis may be less common where those actively professing Christ are a minority (and where their faith is not confused with ethnic allegiance), such that lines of faith demarcation are more self-evident.

99. Again my focus is not on the grammatical debate but simply theological: where specified, Christ and the Father are the normal objects of Pauline faith.

100. For Rom. 6:11 as the summary of 6:1–10, see Hubbard, *New Creation*, 94 (after clearly tracing the passage's structure); cf. Bornkamm, *Experience*, 75. (This structure seems more compelling than the ingenious chiasm proposed in Boers, "Structure.")

101. Origen *Comm. Rom.* on 6:11 (*CER* 3:188; trans. Bray, *Romans*, 162). Cf. Strong, who, however, puts less emphasis on ontological change: "Some prophecies produce their own fulfilment. Tell a man he is brave, and you help him to become so. So declaratory justification, when published in the heart by the Holy Spirit, helps to make men just" (*Systematic Theology*, 860).

Cognitive Reckoning in Other Ancient Sources

Paul was not alone in considering the role of reason and new perspective in overcoming passion. Ancient thinkers emphasized focusing one's mind on what was good (cf. Phil. 4:8).[102] Philosophy was a matter of using reason and contemplating what was necessary.[103]

Right thinking was crucial for Stoics.[104] A Stoic could contend that what matters most is to *think* rightly, being unafraid of fortune and joyful in hardship.[105] By disciplining the mind, people can learn to abstain from any pleasure, to endure any pain.[106] Stoics developed cognitive exercises in order to form habits of interpreting reality according to their philosophic beliefs.[107] Some adopted some Pythagorean exercises, such as taking inventory in the evening of one's reactions during the day.[108] For Stoics, the way things appeared was not necessarily reality; appearances were distorted by wrong thinking about them.[109] Indeed, externals were irrelevant to one's core identity.[110]

The cognitive element in Paul's imperative in Romans 6:11 should not be underestimated. Nor should we underestimate Paul's prior emphasis on identity; self-knowledge, including recognition of one's limitations, was a fundamental issue in ancient philosophy.

Excursus: Self-Knowledge[111]

The Delphic saying "Know yourself" probably originally meant to recognize one's limitations as a human and thus submit to the gods and one's

102. Such as focusing the mind on nature, to live in harmony with it (Mus. Ruf. frg. 42, p. 138.9–11), or on the soul (Plut. *Pleas. L.* 14); the gods would reward a good mind (Max. Tyre *Or.* 8.7). One's thinking (φρόνημα) should always be "turned toward God" (Porph. *Marc.* 20.327–29; trans. O'Brien Wicker, 63); one's speaking would thus be inspired (ἔνθεος, 20.329). Oaths to Caesar could even promise mental loyalty (*CIG* 3.137; *OGIS* 532; Sherk, *Empire*, §15, p. 31).

103. Mus. Ruf. 16, p. 106.3–6, 12–16.

104. Still, Stowers (following Rist, *Stoic Philosophy*, esp. 22–36, 256–72), warns, "It is misleading to overstress the cognitivist character of early Stoic thought" (*Rereading*, 361n22).

105. Sen. Y. *Nat. Q.* 3.pref.11–15.

106. Sen. Y. *Dial.* 4.12.4–5. Lutz, *Musonius*, 28, observes that Musonius also opined that through disciplining one's mind (Mus. Ruf. 6, p. 54.16–25) a wise person would achieve self-mastery (6, p. 54.2–10).

107. See Sorabji, *Emotion*, 165, 211–27. Some techniques remain useful today, e.g., relabeling (222–23). For Cynic practice of virtues, see, e.g., Malherbe, *Philosophers*, 16.

108. Sorabji, *Emotion*, 213.

109. Sorabji, *Emotion*, 165.

110. Mitsis, "Origin," 173.

111. Adapted from Keener, *John*, 236–37.

lot in life.[112] It became one of the most frequently cited maxims of Greek antiquity,[113] and many writers regarded it as one of life's most basic truths.[114] Ancient interpreters applied it in a variety of ways,[115] but some writers applied it in a manner consistent with its original sense. Plutarch, for example, declares that the flatterer violates the maxim by causing others to deceive themselves.[116] Elsewhere, addressing those who would censure others, he admonishes them to "know themselves," that is, search themselves first.[117] A Cynic writer explains that self-knowledge includes diagnosis of one's soul's diseases, moving one to get proper philosophic treatment.[118] One speaker declares that mortals understand who they are only when they study all of nature.[119] A Roman satirist uses the saying to critique those who specialize in esoteric knowledge but are ignorant of daily matters.[120] Aristotle notes that the vain are those who lack self-knowledge.[121] Some of Plato's applications retain the basic sense: virtue must come from knowledge, and true self-control relates to proper self-knowledge.[122] For Philo, self-deification, in contrast to recognizing the creator, can be cured by proper self-knowledge.[123] Such proper self-knowledge prepares one for the proper knowledge of God.[124]

This idea of self-knowledge as humility was not limited to the statement "Know yourself"; as Epictetus points out, "The man who does not know who he is, and what he is born for, and what sort of world this is that he exists in,

112. Nilsson, *Piety*, 47–48; Grant, *Religions*, xxii–xxiii; Marshall, *Enmity*, 192–93, 201; also Plut. *Demosth.* 3.2. Diog. Laert. 1.40 attributes the proverb to Thales.

113. E.g., Plato *Alcib.* 1.129A; *Charm.* 164E–65A; *Lov.* 138A; Xen. *Mem.* 3.9.6; 4.2.24; Diod. Sic. 9.10.2; Epict. frg. 1; Plut. *Flatt.* 25, *Mor.* 65F; *Profit by Enemies* 5, *Mor.* 89A; *Dinner* 21, *Mor.* 164B; *E Delph.* 17, *Mor.* 392A; 21, *Mor.* 394C; Hippol. *Ref.* 1.15. Allusions are also frequent, e.g., Antisthenes in Diog. Laert. 6.1.6; Epict. *Diatr.* 1.2.11; 1.18.17; Cic. *Fin.* 3.22.73; Sen. Y. *Ep. Lucil.* 35.

114. E.g., Epict. *Diatr.* 3.1.18; Plut. *Apoll.* 28, *Mor.* 116CD; *E Delph.* 2, *Mor.* 385D; *Or. Delphi* 29, *Mor.* 408E; *R. Col.* 20, *Mor.* 1118C.

115. For a survey, see Reiser, "Erkenne."

116. Plut. *Flatt.* 1, *Mor.* 49B.

117. Plut. *Profit by Enemies* 5, *Mor.* 89A; cf. a similar sense in Thales, according to Diog. Laert. 1.36.

118. Diogenes *Ep.* 49.

119. One view appears in Cic. *Fin.* 5.16.44; in 5.15.41–43 one offers the view that we come to this knowledge only over time.

120. Juv. *Sat.* 11.23–28.

121. Arist. *N.E.* 4.3.36, 1125a.

122. Plato *Charm.* passim; *Alcib.* 1.129A; *Lov.* 138A. For a fuller discussion of Plato's view of knowledge, cf. Gould, *Ethics*, 3–30.

123. Philo *Spec. Laws* 1.10.

124. Philo *Spec. Laws* 1.264–65; *Migr.* 195; *Dreams* 1.60; cf. *Unchangeable* 161; *Names* 54; *Dreams* 1.211–12.

and whom he shares it with . . . such a man, to sum it all up, will go about deaf and blind, thinking that he is somebody, when he really is nobody."[125]

Other applications became more common in time, however. The magical papyri apparently use the saying as an exhortation to secure power over one's daimon by magical formulas, using it for inquiry.[126] It moved even further from its original sense in the Hermetica, which interpret it into a summons to divinization.[127] Yet long before the Hermetica, Cicero interpreted the maxim as declaring that knowing one's own soul was godlike (*divinum*);[128] by Pompey's day an Athenian inscription announced that recognition of one's humanity produced divinity;[129] Neoplatonic self-knowledge included the reality that the real self did not include the body, inviting divine union;[130] and many philosophers had linked knowledge of God and participation in divinity.[131] This view never became the only one, however; not long after the time of John, Plutarch interpreted the response to "Know yourself" as the fact that only the deity was changeless and mortals were not divine.[132]

As Stowers notes, philosophers believed that the wise "could reconstitute the self on a new basis," allowing it to achieve virtue by mastering "passions and desires." Different philosophies insisted on different ways to bring about the "new self," but all attributed wrong passions to false beliefs about reality. The different schools merely disagreed on which beliefs about reality were false![133]

Stoics taught their disciples a new worldview, moving from youthful self-awareness and self-seeking to a more mature, wider view of the world,[134] where things are valued according to nature rather than according to how they benefit the self.[135] When the mind moves to contemplation of the cosmos, one transcends one's mortality to contemplate divine matters.[136]

125. Epict. *Diatr.* 2.24.19 (trans. Oldfather, LCL, 1:417); cf. quite similarly, Marc. Aur. 8.52.
126. Betz, "Maxim in Papyri."
127. Betz, "Hermetic Interpretation," 465–84; cf. Dodd, "Prologue," 16.
128. Cic. *Tusc.* 1.22.52.
129. Plut. *Pomp.* 27.3.
130. Porph. *Marc.* 32.485–95.
131. Winslow, "Religion," 246.
132. Plut. *E Delph.* 17, *Mor.* 392A and context; see also Meeks, *Moral World*, 43.
133. Stowers, "Resemble," 92. Articulation of divine realities in noetic terms appears from Philo and some patristic writers through medieval Judaism; see Giulea, "Noetic Turn."
134. Engberg-Pedersen, *Paul and Stoics*, 53–54, citing Cic. *Fin.* 3.
135. Engberg-Pedersen, *Paul and Stoics*, 55–59, citing Cic. *Fin.* 3.20–21.
136. Sen. Y. *Nat. Q.* 1.pref.7, 17.

Stoic wisdom focused on *self-cognition*—a new view of one's own identity, a new self-awareness in a "radically cognitive" way.[137] For Stoics, this meant not a replacement of the "I-person" but a new content of that identity.[138] Some suggest that Paul identifies with Christ in a manner analogous to how Stoics identified with reason.[139]

Identifying with Christ

Despite some very limited analogies, Paul's idea of identification with Christ is distinctive. Identification with a deity is attested in some popular texts in an Egyptian context,[140] though in contrast to Paul's approach, many of these texts might be intended to deceptively manipulate spirits, perhaps as sympathetic magic.[141] The practice of a patron or recommender identifying with a client or friend, however, was common; one could request that the receiver grant the requested favor for the person "as if he were myself," or in similar ways.[142] Friends and allies sometimes said, "I am as you are," or "What is mine is yours."[143] One might deem a close friend as another iteration of oneself.[144]

For Paul, however, this identification with another is no mere useful fiction or hyperbole;[145] it reflects a genuine union with Christ on which the cognitive decision is based. As Luke Timothy Johnson observes, believers are to act new in Romans 6 "precisely because they have been given the

---

137. Engberg-Pedersen, *Paul and Stoics*, 65.

138. Engberg-Pedersen, *Paul and Stoics*, 55. Philosophers disagreed as to whether the "I-person" could continue eternally (see Sorabji, *Emotion*, 243–49), but the self could continue during one's life.

139. Engberg-Pedersen, *Paul and Stoics*, 70, 91, 95 (citing, e.g., Phil. 1:20–21). For Philo, the fixed point was not human freedom or choice but God (cf. Levy, "Breaking").

140. E.g., *PGM* 1.178–81.

141. Cf. *Book of Dead*, Spell 30, parts P-1 and 2; Spell 43a, part P-1, 43b; Spell 79, part S-2; Spell 85a, part S-1; Spell 131, parts P-1 and 2, S-1; Spells 145–46; *PGM* 1.251–52; 4.169–70, 216–17, 385–90; *PDM Suppl.* 131–32, 163, 183. Unlike *PGM* and *PDM*, the *Book of the Dead* spells are pre-Christian.

142. E.g., P.Oxy. 32.5–6; Cic. *Fam.* 13.5.3; 13.45.1; 13.46.1; cf. Fronto *Ad amicos* 1.4, 8; 2.6; *Ad verum imp.* 2.7.7; 1 Cor. 16:10; Philem. 17–19; Kim, *Letter of Recommendation*, 7, 37–42.

143. Xen. *Cyr.* 5.4.29; 6.1.47; Sen. E. *Controv.* 8.5; Pliny *Ep.* 1.4.2–3; 6.18.3; 6.26.3; 6.28.3; 6.30.1; 6.32.2; Suet. *Galba* 20.1; 1 Kings 22:4; 2 Kings 3:7; 2 Chron. 18:3; Gal. 4:12. One might also put people on the same level negatively, as in Herodes *Mime* 2.8.

144. E.g., Diod. Sic. 17.37.6; Cic. *Fam.* 7.5.1; 13.1.5; Val. Max. 4.7.ext.2ab; Quint. Curt. 3.12.17; Pliny *Ep.* 2.9.1; cf. Cic. *Fin.* 1.20.70; Sen. Y. *Ep. Lucil.* 95.63; *Let. Aris.* 228; perhaps Cic. *Or. Brut.* 31.110.

145. Cranfield, *Romans*, 1:315: not pretending, "nor a mere ideal, but a deliberate and sober judgment on the basis of the gospel" that "accepts as its norm what God has done in Christ." Cf. also Ladd, *Theology*, 479; Kruse, *Romans*, 267. Some suggest that Paul must emphasize transformation to counter charges or doubts such as appear in Rom. 3:8; cf. Tobin, *Rhetoric*, 216; Moo, *Romans*, 295; elsewhere, cf. Gal. 2:17–20.

power of new life (5:17, 21)."[146] Taking into account God's help offers a different view of reality and thus a motivation to act accordingly.[147] Like Abraham, believers can act with faith in what God speaks more than in the usual patterns of finite existence (Rom. 4:19–21). That human pride or "boasting" would rebel at this approach is not surprising; in Christ, it is God rather than ourselves who gets the credit for our righteousness (cf. 2:17, 23; 3:27; 4:2; 5:11).

Given the reality in Christ, a forced choice between forensic and participationist categories is not necessary.[148] Both instrumental[149] and local, as well as personal and corporate,[150] uses of "in Christ" appear in various contexts.[151] The experiential aspect is accomplished through the Spirit, not through a mystical sense of Christ's body;[152] the body was actually a common ancient metaphor for the state.[153]

Living Out the New Identity

For Paul, "reckoning" offers the link between the justified new identity and the expected new, righteous behavior. Scholars often note a tension or

---

146. Johnson, *Romans*, 105. Cf. Schlatter, *Romans*, 3: true faith brings about true righteousness, not by legalism but by oneness with Christ (cf. 133, 152); Schreiner, *Romans*, 305: "The focus in Rom. 6 is not on the penalty of sin but on its power"; Ortlund, "Justified," 339: "Union with Christ inaugurates not merely external reformation but internal transformation."

147. See, e.g., Jos. *Ant.* 3.44–45; Sir. 7:16 (μὴ προσλογίζου σεαυτόν); *m. Ab.* 2:1. Naturally, such views were effective only to the extent that they reflected genuine reality (1 Sam. 4:3, 6–11).

148. See Wright, *Justification*, 72; Wright, *Faithfulness*, 903, 912; in Reformers, McCormack, "Justification," 171. The reaction against a participationist approach may have been partly because its early twentieth-century supporters indefensibly embedded the approach in mystery cults (Longenecker, *Introducing Romans*, 308) and other conceptual errors (310).

149. E.g., Conzelmann, *Corinthians*, 21; forensic in Parisius, "Deutungsmöglichkeit"; Campbell (*Union*) emphasizes the instrumental use more (but not exclusively).

150. For a corporate sense, see, e.g., Manson, *Paul and John*, 67; Gibbs, *Creation*, 132–33; esp. Robinson, *Body*.

151. See fuller discussions in Büchsel, "In Christus"; Neugebauer, "In Christo"; Robinson, *Body*; Best, *Body*; Davies, "In Christo"; Bouttier, *En Christ*; Toit, "In Christ"; Campbell, *Union* (particularly thoroughly). Following Deissmann (see *Paul*, 135–39), some have also argued for a mystical sense (Hatch, *Idea*, 38–39; Wikenhauser, *Mysticism*, 21–33, 50–65; Mary, *Mysticism*, 15–28; Thuruthumaly, "Mysticism"; Kourie, "Christ-Mysticism"; cf. Pathrapankal, "Christ"), though usually not in the sense of absorption (see Deissmann, *Paul*, 152–54). For the relational aspect, see, further, Dunn, *Romans*, 1:324; Dunn, *Theology*, 396–401.

152. See Judge, *First Christians*, 568–71.

153. Judge, *First Christians*, 581; Keener, *Romans*, 145; Keener, *Corinthians*, 103. The image was first attributed to Menenius Agrippa (Dion. Hal. *Ant. rom.* 6.86.1–5; Livy 2.32.9–12; Plut. *Coriol.* 6.2–4; Dio Cass. 4.17.10–13), but many writers employed it after him (e.g., Sall. *Ep. Caes.* 10.6; Cic. *Resp.* 3.25.37; *Phil.* 8.5.15; cf. Arist. *N.E.* 1.7; *T. Naph.* 2:9–10). See also Stoic use for the cosmos, e.g., Sen. Y. *Ep. Lucil.* 95.52; Epict. *Diatr.* 1.12.26; Marc. Aur. 7.13.

(as I would put it) a complementarity[154] in Paul between the indicative and the imperative.[155] Because believers *are* new in Christ, they should act accordingly. The connection between the changed identity of believers in Romans 6:1–10 and the exhortations of 6:12–23 (which is also full of reminders of changed identity) is the exhortation[156] in 6:11 to account oneself dead to sin but alive to God in Christ.[157]

That is, one must recognize the truth of one's new situation. Although Paul's multiple rhetorical questions in 6:1–3 accumulate rhetorical force, Paul's question in 6:3 might also function as a hypothetical connection between the failure to live out the new life and ignorance of the new reality (ἀγνοεῖτε). Paul also predicates confidence in believers' future destiny in Christ on the knowledge of their death with Christ (γινώσκοντες in 6:6, εἰδότες in 6:9). This cognitive motif climaxes with embracing God's perspective in 6:11 (λογίζεσθε).

An imperative based on a prior indicative, or commandments based on prior redemption, also fits an Old Testament model of exhortation.[158] The concept would have been intelligible to others in antiquity, although Paul would apply their premise of prior goodness[159] only to those first transformed by grace. Compare the early Greek poet Pindar: "Become such as you are, having learned what that is."[160] The same sort of argument makes sense in a Stoic context as well.[161]

Like Stoics, Paul seeks to help believers understand their new identification, an understanding in which they must progress and for which paraenesis is

154. *Pace* Bultmann, Engberg-Pedersen (*Paul and Stoics*, 224, on Rom. 6–8) argues that the indicative vs. imperative is not really a problem in need of a solution. Because the imperative functions as a reminder, and the matter is entirely cognitive, there is no contradiction (233; cf. 225). Engberg-Pedersen—and ancient Stoicism—may play down noncognitive elements too much (cf. Martyn, "De-apocalypticizing"; Stowers, "Self-Mastery," 538), but he offers important insight on the cognitive element of the question in Rom. 6:11 and some other passages.

155. See, e.g., Ridderbos, *Paul: Outline*, 253–58; Goppelt, *Theology*, 2:136–37; Bornkamm, *Experience*, 71; Kümmel, *Theology*, 224–28; Dunn, *Theology*, 626–31; Saldanha, "Rediscovering"; Prasad, "Walking"; Matera, *Romans*, 161–63; Bird, *Colossians*, 95. Cf. Engberg-Pedersen, *Paul and Stoics*, 294: "*reminding* his addressees of what *has* happened and his *appeal* to them to put it into *practice*." But see esp. Horn and Zimmermann, *Jenseits*, including critique.

156. Jewett (*Romans*, 408) reads λογίζεσθε as indicative rather than as imperative, against "most commentators." Context, however, rules firmly against this interpretation.

157. See Tannehill, *Dying*, 77.

158. Rosner, *Ethics*, 86–89, citing, e.g., Deut. 7:5–6; 14:1–2; 27:9–10.

159. Platonists deemed the true being or pure essence of the soul as wholly good (Iambl. *Soul* 8.45, §456; 8.48, §457; cf. Ps.-Simpl. *De an.* 241.16–17).

160. Γένοι᾿, οἷος ἐσσὶ μαθών (Pindar *Pyth.* 2.72; trans. Race, LCL, 1:238–39). Others also sometimes recognized the more general principle that accurate self-confidence would help one's work (e.g., Pliny *Ep.* 1.3.5).

161. Engberg-Pedersen, *Paul and Stoics*, 233.

helpful.[162] In Stoicism, "Once a person had come to the decisive insight and self-understanding that reordered every value in relation to that insight, then one was qualitatively different, even if one still" needed to be exhorted with respect to details.[163] Paul's paraenesis in Romans remains consistent with his prior argument.

Considering Paul's Solution

Paul would not view his approach as merely a mental reform method, analogous to that of philosophers. His understanding of faith in Christ's work of righteousness includes accepting righteous status in Christ and leaving the righteousness-forming work to God. In Romans 7 Paul will argue that mere religion or knowledge of God's standards does not transform the identity of the sinful person in God's sight; it simply reorganizes the flesh in a more orderly and less harmful way.[164] What alternative solution does Paul offer? The mind of faith—the mind that trusts in Christ—recognizes a new identity, in which the past is forgiven and one's bodily impulses do not set one's agenda.

In today's language, Paul would presumably allow that the old triggers may remain, yet he would insist that those who count themselves dead with Christ (Rom. 6:11) can choose not to react to these triggers, which do not belong to their fundamental new identity. In the sight of the true judge, one is justified by Christ and therefore may live from one's new identity defined in him. Thus, both accusations and temptations, framed as charges that one must answer or the belief that one's desires define one's choices, may be dismissed and left with Christ (8:31–34).[165] The patterns need not be denied; they simply need not be embraced as determinative of one's current identity or choices. When they seem too insistent to be dismissed, one may lay claim forcefully to one's identity in Christ based on what Christ has done. This new construction of personal identity is reinforced by one's new social identity as part of the people of God.[166]

---

162. Engberg-Pedersen, *Paul and Stoics*, 238–39.

163. Stowers, "Self-Mastery," 536 (following Engberg-Pedersen).

164. Understanding God's law could help one to fulfill it (Ps. 119:32, 34, 73, 104), and the law provided wider understanding that included a framework for understanding the world (119:130), but ultimately this must include the heart embracing the truth, i.e., faith (cf. 119:10–11, 34, 36, 69, 111–12, 161). Praying for understanding was good (119:125, 144, 169), as was praying for a heart to fulfill God's word (119:80).

165. Presumably, such cognitive reckoning does not preclude prayer for protection from temptation (Matt. 6:13//Luke 11:4; cf. Mark 14:38; Col. 1:9; 1 Thess. 3:10; 2 Thess. 1:11; Philem. 6) or precautions taken to avoid succumbing to it (1 Cor. 7:5; Gal. 6:1; cf. 1 Cor. 10:13).

166. As my colleague Virginia Holeman in Asbury Theological Seminary's school of counseling has brought to my attention (correspondence, Nov. 16, 2014), social reinforcement through relationships is a major factor in constructing social identity.

Is affirmation of one's new identity simply a psychological tool for transformation? Psychologists who work on self-esteem do help people in a sense to embrace a new identity that is less susceptible to old patterns of thinking. Paul would surely affirm the value of viewing oneself as loved by God (Rom. 5:8–11; 8:31–39; Gal. 2:20). Moreover, he would agree that expectations help shape behavior; certainly, there are reasons why Paul reminds believers of their new identity when urging them to live their new way rather than their old way (1 Cor. 6:11).

For Paul, however, the new identity includes a genuine gift of righteousness in Christ: objective forgiveness of the past and a new destiny. Their identity in Christ is distinct from and more fundamental than their self-perception, because it rests on God's verdict. The believer does not achieve the new identity by consciously remembering or reckoning it, but when one does recognize it (as in Rom. 6:11), one's awareness and consequent action are brought into closer alignment with one's identity as righteous in Christ. The believer appropriates this reality in experience by acting on faith in the same gospel that provided the new identity to begin with.

In an exclusively psychological approach a believer can imagine that Christ is living through the believer; one may thus live *as if* God's new character is formed within one (cf. Gal. 2:20; 4:19; 5:22–23). The difference between this approach and Paul's perspective is that for him, this affirmation does in fact correspond with divine reality, on the level of God's verdict and what he calls the believer to share in affirming. The "as if" is grounded in divine justification.[167]

Conclusion

Paul argues for a new identity in Christ, one defined historically in relation to Christ's death and resurrection and eschatologically in relation to believers' ultimate and completed destiny. Whereas existence in the world conceives its identity in terms of the individual's past and present experience, life in Christ derives its identity from Christ—both his past death and resurrection for us and our future destiny in him.

Paul lays out both indicative and imperative elements in Romans 6. The indicative element is Christ's decisive death and resurrection, historically accomplished events, and the believer's new identity in Christ. The imperative

---

167. Cf. the valid protest of Wright (*Faithfulness*, 779) against Bultmann's anthropocentric approach. Wright rightly emphasizes apocalyptic inner transformation here, corresponding to the sort of incipient or partially realized eschatology that Paul sometimes articulates. See also Wright, "Romans," 541, quoted appropriately by Kruse, *Romans*, 267.

invites the believer to believe even more fully—as one has accepted the meaning of Christ's death and resurrection for reconciliation with God, one should also accept its implications for one's new life.

Believers being righted[168] is God's perfect gift in Christ; new behavior may now proceed from a new identity, rather than from trying to achieve a right identity by one's own imperfect behaviors. New behavior is thus achieved not by weighing temptation as if nothing decisive has happened but by regularly recognizing that Christ has already defeated sin, a recognition that Pauline theology also calls "putting on" the new person (Rom. 13:14; Eph. 4:24; Col. 3:12, 14). Insofar as any battle remains, it is a battle of faith in Christ's triumph rather than a self-focused struggle to defeat the flesh by means of the flesh.

168. "Being righted" is traditionally rendered "justified" (sometimes "rightwised" or "put right") in English. I have preferred something of a neologism to allow consideration of its multiple possible dimensions. A single word will not bear the entire concept, far less in translation; my neologism is meant to highlight a sometimes-neglected aspect, but it is not necessarily better than traditional renderings.

3

@@@@

The Mind of the Flesh
(Rom. 7:22–25)

But I witness a different law working in my body's members, warring against the law that's in my mind and taking me prisoner
to the sin-focused law working in my body's members. . . . Thus
I myself am a servant to God's law with my mind, but to a sin-
focused law with my flesh.

—Romans 7:23, 25

In Romans 7:7–25 Paul depicts, in graphically anguished terms, existence
without divine righteousness despite knowledge of the law. In contrast to the
Gentile mind of 1:18–32, which is ignorant of God's special revelation, the
tormented figure of 7:22–25 has this revelation—and thus finds himself all
the more explicitly condemned for his sin.[1]

Because scholars continue to debate the identity of the figure in Romans 7,
I must survey first, and for much of this chapter, questions surrounding this
issue. I will agree with the strong majority of scholars that this passage depicts

1. A gender-neutral pronoun would work best here, but for the sake of selecting one gender
or the other, I fall back on the conventional default masculine pronoun, especially in view of
the teaching role in Rom. 2:18–20, in this period presumably filled by a male.

life under the law. I will further argue that this is only life under the law without life in Christ; with a majority of current scholars, I deny that 7:7–25 depicts Paul's current experience as a Christian. Paul's pre-Christian existence, viewed retroactively as a Christian, could inform his presentation, but autobiography is not his interest here. The recognition that Paul depicts life under the law apart from Christ provides the foundation for the more specific observations regarding the mind later in this chapter.

Depiction of Christian or Pre-Christian Situation?

Scholars have approached Romans 7:7–25 from various perspectives and combinations of perspectives throughout history.[2] My purpose here is not to note all important scholarship on the issue but simply to summarize and provide samples of the different views, and in the process also to advance what I think is the likeliest view, namely, the majority view that Paul depicts existence judged by the law and does not depict his own Christian experience.

Earlier Interpreters

Most of the earliest interpreters, who would have first read Romans as a whole more than piecemeal, understood this passage as referring to someone unconverted.[3] Origen argues that Paul adopts here the persona of someone not yet fully transformed by conversion.[4] Paul is simply becoming as the weak to the weak (1 Cor. 9:22).[5] Like Origen, ancient commentators frequently viewed the narrator's voice as that of a persona different from Paul.[6] They anticipated many modern explanations. Ambrosiaster viewed Romans 7:14 as addressing those under the law.[7] For Pseudo-Constantius, Paul speaks as an

2. For much more detailed summaries, see Schreiner, *Romans*, 380–92; Jewett, *Romans*, 441–45; MacGorman, "Romans 7," 35–38.

3. With, e.g., Morris, *Romans*, 284. For the ancient view that it is autobiographical but pre-Christian, see MacGorman, "Romans 7," 35; Robinson, *Wrestling*, 83–84.

4. Reasoner (*Full Circle*, 69, 84) sees this as one not yet converted but being convicted and thus in the process of conversion; see Origen *Comm. Rom.* 6.9–10 (PL 14:1085–91; Burns, *Romans*, 170–73). In *Comm. Rom.* on 7:17 (*CER* 3:274, 276; Bray, *Romans*, 193), Origen opines that Rom. 7:17 depicts someone who knows right and has Christ but is not yet mature.

5. Origen *Comm. Rom.* on 7:14 (*CER* 3:270; Bray, *Romans*, 190; Burns, *Romans*, 154, 171–73); he compares Paul to the psalmist sometimes identifying with sinners (e.g., Ps. 38:6–8).

6. Stowers, "Self-Mastery," 537; Stowers, *Rereading*, 268; Bray, *Romans*, 189–90.

7. Ambrosiaster *Comm.* on Rom. 7:14 (CSEL 81:233–35; Bray, *Romans*, 190). Cf. Ambrosiaster *Comm.* on Rom. 7:24 (CSEL 81:245; Bray, *Romans*, 197): Paul addresses one born in sin, but in Christ people can "put sin to death." John Chrysostom notes here (*Hom. Rom.* 13 on Rom. 7:24; Bray, *Romans*, 197) that law and even conscience could not save.

adult who earlier had been under law.[8] For Cyril of Alexandria, 7:15 apparently "refers to the ignorant Gentiles, whose thoughts Paul is reproducing."[9] Diodore contends that "Paul is not condemning himself here but describing the common lot of mankind, which he sees in himself."[10] For Pelagius, the carnal, divided person of whom Paul speaks in 7:25 cannot be Paul himself, since God's grace had set him free.[11]

At one time Augustine also recognized that in Romans 7:7–25 Paul depicts "himself as a man set under the law" and adopts that persona.[12] While Augustine originally believed that these verses referred to the unconverted,[13] however, he shifted his opinion in his later works, partly in reaction against Pelagius's perfectionist views on the will.[14] Augustine forthrightly notes that his dispute with the Pelagians occasioned his change of mind.[15] The Western medieval church largely adopted the view that 7:7–25 depicts the life of believers. Compare already Jerome: "If Paul feared the lusts of the flesh, are we safe?"[16] Yet even Augustine would not have taken comfort in all who shared his view. Earlier, for example, the gnostic thinker Valentinus apparently had also applied the passage to the pneumatic person's experience.[17]

Views continued to vary over the centuries. Aquinas applied the passage to both the righteous and the unrighteous.[18] Erasmus applied it to the

8. Ps.-Const. *Rom.* on 7:14, 25 (*ENPK* 49, 52; Bray, *Romans*, 191, 199).

9. Cyril Alex. *Rom.* on 7:15 (PG 74:808–9; trans. Bray, *Romans*, 191; Burns, *Romans*, 176).

10. Diodore of Tarsus, catena on Rom. 7:15 (*PGK* 15:89; trans. Bray, *Romans*, 191); cf. Diodore, catena on Rom. 7:22 (*PGK* 15:89; Bray, *Romans*, 195).

11. Pelagius *Comm. Rom.* on 7:25 (*PCR* 105; Bray, *Romans*, 199).

12. Aug. *Simp.* 1.1 (trans. Bray, *Romans*, 182).

13. Reasoner, *Full Circle*, 70, on an unregenerate Jew's existence prior to law and under law (citing Aug. *Prop. Rom.* 37–48, on Rom. 7:8–8:3; *Div. Q.* 66.4–5; *Simp.* 1.1, 7).

14. Reasoner, *Full Circle*, 84 (on 70 noting a shift already in Aug. *Guilt* 1.27.43 and full change in *Ep.* 6.138–55); Moo, *Romans*, 443–44 (citing Aug. *Retract.* 1.23.1; 2.1.1; *Ag. Pelag.* 1.10–11); Bray, *Romans*, 196, 199 (citing Aug. *Nat. Grace* 55.65, on Rom. 7:23; *Prop. Rom.* 45–46, on 7:25; *Ag. Jul.* 23.73; Burns, *Romans*, 178–79); cf. *Ag. Jul.* 70 (in Bray, *Corinthians*, 172). Talbert (*Romans*, 186) notes that Augustine treated the passage as pre-Christian in *Propositions from the Epistle to the Romans* and *Confessions* but as the Christian life in *Marr.* 28–32; *Retract.* 2.1.1.

15. Aug. *Retract.* 1.23.1 (Reasoner, *Full Circle*, 71, noting on 70–71 that this was a matter of polemic, not of exegesis).

16. Jerome *Hom. Ps.* 41, on Rom. 7:23 (trans. Bray, *Romans*, 197). For Caesarius (*Serm.* 177.4 [Bray, *Romans*, 199]), the deliverance of which 7:24 speaks occurs at the resurrection.

17. Pagels, *Paul*, 32.

18. Berceville and Son, "Exégèse." Aquinas (*Lecture* 3, on Rom. 7:14) shows how the interpretations of both the early Augustine (*Div. Q.* 83) and the later Augustine (*Ag. Jul.* 2.3.5–7) can make sense, though he prefers the latter (Levy, Krey, and Ryan, *Romans*, 163; cf. also 166–67, on 7:17). In a sinner, sin dwells in both flesh and mind; in the righteous it dwells only in the flesh (Aquinas *Lecture* 3, on Rom. 7:24; p. 171).

unregenerate.[19] The Reformers, and especially Luther, followed Augustine's later view of the believer's struggle.[20] More in keeping with the earlier Greek fathers, Pietists such as A. H. Francke and J. Bengel interpreted the passage's character as one convicted but not yet regenerate.[21] Many Pietist thinkers found a process in Romans 7.[22] Wesley viewed the person as unregenerate,[23] arguing that Paul continues to develop the contrast between the Christian and pre-Christian life of the preceding context (5:12–21; 6:1–23; 7:5–6).[24]

Survey of Modern Views

Many significant exegetes do continue to view Romans 7:7–25 or 7:14–25 as a depiction of Christian existence between the times.[25] Some also view 7:7–13 (which uses past-tense verbs) as preconversion experience and 7:14–25 (which uses present-tense verbs) as postconversion.[26] Some recognize Romans 7 as portraying life under the law and view it as a warning to Christians, as to why they cannot succeed under the law.[27] Similarly, some others also hold a mediating position in which the chapter depicts life outside Christ, but that depicted experience remains a threat to Christians if they depend on their own righteousness instead of Christ's.[28]

Others—the majority of scholars today—contend that this section cannot refer to the Christian life.[29] It is, as Rudolf Bultmann notes, "the situation of

19. Morris, *Romans*, 284.

20. Moo, *Romans*, 444; Johnson, *Romans*, 2; Stuhlmacher, *Romans*, 114. Talbert (*Romans*, 186) cites here Luther's *Lectures on Romans* (scholia on 7:7) and Calvin's commentary on Romans.

21. Moo, *Romans*, 444.

22. See Krauter, "Römer 7."

23. Moo, *Romans*, 444. MacGorman ("Romans 7," 35) identifies this as autobiographical but pre-Christian.

24. Wesley, *Commentary*, 501–2.

25. Barth, *Romans*, 240–57 (religion revealing humanity's depravity), 270; Nygren, *Romans*, 284–96; Cranfield, *Romans*, 1:344–47; Bruce, *Romans*, 151–52; Ziesler, *Righteousness*, 203–4; Dunn, "Romans 7,14–25," 267; Dunn, *Spirit*, 312–16; Dunn, *Romans*, 1:405; Dunn, *Theology*, 472–77; Morris, *Romans*, 287; Packer, "Wretched Man"; Packer, "Malheureux"; Combs, "Believer"; Thurén, "Rom 7 avretoriserat" (allowing for Pauline exaggeration); Jervis, "Commandment"; Jervis, "Conversation." This is also the usual popular reading; see, e.g., Watts, *Wisdom*, 70.

26. See Banks, "Romans 7:25A," 41; Morris, *Romans*, 277, 287.

27. Toussaint, "Contrast," 311–12. Toussaint views the conflict in Gal. 5:17 (with the Spirit) as normal for believers, but the conflict in Rom. 7:14–25 (with the new nature) as only when believers try to live under the law (310–12). Clearly Rom. 7 lacks the Spirit.

28. Mitton, "Romans 7," 134; also (following Mitton) Hunter, *Romans*, 74; Caird, *Age*, 119; Stewart, *Man in Christ*, 99ff. Depending on how it is framed, this position does not necessarily conflict with the majority position.

29. Das, *Debate*, 204–14; Deissmann, *Paul*, 178–79; Kümmel, *Römer 7*; Bornkamm, *Paul*, 125; Ridderbos, *Paul: Outline*, 126–28; Dahl, *Studies*, 111; Gundry, "Frustration," 238; Sanders, *Paul*

the man under the law in general that is described here, and described as seen by the eyes of the one freed from the law by Christ."[30] While the majority of scholars believe that the figure depicted here is not Christian, an even greater majority of scholars also argue that the passage clearly depicts life under the law.[31] This is true even for many scholars who believe that Paul depicts the Christian life.[32] For all, it is life under law without the Spirit.

Why would Paul depict life under the law so negatively? For Paul, the law was good (Rom. 7:12, 14, 16, 22),[33] but whereas it could inform[34] about righteousness (3:20; 5:13), as approached by merely human effort it nevertheless could not transform one to become righteous.[35] The law testifies about the activity of the saving God (3:21, 31), but it must be approached by the way of faith in the saving God, not by works (3:27; 8:2; 9:30–32). As Hae-Kyung Chang points out, whereas Romans 6 shows "what Christ can do," Romans 7

---

and Judaism, 443; Achtemeier, "Reflections"; Achtemeier, *Romans,* 120–26; Fee, *Paul, Spirit, People of God,* 134–35; Byrne, *Romans,* 226; Hübner, "Hermeneutics," 207; Talbert, *Romans,* 188–91; Stuhlmacher, *Romans,* 115; Aletti, "Rm 7.7–25"; Keck, *Romans,* 180; Watson, *Gentiles,* 289; Matera, *Romans,* 167; Lamp, "Rhetoric."

30. Bultmann, *Old and New Man,* 33; cf. Bultmann, *Theology,* 1:266. His student Conzelmann contends, "[Paul] is not . . . picturing his feelings before his conversion, but the way in which he later came to know himself through faith" (*Theology,* 163).

31. With, e.g., Nock, *Paul,* 68–69; Bultmann, *Old and New Man,* 33, 41, 45; Bultmann, *Theology,* 1:266; Bultmann, "Anthropology"; Bornkamm, *Paul,* 125; Bornkamm, *Experience,* 93; Schoeps, *Paul,* 184; Goppelt, *Judaism,* 116n7; Ridderbos, *Paul: Outline,* 129–30; Davies, "Free," 162; Manson, "Reading," 159; MacGorman, "Romans 7," 40–41; Nickle, "Romans 7:7–25," 185; Longenecker, *Paul,* 86–97; Deidun, *Morality,* 197–98; Byrne, "Righteousness," 565; Newman, "Once Again"; Blank, "Mensch"; Ladd, *Theology,* 508; Fee, *Paul, Spirit, People of God,* 134–35; Wright, *Romans,* 95, 131; Bony, "Lecture"; Talbert, "Tracing"; Chang, "Life."

32. E.g., Toussaint, "Contrast," 311–12; Dunn, *Baptism,* 146–47; Bruce, *Apostle,* 194; Parker, "Split."

33. Applied differently, cf. the contrast between the righteous law and Israel's wickedness in *4 Ezra* 9:32–33.

34. Like philosophy (with which Hellenistic Jewish thinkers sometimes identified the law), the law informs but (insofar as it remains dependent on human ability to fulfill it) cannot transform. Philosophers often believed that true knowledge and right beliefs transformed; Paul agrees to the extent that the right belief is Christ, but it is still Christ the object of that belief who transforms. Jewish teachers often presented the law as an antidote for sin, although they stressed obedience in addition to knowledge. For Paul, the law transforms only if written in the heart.

35. The weakness of the law with respect to righteousness was not the code itself but rather the flesh (Rom. 8:3); see Sanday and Headlam, *Romans,* 186; Longenecker, *Paul,* 114–16; Keck, *Paul,* 128; cf. Engberg-Pedersen, *Paul and Stoics,* 8. Sanders (*Law and People,* 78) sees inability to keep the law as unique to Rom. 7 (but cf. 8:7; Gal. 3:21; some cite Jer. 18:12; Josh. 24:19; Isa. 64:7d); in any case, merely human righteousness is inadequate in Rom. 3:20; 6:14; Gal. 2:16; 3:10–11, 22; Phil. 3:9. Paul consistently argues that salvation is only through Christ (with, e.g., Sanders, "Romans 7").

shows "what the law *cannot* do."[36] Indeed, the law brings knowledge of, and thus greater responsibility for, sin.[37]

Romans 7:7–25 as the Christian Life

Those who argue that Paul depicts the Christian life (his or generically) in Romans 7:7–25 or 7:14–25 understandably emphasize the present-tense verbs in 7:14–25.[38] I will address this point in a separate section below. Other points supporting this view may be addressed more concisely here. Dunn notes that the present tense of 7:25b appears *after* the triumphal cry of 7:25a,[39] a point that would be more relevant if 7:25b did not function as a concluding summary of the previous section, such as sometimes appears both in Paul (e.g., 1 Cor. 14:39–40) and in ancient sources in general.[40] As is often noted, the triumphal cry is an interjection rather than part of the argument;[41] it probably responds to 7:24b. Some supporters of the Christian-life view very plausibly appeal to Paul's theology that allows for an "already" to be consummated in the "not yet";[42] that the already/not yet allows for such an approach need not, however, *compel* the approach here.[43]

Some contend that Paul's view of the unbeliever is starker in Romans 1:18–3:20 (though the unbeliever does have conflicting thoughts, 2:15).[44] The inability to obey in 7:14–25, however, is quite stark; as Moo puts it, "What is

36. Chang, "Life," 279.

37. Some rabbis also believed that the law did this; Smith, *Parallels*, 168, cites *Mekilta of R. Simon* 20.20. For ignorance as sometimes mitigating a degree of guilt, see, e.g., Num. 15:22–31; 35:11, 15; *L.A.B.* 22:6; *Pss. Sol.* 13:7; *T. Reub.* 1:6; *Jos. Asen.* 6:7/4; 13:11–13; *BGU* 5.65.164–5.67.170. At greater length, see the sources in Keener, *Acts*, 2:1102–4.

38. Morris, *Romans*, 285.

39. Dunn, *Theology*, 474; Dunn, *Romans*, 1:398–99; cf. Morris, *Romans*, 286. No manuscript evidence supports relocating 7:25b before 7:24, as Moffatt and Dodd attempt (Dahl, *Studies*, 85; Fitzmyer, *Romans*, 477), or dismissing 7:25b as a gloss, as Bultmann (and Lichtenberger, "Beginn") attempts (Byrne, *Romans*, 233; Jewett, *Romans*, 457). Thanksgiving could follow lament in the Psalms (Stuhlmacher, *Romans*, 113). Jewett, *Romans*, 457–58, suggests "a Pauline correction," "perhaps in conjunction with a pause in dictation," and on 473 suggests "a marginal gloss added by Paul himself that was probably intended to be placed between v. 23 and v. 24." (On afterthoughts or corrections, see *Rhet. Her.* 4.26.36; e.g., 1 Cor. 1:16; Men. Rhet. 2.9, 414.26.)

40. E.g., Xen. *Hell.* 3.5.25; 4.8.19; Cic. *Fin.* 3.9.31; 4Q270 frg. 11, col. 1.15.

41. Wenham, "Tension," 83. On interjections, see Anderson, *Glossary*, 41; Rowe, "Style," 143. In addition to Paul (cf. Rom. 6:17; 1 Cor. 15:57; 2 Cor. 2:14; 8:16; 9:15), others also employed the interjection χάρις τῷ θεῷ; cf. Philo *Alleg. Interp.* 2.60; Epict. *Diatr.* 4.4.7; Crates *Ep.* 33; Diogenes *Ep.* 34; for papyri, cf. O'Brien, "Thanksgiving," 61.

42. Nygren, *Romans*, 284–96; Dunn, *Theology*, 473–76; Dunn, *Unity*, 195; cf. Morris, *Romans*, 286, citing Rom. 8:23.

43. Cf. Chang, "Life," 257, noting that Paul in context emphasizes the "already."

44. Morris, *Romans*, 285.

depicted in 7:14–25 is not just a struggle with sin but a defeat by sin."[45] The figure in this passage can do only evil and nothing good.[46] The difference between this passage and 1:18–32 is the difference between one informed by the law and Gentiles without the law.

Most scholars recognize that Paul's Christian depictions of his *preconversion* life in other passages differ from his depiction here (Gal. 1:13–14; Phil. 3:6). But those contexts describe Paul's status or outwardly observable characteristics.[47] Here, by contrast, if Paul addresses his pre-Christian existence at all, he is providing a retrospective view of its spiritual inadequacy.[48] The other preconversion passages offer a greater problem for those who contend that Paul depicts his Christian life here than for those who view this passage as his pre-Christian life or as a non-Christian life. Should we actually suppose that Paul is suggesting that he succumbs to sin more now that he has been converted (a suggestion that would subvert his argument in Rom. 6–8 and in Gal. 2:16–21)? The Qumran sectarians were more stringent than the Pharisees, yet "a deep sense of personal sin co-existed with the conviction that they were the righteous (see esp. 1QH, often written in the "I"-style)."[49]

Some argue that Romans 7:14–25 must be the Christian life because Romans 5–8 as a whole addresses the Christian life.[50] But Paul often offers digressions (e.g., 1 Cor. 9:1–27; 13:1–13), so finding one here would not be surprising.[51] The thought of Romans 7:6b—serving by newness of the Spirit—is picked up again in chapter 8.[52] Moreover, appealing to context actually cuts more sharply in the other direction; contextually, 7:7–25 is plainly life under the law, and the context also offers clear contrasts between the Christian and pre-Christian life (see 6:20–21; 7:5–6; cf. 5:12–21).

Supporters of the postconversion view sometimes also appeal to the mention of the speaker's "inner person" in 7:22,[53] but ancient hearers would not think that only believers had an "inner person."[54] Supporters note that the mind serves God's law (7:22, 25), in contrast to 1:28; this observation is true, but only

45. Moo, *Romans*, 445, allowing that believers may struggle with sin. Cf. also Stuhlmacher (*Romans*, 115–16), who recognizes that believers may face temptation.

46. Gundry, "Frustration," 238.

47. Gundry, "Frustration," 234; Moo, *Romans*, 450.

48. Wenham, "Tension," 84; Sanders, *Paul and Judaism*, 443.

49. Gundry, "Frustration," 234; cf. Byrne, *Romans*, 217; see in detail Talbert, *Romans*, 199–220.

50. Morris, *Romans*, 285–86; cf. Ramm, "Double," 17 (Rom. 6–8).

51. Wenham, "Tension," 83; Moo, *Romans*, 424; Chang, "Life," 279.

52. Moo, *Romans*, 424.

53. Elsewhere applied to believers (2 Cor. 4:16; Eph. 3:16).

54. See Wenham, "Tension," 83. The phrase appears elsewhere; see, e.g., Betz, "Concept"; Aune, "Duality"; and the discussion below (pp. 98, 241n28).

because this passage depicts life under the law, not life as Gentiles without it.[55] Supporters also sometimes contend that the passage's "I" serves God's law (7:25), tries to obey (7:15–20), and celebrates the law (7:22).[56] Granted that the figure desires to obey God's law in Romans 7, the speaker fails, whereas for the believer in Christ, the Spirit provides success (8:2, 9).

In an argument that might feel more persuasive to many of us, Dunn notes that the postconversion approach better fits human experience.[57] Since Paul is depicting life under the law, however, Paul might view any correspondence with Christian experience as part of the problem rather than the solution. Still, Paul himself would not have denied that bodily existence offers continuing challenges for believers (cf. Rom. 6:12–13; 8:12–13; Phil. 3:12; perhaps 1 Cor. 9:27);[58] new identity in Christ does not obliterate susceptibility to sin.[59]

Romans 7:7–25 as a Non-Christian Experience

More often scholars argue that Paul's depiction of life under the law cannot represent his current experience in Christ. They rightly note that a postconversion reading of the passage contradicts a straightforward reading of Romans 6:4, 7, 11–14, 17–19,[60] as well as 6:20, 22; 7:6; 8:2–9. As Hans Hübner complains, "Here is an absolute antithesis, unsurpassable, ontologically total."[61] The person of 7:14 is unredeemed, "sold [as a slave] to sin"; by contrast, the believer, formerly a slave to sin (6:6, 14, 19–20), has been liberated from sin and enslaved to God and to righteousness (6:18, 22; cf. redemption in Gal. 3:13). The person of Romans 7:14 is fleshly (σάρκινος; cf. 7:18, 25), but in 7:5 the struggle "in the flesh" is depicted as in the past, and in 8:9 the one who belongs to Christ is "in the [domain of the] Spirit" rather than "in the [domain of the] flesh."[62] Nothing good dwells in the person of 7:18, but the Spirit and

55. Further, Rom. 7:22–23, 25 is irreconcilable with Rom. 12:2 and Phil. 2:13 (Ridderbos, *Paul: Outline*, 128).

56. Noted by Moo, *Romans*, 446 (who views the person as unregenerate, 448–49).

57. Dunn, *Theology*, 476–77.

58. Wenham, "Tension," 84–85.

59. If one may compare modern conversions, they do not usually erase all prior psychological patterns or the hormones and biochemistry to which those patterns are often connected.

60. Jewett, *Romans*, 466, also noting the ethical expectations in Rom. 12–16; Gundry, "Frustration," 238, contrasting 7:14–25 with 6:1–7:6; 8:1–39.

61. Hübner, "Hermeneutics," 207, contrasting Rom. 7:17, 20 with 8:6.

62. As is regularly noted, Paul uses "flesh" in multiple ways (e.g., bodily existence in Gal. 2:20); the context of the term's usage in Romans, however, decides the usage here against a depiction of Christian experience. Yet even in the harsh language of 1 Cor. 3:1, Paul may hesitate to apply σάρκινος to believers, prefacing it with ὡς and in 3:3 preferring the potentially weaker σαρκικός.

Christ live in Paul (8:9).[63] The person of 7:23 is prisoner of the "law of sin," but believers are freed from that law in 8:2; the law aroused passions when they were "in the flesh" (7:5), but now they have been released from the law (7:4, 6; cf. 6:14). Whereas 7:7–25 employs first-person pronouns repeatedly (perhaps twenty-eight times), it lacks mention of the Spirit, but reference to the Spirit pervades chapter 8 (mentioned roughly twenty times). Moreover, the wretched person of 7:24 does not even know the deliverer's name.[64]

The context that introduces the discussion seems decisive. Paul tells his audience that they were under law till they received Christ (Rom. 7:1–4); life under the law thus reflects a pre-Christian status. Paul tells them "we" *were* (Greek imperfect) in the flesh, experiencing sinful desires aroused by law (7:5)—a description that fits 7:7–25 clearly. But now, Paul declares, we have been released (Greek aorist) from the law into the life of the Spirit (7:6). So the law-life and sin-struggle of 7:7–25 is not Christian life. The first section, 7:7–13, *might* draw from Paul's past experiences, but the graphic use of the present tense in 7:14–25 does not refer to his present life, because it depicts a life "of flesh," enslaved to sin (7:14). Paul has already explained that this is the former life (7:5), not the present one (7:6). For Paul, believers in Jesus should expect to experience new life in Christ and the Spirit, not continuing subjection to sin.

Thus, Paul's "Who will free me?" (Rom. 7:24) is hypothetical; Paul knows that Jesus is the answer, and the believer is already freed in Christ. Nevertheless, although Paul's depiction in Romans 7:15–25 is of life under the law, which in Paul's argument is not directly true of Christians, others may be right to note that when professed followers of Christ seek essential status before God based on effort or any means other than Christ, analogous principles apply.[65]

Why Use Present-Tense Verb Forms?

If Paul does not refer to his own present life, why does he employ present-tense verb forms in Romans 7:14–25? Although the majority of scholars agree, based on context, that Paul cannot be depicting his current condition, explanations of the present-tense form in this section vary. Ernst Käsemann suggests

---

63. The contrast also applies to 1 Cor. 6:19 and Gal. 2:20 (recognized already by Origen; see Stowers, *Rereading*, 266–67).

64. Jewett, *Romans*, 472.

65. Cf. Mitton, "Romans 7," 134; Hunter, *Romans*, 74; Caird, *Age*, 119; cf. Stewart, *Man in Christ*, 99ff., regarding anyone who "lets Christ go." This application does not follow from the present tenses, however, since Rom. 7:14–25 is clearly not Paul's condition when writing.

that these verbs present the results of 7:7b–11 "in their cosmic breadth," as in 1:18–3:20; 5:12–21.[66] Citing the Jewish tradition of repentance, Peter Stuhlmacher suggests that the past experience is narrated as present because it remains "real in the present."[67]

Some compare Paul's use of the present tense in his description of his past activity in Philippians 3:3–6 with his use of the present-tense forms here; however, the verses most relevant for the comparison, 3:5–6,[68] employ only participles (one grammatically present and the other aorist). Some cite for Romans 7 the lack of clear temporal transition in the context, observe the weak temporal markers in the text itself, and argue that the present verbs are imperfective; they suggest that Paul merely shifts "from his narration of life under the law in 7:7–12 to a description of the condition or state" here.[69]

Whatever other factors might be involved, scholars who suggest that Paul shifts to the present-tense form to heighten the narration's rhetorical intensity[70] are likely correct.[71] Paul has already established in Romans 7:7–13 the setting that he depicts—a setting that is not Christian—so the shift to present tense may provide a vivid lament within this already-established setting.[72] Certainly, a shift to present tense could communicate vividness.[73] Criticizing Herodotus's presentation of past events, for example, Plutarch suddenly shifts to *addressing* him in the second person, and in the present tense, as if interrogating him.[74]

66. Käsemann, *Romans*, 199.

67. Stuhlmacher, *Romans*, 112, 115. Perhaps he refers to the use of the present tense in Jewish confessions.

68. Gundry, "Frustration," 228–29, relying on the present verbs of Phil. 3:3–4 to establish the implied tense in 3:5–6; cf. Das, *Debate*, 213.

69. Das, *Debate*, 213, on the imperfective aspect focusing additional attention on an event, following Porter, *Idioms*, 30–31; Seifrid, "Subject," 321–22; see also here Seifrid, *Justification*, 230, 234. Grammarians currently debate the extent to which indicative tenses mark not only aspect but time (albeit only generally, since everyone who defines them as having a usually temporal function admits exceptions).

70. E.g., Fee, *Paul, Spirit, People of God*, 134–35.

71. This is the case even though ancient rhetorical critics sometimes critiqued those who were inconsistent in verb tenses (Dion. Hal. *2 Amm.* 12).

72. I am not using "lament" as a technical designation of genre here. Nevertheless, it is noteworthy that the psalmist often lays out the past situation or plea in which he called on the Lord, narrating it as if present (e.g., Pss. 28:1–5; 31:11–18), before narrating and praising God for the deliverance (e.g., Pss. 28:6; 31:22). Cf. discussion of such psalms in Broyles, *Conflict*; Broyles, "Lament," 386–89; Miller, *Cried*; and (with reception history) Waltke, Houston, and Moore, *Psalms*; for some ancient Near Eastern context for laments more narrowly, cf. Gwaltney, "Book"; Hallo, "Lamentations."

73. This is the case whether interpreters prefer the emphasis on imperfective aspect or (usually) temporal marking with respect to present indicative verbs.

74. Plut. *Mal. Hdt.* 26, *Mor.* 861F.

In vivid rhetorical descriptions one could describe a scene as if one were experiencing it at that time.[75] Such techniques were appropriate for past events as well as present ones.[76] In fact, one scholar defines the rhetorical device of *enargeia* as "the description of a situation or action as though it were present."[77] Indeed, Paul sometimes apparently preached this way: Christ was depicted as crucified "before your eyes" (Gal. 3:1);[78] depicting an action or scene as if before hearers' eyes was a common way of describing vivid narration.[79] Although the verbs are not historical presents (which are not usually consistent throughout a narration, in contrast to the consistency evident in Rom. 7:14–25), historical presents in narrative might provide an analogy insofar as they add vividness to scenes.[80] If the Greek present functions more in terms of providing an inside rather than outside perspective, the aspect of these verbs is more relevant than the traditional understanding of their tense.[81]

We may add the observation that in Romans itself Paul uses present-tense verb forms to charge someone who claims to fulfill the law with a number of serious crimes (Rom. 2:21–23). That passage includes hyperbole, caricature, and vividness as here, although its repetition is tighter and the passage more concise. Likewise, Paul shifts from mention of Israel's sin in the aorist tense (3:3; cf. 3:7, 23) to a litany of texts denouncing sinful behavior mostly using the present tense when in the indicative mood (3:10–18).[82]

75. Anderson, *Glossary*, 125, citing Longin. *Subl.* 15.1. Cf. Hermog. *Inv.* 3.15.166–68.

76. Hermog. *Inv.* 3.15.167. Narration could start with either present (Hermog. *Progymn.* 9, "On Ethopoeia," 21–22; Nicolaus *Progymn.* 10, "On Ethopoeia") or past (Hermog. *Progymn.* 10, "On Ecphrasis," 22) action, but shifting the period of time discussed helps maintain attention. Also citing Hermogenes, Tobin (*Rhetoric*, 238) suggests that Paul follows a respectable rhetorical form by using the aorist in Rom. 7:7–12, the present in 7:13–23, and the future in 7:24–25a.

77. Rowe, "Style," 143–44, citing, e.g., Demosth. *Embassy* 19.65; Cic. *Phil.* 2.34.85. This method did not always use present verbs but could include these as well.

78. Though Paul probably has in view his own cruciform life as well as his preaching; see Gal. 2:20.

79. E.g., Arist. *Rhet.* 2.8.14, 1386a; 3.11.1–2, 1411b; *Rhet. Her.* 4.55.68; Cic. *Or. Brut.* 40.139; *Sull.* 26.72; Vell. Paterc. 2.89.5–6; Sen. E. *Controv.* 1.6.12; Quint. *Inst.* 9.2.40; Theon *Progymn.* 7.53–55; Longin. *Subl.* 15.2; Pliny *Ep.* 5.6.40; Hermog. *Progymn.* 10, "On Ecphrasis," 22–23; see, further, Keener, *Acts*, 1:135.

80. For historical presents, see Aune, *Dictionary of Rhetoric*, 215 (who notes that Mark uses these more than 150 times). These appear also in Latin narrative, e.g., frequently in Caesar *C.W.*, e.g., *C.W.* 1.22, 25, 33, 41, 59; 2.21, 25, 26, 30; and occasionally in Cicero (he slips in a present in *Quinct.* 4.14, though the *narratio* is mainly past tense; also in 5.20). Cf. perhaps also Philost. *Vit. Apoll.* 8.1–2.

81. On this approach to verbal aspect, see in an introductory way Campbell, *Advances*, 106–9, and Das's suggestion, above, concerning the imperfective use of the present.

82. The aorist indicative does appear in Rom. 3:12a, 17, and the imperfect in 3:13. The present indicative appears in 3:10–11, 12b, 14, and 18.

Who Is the "I" in Romans 7?

More debated than whether the passage depicts Christian or non-Christian experience is whether the non-Christian experience depicted in this passage reflects Paul's own pre-Christian experience. Most readers historically saw the "I" as Paul's own experience but believed that he used it to typify experience more broadly.[83] Because Paul elsewhere uses a generic "I" only briefly rather than in such an extended way, some continue to argue that at least an element of allusion to Paul's experience remains.[84] By contrast, even some earlier scholars such as Wilhelm Wrede (1859–1906) saw "I" in Romans 7 as a literary device depicting the situation of humanity needing redemption, a view often followed today.[85] Scholars often find here allusions to Adam, to Israel, or to a combination of the two. Whether or not an element of autobiography remains, certainly the generic element invites attention.[86] The same is true whatever other specific figures, if any, Paul has in mind.

Autobiographical?

Many believe that the passage does reflect Paul's preconversion experience to some degree.[87] Usually, supporters of this view emphasize that the passage sees Paul's background from his new Christian perspective.[88] (In light of Phil. 3, most scholars today, whatever their view on Rom. 7:7–25, doubt that before Paul's conversion he viewed himself as a moral failure.)[89]

Not all agree as to whether to call this proposed allusion to Paul's pre-Christian experience autobiographical. Some describe the passage as autobiographical,[90] but many others reject the autobiographical interpretation, regardless of whether they believe that Paul includes insights drawn from his

---

83. Noted by Moo (*Romans*, 425).

84. Moo, *Romans*, 427.

85. Donaldson, *Paul and Gentiles*, 14–15.

86. Cf. Newman, "Once Again": whether or not the chapter reveals Paul's history, it implies others beyond Paul, because Paul is depicting life under the law. Philonenko ("Glose") supports K. G. Kuhn's gnomic interpretation.

87. E.g., Gundry, "Frustration"; Milne, "Experience"; others noted below. Rubenstein (*Paul*, 11), noting his own Jewish experience under the law, thinks that it also would have fit Paul's.

88. E.g., Denney, "Romans," 639 (on 7:7–13); Stewart, *Man in Christ*, 99ff.; Caird, *Age*, 119; Martin, "Reflections"; Kim, *Origin*, 52ff.; Schreiner, *Romans*, 363–65. Contrast Espy ("Conscience"), who thinks that it depicts even Paul's pre-Christian awareness of his inadequacy. Some even read it psychoanalytically (Rubenstein, *Paul*; Sandmel, *Genius*, 32–33). But as Chilton (*Rabbi Paul*, 53) notes (citing 1 Cor. 15:9), Paul's persecution of the church sufficiently explains any "guilt."

89. See, e.g., Goppelt, *Times*, 72; Jewett, *Romans*, 464; Campbell, *Deliverance*, 141.

90. E.g., Sandmel, *Genius*, 28.

background.[91] Certainly, introspection and self-disclosure were not character-istic of ancient autobiography, which emphasized "self-display."[92] Many deny that the passage need be relevant to Paul's preconversion experience at all.[93]

Still others suggest that Paul speaks more generically but can do so persua-sively because of his own background.[94] Paul's audience, after all, probably has heard of his pre-Christian zeal for the law.[95] This approach may be help-ful in explaining why Paul uses the first person here more extensively than in any of the other generic examples (noted below). Certainly, sages could use their own example to illustrate a principle,[96] and Paul does so elsewhere (e.g., 1 Cor. 9:1–27).

On this approach, although Paul's point is not primarily autobiographical, he uses the first person because he can personally identify with his people's experience.[97] Because Paul includes himself among the "we" once under the jurisdiction of the law but now set free in Romans 7:5–6, he depicts an existence that he acknowledges was once his own, even though he did not yet view it then in the way that he depicts in Romans 7. Thus, at the very least, because this passage depicts existence without Christ, its depiction must include Paul's own pre-Christian condition as understood now in light of Christ.[98]

Generic or Projected "I"

Certainly, Paul does use "I" as an example or even generically at times (scholars cite, e.g., 1 Cor. 8:13; 10:29b–30; Gal. 2:18–21);[99] sometimes the generic "I" even extends over a significant span of content (1 Cor. 13:1–3,

91. E.g., Enslin, *Ethics*, 12; Goppelt, *Judaism*, 116n7; Goppelt, *Times*, 72; Dahl, *Studies*, 111; Sanders, *Paul and Judaism*, 478–79; Dunn, *Romans*, 1:382; Longenecker, "Hope," 22. Some who reject the label of autobiography see Paul depicting his pre-Christian experience from a Christian perspective (Goppelt, *Judaism*, 139–40).

92. Judge, *Jerusalem*, 60.

93. E.g., the more existentially directed reading in Bultmann, *Old and New Man*, 16; Bult-mann, *Theology*, 1:266.

94. Robinson, *Wrestling*, 82; Moo, *Romans*, 431; Watson, *Gentiles*, 290; Dunn, *Romans*, 1:382; Hultgren, *Romans*, 681–91. For partly Paul's experience but especially concerning Israel under the law, see Moo, "Israel and Paul."

95. Jewett, *Romans*, 444–45.

96. E.g., Mus. Ruf. 9, p. 74.13–19.

97. Talbert, *Romans*, 201 (noting that Paul identifies with his people also in Rom. 9:3).

98. Campbell, *Deliverance*, 141; cf. Nock, *Paul*, 68–69; Hunter, *Romans*, 71; Prat, *Theology*, 227ff.; Ridderbos, *Paul: Outline*, 129–30; Achtemeier, *Romans*, 124; Byrne, *Romans*, 217. Rhe-torically, whether "I" refers to Paul or not, it invites audience identification (Keck, "Pathos," 90).

99. Byrne, *Romans*, 217; Wright, *Justification*, 120; Wright, *Faithfulness*, 508; Morris, *Ro-mans*, 277 (although Morris applies Rom. 7:13–25 to believers, 287); for Paul identifying with Gentile hearers in Gal. 3:14, cf. Gager, *Anti-Semitism*, 222. Longenecker ("Hope," 22) empha-sizes that Kümmel showed this in Paul and ancient literature already in 1928. Some interpreters

9–12), although rarely as extensively as Paul appears to do here.[100] In Romans itself Paul may use "we" in a general way (as in 6:1) and "I" generically (as in 3:7),[101] although some possible instances reflect Paul's dialogue with an imaginary interlocutor.[102] Ancient hearers could have recognized such usage. Prayers both in some biblical psalms (e.g., Ps. 118:5–14) and in some Qumran hymns (including 1QS 10.6–11.17) employ the first person generically, at least as the prayers were reused by liturgical communities. Israel speaks as "I" in some psalms and other biblical texts (e.g., Exod. 15:1–2; 17:3 [Heb.]; Ps. 129:1–3; Isa. 12:1–2; cf. Egypt in the Hebrew text of Exod. 14:25).

Some point out that Epictetus can speak in the persona of the ideal Cynic; such usage dramatizes his point.[103] This practice is not limited to Epictetus. "When I say that 'I' do nothing for the sake of pleasure," Seneca points out, "I am speaking of the ideal wise man."[104] Seneca similarly employs "I" hypothetically when he claims, "I live according to Nature if I surrender myself entirely to her."[105]

Interpreters as early as Origen suggested that Paul was speaking in a different persona here, that is, using what is often called *prosōpopoiia* (προσωποποιΐα).[106] Other rhetorically educated readers such as Rufinus and Jerome may have agreed, and Nilus of Ancyra independently viewed it similarly.[107] Many scholars today, following especially the observations of Stanley Stowers, appeal to this literary device here.[108]

---

counter by noting that sometimes Paul does use "I" autobiographically (Gundry, "Frustration," 229, citing Phil. 3:4–6).

100. Cf. 2 Cor. 12:2–4, which is usually regarded as the opposite approach—Paul depicting himself as another (see, e.g., Lincoln, *Paradise*, 75; Bultmann, *Corinthians*, 220; Furnish, *Corinthians*, 524, 544–45; Martin, *Corinthians*, 398; Lyons, *Autobiography*, 69; Danker, *Corinthians*, 188; Thrall, *Corinthians*, 778–82; Matera, *Corinthians*, 278).

101. Schlatter, *Romans*, 160, noting that "I" is more suitable here because Paul is depicting "the individual's inner life." The "we" of Rom. 3:5 becomes "I" in 3:7, probably speaking for Israel more generally. In the context leading up to 7:7–25, Paul often uses the first-person plural (e.g., 4:16, 24–25; 5:1, 5–6, 8, 11, 21; 6:4, 6, 23; 7:4–6), including himself but speaking generically.

102. Some explain the "I" in terms of the diatribe style (e.g., Enslin, *Ethics*, 13; Johnson, *Romans*, 115), although some characteristics of diatribal style are debated today.

103. E.g., Talbert, *Romans*, 186; Johnson, *Romans*, 115, citing Epict. *Diatr.* 3.22.10.

104. Sen. Y. *Dial.* 7.11.1 (trans. Basore, LCL, 2:125); that he does not refer literally to himself is clear (7.18.1).

105. Sen. Y. *Dial.* 8.5.8 (trans. Basore, LCL, 2:195).

106. Stowers, *Rereading*, 266–67; Stowers, "Self-Mastery," 537; Reasoner, *Full Circle*, 69, 84; Talbert, *Romans*, 187. Origen may refer to a person under conviction (cf. Reasoner, *Full Circle*, 69). Anderson (*Rhetorical Theory*, 204–5) counters that Origen suggested this approach only tentatively.

107. Stowers, *Rereading*, 268.

108. E.g., Stowers, *Rereading*, 16–17, 264; Édart, "Nécessité"; Tobin, *Rhetoric*, 10, 226–27; Talbert, *Romans*, 187; deSilva, *Introduction*, 620; Bryan, *Preface*, 139–40; Aletti, "Rm 7.7–25"; Aletti, "Romans 7,7–25"; Witherington, *Romans*, 179–80; Keck, *Romans*, 180; Keck, "*Pathos*," 85; Jewett, *Romans*, 443; Kruse, *Romans*, 298, 305; Rodríguez, *Call Yourself*, 134.

Although rhetorical teachers differed somewhat in their nomenclature,[109] the figure we are calling *prosōpopoiia* was widely used.[110] Plato, for example, could offer a funeral oration in the voice of his hearers' ancestors.[111] This device, one ancient teacher noted, energized one's style.[112] Because it was an elementary exercise, Paul could have learned it at an introductory level.[113] With Phoebe's assistance (cf. Rom. 16:1–2), Romans' first hearers may have recognized this device and the voice of interlocutors more easily; some advised orators to distinguish characters by voice changes in how one reads.[114]

Some argue that Paul is not using *prosōpopoiia*, because he does not clearly introduce the device.[115] Although such an introduction was common, however, it was not necessary.[116] Even if some find the comparison between this passage and *prosōpopoiia* less than fully precise, it offers one analogy that helps us understand how ancient audiences could have heard a sudden change in narratorial voice. Since this passage explicitly depicts struggle under the law, and context equally clearly shows that Paul did not see believers as under the law in this sense, seeking analogies remains valuable.

Adam?

If Paul speaks in another persona, in whose voice does he speak? Some scholars suggest that he speaks in his own former voice, evoking his own past under the law, which may be at least part of why he employs "I."[117] But beyond this suggested connection, what other rhetorical possibilities exist?

If Paul speaks generically, it would not be surprising if he speaks for humanity. A majority find in the "I" another reference to Adam (building on

109. Later rhetoric distinguishes *ēthopoeia* (ἠθοποιΐα), when one speaks in the character of another person, as here, from *prosōpopoiia*, in which inanimate objects are meant to speak (Hermog. *Progymn.* 9, "On Ethopoeia," 20); Demet. *Style* 5.265 seems to include both as *prosōpopoiia*. Others distinguished the terms differently (Aphth. *Progymn.* 11, "On Ethopoeia," 44–45S, 34R; Nicolaus *Progymn.* 10, "On Ethopoeia," 64–65).

110. E.g., Proclus *Poet.* 6.2, K198.29–30 (addressing Plato); Tzounakas, "Peroration."

111. As noted in Demet. *Style* 5.266.

112. Demet. *Style* 5.265.

113. Stowers, *Rereading*, 17.

114. Stowers, *Rereading*, 18, citing the first-century rhetorical teacher Quint. *Inst.* 1.8.3.

115. Anderson, *Rhetorical Theory*, 204–5. Aune (*Dictionary of Rhetoric*, 383, following Anderson, *Rhetorical Theory*, 232) suggests that Paul instead uses personal example. Given irregularity in the use of chronology, however, Hock ("Education," 211) wonders whether ancients would still have viewed Paul's figure as *prosōpopoiia*. Jewett (*Romans*, 444) cites for the figure an anecdote from Epictetus's past used to illustrate and advance his argument in Epict. *Diatr.* 1.18.15–16; 1.29.21; but this is not really *prosōpopoiia* even by Jewett's definition on 443.

116. Tobin, *Rhetoric*, 227, citing Quint. *Inst.* 9.2.36–37.

117. Cf. Jewett, *Romans*, 445.

Paul's explicit reference in Rom. 5:12–21).[118] Even some patristic commentators made connections between these figures.[119] Some supporting arguments for this position are as follows:[120]

1. "Alive apart from the law" could evoke Adam being given life (Gen. 2:7–15).

2. God "commands" Adam regarding trees, one being the tree of life (Gen. 2:16–17); here the "commandment" is "for life."

3. Sin brings death (Rom. 7:9; Gen. 3:1–5).[121]

4. Sin has "deceived" me (Rom. 7:11; Gen. 3:13).

5. The serpent uses the command to cause desire (Rom. 7:8); the tree is desirable (Gen. 3:6) or, in some traditions, causes sexual awakening (Gen. 3:7).

6. The outcome is death (mortality, in Gen. 3:19, 22–24; 5:5).

7. Adam (or Adam with Eve) better provides a first-person voice than does an Israelite after Sinai, given Paul's corporate, typological use of Adam.

118. E.g., Davies, *Paul*, 30–32; Hunter, *Romans*, 71–72; Goppelt, *Judaism*, 140; Manson, "Reading," 158; Käsemann, *Romans*, 196 (citing Jewish tradition); Dunn, "Romans 7,14–25"; Dunn, *Romans*, 1:383; Dunn, *Theology*, 98–100; Dunn, "Adam," 133–35; Martin, *Reconciliation*, 57; Deidun, *Morality*, 196; Morris, *Romans*, 282–83; Talbert, *Romans*, 187 (on 187–88 comparing Eve's "desire" in *Apoc. Mos.* 19:3), 191 (with Adam as the model for the self, not the subject); Grappe, "Corps de mort" (comparing *4 Ezra* 3:4–5); Chow, "Romans 7:7–25"; Campbell, *Deliverance*, 141; Matera, *Romans*, 174; cf. Nock, *Paul*, 68; Bornkamm, *Experience*, 93; Cranfield, *Romans*, 1:342–43; Schoeps, *Paul*, 184; Bruce, *Apostle*, 194; Stuhlmacher, *Romans*, 115. Most of these scholars also emphasize the role of the law here. Some focus on "deceived" and emphasize esp. Eve's role here (Busch, "Figure"; Krauter, "Eva").

119. See (in Bray, *Romans*, 184, 186, 188) Ambrosiaster *Comm.* on Rom. 7:13 (CSEL 81:231); Theodoret *Interp. Rom.* on 7:10 (PG 82:117); Diodore of Tarsus, catena on Rom. 7:9 (*PGK* 15:88); Didymus the Blind, catena on Rom. 7:13 (*PGK* 15:4). Origen viewed 7:7–13 as Israel's relationship to the law, whereas 7:14–25 applied to humanity's (Reasoner, *Full Circle*, 69). This could make sense of the shift in imagery, but why a transition from one "I" to another with no explicit demarcation? Further, "for" in 7:14 and "for" in 7:15 clearly connect the persons.

120. Although many have made some of these connections, I follow here the extensive and helpful list in Watson, *Gentiles*, 282–84. To his credit, Watson also recognizes the allusion to Sinai in Rom. 7:9 (p. 282). Given the emphasis on knowledge in Rom. 7, Watson's suggested possible correlation between the Torah and the tree of knowledge of good and evil (*Gentiles*, 285) is more tantalizing, since Jewish tradition identifies the Torah with a tree of life (*Abot* 6:7; *Sipre Deut.* 47.3.2; *Tg. Neof.* 1 on Gen. 3:24). Some compare the warning not to covet (7:7) with the serpent's invitation to become like God (Gen. 3:5–6; Talbert, *Romans*, 187).

121. Some patristic commentators viewed personified Sin here as the devil (in Bray, *Romans*, 186: Didymus the Blind, catena on Rom. 7:11 [*PGK* 15:3]; Ambrosiaster *Comm.* on Rom. 7:11 [CSEL 81:229]). Some Jewish traditions also linked the serpent and the devil (cf. Wis. 2:24; *3 Bar.* 9:7; cf. Rev. 12:9; *Acts John* 94; the devil utilized the serpent in *Apoc. Mos.* 16:1, 5).

(Those who connect Romans 7 with the Jewish tradition of the evil impulse also could cite the connection of the evil impulse with Adam in later Jewish tradition.[122] The connection, however, was not very widespread.)[123]

Others have criticized this position.[124] Even cumulatively, the proposed parallels above (some of which repeat the content of others) are of limited relevance; the only relevant verbal link is the cognate verb translated "deceived" in both passages,[125] and in Genesis Eve, not Adam, is the character who claims that the serpent deceived her.[126] By itself, this one potential verbal link does not constitute a very clear allusion. By contrast, Paul's verb for "covet" (ἐπιθυμέω, Rom. 7:7) does not appear in Genesis 3; it comes instead directly from a commandment to Israel in Exodus and Deuteronomy (Exod. 20:17; Deut. 5:21).[127]

Beyond this limited commonality the case for any deliberate allusion to Adam is weak. First, nearly all of the narrative action in Romans 7:7–25 follows the coming of the law (7:9), not precedes it. Second, whereas "commandment" (ἐντολή) readily applies to the specifically cited biblical command (7:7) or other commands given to Israel, nowhere does the Septuagint version of the Torah apply it to what God commanded Adam.[128] Keeping the commandments of the law was associated with life, as Paul well knew (10:5).[129] Conversely, breaking God's law

122. Noting the two *yods* in Gen. 2:7, some rabbis suggested that God created Adam with two impulses (*b. Ber.* 61a; *Tg. Ps.-Jon.* on Gen. 2:7), though others differed; earlier, 4Q422 1.9–12 probably connects an evil inclination with Adam (though possibly, as in Gen. 6, with Noah's generation; cf. 4Q422 1.12–2.8). Cf. the idea that the serpent infused humanity with lust when he slept with Eve (*b. Yebam.* 103b).

123. Baudry ("Péché") distinguishes emphases on Adam, Satan, or the evil impulse as sin's origin among early Jewish sources.

124. E.g., Moo, *Romans*, 428–29, 437; Schreiner, *Romans*, 360–61; Jewett, *Romans*, 447, 451–52; Das, *Debate*, 216.

125. Ἐξαπατάω in Rom. 7:11 and (with explicit reference to Eve) 2 Cor. 11:3; ἀπατάω in Gen. 3:13; cf. also 1 Tim. 2:14; Philo *Alleg. Interp.* 3.59–66 (using ἀπατάω, which appears seventy-three times in the Philonic corpus; Philo allegorizes in *Creation* 165); Jos. *Ant.* 1.48 (using the same verb as Paul, ἐξαπατάω, which appears twenty-one times in Josephus; Josephus uses ἀπατάω thirty-six times). Paul's usage is not *limited* to Eve (1 Cor. 3:18; 2 Thess. 2:3); the other *Romans* reference to deception involves not Adam and Eve but false teachers (Rom. 16:18, though that context might actually evoke Adam in 16:19–20). Extrabiblical parallels (some noted below) are easier to find because the corpus is so large, but the corpus that Paul unquestionably shared with his first audience is Scripture. Perkins ("Anthropology") finds correspondences between Rom. 7:7–25 and some Adam material in Nag Hammadi sources.

126. With Gundry, "Frustration," 230.

127. As also noted by Gundry ("Frustration," 230).

128. It does appear in Jos. *Ant.* 1.43, but Josephus employs this noun seventy-six times, sometimes (though not usually) also for the laws or stipulations of Moses (*Ant.* 6.133; 7.318, 338, 342; 8.94, 120, 337).

129. See Deut. 8:1; 11:8 LXX; 30:16; Neh. 9:29; Prov. 6:23 LXX; Ezek. 18:21; Sir. 17:11; 45:5; Bar. 4:1; 2 Macc. 7:9, 23.

brought death.[130] Further, Paul may sometimes use Adam typologically, but he can use other forebears as representative figures besides Adam: Abraham (4:12), Isaac (9:7–8; Gal. 4:28), or (admittedly plural) "our ancestors" (1 Cor. 10:1–11).

Most important, Paul earlier explicitly distinguishes the time of Adam from the time of the commandment (Rom. 5:13–14, 20).[131] Adam may be in the background because of his association with sin and death (5:12–21), but the case for Paul speaking here in the *persona* of Adam is not strong.

Israel

More plausibly, although less frequently emphasized, Paul evokes Israel. Paul has specifically identified Israel as under the law (Rom. 3:19–20; cf. 2:12, 20, 23, 25; 7:1–6; 9:4, 31).[132] Like the figure in Romans 7:9–25, Israel has failed to attain righteousness by the law, because they pursued it from the approach of works rather than that of faith (9:30–32). Most interpreters agree that the context is clear that Romans 7:7–25 depicts life under the law; as here, earlier in Romans the law has made people conscious of sin, and it even multiplied sin (5:14, 20).[133] That Paul would identify with his people in this narration is also plausible (cf. his affirmation in 11:1); he becomes under the law for those under the law (1 Cor. 9:20), and elsewhere he can shift from "we [Jews]" (Gal. 2:15–17) to "I," albeit as one who finds Christ (2:18–21).[134]

130. Deut. 30:15–20; Tob. 3:4. Granted, Adam could be viewed as experiencing spiritual death in passions (Philo *Alleg. Interp.* 1.106; cf. 3.107), but Philo does not limit that description to Adam (*Posterity* 61, 73–74; *Drunkenness* 135; *Studies* 87; *Rewards* 159; cf. *Embassy* 14).

131. See Schreiner, *Romans*, 361; Das, *Debate*, 217.

132. Moo, "Israel and Paul"; Moo, *Romans*, 430–31; Karlberg, "History"; Bryan, *Preface*, 140–45; Napier, "Analysis"; Kruse, *Romans*, 299, 305, 319–20. Moo (*Romans*, 426) cites other examples of those who hold this view, including Chrysostom; Hugo Grotius; E. Stauffer; N. T. Wright; Ridderbos; and P. Benoit. Given the emphasis on the law, Talbert (*Romans*, 196) concludes that the "self" here is a Jewish one rather than Gentile; cf. Gorman, *Apostle*, 373: "the frustrated human (and especially Jewish) condition apart from Christ." In 1981, before being familiar with many Romans commentaries, I concluded that Rom. 7:14–25 could not reflect Adamic humanity in general (1:18–32; 5:12–21) but could reflect Adamic humanity under law (2:12–29; cf. Rom. 9–11). Schreiner, *Romans*, 362–63, offers a plausible objection to Israel here but may press the analogy too forcefully.

133. Talbert, *Romans*, 188 (also suggesting that the Jewish boy receiving the Torah may recapitulate Sinai); cf. Schreiner, *Romans*, 343. The idea was intelligible in an ancient context; scholars (Haacker, *Theology*, 126–27; Talbert, *Romans*, 189) cite texts about laws emphasizing vices and making them more tempting (Cic. *Tull.* 9; Ovid *Am.* 2.19.3; 3.4.9, 11, 17, 25, 31; *Metam.* 3.566; Sen. Y. *Clem.* 1.23.1; Publ. Syr. N 17; Tac. *Ann.* 13.12.2; 13.13.1; cf. 4 Macc. 1:33–34; *L.A.E.* 19).

134. If Gal. 2:15–21 reflects or elaborates Paul's words to Peter in 2:14 ("you as a Jew"), then "we" Jews includes all of ethnic Israel, believing or unbelieving. The difference in Rom. 7:15–25 would remain the use of the present tense for depicting life under the law.

Other factors also may support this identification. First, the Jewish interlocutor earlier in Romans has spoken on behalf of Israel.[135] Second, the contrast here between knowing and doing echoes the hypocrite of Romans 2:17–29—the difference being that here the transgressor recognizes his condition rather than boasts in the law (though this figure still rightly delights in it). This speaker is now reduced to his true state, stripped of self-deception with regard to sinfulness.[136] Third, as a supporting argument (favoring the plausibility of, though not specifically indicating, the idea here), Israel sometimes spoke as a character even in the Old Testament (e.g., Ps. 129:1–2; Jer. 4:31; Lam. 1:11–22; 3:59–66). (Similarly, an entire tribe could sometimes speak as "I," as in Judg. 1:3 in the Hebrew.)

Some suggest that Paul has in mind both Adam and Israel here.[137] The problem with this generous approach in this case is that, as noted above, the claimed echoes of Genesis 3 are weak here. Still, on a more implicit level, Adam's sin probably informs all of Paul's anthropology, including here, whether he specifically refers to the story or not. Further, the passage explicitly addresses only those under the law, which would include not only Jews by birth but also proselytes. Many argue that most of the Jesus believers in Rome were now Gentiles (see Rom. 1:5, 13; 11:13), and at least some of these may have felt obligated to observe the law.

It is likely going too far, however, to think that in this chapter Paul has in mind primarily Gentiles and/or God-fearers under the law,[138] given the clear statements in Romans about Israel's status under the law. Granted, Paul elsewhere depicts only the Gentiles as being enslaved by passions and desire (Rom. 1:24, 26–27; cf. 1 Cor. 6:9–11; 1 Thess. 4:4),[139] a common Jewish view.[140] But apart from Paul not necessarily agreeing with his contemporaries, he cites neither idolatry nor specifically sexual sin here, what Jewish people often regarded as the most distinctively Gentile vices (as Rom. 1:23–26 probably

135. Cf. Rom. 3:7; 4:1. Thus Paul responds in 8:2, "set *you* [singular] free."

136. Granted, the figure in Rom. 2:17–23 is addressed in the second-person singular, in contrast to the first-person singular here. There may be special reasons, however, for the first-person usage here; aside from possible identification with Paul's pre-Christian past (mentioned above), see the discussion below.

137. Streland, "Note" (rightly noting Israel but citing Jewish tradition comparing Israel's idolatry in Exod. 32 with Adam's fall); Byrne, *Romans*, 218; Talbert, *Romans*, 188; Dunn, "Search," 331n44; Grieb, *Story*, 72; Kruse, *Romans*, 299; cf. Watson, *Gentiles*, 282.

138. See Stowers, *Rereading*, 39, 273–84, esp. 273–81; Stowers, "Self-Mastery," 536; Tobin, *Rhetoric*, 237; Das, *Debate*, 221–35; Wasserman, "Paul among Philosophers," 82; Rodríguez, *Call Yourself*, 134; cf. Gager, *Anti-Semitism*, 222–23. Regarding Gentiles more generally, cf. Origen's view of law in Rom. 7:7–13 as natural law (Reasoner, *Full Circle*, 68).

139. Stowers, *Rereading*, 273.

140. Cf. Stowers, *Rereading*, 273–75.

presupposes). Instead, Paul specifies coveting here, which was also a Jewish sin specified in the law (which he cites in 7:7; a prohibition that Gentiles did not have, unless innately in the natural law of 2:14–15). Paul applies ἐπιθυμέω and its cognates to Israelites in 1 Corinthians 10:6; the terms presumably include Jewish behaviors in Romans 6:12; 13:9; and Galatians 5:16–17, 24.[141]

Further, Jewish people did not believe that only Gentiles had passions; as noted, Jews also spoke of the Torah as helping them to combat passion. In Romans 2:17, 20, 23, and more clearly in Romans 3:19 and 7:1–4; 9:4, 31, those under the law are Jews, as also in 1 Corinthians 9:20 (see also Paul's use of "circumcision" versus "uncircumcision"). In Romans Paul is probably not addressing Gentiles under pressure to be circumcised, as in Galatians; nor does his mention of "you Gentiles" (Rom. 1:13; 11:13) mean that every member was Gentile (cf. 16:3, 7, 11).

This is not to deny that Paul's depiction of life under the law could serve as a warning to the believers in Rome, many or most of whom were Gentile (Rom. 1:5, 13; 11:13) but who probably originally learned about Jesus through Jewish believers. Of course, Israel's experience under the law is *human* experience under the law,[142] and the struggle to observe the law might prove even greater for proselytes who have not grown up keeping many of the commandments by culture and habit. The corrupted mind of 1:18–32 is the pagan mind; for Paul, the better-informed but powerless mind here is the mind of all under the law without Christ. But Paul continues to illustrate that all—both Gentiles and Jews, both those under the Torah (as here) and those having only more general natural law, are under sin without Christ (2:11–16; 3:9, 19–20).

Survey of the Context and Function of Romans 7:7–25

Paul offers a very curious statement in Romans 6:14: "For sin will not rule over you, because you are not under the law but under grace." How could being "under the law"—the law that Paul acknowledges as good and inspired (7:12, 14)—facilitate the reign of sin? Paul has already noted that the law has increased the transgression involved in human sin, presumably by showing sin more explicitly for what it is (5:13, 20). This explanation fits Paul's overarching argument in the early chapters of Romans: Gentiles have limited

141. Also Eph. 2:3; Titus 3:3; πάθημα appears in Gal. 5:24 as well as in Rom. 7:5, although πάθος appears only here (Rom. 1:26) and in 1 Thess. 4:5 and Col. 3:5. Despite their negative role in some passages, in most passages Paul does not denigrate Gentiles when mentioning them (e.g., Rom. 1:5, 13; 2:14, 24).

142. Cf., e.g., Engberg-Pedersen, *Paul and Stoics*, 242.

knowledge and will be punished for their sins accordingly; those who know the law have greater knowledge and will also be punished for their sins accordingly (1:18–3:31, esp. 2:12, 25; cf. Amos 3:2). Fuller knowledge bequeaths fuller responsibility.

In Romans 7:1 Paul revisits what it means to be "under the law." The law "rules over a person" and thus has jurisdiction over a person, and the right to condemn, as long as the person lives. Those who have died with Christ to sin, however (6:2–11), have also died to the rule of the law (7:4, 6).[143] This comparison occasions for Paul's imaginary interlocutor the question as to whether, in linking the law and sin, Paul is identifying the two (7:7). Paul will respond, in the graphic monologue of 7:7–25, by showing *how* the law has increased transgression. Like Gentiles who do not have the law, both ethnic Jews and proselytes have sinned; but because they have the law, they have sinned more knowingly and hence face stricter judgment (2:12, 23; 3:20; 4:15; 5:13, 20; 7:5–9). The law can inform but not transform—by itself it cannot keep one from sinning.[144]

As already noted,[145] Jewish tradition emphasized that the law empowered people to overcome passions or, in more Judean tradition, the evil impulse. Paul, however, contends in Romans 7:5 that the law in fact arouses sinful passions, perhaps by focusing attention on them and thus revealing mere reason's vulnerability regarding attempts to ward them off. In 7:6 Paul notes that those who are freed from the law no longer serve in the oldness of the letter; this deliverance refers back to the old life in Adam being crucified, freeing from slavery to sin those united with Christ (6:6). Further, those freed from the law serve in the newness of the Spirit (7:6),[146] a description that refers back to the beginning of new life in Christ (6:4) and forward to the renewing of the mind (12:2), as well as to the discussion of the liberating Spirit in 8:2–16, 23, 26–27.

The figure in Romans 7:7–25 is clearly under the law (7:7–9, 14, 23, 25). This figure is in the flesh (7:14, 18, 25), just like the past state Paul described in 7:5 ("while we were in the flesh"; contrast 8:9). Sin works in his members

---

143. I am not devaluing the various points omitted here, but I reserve them for a fuller commentary on Romans, or refer readers to my short commentary on Romans (Keener, *Romans*).

144. That is, it has functioned as any civil law might; the problem for Paul thus is not the law but the human heart (Rom. 7:14). But ideally the matter is different if God writes the law in the heart (Deut. 30:6), as would be the case with the new covenant (Jer. 31:33; Ezek. 36:25–27; 2 Cor. 3:3, 6). Paul believes that this comes only through divine action, through the Spirit (Rom. 8:2; 2 Cor. 3:3, 6, 8, 17–18).

145. See pp. 29, 32, 74; fuller discussion, pp. 77–78, 87–90.

146. Some understood freedom in terms of civic responsibility (cf. the contribution of this idea to Statius *Silv*. 1.6 in Chinn, "*Libertas*").

(7:23), again as in 7:5. This figure is enslaved to sin (7:14), in contrast to one who has been enslaved to God and freed from sin (6:18, 20, 22), and in contrast to the new life described in 7:6. The empowerment of the Spirit that characterizes the new life (7:6) is conspicuously absent in Paul's description until he reaches 8:2–16.

As noted earlier, it is thus clear from the context that Romans 7:7–25 depicts life under the law, the old life of 7:5; the new life in the Spirit of 7:6 is elaborated in chapter 8. Ancient writers sometimes briefly outlined the points they were about to cover;[147] with many commentators, I believe that Paul does so in 7:5–6.[148] Thus, against those who object that Paul cannot describe a figure different from his current life because, they argue, he does not introduce the figure differently, we may note that in fact he does introduce the figure differently.

Because of controversies about the interpretation of Romans 7, it was necessary to survey introductory issues before turning to the central point of this chapter. Now, however, I turn to the question of the mind and passions also raised by Romans 1.

The Problem of Passion

Although some behaviors are more easily avoided, the problem of desiring what one should not runs deeper. It addresses not simply one's behavior but one's character, yet it also raises questions. For example, in defining one's identity, where does one draw the line between a momentary interest in what one should not desire, perhaps prompted by something as fleeting as confusion, and a simmering and even cultivated passion that could well lead to unjust action?

Desire was a problem not only to Gentile philosophers (as noted in chap. 1)[149] but also to many Jewish thinkers. Jewish thinkers, however, had their own distinctive approach, often related to the Torah, and differed in various regards even among themselves, for example, a more Hellenistic approach in 4 Maccabees or Paul than in the rabbis, and a different approach to the Torah in Paul than in most other Jewish sources.

147. See, e.g., Gorg. *Hel.* 6–8, 20 (with 6–19); Pliny E. *N.H.* 33.21.66 (with 33.21.67–78); John 16:8–11; Pliny *Ep.* 6.29.1–2; Dio Chrys. *Or.* 38.8; Tac. *Ann.* 16.21 (with 16.21–32); Arius Did. 2.7.5a, p. 10.6–7 (with p. 10.7–15); Gaius *Inst.* 1.9–12; Men. Rhet. 2.1–2, 375.7–8; 2.1–2, 385.8 (with 385.9–386.10); Apul. *Apol.* 27 (with 29–65), 61, 67; Porph. *Marc.* 24.376–84. Cf. Anderson, *Glossary*, 32–33; Rowe, "Style," 134.
148. With, e.g., Seifrid, *Justification*, 232; Stowers, *Rereading*, 270; Stuhlmacher, *Romans*, 115; Osborne, *Romans*, 173; Barclay, *Gift*, 502n14; cf. Harrison and Hagner, "Romans," 116.
149. Pages 19–23.

Passion and the Law in Hellenistic Jewish Sources

In chapter 1 I addressed Gentile thinkers' opposition between reason and the passions and how Paul contends that depraved reason, against some pagan intellectual expectations, ultimately simply proliferated slavery to passion.[150] Hellenistic Jewish authors, like many philosophers, saw passions as harmful (and, beyond philosophers, as sinful).[151] For the first-century Jewish philosopher Philo, for example, the mind that loves the body and passion, enslaved to pleasure, cannot hear the divine voice.[152] Like most Gentile philosophers,[153] these Jewish thinkers contended that the key to overcoming passions was reason.[154]

For Jewish thinkers, the epitome of this reason that overcomes passion was found in the Torah.[155] There is strong evidence suggesting that the Jewish community in Rome had a highly developed knowledge of the law and its superiority to other ancient legal collections.[156]

Other thinkers had already compared law and reason, although often favoring the latter for the wise. Some defined law in terms of reason agreed on by a state.[157] Some argued that philosophy was better than law, because it taught right living from within.[158] Stoics felt that only the wise could understand and obey

150. Pages 1–29.
151. E.g., 4 Macc. 3:11; *T. Dan* 4:5; *T. Ash.* 3:2; 6:5; also Sir. 18:30–32 (cf. 6:2, 4); desire is seen as the origin of all sin in *Apoc. Mos.* 19:3; sexual desires can be dangerous in *T. Jud.* 13:2; *T. Jos.* 3:10; 7:8; *T. Reub.* 4:9; 5:6. Philo castigates "lovers of pleasure" in *Creation* 157–59; *Alleg. Interp.* 3.161; *Sacr.* 32; cf. sexual "pleasure" in *T. Iss.* 3:5. *T. Reub.* 2:8 maintains the biblical posture that desire for intercourse is good but warns that it can lead to love for pleasure; Philo (*Creation* 152) complains that woman brought man sexual pleasures, introducing sins. Rulers must avoid being distracted by pleasure (*Let. Aris.* 245), for people are prone to pleasure (277; cf. 108, 222).
152. Philo *Unchangeable* 111. This contrasts with the sacred mind uncorrupted by shameful matters (*Unchangeable* 105). For Philo, the garden's serpent is pleasure (e.g., *Creation* 157–60, 164; *Alleg. Interp.* 2.71–74; *Agr.* 97).
153. See discussion on pp. 21–23.
154. E.g., 4 Macc. 1:1, 9, 29; 2:15–16, 18, 21–22; 3:17; 6:31, 33; 7:4; 13:1–2, 7; Philo *Creation* 81; *Alleg. Interp.* 3.156; see also Tobin, *Rhetoric*, 231; Stowers, "Self-Mastery," 531–34; on 4 Maccabees, note Krieger, "4. Makkabäerbuch"; Dijkhuizen, "Pain"; cf. Fuhrmann, "Mother"; Dunson, "Reason." In contradistinction to orthodox Stoicism, 4 Macc. 3:2–5 affirms that reason subdues rather than eliminates passions. Cf. *T. Reub.* 4:9; Jos. *Ant.* 4.328–29. In early Christianity, see, e.g. (in Bray, *Romans*, 195), Pelagius *Comm. Rom.* on 7:22 (PCR 104–5).
155. See 4 Macc. 2:23; see also Campbell, *Deliverance*, 564. For law providing self-mastery over passions in Josephus and Philo, see Stowers, "Self-Mastery," 532–34; also Rodríguez, *Call Yourself*, 129, 155. In principle, good laws were supposed to make good people (Polyb. 4.47.3–4), since law is not ruled by passion (Arist. *Pol.* 3.11.4, 1287a).
156. See Tobin, *Rhetoric*, 28–30. Rome was one of the ancient centers of book publishing and distribution; see White, "Bookshops," 268, 277 (though Pliny mentions other sites).
157. *Rhet. Alex.* pref. 1420a.26–28; the agreement articulates something like a social contract view.
158. Crates *Ep.* 5.

true law.[159] Many thinkers believed that the wise or virtuous needed no law, since they would do what was right without one.[160] Some suggested that if all people were good, honor would provide sufficient restraint without written laws.[161] Such ideas became common even beyond philosophers (cf. Gal. 5:23; 1 Tim. 1:9).[162]

Appealing to a textual authority more compelling for them than the opinions of Gentile thinkers, Jewish thinkers found in the law of Moses explicit warrant against passion. The tenth commandment, "You shall not covet" (οὐκ ἐπιθυμήσεις, LXX Exod. 20:17 and Deut. 5:21, using ἐπιθυμέω), specifically addresses overcoming passion.[163] Citing this very commandment (Rom. 7:7), Paul argues that the law was never meant to eradicate passion; only Christ frees one from sin.[164]

Desire in Romans 7:7

Jewish people were not the only ones who recognized that it was wrong to covet what belonged to someone else; some Gentiles also noted this.[165] The line that Paul specifically quotes here, however, is Jewish, explicitly from "the law," the same law that is the subject of his preceding context (Rom. 7:1–7a).

159. Arius Did. 2.7.11i, p. 76.33–36; cf. 2.7.11d, p. 68.1–3, 6–8. Cf. Mus. Ruf. 2, p. 36.18–19, arguing that all have the *capacity* for such virtue, even if unfulfilled.

160. Dio Chrys. *Or.* 69.8–9; Lucian *Dem.* 59; Diog. Laert. 2.68 (Aristippus); Porph. *Marc.* 27.424–25; cf. Max. Tyre *Or.* 36.5 regarding Diogenes; Ovid *Metam.* 1.89–90, on the primeval world. Those who follow nature's laws will never err (Cic. *Off.* 1.28.100); innate law renders others superfluous (Max. Tyre *Or.* 6.6; cf. Porph. *Marc.* 27.422–23; Philo *Abr.* 16); the virtuous act wisely and hence are free to do what they wish (Philo *Good Person* 59). Cf. also Arist. *Pol.* 3.8.2, 1284a, which some compare with Gal. 5:23 (Bruce, "All Things," 90).

161. Dio Chrys. *Or.* 76.4.

162. "Virtue outranks . . . law" (Menander *Karchedonios* frg. 4, in Stob. *Anth.* 3.9.16; 4.1.21; trans. Arnott, LCL, 2:133); the ideal is for a city not to need laws (Men. Rhet. 1.3, 360.12–13). In practice, of course, many thinkers did praise the value of laws (e.g., Aeschines *Tim.* 4, 13; Polyb. 4.47.3–4).

163. Tobin, *Rhetoric*, 231–32, citing 4 Macc. 2:4–6; Philo *Decal.* 142–53, 173–74; *Spec. Laws* 4.79–131. In Philo *Spec. Laws* 4.80, desire for what one lacks is the most troublesome passion.

164. With Stowers, "Self-Mastery," 536; cf. Engberg-Pedersen, *Paul and Stoics*, 232; for the law's salvific inadequacy, also Romanello, "Impotence." Paul was more pessimistic about human ability to master passions than Philo and esp. 4 Maccabees (Gemünden, "Culture des passions"). Hübner ("Hermeneutics," 208) rightly emphasizes in Rom. 7 the "many verbs of understanding" (7:7, 13, 14, 15, 16, 18, 21, 22, 23) and (on 212–13) verbs of "willing" (7:15, 16, 18, 19, 20, 21), but focuses on the inability to understand in 7:15 (p. 212).

165. See, e.g., covetousness in Thucyd. 3.82.8; Diod. Sic. 21.1.4a; Cato *Coll. Dist.* 54; Mus. Ruf. 4, p. 48.9; 20, p. 126.18, 21; Dio Chrys. *Or.* 13.32; 17; 34.19; Lucian *Charon* 15; earlier, *Instruction of Ptah-hotep* in ANET 413; envy in Hesiod *W.D.* 195; Musaeus *Hero* 36–37; Eurip. *Oed.* frg. 551; Xen. *Mem.* 3.9.8; Thucyd. 2.35.2; Philod. *Prop.* col. 24.7; Corn. Nep. 8 (Thrasybulus), 4.1–2; Cic. *Fam.* 1.7.2; Epict. *Diatr.* 4.9.1–3; Dio Chrys. *Or.* 34.19; 77–78; Fronto *Ad M. Caes.* 4.1; Hermog. *Inv.* 1.1.95; Philost. *Ep. Apoll.* 43. See further sources in Keener, *Acts*, 2:1206–8.

Avoid Overspecifying Desire Here

The sense of such coveting here is likely general, referring to any inappropriate desire. By contrast, some scholars suggest that the sin here is coveting religious honor[166] (an issue elsewhere in Romans, but there typically designated as "boasting"; Rom. 2:17, 23; 3:27; 4:2), or "*covetous* insistence on Jewish priority among Jews in Christ," "the one human sin that the Law cannot help one overcome."[167] Granted that such behavior epitomizes sin under the law in Romans, it is by no means Paul's only illustration of sin here (2:21–22; 13:9), and it is never described exclusively in these terms.

Somewhat more generally, but still probably too specifically, some scholars suggest a sexual reference here, viewing ἐπιθυμία and its cognates as sexual "lust."[168] Experiencing new hormones, an adolescent might experience that aspect of the prohibition against coveting as the most difficult.[169] In the Septuagint, desiring a neighbor's wife appears as the first example of the prohibition. This may be why 4 Maccabees 2:1–6 applies the prohibition (cited in 2:5) especially to a young man's (Joseph's) reason overcoming sexual desires.[170]

Ancient philosophers often did speak of people who simply indulged bodily passions as beasts;[171] the ideal instead was to cultivate the distinctively human gift of the intellect. Dogs could copulate in public (so could Cynic philosophers, but this was not the philosophic norm); philosophers despised humans ruled by their sex drive. That sexual passion was prominent in Paul's consideration of bodily based sinful ways and thoughts is clear from his letters (Rom. 13:13–14; Gal. 5:17, 19; Col. 3:5; 1 Thess. 4:4–5; cf. 1 Cor. 6:9), which correspond with Jewish thought about Gentile behavior on this issue. It is also suggested by the context of the key text cited in Romans 7, although

166. Jewett, *Romans*, 451, comparing Gal. 1:14–15.

167. Nanos, *Mystery*, 358 (cf. 362, 364–65).

168. As in, e.g., Rom. 1:24; 1 Thess. 4:5; 2 Tim. 3:6; Prov. 6:25; Sir. 20:4; Matt. 5:28; Jos. *Ant.* 1.201; *T. Reub.* 5:6; *Did.* 3.3; Ign. *Pol.* 5.2–3; *Herm.* 1.8; 2.4; Mus. Ruf. 7, p. 56.17–18. But this was only part of the term's semantic range; see, e.g., Rom. 6:12; 13:14; Gal. 5:16–17, 24; Eph. 2:3; 4:22; 1 Tim. 6:9; 2 Tim. 4:3; James 1:14–15; 4:2; 2 Pet. 1:4; Mark 4:19; John 8:44; Acts 20:33; Num. 11:4, 34; Prov. 12:12; Sir. 18:30–31; Wis. 16:3; 19:11; 1 Macc. 4:17; 11:11; 4 Macc. 1:32, 34; 3:11–12, 16; *1 Clem.* 3.4; 28.1; *2 Clem.* 17.3; Galen *Grief* 42–44 (esp. 43). God's "commandment" (Rom. 7:8–13) could apply to sexual issues (*T. Jud.* 13:7; 14:6), but again, this was a very narrow part of the term's range (cf., e.g., 1 Cor. 7:19; 14:37; Eph. 2:15; 6:2; Col. 4:10; Gen. 26:5; Lev. 26:3; 4 Macc. 8:29–9:1; 16:24).

169. Gundry, "Frustration," 233, noting that the youth reaches the age of maturity and responsibility under the Torah at the same time he reaches sexual maturity.

170. The analogy with Rom. 7:7 probably simply reflects consideration of the same biblical command (Charlesworth, *Pseudepigrapha*, 78).

171. As noted in chap. 1; see pp. 23–24.

Paul's argument here is more general and by no means exclusively sexual. Paul's specific example of not "coveting" or "desiring," given its first object in Exodus 20:17 (LXX),[172] naturally includes this issue of a mind ruled by sexual desire. The law can make one wish to suppress such desires, but biological impulses are not easily harnessed by suppressing them, since focusing on them feeds their flame.

Some scholars associate the evil impulse in later rabbinic literature especially with sexual sin.[173] Although that association does appear to have been prominent,[174] the impulse had broader associations,[175] often, for example, with idolatry.[176] Others thus demur from a sexual reference here, arguing that this proposal is too specific.[177] The real sense is not likely so specific as in these suggestions; Paul may choose this commandment because it is the one least observable to others, addressing exclusively the heart.[178]

Philo opines that the Decalogue climaxes with the prohibition of coveting, or desire (ἐπιθυμία), because it is the worst threat, originating from within.[179] Some argue that this specific commandment remains in view throughout Romans 7:7–25 and in 8:4.[180] Influenced by Stoicism, some Hellenistic Jewish circles read this commandment as a prohibition of desire more generally.[181]

172. "Your neighbor's wife" appears second in Hebrew, but the LXX transposes it with "your neighbor's house" or "household."

173. Davies, *Paul*, 21; Gundry, "Frustration," 233.

174. See, e.g., *Abot R. Nat.* 16 A; *b. Sanh.* 45a; *Ruth Rab.* 6:4; perhaps *Num. Rab.* 10:10. Marrying was a good defense against it (*b. Qid.* 30b), and unlike the inclination to idolatry, the inclination to sexual immorality was the only one that still tempted Israel (*Song Rab.* 7:8, §1). Cf. the "spirit of intercourse" that, though healthy in itself, made one vulnerable to sins of pleasure (*T. Reub.* 2:8), an idea consistent with the original form of Stoicism (see Brennan, "Theory," 61–62n31).

175. See, e.g., *Sipra A.M. pq.* 13.194.2.11 (general); *Pesiq. Rab Kah.* Sup. 3:2 (suicidal impulses). Rosen-Zvi ("Ysr") argues that only the Babylonian Talmud associates the evil impulse especially with sexual immorality.

176. *Song Rab.* 2:4, §1; *Tg. Ps.-Jon.* on Exod. 32:22; Davies, *Paul*, 30; Urbach, *Sages*, 1:482.

177. Schreiner, *Romans*, 369–70; Jewett, *Romans*, 448, 465; Das, *Debate*, 216.

178. Hunter, *Message*, 86. Its addressing the heart also invites consideration of how to read the other nine (Kaiser, *Preaching*, 65–66; see also the use of the commandment's demands on the heart in Matt. 5:21–28). Both Paul (Rom. 13:9) and, presumably, his source, Jesus (Mark 12:29–31), treat love as the summary of the law. For the tenth commandment as a summary of the law in Philo, see Knox, *Jerusalem*, 131.

179. Philo *Decal.* 142. For it as the root of all sin, Dunn (*Romans*, 1:380) cites Philo *Creation* 152; *Decal.* 142, 150, 153, 173; *Spec. Laws* 4.84–85; *Apoc. Mos.* 19:3; James 1:15. For the emphasis on the heart in some other early Jewish ethics, see, e.g., *m. Ab.* 2:9; *b. Ber.* 13a; *Tg. Ps.-Jon.* on Lev. 6:2; Bonsirven, *Judaism*, 95; Montefiore and Loewe, *Anthology*, 272–94; Pawlikowski, "Pharisees."

180. Ziesler, "Requirement." Some might find this suggestion too specific.

181. Dunn, *Romans*, 1:379, citing 4 Macc. 1:3, 31–32; 2:1–6; 3:2, 11–12, 16; Philo *Alleg. Interp.* 3.15; *Posterity* 26; Stowers, *Rereading*, 60 (cf. 47), citing esp. Philo and 4 Maccabees. It

Unlawful Desire

It is also possible, however, to define desire here too broadly. Unlike the most extreme Hellenistic thinkers,[182] Paul would not demand the conquest of every bodily desire.[183] For example, Paul probably does not oppose sexual desire in marriage[184] or appreciation for food.[185] On such points Paul reflects not the austerity of some Gentile thinkers but thoroughly conventional, mainstream Jewish views (as well as the common views of most ordinary people in antiquity).

When Paul speaks of passions, he does not define them, unlike some philosophers, but his association of forbidden desire with the law's command not to covet probably presupposes what the biblical commandment contextually specifies: desiring what belongs to someone else. What the body desires may even be necessary for survival or the biblically mandated propagation of humanity;[186] but the mind remains responsible to limit the fulfillment of those desires to what God's law permits. A thirsty person's craving for water or a person's reproductive drive are not wrong of themselves, but desiring someone else's well or spouse is wrong. Desire must be harnessed rather than in control.

The problem of conquering desire arises when desires that were created for good if directed by moral reason instead rule the person. As Paul laments,

I see a different law in my [bodily] members, battling against the law in relation to my mind, and taking me prisoner by the law in relation to my members, · the law that provokes sin. . . . Who will free me from the body [thus] doomed to death? . . . Thus, with respect to the mind, I'm emphatically serving the law that comes from God—but, with respect to the flesh, the law in its role of provoking sin. (Rom. 7:23–25)

Whereas a strong-willed intellect might prevent such desires from bearing fruit in outward action, the very attempt to suppress a thought inevitably draws

---

applies even to craving food in a way that brings complaints against God's provision (1 Cor. 10:6; in the LXX, Num. 11:4; Ps. 105:13–14 [106:13–14 ET]).

182. Most opposed excessive desire rather than proper desire (Deming, *Celibacy*, 45, 69n70, 128nn85–86); for Stoics, some desires or interests could be morally indifferent and thus acceptable provided they were kept within natural bounds.

183. Like others, he was even capable of using ἐπιθυμία in a positive way in the right context (Phil. 1:23; 1 Thess. 2:17).

184. See 1 Cor. 7:9 (despite the way that some interpreters understand 1 Thess. 4:4–5). In earlier Jewish sources, see comment in Mueller, "Faces."

185. See Rom. 14:2–3, 6; 1 Cor. 9:4; Col. 2:16; cf. the echo of a traditional Jewish benediction in 1 Tim. 4:3–5.

186. Compare some rabbinic approaches to the *yēṣer*. Kruse (*Romans*, 330) helpfully cites Gal. 5:16–25 (note esp. 5:17) in connection with the sinful frame of mind in Rom. 8:5; Gal. 5:19–21 exemplifies what the flesh desires, and 5:22–23 what the Spirit desires.

attention to it. A merely passing or intrusive thought at most poses a question that may be ignored or rejected as easily as affirmed, but one's resistance can be worn down by the question's continuous exposing of the issue, especially for someone who scrupulously endeavors to suppress or resolve the question on their own rather than leaving the defense of one's righteousness to Christ. The least failure could discourage especially the most scrupulous.[187] Paul has chosen the prohibition of coveting not randomly but because it addresses the heart and as such is the most difficult to regulate. Only the preassurance of one's righteousness can protect one from condemnation by God's standard, and for Paul this preassurance of acceptance is genuine only in Christ.

Thinking about sin to resist it still leaves sin and condemnation framing the question and defining the subject, so that one must settle for resisting it some of the time. As long as one's objective is to overcome sin much of the time, perhaps comparing oneself with the less scrupulous, one may celebrate one's successful performance of commandments. If one's view of God's standard is perfection, however (as apparently in Rom. 3:20–24; 4:2; 5:18; Gal. 3:22), one who is conscious of any failure may fixate on sin and guilt. The new revelation in Christ provides an entirely new frame of reference—not sin, but God's gift of righteousness in Christ; not the flesh, but the Spirit. Romans 7 connects with philosophers' emphasis on self-control and self-mastery, but only to show up how inadequate this emphasis is by itself. The mind may know and will to do what is right, but this ability offers righteousness that is merely relative to more willing capitulation to sin. With respect to sin, informed consent is all the more culpable (cf. 1:32; 2:15; 7:15–18).

Excursus: Ancient Views
concerning Lust and Other Illicit Desires

Ancient summaries of blamelessness sometimes stressed that particular praiseworthy persons never even thought or intended anything dishonorable.[188] Greek philosophers often felt that thoughts and intentions, not merely deeds, could be evil.[189] Thus Thales, a sixth-century BCE philosopher, reportedly believed that the gods knew and required purity even of thoughts.[190] Seneca

187. On Pharisees as particularly meticulous, see Jos. *Life* 191; cf. *War* 1.110; 2.162. Whatever his didactic hyperbole, Paul's standard appears even more exacting.
188. Val. Max. 1.12.3; 2.1.1–2.
189. Boring, Berger, and Colpe (*Commentary*, 58) cite Aelian *Var. hist.* 14.28, 42; Epict. frg. 100; Diog. Laert. 1.36; Plut. *Busybody* 13; Cic. *Fin.* 3.9.32; Arist. *Magna moralia*.
190. Val. Max. 7.2.ext.8; Diog. Laert. 1.36.

condemned as impious a woman whose virtue stemmed merely from fear.[191] Other thinkers argued that a friend of Zeus would not desire anything evil or shameful.[192] Even law could punish known plotting,[193] although not simply inward attitudes. Pharisees emphasized inward attitudes and not merely external behavior.[194] Some Jewish writers condemned even *contemplating* evil.[195]

Many viewed anger as problematic;[196] controlling it was honorable.[197] Anger became dangerous especially when it escalated to the extent of the desire to kill.[198] Some warned that anger could easily lead to murder.[199] Some argued that to lose one's temper was to lose one's mind, that is, experience temporary insanity.[200] Stoics opposed anger;[201] Epicureans viewed it negatively but did not believe, as Stoics did, that it could be eradicated.[202]

Views on sexual desire varied, though most Gentiles at the popular level did not view it as problematic.[203] Even philosophic approaches varied, Epicureans naturally approving passion, with a Neoplatonist such as Porphyry

---

191. Sen. *Y. Ben.* 4.14.1.

192. Dio Chrys. *Or.* 4.43.

193. See Apul. *Flor.* 20.7–8.

194. E.g., *m. Ab.* 2:9; *b. Ber.* 13a; compare rabbinic discussions of *kawwānâ* (on which see Bonsirven, *Judaism*, 95; Montefiore and Loewe, *Anthology*, 272–94; Pawlikowski, "Pharisees"); cf. Jos. *Ag. Ap.* 2.183, 217 in Vermes, *Religion*, 32. Rabbinic documents may appear more legalistic because they are *legal* documents, but this does not represent all of rabbinic, Pharisaic, or Jewish ethics (Davies, "Aboth," 127; Vermes, *Religion*, 195); the covenantal perspective is better represented in early Jewish prayers (Segal, "Covenant").

195. E.g., *Let. Aris.* 132–33; though contrast *b. Hul.* 142a, and avoiding sin in one's thoughts was a high standard (*T. Zeb.* 1:4). Cf. atonement "for the sinful thoughts of the heart" (*Tg. Ps.-Jon.* on Lev. 6:2, trans. Maher, 134).

196. See, e.g., Publ. Syr. 214; Cic. *Quint. fratr.* 1.1.13.37–39; Lucian *Dem.* 51 (quoting Demonax); Diog. Laert. 8.1.23; the many sources cited in Keener, *Acts*, 3:2308–9.

197. See, e.g., Cic. *Phil.* 8.5.16; *Prov. cons.* 1.2; Plut. *Contr. A., Mor.* 452F–464D (entire essay); *Educ.* 14, *Mor.* 10B; Diog. Laert. 1.70.

198. E.g., Matt. 5:21–22; 1 John 3:15; cf. *T. Gad* 1:9; 4:4; Sen. *Y. Ben.* 5.14.2; Davies and Allison (*Matthew*, 1:509) cite *Tg. Ps.-Jon.* and *Tg. Onq.* on Gen. 9:6; *Der. Er. Rab.* 11:13.

199. Cf. Demosth. *Con.* 19; Sir. 8:16; Ps.-Phoc. 57–58; *Did.* 3.2; cf. Hor. *Ep.* 1.2.59–62; Boring, Berger, and Colpe (*Commentary*, 57) cite Plut. *Uned. R.* 6, *Mor.*

200. Cato the Elder 16 in Plut. *S. Rom., Mor.* 199A; Hor. *Ep.* 1.2.61–62; Sen. *Y. Ep. Lucil.* 18.14 (quoting favorably Epicurus); Philost. *Ep. Apoll.* 86.

201. E.g., Sen. *Y. Ep. Lucil.* 123.1–2; *Dial.* 3–5; Mus. Ruf. 3, p. 40.21; 16, p. 104.18 (emphasizing self-control); Epict. *Diatr.* 1.15.1–5; 2.19.26; Arius Did. 2.7.10e, pp. 62–63.15–16; 2.7.11s, p. 100.6–7; Marc. Aur. 6.26.

202. Procopé, "Epicureans," 188–89. For an Epicurean warning against anger, see, e.g., Philod. *Crit.* frg. 12; for Stoics favoring its eradication, see Van Hoof, "Differences."

203. In what follows, I have augmented material from Keener, *Matthew*, 186; cf. also Keener, "Adultery."

wanting to control it.[204] Many schools of philosophic thought, however, viewed it ambivalently or negatively.[205] Some viewed intercourse as positive only for the common good provided by procreation.[206] Some philosophers, especially Stoics, opposed lust because it meant that pleasure rather than virtue dominated one's thoughts,[207] though Stoic philosophers did not condemn sexual arousal in the service of intercourse.[208] Diaspora Jewish intellectual thought often echoed Greek philosophic approaches.[209]

By contrast, many men in the ancient Mediterranean thought lust a healthy and normal practice.[210] Among the most common magical spells were those used to secure love.[211] Some of these describe self-stimulation as a way to secure intercourse with the object of one's desire,[212] even if she is married.[213] Still, even many people who otherwise thought lust acceptable disapproved if the woman was betrothed or married,[214] though it was not legally punish-

204. Sorabji, *Emotion*, 11, 273–80; on Epicurus, see, e.g., Max. Tyre *Or.* 32.8. For diverse views on self-stimulation, see Sext. Emp. *Pyr.* 3.206; masturbation appears negatively already in the Negative Confessions in the Egyptian *Book of the Dead*, Spell 125 (Wells, "Exodus," 230).

205. See, e.g., the condemnation of Paris's choice of the erotic life in Heracl. *Hom. Prob.* 28.4–5; Proclus *Poet.* 6.1, K108.18–19.

206. Sorabji, *Emotion*, 276, citing Philo *Spec. Laws* 3.113; Mus. Ruf. frg. 12 Hense; Porph. *Marc.* 35; Ps.-Ocellus *Nat. Univ.* 4; many early Christian sources. (Sorabji [*Emotion*, 276–77] cites Aug. *Ag. Jul.* 4.14.69 to note that Augustine allows intercourse for health as well as for procreation.) Cf. also Deming, *Celibacy*, 94; Ward, "Musonius," 284.

207. E.g., Epict. *Diatr.* 2.18.15–18; 3.2.8; 4.9.3; Marc. Aur. 2.10; 3.2.2; 9.40; cf. Nock, *Christianity*, 19; Sen. Y. *Ep. Lucil.* 95.37; Arius Did. 2.7.10c, p. 60.14–19. For diverse views among Stoics, see Sorabji, *Emotion*, 281–82.

208. Brennan, "Theory," 61–62n31; Sorabji, *Emotion*, 283; Deming, *Celibacy*, 128.

209. Cf. Luz, *Matthew*, 1:295, for Stoic influence on Hellenistic Judaism. Luz cites Philo *Creation* 152; *Good Person* 159; *Spec. Laws* 4.84; *Decal.* 142; *L.A.E.* 19; Rom. 7:7; and James 1:15. He also parallels the rabbinic use of the *yēṣer haraʿ*.

210. E.g., Ach. Tat. 1.4–6; Apul. *Metam.* 2.8; Philost. *Ep.* 26 (57); Diog. Laert. 6.2.46, 69; Diogenes *Ep.* 35, to Sopolis; Artem. *Oneir.* 1.78.

211. E.g., *PGM* 4.400–405; 13.304; 32.1–19; 36.69–101, 102–33, 134–60, 187–210, 295–311, 333–60; 62.1–24; 101.1–53; charms and formulae in Frankfurter, "Perils"; Jordan, "Spell" (P.Duk. inv. 230); Jordan, "Formulae" (P.Duk. inv. 729); Horsley, *Documents*, 1:33–34. See also Dunand, *Religion Populaire*, 125; Frankfurter, *Religion in Egypt*, 229–30; Graf and Johnston, "Magic," 136, 139; Dickie, "Love-Magic"; Yamauchi, "Aphrodisiacs," 62–63. In written sources, see, e.g., Eurip. *Hipp.* 513–16; Theocritus *The Spell* (GBP 26–39); Virg. *Ecl.* 8.80–84; Pliny E. *N.H.* 27.35.57; 27.99.125; 28.4.19; 28.6.34; 28.80.261; 30.49.141; 32.50.139; Quint. *Decl.* 385 intro.; Philost. *Hrk.* 16.2; Apul. *Metam.* 3.16–18; *T. Jos.* 6:1–5; in farce, Tibullus 1.2.41–58; Lucian *Dial. C.* 1 (*Glycera and Thais*), 281; 4 (*Melitta and Bacchis* ¶1), 286; Lucian *Lover of Lies* 14–15. Regarding the charge against Apuleius, see Bradley, "Magic"; Nelson, "Note."

212. *PGM* 36.291–94.

213. *PDM* 61.197–216 = *PGM* 61.39–71; cf. Eurip. *Hipp.* 513–16.

214. Cf. Ach. Tat. 4.3.1–2 in context; Char. *Chaer.* 2.2.8. Cf. illicit lust for young men in Cic. *Cat.* 1.6.13. In Val. Max. 2.1.5 adulterous eyes (cf. 2 Pet. 2:14) are those that seek intercourse. A

able.[215] Virtuous people wanted to avoid being the object of lust,[216] for which reason married women in many places wore head coverings.[217]

Jewish writers, however, generally viewed lust far more harshly, often warning against gazing on beautiful women.[218] Some writers, in fact, viewed it as visual fornication or adultery,[219] as did many early Christians.[220] A pious rabbi might praise God for a woman's beauty, but he would see it only by accident.[221] Some later rabbis went so far as to praise a predecessor who had never *looked* at his own private parts.[222] Likewise, other Jewish teachers employed the hyperbolic rhetoric that equated the thought with the act or treated the former as worse.[223]

Judean Passions: The Evil Impulse

Although Paul's language resembles especially Hellenistic Jewish thinkers, who in various ways had already bridged earlier Jewish concepts and Greek thought and drawn on the law, somewhat similar concepts already existed in Judean and other traditional Eastern Jewish thought.[224] Thus, in connection with Romans 7 or other Pauline texts, many scholars cite the rabbinic teaching of the two impulses, the *yēṣer hāraʿ* (the evil impulse) and the *yēṣer haṭōb* (the good impulse).[225] Other scholars reject the relevance of this material for

---

leader who controls his passion regarding beautiful women was seen as honorable (Val. Max. 4.3.ext.1; Plut. *Alex.* 21.5; Men. Rhet. 2.1–2, 376.11–13).

215. Char. *Chaer.* 5.7.5–6; 8.8.8.

216. Women in Sen. E. *Controv.* 2.7.6; a young man in Val. Max. 4.5.ext.1.

217. See sources in Keener, "Head Coverings"; more on head coverings in Llewellyn-Jones, *Tortoise*.

218. E.g., Job 31:1, 9; Sir. 9:8; 23:5–6; 25:21; 41:21; Sus. 8; 1QS 1.6–7; 4.10; CD 2.16; 11QT 59.14; 1QpHab 5.7; *Sib. Or.* 4.33–34; *Pss. Sol.* 4:4; *T. Iss.* 3:5; 4:4; *T. Reub.* 4:1, 11; 6:1–3; *T. Jud.* 17:1; *m. Nid.* 2:1; *Abot R. Nat.* 2 A; 2, §9 B; *b. Ber.* 20a; *Yebam.* 63b; *y. Hag.* 2:2, §4; *Gen. Rab.* 32:7; *Pesiq. Rab Kah.* Sup. 3:2; cf. Bonsirven, *Judaism*, 113; Schechter, *Aspects*, 225; Vermes, *Religion*, 32–33; Ilan, *Women*, 127–28. Knowledge of Jewish tradition does appear in some love charms (*PGM* 36.301).

219. *T. Iss.* 7:2; *T. Reub.* 4:8; *b. Nid.* 13b, bar.; *Shab.* 64ab; *y. Hal.* 2:1; *Lev. Rab.* 23:12; *Pesiq. Rab.* 24:2; see Keener, *Marries*, 16–17.

220. Matt. 5:28 (admittedly hyperbolic); 2 Pet. 2:14; Justin *1 Apol.* 15; *Sent. Sext.* 233; Tert. *Apol.* 46.11–12; cf. *Herm.* 1.1.1; lust leads to adultery in *Did.* 3.3.

221. Y. *Ber.* 9:1, §16.

222. Y. *Sanh.* 10:5, §2. Some Tannaim reportedly deemed it wrong for a man to hold his genital organ when urinating (*b. Nid.* 13a; *Gen. Rab.* 95 MSV); handling the organ excessively was deemed worthy of the appendage being amputated (*m. Nid.* 2:1).

223. E.g., *b. Qid.* 81b; Lachs, *Commentary*, 96–97, citing *b. Ned.* 13b; *Yoma* 29a; *Num. Rab.* 8:5.

224. Davies (*Paul*, 23) goes too far by identifying Paul's "flesh" with the rabbis' evil impulse, but the evil impulse does offer an analogy to his more Diaspora-focused approach.

225. Davies, *Paul*, 20, 25–27 (citing Williams, *Fall and Sin*, 150); Marcus, "Inclination" (on esp. Gal. 5:16–17); Martin, *Reconciliation*, 60; Barth, *Ephesians*, 1:230 (on Eph. 2:3); Stuhlmacher,

Romans 7.[226] I view the *yēṣer* as relevant in the sense of providing an analogy native to Judean teachers, though not as directly relevant in this case (at least to Paul's wording) as the Hellenistic Jewish sources.

Jewish Thoughts on the Evil Impulse

Later sources are more diverse than early ones. Later rabbis differed regarding details of the *yēṣer*'s operation,[227] and views became elaborated over time through discussions of various topics and texts.[228] Thus, in some sources this impulse was necessary and could be harnessed for good, for procreation and the like.[229] Perhaps in keeping with the earlier sectarian Jewish understanding of the two spirits, one good and one evil,[230] the rabbis developed the idea of a good *yēṣer* to counter the evil one.[231] Just as reason defeats the passions in many hellenized sources,[232] following the good impulse defeats the evil impulse.[233]

Although rabbinic elaborations about the *yēṣer* are later, the idea of an evil inclination clearly predates Paul's period. It appears at Qumran[234] and

---

Romans, 109; Shogren, "Wretched Man"; this was also what I emphasized in my own earlier years of teaching. Cf. also Marcus, "Inclination in James," on James 1:14; 4:5.

226. E.g., Urbach, *Sages*, 1:472, preferring instead Hellenistic Jewish sources such as 4 Maccabees; Porter, "Concept."

227. Alexander, "Ambiguity." Note the carefully edited composition about the evil impulse in *Abot R. Nat.* 16 A, as discussed by Schofer ("Redaction"); cf. the lengthy collection in *b. Suk.* 51b–52b; more texts in Montefiore and Loewe, *Anthology*, 295–314; Urbach, *Sages*, 1:471–83.

228. For example, the evil impulse deprives one of the present and/or coming world (*m. Ab.* 2:11; *Lev. Rab.* 29:7). God remained sovereign over the evil impulse (*Gen. Rab.* 52:7) but (according to some) regretted having created it (*b. Suk.* 52b; *Gen. Rab.* 27:4; cf. also Schechter, *Aspects*, 284; for its creation, also *Exod. Rab.* 46:4). It grows within one (*b. Suk.* 52ab). Angels lacked this impulse (*Lev. Rab.* 26:5); it desired people like Cain (*Song Rab.* 7:11, §1); Israel was delivered from the inclination to idolatry but still needed to resist the inclination to sexual immorality (*Song Rab.* 7:8, §1).

229. *Gen. Rab.* 9:7; *Eccl. Rab.* 3:11, §3; Kohler, *Theology*, 215; Davies, *Paul*, 22; cf. *y. Suk.* 5:2, §2; good sexual desire in *T. Reub.* 2:8; Mus. Ruf. 14, p. 92.11–12; frg. 40, p. 136.18–19. One should love God with both impulses (*Sipre Deut.* 32.3.1).

230. E.g., *Jub.* 1:20–21; 1QS 4.17–26; 5.5; *T. Jud.* 20:1; *Herm.* 2.5.1; 2.6.2. Cf. the contrast between virtue and vice within, in, e.g., Max. Tyre *Or.* 34.4.

231. E.g., *Sipre Deut.* 32.3.1; *b. Ber.* 61b; *Eccl. Rab.* 2:1, §1; cf. perhaps already *T. Ash.* 1:3–6. Scholars often cite the two-impulses doctrine (e.g., Ladd, *Theology*, 440). The idea of the good *yēṣer* is later than that of the evil one (Rosen-Zvi ["Inclinations"] even suggests that the good *yēṣer* is merely the person oneself).

232. See pp. 21–23.

233. *T. Ash.* 3:2; *Abot R. Nat.* 32 A; *b. Ber.* 60b; *Eccl. Rab.* 4:14, §1. For good works opposing the evil impulse, see *T. Ash.* 3:2; *b. B. Metsia* 32b; for habit opposing sin, cf. *m. Ab.* 4:2; *y. Sanh.* 10:1, §2; for wisdom opposing sin, cf. *1 En.* 5:8.

234. 1QS 5.5; CD 2.15–16 (the same in 4Q266 frg. 2, col. 2.16; 4Q270 frg. 1, col. 1.1); 1QHᵃ 13.8; 4Q417 frg. 2, col. 2.12; 4Q422 1.12; 4Q436 frg. 1a+bi.10; cf. "the inclination of flesh" in

elsewhere.[235] In Genesis 6:5 and 8:21, foundational texts for the later doctrine, God saw that every inclination (*yēṣer*) of the thoughts of the human heart was evil daily, and from humans' youth.[236]

Based on some rabbinic evidence, some scholars have connected the evil impulse with Paul's idea of "flesh."[237] Rabbinic thought did not, however, connect the evil impulse specifically with the body very often.[238] A stronger possible connection would be that these impulses function as the closest rabbinic equivalent to the conflict between reason and passions.

TORAH ENABLES ONE
TO OVERCOME THE EVIL IMPULSE

Overcoming the evil impulse resembled Gentile and Hellenistic Jewish thinkers' emphasis on overcoming passions. Stoics believed that human efforts, cooperating with nature, could overcome inborn impulses.[239] As noted, many philosophers appealed to reason to overcome passions, and Hellenistic Jews likewise often appealed to law-informed reason.[240] Rabbis similarly urged people to overcome their evil impulse,[241] praised those who overcame

---

4Q416 frg. 1.16; 4Q418 frg. 2+2ac.8; also the two spirits in 1QS 3.25–4.1; Seitz, "Spirits"; Price, "Light from Qumran," 15ff.; Baudry, "Péché dans les écrits."

235. Sir. 37:3; *Jub.* 35:9 (= 1Q18 frgs. 1–2.3; 4Q223–224 frg. 2, col. 1.49); *L.A.B.* 33:3; *4 Ezra* 7:92 (cf. Thompson, *Responsibility*, 356); cf. *Jub.* 1:19; Sir. 15:14–15, 17; 21:11; 27:6; Philo *Creation* 154–55; *T. Reub.* 2:8; Bonsirven, *Judaism*, 103. For the two spirits, see *Jub.* 1:20–21; *T. Levi* 19; *T. Jud.* 20:1–2; *T. Gad* 4; *T. Ash.* 1:3–6; 3:2; 6:5 (with ἐπιθυμία); *T. Zeb.* 9:8; *Herm.* 2.5.1; 2.6.2; Bright, *History*, 450. For a similar idea (of two accompanying spirits) in a traditional culture, cf. Mbiti, *Religions*, 114.

236. On the context, cf. Hirsch, *Genesis*, 56–57. Later rabbis thus warned that the *yēṣer* was so evil that even its creator testified how evil it was in Gen. 8:21 (*Sipre Deut.* 45.1.3).

237. Davies, *Paul*, 340, cites a rabbinic source in which the evil impulse ruled over all 248 members of the body. This idea appears (*Abot R. Nat.* 16 A; 16, §36 B; *Pesiq. Rab Kah.* Sup. 3:2; *y. Shab.* 14:3; Urbach, *Sages*, 1:473–74), although is less pervasive than the simpler claim that there were 248 bones or members in the body (*t. Ed.* 2:10; *b. Erub.* 54a; *Gen. Rab.* 69:1; *Tg. Ps.-Jon.* on Gen. 1:27; Cohen, "Noahide Commandments"). Tannaim and later rabbis apparently debate the *yēṣer*'s specific location in the body in *b. Ber.* 61a; the good inclination preserves the body from Gehenna (*Tg. Qoh.* on 9:15). In *Lev. Rab.* 12:3 the Torah is life to all the members.

238. Urbach, *Sages*, 1:472. For rabbis' appreciation for the body, cf., e.g., Kovelman, "Perfection"; for comments about embodiment even in some Diaspora Jewish sources, see Mirguet, "Reflections."

239. Long, *Philosophy*, 184–89, esp. 188. Later, in the Hermetica, divine powers overcome the twelve evil inclinations (Reitzenstein, *Mystery-Religions*, 48–49).

240. E.g., 4 Macc. 1:1, 9.

241. See *Sipra Sh. M. d.* 99.2.3 (following Deut. 10:16); *Pesiq. Rab Kah.* 24:4 (citing Ps. 4:5); *Ruth Rab.* 8:1 (citing Ps. 4:5); also the command to Cain in *Tg. Neof.* 1 on Gen. 4:7; *Tg. Ps.-Jon.* on Gen. 4:7. One could use oaths to overcome it (*Num. Rab.* 15:16; *Ruth Rab.* 6:4), but training it was difficult (*Pesiq. Rab Kah.* 23:7).

it,[242] and prayed for help to overcome it.[243] Some conceded, perhaps tongue in cheek, that if someone was succumbing to the evil impulse, they should commit their sin where no one will know it to prevent the worse offense of profaning God's name.[244] By and large, however, the sages urged people to overcome.

The conflict between reason and passion, or between the good and evil impulse, thus offers an indirect analogy for Paul's contrast between how the law informs one's mind and how it condemns one in connection with one's physical urges (Rom. 7:23). As the law was the common Hellenistic Jewish source of reason for controlling the passions,[245] so in Hebrew and Aramaic Jewish texts the law protected people from the evil impulse;[246] the law was the cure for it.[247] Likewise, the reverse could be true: the evil impulse worked to keep people from studying and believing the Torah.[248]

When did the law come, bringing death to this figure (Rom. 7:9)? Historically, it came in the time of Moses (5:13–14), most relevant to the extent that this figure represents Israel. It would be recapitulated in the life of Jewish children when they became conscious of the law, or of proselytes when they joined the Jewish people and (in the case of a man) were circumcised.

242. Such as Abraham (*y. Ber.* 9:5, §2; *Sot.* 5:5, §3; *Gen. Rab.* 59:7; *Num. Rab.* 14:11); all three patriarchs (*b. B. Bat.* 17a); Moses, David, and Ezra (*Song Rab.* 4:4, §2; others debated David [*b. B. Bat.* 17a] or, more plausibly, denied his victory [*y. Ber.* 9:5, §2; *Sot.* 5:5, §3]); or R. Simeon b. Eleazar (*Deut. Rab.* 2:33). The wise (*Gen. Rab.* 97 NV) and the truly mighty (*b. Tamid* 32a) conquer it; one who overcomes the evil impulse is like one who has conquered a city (*Abot R. Nat.* 23, citing Prov. 21:22).

243. E.g., "May the good inclination have sway over me and let not the evil inclination have sway over me" (*b. Ber.* 60b, Soncino p. 378; cf. prayer for the good inclination in *y. Ber.* 4:2); some construed the blessing of Num. 6:24 to mean, "May God keep you from the evil impulse" (*Sipre Num.* 40.1.3; *Num. Rab.* 11:5); cf. also Ps. 91:10 (*b. Sanh.* 103a). Prayer for the evil impulse to be uprooted, however, would be answered only eschatologically (*Exod. Rab.* 46:4). Already in 4Q436 frg. 1a+bi.10 one thanks God for protecting him from the evil impulse.

244. E.g., *b. Qid.* 40a; *Hag.* 16a. This is likely a homiletical way of emphasizing the horror of profaning God's name, and not all the rabbis concurred even with the illustration.

245. E.g., 4 Macc. 2:23; with, e.g., Stowers, "Self-Mastery," 532–34; Byrne, *Romans*, 219. See Gemünden, "Culture des passions," correctly nuancing the varied approaches of 4 Maccabees, Philo, and Paul.

246. *Sipre Deut.* 45.1.2; *Pesiq. Rab Kah.* Sup. 3:2; *b. Ber.* 5a; *Suk.* 52b; *Lev. Rab.* 35:5; *Pesiq. Rab.* 41:4; Montefiore and Loewe, *Anthology*, 124; Davies, *Paul*, 22; Urbach, *Sages*, 1:472. For the law against sin more generally, see *m. Ab.* 4:2; *Qid.* 1:10; *Pesiq. Rab Kah.* 15:5; Urbach, *Sages*, 1:366; Smith, *Parallels*, 64.

247. E.g., *Abot R. Nat.* 16 A; *b. Qid.* 30b, bar.; *B. Bat.* 16a; *Tg. Qoh.* on 10:4; Moore, *Judaism*, 481, 489–90; Davies, *Paul*, 225n2. Rabbis also considered repentance a cure for the evil impulse (Davies, *Paul*, 23); one could sacrifice the impulse by confessing sin (*b. Sanh.* 43b; *Lev. Rab.* 9:1).

248. *Sipre Deut.* 43.4.1; *b. Tem.* 16a; *Pesiq. Rab Kah.* 4:6; *Num. Rab.* 19:5.

When might someone Jewish first become conscious of violating the Torah? In the line of Jewish tradition followed by later rabbis, a person was born with an evil impulse;[249] a young man became an adult at puberty[250] and thus became responsible for keeping the Torah around age thirteen.[251] That was also when some later rabbis felt that the good impulse entered a boy, in keeping with his responsibility for the Torah.[252] Some thus suggest that Paul refers here to something analogous to the bar mitzvah, which would have occurred at about this age.[253] Against this suggestion, the ceremony as we know it began in the fourteenth century.[254] Nevertheless, coming of age certainly represented a significant transition in ancient Jewish as in some surrounding cultures.[255] Puberty rites are common in many traditional cultures;[256] Romans had a coming-of-age ritual in the mid-teens.[257] In the rabbis, full responsibility for the Torah accompanied coming of age.

Yet the consciousness of sin, of which Paul speaks here, surely could begin earlier than one's social coming of age;[258] certainly, instruction in the Torah

249. *Abot R. Nat.* 16 A; 30, §63 B; *Pesiq. Rab Kah.* Sup. 3:2. Certainly from one's youth (*Exod. Rab.* 46:4), though not from one's conception (*b. Sanh.* 91b; *Gen. Rab.* 34:10).

250. E.g., *y. Ter.* 1:3, §1; cf. discussion in *Gen. Rab.* 91:3. Cf. perhaps twelve in 1 Esd. 5:41. Wishing to emphasize that he was a prodigy, Josephus speaks of exploits when he was fourteen and "like a mere boy" (*Life* 9). Stoics believed that people acquired reason not inherently but near age fourteen (Iambl. *Soul* 2.15, §609).

251. *M. Ab.* 5:21 (a late second-century rabbi); *Gen. Rab.* 63:10. Cf. Nock, *Paul*, 68n1. Other roles also had age requirements (e.g., CD 10.1).

252. *Abot R. Nat.* 16 A; *Pesiq. Rab Kah.* Sup. 3:2; cf. also Davies, *Paul*, 25. Minors were exempted from some commandments (e.g., *m. Suk.* 2:8; *Hag.* 1:1; *b. Ketub.* 50a; *y. Hag.* 1:1, §4; *Suk.* 2:9).

253. Davies, *Paul*, 25; Nickle, "Romans 7:7–25," 184; Martin, *Reconciliation*, 57; Lohse, *Environment*, 184; Gundry, "Frustration," 232–33 (though recognizing, more explicitly than many others, the medieval origin of the current ceremony); Jewett, *Romans*, 451. The phrase "son of the law" appears earlier for all Jacob's descendants (2 *Bar.* 46:4).

254. Sandmel, *Judaism*, 199; Safrai, "Home," 771; Schreiner, *Romans*, 369; Das, *Debate*, 215. Cf. the historic development of Western Christian confirmation, eventually at a similar age.

255. With Safrai, "Home," 2:772; cf. ancient coming-of-age rituals in Wiesehöfer, "Youth," 854. Traditional Greek culture also recognized legal distinctions (e.g., Aeschines *Tim.* 18, 39). Xen. *Cyr.* 1.2.8 claims that Persian boys traditionally became men around sixteen or seventeen years old.

256. E.g., Eliade, *Rites*, 41; Mbiti, *Religions*, 158–73 (esp. 159–60, 171); Dawson, "Urbanization," 309; Kapolyo, *Condition*, 43–44.

257. Suet. *Aug.* 8.1; 38.2; *Calig.* 10.1; *Vergil* 6; Pliny *Ep.* 1.9.2; 8.23.2; 10.116.1; Gardner, *Women*, 14; Dupont, *Life*, 229; Croom, *Clothing*, 122. For legal maturity near puberty, see, e.g., Gaius *Inst.* 1.196; 2.113; 3.208; Schiemann, "Minores." For age classifications, see, e.g., Suder, "Classification"; Binder, "Age(s)"; Overstreet, "Concept"; Keener, *Acts*, 2:1447–48; for the age of puberty, see Wiesehöfer, "Pubertas," 177.

258. Philo (*Rewards* 25) expects the deception of idolatry to infect children from infancy. Deissmann (*Paul*, 92–93), thinking of 1 Cor. 13:11, cites a Jewish tradition regarding a boy's ninth year, although conceding that the source is quite late. For knowledge of right and wrong

did.[259] Paul does not specify the time when the liability function of the law (Rom. 2:12; 4:15; 5:13; 7:9, 23–24; 8:2; 1 Cor. 15:56; 2 Cor. 3:6–7) becomes active; presumably, he would regard it as whenever the person becomes conscious of the demands of the law.[260]

Internal Conflict

Paul here depicts life under the law. A modern psychologist might reasonably diagnose the figure here as struggling with something like an anxiety disorder linked with an obsessive-compulsive disorder and rooted in a religious fixation.[261] Whether or not this is the case, however, Paul's hyperbole draws on the language of struggle current in his day.

Ancient Beliefs about Internal Struggle

Ancient autobiography avoided the sort of introspection that appears in Romans 7:7–25.[262] This observation does not mean, however, that introspection did not occur.[263] Stoics did "look inwards and interrogate themselves."[264] Nor was it likely unfamiliar in Jewish piety.[265]

---

at age twenty, see 1QSa 1.10–11. Before the Torah, one rabbi concluded, accountability began at age one hundred (*Gen. Rab.* 26:2).

259. Jos. *Ant.* 4.211; *Ag. Ap.* 1.60; 2.204 (cf. also 4.209, 309); *m. Ab.* 5:21; Dunn, *Romans*, 1:382. Jewett (*Romans*, 450–51) retorts that a boy was not required to obey the law until initiation; rabbinic sources speak of adult accountability, however, not of earlier knowledge of sin.

260. For this reason, some identify the figure here as a Gentile converting to Judaism (e.g., Tobin, *Rhetoric*, 42) or as humanity's coming of age (e.g., Dunn, *Romans*, 1:382; cf. Gal. 3:23–25; 4:3–4). Cf. Origen in Burns, *Romans*, 68–69; but his use by Augustine brought "age of accountability" into "the exegetical tradition" (Reasoner, *Full Circle*, 71, citing Aug. *Guilt* 1.65–66).

261. For Juan-Luis Segundo's thoughts (1926–96) on anxiety in Rom. 7, see Philipp, "Angst." Beck (*Psychology of Paul*, 122) notes (with van den Beld, "*Akrasia*") some resemblance to splitting but warns that this pathology does not fit Paul's own personality.

262. Judge, *Jerusalem*, 60, contending that Augustine's approach to Rom. 7 led to modern literary and film interest in motivation, moral dilemmas, and the like.

263. See Stramara, "Introspection."

264. Sorabji, *Emotion*, 13, noting that they even had "a special word, *prosokhē*, for the introspective supervision of one's own thoughts and actions" (citing Stob. *Anth.* 2.73.1 Wachsmuth; Epict. *Encheir.* 33.6; *Diatr.* 4.12; frg. 27; Plut. *Progr. Virt.* 12, *Mor.* 83B; *Garr.* 23, *Mor.* 514E).

265. One pre-Christian work might offer this idea: "The righteous person is always inspecting his or her house, to remove unrighteousness done by violations," or, as *OTP* 2:654 translates, "his unintentional sins" (*Pss. Sol.* 3:7–8, here 3:7). Though the Syriac differs (Trafton, *Version*, 50, 55), "the righteous person" is clearly the subject in the Greek sentence; "unintentional" corresponds with "ignorance" (ἄγνοια) in 3:8. Many associate *Psalms of Solomon* with Pharisaic piety (Rost, *Judaism*, 119), or at least with the mainstream Jewish piety to which Pharisaism belonged (Sanders [*Judaism*, 453–55] suggests *non*-Pharisaic piety). Cf. also Yohanan ben Zakkai's premortem questioning of his direction in *Abot R. Nat.* 25 A; *b. Ber.* 28b; *Gen. Rab.* 100:2.

Ancient hearers would not have found the sort of struggle depicted in Romans 7:15–25 strange. In ancient sources the conflict between reason and passions, or between a good and evil impulse, could be intense. Thus, one man decided that his conflicting desires corresponded to two souls, one of which sometimes overcame the other.[266] Another was smitten by a woman's extraordinary beauty; because he was of noble character, he struggled hard, by using his reason, to fight severe passion.[267]

Already committed to overcoming the passions by reason, many philosophers recognized the reality of internal conflicts. Platonists in particular saw the conflicted person as divided, with parts inside warring.[268] Even the good soul experiences a struggle against evil, trying to attain good, because it cannot avoid all association with the world.[269] Some philosophers urged people to internal unity, against being of two minds, having varying opinions, and being at war with oneself.[270] If a Platonist heard Romans 7:7–25, it would sound like the "worst-case scenario where the appetites succeed in storming 'the citadel of the soul' . . . to replace its rightful ruler, reason."[271]

Early Stoics, by contrast, viewed the self, the ruling part of the soul, as unitary.[272] For early Stoics, false beliefs warred against innate virtue.[273] The ideal

266. Araspas in Xen. *Cyr.* 6.1.41, explaining his former slavery to passion for the captive and his new resolve to please Cyrus.

267. Char. *Chaer.* 2.4.4 (ἀγῶνα λογισμοῦ καὶ πάθους).

268. Meeks, *Moral World*, 44 (citing Plut. *Flatt.* 20, *Mor.* 61DF); Stowers, "Self-Mastery," 529, 538; Sorabji, *Emotion*, 303–5 (esp. on Plato's divided soul; more generally, 303–15). Cf. Philo *Alleg. Interp.* 2.91; Stoike, "Genio," 278 (on Plut. *Mor.* 592B); Iambl. *Soul* 2.11, §369; for Plato's tripartite soul, see, e.g., Plato *Rep.* 6.504; 9.580D; *Tim.* 89E; Diog. Laert. 3.67, 90; Lucian *Dance* 70; Iambl. *Soul* 2.11, §369 (cf. discussion in Merlan, *Platonism*, 25–27); for that of Pythagoras, see Diog. Laert. 8.1.30; for Middle Platonists (also drawing on Aristotelians and Posidonius), see Vander Waerdt, "Soul-Division." For intellect, soul, and body, see, e.g., Porph. *Marc.* 13.234–35.

269. Max. Tyre *Or.* 34.2. Cf. Virtue and Vice warring over elements within the soul in Max. Tyre *Or.* 38.6.

270. Iambl. *Letter* 9.4–5, 7, 10 (Stob. *Anth.* 2.33.15).

271. Wasserman, "Paul among Philosophers," 82, citing Philo *Alleg. Interp.* 2.91–92; Plato *Tim.* 70a; *Rep.* 560b. Cf. Wasserman, "Death."

272. Sorabji, *Emotion*, 303, 313–15; Brennan, "Theory," 23. It had merely different capacities rather than parts (Sorabji, *Emotion*, 314). Stoics accepted eight parts in the soul, of which the unified ruling part was only one (315; see Diog. Laert. 7.1.110, 157; Iambl. *Soul* 2.12, §369); the soul was part of the self (Sen. Y. *Ep. Lucil.* 113.5). Aristotle's followers denied that the soul had components (Iambl. *Soul* 2.11, §368); Epicureans saw the soul as united but distinguished rational and irrational functions (Long, *Philosophy*, 52).

273. Chrysippus in Stowers, "Self-Mastery," 529; cf. Hierocles *Love* 4.27.20 (in Malherbe, *Moral Exhortation*, 95); for prior goodness needed to attain virtue in Stoicism, see Stowers, "Resemble," 91; for the potential for virtue but the need to acquire it, see Frede, "Conception," 71. Paul rejected innate virtue, at least in a salvific way (Rom. 3:23; 5:12–21; he might accept intrinsic worth as God's image or objects of God's love). Whereas Chrysippus viewed emotions

virtuous person would always desire only what was right and thus not struggle,[274] but few claimed to achieve perfect virtue.[275] People "do not know what they wish, except at the actual moment of wishing," Seneca opined; no one "ever decided once and for all to desire or to refuse." One must press on "to perfection, or to a point which you alone understand is still short of perfection."[276]

Yet Stoics and others might view any struggle as especially intense for those who have not resolved their allegiance or found ways to subdue their passions.[277] Seneca warns that those who are unwilling to acknowledge the cause of the problem, and simply try to restrain their desires inside them, end up depressed, with "the thousand waverings of an unsettled mind."[278] For the Jewish eclectic Middle Platonist Philo, the passions and desires to do wrong stir within the soul the most violent of wars. When temperance controls the passions, however, it ends the war, establishes peace, and brings proper respect for law.[279]

Envisioning Someone Overwhelmed by Passion

One dramatic depiction of internal anguish attracted frequent attention in antiquity: Euripides's fifth-century BCE portrayal of Medea, when she

---

as the results of reason, Galen suggests that Posidonius accepted more of the Platonic allowance for emotion alongside reason (so Cooper, "Posidonius," 71; Gill ["Galen"] doubts that Galen completely understood Chrysippus).

274. Engberg-Pedersen, *Paul and Stoics*, 52; Engberg-Pedersen, "Vices," 613; cf. Mus. Ruf. 2, p. 36.16–19. Engberg-Pedersen ("Vices," 612) notes that Aristotle allowed for a self-controlled person who experienced some internal conflict but always achieved good, in contrast to the person so conflicted that sometimes they followed irrational desires; cf. van den Beld, "*Akrasia*."

275. See, e.g., Haacker, *Theology*, 128–29, on Seneca. Most people believed that Stoics were wrong to ignore degrees of vice and virtue (Cic. *Fin.* 4.24.66–68; Plut. *Progress in Virtue*), which was the idea that all true wrong was equally wrong (Pliny *Ep.* 8.2.3); Stoics regarded virtues as inseparable (Arius Did. 2.7.5b5, p. 18.15–20). Stoics believed that all offenses were equal but not the same (Cic. *Parad.* 20; Arius Did. 2.7.11k, p. 84.15–17; 2.7.11L, p. 85.34–37; p. 87.1–7, 13–20; 2.7.11o, p. 96.22–29; 2.7.11p, p. 96.30–34; Diog. Laert. 7.1.120; cf. Epict. *Diatr.* 2.21.1–7; contrast Marc. Aur. 2.10); others complained about this view (Cic. *Fin.* 4.27.74–75), especially Epicureans (Diog. Laert. 10.120). Jewish teachers often valued even the least of the commandments like the greatest (e.g., *m. Ab.* 2:1; 4:2; *Qid.* 1:10; *Sipre Deut.* 76.1.1); some Diaspora Jews even echoed the Stoic teaching that all commandments were equal (4 Macc. 5:19–21).

276. Sen. Y. *Ep. Lucil.* 20.6 (trans. Gummere, LCL, 1:135, 137). Cf. *Ep. Lucil.* 52.1–9: "What is this force that . . . does not allow us to desire anything once for all? . . . None of our wishes is free, none is unqualified, none is lasting" (in Malherbe, *Moral Exhortation*, 62).

277. Meeks (*Moral World*, 47) suggests that Stoics and Platonists agreed that one must distinguish real happiness from transient pleasures, and that one learns this by "repeated, deliberate choice, a lifelong struggle for rational mastery."

278. Sen. Y. *Dial.* 9.2.10 (trans. Basore, LCL, 2:219).

279. Philo *Creation* 81. For Philo, the soul has three parts, each divided into two (*Heir* 225; *Alleg. Interp.* 1.70, 72; 3.115; *Conf.* 21); this presumably follows Plato's tripartite soul (Diog. Laert. 3.67, 90). But Philo is not consistent in this regard and elsewhere thinks of two parts (*Studies* 26; Dillon, *Middle Platonists*, 174).

decided to take vengeance on her unfaithful husband Jason by killing her own children.[280] With her mind she understood that the action was wrong, but rage nevertheless controlled her.[281] Although Euripides's account provided the best-known version, Paul's language is even closer to some other retellings of Medea's behavior, especially that of Ovid.[282]

Early philosophers such as Plato and the Stoic Chrysippus deployed this prominent example in discussions about reason and the passions.[283] Many rejected Medea's reported belief. Plato's Socrates questioned Medea's claim, observing that one who genuinely knows what is right will do what is right.[284] Stoics likewise regarded wrongdoing as based on wrong belief and ignorance, rejecting the common Platonic idea that irrational elements vie with reason in the soul.[285] A generation after Paul, one Stoic philosopher, though aware that others use the example of Medea to argue that passions can overwhelm reason, maintains that her conflict arises from mistaken judgment.[286] Also observing that Medea "did not know where the power lies to do what we wish," he advised, in good Stoic fashion, that this power comes only by giving up wanting anything but what God wants.[287]

280. The story was widely known and retold, e.g., Cic. *Tusc.* 4.32.69; Hor. *Epode* 3.9–14; Virg. *Ecl.* 8.47–50; Ovid *Metam.* 7.391–97; Pliny E. *N.H.* 24.99.157; Plut. *Poetry* 3, *Mor.* 18A; Lucian *Hall* 31; Char. *Chaer.* 2.9.3; Paus. 2.3.6–7; Philost. *Ep.* 21 (38); Libanius *Invect.* 7.32; *Speech Char.* 1, 17; *Descr.* 20.1–2; *Gr. Anth.* 7.354; second- and third-century CE sarcophagi in Gessert, "Myth." Cf. further Dräger, "Medea." Cf. an apparently different version in Philost. *Hrk.* 53.4; possibly Apollod. *Bibl.* 1.9.28.

281. Eurip. *Med.* 1077–80 (cf. 1040–48, 1056–58). This is cited by Renehan, "Quotations," 24 (following the 1963 Sather Lectures of Bruno Snell); Stowers, *Rereading*, 260–61; Stowers, "Self-Mastery," 525; Talbert, *Romans*, 193; Tobin, *Rhetoric*, 232; Bendemann, "Diastase"; Bryan, *Preface*, 143; Longenecker, *Introducing Romans*, 370. That Euripides invented this tradition is evident in Arist. *Poet.* 14.12, 1453b. Renehan ("Quotations," 25) cites also Eurip. *Hipp.* 380–83; frg. 220 Nauck; frg. 841 Nauck; Plato *Prot.* 352d; Xen. *Mem.* 3.9.4. Euripides spoke elsewhere of inability to do what is best (Eurip. *Oenom.* frg. 572, from Stob. *Anth.* 4.35.8).

282. Ovid *Metam.* 7.17–21 (esp. 19, 21). See for this point Renehan, "Quotations," 25 (noting that Snell missed this example, and comparing also Hor. *Ep.* 1.8.11; Menander frg. 489 Koerte); Käsemann, *Romans*, 200, recognizing that this passage is often cited; Moo, *Romans*, 457; Byrne, *Romans*, 228; Tobin, *Rhetoric*, 234; Bendemann, "Diastase"; Bryan, *Preface*, 143.

283. Stowers, "Self-Mastery," 525–26; Stowers, *Rereading*, 262; Bendemann, "Diastase"; see Gill, "Galen," 121, 137; Gill, "Did Chrysippus Understand?"

284. Stowers, *Rereading*, 261, citing Plato *Prot.* 352D, and contrasting Arist. *N.E.* 7.

285. See Stowers, *Rereading*, 262–63; Tobin, *Rhetoric*, 234.

286. Epict. *Diatr.* 1.28.6–9, cited in Stowers, *Rereading*, 262; Bryan, *Preface*, 144; Tobin, *Rhetoric*, 234.

287. Epict. *Diatr.* 2.17.21–22 (ποῦ κεῖται τὸ ποιεῖν ἃ θέλομεν; trans. Oldfather, LCL, 1:342–43; cf. also Tobin, *Rhetoric*, 233). Others cite also allusions to Medea in Epict. *Diatr.* 2.26.1–2 (Stowers, *Rereading*, 262; Moo, *Romans*, 457; Byrne, *Romans*, 231; Talbert, *Romans*, 193; Tobin, *Rhetoric*, 234; Jewett, *Romans*, 463–64); Plut. *Virt.* 441–52 (Bryan, *Preface*, 144). Her cutting her children's throats also appears in Epict. *Diatr.* 4.13.14–15.

One need not suppose that Paul read Euripides to recognize that the tradition of thought that he addresses was first popularized by that source.[288] Likewise, one need not assume that Paul is here assuming the persona of Medea[289] to recognize that he is playing on a familiar theme of his milieu. If Paul *is* adopting the persona of Medea, as a male actor in a theater could do, ancient auditors might also view the moral failure in this passage in a feminine way. Some writers in antiquity associated passions with what was feminine, but Paul's undisputed letters do not do so.[290] Full adoption of the persona is unlikely, though, and mere analogies are never precise.

We have reason to doubt that ancient hearers, even highly educated ones, would necessarily think of Medea when they heard Romans 7:15–25, although some undoubtedly did so. Euripides himself, for example, offers a similar depiction of a man about to rape a boy.[291] Stoics could also allude to Euripides's language of overpowering passion with general applicability, without specifically calling attention to Medea herself.[292] Certainly, not all actual ancient auditors heard Paul as referring to Medea. When Cyril of Alexandria warns about a wrong comparison between Romans 7 and Greek mythology, he alludes not

288. Renehan, "Quotations," 26; Tobin, *Rhetoric*, 233, 242.

289. Stowers (*Rereading*, 271–72) appears to treat Medea as the persona Paul adopts; but as Stowers himself has noted, philosophers applied the example of Medea's struggle more widely; she can be an analogy without constituting the persona here. Partly because Galen says that Euripides used Medea to portray "barbarians and uneducated people," whereas Greeks use reason over anger (Galen *Hippoc. and Plat.* 3.189.20–190.1; Stowers, *Rereading*, 276), Stowers argues that the "I" figure here must be a Gentile (277). One could as readily assume that Paul adopts a feminine persona here; see comment below. Jewett (*Romans*, 462–64) questions the allusion to Medea in Paul.

290. Cf. in Lucret. *Nat.* 3.136ff. the rational *animus* versus irrational *anima* (in Long, *Philosophy*, 52); the emphasis on passion's feminine character in Philo *Alleg. Interp.* 3.11; *Sacr.* 103; *Worse* 28, 172; *Giants* 4; *Cher.* 8; or "even" a woman overcoming emotion in 4 Macc. 16:1–2; ancient male views on women's character are discussed in Keener, *Acts*, 1:610–19. Most important, similarities with the portrait of Phaedra (cf. Phaedra in Eurip. *Hipp.* 377–83, cited in Stowers, *Rereading*, 261; and in Sen. Y. *Hippol.* 177, cited in Talbert, *Romans*, 193) and some other examples suggest that some connected such irrational passion more with what was feminine. See esp. Gemünden, "Femme," who argues that, unlike some others in antiquity, Paul does *not* relate reason and passions in gender-specific ways.

291. Eurip. *Chrys.* frg. 841. For reprehensible men doing the opposite of what they should, see, e.g., Pliny *Ep.* 4.2.8. Bad persons cannot live as they wish (Epict. *Diatr.* 4.1.2–5); apparently similar language in Sen. Y. *Ep. Lucil.* 67.2, however, simply refers to partial incapacitation due to old age. Jewett (*Romans*, 463) suggests Paul's subversion of the law by his pre-Christian persecution of Christians, as viewed in retrospect; but Rom. 7:7–25 sounds more *conscious* of the internal struggle than Paul would have recognized before his conversion.

292. See Arius Did. 2.7.10a, p. 56.24–33, esp. 32–33. Similarly, Stoics did not always describe even Medea's struggle in language clearly resembling Rom. 7. Although Paul's Stoic contemporary Seneca depicts Medea's vacillation in Sen. Y. *Med.* 926–30, 988–90, his language is not as close to Paul's as is that of some of the other passages.

directly to Medea but to Fate controlling all human actions.[293] The issue for Paul's immediate audience, then, was not Medea herself but the sort of struggle that various writers used her case, and sometimes other cases, to exemplify.

Bondage of the Will? Wanting to Do Right

Romans 7:15–21 contains many verbs of willing (7:15, 16, 18, 19, 20, 21)[294]—the figure is able to want what is right, but the greater power of sin prevents its execution.[295] What is the point of narrating the figure's unsuccessful willing to do right here? Although Paul's interest is not in constructing a consistent anthropology, understanding some of his culture's options regarding will may prove helpful in establishing a range of thought within which he moves here.[296]

Aristotle addressed ἀκρασία, the weakness of the will.[297] In his thought the fully virtuous person *wants* to do right,[298] but others are divided—both one who does right only by self-control and one who fails because of ἀκρασία.[299] Most thinkers valued deciding for what was right rather than desiring what was wrong. For example, Hellenistic intellectuals recognized the value of willing in the sense of deliberation or discussing before acting, something more rational than mere desire.[300] Stoics considered what was worth wanting.[301] In a sense, one could say that Stoics distinguished the irrational will—"desiring" what one wanted that one should not want—from the rational will, the ruling cognition.[302] Writing later, Augustine believed that Stoics countered desire, the experience of the foolish, with will, the experience of the wise.[303]

---

293. Cyril Alex. *Rom.* on 7:15 (PG 74:808–12; Burns, *Romans*, 175). Cosmic fatalism became an increasing problem in late antiquity.

294. Noted by Hübner ("Hermeneutics," 212–13), though he construes Rom. 7:15 as reflecting "our *basic inability* to understand what we do, *to understand ourselves*" (emphasis his, p. 212).

295. Cf. Keck, *Romans*, 193, noting that the problem is not inability to choose right (Deut. 30:19) but inability to carry out "the right choice."

296. Cf. Löhr ("Paulus"), who addresses briefly human will in ancient sources and then "willing" and "will" in Paul's letters.

297. Engberg-Pedersen, *Paul and Stoics*, 52, citing Arist. N.E. 7.1–10.

298. Engberg-Pedersen, *Paul and Stoics*, 52, citing Arist. N.E. 1.13.17, 1102b26–28.

299. Engberg-Pedersen, *Paul and Stoics*, 52, citing Arist. N.E. 7.8.4, 1151a11–20, in context.

300. *Rhet. Alex.* pref. 1420b.20–21 (βουλεύεσθαι); 1421a.10–11.

301. Arius Did. 2.7.11f, p. 70.3 (distinguishing "what is worth wanting" [βουλητόν] from "what must be wanted"). Epict. *Diatr.* 4.1.2–5 (trans. Oldfather, LCL, 2:244–47) opines that no one wants to live in error; a bad person is thus one who does not live as they wish (θέλει). Yet imperfect people often "do not know what they wish" except when wishing it (Sen. Y. *Ep. Lucil.* 20.6; trans. Gummere, LCL, 1:135).

302. Matheson, *Epictetus*, 31. Platonists and Aristotle also distinguished rational interest in what was good from desire for pleasure (Sorabji, *Emotion*, 319–20), though Aristotle also distinguished rational desire from reason, unlike Platonists (322–23) and Stoics (328–30).

303. Aug. *City* 14.8.

Some others agreed on the importance of wanting what is right; the eclectic Middle Platonic thinker Plutarch suggests that only those who follow reason are truly "free": "For they alone, having learned to wish [βούλεσθαι] for what they ought, live as they wish [βούλονται]; but in untrained and irrational impulses and actions there is something ignoble, and changing one's mind many times involves but little freedom of will."[304] While other components of the later concept of "will" appear in various sources, however (such as reason, free choice,[305] and perversion of the will), it may have been Augustine in particular who brought them together in their later form, making the will central.[306] The Augustinian synthesis of late antiquity should not be read back into Paul.

Many observe that Paul was not writing as a Stoic here. The speaker has reason and cognitive knowledge, yet his passions prevail. Nor was Paul like Philo or the author of 4 Maccabees; the speaker knows the law, yet neither philosophy nor the law delivers this person from conflict and defeat.[307] Commentators who note that Paul, unlike philosophers, did not regard knowledge as enough to liberate a person are technically correct; in Romans, such liberation requires divine action. Nevertheless, there may be a sense in which Paul agreed with philosophers here. The world and especially the biblically informed know enough to be condemned, but saving truth is revealed in the gospel (Rom. 1:17–18). It is not mere information the speaker needs, but this speaker does need a different form of what some might call knowledge: divine truth understood by faith (Rom. 6:11).[308]

Paul's point of emphasizing "willing" here is to underline the failure of not only knowing the law but even of *desiring to obey* the law as sufficient to achieve righteousness. Whereas the Gentiles in Romans 1:18–32 sinned

304. Plut. *Lect.* 1, *Mor.* 37E (trans. Babbitt, LCL, 1:204–7). For condemnations of fickleness in antiquity, see, e.g., Cic. *Fam.* 5.2.10; Vell. Paterc. 2.80.1; Plut. *Cic.* 26.7; Pliny *Ep.* 2.11.22; Fronto *Ad amicos* 1.19; Apul. *Apol.* 77; further, Keener, *Acts*, 1:1037n469; by Stoics, Arius Did. 2.7.11i, p. 78.15–18; 2.7.11m, p. 96.5–14. Aristocrats attributed this disposition especially to the masses (e.g., Lucan *C.W.* 3.52–56; Quint. *Decl.* 352.1; Quint. Curt. 4.10.7; Dio Chrys. *Or.* 66) and sometimes to other peoples (Cic. *Flacc.* 11.24; Caesar *Gall. W.* 4.5; Jos. *Ant.* 18.47) or to women (Virg. *Aen.* 4.569–70).

305. I have surveyed the discussion regarding determinism and free will in late antiquity, including in patristic sources, briefly in Keener, *Acts*, 1:927–36. The issue was probably less dominant in Paul's own era.

306. Sorabji, *Emotion*, 11–12, 335–37. Augustine rejected the Manichaean theory of two souls, but his own "experience of struggling against lust convinces him that we have a spiritual and a carnal will" (Sorabji, *Emotion*, 315–16). Sorabji (*Emotion*, 339) questions whether Augustine's particular configuration of the concept, a configuration that became dominant, is helpful.

307. E.g., Tobin, *Rhetoric*, 235; Jewett, *Romans*, 464.

308. Creation provides Gentiles with some potential knowledge that they are doing wrong (Rom. 1:19–20 [shrouded in 1:28]; 2:14); Jews have greater moral knowledge through the law (here). In Paul's view, only those in Christ have the fuller transforming knowledge of the gospel.

without full knowledge of God's law,[309] the Jewish person of 7:7–25 sins *with* full knowledge of it, and even with desire to obey that knowledge. General revelation in creation (1:19–20) offers some moral truth about honoring God (1:21–23) and others made in his image (1:24–32); special revelation in the Torah reveals more truth even more finely.

By themselves, however, both revelations merely teach moral truth rather than giving life (cf. Gal. 2:21; 3:21); for that, a yet fuller knowledge is needed: knowledge of the good news (Rom. 1:16–17; cf. 10:14–17). That good news was announced in advance through the prophets who foretold the promised era of restoration (Rom. 1:1–2; cf. Isa. 52:7), a restoration now inaugurated in Jesus Christ (Rom. 1:1–4).

Paul may allow that people can perform positive actions in obedience to rational guidelines such as the law, but he regards genuine transformation by the gift of righteousness as inseparable from the new creation in Christ (cf. Rom. 5:12–6:11).[310]

Law in One's Body versus Law in One's Mind (Rom. 7:22–25)

Paul depicts here a divided person. Biblical law informs this figure's mind or inner person, revealing God's righteous standard, but the law operating in the person's (physical) members pulls the person in a different direction, preventing the mind from exercising complete control.

Law in the Mind

The figure here rightly delights in the Torah (Rom. 7:22), as Jewish sources suggest that Jewish people normally did.[311] But one can appreciate moral truth (7:16) and even feel good about mastering intellectual knowledge and yet find oneself unable to suppress contrary desires or inclinations.[312] Whatever others

309. The natural law in the heart (Rom. 2:14–15) is less complete than the Torah.

310. See Odeberg, *Pharisaism*, 60–61, on Rom. 2:17–24; Barclay, *Gift*, 497. Lafon ("Moi," on 7:15–21) connects recognition of one's will with inability to achieve righteousness.

311. Cf. Rom. 10:2; Neh. 8:9–12; Ps. 19:8; Jos. *Ag. Ap.* 2.189; *Pesiq. Rab Kah.* 27:2; *b. Yoma* 4b; *Lev. Rab.* 16:4 (purportedly from Ben Azzai); *Song Rab.* 4:11, §1; *Pesiq. Rab.* 21:2/3; 51:4; Urbach, *Sages*, 1:390–92; Bonsirven, *Judaism*, 95; see especially the Tannaitic sources in Urbach, *Sages*, 1:390; most fully, Anderson, "Joy."

312. Philosophers claimed that one needed self-discipline, not mere knowledge that one should control pleasures (Mus. Ruf. 6, p. 52.15–17); hearing without obeying was unprofitable (17, p. 108.38–39). Later rabbis debated whether learning or implementing Torah took precedence; both were needed (cf. *m. Ab.* 5:14), but many preferred learning because it was the prerequisite for action (*Sipra Behuq. par.* 2.264.1.4; *Sipre Deut.* 41.2.5–6; *b. Qid.* 40b; *y. Hag.* 1:7, §4); rabbis too, however, recognized that one could learn without doing (*Sipre Deut.* 32.5.12;

see outwardly, the desires remain, although the speaker seems ambivalent about owning them as part of the "I," the rational, controlling identity (yes in 7:14–16, 19, 21; no in 7:17, 20, 23–25; perhaps both in 7:18).[313]

Paul contrasts the "inner person" (Rom. 7:22) with the "members" (7:23). From 7:23 it seems clear that Paul equates the law in the inner person (7:22) with "the law of my mind." The inner person here does not specify the new person in Christ (cf. 6:6; Eph. 2:15; 4:22, 24; Col. 3:9),[314] as it might if Paul were depicting Christian existence, but something more like the soul or (in this context) the mind, as opposed to the body (see 2 Cor. 4:16; Eph. 3:16).[315] Plato's language of the "inner person" remained current in Paul's day, although Paul adapted the image for his distinctive purposes.[316] The law in the mind informs him of what is good.

The Law, the Body, and Sin

The law[317] has a different effect on this figure's members[318] than on his mind; he wants to do right but cannot do so,[319] because his body moves him

---

b. Sanh. 106b), and this was inadequate (early sages in m. Ab. 1:17; 3:9, 17; cf. Let. Aris. 127; Abot R. Nat. 24 A).

313. Perhaps the figure increasingly realizes that this is not the identity in God's image the figure was created to be. Stowers ("Self-Mastery," 537–38) compares the divided self in Platonism.

314. The term ἄνθρωπος by itself need not point back to Rom. 6:6 (although the outer person of 2 Cor. 4:16 awaits resurrection; cf. 5:1–5); the term appears some 126 times in Pauline literature.

315. So also ancient interpreters, e.g. (in Bray, Romans, 195–96, 198), the rational soul in Ambrosiaster Comm. on Rom. 7:23 (CSEL 81:243); Pelagius Comm. Rom. on 7:22 (PCR 104–5); Severian of Gabala, catena on Rom. 7:24 (PGK 15:220); the mind in Theodoret Interp. Rom. on 7:22 (PG 82:125).

316. Plato Rep. 9.588A–591B (esp. 588A–589B); Stowers, "Self-Mastery," 526–27; Markschies, "Metaphor"; Betz, "Concept"; Judge, Jerusalem, 60. Aune ("Duality," 220–22) finds analogous phrases rare until the church fathers and Neoplatonists but does identify the expression in Philo, who preceded Paul. Philosophers often warned against concern for "externals" (e.g., Epict. Diatr. 1.4.27; 1.11.37; 2.2.10, 12; 2.16.11; 4.10; Marc. Aur. 7.14). By contrast, Paul probably employs the language in an ad hoc manner (Tronier, "Correspondence," 195).

317. Although some prefer to translate "principle" here (Bergmeier, "Mensch"; Kruse, Romans, 309–10), sometimes comparing the good and evil impulses (Bruce, Apostle, 197) or the Greek idea of an immanent law in nature (Dodd, Bible and Greeks, 37), the context focuses on the law, so there must be at least a play on that sense here (with, e.g., Wright, Faithfulness, 1:506, 510). Paul does, however, play on both universal law and Torah (Rom. 2:14; cf. perhaps Ps. 19:4 in Rom. 10:18).

318. The ideal auditor understands from the term's usual sense that these are members of his body, here and in Rom. 6:13, 19; 7:5 (explicit for Christ's body in 12:4–5; 1 Cor. 12:12, 14, 18–22, 25, 27). Paul might have envisioned different kinds of sins for different members (so Theodore of Mopsuestia, catena on Rom. 7:23 [PGK 15:132]); cf. Rom. 3:13–18.

319. For the compatibility, on different levels, of Paul's portrayal of humans as able to do some good and yet (as here, e.g., Rom. 7:18) not ultimately able to do good, see discussion in Westerholm, Justification, 38–49.

in a different way (Rom. 7:22–23).[320] Thus the law-knower here cries out for deliverance from the body of death (7:24)—presumably meaning the body under sin's sentence of death (5:12–21; 6:16, 21, 23; 7:5, 9–10, 13; cf. 1:32).[321] Because his flesh is vulnerable to sin (cf. 8:3), the law functions for him as a law condemning his sin and consequently as a sentence of death, from which he must be freed (8:2). His mind serves God's law, but his "flesh" serves the law that highlights sin (7:25). His perspective thus is captivated by the flesh rather than by God's Spirit (8:5–8).

Why does Paul contrast the mind here with members, the body, and the flesh? Some ancient interpreters heard in Romans 7 a struggle between the body and the soul.[322] This approach is certainly an oversimplification (not least because Paul never uses the term translated "soul" in this manner); nevertheless, ancient interpreters' recognition that Paul connected the mortal body with vulnerability to vice[323] picks up on an idea in Paul that modern interpreters sometimes seem eager to avoid. Even if Paul is simply playing on an idea in his culture, in this context Paul clearly does in some sense connect sin with the behavior, desires, and mortality of the body:

- the "body of sin" (6:6)
- the "desires" of the "mortal [death-destined] body" (6:12)
- "sinful passions" working in bodily members (7:5)
- sin related to the "flesh" (7:18, 25)
- "the body of this death" (7:24)
- the present body "dead because of sin" (8:10)
- resurrection hope for "mortal bodies" (8:11)
- death for those who live according to the "flesh" (8:13a; cf. 8:6)
- hope of life if one puts to death the body's works (8:13b)

320. Gentile thinkers could also speak of divine law as being inaccessible to those ruled by passion; this was true for the later writer Porphyry (*Marc.* 26.402–4), for whom passions were inextricably linked to the body.

321. With, e.g. (in Bray, *Romans*, 198), Jerome *Ruf.* 1.25; Theodoret *Interp. Rom.* on 7:24 (PG 82:128). Cf. similar phrases for mortal bodies in Epict. *Diatr.* 2.19.27; Marc. Aur. 10.33.3; the body as a corpse in Epict. *Diatr.* 1.9.19; 1.9.33–34; Marc. Aur. 4.4. Bousset, *Kyrios Christos*, 179, associates this with the body of the entirety of the old humanity; association with Adam, based on *4 Ezra* 3:4–5 (Grappe, "Corps de mort"), fits the proposed associations with Adam elsewhere in Rom. 7 but seems too specific. Whether "this" (masculine or neuter) belongs with "death" (Sanday and Headlam, *Romans*, 184; cf. Exod. 10:17) or, less likely, with "body" (Jewett, *Romans*, 472) does not ultimately alter the association between them.

322. Severian of Gabala, catena on Rom. 7:24 (PGK 15:220; Bray, *Romans*, 198).

323. E.g., Ambrose *Death* 2.41; Jerome *Ruf.* 1.25; cf. Ambrosiaster *Rom.* 7:14–25.

That for Paul sin also pervades even the law-informed mind (Rom. 7:23, 25) shows that, whatever role the body might play, the mind too is vulnerable to sin. Paul will not, then, simply present the body as sinful and the mind as good. He allows, with philosophers and Jewish thinkers, that reason *should* choose to control desires when they contravene moral law. For Paul, however, this consistent success of reason appears even more hypothetical than Stoicism's ideal sage—in practice, Stoics did not claim to have attained perfection. (For most Jewish sources the same could almost be said for achieving sinlessness.)[324] Nevertheless, Paul argues that one is *reckoned* as the ideal in Christ; even before one attains full maturity behaviorally, the ideal has somehow become the premise rather than the goal (Rom. 6:1–11; 8:3–11; see chap. 2, above).

Stoics focused not primarily on the bodily character of passions but on the danger of false beliefs.[325] Paul may be closer to the Stoic understanding on this point, though his views are not identical with those of Stoics. Contrary to Stoic expectations, Romans 7 emphasizes that merely correct belief about right and wrong cannot adequately address passion.

This was true even for correct belief based on moral teachings of Scripture. Whereas among Gentiles who lack sufficient revelation the mind ends up party to "fleshly" desires (Rom. 1:25–28; cf. Eph. 2:3; 4:17–19),[326] the law-trained mind can refuse to assent to such desires and yet find itself unable to extirpate them (Rom. 7:22–25). Rational religion falls short of transformation in Christ.

Bodily Desires in Ancient Thinking

As noted earlier, some philosophic approaches highlighted the classic struggle between reason and the passions—passions that were biologically generated and sociologically shaped, not guided by sound reason.[327] In Jewish teaching the law was supposed to liberate or protect one from passion's

---

324. *Jub.* 21:21; 1QS 11.9; 1 Esd. 4:37; *4 Ezra* 7:138–40 (68–70); Moore, *Judaism*, 467–68; Bonsirven, *Judaism*, 114; Sandmel, *Judaism*, 187; Flusser, *Judaism*, 62. Some exempted a few persons from sin, such as perhaps Abraham (Pr. Man. 8; *T. Ab.* 10:13 A), Moses (*b. Shab.* 55b), Jesse (*Tg. Ruth* on 4:22), or Yohanan ben Zakkai (*Abot R. Nat.* 14 A).

325. Stowers, "Self-Mastery," 540.

326. Arguing in a different way, Eph. 2:3 apparently applies the same principle to Jews as to Gentiles.

327. Although the human mind's activity is more connected to neurochemistry than ancient thinkers imagined, and many specific expressions of instinct are influenced by human experience and choices, ancients were right in recognizing sexual instincts, sudden fear reactions, and other innate drives as somehow connected to the body. Of course, they could not have anticipated the complexity of the connectedness in terms of hormones, the amygdala, or even how the brain adapts to new stimuli in conjunction with thinking.

control.[328] Here, however, the law facilitates the identification and thus power of biologically driven passions, perhaps repressed but not eradicated, and likely suppressed but not subdued.

Excursus: Flesh[329]

Paul's use of "flesh" would not be completely novel in a Greek context. Occasionally, Greek sources already spoke of the "flesh" (σάρξ) as worthless.[330] Some scholars suggest that the usage stemmed originally from reaction against Epicurus.[331] Epicureans claimed that those made of flesh (σάρκινον) naturally viewed pleasure positively.[332] For a first-century Stoic, the divine consisted purely of reason, not flesh (σάρξ),[333] and excellence belonged to moral purpose rather than to flesh.[334] For one second-century Stoic, one should "disdain the flesh: it is naught but gore and bones and a network compact of nerves and veins and arteries."[335] Some later sources warned against descending "into the flesh [σάρκα]."[336]

Especially given Paul's contrast between "flesh" and (God's) "Spirit," however, Paul's language echoes Jewish usage much more clearly. Scholars have sometimes jumped too quickly from the usual Old Testament holistic usage to Paul's usage[337] as if Paul were simply writing to ancient Israelites

328. Fourth Maccabees, perhaps with apologetic for potential Gentile hearers in view, depicts the deliverance more strongly than the rabbis' in-house discussions.

329. Although I adopt the conventional English translation "flesh," σάρξ has been translated a variety of ways (Creve, Janse, and Demoen, "Key Words"); for important lexical considerations, see Dunn, *Theology*, 62–73 (esp. the warning on 70); Marshall, "Flesh."

330. Despite the partly correct warning about later usage in Davies, *Paul*, 18. For ὕλη and ψυχή, see, e.g., Philo *Posterity* 61.

331. Epicurus sometimes applied σάρξ to the location of desire (Schweizer, "Σάρξ," 103), and was apparently often followed on this point by Hellenistic Judaism (105).

332. Plut. *R. Col.* 27, *Mor.* 1122D. Plutarch also complains of those who view the entire person as fleshly, i.e., bodily (Plut. *Pleas. L.* 14, *Mor.* 1096E), and notes that the flesh by nature is susceptible to disease (*Pleas. L.* 6, *Mor.* 1090EF). But even as late as Porph. *Marc.* 29.453–57, negative "flesh" pertains primarily to externals, so the issue is more "body" and especially "matter."

333. Epict. *Diatr.* 2.8.2.

334. Epict. *Diatr.* 2.23.30; cf. similarly 3.7.2–3, also against an Epicurean.

335. Marc. Aur. 2.2 (trans. Haines, LCL, 26ff.).

336. Porph. *Marc.* 9.172–73 (trans. O'Brien Wicker, 55); instead, one should flee from the body (ἀπὸ τοῦ σώματος; 10.176), gathering the dispersed elements of one's soul up from the body (10.180–83).

337. See, e.g., Grant, *Judaism and New Testament*, 62; Sandmel, *Judaism*, 178; cf. Davies, *Paul*, 18–19 (appealing to rabbinic thinking for the differences; cf. Davies, *Origins*, 145–77); Hunter, *Gospel according to Paul*, 17.

using equivalent Greek terms.[338] Against the expectations of some, when the Septuagint uses σῶμα, it normally does so with physical connotations.[339] Jewish sources sometimes commented on the difference between bodily and nonbodily parts or aspects of a person;[340] thus, for example, a Tanna attributed the soul to heaven and the body to earth.[341]

Despite some similarities of language elsewhere, Paul's contrasting use of "flesh" and "Spirit" in Romans 8:4–6, 9, 13[342] reflects especially his background in Judean thought, such as in the Dead Sea Scrolls.[343] The contrast appears in the Old Testament in Isaiah 31:3 but most notably in Genesis 6:3,[344] which appears in a highly influential section of Scripture.[345] In these sources the contrast is between humanity as flesh (like other mortal creatures) and God's own Spirit.[346] In the Old Testament, humans as flesh are mortal and prone to weakness.[347]

Paul often uses "flesh" as weakness[348] but also goes somewhat further,[349] yet in a way consistent with some Jewish circles' development of the language. Unlike some other early Jewish sources,[350] the Dead Sea Scrolls develop the

338. Flusser, *Judaism*, 63. Following Bultmann, Conzelmann (*Theology*, 176) emphasizes holism in Paul; nevertheless, on 177 he acknowledges a sort of anthropological dualism.

339. See Gundry, *Sōma*, 16–23. Robinson (*Body*, 31) treats σάρξ as humanity distanced from God but σῶμα as humanity "made for God." Gundry (*Sōma*, 50) sees σῶμα as "the physical body, roughly synonymous with 'flesh' in the neutral sense"; cf. Craig ("Bodily Resurrection," 53–54), who also follows Gundry.

340. See Moore, *Judaism*, 451 (though also the qualification on 502).

341. *Sipre Deut.* 306.28.2; later, cf. *Gen. Rab.* 8:11.

342. See also Gal. 3:3; 4:29; 5:16–17; 6:8; Phil. 3:3; cf. Rom. 7:14; 1 Cor. 3:1. Sometimes in contrast with the Spirit, σάρξ refers simply to the body (John 3:6; 1 Tim. 3:16; 1 Pet. 3:18; 4:6), as it also does when the contrasted spirit is human (Mark 14:38; 1 Cor. 5:5; 2 Cor. 7:1; Col. 2:5; 2 *Clem.* 14.5; Ign. *Magn.* 13.1; *Trall.* pref.; 12.1; *Phld.* 11.2; *Smyrn.* 1.1; *Pol.* 5.1).

343. See Frey, "Antithese"; Flusser, *Judaism*, 64–65. Pryke ("Spirit and Flesh," 358) understands it as good vs. evil spirits.

344. Though the Hebrew is worded differently in 4Q252 1.2, the LXX of Gen. 6:3 uses the same words for "flesh" and "Spirit" that Paul does.

345. With, e.g., Ladd, *Last Things*, 30–31; Ladd, *Theology*, 458; cf. Klausner, *Jesus to Paul*, 486–87. Cf. also *Jub.* 5:8; *1 En.* 106:17. Even in Philo *Heir* 57, the Spirit alongside reason, contrasted with fleshly pleasure, is the divine spirit.

346. Robinson (*Body*, 11–14) argues that the OT is so holistic that it lacks a term for "body" and a distinction between "body" and "soul" (perhaps an exaggeration; cf. Isa. 10:18 in MT and LXX). Humans are flesh also in traditional Jewish sources, such as, e.g., *Jub.* 5:2; Sir. 28:5; physicality seems implied in, e.g., Gen. 17:11–14; Jdt. 14:10.

347. Baumgärtel, "Flesh"; Davies, *Paul*, 18.

348. For flesh as humanity, e.g., Rom. 3:20; 1 Cor. 1:29; Gal. 1:16; for weakness, e.g., Rom. 6:19; 8:3; 1 Cor. 7:28; 2 Cor. 1:17; 5:16; 7:5; Gal. 4:13–14; for mortality, 1 Cor. 15:50; 2 Cor. 4:11; Phil. 1:22, 24. Sheldon (*Mystery Religions*, 79) cites OT language as more relevant than the mysteries.

349. Bornkamm, *Paul*, 133.

350. The decomposition of flesh (*m. Sanh.* 6:6; *Moed Qat.* 1:5), even understood as atoning for sin (e.g., *Pesiq. Rab Kah.* 11:23; *b. Sanh.* 47b), does not suggest that the body was viewed as evil.

sense of weakness in a moral direction, including susceptibility to sin,[351] a sense that the equivalent Greek term often bears in Paul.[352] Clearly, when Paul contrasts flesh and the Spirit in Romans 8:4–9, 13, he speaks of God's Spirit, as the full context shows (cf. also 1:3–4; 7:6; 1 Cor. 5:5; Gal. 3:3; 4:29; 5:17; 6:8), the clear exceptions being 2 Corinthians 7:1 and Colossians 2:5.[353]

Many ancient thinkers connected passions with the body.[354] Socrates, for example, reportedly insisted that a philosopher "disdains the demands of the body and is not enslaved by the pleasures of the body."[355] He also reportedly asked who was less enslaved by passions of the body than he.[356] Plato complains that "the body and its desires" lead to violence for the sake of money and, worst of all, distraction from philosophic study.[357] The Platonist tradition disparaged the body more than did many other thinkers.[358] Bodies distracted people from divine reality.[359]

351. Meyer, "Flesh"; Driver, *Scrolls*, 532; Wilcox, "Dualism," 94–95; Best, *Temptation*, 52; esp. Flusser, *Judaism*, 62–65. See 1QS 3.8; 4.20–21; 9.9; 11.7, 12; 1QM 4.3; 12.12; 1QH^a 5.30; 12.29–32; 17.14–16 (Sukenik 4.29–32; 9.14–16; 13.13); perhaps CD 1.2; 4Q511 frgs. 48–49 + 51.4; as in Scripture, its range of meaning remains extensive, sometimes referring simply to kinship (CD 5.9, 11; 7.1; 8.6) or humankind (1QM 15.13; 17.8; 4Q511 frg. 35.1; 1Q20 1.25, 29) or to physicality alongside the heart (spirit; 1QM 7.5). In Greek, in *T. Job* 27:2 (*OTP*)/27:3 (ed. Kraft), Satan contrasts himself as a spirit with Job as "a fleshly person," i.e., weak and mortal.

352. Dunn (*Romans*, 1:370) correctly notes that "it is precisely the weakness and appetites of 'the mortal body' (= the flesh) which are the occasion for sin." Likewise, "the problem with flesh is not that it is sinful *per se* but that it is vulnerable to the enticements of sin—flesh, we might say, as 'the desiring I' (7.7–12)" (Dunn, *Theology*, 67).

353. Unlike Seneca, Paul uses "Spirit" to refer to God's Spirit in Christ, not a shared possession of humanity (Sevenster, *Seneca*, 79–80); Paul thinks not of "two 'parts'" of people but rather of "two modes of existence" that characterize the old aeon and the new aeon (Ridderbos, *Paul: Outline*, 66). He is not anti-body (*pace* Kohler, *Theology*, 215).

354. E.g., Plato *Phaedo* 66CD; 83CD; Aeschines *Tim.* 191; Cic. *Resp.* 6.26.29; Sen. Y. *Dial.* 2.16.1; Dio Chrys. *Or.* 4.115; 13.13; Max. Tyre *Or.* 7.7; 33.7; Philost. *Vit. Apoll.* 7.26; Proclus *Poet.* 6.1, K121.14–15; Iambl. *Pyth. Life* 31.205; *Letter* 3, frg. 2 (Stob. *Anth.* 3.5.45); Porph. *Marc.* 14.243–44; 33.506–7; Philo *Alleg. Interp.* 3.161. Cf. matter in Iambl. *Soul* 8.39, §385; *Letter* 3, frg. 4.5–6 (Stob. *Anth.* 3.5.47). Even Epicurus thought the mind superior to the flesh (σάρξ), because mind grasped proper pleasure best (Diog. Laert. 10.145–20).

355. Socratics *Ep.* 14 (trans. Stowers and Worley, 257, 259).

356. Xen. *Apol.* 16, ταῖς τοῦ σώματος ἐπιθυμίαις.

357. Plato *Phaedo* 66CD (trans. Fowler, LCL, 1:231).

358. Seneca, for example, thought that the body, though temporary, can be of service to the mind (Sen. Y. *Dial.* 7.8.2). Stoics viewed everything, even spirit (πνεῦμα) and virtues (Arius Did. 2.7.5b7, p. 20.28–30), as "bodies."

359. Plut. *Isis* 78, *Mor.* 382F; Max. Tyre *Or.* 11.10; Iambl. *Letter* 16, frg. 2.1–2 (Stob. *Anth.* 3.1.49). Any particularities weakened the original, universal whole (Proclus *Poet.* 5, K52.7–19, 23–24).

A second-century orator warns that "the function particular to the flesh," which humans share with animals, "is Pleasure," and "that particular to the intelligence is Reason," which mortals share with the divine.[360] Most pervasively in ancient sources, the body, in contrast to true being, was mortal.[361] Many spoke of the body as a prison or chains detaining the soul.[362]

With its limitations, materiality itself sometimes became a problem. Some Stoics envisioned people as souls who did not even own their bodies;[363] whereas the heavens were pure, bad things happened on earth because it consisted of corruptible matter.[364] Later Platonists sought to purify their immortal souls from passions and attention to perishable matter.[365] Some later sources developing the Platonic tradition even presented love of the body as evil.[366]

Such attitudes toward the body, ranging from ambivalent to hostile, naturally led to asceticism. Carneades, a second-century BCE Skeptic, ascetically neglected his body, supposing that this would increase his intellectual concentration.[367] For a mildly ascetic later Christian source, love of pleasure is what makes the body unbearable for the soul.[368]

360. Max. Tyre *Or*. 33.7 (trans. Trapp, 266; cf. 6.1, 4; 41.5); see also Epict. *Diatr*. 1.3.3; cf. *Sipre Deut*. 306.28.2. For the true nature of deity being intelligence rather than "flesh" (σάρξ), see Epict. *Diatr*. 2.8.2. For passions vs. reason ruling lower animals, see, e.g., Arist. *Pol*. 1.2.13, 1254b. Philosophy thus converts a person from a beast into a god (Marc. Aur. 4.16).

361. E.g., Cic. *Resp*. 6.26.29; Sen. Y. *Dial*. 1.5.8; Epict. *Diatr*. 2.19.27; Iambl. *Pyth. Life* 32.228; Marc. Aur. 4.4; 10.33.3. Cf. later Manichaeans and Mandaeans in Reitzenstein, *Mystery-Religions*, 79 (which Reitzenstein wrongly thinks [449] influenced Rom. 7:24).

362. E.g., Plato *Gorg*. 493AE; *Phaedo* 82E; *Cratyl*. 400B; Heracl. *Ep*. 5; Epict. *Diatr*. 1.9.11–12; Max. Tyre *Or*. 7.5 (recalling Plato *Rep*. 514A–516B); 36.4; Philost. *Vit. Apoll*. 7.26; Iambl. *Letter* 3, frg. 2 (Stob. *Anth*. 3.5.45); *Gnom. Vat*. 464 (Malherbe, *Moral Exhortation*, 110). Thus a philosopher being ground to death "declared that he himself was not being ground, but only that thing of his in which, as it chanced, he had been enclosed" (Dio Chrys. [Favorinus] *Or*. 37.45; trans. Crosby, LCL, 4:45).

363. E.g., Epict. *Diatr*. 1.11–12 (though Sorabji [*Emotion*, 215], commenting on 1.22.10, suggests that such ideas may have been Epictetus's innovation).

364. Hierocles *Gods* (Stob. *Anth*. 2.9.7).

365. Iambl. *Soul* 8.39, §385; 8.43, §456. Cf., earlier, Plato *Rep*. 10.611C.

366. Porph. *Marc*. 14.244–50; 25.394–95 (though the real source of evils comes from choices in the soul, 29.453–57). Love of the body is ignorance of God (13.227–29), and one must hold the connection with it lightly (32.485–95). Cf. Plot. *Enn*. 1.8 on the secondary negativity of the body; matter is evil (1.8.4), worthless (2.4), and unreal (3.6.6–7). Many gnostic thinkers also apparently found matter problematic (Hippol. *Ref*. 6.28; 7.20); some cite dualism in Orphism (Tarn, *Civilisation*, 354; Guthrie, *Orpheus*, 82–83, 174).

367. Val. Max. 8.7.ext.5; cf. a later Neoplatonist in Eunapius *Lives* 456 (albeit reported differently in Porph. *Plot*. 11.113). Seneca indulged the body for health but otherwise was hard on it to subdue it to his mind (Sen. Y. *Ep. Lucil*. 8.5); cf. even the rhetorical claim in Fronto *Nep. am*. 2.8.

368. *Sent. Sext*. 139a–139b. Passion is dangerous and must be suppressed in *Sent. Sext*. 204–9. In *Diogn*. 6.5–6 σάρξ wars against the soul (cf. 1 Pet. 2:11). Later Christian asceticism drew from existing trends in late antiquity (see, e.g., Judge, *Jerusalem*, 223).

Hellenistic Jews did not escape the influence of such language. Thus they could associate the body with passions.[369] Philo speaks of the soul entombed within a body in this life;[370] death was an escape.[371] "Flesh" (σάρξ) is alienated from what is divine.[372] The soul was presently enslaved to the body through its passions.[373] For others, drunkenness allowed pleasure to stir the body to adultery.[374] Satan blinded a man "as a human being, as flesh [σάρξ], in my [the man's] corrupt sins" until the man repented.[375]

Paul and the Body

When Paul speaks of the "flesh" or associates passions with the body, he adapts some of the language of his day to argue his point. But did Paul, like later Neoplatonists and many gnostics, view the body as evil? Did he envision a conflict between body and soul? Despite pagan criticisms,[376] and against some gnostic thinkers, even patristic writers defended materiality in the "flesh."[377]

Some earlier Pauline interpreters suggested that Paul desires liberation from the body and its passions in a way resembling the thinking of Platonic philosophers.[378] This comparison certainly risks exaggeration, especially in view of Paul's expectation of the body's resurrection (Rom. 8:11, 13, 23;

369. E.g., Philo *Alleg. Interp.* 2.28; *Sacr.* 48; *Posterity* 96, 155; *Unchangeable* 111; *Agr.* 64; *Plant.* 43; *Abr.* 164; *Mos.* 2.24; *T. Jud.* 14:3.

370. Philo *Alleg. Interp.* 1.108; *Unchangeable* 150; *Conf.* 78–79; *Spec. Laws* 4.188; cf. *Alleg. Interp.* 3.21; *Heir* 85; so also the Christian work *Diogn.* 6.5.

371. Philo *Cher.* 114.

372. Philo *Giants* 29 (usually employing σῶμα in this way, but using σάρξ here because he quotes Gen. 6). It is our fleshly nature (σαρκῶν φύσις) that hinders wisdom's growth; souls "free from flesh and body [ἄσαρκοι καὶ ἀσώματοι]" can celebrate with the universe (*Giants* 30–31; LCL, 2:460–61); flesh prevents people from being able to look up to heaven (*Giants* 31).

373. Philo *Heir* 267–69 in Stuhlmacher, *Romans*, 109, who compares the cry for liberation from the body in Rom. 7:24; see, further, Wolfson, *Philo*, 1:433. In terms of rational command, one would normally envision the body as slave to the mind (Arist. *Pol.* 1.1.4, 1252a; 1.2.10, 1254a; cf. Cic. *Resp.* 3.25.37; Sall. *Catil.* 1.2; Heracl. *Ep.* 9; Philo *Sacr.* 9; reason ruling the senses in Sen. Y. *Ep. Lucil.* 66.32), all the more when some called slaves "bodies" (Deissmann, *Light*, 165; BDAG cites, e.g., Tob. 10:10; 2 Macc. 8:11; Jos. *Ant.* 14.321).

374. *T. Jud.* 14:3.

375. *T. Jud.* 19:4 (*OTP* 1:800; Greek in Charles, *Testaments*, 95). The Lord accepts repentance because people "are flesh [σάρξ] and the spirits of deceit lead them astray" (*T. Zeb.* 9:7; *OTP* 1:807; Charles, *Testaments*, 128).

376. Some pagans critiqued Christians for their high view of the body (e.g., Origen *Cels.* 8.49; Cook, *Interpretation*, 113); but cf. Cyril Alex. on Rom. 6:6 (Burns, *Romans*, 139).

377. Talbert (*Romans*, 162) cites here Tert. *Flesh* 15. Bray (*Corinthians*, 56, 108, and *Romans*, 165) cites Chrys. *Hom. Cor.* 17.1; *Hom. Rom.* 11 (on 6:13); Theodoret *Interp. Rom.* on 6:13 (PG 82:109); and Aug. *Contin.* 10.24. Still, cf. Aug. *Ag. Jul.* 70 (in Bray, *Corinthians*, 172).

378. Schlatter, *Romans*, 3, 157 (but cf. 167).

perhaps 7:24b–25a).[379] Nevertheless, many scholars who have downplayed Paul's distinctions among elements in the human personality have also overstated their case.[380]

In Paul the body, guided by a renewed mind (Rom. 12:2–3), could be used for good (12:1; cf. 6:13); but under other circumstances the body could also be used for sin (1:24; 6:12–13; 7:5) and even be closely associated with it (6:6; 8:10, 13; cf. 7:24). Relevant to our discussion of the "fleshly mind," bodily passions could war against the mind (7:23). Though the mind might disagree with bodily passion (7:23, 25), it could find itself subject to it and corrupted by it (1:28). Thus, the frame of mind shaped by the flesh, by human frailty susceptible to temptation, cannot please God (8:8). In this context only new life in the Spirit could free a person (8:2).

For Paul and for the Jewish tradition he follows, creation and bodily existence are good. One is not delivered from some bodily limitations, such as mortality, until the resurrection (Rom. 8:11), but the presence of the Spirit nevertheless gives life in the present so the body can be an instrument for good rather than evil (6:13, 19). By itself, however, bodily existence is susceptible to a range of drives that in themselves cannot recognize right or wrong. These drives could intersect with what Jewish people considered fundamental behaviors of pagan life, such as sexual impropriety or eating food offered to idols (1 Cor. 10:6–8).[381]

No one, including Paul, would have denied that virtually everyone had such biological passions as hunger, necessary for survival, and procreation, necessary for the propagation of humanity.[382] Nevertheless, whereas in principle reason could veto the proposals raised by passions, the pull of these passions pervaded the functioning of the intellect, a pervasiveness exposed all the more plainly by the law. One might avoid acting on covetousness, but covetousness itself arose in the heart before the law could instruct against it. Indeed, by exposing right and wrong, the law spotlighted it rather than rooted it out.

379. Schlatter himself makes distinctions between Paul and Platonism here (*Romans*, 167). Paul lacks Platonic vocabulary of the "soul" (see appendix A, below), though he does speak of the "inner person."

380. Commentators after Bultmann (with his commendable modern appreciation of the whole person) have often shied away from such non-"Hebrew" ideas. Some scholars have, however, noted some anthropologically dualistic language (e.g., Vogel, "Reflexions"; Pelser, "Antropologie"; earlier, Glover, *Paul*, 20).

381. Cf., e.g., Rev. 2:14, 20; Acts 15:20; *Sib. Or.* 3.757–66; *t. Abod. Zar.* 8:4; *b. Sanh.* 56a, bar.; *Pesiq. Rab Kah.* 12:1.

382. This is not a cultural issue; Confucius, who warned against lust (*Anal.* 9.17; 15.12 [47]), also found no one who loved virtue as much as feminine beauty (*Anal.* 16.7 [82]).

Scholars debate the extent to which Paul and other Jewish contemporaries agreed with wider Greek conceptions and the extent to which they simply appropriated and adapted the language. As noted in my discussion of Romans 6,[383] Paul does not oppose all desire and certainly not all unpleasant emotion; when he provides specific examples of prohibited desire, it refers to desiring to possess or perform what Scripture has already prohibited.

For Paul, the "flesh" and the Spirit generate contradictory desires, though Paul seems more comfortable associating the language of "desire" especially with the predilections of the flesh (Gal. 5:16–17; cf. 5:24; Rom. 6:12; 13:14; Eph. 2:3). Although in principle believers' desires are dead (Gal. 5:24) as one is dead to sin in principle (2:20; Rom. 6:2–10), in practice one must continue to address these desires when they arise (cf. Rom. 6:2–13; Gal. 5:13–16; 6:1; Col. 3:5), perhaps by reckoning them dead (Rom. 6:11). Increasingly identifying with Christ and the Spirit, one may embrace the Spirit's desires; a life with the Spirit would protect one from living merely for physical impulses (Gal. 5:16–17).[384] In any case, Paul is clear that the divided person is not the ideal and that the law, far from unifying the person, in fact divides this person.

Paul affirms the body, whose destiny is resurrected glory, but the flesh is connected to a side of existence dominated by bodily passions, some of which, if unrestrained, lead to violation of God's law. Translating such language into modern terms might help us understand more concretely the sorts of concepts that Paul was articulating, although ancient and modern psychologies lack correspondences at many points. Today we understand that someone who develops a chemical dependency will have a craving for those chemicals on a physical level. In the same way, an adolescent whose habits connect particular sorts of images with sexual arousal will develop a neurochemical pattern of those images regularly triggering such arousal.

Religious convictions do not automatically change patterns in the brain; one may be disgusted by and reject habitual responses on the level of one's conscious will, but the "temptation" remains.[385] Empirically speaking, religious

---

383. See pp. 39, 81–82.

384. I am grateful to Prof. Jim Hernando of the Assemblies of God Theological Seminary for this insight (personal conversation, Feb. 5, 2015).

385. Freud highlighted repressed desires, defense mechanisms, and their development in humans' unconscious minds. Unfortunately, popular culture has sometimes appropriated the recognition of unconscious or barely conscious desires as revealing one's identity and thus shaping one's inevitable choices and destiny; if repression is hypocrisy, resistance seems ultimately futile. (Popular culture also readily embraced his overemphasis on sexual aspects of desire, central as those are in mammals after puberty. Puberty appears later in the physical maturation process for humans than for most other mammals [cf. Stormshak,

practice, of whatever kind, by itself does not ordinarily alter such patterns;[386] Paul was aware of this in his Letter to the Galatians, in which he associates the flesh both with religion (Gal. 3:2–3) and with sinful behavior (5:16–21, 24). The best that mere religion can do is recognize right from wrong, cover over the wrong, and insist on different behavior.[387]

An Image of Defeat

Philosophers often claimed to be soldiers winning victories against passions.[388] In one pseudepigraphic letter Diogenes the Cynic exhorts, "If you are trying to subdue the human passions, summon me, for I can wage war [πόλεμον] against these just like a general [στρατηγεῖν]."[389] Philo exhorts the mind to fight against passions, particularly pleasure.[390] Thus, in Romans 13:12–14 Paul exhorts that, against desires, one put on the armor of light.[391] Later rabbis spoke of using and obeying the Torah to battle against the evil impulse.[392]

In Romans 7, however, the embattled figure concedes defeat. The outcry "Wretched person that I am!" need not reflect a particular persona.[393] Such

---

"Comparative Endocrinology," 157].) In contrast to such approaches dependent solely on human resources, Paul affirms the genuine activity of God's power through the Spirit to transform.

386. Cf. the complaint about many evangelicals' sexual and marital behavior in Sider, *Scandal*.

387. Cf. Odeberg, *Pharisaism*, 66, 72: Jesus would affirm most Pharisaic ethics, but the genuinely Christian approach requires inner transformation.

388. E.g., Xen. *Mem.* 1.2.24; *Oec.* 1.23; Sen. Y. *Nat. Q.* 1.pref.5; Lucian *Phil. Sale* 8. For athletic victories, cf. Dio Chrys. *Or.* 8.11–9.18.

389. Diogenes *Ep.* 5 (trans. Fiore, 96–97). Cf. battling against popular opinion in Diogenes *Ep.* 10; against pleasure and hardship in *Ep.* 12.

390. Philo *Alleg. Interp.* 2.106. Reason also fights against passions in 4 Macc. 3:4–5.

391. For the armor image, see also Eph. 6:11–17; 1 Thess. 5:8; Ign. *Pol.* 6.2; cf. 2 Cor. 10:3–4; 1 Tim. 1:18; 2 Tim. 2:4; Rev. 12:11; comment below (pp. 110–11). Despite the image's possible Cynic roots, some (e.g., Downing, *Cynics and Churches*, 137–41) focus too exclusively on it; but a background in philosophers and moralists (Dibelius and Conzelmann, *Pastoral Epistles*, 32–33; Lincoln, *Ephesians*, 437; Malherbe, *Moral Exhortation*, 159–60) is reasonable.

392. Schechter, *Aspects*, 272–73; for fighting against and subduing the evil impulse, see also, e.g., *m. Ab.* 4:1; *Ruth Rab.* 8:1.

393. Stowers (*Rereading*, 271–72) cites Medea's cry in Seneca's *Medea*. Ancient interpreters generally viewed the wretchedness more generally; see, e.g. (in Bray, *Romans*, 197), Ambrosiaster *Comm.* on Rom. 7:24 (CSEL 81:245); Chrys. *Hom. Rom.* 13 on Rom. 7:24. Smith ("Form") finds parallels in some preconversion liturgical laments (albeit with very limited evidence). If a particular figure is in view, it is probably Israel under the law (with Grieb, *Story*, 76). In Rom. 3:16 Paul employs a cognate for his present term for "wretchedness" for sinners under the law.

laments appear in dramas and elsewhere,[394] apparently because they reflected the way people actually spoke when lamenting their situations.[395] One later first-century Stoic warns an interlocutor, who complains about being wretched in his flesh, that he ought to abandon attention to the flesh.[396]

The plea "Who will free me from this mortal body?" continues the image of the prisoner and resembles some other ancient passages where the answer is only death.[397] The answer here, however, is in Jesus Christ (Rom. 7:25a). This answer is partly developed for people in Christ in 8:1–17, and it ultimately is fully developed in 8:10–11, 13, where the body is dead but the Spirit that raised Jesus will raise those who put the body's works to death.[398]

The law active in the members wages war against the law active in his mind, making him (and thus also his mind) prisoner of war to the law focused on sin (Rom. 7:23).[399] Prisoners of war were usually enslaved or executed.[400] Here the prisoner is a slave to sin (7:25; cf. 6:6, 16–17, 20) and awaiting death (7:24). Other thinkers described one ruled by passions as enslaved and a prisoner of war.[401]

394. E.g., Aeschylus *Ag.* 1260; Ovid *Am.* 1.4.59; *Metam.* 9.474; Terence *Andr.* 882; *Phorm.* 1006; *Moth.* 293; Plut. *L. Wealth* 5, *Mor.* 525D; Apul. *Metam.* 3.25; *Jos. Asen.* 6:2 (*OTP*; 6:5 in Philonenko's Greek text); cf. Lysias *Or.* 24.23, §170; Isa. 33:1 LXX; Mic. 2:4 LXX; 4 Macc. 16:7.

395. Cf. Demosth. *Aphob.* 1.66 (*Or.* 27). The outcry functions almost like a pathetic "Woe is me," Epict. *Diatr.* 1.4.23–24; 3.13.4; 4.1.57; 4.4.21.

396. Epict. *Diatr.* 1.3.5–6; cf. 1.12.28, where Epictetus responds to a similar claim of wretchedness by urging contentment. Epictetus repeatedly levels this label of wretchedness against foolish imaginary interlocutors (*Diatr.* 1.4.11; 2.8.12; 2.17.34; 2.18.27; 3.2.9; 3.22.31; 4.1.21; 4.6.18). Some people criticized others as wretched; see Dio Chrys. *Or.* 34.2 (noting the view of some concerning Cynics); Wis. 3:11; 13:10. In common usage, such language also could express sympathy, such as "Poor fellow!" (Epict. *Diatr.* 4.6.21).

397. Many philosophers considered suicide the appropriate answer to "Who will release me from these pains?" (Diog. Laert. 6.21; cf. Max. Tyre *Or.* 7.5; on philosophers and suicide, see Keener, *Acts*, 3:2498–507, esp. 2503–5). See comments on ancient beliefs about the body as a prison above, p. 104, and below, p. 268 (where death was the means of release, e.g., Epict. *Diatr.* 1.9.16); and Sevenster, *Seneca*, 82–83. Gnostics naturally construed this passage as seeking release from the body (Pagels, *Paul*, 32–34), but Paul is no gnostic here (Bornkamm, *Experience*, 99). Of course, people could also cry for deliverance (Apul. *Metam.* 11.2, preferring, however, death to nondeliverance).

398. That resurrection is the ultimate answer to the body's corruption was also recognized by some ancient commentators, e.g., Caesarius *Serm.* 177.4 (in Bray, *Romans*, 199).

399. Cf. fleshly desires (1 Pet. 2:11) or the flesh (*Diogn.* 6.5) warring against the soul.

400. Jewett, *Romans*, 470–71.

401. Dio Chrys. *Or.* 32.90; Iambl. *Pyth. Life* 17.78; cf. Philo *Sacr.* 26. In popular literature, see Xen. Eph. *Anthia* 1.3–4. The metaphor does appear more widely, e.g., for "captivating" one by beauty (Jdt. 16:9).

Excursus: Ancient Military Metaphors

Military metaphors were naturally common.[402] Orators, for example, often used military metaphors,[403] sometimes for moral issues.[404] When battling against internal temptations, Dio Chrysostom demands, what defense or armor or bodyguards does one have "unless it be words of wisdom and prudence?"[405]

Military imagery was particularly pervasive in philosophers.[406] Thus, one of Socrates's admirers declares that those tempted by desires have found in Socrates an ally, or fellow warrior (συμμάχῳ), against passions.[407] Diogenes the Cynic declares that he has battled against hardships[408] and pleasure.[409] A Cynic sage could fortify his mind like a city ready to withstand siege.[410] Another Cynic could claim to be a soldier like Heracles, battling pleasures.[411] Stoics saw life as a battle against hardships;[412] wisdom arms the wise person for life as weapons arm a soldier.[413] Even an Epicurean could contend that one must fight against vices.[414] Not surprisingly, Hellenistic Jewish writers sometimes also used such warfare language.[415]

---

402. E.g., for love in Ach. Tat. 2.10.3; Catullus 67.21; Lucian *Lucius* 10 (intercourse); Apul. *Metam.* 2.17; hyperbole for verbal arguments in Hor. *Ep.* 1.18.15–16; a comparison for military exhortations in 2 Macc. 15:11.

403. E.g., Dion. Hal. *Demosth.* 32; Cic. *De or.* 3.14.55; Sen. E. *Controv.* 9.pref.4; Pliny *Ep.* 1.20.3; 4.22.5; 7.25.6; Tac. *Dial.* 32, 34, 37; Fronto *Eloq.* 1.16; Lucian *Nigr.* 36; Philost. *Vit. soph.* 2.1.563. For arguments as weapons, see also Hor. *Sat.* 2.3.296–97; Sen. Y. *Ep. Lucil.* 117.7, 25; perhaps Heracl. *Ep.* 7.

404. E.g., Cic. *Fam.* 4.7.2; *Brut.* 2.7. For luxury as the greatest enemy, see Dio Chrys. *Or.* 33.28.

405. Dio Chrys. *Or.* 49.10 (trans. Crosby, LCL, 4:303).

406. E.g., Epict. *Diatr.* 1.14.15; 4.5.25–32. Val. Max. 4.1.ext.2 claims that Plato in moral combat guarded his soul from vice; in 8.7.ext.5, Carneades is a "soldier of wisdom."

407. Xen. *Mem.* 1.2.24; cf. *Oec.* 1.23.

408. Dio Chrys. *Or.* 8.11–16, esp. 13, 15.

409. Dio Chrys. *Or.* 8.20; Diogenes *Ep.* 5; pleasure and hardship in Dio Chrys. *Or.* 9.11–12; Diogenes *Ep.* 12. He also recommends battling popular opinion (Diogenes *Ep.* 10); his wallet is a "shield" (Diogenes *Ep.* 19).

410. An image earlier advanced by the Cynic sage Antisthenes (Malherbe, "Antisthenes"; Malherbe, *Philosophers*, 91–119, esp. here 97–101). Antisthenes reportedly declared, "Wisdom is a most sure stronghold. . . . Walls of defence must be constructed in our own impregnable reasonings" (Diog. Laert. 6.1.13; trans. Hicks, LCL, 2:13).

411. Lucian *Phil. Sale* 8. For the comparison of Diogenes with Heracles, see Dio Chrys. *Or.* 8.28–34.

412. Sen. Y. *Ep. Lucil.* 96.5; Hierocles *Love* (Stob. *Anth.* 4.84.20). Cf. similarly Dio Chrys. *Or.* 16.6.

413. Sen. Y. *Ep. Lucil.* 109.8.

414. Philod. *Prop.* col. 4.6–15.

415. One could speak of sin raising up walls and towers (*T. Levi* 2:3); Moses's armor (ὅπλα) is prayer and his message in Wis. 18:21–22. But see esp. Philo, e.g., in *Alleg. Interp.* 3.14, 155; *Dreams* 2.90; *Abr.* 243; *Mos.* 1.225.

Paul develops this military imagery elsewhere in his letters, including this one. Thus, he uses similar warfare language for his ministry of challenging false ideologies that subvert God's truth (2 Cor. 10:3–5). Most relevant regarding Paul's usage here is his comment about the armor (ὅπλα) of light later in Romans 13:12, alluding back to this text and probably to becoming "instruments" or "weapons" (ὅπλα) of righteousness (Rom. 6:13). In that context one must put aside works of darkness such as excessive feasting, drunkenness, sexual sin, lack of self-control, rivalry, and envy (13:13). Instead, one must put on the armor of light, which is putting on the Lord Jesus Christ (13:14a).[416] This contrasts with premeditating ways to indulge fleshly passions (13:14b), such as those behind the acts just listed in 13:13.

With reference to this book's subject, such a depiction of internal conflict becomes particularly relevant in Romans 7:22–25, regarding the law in the figure's mind. The Jewish mind under the law may delight in the law (7:22, 25) and indeed differs positively in many respects from the pagan mind that has fewer restraints on its passions in 1:28. Nevertheless, it is still a mind that cannot in itself defeat the sin of entertaining misplaced desire but can only await the promised eschatological deliverance from it (7:24).

Thus, Paul illustrates the inadequacy of any approach to the law that depends on flesh—on human ability to fulfill it.[417] One can approach God's law in one of two ways: the way of boasting,[418] or the way of reading it so as to inculcate trust in the God to whom it bears witness (Rom. 3:27; cf. 3:31–4:3). The law may be seen as a moral standard exposing sin and declaring punishment, or it may be seen as the law for which God's Spirit within Jesus's followers empowers the people of the new covenant (8:2). The law may be pursued by human works, or it may be pursued by faith (9:30–32; 10:3–6).

---

416. "Clothing" one with moral attributes or God's Spirit appears in various ancient texts, e.g., *L.A.B.* 27:9–10; also the LXX of Judg. 6:34; 1 Chron. 12:19 (12:18 ET); 2 Chron. 24:20; cf. *Odes Sol.* 25:8; garments of future restoration in Isa. 52:1; *Pss. Sol.* 11:7; *1 En.* 62:15–16; garments of wisdom in *L.A.B.* 20:2–3.

417. Or, on another reading, on ethnic exclusivity. The macrostructure of Romans clearly addresses righteousness for both Jewish people and Gentiles, and its argument climaxes in 15:8–12 with biblical support, from each part of the canon, for welcoming Gentiles. Ethnic possession of the law is relevant in 2:17, 23–24; 3:2; and 9:4. The more specific issue in Rom. 7, however, while supporting the larger discussion of corporate identity, involves moral righteousness and the inability of Jewish people as well as Gentiles to secure this experience as well as status apart from God's gift in Christ.

418. Depending on one's theological framework, this is boasting either in one's achievements or in one's ethnic heritage in the covenant. I see the former emphasis in the particular argument of this passage and the latter with respect to Romans' larger macrostructure.

Conclusion

Romans 7:15–25 depicts neither the ideal Christian law nor Paul's current experience but Paul's graphic dramatization of life under the law. Unlike the lawless Gentiles of 1:18–32, this passage's figure is intellectually enlightened by the truth of God's law. Even such true moral information, however, cannot free one from the verdict of one's passions. One can be freed only by the gift of a new life based on divine righteousness.

Whereas Romans 7:15–25 depicts what Paul goes on to describe as the mind of the flesh, in 8:5–9 Paul offers a stark alternative experience of life with God in terms of the mind of the Spirit.

4

⊚⊚⊚⊚

The Mind of the Spirit
(Rom. 8:5–7)

> People whose lives are oriented around the flesh (and thus the interests of mere bodily existence) think about matters of the flesh, but those who lives are oriented by God's Spirit consider matters of the Spirit. This is because the fleshly frame of mind can expect only death, whereas the Spirit-framed mind has life and peace.
>
> —Romans 8:5–6

In contrast to the way of thinking depicted in Romans 7, which cannot overcome the passions, the new way of thinking in Christ is empowered by God's Spirit that now dwells in believers. Embracing the truth of God's gift of righteousness rather than striving to achieve it by finite flesh, this new approach can fulfill God's will because the Spirit who knows God's will guides, motivates, and empowers the believer.

The New Frame of Mind

Paul contrasts the φρόνημα of the flesh with that of the Spirit. Paul probably employs the term to contrast two dispositions or attitudes toward life, one framed by merely fleshly existence and the other framed by the reality of God's presence, by the Spirit.

Disposition and the Mind

The term φρόνημα has no exact equivalent in English, and even in Greek its semantic range is wide enough that only context will define its sense. Given the semantic range of φρόνημα, the phrases often translated "mind of the Spirit" and "mind of the flesh" can refer to the divergent frames of mind, cognitive dispositions, or cognitive approaches of the Spirit and of the flesh.[1] In today's terms, one might think partly of how outlooks and character are shaped by the different worldviews, or approaches to reality, of these two spheres. One mind focuses on the matters of God; the other is oriented around only matters involving the self and its desires (Rom. 8:5–6).

Philo, who often employs the term φρόνημα, may provide a sample of Diaspora Jewish intellectual usage. He generally uses the term to mean disposition, attitude, or character.[2] As such, it is a settled direction of the personality, not a matter of fleeting thoughts; certainly, this must be true also for Paul, who plainly depicts the corrupted mind of Romans 1:28–31 not as a matter of fleeting thoughts but as a matter of characteristic ones. This disposition may be intelligent,[3] philosophic,[4] untrained and undiscerning,[5] free[6] or slavish,[7] proud[8] or broken,[9] noble,[10] enduring,[11] mature,[12] or brave and courageous.[13] (As one expects from Philo, such aspects of character often correlate with masculinity or with being effeminate.)[14]

1. See BDAG. For something like disposition, see 2 Macc. 7:21; 13:9. For "the direction of the will" as well as thinking, see Schreiner, *Romans*, 411; similarly Sanday and Headlam, *Romans*, 195; for a settled way of thinking or attitude, see Dunn, *Romans*, 1:425 (citing other Pauline texts). Cf. Aquinas, lecture 1 on Rom. 8:5: "the right sense in spiritual matters," and thinking well about God (Levy, Krey, and Ryan, *Romans*, 181). The term is a favorite of Philo's.

2. For attitude, cf., e.g., Philo *Mos.* 1.266; for disposition, cf. also Jos. *Ant.* 1.232; 2.232.

3. Philo *Creation* 17; *Mos.* 1.259; thoughtfulness in *Embassy* 62. Cf. Jos. *Ant.* 12.195 (where the context suggests wisdom, shrewdness, or a sort of business competence).

4. Philo *Good Person* 130. Cf. the outlook in Jos. *Ant.* 2.40.

5. Philo *Drunkenness* 198.

6. Philo *Dreams* 2.79; *Good Person* 62, 111, 119; *Flacc.* 64; *Embassy* 215 (cf. Jos. *Ant.* 4.245).

7. Philo *Good Person* 24 (cf. subdued, Jos. *Ant.* 3.58; 5.186).

8. Philo *Cher.* 64; *Flight* 207; *Names* 176; *Abr.* 223; *Spec. Laws* 1.293; *Virt.* 165, 172; *Rewards* 74, 119; *Hypoth.* 11.16; cf. 2 Macc. 13:9.

9. Discouraged from hardship (Philo *Jos.* 144) or by those who weaken their courage (*Mos.* 1.325; cf. *Hypoth.* 6.1; Jos. *Ant.* 14.355).

10. Philo *Jos.* 4; *Mos.* 1.51, 149; *Virt.* 71, 216; *Good Person* 121.

11. Philo *Mos.* 1.40.

12. Philo *Sober* 20; *Abr.* 26.

13. Philo *Mos.* 1.309; *Virt.* 3; cf. also 2 Macc. 7:21.

14. Masculine associations appear positively in Philo *Dreams* 2.9; *Jos.* 79; *Spec. Laws* 4.45 (thus not led by the crowd to evil); feminine aspects appear negatively in *Posterity* 165; *Giants* 4; also Jos. *War* 2.373.

Because ancient intellectuals often associated such aspects of character with one's way of thinking, it is not surprising that for Philo the term φρόνημα often has cognitive associations, including in ways associated with the sort of intellectual thought elsewhere addressed by Paul. Thus, for Philo φρόνημα ideally contemplates matters beyond heaven rather than lowly ones.[15] It can be divine, viewing matters from a divine perspective and desiring nothing earthly.[16] It can be subject to or avoid pleasure.[17] Ideally, it should think not only of its own locale but with wise knowledge about the cosmos.[18]

Paul certainly includes cognitive associations, because he clearly associates the meaning of this noun with the cognate verb φρονέω, which occurs in Romans 8:5. Yet Paul means even more than exclusively "disposition," "character," "attitude," or "frame of mind," because he uses the same language in relation to the mind of the Spirit[19] (see 8:27), an idea discussed more fully in "Sharing the Divine Mind in Greek Thought," later in this chapter.[20] That is, for Paul, the new way of thinking is empowered by God's own activity.

The mind-frame of the Spirit thus not only contemplates God and shares God's agendas; it depends on God, recognizing the liberation accomplished in Christ (Rom. 8:2) and the consequent power to live a new way (8:3). This is the perspective that Paul has been communicating in previous chapters: believers are righted by Christ, not themselves (cf. 3:21–5:11), and this righting includes a new life in union with Christ (5:12–6:11). Just as Paul depends on Christ for being righted, he depends on God's Spirit for being able to appropriate the cognitive moral character consonant with one who is righted. One who behaves by the new identity is thus walking by the Spirit. For Paul, the new frame for thinking is effective because it depends on the reality of Christ and thus of the new identity in him.

Relation to the Defeated Mind of Romans 7

The fleshly frame of mind and the Spirit frame of mind provide two opposing ways of experiencing reality. As Charles Talbert puts it, the fleshly frame of mind is "an orientation to life in which absolutizing some part of the physical, finite

15. Philo *Drunkenness* 128.
16. Philo *Dreams* 1.140.
17. It can be subject to pleasure (Philo *Heir* 269); not favoring pleasure (in contrast to soft women, *Dreams* 2.9); or masculine and thus avoiding passion (*Jos.* 79).
18. Philo *Dreams* 1.39.
19. For a sense resembling "mind," cf., e.g., Jos. *Ant.* 2.40 (perhaps 2.229).
20. See pp. 128–30.

order is the defining characteristic"; by contrast, Spirit cognition involves "an orientation in which God is one's ultimate concern and one's enabling power."[21]

The contrast between the two ways of thinking in Romans 8:5–9 cannot correspond, as some have suggested, to the internal struggle depicted in 7:15–25; rather, that passage, in which the law-informed mind cannot overcome the fleshly desire for sin, corresponds only to the fleshly mind in 8:5–9. The person of 7:14–25 recognizes the goodness of the law (7:16) but proves unable to fulfill it—like the fleshly mind in 8:7: "The fleshly frame of mind is inherent enmity against God, for it does not subject itself to God's law, nor is it capable of doing so."

The law is fulfilled not in those who depend on the flesh—that is, on themselves—but rather in those who depend on the Spirit (8:3–4). In 7:25 the caricature serves God's law with his "mind" (νοῦς) yet nevertheless fails because of the sin-law active in his members (7:23, 25). In Romans 8 it is this sin-law and its consequent verdict of failure from which the law of the Spirit liberates us (8:2), enabling us to fulfill the law's purpose (8:4). Likewise, the figure of 7:24 is enslaved to a body destined for death, a characteristic of the fallen person of 7:7–25 (7:9–10, 13). By contrast, the frame of mind influenced by the Spirit promises life and peace instead (8:6; cf. 8:2, 13).

As noted above, the fleshly frame of mind in 8:5 summarizes the frame of mind depicted in 7:15–25.[22] Some ancient hearers might also have brought to Paul's language some more general considerations about negative ways of thinking, which they often associated with being ruled by the body's desires. As already noted, Gentile intellectuals sometimes warned against pleasure ruling the mind or soul[23] and sometimes warned against the false ethical views of the ignorant masses.[24] By discipline of the mind, some argued, wise people could learn to abstain from any pleasure, to endure any pain.[25] Later Platonists even wanted to dissociate the mind from the contemplation of matter,[26] though the Stoic thinkers dominant in Paul's day would not have concurred.[27]

21. Talbert, *Romans*, 204–5. Cf. also the citation of Aug. *Spir. Lett.* 19, in Talbert, *Romans*, 209: "Law was given that grace might be sought, grace was given that the law might be fulfilled." Cf. Jesus's contrast between thinking about divine matters and merely human ones in Mark 8:33.

22. Clem. Alex. *Instr.* 6.36 (in Bray, *Romans*, 207) applies the fleshly mind to those still being converted; Origen *Comm. Rom.* on 8:5 (*CER* 3:298; Bray, *Romans*, 207), to Jews under the law (an opinion that would be relevant for most modern perspectives on Rom. 7:7–25).

23. E.g., Max. Tyre *Or.* 33.3. See above, p. 20.

24. E.g., Mus. Ruf. frg. 41, p. 136.22, 24–26.

25. Sen. Y. *Dial.* 4.12.4–5.

26. Iambl. *Soul* 8.39, §385 (on Plotinus and most Platonists).

27. They regarded even mind and soul as material entities; see Arius Did. 2.7.5b7, p. 20.28–30. Contrast Philo and possibly Middle Platonism in Robertson, "Mind."

Although not using Paul's precise terminology, Philo and probably other Hellenistic Jews could have understood a reference to a mind directed toward the flesh. In contrast to the sort of wisdom found in the law of Moses, Philo opines, a different mind loves the body and passions.[28] Philo speaks of a mind that loves the body and would have been perishable if God had not inspired it with the spirit of life.[29] Philo divides humanity into two races: those who live by the divine Spirit and reason, and those who live for the pleasure of the flesh.[30] As noted in the previous chapter,[31] many Judean teachers treated passion for pleasure as functionally roughly equivalent to the evil *yēṣer*.[32] For Paul, this fleshly mind is a mind fixed on earthly, mortal, selfish matters as opposed to the exalted Lord (Phil. 3:19–21)—an autonomous mind that does not acknowledge Jesus as rightful Lord.

Nevertheless, however much Paul's ideas may have connected with Diaspora thought, his specific language, contrasting the spheres of human flesh with God's Spirit, is plainly Judean.[33] It reflects first the Septuagint use of σάρξ (especially in Gen. 6:3, where σάρξ is contrasted with God's Spirit) and more broadly early Jewish usage, including usage of the equivalent Hebrew term, such as is also reflected in the Dead Sea Scrolls.[34] In Judean tradition "flesh" was not by itself evil, but its mortality and finiteness deprived it of moral perfection, making it susceptible to sin.[35]

For Paul, then, the "way of thinking involving the flesh" is a chronic perspective or disposition from mere human, bodily existence as opposed to a life perspective and disposition informed and led by God's presence.[36] Those whose ultimate interests are purely temporal, satisfying their own desires, contrast with those with interest in and divinely provided access to the eternal God.

---

28. Philo *Unchangeable* 110–11 (in 111, φιλοσώματος καὶ φιλοπαθὴς νοῦς). Philo also condemns the body-loving mind in *Abr.* 103; and the passion-loving mind in *Agr.* 83; *Migr.* 62.

29. Philo *Alleg. Interp.* 1.32–33. For the contrast between Philo's heavenly, rational man of Gen. 1 and the earthly man of Gen. 2–3, see my brief discussion below, pp. 192–93.

30. Philo *Heir* 57 (σαρκὸς ἡδονῇ).

31. See pp. 80, 86–88.

32. See, e.g., Davies, *Paul*, 26. Cf. fuller discussion in Moreno García, *Sabiduría del Espíritu.*

33. See, e.g., Davies, *Paul*, 18; Flusser, *Judaism*, 64–65; Frey, "Antithese."

34. Frey, "Antithese"; Flusser, *Judaism*, 64–65; cf. Pryke, "Spirit and Flesh," 358.

35. E.g., 1QHᵃ 7.25; 12.30; 15.40; 1QS 11.9, 12; *T. Jud.* 19:4; *T. Zeb.* 9:7. Cf. Wilcox, "Dualism," 94–95. In Paul, see, e.g., Dunn, *Romans*, 1:370; Dunn, *Theology*, 67–73.

36. Johannine theology also emphasizes God's presence with believers through the Spirit, recognized by faith (see esp. John 14:16–26; 16:13–15; comment in Keener, *Gift*, 27–30; for exegetical details, see Keener, *John*, 932–79, 1035–43, esp. 972–78, 1041–42).

Contrast with the Law-Approach of Romans 7

In Romans as in Galatians, the "flesh" offers an inadequate response to God's righteous standard in the law (Rom. 7:5, 14, 25; 8:3–4, 7; cf. 2:28; 3:20; Gal. 2:16; 3:3, 5; 5:16–19; 6:12–13). The law is good, but flesh is weak (Rom. 7:14); as N. T. Wright puts it, "the material on which" the law "had to work was inadequate" for generating true righteousness.[37] God condemned sin in the flesh by having his Son undergo sin's appropriate condemnation as a sin offering, so that those who walk by the Spirit could fulfill the demands of the law[38] never truly met by those who walk by the flesh (8:3–4).[39] If "walking" evokes here the biblical and Jewish idiom of walking according to the law,[40] the mention of "walking by the flesh" might recall human inability to serve God's law (7:5, 14, 18, 25), an inability explicit in 8:3.[41]

In contrast to the flesh's inability to achieve the ideal of the law, the Spirit empowers true righteousness, providing an internal rather than external law (Rom. 8:2, 4; cf. 7:6; Gal. 3:2, 5; 5:18, 23). The mind of the Spirit, then, is a mind led by righteousness such as appears embodied in the principles of the law (cf. Rom. 8:2), providing obedience (Ezek. 36:27; cf. Deut. 5:29; 30:6) and perhaps also fulfilling the ideal of continuous meditation on, and hence continuous experience of, God's true law (Deut. 6:6; Josh. 1:8; Pss. 1:2; 119:15, 23, 48, 78, 148). This mind directed by the Spirit is presumably at least part of

37. Quoting Wright, *Faithfulness*, 1:507, regarding Rom. 8:3.

38. Some argue for a particular command here, such as not coveting (Rom. 7:7; Ziesler, "Requirement") or the law of love (13:8–10; Gal. 5:14; Sandt, "Research"); others argue instead for the principles of the law as a whole (Dunn, *Romans*, 1:423).

39. Cf. Chrys. *Hom. Rom.* 13 on Rom. 8:1 (in Bray, *Romans*, 200). The issue here probably goes beyond being merely forensic; see Schreiner, *Romans*, 404–5. Against a merely forensic approach (despite Paul's other forensic language), Paul goes on to specify those who walk by the Spirit (Rom. 8:4), involving the law of the Spirit of life (8:2), and to speak of the mind of the Spirit that, in contrast to the mind of the flesh, can submit to God's law (8:5–7, esp. 8:7).

40. See Paul's usage in the context of Gal. 5:16 (and cf. Acts 21:21; 1 John 2:3–6), though he usually employs the phrase for behavior more generally. The language of "walking" evokes the Semitic idiom for behavior (e.g., 2 Kings 21:21; 22:2; 2 Chron. 6:27; 34:2; Ps. 143:8; Prov. 2:20; 10:9; 1QS 4.11–12; 1QH[a] 7.31; 12.22, 25; *1 En.* 82:4; *4 Ezra* 7:122; Tob. 1:3; 4:5) and might evoke the idea of walking according to God's law, as in, e.g., Exod. 18:20; Lev. 26:3; Deut. 5:33; 8:6; 13:5; 26:17; 28:9; 30:16; 1 Kings 2:3; 3:14; Ps. 119:1; Isa. 2:3; *Jub.* 21:2; 25:10; *1 En.* 91:19; 94:1; 1QS 2.2; 3.9, 18; 4.6; 5.10; 9.8–9, 19; 1QSb 3.24; CD 2.15–16; 7.4–7; 4Q524 frgs. 6–13.1; 4Q390 frg. 1.3; 11QT 54.17; 59.16; Bar. 1:18; 2:10; 4:13; Wis. 6:4 (though it may not yet usually be legal; cf. Green, "Halakhah"); and in later halakah (cf., e.g., Hultgren, *Romans*, 248, 300, and his sources). Writing in Greek, the LXX translators and Josephus tend to avoid the idiom, although Gentiles could use walking for meditation (O'Sullivan, "Walking"; O'Sullivan, "Mind") or perambulatory lectures (Sen. Y. *Ep. Lucil.* 108.3; Eunapius *Lives* 481; esp. Aristotle's school, cf. Lucian *Dem.* 54); cf. perhaps Arius Did. 2.7.5c, p. 28.8; 2.7.5g, p. 32.5; 2.7.11e, p. 68.14.

41. Cf., e.g., Hunter, *Gospel according to Paul*, 18; Schlatter (*Romans*, 180) emphasizes the bodily aspect.

what it means to be "led by the Spirit" (8:14; cf. Gal. 5:16–23).[42] It is a mind genuinely directed toward and empowered by God.

Paul does not imply that only the one who continually and infallibly follows the will of the Spirit is justified, and that everyone who has ever been distracted by fleshly desire is condemned. People of the Spirit and people of the flesh are ideal types (see the discussion below). Paul is saying instead that those who have the Spirit, and thus may follow the Spirit at all, have been justified even if they require more training and progress, whereas those who lack the Spirit have only the flesh to depend on.

Living according to righteousness that exceeds mere animal instincts—in other words, supernaturally—thus also demonstrates that God has justified Jesus's followers and (cf. Rom. 3:26) that God was righteous/just in declaring them righteous. God is vindicated, or shown just,[43] if someone can really overcome sin at all by God's Spirit. Christ has done this, and those in union with him also may do it enough to vindicate his righteousness (even if not perfectly). *Any* signs of divine righteousness vindicate the truth of the gospel by demonstrating divinely generated activity; as in Romans 3:3–4, human failures, conversely, do not indict this righteousness. Perhaps often only God knows what believers would be like without his righteousness, but Paul expects that at least often it should be evident that God's work in them goes far beyond what mere effort or conditioning would produce.

Two Ways of Thinking

Scholars have frequently explored the dominant biblical and Jewish motifs of Paul's description of flesh and Spirit,[44] which certainly inform how we should understand Paul's contrast between the "frame of mind of the flesh" (φρόνημα τῆς σαρκός) and the "frame of mind of the Spirit" (φρόνημα τοῦ πνεύματος).[45] Although this Jewish understanding contributes most to our understanding of the passage, I want to explore briefly how an audience

42. Cf. Neh. 2:12; 7:5; Wis. 9:11. A philosopher could speak of being led by God by being of one mind with him (consenting to his will; Epict. *Diatr.* 2.16.42), but Paul describes the Spirit in more active terms than Stoic resignation.

43. For the concern for vindicating God's justice, see, e.g., Rom. 3:3–8; 9:6, 14, 19. Later rabbis similarly expected the righteous members of various groups to vindicate God's justice when he judges unrepentant members of such groups, such as Gentiles (*Lev. Rab.* 2:9; *Pesiq. Rab.* 35:3; cf. Matt. 12:38–42) or the poor and the rich (*Abot R. Nat.* 6 A; 12, §30 B; *b. Yoma* 35b; *3 En.* 4:3).

44. E.g., Flusser, *Judaism*, 62–65.

45. On this sense of φρόνημα, see BDAG. I generally translate it differently below to avoid an awkward double genitive construction in English. In any case, it suggests not every individual thought but a settled way of thinking, a pervasive conviction or direction of thought.

familiar with the sort of language represented in Greek and Roman philosophy would have heard Paul's argument here.[46] This exploration may make available additional nuances for understanding how members of a probably mixed real Diaspora community would have heard Paul's words, as well as surfacing some aspects of his message often overlooked.[47]

Greek and Roman philosophers contrasted two ways of thinking, wisdom and folly, as ideal types (see discussion below). Although they would not have adopted the biblical language of "flesh" (σάρξ) and (God's) "Spirit," some associated folly with bodily passions and true wisdom with transformation that comes from meditating on God. Some elements of Paul's argument (such as the importance of right thinking or of depending on a divine rather than merely personal, human perspective) would have been more intelligible to them than were other elements (such as radical dependence on the one God through Jesus Christ).

The Emphasis on Wise Thinking in Philosophy

Philosophers emphasized the importance of reason. Thus, for example, reason was the element within a human that embraced philosophy;[48] philosophy claimed to offer reason as the cure for the human discontent with nature.[49] In fact, for Stoics (the most popular philosophic school in Greece and Rome in Paul's era) the virtues were themselves types of knowledge.[50] Any ignorance produced defects with regard to virtue. True prudence involved the recognition that the only true good that one could control was virtue, and the only true evil was vice.[51] Thinking rightly also involved not fearing fortune but remaining joyful in hardship, thus controlling the

---

46. Popular philosophy affected popular discourse; we should not presuppose that all Roman Christians were highly educated, despite the sophisticated level of Paul's argumentation (cf. Rom. 15:14). Paul was well educated, but his language coincides at points with popular philosophy that required no particular training in a philosophic school.

47. Most scholars, in fact, recognize that Paul's audience in Rome was predominantly Gentile (cf. Rom. 1:5–6, 13–16; 11:13); see, e.g., Nanos, *Mystery*, 77–84; Dunn, *Romans*, 1:xlv, liii; Tobin, *Rhetoric*, 37; Matera, *Romans*, 7; Jewett, *Romans*, 70. Moreover, Hellenistic anthropology deeply impacted Jewish sources, not only those widely acknowledged as hellenized (e.g., *Let. Aris.* 236; Jos. *Ag. Ap.* 2.203) but even sources normally reflecting a more traditional Semitic perspective (*1 En.* 102:5; *Sipre Deut.* 306.28.2; see discussion below, pp. 274–75). For some dualistic language in Paul, see also, e.g., Vogel, "Reflexions"; Pelser, "Antropologie."

48. Mus. Ruf. 16, p. 106.3–6, 12–16.

49. Lutz, *Musonius*, here 28 (citing Mus. Ruf. frg. 36).

50. Arius Did. 2.7.5b5, p. 18.15–17.

51. Lutz, *Musonius*, 28.

one matter over which one held power, namely, oneself.[52] Stoics felt that falsehood perverted the mind and that this distortion produced the harmful emotions.[53]

Φρόνησις, a cognate to Paul's term in Romans 8:6–7,[54] was one of the four traditional Aristotelian virtues, by Paul's era widely used beyond Aristotelian circles;[55] the term and its cognates often describe the sound thinking appreciated by Stoics[56] and others.[57] For Stoics, this virtue involved right and virtuous thinking.[58] The real heart of philosophy, a Stoic might contend, lies in thinking on (φρονεῖν) the things that are necessary and contemplating them.[59] Perhaps relevant for Paul's comments about the perspective of the flesh involving death (Rom. 8:6) is that for Stoics, thinking (φρονεῖν) the right way included overcoming the fear of death.[60]

Jewish sources composed in the Greek language, especially sources already particularly influenced by Greek intellectual thought, also speak of purifying the mind from evil desires,[61] sometimes by meditating on what is right.[62] Some of these sources speak of meditating on wisdom[63] or on what is good.[64] The Alexandrian Jewish *Letter of Aristeas* concludes by praising its dedicatee for spending most of his time on study that is helpful for the mind.[65] Philo regards

---

52. Sen. Y. *Nat. Q.* 3.pref.11–15; Epict. *Diatr.* 2.19.32; cf. Sen. Y. *Ep. Lucil.* 96.1–2; 123.3; *Dial.* 1.3.1; Mus. Ruf. 17, p. 108.37–38; Epict. *Diatr.* 2.5.4; 2.14.7–8; for a later Platonist, Porph. *Marc.* 30.470–76. For Stoic unconcern with matters not under one's control, see, e.g., Sen. Y. *Dial.* 7.8.3; Epict. *Diatr.* 1.12.23; 1.29.22–29; 4.1.133; Lucian *Phil. Sale* 21; but they did recognize some externals as good (Arius Did. 2.7.5e, p. 30.5–6).

53. Diog. Laert. 7.1.110.

54. This cognate of φρόνημα should not be confused with it, but their semantic ranges overlap significantly (see BDAG).

55. E.g., Mus. Ruf. 4, p. 44.11–12; 4, p. 48.1; 6, p. 52.21; 9, p. 74.26; 17, p. 108.9–10; Arius Did. 2.7.5b1, p. 12.13–22; 2.7.5b2, p. 14.1–4; 2.7.5b5, p. 18.21–35; Men. Rhet. 1.3, 361.14–15; 2.5, 397.22–23; cf. Arius Did. 2.7.5a, pp. 10–11.7–9; 2.7.5b, pp. 10–11.16–21. For rulers and governors, Dio Chrys. *Or.* 3.7, 58; Men. Rhet. 2.1–2, 373.7–8; 2.3, 380.1–3; 2.3, 385.28–386.6; 2.10, 415.24–26; for cities, Dio Chrys. *Or.* 32.37; perhaps even in Josephus's retelling of biblical narratives (Feldman, "Jehu").

56. E.g., Arius Did. 2.7.5f, p. 30.22, 33.

57. The virtue was praiseworthy in cities (Men. Rhet. 1.3, 364.10–16) and rulers (Men. Rhet. 2.1–2, 376.13–23; 2.3, 385.28–386.6; 2.10, 415.26–416.1). See also Aubenque, "Prudence."

58. Arius Did. 2.7.5b1, p. 12.13–16, 22–25; 2.7.5b2, p. 14.4–5, 12–14; 2.7.5b5, p. 18.21–26; 2.7.11e, p. 68.12–16; 2.7.11i, p. 78.12–14.

59. Mus. Ruf. 16, p. 106.16. For focusing thoughts on the nature of the universe, hence accepting necessity, see also Mus. Ruf. frg. 42, p. 138.9–11.

60. Mus. Ruf. 3, p. 42.3. I discuss this perspective further below, p. 136.

61. *T. Reub.* 4:8. Evil enters through the mind (e.g., *T. Iss.* 4:4).

62. *T. Ash.* 1:7–9.

63. Wis. 6:15; 8:17.

64. *Let. Aris.* 236 (cf. 212).

65. *Let. Aris.* 322. Later Gentile intellectuals also spoke of philosophy, literature, arts, and so forth as better concerns for the soul than interest in Aphrodite's ways (Men. Rhet. 2.3, 385.24–28).

as imperishable in humans only their intellect.[66] Just as Stoics emphasized the need to agree with nature's decrees, many Jews emphasized that right thinking recognized God's rule over human affairs.[67]

Ideal Types

Some felt that character was inborn and therefore not readily changed.[68] Others, including many Stoics, felt that training could adjust one's nature.[69] In either case, descriptions dividing humanity into two antithetical categories normally functioned as ideal types and were not meant to take into account a range of mixtures between good and bad.

Two Categories in Humanity as Ideal Types

In terms of literary form, Paul's contrasts here are not unusual.[70] Ancient auditors understood that the rhetoric of absolutes often involved ideal types rather than perfect virtue or vice.[71] As noted below, this structured way of articulating matters fit, and therefore was comprehensible in, both Gentile and Jewish rhetoric.[72]

Traditional Stoics divided humanity into two categories: the wise, virtuous, and otherwise perfect (an extremely small minority); and the foolish and vice-ridden (the masses of humanity).[73] "There is nothing in-between virtue

66. Philo *Unchangeable* 46.

67. *Let. Aris.* 244; cf. Jos. *Ant.* 18.18; *T. Iss.* 4:3. Jewish sources can also tend to emphasize God's sovereignty over the mind (*Let. Aris.* 227, 237–38, 243).

68. E.g., Pindar *Ol.* 11.19–20; 13.12; Quint. *Decl.* 268.6; perhaps Max. Tyre *Or.* 8.7.

69. E.g., Arius Did. 2.7.11m, p. 86.24–28. For acquired vices, see Iambl. *Pyth. Life* 31.205.

70. *Pace* Watson, *Gentiles*, 51–54, 88, 92, 95, 97, we need not envision an especially sectarian context for Paul's contrasts (cf. Segal, *Convert*, 65–66, suggesting conversion as a sociological background for the contrasts), though such an explanation has also been suggested for Qumran (cf. Duhaime, "Dualisme"). Greek dialectic had argued antithetically, using dialectic, since at least Protagoras in the fifth century BCE (Diog. Laert. 9.8.51). For the use of dialectic and antithetical contrasts in rhetoric, see, e.g., Hermog. *Inv.* 4.2.173–76; *Method* 15.431–32; *Rhet. Alex.* 26, 1435b.25–39; Dion. Hal. *Lysias* 14; Anderson, *Glossary*, 21–22; Rowe, "Style," 142.

71. Modern Western thinkers, for whom language often should quantify matters precisely, may struggle with such language until they recognize that it was a familiar rhetorical approach.

72. Although I find Engberg-Pedersen's insights very helpful with regard to Stoicism here, critics are correct to note that some of these insights would apply to many other settings as well (cf. Wright, *Faithfulness*, 1394–95).

73. See Arius Did. 2.7.11g, p. 72.5–24; cf. 2.7.5b8, p. 22.5–14; 2.7.5b10, p. 24.5–17; 2.7.5b12, p. 24.28–30; 2.7.5c, p. 28.3–16. Thus, the good person is as good as Jupiter (Sen. Y. *Ep. Lucil.* 73.12–16).

and vice," they argued.[74] Virtues were inseparable; whoever had one had all[75] (and thus, whoever had virtue could simply act accordingly).[76] There were no degrees of virtue or vice—though this simply meant that all virtue was by definition completely virtue, and all vice was completely vice, not that some virtues and vices were not more beneficial or harmful than others.[77]

At least by this period, however, Stoics, may have often employed these categories as ideal types.[78] The wise man was an ideal, a definition, so that tautologically he was completely virtuous;[79] everything he did, he therefore did well.[80] Thus, for example, he was inerrant, trusting only what was true and never believing unsubstantiated opinion.[81] Likewise, he was complete, having every virtue;[82] the worthless person, by contrast, lacked every virtue.[83]

Stoics might recognize that in practice mental transformation took time,[84] and they often spoke of "progress" in virtue.[85] The Stoic philosopher Seneca, for example, acknowledges that his own progress in virtue is not yet adequate.[86] He speaks of "the ideal wise man," who is ruled by nothing,[87] yet he admits

74. Arius Did. 2.7.5b8, p. 22.5 (trans. Pomeroy, 23).

75. Arius Did. 2.7.5b5, p. 18.17–20; 2.7.5b7, p. 20.25–26. Most ancient philosophic schools agreed that virtue was a settled disposition rather than partial (Engberg-Pedersen, "Vices," 611–13; Engberg-Pedersen, *Paul and Stoics*, 52; cf. Max. Tyre *Or.* 8.7).

76. Diog. Laert. 7.1.125 (reporting the Stoic view).

77. Arius Did. 2.7.11L, p. 85.34–37; p. 87.1–4, 13–20; 2.7.11o, p. 96.22–29; 2.7.11p, p. 96.30–34.

78. For one nuanced portrait, see Engberg-Pedersen, "Vices," 612–13 (on three types of person). For Stoic depictions of the ideal sage as hyperbolic, see also Liu, "Nature," 248.

79. E.g., Arius Did. 2.7.5b8, p. 22.11–14.

80. Arius Did. 2.7.5b10, p. 24.5–6 (just as an ideal flute- or lyre-player plays the flute or lyre well, by definition, 24.6–9); 2.7.11i, p. 78.12; 2.7.11k, p. 84.15–16. By contrast, "the worthless person does everything he does badly" (2.7.5b10, p. 24.15–17 [trans. Pomeroy, 25]; 2.7.11i, p. 78.15–16; 2.7.11k, p. 80.26–31; p. 82.5–18; p. 84.15, 17).

81. Arius Did. 2.7.11m, p. 94.19–35; p. 96.2–14; 2.7.11s, p. 98.34–36; p. 100.1–3. Likewise, a wise person cannot get drunk (2.7.11m, p. 88.34–39).

82. Arius Did. 2.7.11g, p. 70.1–3.

83. Arius Did. 2.7.11g, p. 70.31–33.

84. E.g., Epict. *Diatr.* 1.15.6–8. For continuing memories of the former life, see Engberg-Pedersen, *Paul and Stoics*, 72–73.

85. See, e.g., Cic. *Fin.* 4.24.67; Sen. Y. *Ep. Lucil.* 87.5; 94.50; Epict. *Diatr.* 1.4.1; 2.17.39–40; *Encheir.* 12–13; 51.2; Lucian *Hermot.* 63; Marc. Aur. 1.17.4; Diog. Laert. 7.1.25; Arius Did. 2.7.7b, p. 44.26; Plut. *Progr. Virt.* (protesting the Stoic approach); cf. Motto, "Progress"; Deming, "Indifferent Things," 390; Malherbe, *Moral Exhortation*, 43; Meeks, *Moral World*, 50; Engberg-Pedersen, *Paul and Stoics*, 71. For non-Stoics on progress, see, e.g., Philod. *Death* 17.37–38; 18.10–11; they emphasized progress toward virtue even more than did Stoics (Stowers, "Resemble," 91).

86. Sen. Y. *Ep. Lucil.* 87.4–5. So rare was the ideal sage that Seneca thought one appeared only every half millennium (*Ep. Lucil.* 42.1; Meeks, *Moral World*, 50; cf. Brouwer, *Sage*, 106, 110). Galen (*Grief* 71) questions whether a full passionless (ἀπαθής) wise man exists, recognizing that some extremities could disturb him (72a).

87. Sen. Y. *Dial.* 7.11.1 (trans. Basore, LCL, 2:125).

his own imperfection.[88] Another first-century Stoic, Musonius Rufus, similarly concedes that though we philosophically trained people know better, we still fear loss, and we love temporal things by habit, so we must continue to train ourselves.[89] Even the early Stoic Chrysippus does not consider himself, his associates, or his teachers to be wise.[90] The Stoic ideal may have existed only in theory, but it remained an ideal toward which Stoics would strive;[91] one could be wise enough to be making progress toward the ideal type of perfect wisdom.[92]

Other thinkers sometimes ridiculed this Stoic way of speaking.[93] Lucian points out that Stoic sages themselves do not claim to have achieved this ideal wisdom.[94] Critics opine that since Stoics allow progress toward virtue, they are wrong to deny the possibility of degrees of vice and virtue.[95] Nevertheless, many ancient thinkers did not mind some paradox as a device for communicating a point.[96]

Persian dualism also contrasted good and evil as pure types.[97] In ordinary speech Greeks and others also contrasted good people with shameless ones.[98] In a practical way, writers also could contrast ideal categories, such as wisdom or virtue and pleasure.[99] Allowing for more shades of commitment, Aristotle contrasts the fully virtuous person with the person whose

88. "It is of virtue, not of myself, that I am speaking, and my quarrel is against all vices, especially against my own" (Sen. Y. *Dial.* 7.18.1; trans. Basore, LCL, 2:145). In a different culture, cf. similarly the ideals of Confucius (*Anal.* 91 [14.13]), who humbly acknowledges that he has not yet attained particular virtues (*Anal.* 71 [14.30]; 178 [7.16]).

89. Mus. Ruf. 6, p. 54.35–37; p. 56.1–7.

90. Erskine, *Stoa*, 74, citing esp. Plut. *Stoic Cont.* 1048e (*SVF* 3.668); secondarily Sext. Emp. (*SVF* 3.657), Plut. *Comm. Conc.* 1076bc.

91. Klauck, *Context*, 376; Erskine, *Stoa*, 74; Engberg-Pedersen, *Paul and Stoics*, 61–62.

92. See Engberg-Pedersen, *Paul and Stoics*, 70–72.

93. Cf. Meeks, *Moral World*, 45, citing Plut. *Progr. Virt*, *Mor.* 76B.

94. Lucian *Hermot.* 76–77. Some Greco-Roman thinkers also argued for degrees of virtue and vice, against the Stoic ideal types (Cic. *Fin.* 4.24.66–68); later Platonists averred that the philosopher could be virtuous and wise by nature yet still need guidance in that direction (Plot. *Enn.* 1.3.3).

95. Cic. *Fin.* 4.24.67.

96. For the usefulness of paradox in ancient rhetoric, see Anderson, *Glossary*, 88. For the paradoxical tension between sinless expectation and actual sinning outside Paul, cf. 1 John 1:8–10; 2:1; 3:6, 9.

97. Conzelmann, *Theology*, 14, suggesting this dualism as an influence on early Jewish and Christian dualism (many have suggested influence on the Dead Sea Scrolls; see Fritsch, *Community*, 73). Against this, Gordon (*Civilizations*, 190) suggests dualism even in Canaanite thought, though adducing mostly divine warrior imagery. Some dualism may even appear in Thracian cults (Bianchi, *Essays*, 151–56). For clear Zoroastrian dualism, see Yamauchi, *Persia*, 438–40.

98. Aeschines *Tim.* 31; Max. Tyre *Or.* 8.7.

99. Max. Tyre *Or.* 33.2. Suggestions of dualism in Plato could be developed further by his later auditors (Nock, "Gnosticism," 266–67, citing *Pol.* 269E).

allegiance is divided between reason and desire.[100] Euripides, speaking of extremes, notes, "Those who are without self-control, and in whom the evil of enmity and injustice overflows, are evil, while those in whom the opposites prevail are imbued with virtue"; but Euripides also recognizes explicitly that others are mixed.[101]

Jewish Ideal Types

Jewish sources could also divide humanity into ideal categories, without assuming that individuals behaved perfectly righteously or absolutely wickedly. The biblical wisdom tradition also divided humanity into wise and foolish, again to some extent as ideal types.[102] Sirach, for example, explains that "good is the opposite of evil, and life the opposite of death; so the sinner is the opposite of the godly."[103] The *Testaments of the Twelve Patriarchs* also include such contrasts: "God has granted two ways to the sons of men, two mind-sets, two lines of action, two models, and two goals. Accordingly, everything is in pairs, the one over against the other. The two ways are good and evil; concerning them are two dispositions within our breasts that choose between them."[104] The image of or choice between the Two Ways appears in both Gentile and Jewish sources,[105] and some scholars appeal to its relevance to Paul's portrayal here.[106]

A moral division between righteous and wicked, those with knowledge of God and those who lack it, pervades the Dead Sea Scrolls as well,[107] in which

100. Engberg-Pedersen, *Paul and Stoics*, 52, citing Arist. *N.E.* 1.13.17, 1102b26–28; 6.13.2, 1144b16; 7.8.4, 1151a11–20.

101. Eurip. frg. 954 (trans. Collard and Cropp, LCL, 8:549).

102. Thus, the author of a wisdom psalm praises the wholly righteous (Ps. 119:1–3) and then pleads to be among them (119:5). For the righteous and the wicked, see, e.g., Ps. 1:5; Prov. 10:3, 6–7, 11, 16, 20, 24–25, 28, 30, 32; 4Q511 frg. 63, col. 3.4. For the wise and the foolish, see, e.g., Prov. 10:1, 14; 13:20; 14:1, 3, 24; 4Q301 frg. 2a.1; 4Q548 frg. 1ii 2.12. Ancient Egyptian wisdom tradition had a similar contrast, albeit on somewhat different social grounds (Morris, *Judgment*, 13). For dualism in wisdom and apocalyptic sources, see, e.g., Gammie, "Dualism."

103. Sir. 33:14 (NRSV); see also 33:15.

104. *T. Ash.* 1:3–5 (*OTP* 1:816–17); for the contrasting impulses, see discussion in chap. 3.

105. E.g., Sen. Y. *Ep. Lucil.* 8.3; 27.4; Dio Chrys. *Or.* 1.68–81; Diogenes *Ep.* 30, to Hicetas; Max. Tyre *Or.* 14.1–2; Deut. 30:15; Ps. 1:1; *m. Ab.* 2:9; *T. Ash.* 1:3, 5; Matt. 7:13–14; *Did.* 1.1–6.2; *Barn.* 18.1–21.9; Keener, *Matthew*, 250; other sources in Aune, *Dictionary of Rhetoric*, 478.

106. Talbert, *Romans*, 203.

107. E.g., 1QM 1.1, 11; 13.16; 1Q34bis frg. 3, col. 1.5; 4Q473 frg. 1. Dunn, *Romans*, 1:425, also compares 1QS 3.13–23 (noting parallels to Paul's contrasts in 1QS 3.18, 20–21; 4.6–18), noting that even there "the covenanters themselves belong to *both* groups (1QS 4.23–25 . . .)." Cf. both moral (Flusser, *Judaism*, 25–28; Driver, *Scrolls*, 550–62) and eschatological (see Jeremias,

God's Spirit purifies the righteous remnant community.[108] Yet although the Qumran covenanters apparently did believe that all behavior originated with either the spirit of truth or the spirit of perversity,[109] they acknowledged that only God could justify them fully.[110] Like the Stoics, the community that produced the scrolls also recognized their own imperfection; here the righteous could be called "perfect" in some sense, yet they could recognize their weakness before God.[111] Later rabbis warned against violating the least commandment[112] yet acknowledged that nearly everyone sins.[113]

Paul himself has just divided humanity into those who are in Adam and those who are in Christ (Rom. 5:12–21), but Paul himself recognizes that those in Christ still need to be exhorted not to sin (6:1, 11–13, 15–16; 8:12–13). When Paul contrasts the corporate identities of those born into Adam and those baptized into Christ, the difference is not that the latter group has become incapable of sin. Rather, the difference is that the latter group, now in Christ, is capable of living out God's true (divinely given) righteousness, to the extent that they recognize their identity with Christ, in whom sinfulness was not expected (6:11).

Thus, when Paul divides humanity into those with the character of the flesh and those with the character of the Spirit, he must be addressing ideal types rather than differentiating levels of commitment within those types.[114] All those who have the Spirit are people of the Spirit (Rom. 8:9); all others belong in the sphere of helpless, mortal humanity—that is, in the flesh (or, as many commentators put it, in the sphere of the old Adam). That is, the actual division is based not on the degree of accommodation to the "flesh"

"Significance") dualism in the Scrolls; eschatology and God's sovereignty limit the Scrolls' cosmic dualism (1QS 4.17–20); also cf. the contrast between the two spirits in 1QS 4.2–14 (Duhaime, "Voies").

108. See, e.g., 1QS 3.7; 4.21; 4Q255 frg. 2.1; cf. Chevallier, *Ancien Testament*, 56–57; Keener, *Spirit*, 8–10; Keener, *Acts*, 1:532–34; Coppens, "Don," 211–12, 222.

109. See esp. 1QS 3.19. A portion of both wisdom and truth inhabited everyone, albeit in different measures (1QS 4.24). In context it might be debated whether this was to stop after joining the community, but it seems more likely that the *Manual of Discipline* expects it to cease after the eschaton.

110. E.g., 1QS 11.10–17; 1QHᵃ 5.33–34; 12.30–38; 4Q264 frg. 1.1; cf. 1QHᵃ 11.21–26.

111. For their "perfection" or completeness by some standard, see, e.g., 1QS 4.22; 8.25; 10.22; 1QM 14.7; 4Q403 frg. 1, col. 1.22; 4Q404 frg. 2.3; 4Q405 frg. 3, col. 2.13; frg. 13.6; 4Q491 frgs. 8–10, col. 1.5; 1QHᵃ 8.35; 9.38; but contrast 1QHᵃ 12.30–31; 17.13; 22.33.

112. E.g., *Abot R. Nat.* 35, §77 B; *Sipre Deut.* 48.1.3.

113. Moore, *Judaism*, 1:467–68; Flusser, *Judaism*, 62.

114. Dunn, *Romans*, 1:425; Dunn, *Theology*, 478, favors ideal types yet argues against dividing humanity in a binary way, which is essentially what ideal types do. Still, no one fully met the types in practice, which may be close to Dunn's point.

but on whether or not the Spirit is active and bringing transformation.[115] The Spirit effects true righteousness; ideally, this Spirit-activity produces perfect character, but ancient hearers could recognize that in practice this ideal might not obviate the value of progress.

Sharing God's Mind

Paul contrasts the fleshly mind with the mind of the Spirit. Since this biblical and early Jewish contrast refers to God's Spirit, Paul is speaking of divine empowerment, and in a way that most of his audience likely understood.

Given potential ancient analogies, Paul probably means more than metaphor when he speaks about "the mind of Christ" (1 Cor. 2:16), thinking the way that Jesus did (Phil. 2:5), thinking according to the Spirit (Rom. 8:5), and the like.[116] Besides Romans 8:6, the one other place in his letters where Paul speaks of τὸ φρόνημα τοῦ πνεύματος is later in the same discussion, at 8:27, where the phrase refers to the mind of God's Spirit. God knows the mind of the Spirit, who dwells in believers and intercedes in God's way.[117]

Thus, he speaks of not merely a frame of mind that accords with God's but one that is inspired or activated by God. For Paul, this is part of the promised eschatological outpouring of God's Spirit.[118] Paul may also believe in an inward prompting (if Rom. 8:14 suggests this)[119] and an affective

115. Cf. Chrys. *Hom. Gen.* 22.10 (trans. Bray, *Romans*, 211): "*You are not in the flesh* not because you are not clad in flesh but because in spite of being clad in flesh you rise above the thinking of the flesh." This does not mean that one cannot marginalize the Spirit to a dangerous extent; apostasy remains possible (Lambrecht, "Exhortation"; cf. Rom. 8:13).

116. For the related experience of Christ and of the Spirit, see, e.g., Keck, *Romans*, 200; Toit, "In Christ." That Jesus can at times assume for Paul the divine role played by deity in philosophers seems clear even in the context of Rom. 8, e.g., with the "Spirit of Christ" (8:9; see Turner, "Spirit of Christ," esp. 436; Fee, "Christology and Pneumatology," esp. 331; Hamilton, *Spirit and Eschatology*, 28–29) and possibly the sending of the Son (8:3; see discussions in Adinolfi, "L'invio"; Wanamaker, "Agent"; Byrne, "Pre-existence"; elsewhere, cf. Howell, "Interchange").

117. Whether or not all of Paul's Roman audience would have understood him on their first hearing of 8:6, they would quickly hear 8:27, and both Phoebe and Paul's former colleagues in Rome could probably explain his usage to them (cf. esp. Rom. 16:1–5, 7). Like literary criticism's ideal reader (with Johnson, *Romans*, 19–20), ancient readers and auditors often heard a passage in light of the entire work, which they would read or hear multiple times (Quint. *Inst.* 10.1.20–21; Sen. Y. *Ep. Lucil.* 108.24–25; Hermog. *Method* 13.428; Philost. *Hrk.* 11.5).

118. E.g., Joel 2:28–29; esp. Ezek. 36:27 with Jer. 31:33. Cf. 1QS 4.21 with Ezek. 36:25–27.

119. Ancient hearers could understand a divine intuition or voice that could supplement the more ordinary divine gift of wisdom; see Apul. *De deo Socr.* 162–66. Cf. Neh. 7:5.

assurance of relationship with God from the Spirit (8:16),[120] but he also expects God's Spirit to help shape the *thinking* of those who are in Christ, as in 8:5–7.[121] This perspective becomes obvious again in 1 Corinthians 2:16, where believers who have the Spirit also experience some of the mind (νοῦς) of Christ.[122]

Sharing the Divine Mind in Greek Thought

Paul's reasoning comes from Scripture, but his language would also have resonated with educated Gentiles. Indeed, some might have overcontextualized his language, as if he were speaking of the mind's divinity.[123] Although some thinkers spoke of mortal minds that did not know what was good the way the gods did,[124] others spoke of the mind's divinity or ability to achieve some divinity. A fragment from the fifth-century BCE tragedian Euripides suggests that the individual mind was a god.[125] Gentile thinkers often associated the mind with what was divine.[126] Some claimed that of all human benefits, reason alone shared in the nature of the divine.[127]

120. Paul distinguishes the human spirit, apparently an affective element of the human personality, from the rational element in 1 Cor. 14:14–15 (in the context of 14:13–16, Paul refers to prayer in tongues with one's spirit and interpretation through the understanding, both inspired, in light of 12:7–11, by the same Spirit); cf. Marc. Aur. 12.3; Ridderbos, *Paul: Outline*, 121.

121. Cf. Edwards, "Light," 139 (delivered in 1733 and influenced by Locke's psychology): "The Spirit of God . . . may indeed act upon the mind of a natural man, but he acts in the mind of a saint as an indwelling vital principle. . . . [H]e unites himself with the mind of a saint, takes him for his temple, actuates and influences him as a new supernatural principle of life and action . . . exerting his own nature in the exercise of their faculties." This was not revealing new doctrine, Edwards warns (in opposition to certain movements of his day, probably including contemporary elements of the Quakers); instead, the Spirit provided a sense of God's holiness, moved the saint's reason toward truth, and generated understanding and faith. Cf. here also McClymond and McDermott, *Theology of Edwards*, 416–17, 420–21; for Edwards, the affections holistically include intellect and will, as well as emotions (312–13). Cf. Calvin, *Commentary on Galatians* 2:20, in Bray, *Galatians, Ephesians*, 80–81; esp. Rudolf Gwalther, *Sermons on Galatians*, on Gal. 3:5 (ibid., 94).

122. Paul cites "the mind of the Lord" from Isa. 40:13 LXX, but the context of Paul's own argument (1 Cor. 2:11–12) suggests that he is aware of the Hebrew reading in Isaiah, namely, "the Spirit of the Lord."

123. See discussion on pp. 196, 201–6.

124. Val. Max. 7.2.ext.1a.

125. Eurip. frg. 1018. Collard and Cropp (LCL, 8:577n1) suggest another possible interpretation but note that we (and probably many ancient interpreters) lack the saying's context.

126. Sen. Y. *Ep. Lucil.* 124.23; Porph. *Marc.* 11.191–93; 26.409–10; cf. Mus. Ruf. 17, p. 108.8–22.

127. Ael. Arist. *Def. Or.* 409–10, §139D. Deliberation was the most divine part of human matters (*Rhet. Alex.* pref. 1420b.20–21).

For a Stoic, the ideal was to be of "one mind" with God and hence to accept reason and the will of fate;[128] a person who had progressed this far had become virtually divine, though such a person was difficult to find.[129] One can approach God only rationally, Stoics opine, because God is pure Intelligence.[130] The first-century Stoic Seneca opines that the human soul is divine;[131] God is superior in that he is *completely* reason or soul, without admixture with other elements.[132]

Such interests were widespread among Greco-Roman intellectuals. A friend of Zeus, one orator decides, would think like Zeus, by which the orator means desiring what is virtuous rather than what is shameful.[133] A much earlier orator advises hearers to "cultivate the thoughts of an immortal."[134] The Stoic philosopher Epictetus urges being "of one mind" with God.[135] For Seneca, this could include contemplating questions about what God does with the universe, thereby transcending one's "own mortality."[136] Later Platonic thinkers suggest that "the god-filled intellect . . . is united to God, for like must gravitate to like."[137] Further, only the mind knows the divine law, which is stamped on it.[138] Through virtue, one should make one's "thought like God."[139] The mind should obey God because like a mirror it reflects his image.[140] For Philo, a Jewish Middle Platonist, intelligence represents a divine element in humanity (though mortals are not thereby

128. See Mus. Ruf. frg. 38, p. 136.4–5 (Lutz's translation captures the sense, although Musonius here says simply τῷ θεῷ); Epict. *Diatr.* 2.16.42 (ὁμογνωμονῶ); 2.19.26–27 (where it corresponds to seeking to become divine). On thinking like Zeus, cf. Dio Chrys. *Or.* 4.42–43. One should follow the wisdom of the gods and be "of one mind" (ὁμογνώμονας) with them (Libanius *Thesis* 1.3).

129. Epict. *Diatr.* 2.19.26–27.

130. Epict. *Diatr.* 2.8.2.

131. Sen. Y. *Ep. Lucil.* 41.4–5 (trans. Gummere, LCL, 1:274–75): Souls that disregard this world's troubles or pleasures are divine, stirred from heaven (*caelestio potentia agitat*). Cf. the divine law stamped on the soul in Porph. *Marc.* 26.419–20.

132. Sen. Y. *Nat. Q.* 1.pref.14.

133. Dio Chrys. *Or.* 4.43. For Zeus as "the supreme Mind," see Max. Tyre *Or.* 4.8.

134. Isoc. *Demon.* 32 (trans. Norlin, LCL, 1:23, 25), though also advising contemplating mortality in the right ways.

135. Epict. *Diatr.* 2.16.42; 2.19.26–27.

136. Sen. Y. *Nat. Q.* 1.pref.17 (trans. Corcoran, LCL, 1:13).

137. Porph. *Marc.* 19.314–16 (trans. O'Brien Wicker, 63). Line 314 reads ἔνθεον φρόνημα, probably suggesting inspiration. In 19.318–19 he urges that the mind (νοῦς) be a temple (νεώς—Attic for ναός) for God, possibly playing on words; cf. 11.191–93, 196–98.

138. Porph. *Marc.* 26.409–10.

139. Porph. *Marc.* 16.265–67 (trans. O'Brien Wicker, 59). On Platonists desiring to be like God, see Nock, *Christianity*, 55.

140. Porph. *Marc.* 13.233–34 (in turn, the soul should obey the mind, and the body the soul; 13.234–35).

identified with God).[141] One's disposition could be divine and focused on divine matters.[142]

Not only did one need to think like God and think about him; a few thinkers also recognized the need to depend on God for this power. One could learn philosophy, but mere recitation of information was not enough. Only divine indwelling, Seneca recognizes, can make one good: "God is near you, he is with you, he is within you. This is what I mean, Lucilius: a holy spirit indwells within us,[143] one who marks our good and bad deeds, and is our guardian. As we treat this spirit, so are we treated by it. Indeed, no man can be good, without the help of God."[144] God comes into people, and no mind that lacks his presence is good.[145]

Thus, for Platonists one experienced the divine mind through meditating on God's perfection, and Stoics accepted the divine mind by embracing fate. By contrast, for Paul, as we have mentioned, the Spirit internalizes God's law (Rom. 8:2–4), as the prophets have promised.[146] The new mind exists by virtue of being in Christ, and one accesses the divine mind through the experience of the Spirit. Like Philo,[147] Paul would have rejected any notion of reaching God by pure reason apart from revelation. Like Philo and some other Diaspora Jews, however, he may have allowed for divine inspiration of reason at times.[148]

Indwelling Deity in Gentile and Jewish Thought

Despite some exceptions, Jewish monotheists generally were much more careful than Gentiles about depicting themselves as divine;[149] their reverence for the one God precluded it. Being moved by divine agency, however, was

141. E.g., Philo *Alleg. Interp.* 2.10, 23; *Unchangeable* 46–48.

142. Philo *Dreams* 1.140.

143. Lat.: *sacer intra nos spiritus sedet.*

144. Sen. Y. *Ep. Lucil.* 41.1–2 (trans. Gummere, 1:273). Some others also recognized the need for God to help virtue prevail in mortals' souls (Max. Tyre *Or.* 38.6). In Porph. *Marc.* 12.207 God is "responsible for all the good that we do," whereas (12.208) we are responsible for our evils.

145. Sen. Y. *Ep. Lucil.* 73.16.

146. In light of 2 Cor. 3:3, 6 (cf. Rom. 7:6), a midrashic combination of Ezek. 36:26–27 and Jer. 31:31–34 informs Paul's understanding (cf., e.g., Bruce, *Apostle*, 199; Dunn, *Romans*, 1:417). The LXX of Jer. 31:33 (ET) has the law in the διάνοια (mind, understanding) and καρδία (also including cognitive elements) as well as "knowing" (both γινώσκω and οἶδα) God in 31:34 (ET; 38:33–34 LXX).

147. Philo *Abr.* 80; cf. Isaacs, *Spirit*, 50; Dillon, "Transcendence in Philo"; Hagner, "Vision," 89–90.

148. Cf. 1 Cor. 2:16; 12:8. For a case for this idea in *Letter of Aristeas*, see Scott, "Revelation." Cf. perhaps Ign. *Trall.* 4.1: "φρονῶ ἐν θεῷ."

149. See again discussion on pp. 201–6.

far less questionable, since it was supported in Scripture itself.[150] Both Jews and Gentiles entertained notions of deity dwelling with or in people. Gentile references to deities dwelling in or affecting mortals' minds are not, of course, as relevant to Paul's discussion as Jewish sources concerning the Spirit of the one true God, but they illustrate that Paul's imagery need not have been unfamiliar or unintelligible to even some of the less biblically literate members of his real audience.

Although in Scripture Gentiles might sometimes recognize that the divine Spirit was in Israelite servants of God (Gen. 41:38; Dan. 4:9, 18; 5:14), the more common Hebrew idiom noted the Spirit coming "on" someone, especially for a divine task.[151] Sometimes the expressions could be equivalent, at least for someone who would bear the Spirit long-term and not simply temporarily (Num. 27:18; Deut. 34:9). Eschatologically, God would put his Spirit within his people to transform them (Ezek. 36:27) and on them to empower them (Joel 2:28–29). Probably partly for theological reasons, Paul more often speaks of the Spirit working in and among God's people (e.g., 1 Cor. 3:16; Gal. 6:8).

How could Gentiles and Diaspora Jews have understood Paul's language about God's or Christ's Spirit dwelling in believers? Some writers claim that Socrates had a god within him.[152] Plutarch stresses that the divine νόμος should always dwell within the good ruler.[153] A Neoplatonist poses an alternative in which either the divine or an evil demon dwells in the soul.[154] Denying that a person is ever alone, Epictetus speaks of the presence of the deity in all people: "God is within, and your own genius [δαίμων] is within."[155] Likewise, "you are a fragment of God; you have within you a part of Him. Why, then, are you ignorant of your own kinship?"[156] The Roman Stoic Seneca similarly insists that God comes into people (*in homines venit*), divine seeds being sown (*semina . . . dispersa*) in them.[157] Such language was not pervasive, but it was intelligible.

150. See the discussion in Keener, *Acts*, 1:532–37; for the biblical background, see, e.g., Keener, "Spirit," 485–87.
151. See fuller discussion in Keener, *Acts*, 2:1810.
152. Apul. *De deo Socr.* 157.
153. Plut. *Uned. R.* 3, *Mor.* 780CD. This reference could easily be figurative.
154. Porph. *Marc.* 21.333–36; cf. 19.321–22; 21.331–32, 336–39 (ἐνοικέω); cf. demons in the souls as the cause of wickedness in 11.201–2.
155. Epict. *Diatr.* 1.14.13–14 (trans. Oldfather, LCL, 1:104–5); cf. *Diatr.* 2.8.14; Marc. Aur. 2.13, 17; 3.5–6; 3.12; 3.16.2; 5.10.2. These passages probably also involve the mind's divinity.
156. Epict. *Diatr.* 2.8.10–11 (trans. Oldfather, LCL, 1:260–61). One could beseech Mithras to "dwell" in one's ψυχή (*PGM* 4.709–10), an entreaty that might have erotic overtones (so Betz, *Magical Papyri*, 52) or might even reflect Christian influence.
157. Sen. Y. *Ep. Lucil.* 73.16 (after arguing that good people are divine, 73.12–16). In a different vein Ovid (*Fast.* 6.5–6) claims that a god is in mortals, leaving them seeds (*semina*) of inspiration; cf. divinizing intimacy and union in Iambl. *Pyth. Life* 33.240.

Following the Old Testament, Jewish people sometimes referred to God or his Spirit dwelling in or among his people. In the Wisdom of Solomon, Wisdom enters into holy souls to make them both friends of God and prophets.[158] In Pseudo-Philo, "a holy spirit" (*spiritus sanctus*) not only "came upon" but also "dwelled in him," inspiring prophecy.[159] The *Testaments of the Twelve Patriarchs* speaks similarly. Thus, Joseph had the Spirit of God in him and therefore did good (cf. Gen. 41:38).[160] In the eschatological time God will dwell in (or with) any compassionate person he finds.[161] God's people must avoid sin so "that the Lord may dwell among you,"[162] and "the Lord will dwell among" those who do right.[163] Philo too offers some analogies for helping us grasp how Paul's Diaspora audiences may have understood him speaking about God indwelling those devoted to him.[164]

Paul's idea does not depend on Greek thought: his mention of both the law and God's Spirit more directly echoes the biblical prophets, according to whom it was ultimately God's Spirit that would enable God's people to serve him fully (Ezek. 36:25–27).[165] Paul also limits this divine activity to participants in God's covenant (Rom. 8:9), and they remain fully human, though agents of the divine. But some of Paul's thought would nevertheless have been intelligible in a Gentile milieu.

Experiencing the Spirit

As is widely acknowledged, the Spirit is a central element in Paul's theology;[166] for Paul, the gift of the Spirit is the defining mark of believers.[167] Although the academic or anthropological approach commonly found in Gentile philosophy overlaps with Paul's concerns at various points, it cannot parallel Pauline thought fully. For Paul, divine initiative itself, rather than some

158. Wis. 7:27; see also 1:4, 8:9, 16; 10:16.
159. *L.A.B.* 28:6 (*OTP* 2:341; Latin in Kisch, p. 195).
160. *T. Sim.* 4:4.
161. *T. Zeb.* 8:2.
162. *T. Dan* 5:1 (*OTP* 1:809; Greek in Charles, *Testaments*, 136: κατοικήσει ἐν ὑμῖν).
163. *T. Jos.* 10:2 (*OTP* 1:821; Charles, *Testaments*, 196: κατοικήσει ἐν ὑμῖν).
164. Cf. Sellin, "Hintergründe." See, e.g., Philo *Cher.* 98, 100; *Dreams* 1.149; *Mos.* 1.277. Philo speaks elsewhere of the body as the soul's dwelling place.
165. Davies, *Paul*, 341, cites *Yalqut* on Gen. 49 for the righteous doing everything in the Holy Spirit; this language appears rare in rabbinic sources, but in the Dead Sea Scrolls God's Spirit purifies a person (1QS 3.6–9; 3.25–4.5; 4.21; 1QH^a 8.30; cf. 4Q444 frgs. 1–4i + 5.3–4). The idea that God enables one to perform good appears more widely; see, e.g., *Jub.* 1:19; *Let. Aris.* 243, 252, 274, 276, 278, 282, 287, 290.
166. With, e.g., Fee, *Presence*; Schreiber, "Erfahrungen"; Stegman, "Holy"; Jervis, "Spirit."
167. Dunn, "Gospel," 148–51; Dunn, *Romans*, 1:429–30; Matera, *Romans*, 208–9.

innate divinity accessible simply by human reason, activates divine reality in one's life.

Whereas one may try to embrace a new identity cognitively, one experiences this reality by the Spirit. Responding to the Spirit includes cognitive embrace, but the embrace must acknowledge the divine initiative rather than fail to recognize and express gratitude, as did those who abandoned the knowledge of God in Romans 1:18–32.

The Spirit adds a subjective, relational element that the human mind and will, empowered by the Spirit, may serve but not control. Although in Romans 6 Paul speaks of walking in newness of life (an aorist subjunctive in 6:4, the meaning of which is debated),[168] he speaks more of believers' identification with Christ in terms of Christ's past death and resurrection and their past baptism. That is, this aspect of his argument may be approached objectively.

Although Christ's death and resurrection have been completed, God's Spirit applies this reality to believers in the present. God's Spirit appears here as continuing to act, so that believers' experience of the Spirit remains present. The Spirit continues to activate the new and continuing life in Christ (cf. Rom. 7:6; 8:2, 10) and will someday transform believers' bodies (8:11, 23) as God through the Spirit raised Jesus (1:4). The Spirit presently and continually dwells in believers (8:9, 11), empowering believers to actualize the death of sin (8:13), leading God's children (8:14), and instilling confidence that we are in fact God's children (8:15–16). The Spirit inspires believers' experience of relationship with God as Father (8:15), interceding within us on our behalf (8:26).

The subjective or relational dimension of the Spirit's activity is evident in many of the Spirit's works. The Spirit, for example, distributes gifts among believers (1 Cor. 12:7–11) and produces moral fruit within them (Gal. 5:22–23). That is, the Spirit is more than a doctrine to confess or to abstractly explain God's activity; the Spirit is active in believers' lives. The Spirit attests and communicates the message of the cross (1 Cor. 2:4); without the Spirit the message will not be understood (2:10–15).[169] Nevertheless, the full activity of the Spirit is not automatic: believers might forget that the Spirit dwells among them (1 Cor. 3:16) and in them (6:19) or has righted them (6:11). This

---

168. Despite the parallel with what may be the future resurrection in Rom. 6:5, the aorist subjunctive in 6:4 probably invites present behavior; possibly contrary to traditional understandings of tense forms here, compare the present subjunctive of ἐπιμένωμεν with the aorist subjunctive for πλεονάσῃ in 6:1 and perhaps the aorist indicative with the future indicative in 6:2.

169. Likewise, only some hearers would genuinely recognize the inspired message of the gospel as truly God's message (1 Thess. 2:13; cf. Mark 4:15–20).

neglect does not stop the Spirit from dwelling in believers, but it may impede a degree of the Spirit's activity.

At the same time, the Spirit does not only work in ways that exclude potential alternative or complementary natural explanations; that is a modern conception popularized in the aftermath of Hume's essay on miracles.[170] A way of thinking pervaded by the Spirit's activity might be indistinguishable from a mind renewed to discern God's will (Rom. 12:2) or a mind that understands the wisdom of the cross (1 Cor. 1:18, 24; 2:15–16). The Spirit touches us in multiple ways and through different aspects of our personality.[171] Paul speaks not only of the Spirit bearing witness with the human spirit that believers are God's children (Rom. 8:16) but also of the Spirit's activity regarding thinking (8:5–7; cf. 12:2). Some Christian individuals and groups may gravitate toward one of these emphases or the other, but we are most complete when we welcome all the Spirit's activities.

Paul's emphasis on God's Spirit in Romans 8 reveals that more than mere academic judgments about a text or theology is needed; genuine faith in (i.e., full recognition of) the real activity of God in one's life enables one to live out the reality Paul describes. Such faith recognizes the present reality of God's activity in one's own life and community. Yet it is not simply a self-improvement technique or a matter of self-discipline; it is God's gift in the sense that it acknowledges and so welcomes the divine initiative in Christ.

The one who trusts in Christ's work for being put right forensically should also trust in Christ's work for being put right behaviorally. Instead of merely trying to control their sinful impulses (though self-control is also a fruit of the Spirit, Gal. 5:23), believers may be conscious that Christ is living through them. In Pauline theology the Spirit of Christ lives in believers (Rom. 8:9–10), Christ lives in them (8:10; Gal. 2:20), and Christ is "our life" (Col. 3:3–4; cf. Phil. 1:21).[172]

Charles Sheldon's late nineteenth-century question, "What would Jesus do?" is an apt one for Pauline theology, but perhaps even more fully, Paul would urge believers to consider "What is Jesus like?" and to confidently expect that same moral character to be expressed in them. Thus, we read about the "fruit" of God's presence in believers by the Spirit (Gal. 5:22–23, 25; cf.

---

170. See Keener, "Reassessment"; Keener, *Miracles*, 83–208, and sources cited there.

171. Note, for example, that both tongues and interpretation of tongues—both praying with one's spirit and praying with one's understanding (1 Cor. 14:13–15)—are gifts inspired by God's Spirit (12:10–11). God's Spirit deals not only with the human spirit but also with the mind, often through wisdom and the like (1 Cor. 2:16). For various aspects of the Spirit's wisdom, cf. also Moreno García, "Sabiduría del bautizado"; Moreno García, "Sabiduría del Espíritu."

172. Cf. perhaps also the "divine life" in Eph. 4:18, depending on the sense of the genitive construction there.

Rom. 15:30; Eph. 5:9; Phil. 1:11), in contrast with the works that express the natural predilections of the flesh (Gal. 5:19–21).[173]

The Frame of Mind of the Spirit Is Peace (Rom. 8:6)[174]

In light of Paul's previous argument in Romans, the general point of his mention of "death" and "life" in 8:6 seems clear enough: whereas sin results in a sentence of death, those who are in Christ receive eternal life. But what does Paul mean by "peace"? Most obviously, he means "peace with God"—reconciliation that ends one's enmity in relation to God (Rom. 5:1, 10–11); this contrasts with the frame of mind hostile toward God in 8:7.[175]

Because of the ancient context in discussions of the mind, I will explore here a potential additional nuance, namely, internal peace, although it appears less explicit than peace with God. When ancient writers spoke of something like "peace" (quietness, lack of disturbance) in connection with the mind, they could refer to inner harmony or tranquility. (The information provided here, especially that from ancient philosophy, will also inform the discussion of Phil. 4:7 in chap. 7.[176] It may be more relevant there than here, but it is treated here because it occurs earlier in the book.) While Paul undoubtedly thinks of more than tranquility (as I suggest below), discussions of internal tranquility among ancient philosophers could suggest that this is part of the sense that Paul and his real audience would hear in this context. At the very least, "peace" certainly ends the internal "warring" of the fleshly mind in Romans 7:23, just as "death" echoes the state of the figure in 7:10, 13, and 24 (and 5:12–21; 6:16, 21, 23; 7:5).[177]

Tranquil Minds in the Philosophers

Given differences in wording, Paul's language of "peace" need not correspond with philosophic ideals of tranquility or of ending the war of passions, but the association merits consideration. Stoics valued tranquility and peace

173. See, e.g., discussion in Keener, *Gift*, 74–82 (esp. 74–77).
174. In most of this section I am adapting Keener, "Perspectives," 222–25.
175. The term ἔχθρα here recalls ἐχθρός in 5:10.
176. See pp. 218–19.
177. Cf. Philo *Alleg. Interp.* 3.117, where war in the soul subjects the mind and disturbs its peace; or 3.130, where eradicating passions brings internal peace; passion brings war to the soul, but God can give peace to the mind (3.187; cf. *Creation* 81; *Good Person* 17; *Spec. Laws* 4.95; *Dreams* 2.250; *Conf.* 43; *Abr.* 26). Wickedness prevents tranquility in the soul (*Alleg. Interp.* 3.160; *Conf.* 46); it disorders the soul (e.g., *Studies* 176; *Mos.* 2.164).

of mind,[178] as did Epicureans[179] and others.[180] For Stoics, following Aristotle, "A virtue is a state (*hexis*) of mind, one that need not always be active but may precisely be activated in the appropriate circumstances."[181] Both Stoics and Epicureans sought tranquility through understanding truth.[182] Not just Stoics but also others warned that ignorance and desire for pleasure caused most mortals to be perturbed in mind.[183]

Various philosophies claimed to provide peace and tranquility;[184] this promise could contrast, as in Romans 8:6, with preoccupation with "death." Epicureans, for example, claimed to establish peace of mind by banishing superstition and fear of death.[185] Many thinkers,[186] including Stoics[187] and Epicureans,[188] claimed that the fear of death was irrational. How bravely a philosopher dies, ancient observers often maintained, is a real test of that philosopher's beliefs and character.[189] A philosopher should remain unafraid when facing dangers.[190]

178. Sen. Y. *Dial.* 4.12.6; 4.13.2; 5.6.1; 9 passim; *Ep. Lucil.* 75.18; Mus. Ruf. frg. 38, p. 136.1–3; Epict. *Diatr.* 1.4.1; Arius Did. 2.7.5b1, p. 12.31–33; 2.7.5k, p. 34.1–4; 2.7.11s, p. 100.7.

179. Lucret. *Nat.* 5.1198–1206; Cic. *Fin.* 1.14.47; Lucian *Alex.* 47; Diog. Laert. 10.131; 10.144.17. Epicurus's chief goal was peace of mind (in the sense of lack of disturbance; Diog. Laert. 10.85; cf. 10.144.17).

180. Iambl. *Pyth. Life* 2.10; cf. Cic. *Amic.* 22.84; Hossenfelder, "Ataraxia."

181. Engberg-Pedersen, *Paul and Stoics*, 51, citing Arist. *N.E.* 2.5.

182. See Bett, "Emotions," 212, who notes that Skeptics sought the opposite, recognizing that such absolute truth did not exist.

183. Dio Chrys. *Or.* 13.13.

184. On the importance of peace of mind (ἀταραξία) in philosophy, see Hossenfelder, "Ataraxia."

185. Cic. *Fin.* 1.18.60; Lucian *Alex.* 47; for lack of disturbance in the mind, see Lucret. *Nat.* 5.1203; Diog. Laert. 10.144.17. Epicureans advised temperance as a means for achieving this objective (Cic. *Fin.* 1.14.47).

186. E.g., Cic. *Leg.* 1.23.60; Diogenes *Ep.* 28; Max. Tyre *Or.* 11.11; 36.2; Iambl. *Pyth. Life* 32.228. Cf. Val. Max. 9.13.pref.; 9.13.3; Plut. *Poetry* 14, *Mor.* 37A; Sir. 40:2, 5; Heb. 2:14–15; *Mart. Pol.* passim.

187. Sen. Y. *Ep. Lucil.* 80.6; 82 passim; 98.10; *Nat. Q.* 1.pref.4; 2.58.3; 6.32.12; *Dial.* 9.11.4–5; Mus. Ruf. 1, p. 34.31–33; 3, pp. 40.35–42.1; 3, p. 42.3; 4, p. 48.5–6; 17, p. 110.1, 12–13; Epict. *Diatr.* 1.17.25; 2.1.13; 2.18.30; Marc. Aur. 9.3; 12.35; cf. 8.58. But even philosophers could admit to struggling with this fear (Mus. Ruf. 6, pp. 54.35–56.7, esp. 56.2).

188. Perhaps *especially* Epicureans; see, e.g., Lucret. *Nat.* passim (esp. 1.102–26; 3.1–30, 87–93; cf. O'Keefe, "Lucretius"; Warren, "Lucretius"); Cic. *Fin.* 1.18.60; 4.5.11; *Nat. d.* 1.20.56; Diog. Laert. 10.125.

189. E.g., Cic. *Fin.* 2.30.96–98; cf. tested bravery in Sen. Y. *Ep. Lucil.* 66.50. For failure in this regard exposing a false philosopher, see Lucian *Peregr.* 42–44.

190. Mus. Ruf. 8, p. 66.10; cf. Iambl. *Pyth. Life* 32.224–25. On philosophers against fear, see, further, Val. Max. 3.3.ext.1; Sen. Y. *Ben.* 4.27.1; *Ep. Lucil.* 13; 98.6; Dio Chrys. *Or.* 1.13; 3.34; Crates *Ep.* 7; Arius Did. 2.7.5a, p. 10.11; 2.7.5b, p. 12.6; 2.7.5b1, p. 12.27–29; 2.7.5c, p. 28.14–15; Philost. *Vit. Apoll.* 1.23.

Consequently, one sign of true philosophers in general was to be their tranquility even in hardship.[191] Granted, philosophers often fell short of this standard;[192] yet they did not believe that this failing negated the value of their ideal. Many averred that uncontrolled negative emotions were harmful[193] and that philosophy was instrumental in conquering useless emotions.[194] Subduing the passions brought calmness of soul, without the "mental excitement" that stirred anger, wrong desire, and so forth.[195] Paul's approach to suffering is different here (Rom. 8:17–18, 35–39), but it is possible that he could have accepted a contrast between tranquility and anxiety about death if some of his first audience understood him this way (cf. 1 Cor. 15:58; 2 Cor. 4:13–14; 5:6–8; Phil. 1:20–21; 1 Thess. 4:13).

Stoics in particular emphasized tranquility and lack of internal disturbance;[196] the ideal wise person was tranquil.[197] For Seneca, the reward for disciplining the mind for endurance was tranquility of the soul;[198] this was the opposite of such disturbing passions as anger.[199] Truth liberates from error and fear and hence provides tranquility in the soul.[200] The mind should be as tranquil and restful as the highest heavens.[201] Another Roman Stoic, Musonius Rufus, emphasizes that the correct use of reason can lead to serenity and freedom.[202] One achieves serenity by gaining the object of the only desire one can be certain to gain by seeking it exclusively—namely, virtue[203]—or by wishing for no more than what actually happens.[204]

191. E.g., Sen. Y. *Nat. Q.* 6.32.4; Epict. *Diatr.* 2.19; Iambl. *Pyth. Life* 2.10; 32.220; Philost. *Vit. Apoll.* 1.23; cf. further Stowers, "Resemble," 93; Keener, *Acts*, 4:3627–29. Other factors, like friendship, could bring the soul tranquility (Cic. *Amic.* 22.84).

192. Mus. Ruf. 6, pp. 54.35–56.7 (esp. 56.2); Aul. Gel. 19.1.4–21; Diog. Laert. 2.71 (on Aristippus).

193. E.g., Cic. *Off.* 1.38.136; Diog. Laert. 7.1.110; Iambl. *Pyth. Life* 32.225. To restrain passions was part of virtue (Cic. *Off.* 2.5.18).

194. E.g., Val. Max. 3.3.ext.1.

195. Cic. *Off.* 1.29.102; 1.38.136.

196. Arius Did. 2.7.5k, pp. 34–45.1–3; at length, Sen. Y. *Dial.* 9. A virtuous soul was in harmony with itself, lacking contradictory impulses (Arius Did. 2.7.5b1, p. 12.31–33).

197. Arius Did. 2.7.11s, p. 100.7–10.

198. Sen. Y. *Dial.* 4.12.6. This may be distinguished from simple relaxation, useful as that was (as in Sen. E. *Controv.* 1.pref.15). Seneca the Younger also valued the ability to avoid distraction (Sen. Y. *Ep. Lucil.* 56).

199. Sen. Y. *Dial.* 4.13.2. For such disturbances of the soul, cf., e.g., Dio Chrys. *Or.* 13.13.

200. Sen. Y. *Ep. Lucil.* 75.18. For overcoming fear, see also Epict. *Diatr.* 2.16.11; 2.17.29.

201. Sen. Y. *Dial.* 5.6.1. On the relation of the mind to the heavens, see discussion above. Contrary to a literal reading of the myths, the gods had peace and tranquility, without strife (Proclus *Poet.* 6.1, K87.16–17, 21–22; Libanius *Invect.* 7.2).

202. Mus. Ruf. frg. 38, p. 136.1–3.

203. Epict. *Diatr.* 1.4.1, 3.

204. Epict. *Encheir.* 8.

Diaspora Jews also spoke of "peace," or tranquility in the soul, even during difficult times.[205] More relevant, Philo could contrast peace (εἰρήνη) for the mind with war within a passion-stirred soul.[206] Likewise, the wise person's thinking liberates one from wars and internal turmoil, providing calm and peace (εἰρήνη).[207]

Fear (discussed above) was not only a concern of philosophers. In Romans 8:15 Paul contrasts the reception of the Spirit of adoption as God's children with the former spirit of slavery in fear; certainly, the depiction of inner chaos in 7:15–25 resembles fear much more than peace.[208] In another Pauline letter, divine peace guarding the mind (Phil. 4:7) contrasts with anxiety (4:6).[209]

Possible Exegetical Basis for the Peaceful Mind

While such tranquility may be partly in view here, Paul may also have exegetical reasons for his view and wording, if he has access to an exegetical tradition here that bypasses the Septuagint.[210] Paul would know that in Isaiah 26:3 the mind of *faith* has peace.[211] Paul elsewhere draws on Isaiah to address the new mind (1 Cor. 2:16), and his meditation on Isaiah seems to form a significant substratum for his language elsewhere in his letters, especially Romans.[212] Paul's "life" (Rom. 8:6) could draw on various sources, but one possible source appears in the same context in Isaiah, which Paul would understand as announcing the coming resurrection (Isa. 25:8–9; 26:19), just as "life" in his own literary context involves resurrection (Rom. 8:11).[213]

205. *Let. Aris.* 273. In *T. Sim.* 3:5 the mind is eased when one flees to God and the spirit of envy is driven out. For unmixed peace (cf. James 3:17), see Philo *Flight* 174.

206. Philo *Alleg. Interp.* 3.187.

207. Philo *Dreams* 2.229 (cf. also the mind at rest in 2.228).

208. Also compare the fear of death in some philosophers cited above with Rom. 7:24 and 8:6. The sort of anxiety depicted in Rom. 7 readily feeds on itself, rendering fear compulsive. Paul would not, however, endorse someone making their experience of fear or anxiety as itself an object of anxiety about their condition; his preceding discussion in this letter makes clear that the object and grounding of one's trust is in the objective reality of justification in Christ, not one's subjective emotional state. Cf. in Paul's own letters, e.g., 2 Cor. 7:5; 11:28–29; 1 Thess. 3:5.

209. The peace is undoubtedly partly corporate also in Philippians (see 2:2; 4:2–3; cf. 4:9), but the individual mind must also be partly in view (4:8).

210. Although the LXX has εἰρήνη here, the sense of the LXX is completely different, so any influence must be through the MT (or a Greek version other than what became the majority of readings that we generalize as the LXX text).

211. In the larger context this "peace" also is relational (Isa. 26:12; 27:5), as usually in Paul.

212. On Paul's use of Isaiah, see, e.g., Wagner, *Heralds*; Hays, *Conversion*, 25, 46–49; Oss, "Note"; Haacker, *Theology*, 100. This usage also accords with the prominence of Isaiah among some other "eschatological" interpreters of his era (cf. Fritsch, *Community*, 45).

213. Paul *might* even infer the "Spirit" from Isa. 26:9, but there it is the spirit of the person praying (*my* spirit), paralleled with his soul. More likely, he simply attributes resurrection, and

The Hebrew term usually translated "mind" in Isaiah 26:3 is *yēṣer*;[214] aside from its development in Jewish usage noted in my previous chapter,[215] the term often meant something like "intent" or "plan."[216] The term elsewhere appears relevant to the mind or to the "intent" and "inclination" of one's thoughts;[217] as such, it could apply to something one sets one's thought on, something like Paul's "mind-frame" in Romans 8:5–7.

The term often translated "steadfast" (e.g., NRSV, NASB, NIV), describing the mind, probably occurs in relation to trust (trusting in the Lord appears in the verse's following line).[218] The cognate verb for "trust" here appears elsewhere in Isaiah for putting one's trust in the Lord or others,[219] including in the following verse (Isa. 26:4). The term appears parallel to faith in Psalm 78:22, where Israel in the wilderness did not believe in God or trust his salvation.[220]

The sense is something like, "You will guard/keep/watch over in full peace (prosperity, well-being) the one whose thoughts depend on you, because that person trusts in you." Thus, a mind established by faith, trusting God, secures peace.

The context in Isaiah also supports this reading. The "righteous" nation keeps fidelity, that is, is "faithful" (Isa. 26:2); one should trust the Lord, for

presumably the life of faith, to the Spirit; for the Spirit and resurrection in early Judaism, see Philip, *Pneumatology*, 137–38.

214. Isaiah's text might include a wordplay; two words later the text says, "you will keep" (*tiṣōr*).

215. See pp. 85–90.

216. Usually, in Isaiah the term and its cognates involve pottery or whatever is formed (with God forming, Isa. 29:16; 43:1, 7, 10, 21; 44:2, 21, 24; 45:7, 9, 18; 64:8; humans forming carved images, 44:9–10, 12), but it can also mean what the mind forms (plans, imagination; cf. 22:11; in Isa. 37:26, it could mean what God planned or what he formed).

217. Cf. Gen. 6:5 (cf. LXX); 8:21; Deut. 31:21; 1 Chron. 28:9; 29:18. It is just possible that Rom. 8:26–27 echoes God searching hearts in 1 Chron. 28:9; an echo there of ἀντιλαμβάνομαι from Isa. 26:3, however, is unlikely, since it is not used the same way and the term is common in the LXX. Paul may echo 1 Chron. 29:18 in Phil. 4:7.

218. The same verb for "lean" and the cognate verb for "trust" appear together in Isa. 36:6, which warns against leaning on or trusting in Egypt; the only other place where these verbs appear together is 2 Kings 18:21 (= Isa. 36:6). In Isa. 48:2 people lean (depend) falsely on the Lord, but the dependence is genuine in 26:3.

219. For the term or cognates, see Isa. 12:2; 30:12; 31:1 (misplaced trust in Egypt and their horses, which horses in 31:3 are "flesh and not spirit"); 32:17 (vs. misplaced trust and dwelling securely in 32:9–11); 36:4–9 (the Rabshakeh's challenge: don't trust in Egypt); 36:15 and 37:10 (further challenge: don't trust the Lord); 42:17 (warning not to trust idols); 50:10 (trust the Lord); 59:4 (misplaced trust in confusion). It also communicates security (Isa. 14:30) or false security (Isa. 32:9–11; 47:8, 10). Although the root appears 155 times in the MT, only eight are in the Pentateuch, where they address "security" or (Deut. 28:52) misplaced trust.

220. In the Psalms the term often expresses trust, e.g., Pss. 55:23; 56:3–4, 11. One might also compare Mic. 7:5, where one must not trust one's neighbor or be confident in a friend, in contrast with 7:7: "I will look for the LORD and wait for God of my salvation."

he is trustworthy (26:4), and God the righteous one will be with the "righteous" ones (26:7), who *wait for* him (26:8). God will establish "peace" for them (26:12).[221] In Isaiah 26:3 the mind that leans on God, trusting in him (thus, the mind of faith), is the mind that will have "peace."[222] Why would Paul not simply quote a text so fertile for discussing faith (as he quotes both texts linking faith and righteousness in Rom. 1:17; 4:3; Gal. 3:6, 11)? If he reasons from midrashic exegesis here, he may nevertheless see little value in quoting directly a version of the text that his hearers could not recognize.[223]

Community Tranquility

Given the context about the mind, Paul might intend "peace" to include internal tranquility.[224] Nevertheless, his usage elsewhere suggests that it involves more than this; often Pauline "peace" involves nonhostility, reconciliation, or unity (with God or humans).[225] Indeed, the normal semantic range of the term involves peace with others or wholeness, more than internal tranquility,[226] and Paul's audience would probably envision the relational dimension, especially given the context of this letter and its likely setting of Jewish-Gentile conflict. Peace should be with all (Rom. 12:18), but Paul emphasizes peace with others especially when he addresses differences in the community (14:17, 19; 15:13).

Most important in this context, in contrast to the mind-frame of the Spirit that involves peace, the mind-frame of the flesh involves enmity with God (Rom. 8:7). Indeed, given this context, Paul could even deliberately emphasize objective peace with God over the subjective tranquility sought by

221. Resurrection appears to be promised in Isa. 26:19.
222. The Hebrew repeats "peace" twice (as recognized in the NRSV); this is undoubtedly an idiom (cf. KJV, ASV, NASB, NIV: "perfect peace"). The same construction appears in Isa. 57:19 (where God brings peace to the lowly [57:15; to fallen Israel, 57:16–18] far and near and heals; but no peace for the wicked, 57:21); false prophets say, "Peace, peace," when there is none (Jer. 6:14; 8:11); and warriors bless David with "Peace, peace to you" (1 Chron. 12:18).
223. By contrast, in Rom. 1:17 his audience may at least recognize the quotation without the pronoun, which differs in the standard Greek and Hebrew versions.
224. Such a connection need not exclude moral connotations; in *T. Sim.* 3:5 the mind is eased when God expels the spirit of envy. Similarly, in Iambl. *Letter* 9 (Stob. *Anth.* 2.33.15), ὁμόνοια (9.1) applies to "cities and homes" (9.3; trans. Dillon and Polleichtner, 29) and also to unity with oneself (9.4–5); for one "in two minds toward himself . . . is in conflict with himself" and "at war with himself" (9.7, 10; trans. Dillon and Polleichtner, 29).
225. E.g., with humans, Rom. 3:17; 12:18; 14:19; 1 Cor. 7:15; 14:33; 16:11; 2 Cor. 13:11; with God, Rom. 5:1. Even in the sparsely worded Rom. 15:33, some of the earliest interpreters found the relational emphasis (Theodoret *Interp. Rom.* [PG 82.217]; Pelagius *Comm. Rom.* [PCR 150]; cf. Ambrosiaster *Comm.* [CSEL 81:477]; all in Bray, *Romans*, 367–68). One could argue for the meaning of tranquility in Phil. 4:7, though cf. the issue of unity in Phil. 4:2–3.
226. Even most of the "tranquility" terms used by various writers above involve "quietness" or "lack of disturbance."

philosophers. Given Paul's language of internal warring in 7:23, however, Paul may well mean both senses, and certainly they are not incompatible.

Contemporary analogies suggest that at least many urban hearers would have found Paul's claim of peace with God to be intelligible. For Stoics, any wrong act was impiety against the gods,[227] and those ruled by folly were enemies of the gods,[228] always in disharmony against them.[229] Paul's ideal types or spheres involve the two kinds of humanity with their contrasting statuses before God. Paul's reference to the fleshly mind's inability to submit to God's law (Rom. 8:7) alludes to the mind's failure in 7:23, 25; only the Spirit can inscribe the law in the heart (8:2–4).

Conclusion

Believers should embrace not only the reality of their own new identity in union with Christ but also the reality that Christ and God's own Spirit live inside them. These are greater resources for achieving moral and civic good than the sorts of cognitive resources to which most other thinkers appealed. Still, dependence on divine peace was intelligible to Paul's contemporaries, though not pervasive.

For Paul, the "frame of mind involving the flesh" is the disposition or habitual way of thinking dominated by worldly, purely human concerns. Self-focused on one's personal bodily existence, this mental lifestyle is incapable of fulfilling the righteous purpose of God's law. Even its best efforts yield only the sort of self-consumed struggle depicted in Romans 7:15–24 (especially in 7:22–23, where even the law-informed mind is helpless to defeat bodily passions).

By contrast, the "frame of mind involving the Spirit" is a righteous mental lifestyle in which God's presence by the Spirit makes the decisive difference. This frame of mind involves life and peace, possibly evoking the context of Isaiah 26:3 (though the allusion remains uncertain). "Peace" may partly involve tranquility, an emphasis in some ancient discussions of thinking (also contrasted by some ancient thinkers with fear of death and the restless mind of divided allegiances such as appears in Rom. 7:15–25). Paul's emphasis in the context of Romans itself probably especially also seeks peace in relationships in the wrongly divided Christian community.

227. Arius Did. 2.7.11k, p. 84.4–6.
228. Arius Did. 2.7.11k, p. 84.23–24, 29, 33. Zeno reportedly taught that all bad persons were naturally at enmity with other persons (Engberg-Pedersen, *Paul and Stoics*, 74–75).
229. Arius Did. 2.7.11k, p. 84.27–28.

5

A Renewed Mind
(Rom. 12:1–3)

Don't follow the pattern of this age; instead, be transformed by your mind being made new. This way you'll be qualified to evaluate what is good, pleasing, and perfect—and so recognize God's will.

—Romans 12:2

In Romans 12 Paul revisits the issue of proper thinking.[1] Whereas humanity did not judge it valuable to keep knowing God, and God therefore gave them over to a mentality that failed his own evaluation (1:28), God here renews the minds of those devoted to him so that they can truly evaluate the good things that are his will (12:2).[2]

1. This passage (Rom. 12:1–2) also appears as strategic for the section; many or most scholars view it as the thesis statement for 12:1–15:13 (Crafton, "Vision," 333–35, esp. 335; for a summary of the consensus, see Jewett, *Romans*, 724). Some even view it as one of Paul's two key exhortations in the letter, revealing its joint purpose (Smiga, "Occasion"). Most scholars recognize the importance of cognition here (e.g., Keefer, "Purpose").

2. As noted above on pp. 26–27, Rom. 1:28 plays on cognates of δοκιμάζω: ἐδοκίμασαν and an ἀδόκιμον νοῦν; here the νοῦς is renewed so that it may instead δοκιμάζειν. Cf. 1 Cor. 2:15–16, where (in different words) a person of the Spirit may evaluate all things because she has the mind of Christ.

This chapter surveys elements of Romans 12:1–3 relevant to Paul's interests in the mind there. Paul introduces the matter of reason already when exhorting believers to offer their bodies as spiritual sacrifices for God's work (12:1). Paul develops this theme further when he warns believers not to follow the pattern of the present age, a fallen age in which sinful choices have corrupted moral discernment (12:2; cf. 1:28). Instead, believers are transformed as their minds follow the pattern of a new age; thus, they become able to evaluate what is truly good, so discerning God's will (12:2). The renewal of their minds evokes the divine mind of 11:34. It also enables them to think (12:3) in the wider context of Christ's diversely gifted body (12:4–6).

Ideally, even admonitions ordinarily should be gentle.[3] Παρακαλέω (12:1, translated in the NRSV as "I appeal"; the NIV and NASB as "I urge"; in the KJV and ASV as "I beseech") appears often with requests in letters.[4] It has a wide range of meaning, including not only "strongly urge" or "exhort," as here, but also even "comfort." As such, it served as a much gentler term than terms usually translated "admonish" or "warn."[5]

Paul is surely gentle here, exhorting the Roman believers not as one assuming authority but as one gifted to exhort. "Through the grace given me" (12:3) evokes the grace given to each believer for their varied gifts in 12:6. Most important, "exhort" appears in the list of gifts in 12:6–8 (v. 8). Paul exhorts them as "siblings"[6] and as one whose act of exhortation reflects a God-given ministry shared by some others in Christ's body (12:8).[7]

---

3. Cf. Rom. 15:14; Gal. 6:1; Plut. *Old Men* 22, *Mor.* 795A; 23, *Mor.* 795BC; Iambl. *Pyth. Life* 22.101; 33.231; 1QS 5.25; *b. Sanh.* 101a; cf. even harsher genres in *Rhet. Alex.* 37, 1445b.17–19; *t. Kip.* 4:12.

4. Aune, *Environment*, 188; Stowers, *Letter Writing*, 24, 78.

5. Following categories articulated in later handbooks, protreptic or hortatory correspondence (Stowers, *Letter Writing*, 112–25) did not require the level of harshness found in letters of admonition (125–32) and especially rebuke (133–38) and, most harshly, reproach (139–41). Urgent requests could be worded as entreaties. Thus, e.g., even honorable people could "beg" on behalf of another, as in Cic. *Fam.* 13.14.2; 13.20.1; 13.24.3; 13.26.2; 13.30.2; 13.32.2; 13.35.2; 13.54.1; 13.72.2; 13.74.1; or "I beg of you again and again" (13.28b.2; 13.41.2; 13.43.2; 13.45.1; 13.47.1; 13.73.2; 13.76.2). Cf. a loving exhortation in a nonrecommendation letter: "I implore you again and again, my dear brother, to keep well" (Cic. *Quint. fratr.* 3.1.7.25; trans. W. G. Williams). Longenecker (*Introducing Romans*, 218) similarly cites affectionate or urgent request formulas (*BGU* 846.10; *P.Mich.* 209.9–10). On Paul's gentleness here, see, e.g., Aquinas, lecture 1 on Rom. 12:1, cited in Levy, Krey, and Ryan, *Romans*, 247.

6. Also in Rom. 1:13; 7:1, 4; 8:12; 10:1; 11:25; 15:14, 30; 16:17; also applied to the Jewish people in 9:3. For the range of senses, see Keener, *Acts*, 2:1663–64, with references from ancient sources; here it expresses affection to fellow believers, as often in early Christianity (cf. Rom. 14:10, 13, 15, 21). Paul opens this section of the letter with "two rather standard epistolary conventions . . : a *request formula* . . . and a *vocative of direct address*" (Longenecker, *Introducing Romans*, 422).

7. Elsewhere in Romans, the verb appears only in 15:30; 16:17.

Presenting Bodies as Sacrifices

Believers here not only are priests offering sacrifices (cf. Paul's role in Rom. 15:16 and his doxology in 11:33–36)[8] but are themselves the sacrifices to be offered up.[9] The image of spiritual sacrifices was a familiar one, and the language of "presenting" (12:1) is appropriate for sacrifices,[10] but the verb must also be taken with Paul's earlier usage in the letter. Presenting one's body continues the image of presenting one's members as instruments or weapons for God in 6:13, 19 (cf. 6:16).[11] They are thus to be totally consecrated for God's purposes.[12]

Presenting bodies for good purposes confirms that for Paul, the body is an instrument that can be used for good (Rom. 6:13; cf. 8:11, 23; 1 Cor. 6:13, 15, 19–20; 2 Cor. 4:10; 5:10; Phil. 1:20; 3:21; Col. 2:23) as well as for evil (Rom. 1:24; 6:6; 7:24; 8:10, 13; 1 Cor. 6:16; 2 Cor. 5:10).[13] The body is not itself evil; it is simply that Christ- and Spirit-enlightened minds, rather than morally directionless physical desires (Rom. 1:24; 6:12), should control one's behavior (cf. possibly 1 Cor. 9:27, depending on how far one wants to press Paul's illustration).

Ultimately, the purpose of our body is not to fulfill its autonomous desires but to serve Christ's greater body (Rom. 12:4–6; cf. 7:4), just as the renewed mind (12:2) thinks in terms of the greater body (12:3).

8. Others also connect Rom. 12:1 and 15:16; see, e.g., Dillon, "Priesthood"; cf. 1 Pet. 2:5. In Roman religion, in contrast to Israel's Levitical class, any person of status could be a priest, and cultic practices were open to all; see Rives, *Religion*, 43. Sacrifice was an individual matter; see Judge, *First Christians*, 614. Still, killing of sacrifice was "typically performed by a professional" (Rives, *Religion*, 25).

9. Cf. Aker, "*Charismata*," who also connects the ministries of Rom. 12:6–8 with spiritual temple imagery here. Grieb (*Story*, 117) plausibly suggests that Paul revisits a cultic metaphor (sacrifice, atonement) used in Rom. 3:21–26. For cultic metaphors in Paul, see especially Gupta, *Worship*.

10. On "presenting" with sacrifices, see Jos. *Ant.* 7.382; Sanday and Headlam, *Romans*, 352 (citing Jos. *Ant.* 4.113); Dunn, *Romans*, 709 (citing Moulton and Milligan, *Vocabulary*; and BDAG).

11. The verb παρίστημι connects the texts; its other two uses in Romans bear an unrelated sense. See also other scholars, e.g., Dunn, *Theology*, 58. The aorist infinitive may invite an act of commitment (cf. 2 Cor. 11:2; Col. 1:22; 2 Tim. 2:15), though perhaps as one always appropriate rather than implying a once-for-all moment. This construction need not suggest a once-for-all single event; cf. Combs, "Doctrine." (Jewett [*Romans*, 728–29] reads the aorist here too specifically, for Paul seeking help for his mission to Spain; the aorist imperative of the same verb in Rom. 6:13, 19 has broader ethical connotations.)

12. Cf. the ideal in the Dead Sea Scrolls community, namely, devoting one's resources, bodily strength, and attitudes to God (Betz, *Jesus*, 72, cites 1QS 1.11–13; 5.1–3; 6.19).

13. Because "bodies" is plural here, Jewett (*Romans*, 728) argues that Paul is calling for a communal sacrifice; Paul could have made the argument even more forcefully, however, had the term been singular. When he employs the plural for "bodies" in 1 Cor. 6:15, he refers to individual bodies (see 6:16–18), even though his argument also has corporate implications.

Sacrifices in Antiquity

Sacrifices, including animal sacrifices, characterized ancient religion; most temples required animal sacrifices.[14] Sacrifices appear commonly, for example, on coins[15] and on reliefs.[16] Many Gentiles viewed sacrifice as an exchange with the gods, who were expected to reciprocate with benefits;[17] as a later orator puts it, "Sacrifices elicit the goodwill of the gods."[18]

Some intellectuals did, however, oppose sacrifices.[19] Scholars debate whether Zoroaster opposed them or merely opposed their abuse.[20] Some thinkers opposed sacrifices in principle, though not always in practice.[21] Others were more consistent. Pythagoras and Pythagoreans opposed animal sacrifices (and eating meat);[22] they felt that even the less committed ought to avoid sacrificing (and eating) higher, ensouled animals.[23] Apollonius of Tyana reportedly followed Pythagorean practice on this matter.[24] Some mythographers and later intellectuals believed in a primeval golden era before animal sacrifices.[25]

Some valued thank offerings more highly than danger-averting sin offerings.[26] *True* piety, some aver, would expend less on so many sacrifices and so much frankincense.[27] A classical orator opines that the gods are more

14. On sacrifices, see, e.g., Burkert, *Religion*, 68–70; Smith, *Symposium*, 67–69; Siebert, "Immolatio," 745; most intellectuals practiced sacrifices, e.g., Pliny *Ep*. 9.10.1. Not all sacrifices, of course, were of animals; cf., e.g., Malkin, "Votive Offerings," 1613; earlier, e.g., *ANET* 420.

15. Williams, "Religion," 150–54.

16. Moede, "Reliefs," 165–68, 173–75.

17. Klauck, *Context*, 38. On the principle of reciprocation in ancient Roman ethics, see, e.g., Pliny *Ep*. 6.6.3; Statius *Silv*. 4.9; Libanius *Anec*. 1.20; Symm. *Ep*. 1.104; more fully, Keener, *Acts*, 3:3314n1610.

18. Libanius *Maxim* 3.4 (trans. Gibson, 103). Greeks shrewdly waited to sacrifice sheep until they were shorn and had borne young (Androtion *Atthis* frg. 55).

19. Lucian ridicules the practice in *Sacrifices*. He presents Demonax as opposing sacrifice in Lucian *Dem*. 11. Porph. *Marc*. 19.316–17 denounces the sacrifices of the ignorant.

20. Yamauchi, *Persia*, 448.

21. E.g., Plut. *Stoic Cont*. 6, *Mor*. 1034C. Some regarded even images to be valuable only as reminders of deity (Max. Tyre *Or*. 2.1–2); deities do not need human service (Sen. Y. *Ep. Lucil*. 95.48).

22. Diog. Laert. 8.1.22; Philost. *Vit. Apoll*. 1.1; 6.11; Iambl. *Pyth. Life* 11.54; 24.108. See also Aristotle's student Theophrastus (as cited in Porph. *Abst*. 2.32; so Ferguson, *Backgrounds*, 271).

23. Iambl. *Pyth. Life* 18.85; 28.150. Ethiopia's sages disapprove of animal sacrifice in Heliod. *Eth*. 10.9.

24. Philost. *Ep. Apoll*. 27; *Vit. Apoll*. 1.31–32; 2.38; 4.11; 5.25; 8.7. He preferred Helios worship (*Vit. Apoll*. 2.24, 32, 38, 43; 3.15, 48; 7.10, 31).

25. Ullucci, "Sacrifice."

26. Fronto in *Ep. graec*. 8.3. Cf. sacrifices of praise in Philost. *Vit. Apoll*. 1.1. According to some later Jewish traditions, other offerings will become unnecessary, but the thank offering will remain forever (*Pesiq. Rab Kah*. 9:12).

27. Dio Chrys. *Or*. 13.35.

pleased with goodness and justice than with many sacrifices; such virtue is the best sacrifice.[28]

Figurative or metaphoric sacrifices appear frequently in ancient sources. (For corresponding spiritual *temples*, see 1 Cor. 3:16–17; 6:19; 2 Cor. 6:16; Eph. 2:18–22; 1 Pet. 2:5; Rev. 3:12; cf. John 4:23–24; Rev. 21:2; and esp. 21:22.)[29] Although Stoics participated in public cults, in principle they affirmed that the wise "are the only [genuine] priests; for they have made sacrifices their study, as also the building of temples, purifications, and all the other matters appertaining to the gods."[30]

Similar ideas appear in the *Pythagorean Sentences*: "The wise man alone is a priest, alone is dear to the gods, and alone knows how to pray."[31] Likewise, "Votive gifts and sacrifices do not honor God; offerings are not an honor to God. But the inspired mind which is completely secure meets God, for like must come to like."[32] For Porphyry, a Neoplatonist, the true temple of the divine is the wise man's mind;[33] God is honored not by sacrifices but by a God-filled frame of thinking.[34]

Certainly, the priority of spiritual sacrifices was biblically supportable, already appearing in the Old Testament.[35] In early Jewish circles, praise,[36] alms,[37] and other righteous deeds[38] were sacrifices. Some Jews also opposed animal sacrifices, though perhaps especially to critique pagan ones.[39] Some Diaspora Jews, who had less access to the Jerusalem temple, may have

28. Isoc. *Ad Nic.* 20. Cf. Porph. *Marc.* 17.282–84, 287–88: pious deeds and a disposition resembling the divine matter more than sacrifices.

29. See, e.g., 1QS 8.5; 4Q511 frg. 35.2–3; *Let. Aris.* 234; Philo *Rewards* 123; Tac. *Ann.* 4.38.2 (in Sinclair, "Temples"); Porph. *Marc.* 19.318–19; the universe as a temple in Cic. *Resp.* 6.15.15; cf. Davila, "Macrocosmic Temple"; one's home figuratively as a temple in Hierocles *Marr.* (Stob. *Anth.* 4.79.53); further information in Gärtner, *Temple*; Keener, *Acts*, 1:1033–34; 2:1323, 1417; 3:2639–40, 2643, and esp. 3151–52. My doctoral student Philip Richardson has begun to research this question further.

30. Diog. Laert. 7.1.119 (trans. Hicks, LCL, 2:225). Hierocles *Marr.* (Stob. *Anth.* 4.79.53, p. 83) urged that parents be honored as deities, making their children thus like priests ordained by nature.

31. *Pyth. Sent.* 15 (in Malherbe, *Moral Exhortation*, 110).

32. *Pyth. Sent.* 20 (in Malherbe, *Moral Exhortation*, 111). For the purity of soul as well as body that was required in some sanctuaries, see the sources in Nock, *Christianity*, 18–19.

33. Porph. *Marc.* 11.191–93, 196–98; 19.318–19.

34. Porph. *Marc.* 19.313–16.

35. E.g., Kelly, *Peter*, 91, cites Pss. 50:14; 51:16–19; 69:30–31; 141:2; Hosea 6:6; Mic. 6:6–8; cf. also 1 Sam. 15:22; Isa. 1:11–17; 58:3–7; Amos 5:21–24. Fearing God is better than mere sacrifice (Jdt. 16:16).

36. Ps. 154:10–11 (11QPsᵃ 154); 4Q403 frg. 1, col. 1.39–40.

37. Sir. 3:30; 29:12; 35:4. Cf. also alms in Islam (Mbiti, *Religions*, 330).

38. Sir. 35:1–5.

39. See *Sib. Or.* 4.29–30, possibly from the Hellenistic age.

adopted wider arguments for praise being the only true sacrifice.[40] For Philo, piety,[41] or the mind devoted in love to God,[42] or truth from the soul,[43] was the best sacrifice.[44]

Outsiders differed as to whether Essenes offered their own sacrifices away from the temple[45] or did not sacrifice at all, dedicating their minds in reverence instead.[46] Although the covenanters probably did value literal sacrifices,[47] the Qumran texts also suggest spiritual sacrifices.[48] The sectarians may have believed that their spiritual sacrifices functioned as the true equivalent of temple sacrifices until the expected new temple of the future era.[49]

Already in the Hellenistic era, Aristotle's student Theophrastus apparently knew of the spiritualization of Jewish sacrifices.[50] Such an attitude appears in the *Letter of Aristeas*: "To honor God . . . not by offerings and sacrifices but by purity of spirit."[51] In the Wisdom of Solomon, God accepts martyrs as sacrifices.[52] The idea of spiritual sacrifices was thus by no means merely an accommodation to the temple's destruction.[53] Nevertheless, the idea necessarily became more central after the temple's destruction.[54] Jewish teachers

40. Cf. Philo *Plant.* 126; cf. Knox, *Gentiles*, 32. Philo's interest, however, may be especially in opposing the futile sacrifices of the wicked (*Plant.* 108, 124), since elsewhere he does speak favorably of pious sacrifices. Philo attests that some others allegorize all the laws, a practice of which he disapproves (*Migr.* 89–93; Sanders, *Judaism*, 53).

41. Philo *Mos.* 2.108.

42. Philo *Spec. Laws* 1.201, 271–72, 290; cf. *Alleg. Interp.* 2.56; *Unchangeable* 8.

43. Philo *Worse* 21; cf. *Sacr.* 27; *Dreams* 2.72. The soul of the one who sacrifices must be free from passions (*Spec. Laws* 1.257).

44. See now more fully also Richardson, "Sacrifices," 9–14.

45. So Jos. *Ant.* 18.19; some think that Josephus merely wished to present the Essenes as having a positive attitude toward the temple, which he valued (Nolland, "Misleading Statement"). Some suggest that the animal bones at Qumran, which others attribute to sacrifice, come instead from a communal meal (Laperrousaz, "Dépôts") or merely a rare sacrifice, such as an annual covenant renewal (Duhaime, "Remarques"). There is no clear evidence that the bones found there were used in ritual (Donceel, "Khirbet Qumrân").

46. Philo *Good Person* 75. This may be Philo's idealization. Heger, "Prayer," argues that the idea that prayer replaced sacrifice is a case of reading later rabbis into the Dead Sea Scrolls.

47. See CD 9.14; 11.17–19; 16.13; Davies, "Ideology."

48. 1QS 9.4–5; CD 11.21; Gärtner, *Temple*, 30, 44–46. For offerings of praise, see, e.g., 1QS 10.6.

49. Flusser, *Judaism*, 39–44. Cf. Arnaldich, "Sacerdocio."

50. Stern, *Authors*, 1:8–11.

51. *Let. Aris.* 234 (trans. Hadas, 193).

52. Wis. 3:6; see also 4 Macc. 17:22.

53. Gathercole, *Boasting*, 205; cf. Sanders, *Judaism*, 253. Roetzel (*Paul*, 7) even suggests Pharisaic influence on Paul's idea of spiritual sacrifice. Pharisees were meticulous about purity but did not try to achieve it on the priestly level (Sanders, *Jesus to Mishnah*, 131–254).

54. Judaism already affirmed spiritual sacrifices, but Guttmann ("End") probably overstates Pharisaic distaste for the temple establishment.

then continued the tradition of prayer,[55] confession of sin,[56] a contrite heart,[57] potential martyrdom,[58] suffering,[59] acts of mercy,[60] study of the Torah,[61] and other activities as spiritual sacrifices.[62]

But whereas among Gentiles only some members of the intellectual elite really eschewed sacrifices, Christian groups lacked the physical sacrifices typically associated with religion.[63] In this respect they more resembled a philosophic school than what outsiders normally considered a religion.[64] Whereas Jesus's Judean followers in this period retained access to sacrifices in the temple,[65] his followers in the Diaspora lacked anything of the sort.

A Living Sacrifice

In Romans 12:1 Paul describes the sacrifice of their bodies with three adjectives: living, holy, and pleasing or acceptable to God.

That the sacrifice is living might allude to a special kind of Old Testament offering[66] but more likely functions here as an oxymoron or paradox meant to grip attention.[67] Greeks had stories of animals that offered themselves willingly for sacrifice,[68] but human sacrifice was abhorrent to most peoples.[69] Martyrdom

---

55. E.g., *b. Ber.* 15a.
56. *B. Sanh.* 43b.
57. *Pesiq. Rab Kah.* 24:5.
58. *Gen. Rab.* 34:9.
59. *Sipre Deut.* 32.5.2.
60. *Abot R. Nat.* 4 A; 8, §22 B. Among Christians, cf. *Sent. Sext.* 47.
61. *Abot R. Nat.* 4 A; *Pesiq. Rab Kah.* 6:3; *Pesiq. Rab.* 16:7; cf. *Sipre Deut.* 306.20.3.
62. Cf. the continuing thought among Christians, e.g., Jerome *Hom. Ps.* 1 (trans. Bray, *Corinthians*, 102): "If I do what is prescribed, I am praying with my whole body what others are praying with their lips." For a different but useful list of spiritual sacrifice language in antiquity, see Talbert, *Romans*, 283–84.
63. With Dunn, *Romans*, 710; Witherington, *Acts*, 398; cf. also Nock, "Vocabulary," 134.
64. Wilken, "Christians," 107–10 (yet also as a religious association devoted to Christ, 110–18); Wilken, "Social Interpretation"; Keener, *Acts*, 3:2610–11. By the second century many viewed Christianity as a philosophic school; see Wilken, "Social Interpretation," 444–48; Schmeller, "Gegenwelten."
65. As in Acts 21:23–26; cf. Luke 24:53; Acts 2:46; 3:1; 5:42.
66. For the Azazel goat, see Kiuchi, "Azazel-Goat." This is the likeliest option among the OT sacrifices that do not require death (such as grain offerings or libations, e.g., Jewett, *Romans*, 729); sacrifices that require death would less easily be depicted as "living."
67. E.g., Krentz, "Oxymora." On oxymora, see Rowe, "Style," 143; Aune, *Dictionary of Rhetoric*, 327; in Paul, see Anderson, *Rhetorical Theory*, 227; Porter, "Paul and Letters," 582.
68. E.g., Philost. *Hrk.* 17.4; 56.4.
69. E.g., Sil. It. 4.791; Plut. *Cic.* 10.3; *Themist.* 13.2–3; Lucian *Dial. G.* 274 (3/23, *Apollo and Dionysus* 1); Philost. *Vit. Apoll.* 8.7; Rives, "Human Sacrifice"; Garnsey and Saller, *Empire*, 169. Accounts of the practice appear in, e.g., Hom. *Il.* 23.175–76; Aeschylus *Ag.* 205–26; Apollod. *Bibl.* 2.5.11; 3.15.8; Lycophron *Alex.* 229; Ovid *Metam.* 13.447–48; Virg. *Aen.* 10.517–20; Livy 22.57.6; Sen. Y. *Troj.* 360–70; Quint. Curt. 4.3.23; Appian *C.W.* 1.14.117; Arrian *Alex.* 1.5.7;

would be an acceptable sacrifice,[70] but Jesus's followers must live each day as if their lives are forfeit for his cause, showing the same commitment as martyrs not only by how they die but by how they live.[71]

People often spoke of what was "pleasing" to a deity,[72] and sacrifices had to be "acceptable" or pleasing to a deity.[73] Scripture sometimes declares, using various expressions, that God accepted or was pleased with sacrifices offered to him[74] or, conversely, that he found them unacceptable.[75] Paul also speaks figuratively of an acceptable sacrifice to God, in this case of a gift for Paul, in Philippians 4:18.

Because Paul employs this same adjective ("pleasing") among his three descriptors of God's will in Romans 12:2, it seems clear that Paul ties the acts together: God's will in verse 2 is the purpose for which we present our bodies. Likewise, our minds are renewed to discern God's will in terms of how we can use our bodies on behalf of his greater body.

A Rational Sacrifice

The Greek term λογικός has a wide semantic range and can be translated various ways in various contexts; the RSV, NRSV, ASV, the revised version of the NAB, and the ESV render it "spiritual" both here in Romans 12:1 and in 1 Peter 2:2; the NIV renders it "true and proper" in Romans 12:1 and

---

Dio Chrys. *Or.* 8.14; Tac. *Ann.* 14.30; Plut. *Par. St.* 35, *Mor.* 314CD; Tert. *Apol.* 9.2. In Jewish thought, individual death might atone on behalf of others (see, e.g., Schenker, "Martyrium"; Baslez, "Martyrs"; Thoma, "Frühjüdische Martyrer"; Haacker, *Theology*, 133–34; *Mek. Bah.* 6.142–43; *Sipre Deut.* 32.5.2, 5; 310.4.1; 311.1.1), but "sacrifice" (as here) is a larger category than atonement.

70. In Pauline literature, cf. Eph. 5:2; Phil. 2:17; 2 Tim. 4:6; perhaps 1 Cor. 5:7.

71. Cf. Jesus's teaching portrayed in Mark 8:34 and especially the application in Luke 9:23; cf. also the language of sharing Jesus's baptism and cup of suffering (Mark 10:38–39; cf. 14:23–24, 36; Luke 12:50) and Paul's image of baptism into Christ's death (Rom. 6:3–4; cf. the cup in 1 Cor. 10:16; 11:26). For sacrificing here by how one lives, see Chrysostom *Homily* 20.1 (on Rom. 12:1), cited in Burns, *Romans*, 292.

72. E.g., Epict. *Diatr.* 2.14.12; 4.12.11; in Judaism, e.g., *Jub.* 2:22; 23:10; Tob. 4:21; Wis. 4:10; 9:10; *T. Dan* 1:3; *T. Ab.* 15:14 A; cf. Sir. 2:16.

73. In Gentile religion this could be determined by examining the sacrificed animal's internal organs after the sacrifice (deSilva, *Honor*, 252). The phrase "acceptable to God" is not uncommon Koine (Moulton and Milligan, *Vocabulary*, 259, citing *Priene* 114.15; and, later, P.Fay. 90.17; P.Flor. 1.30.30; P.Stras. 1.1.9; P.Gen. 1.15.2; Jewett, *Romans*, 729, following Foerster, "Εὐάρεστος," 456). For this and related language applied to sacrifices, see Porph. *Marc.* 17.282–86; for unacceptable sacrifices, see Lucian *Sacr.* 12–13 (sarcastically); *Runaways* 1.

74. E.g., Gen. 8:21; Exod. 29:18, 25, 41; Lev. 1:9, 13, 17 and passim; Num. 15:3; Ezra 6:10; Pss. 20:3; 119:108; Isa. 56:7; cf. also 1 Esd. 1:12; Sir. 35:8; 45:16; 50:15; *Jub.* 6:3; 7:5; 21:7, 9; 49:9; 1QS 3.11; 8.10; 9.4; 2Q24 frg. 4.2; 11QT 27.4; Philo *Spec. Laws* 1.201; Jos. *Ant.* 4.34, 311; 6.149; 7.334; 10.64; 12.146.

75. E.g., Gen. 4:4–5; Jer. 6:20; 14:12; Ezek. 43:27; Amos 5:22; Mal. 1:10; 2:13; *Jub.* 4:2; Philo *Spec. Laws* 1.223; Jos. *Ant.* 5.266.

"spiritual" in 1 Peter 2:2; the CEB as "appropriate" in the former and "of the word" in the latter; both the NASB and the earlier version of the NAB preserve "spiritual" in the former and "of the word" in the latter (the NASB retaining the KJV rendering in the latter); the GNT renders it as "true" in the former and "spiritual" in the latter; the NCV renders it "spiritual" in the former and "simple" in the latter; the KJV renders it "reasonable" in the former and "of the word" in the latter (retaining the connection with λόγος in 1 Pet. 1:23); and the Douay-Rheims "reasonable" in the former and "rational" in the latter.

Translations of λογικός in Romans 12:1 and 1 Peter 2:2

Bible Version	Romans 12:1	1 Peter 2:2
RSV, NRSV, ASV, ESV, NAB	spiritual	spiritual
NIV	true and proper	spiritual
CEB	appropriate	of the word
NASB	spiritual	of the word (retaining the KJV reading)
GNT	true	spiritual
NCV	spiritual	simple
KJV	reasonable	of the word (retaining the connection with λόγος in 1 Pet. 1:23)
Douay-Rheims	reasonable	rational

In contexts referring to the mind, however, like this one (Rom. 12:2–3), the term often implies reason (i.e., the rational element), in this case unexpectedly captured by the older KJV rather than by many of the newer translations.[76] Thus, for Stoics, for example, any act that was not appropriate was wrong for a "rational" (λογικῷ) being,[77] by which they meant humans.[78] Stoics saw a relation between humans as λογικός and God as λόγος—in other words, between human reason and the reason that structured the cosmos.[79] On this basis, some Stoics viewed "only *logikos* [i.e., rational]

76. For the rational element, connected with the mind in Rom. 12:2, see also, e.g., Cranfield, *Romans*, 2:602 (noting Stoic usage); Byrne, *Romans*, 366; Schreiner, *Romans*, 645; Cobb and Lull, *Romans*, 161; Bryan, *Preface*, 195n5 (citing Epict. *Diatr.* 2.9.2); Hultgren, *Romans*, 440; Kruse, *Romans*, 463; Barclay, *Gift*, 509; earlier, see, e.g., Aquinas, lecture 1, on Rom. 12:1, cited in Levy, Krey, and Ryan, *Romans*, 249. Some cite instead ancient usage supporting merely "spiritual" sacrifice as opposed to animal sacrifice (Hunter, *Romans*, 108) or think it refers to the entire life (Bornkamm, *Experience*, 41, opposing Stoic-like usage here).

77. Arius Did. 2.7.8a, p. 52.21–22. Only an appropriate act can have "a reasonable defence [εὔλογον ἀπολογίαν]" (2.7.8, pp. 50.36–52.1; trans. Pomeroy). Cf. 2.7.10a, p. 56.23–25 (though this passage notes that Stoic technical usage of terminology differs from common usage).

78. Epict. *Diatr.* 4.7.7; Arius Did. 2.7.6, p. 36.25; cf. 2.7.11m, p. 90.9–10.

79. Thorsteinsson, "Stoicism," 23. Jewett (*Romans*, 730) rightly follows Cranfield (*Romans*, 2:602, citing Epict. *Diatr.* 1.16.20; 2.9.2; Marc. Aur. 2.16) in translating with respect to reason

worship" as genuine worship, in contrast to the masses' superstitions.[80] Nor was such language limited to Stoics,[81] although as the most popular philosophic school of Paul's day they remain relevant as a reflection of the period's intellectual milieu. Some Diaspora Jews thus also applied the language to appropriate sacrifice.[82]

In other words, in Romans 12:1 the way one offers one's body as a sacrifice to God is rationally, through reason—one's mind dictates how the body will serve.[83] In view of 12:2–3, this means that one's renewed mind discerns God's will (12:2), including one's useful place in Christ's body (12:3–8).

Transformed versus Conformed

Paul opposes two antithetical models for life: being conformed to this present age or being transformed in connection with the new age in Christ.[84] Some infer from the present tenses of each of the verbs that they refer to "an ongoing process"[85] and also note that they are passive,[86] perhaps suggesting natural socialization in the former case and God's work in the latter case.[87] Thinkers

here, as in Stoicism, but unfortunately, Jewett then applies this too narrowly to the mission in Spain (731); contextually, it could apply more generally to unity (as in Rom. 12:4–6).

80. Moo (*Romans*, 752) cites here Kittel, "Λογικός," 142; Ortkemper, *Leben*, 28–33.

81. Middle Platonists could distinguish "rational" and "irrational" parts of the soul (Dillon, *Middle Platonists*, esp. 174, on Philo); later, in Porphyry the "body" of the "mind" (νοῦς) is "the rational soul" (ψυχὴν λογικήν; Porph. *Marc.* 26.412). Philo speaks of the "rational" soul made in God's image (*Plant.* 18) and "rational spirit-force within us which was shaped according to the archetypal form of the divine image" (*Spec. Laws* 1.171; trans. Colson, LCL, 7:197). In Plato, though developed far more in Philo, cf. Aune, "Duality," 221.

82. Moo (*Romans*, 752) cites here Philo *Spec. Laws* 1.277. Cf. rational piety in 4 Maccabees (with Janzen, "Approach," although the suggestion of dependence seems too optimistic).

83. For "rational" worship, though using different Greek terminology, see, e.g., Iambl. *Pyth. Life* 33.229: friendship "of gods with human beings through piety and scientific worship" (trans. Dillon and Hershbell, 227).

84. The two verbs do not include a wordplay as in English, but Paul might be using cognate roots as synonymous or close in sense (cf. both μορφή and σχῆμα, Phil. 2:7).

85. Bryan, *Preface*, 196. Cf. the Stoic Epictetus, who opines that no one's mind changes instantly; it takes time to transform a person (Epict. *Diatr.* 1.15.6–8). Stoics still experienced the pull of old memories but were committed to retaining the right perspective (Engberg-Pedersen, *Paul and Stoics*, 72–73). Greek verb tenses are notoriously difficult to translate into English temporal categories, but the observation could be correct here.

86. Bryan, *Preface*, 196.

87. The verb "conformed" (συσχηματίζω), however, may function more as an active (cf. BDAG). For God's work with human yielding or cooperation in transformation, see e.g., Cranfield, *Romans*, 2:607; Kruse, *Romans*, 464; Gorman, *Cruciformity*, 134. Cf. also the aorist passive subjunctive in Gal 4:19 (with Gorman, *Inhabiting*, 169, citing Bonhoeffer, *Discipleship*, 284-85).

often valued not being like the masses or sharing their values.[88] To hold their beliefs revealed ignorance.[89]

The New Age versus the Old

Interpreters often rightly contrast "this age" in this passage with the promised messianic age to come.[90] Paul's usage would have been particularly clear to those familiar either with Judean tradition or with Paul's own teachings. Traditional Judean thought often distinguished the present age of evil and suffering from the coming age of deliverance,[91] emphasizing an eschatological reversal of roles.[92] Thus, elsewhere Paul declares that Christ has delivered us from the present evil age (Gal. 1:4) and that the Spirit provides a foretaste of the coming age (1 Cor. 2:9–10; 2 Cor. 1:22; 5:5; Gal. 5:5). Elsewhere in Romans Paul employs αἰών ("age") as simply part of the idiom "forever," but in other letters he devalues the wisdom of this age (1 Cor. 1:20; 2:6, 8; 3:18) and the hostile "god of this age" (2 Cor. 4:4).[93] In Pauline language, not being "conformed" (συσχηματίζεσθε) to this age may include not investing heavily in the transitory values of "this world" that is passing away (1 Cor. 7:31, speaking of the "form" [σχῆμα] of this world).[94]

Paul's use of ἀνακαίνωσις in this connection reinforces the point. Of course,

88. E.g., Philo *Abr.* 38; Max. Tyre *Or.* 1.7–8.

89. E.g., Mus. Ruf. frg. 41, p. 136.22, 24. Many philosophers believed that the nonphilosophic masses were "mad," not thinking soundly; see, e.g., Epict. *Diatr.* 1.12.9; 1.21.4; Arius Did. 2.7.5b13, p. 26.28–30; 2.7.5b13, p. 28.1–2.

90. E.g., Sanday and Headlam, *Romans*, 353; Taylor, *Romans*, 92; Nygren, *Romans*, 418; Furnish, "Living," 194–95; Gorman, *Cruciformity*, 354, 365; Hultgren, *Romans*, 441; cf. Cullmann, *Time*, 45.

91. See, e.g., 1QS 3.23; 4Q171 frgs. 1–2, col. 2.9–10; 4Q215a frg. 1, col. 2.4–6; *4 Ezra* 4:35–37; 6:7–9, 20; 7:31, 47, 50, 113–14; 8:1, 52; *2 Bar.* 15:8; *t. Ber.* 6:21; *Peah* 1:2–3; *Sipre Num.* 115.5.7; *Sipre Deut.* 29.2.3; 31.4.1; 32.5.10; 34.4.3; 48.7.1; *Abot R. Nat.* 5, 9 A; 22, §46 B; *Pesiq. Rab Kah.* 4:1; *b. Hag.* 12b; *y. Hag.* 2:1, §16; *Pesiq. Rab.* 16:6; 21:1; 25:2; *Gen. Rab.* 1:10; 53:12; 59:6; 66:2, 4; 90:6; 95 (MSV); *Exod. Rab.* 47:3; *Lev. Rab.* 2:2; 3:1; *Deut. Rab.* 1:20; 2:31; 3:4; *Eccl. Rab.* 4:6, §1; *Song Rab.* 2:2, §6; *Lam. Rab.* 1:5, §31; 3:3, §1; 3:18, §6; 3:22, §8; *Tg. Ps.-Jon.* on Gen. 25:32; cf. *Sib. Or.* 3.367–80; Pryke, "Eschatology," 48; Ferch, "Aeons"; Charlesworth, *Jesus within Judaism*, 43; Grant, "Social Setting," 140. Later, cf. also Qur'an 16.107, 122; 29.64. For the present age of evil, see, e.g., CD 4.8, 10, 12; 6.10, 14; 12.23; 14.19; 15.7, 10; 1QS 4.18; 4Q271 frg. 2.12; 4Q301 frg. 3ab.8; 4Q510 frg. 1.6; *4 Ezra* 4:27.

92. For eschatological inversion, see, e.g., 1QM 14.4–7, 10–15; 4Q215a frg. 1, col. 2.3–6; *1 En.* 46:5–6; 96:8; 104:2; *Sib. Or.* 3.350–55; *2 Bar.* 83:5; *t. Taan.* 3:14; *Sipra Behuq. pq.* 3.263.1.8; *Sipre Deut.* 307.3.2–3; *Abot R. Nat.* 39 A; 22, §46; 44, §123 B; *Pesiq. Rab Kah.* 6:2; 9:1; *b. Yoma* 87a; *y. Sanh.* 6:6, §2; *Gen. Rab.* 21:1; *Exod. Rab.* 30:19; *Lev. Rab.* 13:3; 23:6; 33:6; 36:2; cf. *4 Ezra* 6:20–24; *T. Jud.* 25:4.

93. It is possible that Paul also speaks of believers as being at the meeting of the ages (1 Cor. 10:11); see Epp, "Imageries," 104; but for a different interpretation, cf. Ladd, *Theology*, 371.

94. For the connection with 1 Cor. 7:31, see also Jewett, *Romans*, 732, although he overspecifies the application here. Cf. Theodoret *Commentary* 12.2 (on Rom. 12:2), cited in Burns, *Romans*, 293.

philosophers also spoke of becoming new in some respects through conversion to philosophy,[95] but Paul's use of such language elsewhere suggests that he may also use renewal language in light of the eschatology prominent in his Jewish heritage. In 2 Corinthians 4:16 Paul employs the verb cognate of this noun (ἀνακαινόω) for inner renewing in contrast to outer deterioration; the context contrasts the temporal with the eternal (4:17–18) and the present body with the future resurrection body (5:1–5).[96] Earlier in Romans Paul employs the cognate καινότης for new life in Christ (Rom. 6:4), which promises future resurrection (cf. 6:5) and new life in the Spirit (7:6).

Thus, Paul may evoke the new creation in Christ (2 Cor. 5:17; Gal. 6:15), which in the present includes a new worldview or approach to current reality (2 Cor. 5:16).[97] This new worldview is based on being dead with Christ so that believers may live for Christ, who died and rose for them (5:14–15).

Some also connect "renewing" or the implied new era here with being in Christ, the new Adam.[98] Paul has earlier connected what is "old" not only with an approach to the law (Rom. 7:6; cf. 2 Cor. 3:14) but with the old humanity in Adam (Rom. 6:6; cf. Col. 3:9). In Colossians 3:10 the new person is being renewed according to the image of the one who created it, thus probably evoking Genesis 1:26–27.[99]

Renewal for a New Age

Paul's choice of words regarding the reorientation of the mind is not accidental. The new mind is affected by its foretaste of the coming world in Christ. As noted above, "renewing" (ἀνακαινώσει) undoubtedly alludes to the "new" life obtained by union with the risen Christ (cf. καινότης in Rom. 6:4; contrast the "old person" in 6:6) and by the Spirit (cf. καινότης in 7:6; contrast the oldness of the written code also in 7:6).

The renewed mind thus views the world from the standpoint of the coming age (cf. 1 Cor. 2:6–10); present actions and inactions must be evaluated in light of their eternal consequences (Rom. 13:11–14, esp. in light of 1 Thess.

95. See Stowers, "Resemble," 92; on philosophic conversion, esp. Nock, *Conversion*.

96. I understand the present "have" in 2 Cor. 5:1 in connection with the certainty of possession in view of the presence of the eschatological Spirit in 5:5; see Keener, *Corinthians*, 179.

97. With Byrne, *Romans*, 366; Schreiner, *Romans*, 647.

98. E.g., Matera, *Romans*, 287.

99. The LXX can apply a cognate to renewing a former state (Ps. 102:5 [103:5 ET]; Lam. 5:21) and use in parallel with God's re-creative activity (Ps. 103:30 [104:30 ET]); Josephus applies it to rebuilding or repairing (*Ant.* 9.161; 11.107; 13.57). Dunn (*Romans*, 714) suggests that "renewing" indicates a measure of continuity in the personal identity as well as transformation of perspectives.

5:2–9; cf. Rom. 2:6–10; 14:10–12).[100] More than this, however, it experiences a foretaste of the coming world, an experience that Paul associates with those in whom the Spirit dwells (1 Cor. 2:9–10; 2 Cor. 1:22; 5:5).

The renewed mind of Romans 12:1–3 contrasts starkly with the corrupted mind of Romans 1.[101]

Romans 1:18–32	Romans 12:1–3
Humanity failed to thank God (1:21) and eventually worshiped idols (1:23)	Believers worship God, dedicating themselves as sacrifices (12:1)*
They corrupted their bodies (1:24)	They offer their bodies (12:1) to serve Christ's body (12:4–8)
They belong to the present age (cf. verb tenses in 1:18–32)	Not conforming to this age, their minds are made new (12:2)
They did not approve knowledge of God, so God allowed their minds to be corrupted (1:28)	God renews their minds so they may approve his will (12:2)
Their corrupted minds yielded selfish vices (1:28–31)	The renewed mind yields acts of service to Christ's body (12:1–8)

*For the contrast between reasonable worship here and irrational worship in Rom. 1, cf. also Palinuro, "Rm 12,1–2."

The renewed mind accomplishes what the law intended; the person who in Romans 2:17–18 boasts in the law is confident that he knows God's will, but the renewed mind in 12:2 truly recognizes and lives by God's will. It is not the self-focused struggle under the law in 7:14–25 but rather the others-focused character of love in 13:8–10 that fulfills the law.

A renewed mind, then, evaluates matters of this age in light of the coming age, valuing God's opinions rather than the world's and valuing what counts eternally. Perhaps because some Corinthian Christians understand Paul's teaching in light of typical Greek incomprehension of a future resurrection, Paul often calls believers to an eschatological perspective especially in the letter that we call 1 Corinthians (cf. 1 Cor. 3:4–15; 4:5; 5:5; 6:2–3; 7:26, 29–31; 9:22, 24–27; 10:33; 11:26, 32; 13:8–13; 15:20, 30–32).[102] This approach will invite further comment in my treatment of 1 Corinthians 2 in chapter 6.[103] Such an interest is clearly not, however, limited to that letter.

100. Cf. cherishing eternal values in Epicurus *Let. Men.* 135 (in Grant, *Religions*, 160), though Epicurus rejected an afterlife (124–26).

101. Others have also noted some contrasts with Rom. 1, e.g., Kim, "Paraenesis," 124; Gorman, *Inhabiting*, 89.

102. A generation ago scholars often spoke of "overrealized eschatology" without always articulating the wider ancient intellectual factors that made such a perspective more appealing than Paul's approach, which allows for both realized and future elements.

103. For the Spirit and the partial foretaste of eschatology in 1 Cor. 2:9–10, see the discussion on pp. 176–79, below.

The Mind and Transformation

The means of transformation is the renewal of the mind. This suggests that the mind itself is somehow transformed in a manner that facilitates the transformation of one's life. Some have suggested Hellenistic backgrounds for the idea of the mind "being transformed."[104] The most relevant Gentile ideas regarding a transformed mind appear in philosophers, who were the ones who addressed such issues. Thus, for example, Seneca insists that merely learning what to do and not to do is insufficient; one becomes a true wise person only when one's "mind is metamorphosed [*transfiguratus est*] into the shape of that which he has learned."[105] The Platonic tradition also valued being conformed to the divine likeness.[106] The wise person became good only "by thinking the good and noble thought which emanated from the divine."[107] Like some other philosophers,[108] the Jewish philosopher Philo emphasizes being conformed to God.[109]

Ancient philosophic language would allow Paul's audience to understand some of his language, but they might also have recognized that he employs it somewhat differently. Stoics too recognized that wisdom should "transform" one's mind, conforming it to wisdom.[110] For Paul, of course, the transformation is into Christ's image (cf. Rom. 8:29; 2 Cor. 3:18).[111] Imitation of God is

104. This term does not appear in the LXX and therefore has sometimes been attributed to the mysteries (Reitzenstein, *Mystery-Religions*, 454, on 2 Cor. 3:18); the sense, however, is quite different in the mysteries (Sheldon, *Mystery Religions*, 86). The language was often used for transformation of deities and others in mythology (noted by Jewett, *Romans*, 732; see Blackburn, "ΑΝΔΡΕΣ," 190; a range of transformation sources cited in Keener, *John*, 1189–90; Keener, *Acts* 1:667–68, 720; Keener, *Matthew*, 437). This meaning does not fit the present context as well as closer Jewish conceptions do.

105. Sen. Y. *Ep. Lucil.* 94.48 (trans. Gummere, LCL, 3:42–43). In *Ep. Lucil.* 6 (in Malherbe, *Moral Exhortation*, 64), Seneca claims that he is experiencing a transformation, though it is not yet complete. Stoics emphasized transformed thinking (Thorsteinsson, "Stoicism," 24–25). Vining ("Ethics") views Paul's emphasis on reason and ethics as parallel to, yet not dependent on, the same Stoic emphasis.

106. See Nock, *Christianity*, 55, regarding cognitive ideals, against the mystery religions idea. One honors God by making one's thought like him (Porph. *Marc.* 16.265–67), through virtue, which draws the soul to what is like it (16.267–68); a mind like God gravitates toward him (19.315–16; for the divine law stamped in the mind, see 26.410–11, 419–20). Much less relevant is transformation through Platonic reincarnation (Athen. *Deipn.* 15.679A).

107. Porph. *Marc.* 11.199–201 (trans. O'Brien Wicker, 55).

108. E.g., Marc. Aur. 10.8.2 (and comparable sources cited by Haines in LCL, 270n1).

109. Philo *Creation* 144; cf. *Abr.* 87; *Decal.* 73; *Virt.* 168. Philo uses the verb ἐξομοιόω and its cognate noun forty-six times, sometimes with reference to nature's conformity to God's nature. Judeans also could emphasize the importance of right thinking about the law (e.g., 1QS 9.17; 4Q398 frgs. 14–17, col. 2.4).

110. Sen. Y. *Ep. Lucil.* 94.48.

111. These texts about Christ's image employ cognate terms in a relevant manner. On Christ as God's image embodying expectations for divine wisdom (cf. 2 Cor. 4:4; Wis. 7:26), see, e.g., discussion in Keener, *Corinthians*, 169–71, 174; cf. the *logos* in Philo *Dreams* 2.45.

also prominent in philosophic discourse;[112] but in the context of Romans, it is the Spirit rather than human ability that effects the transformation. Most philosophers emphasized that one should not follow the views of the masses;[113] but for Paul, lack of conformity to this "age" belongs to his realized approach to the traditional Jewish "two ages" schema (cf. Rom. 8:11, 23; 1 Cor. 2:9–10; 10:11; 2 Cor. 1:22; Gal. 1:4).

Some sought to discipline their minds toward God. Thus, for Stoics right thinking about what truly mattered was paramount.[114] Both Stoics and Platonists believed that self-mastery was necessary to achieve happiness;[115] disciplining the mind was needed for self-mastery.[116] Pythagoras "purified his intellect."[117] A later Platonist advises focus on mathematics to accustom a student to thinking about immaterial matters.[118] Whereas for some thinkers such transformation was a matter of self-discipline, not bad in itself (cf. Gal. 5:23), the context of Romans also suggests dependence on God. This idea should have been intelligible to Paul's audience. Some Diaspora Jews recognized that only God could dispose the mind toward wisdom; only God could guide the mind toward what was best.[119]

Although Paul's language relates to some philosophic ideals,[120] his thinking here also fits apocalyptic conceptions, since he applies related language to eschatological transformation (Rom. 8:29; Phil. 3:21). The image of eschatological transformation was at home especially in Jewish apocalyptic sources.[121] In

112. See, e.g., Cic. *Tusc.* 5.25.70; Sen. Y. *Dial.* 1.1.5; Epict. *Diatr.* 2.14.12–13; Marc. Aur. 10.8.2; Heracl. *Ep.* 5; Plut. *Borr.* 7, *Mor.* 830B; *Let. Aris.* 188, 190, 192, 208–10, 254, 281; Philo *Creation* 139; *T. Ash.* 4:3; *Mek. Shir.* 3.43–44; *Sipra Qed. par.* 1.195.1.3; *Sent. Sext.* 44–45; Rutenber, *Doctrine*, chaps. 2–3; cf. Eph. 5:1.

113. E.g., Mus. Ruf. frg. 41, p. 136.22–24; Philo *Abr.* 38.

114. E.g., Sen. Y. *Nat. Q.* 3.pref.11–15; for a non-Stoic, see, e.g., Porph. *Marc.* 5.86–94.

115. Meeks, *Moral World*, 47; cf. Lutz, *Musonius*, 28, on Musonius Rufus.

116. Lutz, *Musonius*, 28, on Mus. Ruf. 6, p. 24.

117. Iambl. *Pyth. Life* 16.70. Others might seek to do the same (e.g., Libanius *Speech Char.* 18.3).

118. Plot. *Enn.* 1.3.3.

119. *Let. Aris.* 237–39. God rules human minds (227), and God directs the mind so it does good (243). God leads the mind of the king (the addressee of much of the book's wisdom) in 246; cf. 251, 255, 267, 270, 276. One needs God's help to behave rightly (252); to be a doer of good is a gift of God (231; cf. 278), for he guides human actions (195). God provides insight (Wis. 8:21; 1QS 4.22; 1QH^a 18.29; 19.30–31; 20.16; 4Q381 frg. 15.8; 4Q427 frg. 8, col. 2.18).

120. See, further, the discussion on 2 Cor. 3:18 below on pp. 206–15.

121. Dunn (*Romans*, 713) cites here, with regard to future resurrection, Dan. 12:3; *1 En.* 104:6; 1 Cor. 15:51–53; Phil. 3:21; Mark 12:25; *4 Ezra* 7:97; *2 Bar.* 51:5; and also an occasional transformation "consequential upon one being taken up to heaven while still alive, particularly Enoch (*1 En.* 71.11; *2 En.* 22.8; *Asc. Isa.* 9.9)." Jewett (*Romans*, 732) cites apocalyptic parallels as more distant than Greek mythical ones; the distance, however, is primarily lexical (because most of these sources are not written in Greek), whereas conceptually they better fit Paul's usage. Although the sense here may not involve future eschatology (Jewett, *Romans*, 733), it involves realized eschatology. Segal (*Convert*, 63–65) opines that Paul's emphasis on present and future

a Diaspora Jewish source a martyr seems "transformed" (μετασχηματιζόμενος) by suffering for immortality (4 Macc. 9:22).[122] (Paul's understanding of transformation also draws conceptually on the experience of Moses, although he does not articulate this connection for the believers in Rome; see discussion of 2 Cor. 3:18 in chap. 6.)[123]

To whose mind are believers' minds to be conformed? Eschatologically, believers are conformed to Jesus in Philippians 3:21; in the present they are transformed to share his glory within in 2 Corinthians 3:18; and Paul refers to the mind of Christ in 1 Corinthians 2:16.[124] The same verb (μεταμορφόω) that Paul uses in Romans 12:2 and 2 Corinthians 3:18 appears in another early Christian source for Jesus's transfiguration (Mark 9:2; also Matt. 17:2), thus revealing glory as in 2 Corinthians 3:18.[125]

Suffering may facilitate the process. Paul applies cognate terms for ultimate conformity to Jesus in Romans 8:29 (in a context of preceding suffering) and (with respect to bodily resurrection) Philippians 3:21, and to present conforming to Jesus's suffering and death (Phil. 3:10) to prepare to share his resurrection (cf. 3:11).[126] That is, sufferings often facilitate external opportunities for conformity, just as internal submission to the transformation process does. The end product will be full conformity to Christ when God raises the dead, but the process itself also constitutes an opportunity.

Discerning God's Will

When Paul expects the believer's mind to be renewed to evaluate the good things that are God's will, he counters the false claim of the hypocritical law-expert in Romans 2:18, who supposedly knows God's will and thus evaluates what is best. Romans 2:18 and 12:2 are the only two uses of θέλημα ("will")

---

transformation probably reflects apocalyptic models. For transformation to the divine image in Jewish mysticism, see Morray-Jones, "Mysticism."

122. The writer may adapt Greek mythological language for this purpose (cf. Philo *Embassy* 80). Paul employs the same term (μετασχηματίζω) for false appearances (2 Cor. 11:13–15) but also for eschatological transformation to be like Christ (Phil. 3:21); the term is cognate to Paul's term for "conformed" in Rom. 12:2.

123. See again pp. 206–15 below, esp. 210–14.

124. Johnson, *Romans*, 191. See also Phil. 2:5.

125. Philo applies it to Moses's inspiration in Exod. 2:17 (Philo *Mos.* 1.57) and for Gaius Caligula pretending to be a deity (*Embassy* 95), but not to Moses's transfiguration, to which Paul alludes in 2 Cor. 3:18.

126. Possibly it also contrasts with mere religious "form" (Rom. 2:20); Paul uses cognates for Christ being formed in believers (perhaps in conversion, Gal. 4:19), and for the contrast between Christ's divine and human "form" or "likeness" in Phil. 2:6–7.

in Romans besides the framing verses about Paul's desire to visit the believers in Rome (1:10; 15:32). These are also two of the only four uses of δοκιμάζω ("evaluate") in Romans—one of the others being 1:28, to which 12:2 also alludes by way of contrast. Thus, the renewed mind of 12:2 contrasts with both the pagan mind uninformed by the law (1:28) and the fleshly mind informed but not transformed by the law (2:18; see also 7:23, 25, which offer two of the other uses of νοῦς besides 1:28; 11:34; 12:2; and 14:5).[127]

Doing God's will was a paramount emphasis in early Judaism.[128] Some felt that mortals could discern God's will only by the gift of divine wisdom.[129] Stoics emphasized readiness to submit to God's will.[130] Often this submission meant embracing their situation with a positive outlook, but knowing truth also could dictate action: a virtuous person would immediately know what they should do.[131]

How does the renewed mind think? Here the renewed mind recognizes God's will as that which is good, acceptable, and perfect.[132] Paul here uses conventional language for moral criteria.[133] For Stoics, the mind was essential; only the reasoning faculty could actually examine and understand itself.[134] Reason was from the gods and provided the means to evaluate whether something was good or bad, good or shameful.[135]

Evaluative Criteria

The renewed mind is able to "evaluate" what is good[136]—a clear contrast with the failed minds of Romans 1:28 that refused to judge God's knowledge as

127. The term νοῦς, which Paul finds in Isa. 40:13, appears often enough in the LXX (Dafni, "ΝΟΥΣ," compares Homeric usage), most frequently in 4 Maccabees (1:15, 35; 2:16, 18, 22; 3:17; 5:11; 14:11; 16:13).

128. E.g., *Jub.* 21:2–3, 23; CD 3.11, 15–16; *T. Iss.* 4:3; *m. Ab.* 5:20 MSS; *Sipre Num.* 42.1.2; *Sipre Deut.* 47.2.9; 306.28.2; Israel faces judgments in the present when they disobey God's will (*Sipre Deut.* 40.4.1; 40.6.1; 305.2.1; cf. 114.1.1; 118.1.1; *Abot R. Nat.* 34 A).

129. Wis. 9:13 in context (esp. with 9:17).

130. Sorabji, *Emotion*, 219; for submission to God's (Fate's) will, see, e.g., Sen. *Y. Dial.* 7.15.4; Epict. *Diatr.* 1.6.1; 1.14.16; Marc. Aur. 6.16, and some other texts in Keener, *Acts*, 3:2491–92; in Judaism, cf. 1 Macc. 3:59–60. For doing God's will in philosophy outside Stoicism, see, e.g., Socrates *Ep.* 1; (later), Proclus *Poet.* 6.1, K107.16–17.

131. Diog. Laert. 7.1.125, recounting the Stoic view.

132. For Stoics too, reason enabled one to distinguish good from bad (Mus. Ruf. 3, p. 38.26–30). Such discernment was necessary to prevent utter folly (see Epict. *Diatr.* 2.24.19).

133. For moral criteria more broadly, see, e.g., *Rhet. Alex.* 1, 1421b.25–26.

134. Epict. *Diatr.* 1.1.

135. Mus. Ruf. 3, p. 38.26–30.

136. For δοκιμάζω here as "test," "evaluate," see Byrne, *Romans*, 366. Baumert ("Unterscheidung") applies the passage to discernment but focuses on 12:6, which I understand differently (Keener, *Romans*, 146, regarding ἀναλογίαν τῆς πίστεως as equivalent here to μέτρον πίστεως

appropriate.[137] Evaluating worth was an essential element of ancient philosophy, not least in Stoicism, the dominant philosophy in northern Mediterranean cities in this period. Some things are intrinsically good; others are simply to be preferred to their alternative.[138] Once one knows which things are preferred, these are close to what is intrinsically "good."[139] One who cannot discern good from evil is morally blind and ignorant.[140] It is the mind that must engage in discernment,[141] and this discernment therefore should characterize those trained in philosophy.[142]

Paul lists adjectives that describe what is positive, characteristics that identify and thus allow one to discern God's will. Some of these adjectives also appear among philosophers and rhetoricians as ethical or legal criteria (other criteria not mentioned here include terms for "profitable," as in 1 Cor. 6:12 and possibly Rom. 3:1,[143] and "lawful," as in 1 Cor. 6:12);[144] others are more common in biblical idiom.

---

in 12:3, with, e.g., Fuller, "Theology," 210n13; Harrison and Hagner, "Romans," 187; Dunn, *Romans*, 728; Moo, *Romans*, 765–66; Osborne, *Romans*, 323–24; Schreiner, *Romans*, 656; Kruse, *Romans*, 469–71; I understand it to apply to the diverse applications of faith to different gifts rather than to diverse amounts).

137. Just as the right opinion here must be distinguished from that of "this age" (Rom. 12:2), ancient thinkers often recognized that one could reason more clearly without the emotionally driven views of the masses (Pliny *Ep.* 2.11.6–7).

138. Arius Did. 2.7.7f, p. 48.19–22.

139. Arius Did. 2.7.7f, p. 48.24–26.

140. Epict. *Diatr.* 2.24.19.

141. Porph. *Marc.* 26.413.

142. Mus. Ruf. 16, p. 106.10–12. Such intellectual discernment was not in principle incompatible with divine intuition or revelations (cf. Apul. *De deo Socr.* 162; in Paul, perhaps Rom. 8:14).

143. In philosophy, Plato *Alcib.* 1.114E; *Hipp. maj.* 295E; Xen. *Mem.* 4.6.8; Cic. *Fin.* 3.21.69; Philod. *Crit.* col. 20 b; Sext. Emp. *Eth.* 2.22 (Stoics); Sen. Y. *Dial.* 7.8.2; *Ben.* 4.21.6; Mus. Ruf. 4, p. 46.36–37; 8, p. 60.16–17; 15, p. 96.25; 16, p. 102.33–35; 17, p. 108.35–36; 18B, p. 116.10–11; frg. 27, p. 130; frg. 40, p. 136.8–9; Epict. *Diatr.* 1.2.5–7; 1.6.6, 33; 1.18.2; 1.22.1; 1.28.5–6; 2.7.4; 2.8.1; 4.7.9; Arius Did. 2.7.5b2, p. 14.20–22; 2.7.10a, p. 56.26–27; 2.7.11h, p. 74.23–24, 29–30; Marc. Aur. 6.27; 9.1.1; Diog. Laert. 7.1.98–99 (Stoics); 10.150.31 (Epicurus); 10.151.36; 10.152.37; 10.153.38; Iambl. *Pyth. Life* 22.101; 31.204; in Plato, cf. Lodge, *Ethics*, 62–63; in rhetoric, Arist. *Rhet.* 1.7.1, 1363b; *Rhet. Alex.* 6, 1427b.39–1428a.2; Ael. Arist. *Leuct. Or.* 5.11–16; Theon *Progymn.* 8.45; Hermog. *Issues* 77.6–19; *Progymn.* 6, "On Commonplace," 14; Hermog. *Progymn.* 11, "On Thesis," 25–26; nontechnically, Arist. *Pol.* 1.2.8, 1254a; Phaedrus 3.17.13; Epict. *Diatr.* 3.21.15; 4.8.17. For the inexpedient or unhelpful, see *Rhet. Alex.* 4, 1426b.32; 34, 1440a.1–2; Quint. *Decl.* 261.6; Mus. Ruf. 18B, p. 116.23–25; Arius Did. 2.7.5d, p. 28.21; Hermog. *Progymn.* 5, "On Refutation and Confirmation," 11. Cf. traditional Jewish wisdom in Sir. 37:28.

144. *Rhet. Alex.* 4, 1426b.32; 6, 1427b.39–1428a.2; Mus. Ruf. 12, p. 86.7–8, 12, 15; Epict. *Diatr.* 1.1.21–22; *Encheir.* 51.2; Hermog. *Progymn.* 6, "On Commonplace," 14; *Progymn.* 12, "On Introduction of a Law," 27; Aphthonius *Progymn.* 7, "On Commonplace," 35S, 20R; *Progymn.* 14, "On Introduction of a Law," 53S, 47R; Commentary on Aphthonius's *Progymnasmata* Attributed to John of Sardis, 13, "On Thesis," 240, 5; Nicolaus *Progymn.* 7, "On Commonplace," 44; for custom, Ael. Arist. *Leuct. Or.* 5.6–11; for "permissible," e.g., Hermog. *Issues* 67.2–6. For adequacy and self-sufficiency, see Lodge, *Ethics*, 68–72.

In biblical idiom one could use multiple adjectives virtually synonymously,[145] which seems likely here.[146] Gentiles could also accumulate positive characteristics; thus, for example, Pythagoras allegedly started a group in Samos where people contemplated "things noble, just, and advantageous."[147] Plato says that what is just is what is honorable, good, and expedient.[148] Rhetorical handbooks could list various such criteria that would be widely accepted.[149] An orator might seek to demonstrate that the proposed actions are "just, lawful, expedient, honourable, pleasant and easily practicable."[150] Through wisdom or prudence, which is shared with deities,[151] "we acquire discernment of what is good and advantageous and noble and their opposites."[152]

Good, Pleasing, and Perfect as Criteria

One common ethical criterion was what was good,[153] and this was often stressed among Stoics,[154] who often emphasized seeking the supreme good.[155]

145. Such as "right and good" in Deut. 6:18 and 12:28; 1 Sam. 12:23; 2 Chron. 14:2; 31:20 (the combination is idiomatic, not distinctly theological—see Josh. 9:25; 2 Sam. 15:3; Jer. 26:14; 40:4; Jos. Ant. 13.431; parallelism in Job 34:4; Ps. 52:3). Their function in these passages is cumulative even if a slight difference of nuance is possible.

146. Some might place the three in ascending order here, but it seems difficult to rank the words hierarchically. Note, for example, that "good" is either identical with or superior to "righteous" in Rom. 5:7; cf. esp. Paul's trio of adjectives "holy, just, and good" in 7:12, with "good" there taking the final position.

147. Iambl. Pyth. Life 5.26 (trans. Dillon and Hershbell, 49).

148. Plato Alcib. 1.115–27; see esp. 118A (just, noble, good, and expedient).

149. Rhet. Alex. 6, 1427b.39–41 and 1428a.1–2, listing justice, lawfulness, profitability, and pleasantness.

150. Rhet. Alex. 1, 1421b.25–26 (trans. Rackham, LCL, 277); or at least necessary (1421b.28); cf. also Rhet. Alex. 4, 1427a.26–27. Later, cf. categories for rhetorical use in Hermog. Issues 76.5–6 (trans. Heath, 52): "legality; justice; advantage; feasibility; honour; consequence"; Hermog. Progymn. 12, "On Introduction of a Law," 27; Aphthonius Progymn. 7, "On Commonplace," 35S, 20R; Aphthonius Progymn. 14, "On Introduction of a Law," 53S, 47R; Nicolaus Progymn. 7, "On Commonplace," 44.

151. Iambl. Letter 4.1–9 (Stob. Anth. 3.3.26).

152. Iambl. Letter 4.9–10 (Stob. Anth. 3.3.26; trans. Dillon and Polleichtner, 13).

153. Rhet. Alex. 1, 1421b.16–22; Cic. Fam. 15.17.3 (citing a Stoic maxim).

154. See, e.g., Mus. Ruf. 4, p. 46.36–37; 7, p. 58.25; 8, p. 60.10; 15, p. 96.25; 16, p. 102.35; 16, p. 104.35–36; Epict. Diatr. 1.22.1; 4.7.9; Arius Did. 2.7.5b1, p. 12.15; 2.7.5e, p. 30.1–2; 2.7.5g, p. 32.1–9; 2.7.5h, p. 32.19–24; 2.7.5i, p. 32.25–32; 2.7.5k, p. 32.33–34; p. 34.1–6; 2.7.5L, p. 34.17–20; 2.7.5m, p. 36.10–12; 2.7.6d, pp. 38.34–41.3; 2.7.7g, p. 50.23–26; Marc. Aur. 5.15; Diog. Laert. 7.1.92; Sext. Emp. Eth. 2.22 (on Stoics). For the good as a Stoic goal, see also Murray, Philosophy, 28–30, 36–38, 43.

155. E.g., Sen. Y. Ep. Lucil. 71. Only what is morally noble is good (Cic. Parad. 6–15, agreeing with Stoics); what is honorable is what is good (Sen. Y. Ep. Lucil. 87.25). In a nontechnical sense, one might claim that moral good rarely coincides with expediency (Polyb. 21.32.1), and in Soranus Gynec. 1.11.42, not everything useful is helpful; certainly not everything pleasant

(Plato also emphasized the supreme good.)[156] For Stoics, Virtue necessarily belongs to the chief good;[157] it could be described as "good" and "pleasing" (among other positive adjectives).[158] The sensible could distinguish good from bad;[159] thus, "the good which true reason approves is solid and everlasting."[160] "All good (they say) is expedient, binding, profitable, useful, serviceable, beautiful, and just or right."[161] In the Cynic epistles, wisdom is defined as the ability to know the good.[162] In the Alexandrian Jewish *Letter of Aristeas*, showing others goodwill and being rewarded by God is "the highest good" or "the best."[163] In Philo, God is the source of what is good[164] but is above what is good.[165] In various Jewish circles, God[166] and Torah[167] were good.

"Pleasing"[168] also appears at times as an ethical criterion,[169] although not as frequently; Paul borrows this term from his depiction of the sacrifice in Romans 12:1. It could often apply, as here, to what is pleasing to God.[170] Hellenistic

---

is helpful (Dio Chrys. *Or.* 3.9). But many philosophers defined the terms differently and as coinciding (Mus. Ruf. 8, p. 60.10–12; Epict. *Diatr.* 1.22.1; 2.8.1; Arius Did. 2.7.5d, p. 28.17–19, 25–29; 2.7.11i, p. 74.38; cf. again Plato *Alcib.* 1.115–27; also Aeschines *Tim.* 6).

156. See Lodge, *Ethics*, 343–477, esp. 442–55; for the relation between beauty and the highest good in Plato, see Gilbert, "Relation," 290; Lodge, *Ethics*, 61. For good in a later moralist with Middle Platonist sympathies, see Plut. *L. Wealth* 10, *Mor.* 528A. Opposing Plato's idea of the good, see Arist. *N.E.* 1.6.1–7.2, 1096a ff.; *E.E.* 1.8.1–22, 1217b–1218b.

157. Cic. *Fin.* 2.12.35–13.43; cf. also Long, *Philosophy*, 199; Frede, "Conception," 71. Cicero agrees that virtue must belong to the chief good (Cic. *Fin.* 3.1.2), although thinkers could debate whether it was (3.7.26–9.31; 3.10.33–11.36) or was not (against the Stoics, 4.16.43) the only good. Epicurus made pleasure the chief good (Cic. *Fin.* 1.9.29); Stoics rejected that as a good (Mus. Ruf. 1, p. 32.22), though they could use it to advocate self-control (Mus. Ruf. frg. 24, p. 130).

158. Arius Did. 2.7.11h, p. 74.15–17.

159. Mus. Ruf. 3, p. 38.26–30; Arius Did. 2.7.5b2, p. 14.27–29.

160. Sen. Y. *Ep. Lucil.* 66.31 (trans. Gummere, LCL, 2:21).

161. Diog. Laert. 7.1.98 (trans. Hicks, LCL, 2:205).

162. Anacharsis (to Solon) *Ep.* 2.9–11.

163. *Let. Aris.* 225 ("the highest good," trans. Shutt, *OTP* 2:27; "the best," trans. Hadas, 189). Cf. καλός in *Let. Aris.* 7, 236 (esp. in Hadas); and esp. the best in 195, 212, 238, 322; cf. 287. For a good man, cf. *T. Sim.* 4:4; *T. Benj.* 3:1 (also a concern of Stoics, e.g., Epict. *Diatr.* 1.12.7; 3.26.27–28; 4.10.11; Marc. Aur. 6.30.1; 10.17, 32; 11.5; and others, e.g., Antisthenes, Diog. Laert. 6.12).

164. Isaacs, *Spirit*, 30, citing Philo *Sacr.* 54; *Flight* 131.

165. Isaacs, *Spirit*, 30, citing Philo *Creation* 8. She contrasts this with Plato, who identified the good with God (citing *Rep.* 6.504D; 508E); cf. Wolfson, *Philo*, 1:201–2.

166. Philo *Names* 7; *m. Ber.* 9:2; *b. Ber.* 45b, 46a, 48b, 49a, 59b, 60b; *y. Taan.* 2:1, §10; *Gen. Rab.* 13:15; 57:2; Oesterley, *Liturgy*, 61. For the suggestion that the "good" is God in Rom. 5:7, citing also other texts, cf. Martin, "Good."

167. E.g., *b. Ber.* 5a; *y. Rosh Hash.* 3:8, §5; *Pesiq. Rab Kah.* 15:5; Abrahams, *Studies* (2), 186.

168. As with "good" but even more often here, I group together terms within the same semantic domain.

169. See, e.g., Arius Did. 2.7.5i, p. 32.25–26.

170. E.g., Sir. 2:16. See discussion concerning Rom. 12:1 above, p. 150.

Jewish thinkers probably presumed that true wisdom could discern what met this criterion; in Wisdom 9:10, Wisdom shows what is "pleasing" to God.

Τέλειος (Rom. 12:2) has a wide range of meaning; Paul's contemporaries often used it for what was "complete" or (within its designated sphere) "perfect."[171] (No one word in English encompasses its range of meaning.) Stoics valued what was τέλειος, perfect or complete, as superior;[172] the ideal sage could be so described,[173] though real sages normally did not claim to have met the ideal.[174]

Later Platonists emphasized intellect for achieving the perfect life.[175] Still, finding a perfect life or person was difficult.[176] Those in the Platonic tradition observed that nothing mortal contributes to the perfect life;[177] self-control makes perfect by removing susceptibility to passion;[178] virtue is "the perfection [τελειότης] of the soul."[179] The perfect mind yields perfect wisdom.[180] In its ultimate form full perfection is changeless.[181] The gods, deemed perfect,

171. Cf. "perfect" love in marriage (Mus. Ruf. 13A, p. 88.21), perfect character (Marc. Aur. 7.69), or perfect happiness (Diog. Laert. 7.1.9). The old, narrow association with the mysteries (as in Conzelmann, *Corinthians*, 60; Héring, *First Epistle*, 16; Ladd, *Theology*, 361) reflects inadequate acquaintance with wider usage and ignores the lack of key mystery terms in Paul (so also Sheldon, *Mystery Religions*, 77–78; Nock, "Vocabulary," 134; Pearson, *Terminology*, 28). Appeal to the gnostic use (Schmithals, *Gnosticism in Corinth*, 179, citing Iren. *Her.* 1.13.6) is anachronistic.

172. Arius Did. 2.7.5b4, p. 16.29–31; 2.7.8, p. 52.7, 11; 2.7.11a, p. 63.31; 2.7.11b, p. 64.14; 2.7.11L, p. 87.18. Thus Sen. Y. *Ep. Lucil.* 66.8–12: true virtue is perfect and therefore, being superlative, cannot improve or be surpassed.

173. Sen. Y. *Ep. Lucil.* 109.1; Arius Did. 2.7.5b8, p. 22.13; 2.7.11g, p. 70.1–3 (for the converse, see 70.31–33); 2.7.11m, p. 94.13–16. Seneca notes that even Epicurus could speak in terms of an *ideal* sage (*Ep. Lucil.* 66.18). In principle, Zeno thought that perfection in virtue was attainable (Diog. Laert. 7.1.8). Cf. the ideal king as "perfect" in word and action (Mus. Ruf. 8, p. 64.11).

174. Engberg-Pedersen, *Paul and Stoics*, 61–62; Meeks, *Moral World*, 50; in earlier Stoicism, only the world is perfect and divine (so Cic. *Nat. d.* 2.13.35–2.14.39). Though the ideal wise person has achieved perfection (Sen. Y. *Ep. Lucil.* 109.1), every wise person still has other things to learn (109.3). One cannot be completely faultless, though one can strive to be (Epict. *Diatr.* 4.12.19); the mind is not instantly perfected (Epict. *Diatr.* 1.15.8), but those who are not perfect can make progress toward perfection (Sen. Y. *Ep. Lucil.* 94.50; Epict. *Diatr.* 1.4.4). The terminology may not always be consistent; Epictetus speaks of a person as both being mature (τέλειος) and making progress (Arrian's summary in Epict. *Encheir.* 51.2), and other Stoics could name someone as "perfect," i.e., without blame (Marc. Aur. 1.16.4).

175. Plot. *Enn.* 1.4.4.

176. Max. Tyre *Or.* 15.1 (noting in 15.2 that philosophers are less imperfect than others).

177. Iambl. *Letter* 8, frg. 7 (Stob. *Anth.* 2.8.48), because the soul's genuine essence is perfection.

178. Iambl. *Letter* 3, frg. 3 (Stob. *Anth.* 3.5.46).

179. Iambl. *Letter* 16, frg. 1.1 (Stob. *Anth.* 3.1.17; trans. Dillon and Polleichtner, 47).

180. Iambl. *Letter* 4.5–6 (Stob. *Anth.* 3.3.26).

181. Apul. *De deo Socr.* 146; for God as changeless, see Max. Tyre *Or.* 8.8; Proclus *Poet.* 6.1, K109.12–14; possibly James 1:17. Cf. what is "perfect" (the ultimate) in Aristotle in Engberg-Pedersen, *Paul and Stoics*, 48. That which is *most* perfect is in the highest heaven; the closer to highest, the more perfect something is (Arist. *Heav.* 2.12, 291b.24–293a.14).

thus could not have direct contact with the imperfect world.[182] In Platonism God was necessarily perfect, by definition.[183]

In Jewish circles only the more hellenized sources adopt some of the nuances of the Platonic usage. For Philo, irrational elements make people imperfect, but philosophic pursuit can lead to perfection.[184] "Perfect" could depict the ultimate ideal, as it often did among some Gentile philosophers.[185] Thus, biblical heroes functioned as ideal types of perfect virtue.[186] In another Hellenistic Jewish work it was martyrdom that perfected a godly man in spite of his lifelong obedience to the law.[187]

Despite such ideal uses, "perfect" could also simply mean complete or without deficiency in the matter at hand.[188] Some used such language for those who attained the most advanced stage in philosophy.[189] The best students can be "perfected" in their skills.[190] Jewish tradition also spoke of the blameless person as "perfect," meaning that the person could not be charged with moral transgression.[191] The Hebrew term that often is rendered this way appears frequently in the Dead Sea Scrolls, often with reference to the way of life;[192] especially in prayer, however, the community recognizes their need for

182. Apul. *De deo Socr.* 127.
183. Max. Tyre *Or.* 38.6; Iambl. *Letter* 16, frg. 4 (Stob. *Anth.* 4.39.23), encouraging likeness to God. So also other thinkers, e.g., Marc. Aur. 10.1; cf. Ael. Arist. *Def. Or.* 130, §41D; Lutz, *Musonius*, 27n111, on Mus. Ruf. 17, p. 108.11–13.
184. See Satlow, "Perfection"; for the logos guiding toward perfection, see, e.g., *Migration* 174. Philo speaks of the "perfect person" (*QG* 4.191); for him, the ideally wise person is also the "perfect" person (*Sacr.* 8). The Philonic corpus employs the adjective more than four hundred times, the cognate verb more than fifty times, and the noun τελειότης some thirty-five times. Pearson, *Terminology*, 28–30, emphasizes Philonic usage.
185. E.g., Sarah representing "perfect virtue" in Philo *Posterity* 130 (for perfect virtues, see also, e.g., *Unchangeable* 154; *Drunkenness* 148; *Sober* 8; *Dreams* 1.177, 200; *Abr.* 100, 116; *Mos.* 1.159). Cf. "perfect wisdom" in *Posterity* 174; *Migr.* 166; *Dreams* 1.39; *Spec. Laws* 2.231; *Virt.* 129; "perfect" understanding in Wis. 6:15.
186. Dey, *World*, 72–74.
187. 4 Macc. 7:15.
188. E.g., Philo *Creation* 42, 59; *Spec. Laws* 2.204; Dio Chrys. *Or.* 8.16; 77/78.17; Plut. *Educ.* 10, *Mor.* 7C; Men. Rhet. 2.1–2, 376.31; 2.1–2, 377.2. So also with the Latin *perfectus*, e.g., Fronto *Ad M. Caes.* 4.1.
189. Philod. *Death* 34.10; *Crit.* col. 4 b.5–6, 8a. In Stoic ideals, however, such "perfection" was in practice unattainable (Lucian *Hermot.* 76); cf. Arius Did. 2.7.11g, p. 74.11–13.
190. Men. Rhet. 2.14, 426.27–32; cf. Epict. *Diatr.* 2.19.29.
191. E.g., *L.A.B.* 4:11 (*perfectus*); Noah in Gen. 6:9 LXX and Sir. 44:17; Abraham in *Jub.* 15:3 (cf. Gen. 17:1); Jacob in *Jub.* 27:17; Leah in *Jub.* 36:23; cf. perhaps *Apoc. Zeph.* 10:9. One comparatively perfect by human standards still needs God's wisdom (Wis. 9:6).
192. See, e.g., "perfect holiness" (CD 7.5; 20.2, 5, 7; 1QS 8.20), related to "perfect" behavior (CD 2.15–16; 1QS 1.8; 2.2; 3.9; 5.24; 8.1, 9, 10, 18, 21; 9.2, 5, 6, 8, 9, 19; 10.21; 11.2; 1QSa 1.17, 28; 1QSb 1.2; 5.22; 1QM 7.5; 14.7; 1QHᵃ 9.38; 4Q255 frg. 2.5; 4Q259 2.18; 3.1; 4Q266 frg. 5, col. 1.19; 4Q403 frg. 1, col. 1.22; 4Q525 frg. 5.11); the "perfect way" of behavior (1QS

divine mercy.[193] Thus, one can recognize that one's way cannot be "perfected" without God's help.[194] Humans are sinful and do not walk in the perfect way, although God's Spirit may perfect the way for them.[195]

For Paul, the adjective τέλειος and its cognates can mean "mature" (1 Cor. 2:6; 14:20; Eph. 4:13; Phil. 3:15), morally blameless (Col. 4:12), or "perfect" (Col. 3:14) and can refer to an ideal or goal (Phil. 3:12; Col. 1:28). In any case, ancient thinkers could recognize that Paul was employing a criterion appropriate to God's will.

One thus can discern God's will by discerning what is good, what pleases God, and what is "perfect" or "complete" in a positive way. As in much philosophic discourse, Paul speaks here in general terms, but he will define (or provide examples of) this way of thinking more concretely in the following context. Although this context includes all of the following paraenesis, my focus below will be how this relates to thinking in Romans 12:3.

The Literary Context for This Renewing of the Mind

Although reading Paul's vocabulary here in light of his usage elsewhere is helpful,[196] Paul obviously did not expect the believers in Rome to perform a concordance search of his other letters that would later remain extant. Although he probably expected his ideal audience to recognize the theme of the mind in his letter to the believers in Rome, he would not have expected them to only trace isolated words even within this letter. Instead, he expected them to hear the flow of thought in the letter as a whole.[197]

In view of the preceding context, Paul thinks partly of God's own mind or wisdom revealed in salvation history reported in Scripture. God provides believers some retroactive insight into his purposes.[198] If the preceding context

---

4.22). It can also mean "complete" (as in "a complete year"; CD 15.15; 4Q252 2.5; 4Q266 frg. 8, col. 1.6).

193. E.g., 1QS 11.3, 14; 1QM 11.4; 1QH^a 8.30, 34; 15.32–16.3; 17.7; 18.23; 19.32–34; 4Q504 frg. 4.5–7. Cf. also Kim, *New Perspective*, 150.

194. See 1QS 11.17.

195. 1QH^a 12.30–33.

196. Skilled ancient readers also took into account authors' vocabulary elsewhere; see, e.g., Sen. Y. *Ep. Lucil.* 108.24–25; Philost. *Hrk.* 11.5; cf. Dion. Hal. *Demosth.* 46.

197. Intellectuals expected attention to context, e.g., Quint. *Inst.* 10.1.20–21; Apul. *Apol.* 82–83; Hermog. *Method* 13.428–29.

198. Cf. the pesher hermeneutic in the Dead Sea Scrolls (see, e.g., Dimant, "Pesharim"; Brooke, "Pesher"; Brooke, "Pesharim"; Brooke, "Interpretation"; Aune, *Dictionary of Rhetoric*, 347–50; Longenecker, *Exegesis*, 31, 38–45; Fitzmyer, "Quotations," 325–30; Brownlee, "Interpretation," 60–62; Lim, "Orientation"), although a hermeneutic of hindsight is in no way

offers God's sovereign plan as a foundation for transforming the mind, the following context offers one objective of this transformation. The right way of thinking puts each of us and our gifts in the wider context of Christ's body.

Stoic reasoning sought to transcend embodied individual limitations through recognizing God's mind in the cosmos, viewing the universe and even the state as a body. For Paul, both salvation history and God's people offer a context beyond ourselves. Unlike many modern Western expositors, however, Paul was not addressing a highly individualistic audience, although an individualistic perspective would be more common among Greek-speaking Gentiles in Rome than among Jesus's Galilean hearers. Paul's point is not simply a context beyond our own limited personhood, as in Stoicism, but rather a life beyond human autonomy in its willful rejection of God's perspective.

For Paul, Christ dwells in his body, working through all believers. Although God works in the cosmos (Rom. 1:19–20; Col. 1:15–16) and in all of history, he is revealed most fully in the history of his people and in his current work among his people in Christ. Although Paul does not emphasize the point here in this connection, however, because greater revelation demands greater responsibility (Rom. 2:12; 5:13; 7:7), one might expect Paul to challenge believers with higher demands than outsiders to the faith (e.g., 1 Cor. 6:1–5, 15, 19).[199]

God's Own Mind in the Preceding Context

"Therefore" (the postpositive conjunction οὖν in Rom. 12:1) connects the exhortation of 12:1 with the preceding context.[200] Although Paul uses a different term in 12:1, God's "mercies" or "expressions of compassion" there may well evoke the theme of God's "mercy" in Romans 9:15–16, 18, 23 and 11:30–32.[201] (Paul may exhort here by God's mercies; one could exhort someone

---

limited to the Dead Sea Scrolls. Cf. also the Spirit's role in providing insight in the scrolls (1QS 4.3; 1QH^a 20.15; 4Q427 frg. 8, col. 2.18).

199. For the concept of greater knowledge demanding greater responsibility, see also, e.g., Philost. *Vit. soph.* 1.16.501; Amos 3:2; *2 Bar.* 15:5–6; 19:3; *Sipre Deut.* 43.14.1; *b. Shab.* 68ab; *Yoma* 72b; Luke 12:47; James 3:1; 4:17.

200. As often noted, e.g., in Dunn, *Romans*, 708. Admittedly, Paul uses the conjunction freely (more than thirty times in Romans), but it carries its normal meaning in these instances, and conjoined with a fresh exhortation (as also in 1 Cor. 4:16), the element of consequence is important. Sometimes Paul uses "therefore" when developing an ethical section that follows more theological groundwork (Marshall, *Thessalonians*, 104), and some commentators envision its function thus here (Moo, *Romans*, 748). Writers often transitioned even by restating a point and then setting forth what would follow (*Rhet. Her.* 4.26.35).

201. Many view "mercies" here as referring back to Rom. 9–11, e.g., Schreiner, *Romans*, 639. Cranfield (*Romans*, 2:448) regards the keyword of Rom. 9–11 as "mercy." The LXX employs Paul's term for "mercies" here for God's mercy with respect to God's covenant faithfulness (Gupta, "Mercies"). Furnish ("Living," 194) applies it also to all claims about God's love in

by a deity.)[202] God has revealed his mercy in the history of salvation, dealing with both Jews and Gentiles, so believers should respond by giving themselves. This history of salvation emphatically reveals God's wisdom (11:33–36).[203]

The connection between God's wisdom in Romans 11:33–36 and the present text is important. As in 8:5, here again Paul probably implies more than a figurative reference to the divine mind as an example; the renewed mind recognizes God's will in part because it is influenced by (or, ideally, suffused with)[204] God's own mind. That divinely influenced mind becomes explicit in 1 Corinthians 2:16, where Paul applies Isaiah 40:13 to Christ's followers having the mind of Christ. Especially because 1 Corinthians 2:16 provides us access to Paul's interpretation of the Isaian verse, we should expect that Paul, like his contemporaries we have surveyed earlier, did in fact believe that the divine mind was at work in renewing the minds of the wise.

Paul employs this particular term for "mind" (νοῦς) only six times in Romans (in five paragraphs: 1:28; 7:23, 25; 11:34; 12:2; 14:5), and one (11:34) is a quotation of Isaiah 40:13 just four verses before his present remark about renewing the mind. This proximity is likely no coincidence. In Romans 11:34 Paul's point is that God's plans in history (surveyed in 11:25–32, introduced with a "mystery") are marvelously wise, beyond what humans would have designed.[205] At the same time, in a manner consistent with his use in 1 Corinthians of the same Isaian verse to affirm believers having Christ's mind, he here speaks of believers' minds being renewed to discern God's will.

A Mind for the Body of Christ in the Following Context

Believers offer up their bodies as sacrifices for God's purposes (Rom. 12:1–2)—ultimately, their bodies for Christ's body (12:4–6). In context, the new way of thinking articulated in 12:2 forms how believers think about themselves in

Christ (including Rom. 5:8; 8:35, 39). Some suggest instead that mercies here are empowerment for presenting oneself, as by the Spirit (Talbert, *Romans*, 282–83, citing Rom. 8:4 and Phil. 2:1–2); but Paul could easily specify the Spirit here, and even Phil. 2:1–2 may be a response to God's mercies shown in his acts.

202. See, e.g., Isaeus *Menec.* 47; *Rhet. Alex.* 15, 1432a.1–2; Dio Chrys. *Or.* 33.45; Rowe, "Style," 139; for invoking deities in other ways, see, e.g., Mus. Ruf. 2, p. 38.17; 3, p. 42.2; Dio Chrys. *Or.* 47.14; in letters, Fronto *Ad Ant. Pium* 2, 4; *Ep. graec.* 1.5; 2.1; 5.4.

203. See appendix B.

204. Cf. also the idea of internalizing here Jesus's model in Murphy, "Understanding."

205. Historians often attributed the process of history to fate or providence, although often deeming it intelligible only in retrospect; see, e.g., discussions in Grene, *Political Theory*, 75–79; Squires, *Plan*, esp. 15–20, 38–51, 121–37, 154–66; Squires, "Plan"; Brawley, *Centering on God*, 86–106; Walbank, "Fortune," 350–54; Brouwer, "Polybius and Tyche."

the context of the Christian community, shaping their relationships there.[206] Continuing his interest in the mind from 12:1–2, Paul goes on in 12:3 to emphasize "sober" thinking, playing on φρονεῖν and σωφρονεῖν.[207] Although the verb σωφρονέω need not imply the cognate noun σωφροσύνη, the semantic ranges overlap considerably. The usage of σωφροσύνη and its cognates in moral discourse extended far beyond philosophers, but in keeping with our discussion of philosophy, some summary comments about typical philosophic usage may be in order here. Plato's Socrates was known for emphasizing this virtue,[208] as were philosophers in the early empire.[209] Like "prudence," σωφροσύνη was one of the four chief Aristotelian virtues,[210] and Stoics continued to treat it as one of the traditional virtues.[211]

Stoics employed this word group especially for self-control over the passions, the baser emotions.[212] It could be used to summarize virtue.[213] It should characterize the reign of the ideal ruler[214] but particularly should typify the

206. Jewett (*Romans*, 733) goes too far when he suggests that the focus in Rom. 12:2 is "on group decision making." This is not the perspective one would gain reading the text in light of ancient philosophy. This interpretation could fit 12:3–6, but the only necessary point is that one takes the group into account in making the decision, whether it is the individual or the group hearing and deciding. Thus, it does require the larger context of Christ's body, but Paul expects individuals to apply the counsel as well as groups. Note the "individual" responsibility as well in 12:5.

207. He also plays on ὑπερφρονεῖν, creating rhetorically pleasant repetition (with Longenecker, *Introducing Romans*, 423; cf. Furnish, *Corinthians*, 308). Many note the connection regarding cognition between 12:2 and 12:3 (e.g., Rodríguez, *Call Yourself*, 237).

208. See esp. Plato *Charm.* 159B–176C; cf. Xen. *Mem.* 1.2.23.

209. See, e.g., Mus. Ruf. 18B, p. 116.20; Arius Did. 2.7.5f, p. 30.23; 2.7.11g, p. 72.15; Lucian *Icar.* 30 (Zeus complaining that they were not living accordingly). Cf. also the moralist Plutarch in *Poetry* 11, *Mor.* 32C.

210. Though ultimately said to derive from Socrates (Plato *Rep.* 4.428–34).

211. E.g., Mus. Ruf. 4, p. 44.10–22, esp. 16–22; p. 48.1, 4, 8, 13, esp. 4; 6, p. 52.15, 17, 19, 21, esp. 15; 7, p. 58.25–26 (minus "courage"); 8, pp. 60.22–64.9, esp. 62.10–23; 8, p. 66.7–8, esp. 8; 17, p. 108.9–10; Marc. Aur. 3.6; Arius Did. 2.7.5a, p. 10.7–9 (Zeno's views); 2.7.5b1, p. 12.13–22 (and their converse in lines 22–29; as *samples* of virtues and vices—see lines 29–30); 2.7.5b2, p. 14.1–4 (esp. 3); 2.7.5b5, p. 18.27–31 (with lines 21–26, 32–35). Cf. Mus. Ruf. 7, p. 58.25–26 (esp. 26); 16, p. 104.32–34, esp. 33; frg. 38, p. 136.3. See discussion in Lutz, *Musonius*, 27, including n. 113. Cf. lists of virtues including at least three of these, e.g., Arius Did. 2.7.5b, p. 10.16–21 (esp. 17); 2.7.11e, p. 68.12–16; Philost. *Vit. Apoll.* 1.20.

212. E.g., cf. Mus. Ruf. 3, p. 40.20–22; 4, p. 44.18–22; 6, p. 52.15–17; 8, p. 62.14–17; 16, p. 104.33–35; 17, p. 108.11–14; frg. 24, p. 130; Arius Did. 2.7.5b2, p. 14.6. Against sexual indulgence, see, e.g., Mus. Ruf. 12, p. 86.13–16; against gluttony, e.g., Mus. Ruf. 18A, p. 112.6–7 (cf. 112.29); 18B, p. 116.4–22, esp. 19–20; 18B, p. 118.4–7, esp. 5; p. 120.2–7, esp. 6–7; against grief, e.g., Arius Did. 2.7.5L, p. 36.3–5. See, further, Lutz, *Musonius*, 28 (noting esp. 6, p. 54.2–25). For the fullest definition, see Arius Did. 2.7.5b1, p. 12.18–19; 2.7.5b2, p. 14.15–16, 31–35; p. 16.1–3; cf. also 2.7.5b, p. 10.21–25 (esp. 23); p. 12.1–2.

213. Mus. Ruf. 5, p. 50.22–26.

214. Mus. Ruf. 8, p. 60.10–23; 8, p. 62.10–21; Dio Chrys. *Or.* 3.7; Philost. *Vit. Apoll.* 5.35, 36.

philosopher.[215] In women, philosophers associated this virtue with chastity and avoiding unlawful relations.[216] The virtue was widespread among philosophers far more broadly than in Stoicism[217]—for example, among Pythagoreans.[218] Although outsiders might question the σωφροσύνη of someone who abandoned everything for philosophy, many intellectuals countered that such a person was genuinely wise.[219]

How does Paul apply σωφρονέω specifically in Romans 12:3? The renewed mind of 12:2 does not view itself more highly than it ought (ὑπερφρονεῖν,[220] 12:3; cf. 12:16);[221] wisdom often was opposed to arrogantly overstepping one's bounds.[222] Instead, the renewed mind should view itself in the context of Christ's body (12:4–6) and hence ultimately in a way that supports believers' unity (cf. 15:5). This renewed mind recognizes that each believer has been apportioned faith for particular activities (12:3, 6),[223] so that no member is more or less valuable than any other member. Specific roles may differ, but each member is gifted for serving the rest of the body of Christ. The renewed mind should thus look for

215. E.g., Mus. Ruf. 8, p. 66.8; Dio Chrys. *Or.* 35.2.

216. E.g., Mus. Ruf. 3, p. 40.17–18, 20; 4, p. 44.16–18. For the virtue as appropriate for women, see also Mus. Ruf. 4, p. 48.4; for philosophy teaching women this virtue, see also Mus. Ruf. 3, p. 42.26–28. See more broadly North, "Mare."

217. Cf. even Epicureans in Cic. *Fin.* 1.14.47 (*temperantiam*), a concession Stoics were ready to exploit (Mus. Ruf. frg. 24, p. 130, with Lutz's note, p. 131). Cf. Lucian *Nigr.* 6.

218. Cf., e.g., Philost. *Vit. Apoll.* 5.36; 6.11; Iambl. *Pyth. Life* 1.1; ruling the tongue, 31.195; concerning the temptations of youth, 8.41; 31.195 (sexual).

219. Dio Chrys. *Or.* 80.1.

220. Thinking "above" one's role (on which see, helpfully, Jewett, *Romans*, 739–41) was often expressed in arrogance (e.g., for Chrysippus in Diog. Laert. 7.7.183, 185; boasting beyond one's strength in Hom. *Il.* 17.19; the object of Socrates's critique in Diog. Laert. 2.38). It should not be confused with positive ancient comments about noble-mindedness or great-mindedness, on which cf. Galen *Grief* 50b; Iambl. *Letter* 6, frg. 2 (Stob. *Anth.* 4.5.75). Nevertheless, in view of Rom. 12:16, part of what Paul clearly has in mind is setting aside considerations of social status (cf. Taylor, "Obligation"), and that verse also evokes Rom. 11:20, which warns God's people against ethnic prejudice.

221. Cf. some philosophers' practices of self-evaluation and self-improvement (Sorabji, *Emotion*, 211–27, Stoics on 213–14). Against inappropriate pride, see, e.g., Eurip. frg. 963 (from Plut. *Mor.* 102e); frg. 1113a (= 1040 N; from Stob. *Anth.* 3.22.5).

222. See Marshall, *Enmity*, 190–94 (for "beyond measure" in 2 Cor. 10:13, see 369). Cf. also North, "Concept"; North, *Sophrosyne*.

223. Treating μέτρον πίστεως (12:3) as roughly equivalent to ἀναλογίαν τῆς πίστεως (12:6), with, e.g., Dunn, *Romans*, 727–28; Byrne, *Romans*, 371; Schreiner, *Romans*, 652; *pace*, e.g., Cranfield, "ΜΕΤΡΟΝ ΠΙΣΤΕΩΣ," 351; Bryan, *Preface*, 197. In support of faith apportioned for gifts, cf. (in Bray, *Romans*, 309–12) Origen *Comm. Rom.* on 12:3 (*CER* 5:46); Basil *Baptism* 8; *Rules* 7 (on Rom. 12:6); Chrys. *Hom. Rom.* 21 (on Rom. 12:6); Ps.-Const. *Rom.* (on Rom. 12:6); Pelagius *Comm. Rom.* on 12:6 (*PCR* 133); Gennadius of Constantinople, catena on Rom. 12:6 (*PGK* 15:404). The point here, however, is not the *amount* of faith God apportions to a believer but the distinctive *purpose* (a particular gift) for which he apportions it.

ways to serve others, not boasting[224] but fulfilling our role from God faithfully as his gift to the body. That is, Paul's emphasis on the right way to think in Romans fits his larger emphasis on unity, as he probably seeks to reconcile Jewish and Gentile believers (an emphasis that many scholars find in this letter).[225]

This larger context of Romans reinforces my earlier suggested additional meaning of "peace" beyond "tranquility," despite the plausibility of emphasis on the latter in ancient discussions of the mind. Presumably for Paul, the mindframe of the Spirit also leads believers to peace with one another, whether across ethnic lines (as in Romans as a whole) or in the diversity of believers' ministry gifts (as in Rom. 12:4–8).

Paul's image of the body[226] would not be lost on believers in Rome; both philosophers and orators had long employed the image.[227] Thinkers sometimes depicted the entire cosmos[228] or humanity[229] as a body, emphasizing its unity. Orators[230] and philosophers[231] also depicted the state in this way, sometimes

224. Neither should one underestimate one's role (cf. the relation between σωφροσύνη and self-respect in Thucyd. 1.84.3; avoiding low thoughts about oneself by reckoning ourselves as children of God, Epict. *Diatr.* 1.3.1), but of course Paul's greater concern in Romans is boasting and looking down on others (e.g., Rom. 2:17, 23; 3:27; 4:2; cf. 1 Cor. 1:29; 3:21; 4:7); to boast about God's grace is different (Rom. 5:2, 3, 11; 15:17; 1 Cor. 1:31). On the value of modest self-esteem as the correct mean between being vain and being of small soul, see Arist. *E.E.* 3.5.16–20, 1233a.

225. E.g., Dunn, *Romans*, lvii; Lung-Kwong, *Purpose*, 413–14; Haacker, *Theology*, 48–49; Grieb, *Story*, 7.

226. Some see this as Paul's primary image (Manson, *Paul and John*, 67; Robinson, *Body*, 9); this verdict may be overstated (cf. Daines, "Use"; Ridderbos, *Paul: Outline*, 366; Judge, *First Christians*, 568–73), but it is certainly important to Paul (1 Cor. 10:17; 11:29; 12:12–27; Eph. 1:23; 2:16; 3:6; 4:4, 16; 5:23, 30; Col. 1:18, 24; 2:19; 3:15; cf. Rom. 7:4). Later, see *1 Clem.* 37.5; 38.1; 46.7; *2 Clem.* 14.2; Ign. *Smyrn.* 1.2; *Herm.* 95.4.

227. The metaphor is a natural one; in Confucian tradition, see Jochim, *Religions*, 80. Some also cite Jewish mysticism (*2 En.* 39:6 A; Kim, *Origin*, 252–54; cf. Schweizer, "Kirche") or even Diaspora Judaism (Quispel, "Mysticism"). Political comparisons in the latter case (Grant, *Christianity and Society*, 37, citing Philo *Spec. Laws* 3.131; *Virt.* 103; Jos. *War* 1.507; 4.406) may be natural or may reflect wider Mediterranean usage.

228. E.g., Diod. Sic. 1.11.6; most often among Stoics: Cic. *Fin.* 3.19.64 (providing the Stoic view); Sen. Y. *Ep. Lucil.* 95.52; Epict. *Diatr.* 1.12.26; cf. Marc. Aur. 4.14, 40; 10.6.2; Long, "Soul." Lincoln (*Ephesians*, 70) notes that the image may have originated with Plato (*Tim.* 30B–34B, 47C–48B; cf. Schweizer, *Colossians*, 58) and that it appears in Philo (*Plant.* 7; *Spec. Laws* 1.210; cf. *Creation* 82; *Migr.* 220; *Spec. Laws* 2.127, 133, 134).

229. Marc. Aur. 7.13. For the body image used for human unity in other ways, see Mitchell, *Rhetoric of Reconciliation*, 119, 158–59; cf. family members in Hierocles *Love* (Stob. *Anth.* 4.84.20; also cited in Sandnes, "Legemet"), though ancient writers connected household and civic management; to some extent friends in Lucian *Tox.* 53; Philost. *Hrk.* 48.22.

230. Cic. *Phil.* 8.5.15 (recommending amputation of a harmful member); *Resp.* 3.25.37; Sall. *Ep. Caes.* 10.6; Dio Chrys. *Or.* 34.22; Max. Tyre *Or.* 15.4–5; cf. Catiline in Cic. *Mur.* 25.51; Plut. *Cic.* 14.4–5.

231. Note the early comparison already in Arist. *Pol.* 1.1.11, 1253a; cf. Philo *Spec. Laws* 157; *T. Naph.* 2:9–10. Note also the early Aesopic fable *The Belly and the Feet* (cited variously

showing how all parts were necessary for the whole.[232] (As has long been observed,[233] this image had been popular in Roman political usage since the speech of Menenius Agrippa in which he exhorted the plebeians to value their productive—yet subordinate—role in the state.)[234]

Contrary to the views of some scholars,[235] points where Paul's depiction differs do not argue against his drawing on this wider usage; they suggest instead that he adapted it for his own purposes, as various other writers also did. Nevertheless, Paul's purposes are surely distinctive in applying the image not to a political or natural body but to those united with Christ. Scholars also often note his reorientation of an originally hierarchical political image to emphasize interdependence without a note of hierarchy.[236]

Paul ideally wanted believers to care for and live for God's concerns rather than for their own (2 Cor. 5:14–15; Phil. 2:20–21; cf. 1 Cor. 4:11–16; 7:29–35; Mark 8:33–38). Granted, most believers in Paul's churches did *not* live this way, and Paul did not therefore deny that they were in Christ. For example, Paul praises Timothy to the faithful Philippian church by noting that Paul has no one like him, since others care for their own concerns rather than those of Christ (Phil. 2:20–21).

There undoubtedly is hyperbole in Paul's exclusion of all others in that praise; writers of letters of recommendation could occasionally indulge in superlatives for more than one person,[237] just as rabbis could.[238] Moreover, it

---

as fable 159/132/130) in Wojciechowski, "Tradition," 108; cf. the similar fable in Dio Chrys. *Or.* 33.16. In rabbinic sources, cf. later *Song Rab.* 4:1, §2; 7:5, §2.

232. Widely noted (e.g., Allo, *Première Épitre*, 328; Horsley, *Corinthians*, 171); see, further, Grant, *Christianity and Society*, 36–37; Lindemann, "Kirche"; Judge, *First Christians*, 568–95 (esp. 581–95). Besides references above, commentators (e.g., Conzelmann, *Corinthians*, 211; Lincoln, *Ephesians*, 70) cite Plato *Rep.* 5.464B; Arist. *Pol.* 1.1, 2; Cic. *Phil.* 8.5.16; *Off.* 1.25, 85; 3.5.22; Livy 26.16.19; Sen. Y. *Clem.* 1.5.1; *Ira* 2.31.7; Quint. Curt. 10.6.8; 10.9.2.

233. E.g., Moffatt, *Corinthians*, 183–84; Knox, "Parallels"; Héring, *First Epistle*, 129–30; Cerfaux, *Church*, 266. As Oster (*Corinthians*, 301) points out, the correspondence with Paul was already recognized by John Calvin, who was a humanist scholar as well as a Reformer.

234. See Livy 2.32.9–12; Dion. Hal. *Ant. rom.* 6.86.1–5 (climaxing the speech of 6.83.2–86.5); Plut. *Coriol.* 6.2–4; Dio Cass. 4.17.10–13; cf. Val. Max. 4.4.2; Sen. Y. *Dial.* 12.12.5.

235. Some generally helpful discussions may overemphasize differences, e.g., Sevenster, *Seneca*, 170–72; Jewett, *Romans*, 744.

236. See, e.g., Robertson and Plummer, *Corinthians*, 269; Kim, *Introduction*, 27; Witherington, *Corinthians*, 254, 259; cf. Troeltsch, *Teaching*, 1:76–77. It should be noted, however, that the notion of hierarchy was not always present in ancient use of the image. On Paul's inversion of the conventional hierarchical function in ancient speeches on concord, some of which exploited this image, see Martin, *Body*, 38–68, esp. 39–47.

237. E.g., Cic. *Fam.* 3.1.3; 13.1.5; 13.5.3; 13.18.2; 13.19.1; 13.26.1; 13.32.2; 13.34.1; 13.35.1; 13.36.1–2; 13.39.1; 13.45.1; 13.51.1; 13.78.2. Cf. even 2 Kings 18:5; 23:25.

238. Kraeling, *John the Baptist*, 139, citing the *Mekilta*. Hyperbole was common in Semitic speech (Caird, *Language*, 133).

is clear from the same context that Epaphroditus risked his life for the work of Christ (Phil. 2:30). Still, Paul seems convinced that most believers fall short of single-minded devotion to Christ, and Paul is disappointed by this state of affairs.

Despite these caveats, however, several points remain clear: first, Paul especially values living wholly for Christ's concerns (Phil. 2:21); second, Christ's concerns in the context in Philippians refer especially to the welfare of God's people (2:20); and third, such concern was praiseworthy because it was, unfortunately, unusual.[239]

Conclusion

Paul exhorts his hearers to decide "rationally" to present their bodies as sacrifices that please God in how they live. He goes on to describe the rational element more fully. Believers will be transformed by the renewing of their minds; this renewal enables them to evaluate the present age from the values of the perfect world to come, and thus not to be pressured into conformity with the character of the present age. A believer can often identify God's will rationally by recognizing what is good, pleasing, and perfect in God's sight.

The preceding context reveals God's mind in his plan in history, which provides a basis for how believers should express devotion to him. The following context also reveals how the renewed mind should think: each one should consider how he or she can best serve Christ's body, and every member should value every other member. Each one thus offers up her or his own body to serve Christ's body.

Neglecting the critical role of the renewing of the mind (Rom. 12:2) can leave believers with a legalistic anxiety or fear of the power of the "flesh"—fear of old patterns or impulses (cf. Rom. 8:15). The renewing of the mind occurs alongside growing in God- and Christ-directed faith, or trust, which inherently involves a relationship with God and Christ. As is particularly emphasized in 2 Corinthians 3:18 (see chap. 6),[240] such trust and renewal in God's likeness grow in proportion to a living experience of God.

---

239. Jesus's chief disciple in the gospel tradition similarly sets his mind on (φρονέω) human interests rather than God's; ultimately, this is a satanic perspective (Mark 8:33; cf. Matt. 4:10; 16:23). The ideal standard and goal do not change, but neither do the disciples always match it, at least within the period narrated in the Gospels.

240. Pages 206–15 below.

6

The Mind of Christ (1 Cor. 2:15–16)

For [Scripture says,] "Who has known the Lord's mind and is thus able to advise him?" But *we have* Christ's mind.

—1 Corinthians 2:16

In 1 Corinthians 1–2 Paul urges believers to grow mature in true, divine wisdom. He also spells out this wisdom's content: the message of the cross that inverts the world's values and invites us to view everything in this age in light of the coming age (2:6–10), when God's wisdom prevails unchallenged.

Paul further recognizes that people receive divine wisdom only because it is revealed by God's own Spirit (1 Cor. 2:10–13). Those without the Spirit cannot properly understand or evaluate the decisions of those who follow divine truth, but those who follow the Spirit's insight have the right vantage point for evaluating the world (2:14–15). Those who have God's Spirit have the mind of Christ (2:16); Christ's body may experience this mind in multiple ways through various gifts, though the true message will always be consistent with the message about the crucified Lord (1:17–24; 2:1–5). Those who, based on worldly philosophies, think themselves divine should instead cultivate a true embrace of the divine perspective (3:3–4).

A passage in 2 Corinthians helps to explicate some of what Paul means by sharing the divine mind, although it does not speak explicitly of cognitive processes. Believers can be transformed more into the divine image through focusing on the glory of Christ (2 Cor. 3:18), who is God's supreme image (4:4). Many ancient thinkers sought transformation through envisioning the divine; Jewish mystics also strove to see what they could of God enthroned, but the fundamental example of transformation through seeing the true divine glory is Moses (3:7–16). What Moses experienced in a partial way, new covenant ministers experience more fully by God's own Spirit living in them (3:3, 6, 8, 17–18).

True Wisdom (1 Cor. 1:18–2:10)

A biblical proverb may summarize an aspect of Paul's perspective on wisdom: "Put your trust in the LORD with all your heart, and do not depend on your own understanding" (Prov. 3:5). Paul urges believers to embrace true wisdom, wisdom that rests on the fear of the Lord.[1] This means recognizing that the ultimately reliable source of counsel is the all-knowing one, whose ways are very different from what is expected by the limited knowledge of mortals.

As in Romans 12:2, so also in 1 Corinthians 1–2 Paul cultivates a wisdom shaped not by the world's values but by the perfectly divine values of the coming age. In the clarity on God's plan afforded by the vantage point of eternity, what the world saw as merely the elites' execution of Jesus for treason becomes instead the climax of salvation history, the prelude to God's triumph by the resurrection.

The Wisdom of the Cross (1 Cor. 1:17–2:5)

In 1 Corinthians 2:6–13 Paul develops his contrast between the inadequate wisdom of the world and the true wisdom that comes from God (cf. James 3:13–18). Paul notes that wisdom about divine matters comes only through the Spirit (1 Cor. 2:10–11) and hence is available only to people of the Spirit (2:12–16).

Paul shows that the wisdom he preaches, the wisdom by which they have been converted, is the message of the cross (1 Cor. 1:17–18, 21, 24, 30; 2:1–5). This message seems like foolishness to the world (1:18, 21, 23, 27), but those who have experienced its transforming power know better (1:18). The world obviously would have done things differently, Paul recognizes, but recent events in history, especially Jesus's death and resurrection, reveal God's greater wisdom. In the light of God's eternal plan, the world's version of theological wisdom amounts to nothing (1:19–20; 3:19–20).

---

1. See Job 28:28; Ps. 111:10; Prov. 1:7; 9:10; 15:33; Sir. 1:18, 27; 19:20; 21:11; cf. *1 Clem.* 57.5.

Paul addresses here not only wisdom but power—translating from Paul's setting to our closest equivalent, not only education but the closely connected issue of status and social influence. The cross lays bare human weakness yet reveals God's power. Signs and wonders may display God's power (1:22; cf. 2 Cor. 12:12), but the cross reveals it still more deeply (1 Cor. 1:18, 24; 2:4–5; 2 Cor. 13:4). Ignorant of God's wisdom and power, the elites that appear so powerful in this age[2] executed as a criminal the true and eternal Lord (1 Cor. 2:6–8). Practicing the nonresistance he preached, Jesus entrusted himself wholly to his Father, depending on the Father to raise him up.[3] Paul likewise embraces weakness by following the way of the cross so that God's power will be honored (2 Cor. 4:7, 10; 12:9; 13:3).

Paul's approach is counterintuitive to human instincts and was certainly countercultural in his setting. Corinthian society valued learning and status,[4] but the backgrounds of most of the Corinthian believers themselves showed that God did not need the world's wisdom or power to accomplish his purposes (1 Cor. 1:26–29, echoing Jer. 9:23–24, part of which is quoted in 1 Cor. 1:31).[5] The Corinthian Christians were emulating the values of a world that exalted people whom God had not chosen over themselves, whom God had chosen.[6]

2. Some scholars understand the rulers here as heavenly or spiritual rulers (e.g., Dibelius, "Initiation," 94; MacGregor, "Principalities," 22–23; Cullmann, State, 63; Héring, First Epistle, 16–17; Berkhof, Powers, 14; Manson, Paul and John, 61; Whiteley, Theology, 26; Lee, "Powers," 63; Conzelmann, Corinthians, 61; Adeyemi, "Rulers"; cf. Ambrosiaster Comm. [CSEL 81:24; Bray, Corinthians, 22]), as probably in Rom. 8:38; certainly in Col. 1:16; 2:15; Eph. 3:10; 6:12; cf. Dan. 10:13, 20; Jub. 15:31–32; 35:17; 1 En. 61:10; 75:1. Some did believe that angels could not understand all of God's work (cf. 4Q402 frg. 4.14–15 [reconstructed]; Eph. 3:10; 1 Pet. 1:12; Daniélou, Theology, 206–14), or that God kept some things secret to circumvent Satan (b. Sanh. 26b). Given the present context, the reference here more likely is simply to earthly rulers (with Miller, "APXONTΩN," 528; Carr, Angels, 120; Fee, Exegesis, 87–91; Fee, Corinthians, 104; Thiselton, Corinthians, 233–39; Allison, Constructing Jesus, 396; cf. Oecumenius, catena on 1 Cor. 2:12 [PGK 15:432; Bray, Corinthians, 23]), as in Rom. 13:1–3; Titus 3:1; and possibly 1 Cor. 15:24—though not because the angelic use is post-Pauline (pace Carr, "Rulers," 30).

3. Note the preaching of the kingdom early in Mark's Gospel and its climax in Mark's passion narrative; although this narrative still envisions a future kingdom (14:25; 15:43), its focus on Jesus's kingship is Jesus being mocked as king by those who are killing him (15:2, 9, 12, 18, 26, 32).

4. Corinth was known for its wealth and trade (e.g., Mart. Epig. 5.35.3; Favorinus in Dio Chrys. Or. 37.8, 36; Thiselton, Corinthians, 6–12; Engels, Roman Corinth, 33–52) but also for its stratification (Alciph. Paras. 24 [Chascobuces to Hypnotrapezus], 3.60, ¶1). For status issues in the urban empire, cf. Meeks, Moral World, 32.

5. Although few Christians there belonged to the upper class (e.g., Gager, "Class," 99; Gager, "Review," 180; Judge, Pattern, 52), some apparently were of high status; a numerical minority within the congregation, they nevertheless exerted disproportionate influence (e.g., Theissen, "Schichtung"; Judge, Rank, 9–10; Malherbe, Social Aspects, 29–30, 118–19). Corinth may have been idiosyncratic in its proportion of higher-status believers (see Friesen, "Prospects," 353–58).

6. From a postcolonial political perspective, we might say that they had internalized the false narrative of the elites.

Paul challenges the Corinthians in the very matters in which they are boasting (cf. 1 Cor. 1:29–31; 3:21; 4:7; 5:6; 6:5; 10:15). The world's philosophies[7] might advocate mental discipline or achieving divine wisdom through depending on innate, natural divinity.[8] For Paul, however, God's wisdom is revealed in his plan in history (as in Rom. 11:30–34), which climaxes in the cross, the epitome of human brokenness. The heart of divine wisdom, and hence the heart of what it means to share the mind of Christ (1 Cor. 2:16), is the way of the cross. Far from embracing the wisdom of this age, it trusts God's greater plan, which the world despises as nonsensical. The truly wise should boast in their weakness and depend on God's power (cf. 1 Cor. 3:18; 2 Cor. 12:9–10); they should give all honor (or, in modern Western terms, all the credit) to God. Such wisdom that depends on God fits Paul's theology, for example, in what I have called the mind of faith.[9]

Wisdom of the Future Age (1 Cor. 2:6–10)

Even more clearly than in Romans 12:2, God's wisdom in 1 Corinthians 2 is eschatological wisdom.[10] Although Paul eschews human wisdom when reaching the unconverted (1 Cor. 2:5), refusing to water down the offensive message of the cross, he does not oppose true understanding. Thus, he speaks wisdom[11] among the mature (2:6a)—a maturity the Corinthian Christians have not attained.[12] Their fixation on status and competition has kept them too immature for Paul to teach them the deeper things[13] (3:1–2) of the Spirit—God's eschatological promises about their future glory (2:7, 9; cf. Rom. 8:16–17;

---

7. Scholars rightly notice the emphasis on speaking—and thus concerns regarding rhetoric among the congregation's more elite members—in 1 Cor. 1:17–18, 20; 2:1, 4, 13; 4:19–20 (including the "wisdom" of skilled speech in 1:5, 17; 2:4); see, e.g., Pogoloff, *Logos*, 109–12; Litfin, *Theology*, 119–24, 245–46. Some, however, have neglected the likely influence also of the other advanced discipline of Greco-Roman antiquity—namely, philosophy—when Paul speaks of wisdom or knowledge (1:5, 19–22, 26–27; 2:1, 4–6, 13; 3:18–20; cf. Clem. Alex. *Strom.* 1.90.1; Ambrosiaster *Comm.*, proem [CSEL 81:3–4]; Chrys. *Hom. Cor.* 4.4, 6; 5.5; Bray, *Corinthians*, 14, 16–17). Paul's contrast between divine wisdom and human philosophy is still more explicit in Col. 2:3, 8.

8. See discussion below on pp. 204–5.

9. See esp. pp. 44–45.

10. The wisdom of the coming age, then to be publicly vindicated (with Ambrosiaster *Comm.* [CSEL 81:23]; Bray, *Corinthians*, 21]); but probably also eschatological in content (see below, pp. 178–79).

11. Paul's repetition of "wisdom" twice in 1 Cor. 2:6 is rhetorically suitable (on such repetition, see, e.g., Cic. *Or. Brut.* 39.135; cf. Anderson, *Glossary*, 18, 37).

12. For the sense "mature" here, as often in Paul, see, e.g., Allo, *Première Épitre*, 91; Garland, *1 Corinthians*, 93.

13. Cf. probably also "depths" in 1 Cor. 2:10.

Eph. 1:13–14). Although lacking Paul's future eschatology, philosophers also valued the eternal far above the temporal.[14]

In connecting wisdom and maturity, Paul might evoke Wisdom 9:6, which also connects the two concepts, although differently: "For even the most mature [τέλειος] among people will be considered as nothing without the wisdom that is from" the Lord.[15] This latter passage emphasizes that no one can learn God's counsel without God giving wisdom and sending his Spirit (Wis. 9:17). Likewise, Paul was able to give them divine wisdom because God's Spirit had inspired him (1 Cor. 2:4–5, 13).[16]

Paul specifies that the wisdom he speaks is not human wisdom (1 Cor. 2:5)—not a wisdom that belongs to the present age (2:6). Like the present age itself (7:31), the rulers of this age are ephemeral and are coming to nothing (2:6); because they lacked eternal wisdom, they executed the most honorable and glorious ruler of all, the true king (2:8).[17] Presumably, Paul has in mind here the members of both Jewish and Roman elites involved in Jesus's execution (cf. Mark 15:1; 1 Cor. 1:23; 1 Thess. 2:14–15).[18]

Yet Paul looks beyond the immediate members of the elite directly responsible and envisions in general those honored and esteemed in this age. That the rulers are "passing away" (καραργουμένων, 1 Cor. 2:6) recalls the esteemed whom God brings to nothing (καταργήσῃ) in 1:28. Paul's example warns the status-conscious Corinthian Christians: their desire for human power (1:26–28) aligns them with those who are powerful by the standards of this age. Instead of honoring the true king's cross, they embrace the foolish

14. E.g., Sen. Y. *Ep. Lucil.* 66.31; Epict. *Diatr.* 2.12.21–22; Marc. Aur. 11.1.2; in 4 Maccabees, cf. Fuhrmann, "Mother." Those with apocalyptic sympathies would understand still more clearly (Mark 8:36–37; 2 *Bar.* 51:15–16; cf. *b. Tamid* 32a).

15. Probably also the source for Philo *QG* 4.191. Paul might omit a citation formula (1 Cor. 1:19, 31; 2:9; 3:19) out of knowledge of the different Judean canon; perhaps Apollos had used such wisdom texts as part of his Alexandrian canon, or they were in use in Corinth's synagogue before Paul's arrival.

16. Paul's wisdom language reflects especially Hellenistic Jewish wisdom tradition; see, e.g., Conzelmann, *Corinthians*, 8; Scroggs, "ΣΟΦΟΣ," 37, 54 ("apocalyptic wisdom teaching"). For Wis. 9 here, see also Scroggs, "ΣΟΦΟΣ," 51; deSilva, "Wisdom," 1274.

17. "Lord of glory," or "glorious Lord" (1 Cor. 2:8), probably contrasts with worldly honor and may evoke believers' future "glory" in 2:7. Similar language appears as a divine title in *1 Enoch* (22:14; 25:3; 27:3, 5; 36:4; 40:3; 63:2; 75:3; 83:8), as Grant (*Gnosticism*, 158) notes; cf. also Ps. 24:7–10 (23:7–10 LXX). *Pace* some (e.g., Pearson, *Terminology*, 34), there is no reason to attribute the phrase to Paul's "opponents" (although "the Lord of glory" is also "Lord of wisdom" in *1 En.* 63:2, with deep secrets in 63:3).

18. Against the idea (articulated in, e.g., Setzer, *Responses*, 16–19; Schmidt, "Linguistic Evidence") that 1 Thess. 2:14–16 is a post-Pauline interpolation, see Das, *Paul and Jews*, 129–36; Schlueter, *Measure*; Donfried, "Test Case"; Donfried, *Thessalonica*, 198–99; Collins, "Integrity."

values of those who executed him.[19] Indeed, they have transferred the world's values about leaders onto the leaders in the church, boasting in them (3:21) and creating elite Christian celebrities (3:4).

Paul must warn his hearers that he and Apollos are merely servants of God's purposes (1 Cor. 3:5–9; 4:1–2) and that only the future day of judgment and reward will reveal the value of each person's work (3:10–15; 4:4–5). The Corinthian Christians had the matter of status precisely backward: not only Christian leaders but in fact everything in the present and future world was for the sake of the church (3:21–23). By following the values of the world's wisdom, the Corinthian Christians missed a deeper wisdom that promised them something far more glorious than they imagined.[20]

In contrast to the transitory wisdom of this age, Paul communicates divine wisdom planned before the present and even any past ages of the world (1 Cor. 2:7).[21] This wisdom has been "hidden" (2:7),[22] concealed from even the most educated and elite persons of the world (2:6, 8); thus, it was not discerned by sight or sound or human imagination (2:9). The subject

19. Cf. the downfall of the world's rulers who valued power over God's wisdom in Bar. 3:14–19; cf. LXX Ps. 104:22 (105:22 ET); Isa. 19:11; Ezek. 27:8; Dan. 1:20; 2:48; 4:18; *Pss. Sol.* 8:20.

20. On a theological level, one might compare God's creation of humanity as vizier over his creation (Gen. 1:26–28) and the abandonment of this almost-supreme status for an empty promise of being "like God" (Gen. 3:5–6). Many thinkers rejected the wisdom of the majority, but whereas Paul's approach defies the values of the social elite, intellectuals disdained the views of the uninformed masses (e.g., Eurip. *Hipp.* 988–89; Aristoph. *Acharn.* 371–73; *Frogs* 419, 1085–86; among philosophers, see, e.g., Arist. *Pol.* 3.6.4–13, 1281a–1282b; 4.4.4–7, 1292a; 5.4.1–5, 1304b–1305b; 6.2.10–12, 1319b; *Rhet.* 2.20.5, 1393b; Epict. *Diatr.* 1.2.18; 1.3.4; 1.18.4, 10; 2.1.22; 4.8.27; Sen. Y. *Ep. Lucil.* 66.31; 108.7; Marc. Aur. 11.23; Mus. Ruf. 41, p. 136.22–26; Iambl. *Pyth. Life* 31.200, 213; Porph. *Marc.* 17.291–92; 30.475; Diogenes the Cynic in Diog. Laert. 6 passim; among rabbis, e.g., *m. Git.* 5:9; *Hag.* 2:7; *t. Demai* 2:5, 14–15, 19; 3:6–7; 6:8; *Maas.* 2:5).

21. For Wisdom's preexistence, see Prov. 8:22–23; Sir. 24:9; Wis. 7:22; 9:1–3; *L.A.B.* 32:7; *t. Sanh.* 8:9; *Sipre Deut.* 37.1.3; *2 En.* 30:8; 33:3. On preexistent wisdom in 1 Cor. 2:6–9, see esp. Hamerton-Kelly, *Pre-existence*, 116–17; discussion in Keener, *John*, 352–55, 367–68, 379–80.

22. The idea of hidden or esoteric wisdom was common (e.g., Val. Max. 8.7.ext.2; 1QS 11.6), though sometimes open to challenge (e.g., Isoc. *Antid.* 84). Against some older commentators who viewed μυστήριον here as related to the mystery cults (as it is in Wis. 14:15, 23; Philo *Spec. Laws* 1.319; 3.40; Jos. *Ant.* 19.30, 71, 104; *Ag. Ap.* 2.189, 266), the language had already acquired a strong home in Jewish wisdom (Wis. 2:22; 6:22; cf. ordinary usage in Sir. 22:22; 27:16–17, 21) and revelatory passages (Dan. 2:19, 27–30, 47). Philo often borrows language of the mysteries figuratively for divine mysteries (*Alleg. Interp.* 3.3, 27, 71, 100; *Cher.* 48–49; *Sacr.* 60; *Unchangeable* 61; *Contempl.* 25). The comparable Hebrew term is pervasive in the Dead Sea Scrolls (more than 150 times); cf. also secrets of wisdom in *1 En.* 51:3 (negatively, 69:8). See discussion in Brown, "*Mysterion*"; Brown, *Mystery*; Caragounis, *Mysterion*; in this context, Casciaro Ramírez, "Misterio"; Jódar-Estrella, "Misterio"; Horsley, *Corinthians*, 58–59.

of this wisdom is the eternal glory God planned for his people in the future (2:7),[23] "the things God prepared for those who love him" (2:9). (The idea of unfathomable future blessings also appears in Pauline thought in Eph. 2:7.)[24] These are matters that can be revealed neither by the senses nor by human reasoning (1 Cor. 2:9)[25] but only by the experience of the Spirit (2:10). That is, the Spirit provides an experiential foretaste of the life of the coming world, an experience also recognized by some other early Christians (see esp. Heb. 6:4–5).[26]

The Spirit's Insight (1 Cor. 2:10–13)

Because only God's Spirit truly knows his mind (1 Cor. 2:11), only God's Spirit can reveal eschatological truth (2:9–10) and the depths of God's heart (2:10). Because believers have received God's Spirit, they can know their promised inheritance (2:12) and communicate it by the Spirit among the spiritually mature (2:13).

Those who have only the spirit of the world (2:12) cannot recognize what spiritual truth is (2:14). They cannot embrace and live by spiritual truth, because that level of understanding comes only to those with the perspective inspired by God's Spirit. Thus, they cannot understand the choices of people of the Spirit, though people of the Spirit understand why people of the world are the way they are (2:15). Only people of the Spirit have the ultimate interpretive grid for reality, the grid provided by the creator.

The Spirit as Revealer (1 Cor. 2:10–11)

God revealed these eschatological realities to believers by the Spirit (1 Cor. 2:10), presumably on a level deeper than human understanding or language by itself could communicate.[27] The Spirit can reveal God's truths because the

23. Cf. Origen's comment on 1 Cor. 2:9: "How great the splendor, the beauty and the brightness of a spiritual body" (*Princ.* 3.6.4; trans. Bray, *Corinthians*, 23). It was widely applied to future blessings (e.g., *1 Clem.* 34.7–8; *Mart. Pol.* 2.3; Tert. *Spec.* 30).

24. For future blessings prepared for the righteous, cf. also, e.g., Matt. 25:34; *1 En.* 25:7; 103:3; *4 Ezra* 8:52.

25. Paul adapts here Isa. 64:3 LXX (64:4 ET), which also became a popular eschatological text among later rabbis (e.g., *b. Ber.* 34b; *Sanh.* 99a; *Shab.* 63a; *Exod. Rab.* 45:6); cf. the phrasing close to Paul's in *L.A.B.* 26:13. Some early interpreters recognized that Paul paraphrases Isa. 64 (cf. the blended wording in *1 Clem.* 34.8; Bray [*Corinthians*, 23] cites Ambrosiaster *Comm.* [CSEL 81:26]); some others suggest a source no longer extant (Chrys. *Hom. Cor.* 7.6).

26. Cf. Arrington, *Aeon Theology*, 132–33.

27. "Revealed wisdom" also appears occasionally in apocalyptic texts, such as *1 En.* 48:7.

Spirit can search even the very depths of God's heart (2:10).[28] Among Jewish thinkers the unfathomable, "deep things" of God already evoked motifs of secret wisdom, especially concerning God's heart and his plan for the world (cf. Rom. 11:33).[29] This connection is clear especially in Job 11:6–8, where the "deep things of God" are higher than heaven and deeper than Sheol, secrets of wisdom inaccessible to mortals. Such language can depict God's inaccessible thoughts.[30] Similarly, in Daniel 2:22 God reveals deep, hidden matters, fitting a Danielic motif concerning the revealing of mysteries, also developed in the Dead Sea Scrolls.[31]

Paul thus speaks here of how the Spirit provides believers a deep connection with God and his wisdom. Most fundamentally, this involves experiencing God's character and his relationship with and heart toward believers; thus, in Paul's theology the Spirit emphasizes God's love in the cross (Rom. 5:5–10, esp. 5:5; 8:15–16).

On both ends, so to speak, the Spirit provides the intimate connection between believers and God. Paul notes elsewhere that God, who searches all hearts, knows the mind of the Spirit within believers (Rom. 8:26–27). In Romans 8 the Spirit praying for believers goes beyond their conscious prayers to their needs; just as creation groans by virtue of its condition rather than deliberately (8:22), so the Spirit interprets the inner groans of believers for God (8:23, 26).[32] Here the Spirit searches God's heart to reveal it to believ-

---

28. The language of "deep things" was appropriate not only to physical depths but also to the hidden or humanly unsearchable regions of the heart or mind; see LXX Ps. 63:7 (64:6 ET); Prov. 20:5; 25:3; Jer. 17:9. Especially relevant is Jdt. 8:14, which compares the unfathomable depths of the human heart with the even greater impossibility of searching out God.

29. See, further, Prov. 18:4; Sir. 1:3; Philo *Drunkenness* 112; depths of knowledge in *Dreams* 1.6; 2.271 (by analogy); *Posterity* 130; cf. *Flight* 200; *3 En.* 11:1; derivatively, God's love in Eph. 3:18; for the suggestion of wisdom language here, see Scroggs, "ΣΟΦΟΣ," 51. Some used "deep" to mean "profound" (e.g., βάθος in Longin. *Subl.* 2.1) or "unknown" (Eccles. 7:24 LXX), or applied "depths" to special mysteries (*1 En.* 63:3; Rev. 2:24; cf. the contrast with the true searcher of hearts in Rev. 2:23).

30. Cf. similar language in *2 Bar.* 54:12, addressing God: "Who understands your deep thoughts of life?" (trans. A. F. J. Klijn, *OTP* 1:640; Charles's older translation reads, "Who comprehendeth Thy deep thought of life?" [*APOT* 2:511]). Cf. also, similarly, Sir. 1:2–3, praising the unsearchable greatness of wisdom.

31. For mysteries in Daniel and early Judaism, esp. in the Dead Sea Scrolls, see more fully, e.g., Brown, "*Mysterion*"; Brown, *Mystery*; Caragounis, *Mysterion*; and most recently, Beale and Gladd, *Hidden*, 29–55.

32. Further exposition would explain backgrounds in the exodus (Exod. 2:23) and eschatological birth pangs (Rom. 8:22), as well as the connection with the intercession of Jesus the justifier (8:34; see, further, Keener, *Romans*, 106–8). I have briefly argued against identifying this with tongues (107–8n37), but Fee makes a noteworthy and perhaps compelling case for their identification (*Listening*, 105–20). At the least, they reflect analogous functions in Paul's theology. The groans are not cognitive and may be Spirit-inspired prayer that occurs by virtue

ers (1 Cor. 2:10). To paraphrase some language more dominant in works on Johannine theology, the Spirit is the means of mutual indwelling.

Revealing God's heart is a role that only God's Spirit can fulfill. No one else fully knows one's experience of oneself, or even one's thoughts, except oneself,[33] and in the same way, only God's own Spirit fully knows God's heart (1 Cor. 2:11; cf. 2:16).[34] (The analogy would be familiar to many Diaspora Jewish hearers: Judith warns her hearers that they cannot search the depths even of human hearts, so how can they expect to search and understand God's mind?)[35] Job complains in a later testament that since his critics do not understand how the body works, they should not claim to understand heavenly matters.[36]

Some thinkers, especially those in the Platonic tradition, considered the highest deity ineffable[37] or at least beyond human grasp,[38] and other writers warned that mortal minds could never grasp the plans of the gods.[39] Given Paul's marked biblical citations in the context, Jewish sources may be more relevant. Traditional Jewish meditations on wisdom already understood that only God is fully wise, and therefore his wisdom must be "revealed" (Sir. 1:6–9).[40] Paul

---

of the Spirit within believers, rather than believers' deliberate, and perhaps often conscious, work (cf. similarly the Abba prayer of Rom. 8:15).

33. The idea was common enough (e.g., Dio Chrys. *Or.* 3.18; Prov. 14:10; perhaps also relevant here is Prov. 20:27, though understood quite differently in *1 Clem.* 21.2; *Pesiq. Rab.* 8:2). In other contexts one might claim that no one knows man (*Ahiq.* 116, saying 33), or one might claim to know the mind of a friend, because a friend was a "second self" (Papyrus Merton 12 in Stowers, *Letter Writing*, 61; more generally for a friend as a "second self," see Diod. Sic. 17.37.6; Cic. *Fam.* 7.5.1; 13.1.5; cf. P.Oxy. 32.5–6; Cic. *Fin.* 1.20.70; Sen. Y. *Ep. Lucil.* 95.63). Hellenistic Jewish writers employed πνεῦμα, as here, for the human element that Koine more often depicted as ψυχή (Isaacs, *Spirit*, 35–36; cf. Allo, *Première Épitre*, 104); Philo associates it with human reason and conscience (Isaacs, *Spirit*, 38–41).

34. Cf. Bar. 3:31–32: no one except God knows Wisdom's way.

35. Jdt. 8:14, using a cognate form of the verb ἐραυνάω that Paul employs in 1 Cor. 2:10. Cf., later, Diogenes in Dio Chrys. *Or.* 10.22 (cf. 10.27): in violation of the Delphic inscription "Know yourself," most people do not know themselves; how then can they know the gods? (Why, he is arguing, should they consult the oracle?)

36. *T. Job* 38:5 (*OTP* 1:858). One of his critics responds, "We are not investigating the things beyond us" (38:9, trans. Kraft; 38:6 in *OTP* 1:858, trans. Spittler).

37. E.g., Plato *Tim.* 28C; *Ep.* 2.312E; Max. Tyre *Or.* 2.10; 11.9; 21.7–8; Apul. *Apol.* 64; *De deo Socr.* 123–24. Cf. also Philo *Names* 15; Shibata, "Ineffable."

38. God's realm was beyond that of mortals (Sen. Y. *Dial.* 12.8.5); Pythagoreans invoked divine aid in understanding their divine philosophy, for "it cannot be comprehended without the gods' aid" (Iambl. *Pyth. Life* 1.1; trans. Dillon and Hershbell, 31).

39. Pindar *Paean.* 21, frg. 61, in Stob. *Anth.* 2.1.8 (using in line 4 a cognate form of ἐραυνάω, as here). Cf. also Hesiod *Melamp.* 9 (in Clem. Alex. *Strom.* 5. p. 259): "There is no seer among mortal men such as would know the mind of Zeus" (trans. Evelyn-White, LCL, 271).

40. Sir. 1:6–9 is the only LXX passage that includes both "wisdom" and "reveal"; cf. Bar. 3:31–32. For true wisdom as only a gift from God in Sirach, see, further, Boccaccini, *Judaism*,

explains that the world cannot understand God, but God's own Spirit, who understands him, can reveal him to those who accept his wisdom (1 Cor. 2:12, 16).

Understanding by God's Spirit versus the World's Spirit (1 Cor. 2:12–13)

The Spirit that believers have received is not[41] the spirit of the world system (1 Cor. 2:12; cf. 2:6),[42] whose rulers crucified the Lord (2:8).[43] Instead, all believers have received the Spirit from God, the Spirit that knows God's heart (2:11). This Spirit enables believers to know what God has freely given (2:12), in this context undoubtedly including the prearranged promise of eternal glory (2:7, 9). This knowledge of eschatological reality is available in the present, because believers have already received the Spirit that makes this knowledge available (in Paul's nomenclature, believers apparently "receive" the Spirit at conversion; Gal. 3:2; cf. 2 Cor. 11:4; Gal. 3:14).

Since people could fully apprehend eschatological hope and an eschatological perspective only through the Spirit (1 Cor. 2:9–11), how could Paul's preaching communicate it? Paul has already claimed that he speaks not human wisdom but the message of the cross (2:2) and the hidden wisdom (2:7) through the Spirit (2:4–5). Now he reiterates that he communicates not human wisdom but wisdom conveyed by the Spirit (2:13).

82–83. Paul's use of "those who love him" in 1 Cor. 2:9 could allude to this passage, since Sir. 1:10 so describes those who receive the gift of wisdom and Paul uses these words to midrashically adapt the language of Isa. 64:3 LXX (64:4 ET). Admittedly, the phrase "those who love" God was familiar in Scripture (cf. Exod. 20:6; Deut. 5:10; 7:9; Neh. 1:5; Pss. 91:14; 119:132; 122:6; 145:20; Dan. 9:4) and beyond it (e.g., 1 Macc. 4:33; *Pss. Sol.* 4:25; 6:6; 14:1; 4Q176 frg. 16.4; 4Q525 frg. 5.13; *T. Ab.* 3:3 A), including in Sirach (Sir. 2:15–16; 34:19). Others suggest theological reasons for the change (Bauer, "ΑΓΑΠΩΣΙΝ").

41. In Rom. 8:15, as well as here, Paul contrasts the spirit believers have not received with the Spirit they have received. For Paul, "receiving" the Spirit probably coincides with conversion (Gal. 3:2, 14), at least in principle.

42. Some suggest that "spirit of the world" here refers to Satan (cf. Isaacs, *Spirit*, 105; Eph. 2:2), or plausibly compare the spirit of error that opposes the spirit of truth in the Dead Sea Scrolls (Levison, *Filled*, 281–82, citing 1QS 4.3–6, 9–11; noting also differences, Flusser, *Judaism*, 68) or the related contrast in *Jub.* 1:20–21. At the same time, Jewish writers in Greek use πνεῦμα even for psychological dispositions or inclinations (Chevallier, *Ancien Testament*, 39; Isaacs, *Spirit*, 71); cf. the parallel Pauline construction in Rom. 8:15.

43. Although they would have differed with Paul over criteria distinguishing true and false wisdom (though usually the criteria were their own school's doctrine, as here), many thinkers made such distinctions; see, e.g., Sen. Y. *Ep. Lucil.* 88.44; *Nat. Q.* 1.pref.14–15; Aul. Gel. 10.22; Lucian *Carousal* 30, 34; *Dial. D.* 329 (1/1, *Diogenes* 1); 332 (1/1, *Diogenes* 2); Fronto *Ad M. Caes.* 4.3.1; Porph. *Marc.* 25.394–95; 27.425–31; cf. Prov. 3:5–7; 1 Tim. 6:20; *Sib. Or.* 5.86–87; *Diogn.* 12.4–7. Likewise, the community that produced the Dead Sea Scrolls believed that they alone possessed the Spirit of truth (Flusser, *Judaism*, 54) that would give them true insight (1QS 4.21–23).

There are two possible ways to understand 1 Corinthians 2:13, depending on whether the adjective πνευματικοῖς is taken as neuter or masculine (the dative form can be understood either way). If it is understood as neuter, Paul is saying that one can interpret matters of the Spirit not in the context of a purely natural framework but only in the context of other matters of the Spirit.[44] (Certainly, Paul does believe that his message is "spiritual," i.e., from the Spirit.)[45] By contrast, the Corinthian Christians have been trying to interpret matters of the Spirit (2:13) within a human framework. By comparing[46] Paul and Apollos by human standards (3:4), the Corinthians fail to evaluate spiritually (2:14–15).[47]

Alternatively, and more likely, Paul communicates eschatological promises, beyond the basic message of the cross, only to those who can receive them.[48] Unbelievers cannot understand *spiritually*, because such understanding includes embracing the truth (by virtue of which one is no longer an unbeliever), not simply explaining the message's grammar.[49] Paul communicates not by trying to explain matters of the Spirit (πνευματικά, neuter, 2:13) to those with a purely natural framework, for whom such matters would prove unintelligible (2:14), but by

44. With Chrys. *Hom. Cor.* 7.8 (in Bray, *Corinthians*, 25).

45. A "spiritual" word might mean "allegorical," as some suggest for Rev. 11:8 (Beale, *Revelation*, 592), though probably wrongly in that case (see Bruce, "Spirit in Apocalypse," 339; Roloff, *Revelation*, 133; Bauckham, *Climax*, 168–69)—though it could mean "figuratively," a communicative form in Revelation common in the preexilic prophets, who prophesied in poetry. But Paul elsewhere normally associates "spiritual" with the Spirit (with, e.g., Fee, *Presence*, 28–31; Fee, *Listening*, 5). The message of the cross itself is "spiritual" and remains God's word revealed by the Spirit (1 Cor. 9:11; 2 Cor. 2:17; 4:2; 5:19; 1 Thess. 2:13); perhaps broken dependence on the Spirit also facilitates its communication through its messengers (cf. 2 Cor. 4:7–10).

46. Paul's term for interpreting or understanding in 1 Cor. 2:13 (συγκρίνω) applies especially to comparing (objects or persons). Relevant to the issue in 3:4–7, the term and its cognates applied frequently to comparisons used in evaluation, including in rhetoric; see Philo *Virt.* 85 (cf. also Martin, "Philo's Use"); Jos. *War* 1.13; Plut. *Comparison of Alcibiades and Coriolanus* (and his other parallel lives); Hermog. *Inv.* 4.14.212; *Progymn.* 8, "On Syncrisis," 18–20; Men. Rhet. 2.3, 381.31–32; 2.10, 416.2–4; 2.14, 427.1–3; 2.10, 417.5–9; Libanius *Comp.* passim; Nicolaus *Progymn.* 9, "On Syncrisis," 59–62; Gärtner, "Synkrisis"; Aune, *Dictionary of Rhetoric*, 110. In Paul, see 2 Cor. 10:12.

47. Comparison did not necessarily denigrate one person to exalt another (Men. Rhet. 2.6, 402.26–29; 403.26–32; 404.5–8; 2.10, 417.5–17; e.g., Plut. *Comparison of Aristides and Marcus Cato*; *Comparison of Lucullus and Cimon*), but sometimes it did (e.g., Cic. *Ag. Caec.* 12.37; *Brut.* 93.321–22; *Pis.* 22.51; in rhetoric, cf. Demosth. *Embassy* 174; see comment in Keener, *John*, 916–17, 1183–84), and the partisan divisions probably suggest that some denigration happened in this case.

48. Cf. Witherington, *Corinthians*, 128: "We . . . interpret spiritual matters to spiritual people," construing the verb as "interpret," as in Gen. 40:8, 22; 41:12; Dan. 5:12. This approach does not rule out the nuance of comparison noted above; Paul's only other use of the term συγκρίνω is in 2 Cor. 10:12, although only the latter is a clearly rhetorical use (Forbes, "Comparison," 152).

49. These levels of understanding are different. By way of analogy, there is a difference between explaining the chemical properties of ink on a page and reading the message.

explaining them to those who have received the Spirit (i.e., πνευματικοῖς under-stood as masculine, as the noun is in 2:15). Precisely because the Corinthian Christians are not yet acting like people of the Spirit themselves (note πνευματικοῖς in 3:1),[50] Paul has refrained from sharing deeper spiritual truth with them.[51]

To some degree, it does not matter which of these two readings one prefers. Because the passage shares the same context, both readings lead to roughly the same application. As in Johannine theology, merely human wisdom cannot grasp the things of the Spirit (John 3:3, 8, 10); John allows the use of earthly analogies, but even these analogies appear as little more than a sage's riddles to someone unfamiliar with heavenly matters (3:12).

Paul here develops a theme already present in Jesus's teaching and consistent with earlier biblical ideas. Jesus teaches that God has concealed his truths from the wise and sensible but revealed them to infants (Matt. 11:25//Luke 10:21), presumably implying the disciples (Matt. 12:1–2; 18:3; Luke 10:23–24). In the same tradition, no one can know God except through divine revelation in Christ (Matt. 11:27//Luke 10:22; cf. Matt. 16:17). Earlier biblical sages and prophets also recognized the importance of depending on God's greater wisdom rather than one's own (e.g., Deut. 4:6; Prov. 2:1–6; 3:5, 7, 11–13; 26:12; Isa. 5:21; 29:14; Jer. 8:9; 9:23–24).[52] Elsewhere the Spirit inspires wisdom, such as for artistic skill to glorify God (Exod. 28:3; 31:3; 35:31) or for leadership (Deut. 34:9; Isa. 11:2).

Spiritual Competence to Assess Truth (1 Cor. 2:14–15)

Spiritual truth could be communicated only by the Spirit (1 Cor. 2:10–11) and only among those receptive to the Spirit (2:12–13). Because the world's wisdom cannot recognize God's true wisdom (1:21, 23–25; 2:8, 12–13), humans

50. Paul probably challenges their self-perception here; cf. 1 Cor. 14:37. Some tie the situation especially to prophetic figures (Wire, *Prophets*, 39–71); others demur (Hill, *Prophecy*, 130, against Dautzenberg, "Botschaft"). Some suggest that the self-perceived πνευματικοί may belong to the "of Christ" faction in 1 Cor. 1:12 (Snyder, *Corinthians*, 36). Paul probably employs the term positively in Gal. 6:1 (cf. 5:16–18, 22–23, 25; 6:8).

51. The gospel that he has shared, however, can also be described as "spiritual things" or "matters of the Spirit," as is clear from 1 Cor. 2:4–5 and 9:11. Both Paul's "milk" and solid "food" (3:2) are matters of the Spirit, but some require a deeper level of openness to the Spirit than others do. Later in the letter the expression "things of the Spirit" also seems to apply to ministry empowerments from the Spirit (12:1; esp. 14:1; cf. Rom. 1:11).

52. Proverbs does include much wisdom shared with Egyptian sages; intelligence and some kinds of wisdom are a common gift for all humanity (cf. *Diogn*. 10.2). But the fear of the Lord is the starting point for wisdom about divine and moral matters, on which God has provided instruction (Ps. 111:10; Prov. 1:7, 29; 9:10; 15:33). Human wisdom as a worldview or interpretive grid for reality is corrupted by human rebellion especially to the degree that it addresses divine matters and is shaped by personal or corporate sin.

without the Spirit are in no position to evaluate spiritual matters or people who follow the eternal wisdom of the Spirit (2:14–15). Having received the spirit of the world rather than God's Spirit (2:12), those without the Spirit cannot receive matters of the Spirit (2:14).

In the same way that Jesus's identity and cross are unintelligible to the world because of its values (2:8), those acting according to the mind of the Spirit are unintelligible in terms of the world's wisdom (cf. John 3:8). Spirit-moved behavior and eschatologically motivated choices in the present make little sense to those accustomed to the world's values.

Yet Corinthian Christians were employing the world's standards to evaluate the message of Paul (1 Cor. 1:18–2:5) or compare him with his colleagues (1:12; 3:4)! That some were "evaluating" Paul is clear; the same verb that Paul employs here for outsiders unable to understand the wise (ἀνακρίνω, 2:15) appears afterward for the Corinthian Christians' worldly evaluations of Paul (4:3; 9:3).[53] They are judging his teaching by Greek rhetorical criteria[54] or by popular philosophic beliefs they deem self-evident. Yet by the world's standards, the cross is the antithesis of power, status, and a sensible message.

A Pervasive Culture of Evaluation

Greco-Roman elite culture valued the ability to evaluate clearly, to appraise both cities and individuals.[55] This behavior carried over into other relationships.[56] Thus, for example, Cicero advises that one "should love your friend after you have appraised him; you should not appraise him after you have begun to love him."[57] That is, one should choose whom to befriend based on their character. Affection might even be thought to make one more critical, for the other's benefit.[58]

Evaluating speeches was pervasive, and the ability to do so was valued.[59] Rhetorical critics evaluated even past orators.[60] One might compete rhetorically with written passages, afterward comparing one's performance with them

---

53. With also Horsley, *Corinthians*, 61. For the situation, see also the discussion in Keener, "Corinthian Believers."

54. See, e.g., Witherington, *Corinthians*, 47; Grindheim, "Wisdom."

55. See Savage, *Power*, 19–53 passim; also, e.g., Pliny *Ep*. 1.21.1.

56. Slaveholders were interested in evaluating slaves (Pliny *Ep*. 1.21.2).

57. Cic. *Amic*. 22.85 (trans. Falconer, LCL, 20:190–93).

58. Pliny *Ep*. 6.26.2. Pliny seemed ready to both offer criticism to (Pliny *Ep*. 3.15.1–2; 7.20.1) and welcome criticism from (3.13.5; 5.3.8; 5.12.1; 7.17.1–3; 7.20.2; 8.19.2) friends and peers, especially to catch lapses before publication. This setting, of course, differs from hostile public exchanges.

59. E.g., Fronto *Ad M. Caes*. 1.8; Apul. *False Preface* 1.104–5.

60. Dio Chrys. *Or*. 18.11. Lucian ridicules the masses, who cannot evaluate speakers wisely (Lucian *Prof. P.S.* 20, 22).

to improve one's own skills.[61] Evaluating speech is relevant to this context (1 Cor. 2:1–7, 13) and became an even greater issue for Paul later in the face of rhetorically skilled outside critics (2 Cor. 10:10; 11:5–6). Hearers could also evaluate content; thus, a rhetorician was ready to appraise a philosopher's philosophic skill.[62] The ideal Stoic sage never expresses a mere opinion but embraces only certain knowledge.[63]

Partly because of the competition for honor that such appraisals of others invited, rivalry and division were rife in ancient urban Mediterranean society.[64] Continuing the deeply ingrained habits characteristic of their culture, even God's people in Corinth also engaged in rivalry and division. It was their division (1 Cor. 1:10–12; 3:3b–4), probably in part rivalry over different teachers' wisdom and/or rhetorical skill,[65] that provoked Paul's lengthy digression about the true, divine wisdom in his message about the cross (1:17–3:3a).

Such division, even about "spiritual" matters or leaders, reflected the character of the surrounding world (and continues in much of today's church, not least in much of sectarian Protestantism). For Paul, the practice of weighing people's worth to Christ's body by status, education, communication skills, or other criteria of the world misses how Christ feels toward his own body.

Evaluation Criteria

Paul may be more interested in ethical and spiritual discernment. Stoic philosophers expended attention on distinguishing and choosing preferable matters over those that were less to be preferred.[66] More important—since preferences often could be indifferent as opposed to right and wrong[67]—some

61. Pliny *Ep*. 7.9.3.
62. Symm. *Ep*. 1.29 (in this case, favorably), opining that "a man may judge skills he does not himself possess" (trans. Salzman and Roberts, 68).
63. Arius Did. 2.7.11m, p. 94.5–18.
64. Among cities, e.g., Heracl. *Ep*. 9; Babr. 15.5–9; Hdn. 3.2.7–8; in partisan politics, e.g., Corn. Nep. 7 (Alcibiades), 4.1; 25 (Atticus), 7.1–11.6; Sall. *Jug*. 73.5; Plut. *Sulla* 4.4; 7.1; Aul. Gel. 6.19.6; in rhetoric, e.g., Dio Chrys. *Or*. 24.3; Lucian *Prof. P.S*. 22; Eunapius *Lives* 493–94; in literary competition, e.g., Plut. *Cim*. 8.7; Aul. Gel. 17.4.3–6; and so forth. See, further, Keener, *Acts*, 3:2287–88.
65. Students of different schools often viewed themselves as rivals (Suet. *Tib*. 11.3; Philost. *Vit. soph*. 1.8.490; Pogoloff, *Logos*, 175; Winter, *Philo and Paul*, 170–76; Winter, *Left Corinth*, 38–39), including in Corinth (Dio Chrys. *Or*. 8.9; Winter, *Left Corinth*, 37, 39–40); this pattern continued even in medieval schools (Shelley, *Church History*, 198). This could be the case even when the teachers themselves were friends, as Paul and Apollos apparently were (cf. 1 Cor. 16:12; Mihaila, "Relationship"), and as was the case later with Whitefield and the Wesleys (Cragg, *Church*, 145).
66. See, e.g., Arius Did. 2.7.7f, p. 48.19–22; 2.7.7g, p. 50.11–16.
67. E.g., Arius Did. 2.7.7g, p. 50.23–26.

Stoics argued that the heart of philosophy was distinguishing good from evil,[68] and Stoic philosophy regularly addressed this issue.[69] Not unrelated, they insisted on distinguishing what was true from what was false.[70] For Stoics, only good people could distinguish good from evil,[71] and reason was the means of evaluating critically.[72]

The right means were necessary for such evaluation, however. In some traditional Jewish sources, one distinguished good from evil based on wisdom that was God's gift.[73] Philosophers believed that philosophy was meant to distinguish truth from falsehood,[74] and philosophers regularly emphasized discerning truth from falsehood[75] and good from evil or what is harmful.[76] Reason enables proper discernment,[77] enabling one to choose good and reject evil.[78]

Philosophic schools varied in their views regarding the senses in discernment. For Stoics, reason should rule rather than serve the senses;[79] as Seneca complains, "The senses do not decide upon things good and evil."[80] Nevertheless, Stoics affirmed that sense organs were beneficial and played an epistemic role.[81] Some others agreed, allowing that the senses can play a

68. Sen. Y. *Ep. Lucil.* 71.7; Mus. Ruf. 8, p. 60.16–17. Distinguishing good from evil is "the function of wisdom" (Cic. *Off.* 3.17.71; trans. Miller, LCL, 21:341), and a philosopher should be a proper judge of the things that are just and fitting (Mus. Ruf. 8, p. 66.7–8).

69. E.g., Sen. Y. *Ep. Lucil.* 45.6; Mus. Ruf. 8, p. 60.10–12; Epict. *Diatr.* 2.3.1 and passim; Marc. Aur. 6.41 (regarding what is in our power to control). Only humans, not the animals, need the ability to differentiate between various external expressions (Epict. *Diatr.* 1.6.18).

70. Epict. *Diatr.* 1.7.8.

71. Diog. Laert. 7.1.122.

72. Mus. Ruf. frg. 36, p. 134.11–12. Differentiation was a distinctively human gift (Epict. *Diatr.* 1.6.18).

73. E.g., 1 Kings 3:9–12; 4Q417 frg. 1, col. 1.6–9; cf. 1QS 4.22–5.2; based on God's laws in Ezek. 44:23–24. Contrast inability to distinguish good from evil among young children (Deut. 1:39; Isa. 7:15–16) and among the wicked (Isa. 5:20).

74. Mus. Ruf. 8, p. 60.16–17; 8, p. 62.39–40; Iambl. *Letter* 13, frg. 2 (Stob. *Anth.* 2.2.7); cf. the definition of wisdom in Cic. *Inv.* 2.53.160. Sen. Y. *Ep. Lucil.* 71.7 opines that Socrates brought philosophy back from wordplay to distinguishing good from evil.

75. E.g., Epict. *Diatr.* 1.7.8; Marc. Aur. 9.1.2. The elite complained that the masses lacked this capacity (Tac. *Hist.* 2.90).

76. Sen. Y. *Ep. Lucil.* 45.6; Mus. Ruf. 8, p. 60.10–12; Epict. *Diatr.* 1.4.1; 2.3.1–3; 2.24.19; Marc. Aur. 2.1, 13. This distinction was limited to what one could control (Marc. Aur. 6.41).

77. Mus. Ruf. frg. 36, p. 134.11.

78. Cic. *Leg.* 1.23.60.

79. Sen. Y. *Ep. Lucil.* 66.32; *Dial.* 7.8.4.

80. Sen. Y. *Ep. Lucil.* 66.35 (trans. Gummere, LCL, 2:23). For discussion of the "senses" in Stoicism, see Rubarth, "Meaning"; Diog. Laert. 7.1.110, 157. The soul itself was a sensory faculty (Hierocles *Ethics* 4.23–24; Arius Did. 2.7.5b7, p. 20.32–33; cf. Plut. *Pleas. L.* 14).

81. Mus. Ruf. 3, p. 38.30–31; Sen. Y. *Dial.* 5.36.1; 7.8.4; Stoics in Diog. Laert. 7.1.52; see, further, Murray, *Philosophy*, 26; Long, *Philosophy*, 123–31. Health of the senses, like other

role in moral discernment (Heb. 5:14).[82] By contrast, Platonists emphasized reason over the senses more adamantly.[83] Most suspicious regarding the senses were the Skeptics,[84] who also denied any distinction between good and evil.[85]

Paul values faith in eternal things over physical sight of temporal things (2 Cor. 4:18; 5:7; cf. 1 Cor. 2:9–10), but he also recognizes that physical senses are the normal means through which a person with understanding apprehends these matters (Rom. 1:19–20; 10:14; 1 Cor. 9:1; 15:5–8; Phil. 1:30; 4:9; 1 Thess. 2:17; 3:6).

For philosophers, their philosophic grid provided the basis for moral discernment. For Paul, God's wisdom expressed in the gospel and communicated by the Spirit enables moral discernment. People without the Spirit are not qualified to understand people of the Spirit. Fleshly critical evaluation stands outside dependence on Christ and suspends belief, working from other, often unacknowledged, worldviews; Spirit-filled evaluation starts with the premise of faith and critically evaluates what is not in accordance with God's trustworthy revelation.

Many protested that others were not qualified to evaluate them because the others lacked the requisite knowledge or ability.[86] Assemblies must depend on majority vote by necessity, Pliny the Younger observes,[87] but unfortunately "the same right to judge" does not confer "the same ability to judge wisely."[88] When one philosopher opines that one can never find a wise person, another responds, "Naturally . . . for it takes a wise man to recognize a wise man."[89]

---

physical health, was indifferent but preferred, as what is normal in nature (Arius Did. 2.7.7a, p. 42.34; 2.7.7b, p. 44.30). Sensory knowledge was key to Epicurean epistemology; see Long, *Philosophy*, 21; on the senses, cf. also Arist. *Soul* 3.1, 424b.

82. See, e.g., the view in Max. Tyre *Or.* 10.8. For the senses as a good divine gift, see Xen. *Mem.* 4.3.11. See also the value of senses for turning people toward God in *Let. Aris.* 156.

83. Plato *Phaedo* 83A; cf. Max. Tyre *Or.* 11.7, 10–11; Porph. *Marc.* 8.147–50 (though cf. also 10.185–86); for Pythagoreans, Iambl. *Pyth. Life* 32.228. For reality transcending the senses, see Plato in Diog. Laert. 6.2.53. For the senses' real but lesser role, cf. also Philo in, e.g., Baer, *Categories*, 65–66; Mattila, "Wisdom"; the senses were meant to guard the soul and mind (*Alleg. Interp.* 3.15; *Worse* 33, 85; *Drunkenness* 201; *Conf.* 19–20; *Dreams* 1.27, 32; *Spec. Laws* 3.111; 4.92, 123). Others recognized that pleasure could exploit the senses (Dio Chrys. *Or.* 8.23; *T. Reub.* 3:3).

84. Murray, *Philosophy*, 26.

85. Diog. Laert. 9.11.101.

86. E.g., Corn. Nep. pref.2–3; Pliny E. *N.H.* pref.29–30. Reitzenstein (*Mystery-Religions*, 33; cf. 74), who offers no primary source at this point, appeals narrowly to the mysteries; the idea, however, was much more common.

87. Pliny *Ep.* 2.12.5.

88. Pliny *Ep.* 2.12.6 (trans. Radice, LCL, 1:121).

89. Diog. Laert. 9.2.20 (trans. Hicks, LCL, 2:427), recounting Xenophanes's reported reply to Empedocles. Cf., similarly, Lucian *Dem.* 13: one cannot discern who is a true philosopher unless one is a true philosopher oneself.

One intellectual complains that the court that condemned Socrates could not genuinely evaluate him rightly because it was unskilled in virtue.[90] The impious cannot properly judge the pious, a Cynic observes: "If the blind were to determine what is sight, they would call seeing blindness."[91] In the Dead Sea Scrolls those who are careless in discernment should not be given authority to judge the pursuers of knowledge.[92]

Paul recognizes the importance of evaluation but insists that believers must depend on true wisdom (1 Cor. 6:2–3; 10:15; 11:31) and the prophetic Spirit (14:24, 29), not worldly criteria. The person of the Spirit (ὁ πνευματικός) is qualified to examine all things, but this person's values cannot be evaluated by those who understand only natural things (2:15).[93] On this reading, the Corinthians fail to properly discern people of the Spirit because they are trying to compare and evaluate Paul and Apollos by natural means (3:4).

Inability to Understand Spirit Matters (1 Cor. 2:14–15)

In 1 Corinthians 2:14–15 Paul contends that the unspiritual cannot apprehend what is revealed only by the Spirit. Just as in Romans 8:3–11, Paul divides humanity into two groups.[94] As in both Greek philosophy and the Jewish wisdom tradition, a major line of demarcation here is between the wise and unwise. But also as in Romans 8:3–11, Paul divides these groups into "fleshly" (cf. 1 Cor. 3:1, 3)—that is, those dependent on themselves, without God's empowerment—and "spiritual"—that is, those who have access to God's Spirit.[95]

Paul explains that a natural person does not receive the matters of God's Spirit; whether Paul speaks the basic message of the cross (1 Cor. 1:17–21, 23) or God's future promises (2:9–10), these matters seem foolish to the natural person. They can be embraced only by the Spirit (2:14).

Excursus: "Natural" and "Spiritual" Persons

The person who lacks the Spirit in 1 Corinthians 2:14 is ψυχικός, a term translated variously as, for example, "unspiritual" (RSV, NRSV; cf.

---

90. Max. Tyre Or. 3.1, 5.
91. Heracl. Ep. 4 (trans. Worley, 190–91).
92. 4Q424 frg. 3.2, in the context of frg. 3.1–7.
93. Cf. John 3:8.
94. Two groups rather than three; with, e.g., Héring, First Epistle, 22; Ridderbos, Paul: Outline, 120.
95. "Spiritual" usually relates to the Spirit of God (see Fee, Presence, 28–31).

NLT), "natural" (KJV, ASV, NASB, NKJV, ESV), "the person without the Spirit" (NIV), "whoever does not have the Spirit" (GNT), or even simply "the unbeliever" (NET). English translations vary considerably because no single English word corresponds well to the Greek term ψυχικός, which I render above as "natural" but which someone might render "soulish" to retain a connection with ψυχή (see appendix A, "The Soul in Ancient Mediterranean Thought").

Suggested Sources of the Language

The contrast between "natural" and "spiritual" persons appears in some later gnostic sources,[96] but these sources are interpreting Paul or traditions that interpreted him.[97] By contrast, the language has a plausible context in Hellenistic Jewish thought.[98]

Not all sources are equally helpful, though even the less helpful sources often offer at least some help. Josephus speaks of Herod's "body" and "soul" and of how he flourished both bodily and, one might say, "with regard to soulish matters" (ψυχικοῖς).[99] Nevertheless, Josephus is not thinking of ψυχή in Platonic terms or other frequent nuances of the English term "soul"; Josephus may refer simply to his generous behavior.[100]

Likewise, Paul's own usage is hardly Platonic. A human can be a ψυχή (e.g., Gen. 2:7, quoted in 1 Cor. 15:45); when Paul uses the term, he often uses it for a person or life (Rom. 11:3; 13:1; 16:4; 2 Cor. 12:15; Phil. 2:30; probably Rom. 2:9; 2 Cor. 1:23). Paul employs it only once clearly for a part or aspect of a person, and there in connection with the entire person (1 Thess. 5:23); whether his distinction there between the terms usually rendered "spirit" and "soul" is rhetorical and random or reflects a deeper theological distinction is debated, but Paul may make distinctions more

96. See, e.g., Thiselton, *Corinthians*, 268, citing Iren. *Her.* 1.8.1, 3. According to Irenaeus, many gnostics viewed only themselves as spiritual, with ordinary Christians having just two natures (Iren. *Her.* 1.6.2). Some commentators have appealed to gnostic background for the early Christian vocabulary (e.g., Bultmann, *Christianity*, 166; Dibelius, *James*, 211–12, while differentiating the concepts), but this is highly unlikely (see Pearson, *Terminology*, 9–11).

97. Pagels, *Paul*, 59, 163–64; Sheldon, *Mystery Religions*, 82; Wilson, *Gnostic Problem*, 211; Thiselton, *Corinthians*, 268. Although some terminology may appear in the mysteries, the contrast between "natural" and "spiritual," using these terms, is not attested before Paul (Sheldon, *Mystery Religions*, 82; Moffatt, *Corinthians*, 35).

98. Pearson (*Terminology*) recognizes this context, but Paul's exact terminological distinctions are more difficult to attest (see Horsley, "Pneumatikos," 270–73, although he also values the Hellenistic Jewish context).

99. Jos. *War*. 1.429–30, including Josephus's only use of the term ψυχικός.

100. Note the context in Jos. *War* 1.426–28.

for addressing particular issues rather than employing a thoroughgoingly consistent vocabulary.

Fourth Maccabees distinguishes "bodily" desires from "soulish" ones (ψυχικαί), expecting reason to dominate them both (4 Macc. 1:32).[101] More important, the adjective appears more than forty times in the Philonic corpus, perhaps suggesting its popularity in Hellenistic Judaism—at least with Philo and those influenced by him. Sometimes Philo contrasts it with what is bodily (σωματικός).[102] Certainly, Philo regularly distinguishes soul and body and sees them as the two primary elements in humans.[103]

Mortals in Adam versus the Spirit of Christ

In his extant correspondence Paul revisits the term ψυχικός in only one other passage, which appears later in the same letter (1 Cor. 15:44, 46).[104] Here the adjective modifies σῶμα, "body"—a correlation that may grab attention no less firmly than his mention of a σῶμα πνευματικόν, a "spiritual body."[105] Paul presumably does not speak of bodies consisting of "soul" and "spirit," despite Stoic thought about the essential materiality of spirit. As Anthony Thiselton notes, -ικος suffixes (as opposed to -ινος suffixes) typically involve *modes of existence or of life* rather than "substances."[106]

Since Paul elsewhere sometimes uses "spiritual" to mean "related to the Spirit" (1 Cor. 2:11–15; 12:1–4), and since he associates the Spirit with resurrection (Rom. 1:4; 8:11) and the future (Rom. 8:23; 1 Cor. 2:9–10), and since resurrection in a Jewish context involved bodies, Paul probably uses "spiritual body" to designate a future body raised by God's Spirit. "Spiritual bodies" are bodies fitted for the full life of the Spirit, of which

101. The adjective ψυχικός functions negatively in Porph. *Marc.* 9.157, but only because it modifies πάθη, "passions"; Porphyry views the soul favorably (e.g., *Marc.* 32.494–95; 33.506–7).

102. Philo *Creation* 66; *Names* 33; *Abr.* 219.

103. E.g., Philo *Creation* 119, 134–36, 139–41, 145, 164; *Alleg. Interp.* 1.105–8; and passim.

104. Elsewhere in early Christianity, see the uses, both negative, in James 3:15; Jude 19.

105. In antiquity as today, a shocking statement could command attention (see Anderson, *Glossary*, 88). Although this is a phrase rather than a term, speakers sometimes used word coinage (cf. Anderson, *Glossary*, 75, 83; Fronto *Ad M. Caes.* 3.13.1), although critics might complain (cf. Rowe, "Style," 123–24; Fronto *Eloq.* 1.4). Paul may sometimes coin some terms, although our limited data from antiquity leaves this uncertain (Anderson, *Rhetorical Theory*, 228–29, 239n105). Paul's adaptation might be closer to what some thinkers called catachresis (cf. Anderson, *Glossary*, 66).

106. See Thiselton, *Corinthians*, 1276–77. Thiselton's fuller argument (1275–81) is also followed by Wright, *Faithfulness*, 1401–2. Cf. also Fee, *Corinthians*, 124; Witherington, *Corinthians*, 132.

the present experience of the Spirit is a foretaste (cf. 2 Cor. 1:22; 5:5), "heavenly" bodies of "glory" (1 Cor. 15:43, 49) fitted for the sort of pure existence that was believed to characterize the heavens (cf. 15:40–41).[107] This understanding also fits the context in 1 Corinthians 2, where a "spiritual" person is one receptive to divine revelation, not a person consisting entirely of spirit.[108]

Certainly, in Paul's immediate context in 1 Corinthians 15, the ψυχικός body corresponds exegetically to the life of the first Adam—Adam is not made out of an immaterial substance but is a "living soul" (1 Cor. 15:45, quoting Gen. 2:7). The Septuagint applies the same phrase to animals (e.g., Gen. 1:20, 24; 2:19); thus, present mortal existence, shared with animals, differs from a new life empowered by the Spirit.

Probably relevant to Paul's usage in 1 Corinthians 15 is Philo's exegesis of God breathing the breath (πνοή)[109] of life into Adam so that he became a living ψυχή (Gen. 2:7 LXX).[110] Philo was too distinctive socially to be generally representative of Hellenistic Jewish thought,[111] but given our limited extant sources, his work provides a key source for understanding some of Paul's context.[112] In Philo, in contrast to 1 Corinthians 15, the

107. Most people considered the fiery stars to be celestial beings; see, e.g., Sen. Y. *Ben.* 4.23.4; *1 En.* 80:6–8. For stars and fire, the lightest and thus highest element, see, e.g., Cic. *Nat. d.* 2.36.92; Pliny E. *N.H.* 2.4.1; Apul. *De deo Socr.* 138; Philost. *Vit. soph.* 2.8.580; 2.20.602; Heracl. *Hom. Prob.* 36.3; *Pesiq. Rab Kah.* 1:3; views in Hippol. *Ref.* 1.5, 7.

108. Concurring with the interpretation of 1 Cor. 2 in Iren. *Her.* 5.6.1, drawn to my attention by Palma ("Glossolalia," 42). Cf. one open to God's Spirit and God's revelation in Robinson, "Spiritual Man."

109. Although the LXX does not use πνεῦμα here, in 1 Cor. 15:45 Paul might identify Jesus with the life-giving spirit or breath of Gen. 2:7. Others have argued that Paul identifies Jesus with the Spirit on the level of Christian experience, as some have argued for 2 Cor. 3:17.

110. See Pearson, *Terminology*, 18–20, for the relevance of Gen. 2:7 to some Hellenistic Jewish concepts of immortality; Pearson argues (17) that Paul's "opponents" in Corinth affirmed immortality but not resurrection. More recent scholarship concludes that reconstructing opponents can be quite difficult (Longenecker, *Introducing Romans*, 78; see esp. Sumney, *Opponents*, esp. 85–86, 142), and 1 Corinthians addresses especially parties rather than explicit opponents (Mitchell, *Rhetoric of Reconciliation*, 302; Pogoloff, *Logos*, 102). Still, Paul may well respond here to the Philonic-like views of his critics in the church; see, e.g., Davies, *Paul*, 52; Isaacs, *Spirit*, 78; cf. Wedderburn, "Heavenly Man."

111. By the time Philo was old, few if any, even among the elite of Alexandrian Jews, would have rivaled his intellectual and social status (Jos. *Ant.* 18.259).

112. The present material could represent a tradition to which Philo bears witness, or possibly a tradition stemming from Philo's own exegesis, given his recent influential place in Alexandrian Judaism (Jos. *Ant.* 18.259) and the connection between Alexandrian Jewish-Christian teaching and the Corinthian church (Acts 18:24–28). In any case, Philo attests traditions that do appear relevant to 1 Cor. 2 (see Sterling, "Wisdom"; Nordgaard, "Appropriation").

"heavenly" man, whom Philo connects with the Logos,[113] comes first (using Gen. 1:26–27), whereas the "earthly" man, the "living soul" (Gen. 2:7), comes afterward.[114] (Paul's reverse arrangement would make sense, though, especially since everyone who believed in resurrection understood that it would follow rather than precede present bodies.) Paul probably was also familiar with Judean exegesis associating Genesis 2:7 with the future resurrection that Jewish interpreters found in Ezekiel 37.[115] (As noted earlier in the book, Gen. 1–3 was a frequent focus of Jewish discussion in early Jewish thought;[116] the Corinthian Christians certainly knew the story, as attested in 1 Cor. 11:7–9.)

If a Diaspora Jewish exegesis of the passage probably stands behind Paul's explanation in 1 Corinthians 15:44–46, it is fairly reasonable to assume that Paul's audience in 2:13–3:3 was familiar with this language.

Paul seems to use "natural" (ψυχικός, 1 Cor. 2:14) and "fleshly" (σάρκινος, 3:1) in closely connected ways, in contrast to "spiritual," that is, a person of the Spirit.[117] The person of the Spirit has true discernment from the Spirit, the true wisdom from the mind of Christ (1 Cor. 2:14–16). Such a person is "mature" (2:6) rather than a spiritual infant (3:1).

By contrast, the Corinthian Christians were like babies with respect to Christ and were like people who were "fleshly" (σάρκινος). (Because they have received the Spirit through conversion, Paul hesitates to call them fully "fleshly," prefacing the term with ὡς. By contrast, his cognate term in 3:3, σαρκικός, is not quite as harsh, at least if Paul uses it distinctly.)[118]

113. Philo *Conf.* 41, 146. The heavenly man bears God's image and is imperishable (*Creation* 134; *Plant.* 44). Others concurred that part of being made in God's image was immortality (Wis. 2:23) but thought this immortality ruined by sin (2:24; but cf. 6:18–19).

114. Philo *Alleg. Interp.* 1.31–32; 2.4–5.

115. See *Gen. Rab.* 14:8, although the tradition could be later; Grassi, "Ezekiel xxxvii," esp. 164. Pharisees preferred to prove the resurrection from pentateuchal texts, since Sadducees often demanded these; for rabbinic ingenuity in finding relevant passages, see, e.g., *Sipre Deut.* 306.28.3; 329.2.1. Paul also supports his argument with clearer prophetic texts in 1 Cor. 15:54–55.

116. See, e.g., sources on p. 211.

117. Paul may vary terms rhetorically rather than depicting three types of people, as postulated later by Valentinian gnostic interpreters. For appreciation for such variation, see, e.g., Lee, "Translations: Greek," 776–77, on μεταβολή.

118. Fee, *Corinthians*, 124. Paul's rhetoric here is thus less harsh than in 2 Cor. 5:20–6:2, where he invites the Corinthian Christians to be converted (cf. Gal. 4:19; 5:4).

Although Jesus offered God's revelation to children (Matt. 11:25//Luke 10:21), Paul's point here is to reprove the Corinthian Christians' spiritual childishness (cf. 1 Cor. 14:20). For Philo, the perfect, or mature (τέλειος), ideal person needs no instruction, but the wicked person is like a baby (νήπιος, 3:1) who needs teaching;[119] the former is wise, but the latter requires training.[120] Infants provide a ready image for mental or intellectual immaturity[121] and a contrast with an ideal wise person.[122] Thinkers sometimes chide those content with elementary knowledge.[123]

If the Corinthians want something deeper than the milk that Paul gave them, he suggests, they need to realize that he gave them milk because they were, and remain, like infants.[124] Some writers naturally used milk as an image for elementary studies, suitable for new learners.[125] Similarly, Paul explains that the only reason that he has not given the Corinthian Christians "deeper" wisdom is that they have showed themselves too immature for it. (One may compare how a subsequent Stoic thinker complains about immature people who worry about what they cannot control: "Are you not willing, at this late date, like children, to be weaned and to partake of more solid food, and not to cry for nannies?")[126]

For Paul, the Corinthian Christians' present divisions openly demonstrate their immaturity (1 Cor. 3:1–4). Giving milk is a parental or nursing image,[127]

119. Philo *Alleg. Interp.* 1.94. Cf. the comparison for idolaters' foolishness in Wis. 12:24; cf. also 15:14. On Hellenistic Jewish language as the context for Paul's language here, see esp. Pearson, *Terminology*, 28–30. Earlier scholarship wrongly associated the common term τέλειος narrowly with the mysteries (e.g., Lightfoot, *Colossians*, 170; Héring, *First Epistle*, 16; Conzelmann, *Corinthians*, 60; Bruce, *Corinthians*, 38; see criticism in Sheldon, *Mystery Religions*, 77–78).

120. Philo *Migr.* 46. One in this state could learn and thus move away from fixation with the body (*Heir* 73).

121. E.g., Philo *Cher.* 63, 73; *Embassy* 1; cf. *Plant.* 168; *Sober* 10; *Mos.* 1.20; children in Aristoph. *Clouds* 821; Max. Tyre *Or.* 36.5; emotional immaturity in Hom. *Il.* 16.7–8. For infants not yet embracing either virtue or vice, see Philo *Alleg. Interp.* 2.53, 64; not yet sharing the capacity for reason, *Alleg. Interp.* 3.210. People often warned against acting like infants, e.g., Hom. *Od.* 1.296–97.

122. Philo *Sober* 9.

123. E.g., Sen. Y. *Ep. Lucil.* 48.11; Heb. 5:12.

124. A second-century bishop in Crete echoes Paul's words here in a letter to the bishop of Corinth, subsequently cited in Euseb. *H.E.* 5.23; earlier, see Ign. *Trall.* 5.1.

125. Quint. *Inst.* 2.4.5–6; Philo *Good Person* 160; *Agr.* 9; *Prelim. St.* 19; *Migr.* 29; *Dreams* 2.10; for a child image in connection with elementary education, cf. also *Studies* 154; for even an infant understanding the basic truth that the creator is greater than his creation, see *Decal.* 69. More positively, cf. Torah as milk in *Sipre Deut.* 321.8.5; God's message in 1 Pet. 2:2; Scripture in Caesarius *Serm.* 4.4 (in Bray, *Corinthians*, 27); God's word in *Barn.* 6.17; see Keener, "Milk," 708.

126. Epict. *Diatr.* 2.16.39 (trans. Oldfather, LCL, 1:333).

127. Many believed that mothers should nurse their own children (Mus. Ruf. 3, p. 42.7; Plut. *Educ.* 5, *Mor.* 3CD; Tac. *Germ.* 20; *Dial.* 28–29; Aul. Gel. 12.1; Osiek and MacDonald,

sometimes used for teachers.[128] Paul continues the parental image in the following context, where he is their father (4:15; cf. 4:17), they should imitate him (4:16–17), and he may need to discipline them (4:21).

What the Corinthian Christians consider "deeper" teaching clearly differs from what Paul himself has in view, although interpreters disagree regarding exactly what Paul had in view.[129] Some think that for Paul the solid food, like the milk, remains the message of the cross;[130] certainly, it is inseparable from that, even if it develops the implications more fully. The distinction between elementary and advanced teachings is not as explicit here as in Hebrews 5:11–6:8; Paul is more interested here in reminding his hearers that division demonstrates their lack of mature wisdom. Their divisions show that, for all their other gifts, they lack the deepest and truest sign of spiritual maturity: the fundamental Christian virtue of love (1 Cor. 13:1–13).[131]

We Have the Mind of Christ (1 Cor. 2:16)

Paul's point is not merely that human wisdom cannot fathom God; he also argues the converse, namely, that by the Spirit believers *can* understand God. The full knowledge of God is eschatological (1 Cor. 13:12), but believers can experience a foretaste of that knowledge in the present. We might describe

---

Place, 64; Garnsey and Saller, *Empire*, 139; Dixon, *Roman Mother*, 3, 105), but nurses were common (for their influence, see, e.g., Quint. *Inst.* 1.1.4–5; Plut. *Educ.* 5, *Mor.* 3DE; Soranus *Gynec.* 1.1.3; 2.12.19 [32.88]; Bradley, "Wet-Nursing"; Treggiari, "Jobs," 87; Ilan, *Women*, 119–21).

128. For comparisons of teachers with fathers, see, e.g., Epict. *Diatr.* 3.22.82; Philost. *Vit. soph.* 1.490; 1.25.536, 537; Eunapius *Lives* 486, 493; Iambl. *Pyth. Life* 35.250; Porph. *Marc.* 1.6–8; *t. B. Qam.* 9:11; *Sanh.* 7:9; *Sipre Deut.* 34.3.1–3, 5; 305.3.4; for the nursing image, cf. Malherbe, "Gentle as Nurse," 212; 11Q5 21.14; Fronto *Ad Ant. imp.* 1.5.2. Because they understood the limits of comparisons, ancients were sometimes ready to employ feminine images for males (cf., e.g., Hom. *Il.* 8.271–72; *Od.* 20.14–16).

129. Severian of Gabala (catena on 1 Cor. 3:2, *PGK* 15:236; trans. Bray, *Corinthians*, 27–28) construes the elementary teachings as "moral teaching and miracles," as opposed to "the proclamation of the doctrines of God."

130. Hooker, "Hard Sayings"; cf. Litfin, *Theology*, 215, 218; Willis, "Mind." In any case, it does not likely refer to hidden teachings that Paul communicated to a spiritual elite (*pace* Baird, "Mature"); he is demeaning the Corinthians, not exalting a secret group. Degrees of initiation do appear in many societies (Eliade, *Rites*, 37–40, 44–47; Mbiti, *Religions*, 164).

131. Although some other sages ranked love highly (*Jub.* 36:4, 8; *m. Ab.* 1:12; for R. Akiba, love of neighbor was the greatest commandment; *Sipra Qed. pq.* 4.200.3.7; *Gen. Rab.* 24:7), the only ancient movement that unanimously ranked it the chief virtue (Rom. 13:8–10; Gal. 5:13–14; James 2:8; *Did.* 1.2; Poly. *Phil.* 3.3; cf. John 13:34–35; 1 Pet. 1:22; 4:8; 1 John 2:7–11; 1 *Clem.* 49.1–50.5; Ign. *Magn.* 1.2) also stemmed from one teacher who expressly made love of God and neighbor the chief commandments (Mark 12:29–31; cf. Luke 10:27–28).

this knowledge as quantitatively finite,[132] given the finiteness of the human recipients, but qualitatively perfect (in its pure form), because it comes from the Spirit of the infinite God. (For comments on the range of meaning involved when ancient thinkers spoke of sharing the divine mind, see the discussion in chaps. 4 and 6.)[133]

Paul's Biblical Basis

In this passage about revealed divine wisdom, Paul quotes two texts from Isaiah, both of which articulate the inability of mortals to fathom God's infinitely greater ways (Isa. 64:3 LXX [64:4 ET] in 1 Cor. 2:9,[134] and Isa. 40:13 in 1 Cor. 2:16a). Elsewhere Paul quotes the second passage at slightly greater length regarding God's unexpected plan in history (Isa. 40:13 in Rom. 11:34); he is presumably familiar also with the same theme in the passage's wider context (Isa. 40:12, 14, 18–26).[135] The inability to know God's mind or advise him (Isa. 40:13) justifies Paul's position that those without the Spirit cannot understand or evaluate those whose lives are directed by God (1 Cor. 2:14–15).

Immediately after quoting both passages, however, Paul qualifies them. Although humans cannot understand God's ways by themselves, they can do so through God's Spirit (1 Cor. 2:10, 16b). Many Greek philosophers affirmed that humans could have a share in the divine mind because of an innate spark of divinity, identified with reason; for Paul, by contrast, the connection with the Lord's mind comes through the gift of his Spirit. Paul uses the Septuagint of Isaiah 40:13, which speaks of God's mind (νοῦς), but the entire course of his argument presupposes dependence on God's Spirit (1 Cor. 2:10–14). Paul undoubtedly knows, although at least new adherents to the Corinthian Christian community would not,[136] that the Hebrew term translated as "mind" here is *ruakh*—referring to God's Spirit.

132. Cf. Chrys. *Hom. Cor.* 7.12 (trans. Bray, *Corinthians*, 26): "This does not mean that we know everything which Christ knows but rather that everything which we know comes from him and is spiritual."

133. See pp. 128–30, 201–6.

134. Paul might midrashically blend "not enter their heart" from the new-creation context in Isa. 65:16 LXX; see discussion in Robertson and Plummer, *Corinthians*, 42; Thiselton, *Corinthians*, 250–52; differently, Soards, *Corinthians*, 59–60; for extrabiblical sources, cf., e.g., Berger, "Diskussion"; an apocryphal quotation from Paul's opponents, Pearson, *Terminology*, 34–35 (noting *L.A.B.* 26:13; alternatively, it could be a Christian scribal expansion).

135. Indeed, the theme appears often in this section of Isaiah (e.g., Isa. 55:8–9). Cf. Sir. 1:2–3.

136. Especially in view of Paul's use of the passage elsewhere (Rom. 11:34), it is not improbable that he had expounded this passage at some point during his eighteen months (Acts 18:11) in Corinth. The founding core of the congregation began in a synagogue (Acts 18:4–8).

Paul interprets the mind of God in the Septuagint of Isaiah as Christ's mind; this seems to fit a pattern of Paul applying Septuagint texts about the divine κύριος to Jesus (e.g., Rom. 10:9–13; 1 Cor. 8:6; Phil. 2:10; 1 Thess. 3:13).[137] Paul's application here also fits the similar identification of the Spirit of God with the Spirit of Christ in Romans 8:9.[138] It is thus not too surprising that the mind of Christ functions here the way the divine mind does in many ancient sources (again, see the discussion in chaps. 4 and 6).[139] One does not find some philosophic school claiming that the spirit or mind of a particular deified Greek hero lived in them the way that one finds many of them speaking of the more omnipresent divine mind. Christ's mind here is the divine mind, communicated by the Spirit.

Revealing God's Mind

Possible hints of sharing elements of the divine mind appear elsewhere in this context. In 1 Corinthians 2:10 Paul notes that the Spirit reveals believers' future glory because the Spirit searches God's depths. Paul could mean that the Spirit knows God's hidden plans because the Spirit knows the depths of God's heart; yet Paul also could identify the future glory with the depths of God—that the glory itself involves ever-deeper intimacy with the heart of God. Neither grammar nor Paul's theology decides the matter fully either way; Paul may regard both as true. In any case, the context is clear that believers do experience the Spirit and thereby God's heart (2:11–12, 16).

Beyond this context, Paul probably understands even the "mind-frame of the Spirit" in Romans 8[140] as implying the activity of God's mind on that of his children. Thus, later in the same context of Romans 8, God knows the mind of the Spirit and hears the Spirit's intercession within believers (Rom. 8:26–27). Although the terminology is the same as in 8:6 (τὸ φρόνημα τοῦ πνεύματος), in 8:27 it must mean more than simply "frame of mind." This suggests that Paul's expression of this way of thinking characterizing believers in 8:6 encompasses not only a perspective but also the direct influence of the

137. With Collins, *Corinthians*, 137. Cf. also 1 Cor. 1:8; 5:5 (in some MSS); 2 Cor. 3:18 with 4:4; Phil. 1:6.

138. Cf. Turner, "Spirit of Christ," esp. 436; Fee, "Christology and Pneumatology," esp. 331; Hamilton, *Spirit and Eschatology*, 28–29. This is more, and more pervasive in Paul, than a simple overlap as in the later *Gen. Rab.* 2:4 (based on Isa. 11:2); the divine Spirit is characteristically God's (e.g., CD 2.12), and there is no thought in early Judaism of the divine Spirit that is on the Messiah subsequently dwelling in his followers through him.

139. See pp. 128–30, 201–6.

140. See chap. 4, above.

Spirit on the believer's mind. That is to say, God's Spirit influences not only the believer's spirit, as in 8:16, but also the believer's mind.

What many Christians call being led by the Spirit or receiving divine insight may be related to the processes described here. Granted, to some extent Paul may refer again to the believer's new worldview, through which knowledge is understood in its correct theological framework (e.g., creation testifies to God, rather than inert nature itself being divine or meaningless). Thus, a person of the Spirit can evaluate both natural and spiritual matters on the right basis (1 Cor. 2:15), whereas someone who does not have the Spirit cannot fathom spiritual matters or the values of one moved by the Spirit (2:14–15).

The language here, however, goes beyond exclusively addressing a settled worldview; it also implies a continuing experience. Paul speaks of the Spirit's inspiration for teaching truth (2:13);[141] he knew that Jewish people associated such inspiration with special insight[142] (particularly in the Dead Sea Scrolls)[143] and especially prophetic enablement.[144] More tellingly, in the Spirit believers experience a foretaste of eschatological glory (2:9–10). Paul speaks of knowing God's thoughts (2:11); in a Hellenistic context, such language communicated the idea of actively sharing part of the divine mind. Paul speaks here of a continuing experience, one that might be described in terms of illumination

141. For inspired learning or teaching, see, e.g., Abraham in *Gen. Rab.* 61:1; 95:3. Philo "preferred the speech which was prompted by God" (Litfin, *Theology*, 232). Paul may be preparing his audience for the discussion of inspired speech in 1 Cor. 14; cf. Boring, *Sayings*, 66. Early Christians could employ Paul's verb ἐραυνάω, found in 1 Cor. 2:10, not only for God's activity (Rom. 8:27; Rev. 2:23; cf. the cognate form in *1 Clem.* 21.2, apparently cited from memory or depending on a version of Prov. 20:27) but also for prophetic activity by the Spirit (1 Pet. 1:10–11).

142. E.g., Sir. 39:6; John 14:26. Some sources identify wisdom and the Spirit (Wis. 1:5–7; 7:22; 9:17; Keener, "Pneumatology," 256–57; in the Dead Sea Scrolls, cf. Menzies, *Development*, 84–87; Isaacs, *Spirit*, 136–37; cf. 1QS 4.3). Later interpreters also could identify the biblical "Spirit of wisdom" with the Holy Spirit; see, e.g., *Tg. Neof.* 1 on Exod. 35:31.

143. E.g., 1QS 4.3; 9.3–4; 1QHᵃ 6.24; 20.15–16; 4Q213a frg. 1.14; 4Q444 frgs. 1–4i + 5i; 4Q504 frg. 4.4–5; for comparison with early Christians, see, e.g., Flusser, *Judaism*, 67–68; Wooden, "Guided." For the Dead Sea Scrolls, this revelation certainly included revelation to the founder and to the community as a whole.

144. Num. 11:25–26, 29; 1 Sam. 10:6, 10; 19:20, 23; Neh. 9:30; Joel 2:28; Zech. 7:12; CD 2.12; 1QS 8.16; 4Q266 frg. 2, col. 2.12; 4Q270 frg. 2, col. 2.14; 4Q381 frg. 69.4 (perhaps also 1Q34bis frg. 3, col. 2.7); *1 En.* 91:1; *Jub.* 25:14; 31:12; Sir. 48:24; *L.A.B.* 28:6; *4 Ezra* 14:22; Philo *Flight* 186; *Heir* 265; *Mos.* 1.175, 277; 2.265; *Decal.* 175; *Spec. Laws* 4.49; Jos. *Ant.* 6.166 (cf. *Ant.* 6.56, 222–23; 8.408); *T. Job* 48:3; *t. Pisha* 2:15; *Sipre Deut.* 22.1.2; Chevallier, *Ancien Testament*, 27–29; Best, "Pneuma," 222–25; Bruce, "Spirit in Qumran Texts," 51; Johnston, "Spirit," 33–35, 39–40; Isaacs, *Spirit*, 47–48; Ma, *Spirit*, 30–32, 202–3, 206–7; Menzies, *Empowered*, 49–101; Menzies, *Development*, 53–112; Turner, *Power*, 86–104; Keener, "Spirit," 486–87; Keener, *Spirit*, 10–13, 31–33. In early Christian sources, see, e.g., Luke 1:67; Acts 19:6; Eph. 3:5; 2 Pet. 1:21; *Did.* 11.7–9; Ign. *Magn.* 9.2; *Herm.* 43.2, 7, 12; Justin *Dial.* 32–34; *1 Apol.* 31, 44, 47, 63; Athenag. *Plea* 7; Theoph. 2.33.

or transformation, not exclusively of believers' initial reception of divine wisdom when they embraced the gospel.

In practice, having the mind of Christ or acting on the basis of Christ living in one (Rom. 8:10; Gal. 2:20) probably includes a range of elements: moral empowerment (as in the context of Gal. 2:20); a theocentric, Christocentric, ecclesiocentric, and missional framework for thinking; periodic personal direction from, or being moved by, the Spirit; periodic experiences of acknowledged divine wisdom; periodic revelatory insights; and so on. One may facilitate such experiences in faith, though diversity of gifts means that some will experience some aspects of this (such as wisdom or revelatory insights) more than others.

For a literary/rhetorical purpose, Paul identifies with and adopts the persona of fallen humanity in Romans 7:7–25, but here he invites believers by faith to identify with Christ. This identification means not being Christ (see discussion below)[145] but depending on Christ and what believers trust his heart to be in and through them. The idea may also include some experiences such as those that Luke, whose dominant interest is in mission, depicts on a narrative level: people filled with God's Spirit (e.g., Acts 4:8, 31) and acting confidently "in the name of Jesus" (Acts 3:6; 9:34; 16:18). Paul himself may also allude to some concrete examples of such experience, including elsewhere in 1 Corinthians. Sharing God's heart may be expressed most fully in the fruit of the Spirit, particularly love, but God's heart is also communicated in cognitive ways.

Ministry Gifts and God's Mind

Some ministry gifts communicate God's wisdom (1 Cor. 2:13; 12:8–10). Some scholars have suggested that the revealed wisdom in 1 Corinthians 2:10 comes from revelations in "altered states of consciousness."[146] Paul himself did experience visions and special revelations (2 Cor. 12:1, 7), the content of which usually remained secret (12:4), but we should not assume that this was the only setting in which Paul and others experienced God revealing himself or giving believers a Spirit-directed perspective (1 Cor. 2:15) or the mind of Christ (2:16).

Although Paul's language here is individual and not merely communal (1 Cor. 2:14–15), it probably also has a communal dimension.[147] The larger

145. See pp. 201–2, 205–6.
146. Malina and Pilch, *Letters*, 71. For studies on altered states of consciousness, see discussion in, e.g., Pilch, *Visions*, passim; Keener, *Miracles*, 789–94 passim, 821–22, 871.
147. The primary contextual example of the "person of the Spirit" here is Paul himself, who is being wrongly evaluated (1 Cor. 2:13–15); but clearly it is Paul's ideal that the Corinthians should also act as people of the Spirit, not like people of the flesh (3:1).

context of Paul's letter to the Corinthians may also suggest that the mind of the Spirit may be communicated to others open to the Spirit. Thus, Paul expects to communicate the Spirit's wisdom through teaching (2:13).

Earlier, Paul cited as a reflection of God's grace among the Corinthian believers (1:4) the fact that they were enriched in every kind of speech and knowledge (1:5);[148] he presumably viewed such speaking and knowledge as among the grace-gifts (χαρίσματα) he envisions in 1:7. Some of the ministry empowerments, or spiritual gifts, that Paul later lists do communicate cognitively.[149] Whereas the Spirit inspires prayer in tongues as affective prayer from one's spirit, interpreting such affective prayer in the vernacular language communicates cognitive content and also is a gift from the Spirit (12:9–11; 14:13–15).[150]

Likewise, the gift for building up the body of Christ that Paul emphasizes most extensively in 1 Corinthians 14 is prophecy, which also communicates on the level of understanding. One expression of prophecy can include revealing the secrets of people's hearts (14:25), which presupposes divine revelation (since God is the one who searches hearts, Rom. 8:27).[151] With the exception of tongues, all of the corporately edifying activities in 1 Corinthians 14:26— worship in the vernacular, teaching,[152] and prophetic revelation—communicate cognitively at least in part. Coupled with interpretation, as Paul expects in public assemblies, even prayer in tongues can facilitate communal cognition (14:13, 27–28).

148. A culture that valued rhetoric (including the knowledge to lecture extemporaneously on random topics) and knowledge (including through education and sometimes philosophic principles) naturally would place a premium on cultivating such gifts.

149. Irenaeus (*Her.* 5.6.1) describes those who prophesy, reveal mysteries, speak all languages, and the like as positive examples of those who are "spiritual" in 1 Cor. 2 and his own day.

150. In contrast to beliefs about Greek ecstatic prophecy, Paul also believed that Christian prophets could control themselves and limit even the expressions of their inspiration for the greater good of the body (1 Cor. 14:27–32).

151. Cf. also Ps. 7:9; Jer. 17:10; Wis. 1:6; Philo *Spec. Laws* 3.52; *m. Ab.* 2:1; later, often in the Qur'an (e.g., 5.7); for "searcher of hearts" as a divine designation, see *t. Sanh.* 8:3; Marmorstein, *Names*, 73, 79, 86; see, further, Keener, *Acts*, 1:771–72.

152. With many scholars, including many Pentecostal and charismatic scholars (e.g., Horton, *Spirit*, 272–73; Williams, *Renewal Theology*, 2:355–57; Lim, "Gifts," 464–65; less certainly, Storms, *Guide*, cf. 42–44), I understand the "message of knowledge" in 1 Cor. 12:8 as the gift of communicating knowledge about God, i.e., teaching (which also appears in 12:28; 14:6, 26; cf. also Carson, *Spirit*, 38; Bultmann, *Theology*, 1:154; Cullmann, *Worship*, 20). This fits the sense of "knowledge" in 1 Cor. 1:5; 13:2, 8–9 (γνῶσις; cf. also, e.g., 8:1, 7, 10–11; 14:6) and of "speech" (λόγος; e.g., 1:5, 17–18; 2:1, 4, 13) elsewhere in the letter. In my understanding, what is often *popularly* called "word of knowledge," when genuine, may function as a particular form of the prophetic gift (cf., e.g., 1 Sam. 10:2–7; 2 Kings 4:27; 5:26; 6:12).

That the Spirit may inspire cognitive communication in a variety of ways—such as wisdom, prophecy, teaching, or worship—would not surprise early Christians. They believed that they were in the age of the outpoured prophetic Spirit (Acts 2:17–18) and shared with their Jewish contemporaries the belief that God's Spirit had inspired the Scriptures,[153] the genres of which included narrative, law, prophecy, song, and other elements.

What Paul here adds to this belief is the recognition that the Spirit gifts different individuals in different ways; each one knows or prophesies in part (1 Cor. 13:9), and each one may communicate different aspects of God's heart. Any brief survey of ancient Israelite prophets will demonstrate that even among them, divine revelations came in different ways, for example, through visions, dreams, hearing God's voice, communications from angels, or the divine message overflowing and compelling one to speak.[154]

God may reveal his wisdom in a variety of complementary ways, and each member of Christ's body should be respectful toward those members who bring gifts in forms different from their own. Of course, the more abundant the gifts, the greater the need for discernment, which Paul clearly connects with gifts (and especially prophecy; 1 Cor. 12:10; 14:29; 1 Thess. 5:20–21). But as noted earlier, part of true wisdom in Christ's body is viewing one's own gifts within the larger context of Christ's body and not treating one's own gift as the greatest (or, as some seem tempted to do today, the only legitimate) gift (Rom. 12:3–8, esp. 12:3).

Divine Inspiration and Empowerment, Not Divine Identity (1 Cor. 3:3–4)

The presence of the divine mind within believers contrasts with how Paul specifically and perhaps ironically depicts believers in Corinth. Paul chides the Corinthian Christians for acting like humans (1 Cor. 3:3–4), perhaps in the sense of acting like mortals. In Greek thought the line between human and divine was sometimes thin. Many philosophers believed that by cultivating reason, they liberated the divine spark within them, or that experiencing the

---

153. E.g., 1QS 8.16; Jos. *Ag. Ap.* 1.37; *4 Ezra* 14:22; *Sipra VDDen. par.* 1.1.3.3; 5.10.1.1; *Sh. M. d.* 94.5.12; *Behuq. pq.* 6.267.2.1; *Sipre Deut.* 355.17.1–3; 356.4.1 (repeating 355.17.2); *1 Clem.* 47.3; *Barn.* 9.2; 14.2, 9; *Herm.* 43.9; Justin *Dial.* 25. See, further, e.g., Isaacs, *Spirit*, 51; Foerster, "Geist," 117; Büchsel, *Geist*, 57–58.

154. As in 1 Kings 22:19–23 and 2 Kings 6:16, the *true* perspective was the one informed by heavenly reality, fully available only to those with revelatory insight. Most biblical prophets, however, do not recount experiencing this particular dimension of revelation. Presumably, others who know the revelation that there is a heavenly dimension can accept it by faith without experiencing, e.g., a vision.

divine through reason divinized them. For Paul, by contrast, the greatest sign of God's character, and thus of his presence in believers, is love (e.g., Rom. 5:5–8; 8:35–39; 13:8–10; 14:15; 15:30; 1 Cor. 13:13; 14:1; 16:14; 2 Cor. 5:14; 13:11; Gal. 2:20; 5:14; 1 Thess. 4:9; see esp. Gal. 5:22).

Excursus: Divinization in Greek and Roman Tradition

In contrast to the Jewish monotheistic tradition, boundaries between exalted humanity and incipient divinity in the Greek and Roman tradition by this period often proved fluid[155] (this fluidity was widespread, against some earlier scholars who connected divinization too narrowly with the mysteries).[156]

For example, popular tradition divinized many heroes,[157] such as Dionysus,[158] Heracles,[159] the Dioscuri,[160] Asclepius,[161] Achilles,[162] Trophonius,[163]

155. Cf., e.g., Epict. *Diatr.* 2.19.26–28; Ovid *Metam.* 8.723–24; cf. Jos. *Ag. Ap.* 1.232.

156. Although divinization is alleged to occur in some other groups' initiations (Eliade, *Rites*, 71), the common view that it occurred in mystery cults in the NT period (Reitzenstein, *Mystery-Religions*, 70, 200; Angus, *Mystery-Religions*, 108; Dibelius, "Initiation," 81; cf. Tarn, *Civilisation*, 354–55; Avi-Yonah, *Hellenism*, 42) has come under challenge in recent years (see Ferguson, *Backgrounds*, 239). Given the frequency in Greek culture in general, however, claims for some cults (e.g., Tinh, "Sarapis and Isis," 113) are possible. Certainly, divinization is clear in the later Hermetica (Reitzenstein, *Mystery-Religions*, 70–71; Conzelmann, *Theology*, 11; Wikenhauser, *Mysticism*, 179) and other gnosticizing (Ménard, "Self-Definition," 149; Jonas, *Religion*, 44–45) and later Christian sources (Tatian *Or. Gks.* 7; Taylor, *Atonement*, 206, cites Iren. *Her.* pref.; Athanas. *Inc.* 54.3). In magic, see *PGM* 1.178–81; Frankfurter, *Religion in Egypt*, 229.

157. E.g., Eurip. *Andr.* 1253–58; Cic. *Nat. d.* 2.24.62; 3.15.39; Virg. *Aen.* 7.210–11; Ovid *Metam.* 9.16–17; Lucan *C.W.* 9.15–18, 564; Paus. 8.9.6–8; 9.22.7; Philost. *Hrk.* 2.11. On the deification of heroes, cf. Nock, *Paul*, 96; Hadas and Smith, *Heroes*; Edson and Price, "Ruler-Cult"; Graf, "Hero Cult." Greek veneration of departed heroes may have begun in the eighth century BCE (Antonaccio, "Hero Cult"), though the cults may have flourished especially in the third and late second century CE. Lucian mocks the notion of heroes compounded of human and divine elements in *Dial. D.* 340 (10/3, *Menippus, Amphilocus, and Trophonius* 2) (revealing some of the sort of conceptions that subsequent Eastern Christian Christologies sought to address; for the compounding idea elsewhere, see, e.g., Max. Tyre *Or.* 6.4).

158. E.g., Apollod. *Bibl.* 3.5.3.

159. Apollod. *Bibl.* 2.7.7; 2.8.1; Cic. *Tusc.* 1.12.28; 2.7.17; Sen. E. *Suas.* 1.1; Men. Rhet. 2.9, 414.23–24. See, further, Graf, "Heracles: Cult."

160. See, e.g., Cic. *Sest.* 15.34; 37.79; 38.83; 39.85; Hor. *Ode* 3.3.9–10; 4.5.35–36; *Epode* 17.40–44; Ovid *Fast.* 5.715–20; Val. Max. 1.8.1; Suet. *Tib.* 20; *Calig.* 22.2; Quint. Curt. 8.5.8; Arrian *Alex.* 4.8.2–3; Paus. 1.18.2; 3.13.6; 5.15.5; Parker, "Dioscuri"; Purcell, "Castor"; Keener, *Acts*, 4:3695–99.

161. E.g., Paus. 6 (Elis 2).11.9.

162. E.g., Philost. *Hrk.* 53.8. The ghost of Patroclus also attends the sacrificial feast (*Hrk.* 53.12–13).

163. Max. Tyre *Or.* 8.2; Philost. *Vit. Apoll.* 8.19; contrast Lucian *Dial. D.* 340 (10/3, *Menippus, Amphilocus, and Trophonius* 2).

Palamedes,[164] and sometimes any memorable protagonist of ancient narratives.[165] Homer regularly describes heroes as "peers of gods" or "godlike."[166] Heroes constituted an intermediate category between deities and mortals,[167] in other words, demigods;[168] this intermediate class comprised the deified dead invoked by the living.[169] Ancient heroes, especially those supposed to have been literally sprung from divine seed, were also often sons of gods[170] (though most often in a figurative or distant sense,[171] such as the "Zeus-born" son of such-and-such a human father),[172] or "nurtured" by gods.[173]

Even a particularly eloquent orator might be compared to gods or titled "divine."[174] The same could be done with poets, especially "godlike Homer."[175] Romans offered sacrifices to spirits of the deceased but deified their founder, Romulus, only after the fourth century BCE, due to Greek influence.[176]

Deification of rulers was a particularly dominant public expression of this pattern. Greeks had divinized Hellenistic rulers;[177] the practice began in earnest under Alexander of Macedon, after his conquests invited influence from Eastern traditions.[178] In the late republic, Cicero caricatured Greeks as

164. Philost. *Vit. Apoll.* 4.13; 33.48; cf. *Hrk.* 20.4–21.8.

165. E.g., all of Odysseus's family in *Telegony* Bk. 4; cf. invocations of deceased Ajax in Philost. *Hrk.* 31.7. But Diomedes disqualifies himself by needless brutality (*Thebaid* frg. 9, from scholiast D on Hom. *Il.* 5.126).

166. E.g., Hom. *Il.* 2.407; 7.47; 13.295, 802; *Od.* 3.110; 17.3, 54, 391; 19.456; 20.369; 21.244; cf. also Soph. *Oed. tyr.* 298; Philost. *Hrk.* 21.9; 26.11; 48.15, 19; "godlike Telamon" (while he is killing someone) in *Alcmeonis* frg. 1 (in scholiast on Eurip. *Andr.* 687).

167. E.g., Philost. *Hrk.* 16.4.

168. E.g., Philost. *Hrk.* 23.2 (ἡμιθέοις); cf. Eunapius *Lives* 454.

169. Kearns, "Hero-Cult."

170. E.g., Hom. *Il.* 2.512; see esp. Heracles (Epict. *Diatr.* 3.26.31; Grant, *Gods*, 68–69).

171. E.g., Hom. *Il.* 4.489; 16.49, 126, 707; *Od.* 10.456 (MSS), 488, 504; 11.60, 92, 405, 473, 617; 13.375; 14.486; 16.167; 18.312; 22.164; 23.305; 24.542. For divinity in this figurative sense, Aeschylus *Suppl.* 980–82.

172. E.g., Hom. *Il.* 4.358.

173. Hom. *Il.* 17.34, 238, 685, 702; 21.75; 23.581; 24.553, 635, 803; *Od.* 4.26, 44, 63, 138, 156, 235, 291, 316, 391, 561; 5.378; 10.266, 419; 15.64, 87, 155, 167, 199; 24.122. The title was often bestowed cheaply (*Od.* 22.136) but sometimes applied to a deity (*Il.* 21.223).

174. E.g., Cic. *De or.* 1.10.40; 1.38.172; Pliny E. *N.H.* pref.29.

175. E.g., *Contest of Homer and Hesiod* 316, 325; Men. Rhet. 2.15, 430.13; 2.16, 434.11; together with Hesiod in *Contest of Homer and Hesiod* 313.

176. Hammond and Price, "Ruler-Cult," 1338.

177. Perhaps as early as Philip of Macedon (Diod. Sic. 16.95.1); but philosophers such as Diogenes the Cynic could mock this practice (Diog. Laert. 6.2.63; cf. 6.9.104). On ruler and emperor cults, see in detail Klauck, *Context*, 250–330; Thomas, *Revelation 19*, 45–55; for Hellenistic rulers, Klauck, *Context*, 252–60; cf. Lucian *Cock* 24.

178. For Alexander as a divine son, see Arrian *Alex.* 7.29.3; Diod. Sic. 17.51.1–2; Dio Chrys. *Or.* 32.95; Plut. *S. Kings, Alexander* 15, *Mor.* 180D; *Alex.* 2.2–3.2; 27.5–11; 28.1; also

viewing benevolent governors as divine;[179] but the language so pervaded
the culture of the empire that a late first-century CE Roman could poetically
depict the senate as rivaling deities with their virtue.[180] It became common
in the imperial cults.[181]

More relevant to discussions of the mind, philosophy[182] was held
to divinize people,[183] as was philosophy's goal, virtue[184] or happiness.[185]
Likewise, divinization could stem from proper knowledge of one's
humanity,[186] faithfulness,[187] or, in some views or eulogistic rhetoric, simply death.[188] Philosophers and other sages too were often divinized
or said to be divine in some sense,[189] including Democritus,[190] Pythagoras,[191] Empedocles,[192] Epicurus,[193] Theophrastus,[194] Theodorus,[195]

known by Egyptian Jewry in the centuries immediately surrounding the birth of Christianity
(*Sib. Or.* 5.7; 11.197–98; 12.7). Some believe that Alexander used the notion only as political
propaganda (Plut. *Alex.* 28.3; Lucian *Dial. D.* 395 [12/14, *Philip and Alexander* 1]). Lucian
denies his divinity in *Dial. D.* 397–98 (12/14, *Philip and Alexander* 5); 390 (13/13, *Diogenes
and Alexander* 1).

179. So Cic. *Quint. fratr.* 1.1.2.7; Romans in his day drew the line between deity and mortal
more strictly. In Latin, at least by the beginning of the empire, one could distinguish between
an immortal god who had never been mortal (*deus*) and a mortal who had been posthumously
deified (*divus*).

180. Sil. It. 1.611.

181. For comments on ruler cults, including the emperor cult, see Keener, *Acts*, 2:1784–86.

182. This paragraph is adapted from Keener, *Acts*, 2:1784; see also 1782–86.

183. Sen. Y. *Ep. Lucil.* 48.11; Marc. Aur. 4.16; Iambl. *Pyth. Life* 16.70; Porph. *Marc.* 17.286–88;
cf. Epicurus *Let. Men.* 135; Cic. *Tusc.* 5.25.70; Crates *Ep.* 11; some claimed that "divine" was
applicable to every good person (Sen. Y. *Ep. Lucil.* 73.12–16; 124.14, 23; Max. Tyre *Or.* 35.2;
38.1; Philost. *Vit. Apoll.* 8.5). In Neoplatonism, see Klauck, *Context*, 214, 424; for the ideal in
Stoicism, see Engberg-Pedersen, *Paul and Stoics*, 62.

184. Sen. Y. *Dial.* 1.1.5; Epict. *Diatr.* 2.19.26–28; Philost. *Vit. Apoll.* 3.18, 29; 8.5; Plot. *Enn.*
1.2.7 ("On Virtue"); cf. also Koester, *Introduction*, 1:353; divine virtue within, in Arius Did.
2.7.11m, p. 92.15–16.

185. Εὐδαιμονία, "blessedness"; cf. Arius Did. 2.7.11g, p. 70.36; Max. Tyre *Or.* 26.9.

186. Plut. *Pomp.* 27.3.

187. *Sent. Sext.* 7ab, a Hellenistic Christian source.

188. E.g., (Ps.-)Dion. *Epideictic* 6.283; Cic. *Leg.* 2.9.22; 2.22.55; *Att.* 12.36; 37a; Men. Rhet.
2.9, 414.23, 25–27; 2.11, 421.16–17; cf. *PGM* 1.178–81; later in Poimandres, see Wikenhauser,
Mysticism, 179.

189. E.g., Longin. *Subl.* 4.5; Diog. Laert. 6.2.63 (Diogenes's claim); 6.9.104.

190. Diog. Laert. 9.7.39.

191. Diog. Laert. 8.1.11; Philost. *Ep. Apoll.* 50; Iambl. *Pyth. Life* 2.9–10; 5.10; 10.53; 28.143–
44; 35.255 (cf. the intermediate category in Iambl. *Pyth. Life* 6.31; his golden thigh in 19.92;
28.135, 140). Cf. Abaris in Iambl. *Pyth. Life* 19.91. See also Thom, "*Akousmata*," 103.

192. E.g., Philost. *Vit. Apoll.* 1.1; Diog. Laert. 8.2.68.

193. Cic. *Pis.* 25.59 (ironically also noting Epicurus's skepticism about gods' concern for
the world).

194. Cic. *Or. Brut.* 19.62.

195. Diog. Laert. 2.100.

Apollonius,[196] Indian sages,[197] a divine lawgiver like Lycurgus,[198] and especially "the divine Plato."[199] Greeks bestowed such honorary language still more freely, and many regarded the human soul or rational mind as divine,[200] or even the cosmos as divine.[201]

For the Jewish Middle Platonist Philo, intelligence represents a divine element in humanity.[202] But although divinization language influenced Judaism,[203] even Philo employs it only "in a highly qualified sense."[204] Indeed, in more traditional Palestinian Judaism such promises still belonged to the serpent (Gen. 3:5; Jub. 3:19).[205] Fearing the Lord precluded claims of full divinization.

Tellingly, Paul, despite his subject, does not use the Greek language of deification; he appears even more conservative in his monotheistic expression than Philo.[206] Paul never calls the human mind divine, or speaks of an innate

196. Philost. *Vit. Apoll.* 8.5, 15; *Ep. Apoll.* 44; 48; Eunapius *Lives* 454; also a probably third- or fourth-century inscription; see Jones, "Epigram"; a demigod in Eunapius *Lives* 454. Apollonius looks "godlike" in Philost. *Vit. Apoll.* 7.31 but denies his divinity in 7.32.

197. Philost. *Vit. Apoll.* 3.29; 7.32. Also, to a lesser extent, the magi in Philost. *Ep. Apoll.* 16–17.

198. Hdt. 1.65–66; Val. Max. 5.3.ext.2; Plut. *Lyc.* 5.3. Lawgivers are "godlike" in Mus. Ruf. 15, p. 96.24.

199. Cic. *Opt. gen.* 6.17; *Leg.* 3.1.1; *Nat. d.* 2.12.32; Plut. *Profit by Enemies* 8, *Mor.* 90C; *Apoll.* 36, *Mor.* 120D; Philost. *Ep.* 73 (13); Porph. *Marc.* 10.185–86; Athen. *Deipn.* 15.679A. Cf. patristic sources in Grant, *Gods*, 63–64.

200. Cf. Plato *Rep.* 10, 611DE; Cic. *Parad.* 14; *Resp.* 6.24.26 (Scipio's dream); *Tusc.* 1.24.56–26.65; *Leg.* 1.22.58–59; *Div.* 1.37.80 (citing a Stoic); Sen. Y. *Ep. Lucil.* 32.11; 78.10; *Nat. Q.* 1.pref.14; Mus. Ruf. 18A, p. 112.24–25; Epict. *Diatr.* 1.1; 1.9.6–11, 22; 1.14.6; 1.12; 1.17.27; 2.8.10–11, 14; (Ps.?)-Plut. *Face M.* 28, *Mor.* 943A; Ael. Arist. *Def. Or.* 409–10, §139D; Max. Tyre *Or.* 2.3; 6.4; 33.7; 41.5; Marc. Aur. 2.13, 17; 3.5, 6, 12; 3.16.2; 5.10.2; 5.27; 12.26; Men. Rhet. 2.9, 414.21–23; Iambl. *Pyth. Life* 33.240; cf. *Rhet. Alex.* pref. 1420b.20–21. For a historical survey of divinization of humans, cf. Koester, "Being."

201. In Stoic pantheism (e.g., Cic. *Nat. d.* 2.7.19–20), a view ridiculed by Epicureans (e.g., Cic. *Nat. d.* 1.10.24).

202. E.g., Philo *Alleg. Interp.* 2.10, 23; *Unchangeable* 46–48.

203. Philo *Mos.* 1.279; Jos. *War* 3.372 (Urbach, *Sages*, 1:222); cf. Tabor, "Divinity"; postmortem deification in *T. Adam* 3:2–3 (possibly Christian material); at the resurrection in Ps.-Phoc. 104; cf. immortality or divine character in *Jos. Asen.* 16:16; *L.A.E.* 14:2–3; *Pr. Jos.* 19; *y. Suk.* 4:3, §5; perhaps 4Q181 frg. 1.3–4.

204. Holladay, *Theios Aner*, 236; see Philo *Virt.* 172; *Creation* 135. Cf. Lycomedes's use of the term for benefactors like an apostle, while acknowledging only the true God (*Acts John* 27).

205. See also *Apoc. Mos.* 18:3; cf. Gen. 11:4; Exod. 20:3–5; Isa. 14:14; *Jub.* 10:20; *Exod. Rab.* 8:2.

206. Litwa (*Transformed*, as noted in Costa, "Review") does argue for deification language in Paul, but he is arguing for sharing limited elements of the divine character such as immortality, not elements limited to the one God and not full absorption into God. To this extent,

divine spark in all humans, or says that believers are or become part of God. We "have" the mind of Christ, but our mind is not said to "be" the mind of Christ. That is, he may be avoiding deliberately some language that some of his contemporaries employed when touching on his topic.

Nevertheless, Paul does recognize that God dwells among his people (1 Cor. 3:16), and part of what it means for Christ and the Spirit to live in God's people is that Christ's mind is active in them.[207] The fruit of the Spirit (Gal. 5:22–23), contrasted with works of the flesh (5:19–21), is the fruit, the natural result, of God's moral nature through the Spirit acting within the believer.

For Paul, restoration to Christ's image (Rom. 8:29) apparently entails even more than the original creation in God's image (Gen. 1:26–27). The first humans apparently had periodic communion with God (Gen. 2:16–22; 3:8), but in Christ believers have not only access to God (Rom. 5:2) but even God's Spirit living inside them (Rom. 8:9). The Spirit influences both their spirits and minds (Rom. 8:5–6, 16; 1 Cor. 14:13–15 with 12:10–11). Ideally, many divine insights directly influence the mind that follows the divine frame of thought.

Transformation through Vision (2 Cor. 3:18)

We may more fully understand Paul's message to the Corinthians, as well as his message more generally, by examining other examples of his teaching in the Corinthian correspondence. Here I focus briefly on one passage in 2 Corinthians.[208] The climax of Paul's passage comparing new covenant ministry

---

the difference between deification and nondeification may be semantic, since *Greek* thinkers did sometimes describe such participation in terms of divinization. Nevertheless, I question whether Paul, who is more conservative in most respects than Philo, would have gone as far as such Greek thinkers in describing such sharing in divine nature as deification, since he specifically avoids describing believers in exclusively divine language, never calling them θεοί (note Costa, "Review") or even using the more malleable θεῖος (though cf. its fuller use in 2 Pet. 1:4). Others have developed the language more freely, as in the Eastern Orthodox tradition. Although avoiding the term "divinization," Jonathan Edwards embraced participation, union, and mutual indwelling with God (McClymond and McDermott, *Theology of Edwards*, 422–23; for Neoplatonic connections, see 413–16; see also Hastings, *Edwards and Life of God*). For the idea in Bonhoeffer, see Gorman, *Inhabiting*, 168–70.

207. That is, although I believe that Paul avoids deification language, I am not denying the heart of what the Eastern Christian tradition has called *theosis* (on theosis and holiness in the Fathers, see Blackwell, *Christosis*), insofar as we define theosis in terms of the genuine Pauline emphasis on "transformative participation in the kenotic, cruciform character and life of God through Spirit-enabled conformity to the incarnate, crucified, and resurrected/glorified Christ, who is the image of God" (Gorman, *Inhabiting*, 7, 125; cf. Wright, *Faithfulness*, 781, 1021–22).

208. Other passages in the Corinthian correspondence, such as 2 Cor. 5:13, 16–17, are also relevant, but I can focus only on limited passages in this book. I treated 2 Cor. 5:16–17 briefly

by the Spirit with Moses's ministry of the law highlights Paul's interest in transformation through experiencing Christ's glory (2 Cor. 3:18).

The passage does not directly address either the form of divine revelation mentioned or the question of deification (most Jewish people did not use deification as a description for Moses's glorification). Nevertheless, it remains relevant to this chapter's discussion in that it does address one way that Paul expected believers to experience God, mature, and be transformed. This passage is also relevant in helping us understand Romans 12:2, since 2 Corinthians 3:18 is the only other extant passage where Paul employs the verb μεταμορφόω ("transform").

Hellenistic Vision of the Divine

Vision was a frequent analogy for knowing[209] and often was used for spiritual sight.[210] Plato emphasized the vision of the mind, which could see ideal forms;[211] the physical senses were deceitful, so the soul should depend only on itself and "see" invisible abstractions perceptible only to the mind.[212] Eventually many writers emphasized the mind's or soul's ability to see;[213] Philo spoke repeatedly of the "eyes" of the soul.[214] Stoics such as Epictetus[215] and Marcus Aurelius[216] viewed the ignorant masses as "blind"; likewise, Seneca believed that only the pure mind could comprehend God.[217]

---

above on p. 43. Others have also elaborated the theme of transformation and conformity to the divine here; see esp. now Litwa, "Implications"; Litwa, *Transformed*.

209. E.g., Max. Tyre *Or.* 6.1.

210. I adapt most of the material on spiritual vision here from Keener, *Acts*, 4:3519–22; see at somewhat greater length Keener, *John*, 247–50; more briefly, Keener, "Beheld." For vision mysticism in antiquity, see, further, DeConick, *Voices*, 34–67.

211. E.g., Plato *Phaedo* 65E; 66A; noted also by subsequent writers, e.g., Diog. Laert. 6.2.53; Justin *Dial.* 2; 4.1. On Plato and the vision of God, see Kirk, *Vision*, 16–18.

212. Plato *Phaedo* 83A. Cf. also Iambl. *Pyth. Life* 6.31; 16.70; 32.228. Later writers continued to find in Plato's Socrates an appeal for intellectual vision into the invisible world (Lucian *Phil. Sale* 18).

213. E.g., Cic. *Tusc.* 1.19.44; Marc. Aur. 11.1.1 (cf. 10.26).

214. For the opening of the soul's eyes, O'Toole, *Climax*, 72, cites Philo *QG* 1.39. Philo also speaks of the soul's eyes in *Spec. Laws* 1.37; 3.4, 6; *Unchangeable* 181; *Sacr.* 36, 69, 78; *Posterity* 8, 118; *Worse* 22; *Plant.* 22; *Drunkenness* 44; *Sober* 3; *Conf.* 92; *Migr.* 39, 48, 165, 191; *Heir* 89; *Prelim. St.* 135; *Names* 3, 203; *Abr.* 58, 70; *Dreams* 1.117; 2.160; *Mos.* 1.185, 289; *Rewards* 37; elsewhere, e.g., *Rhet. Alex.* pref. 1421a.22–23.

215. Epict. *Diatr.* 1.18.4, 6; 2.20.37; 2.24.19; cf. 4.6.18.

216. Marc. Aur. 4.29.

217. Sen. Y. *Ep. Lucil.* 87.21, cited in Cary and Haarhoff, *Life*, 335. Seneca the Younger (*Ep. Lucil.* 115.6) uses physical vision as an analogy for the mind seeing virtue. Even a mythographer could speak of Numa seeing the heavenly deities through his mind (Ovid *Metam.* 15.62–64). Association with the mysteries (e.g., Apul. *Metam.* 11.15, 23–24, 30; Reitzenstein, *Mystery-Religions*, 454–56; Dibelius, "Initiation," 81; Strachan, *Corinthians*, 90) is thus far too narrow.

Such views flourished particularly among those most deeply engaged with Platonic tradition, in which the mind was used to envision God.[218] In the mid-second century CE the eclectic Platonist orator Maximus of Tyre stressed vision by the intellect.[219] He noted that at death those who love God will see him, ideal Beauty and pure Truth.[220] In the meantime one could prepare for such perfect vision of the divine by focusing one's mind on the divine. The soul can recall its prenatal vision of divine beauty only vaguely;[221] while such beauty remains perfect in the unchanging heavens, it grows faint in the lower realms of the senses.[222] For an orator with Middle Platonic affinities, removing layers of sense perception helps one to see God;[223] meditating on true divine beauty frees the soul from the lower realms' corruption.[224] Although divine beauty was perfect in the heavenly realms, only intellect could penetrate it in the lower, sensory realms.[225]

In a later period the third-century founder of Neoplatonism sought such vision: Plotinus allegedly "experienced in a trance actual visions of the transcendent God."[226] Developing his views according to the Platonic model, Plotinus declares that the soul's vision, a sort of inner sight, contemplates the beauty of the Good in the realm of Ideas.[227] His followers, however, retained older popular mythology alongside such views.[228] His disciple Porphyry, by contrast, opines that the wise soul is always beholding God.[229] This is pos-

---

218. E.g., Plut. *Isis* 78, *Mor.* 382F; Iambl. *Letter* 4.5 (Stob. *Anth.* 3.3.26); *Soul* 8.53, §458. Middle Platonism includes much Stoic influence but was more transcendental in the early empire than in much of the first century BCE (Dillon, "Plato," 806); it became still more transcendental in Neoplatonism (below).

219. Max. Tyre *Or.* 11.9; 38.3. He allegorized Odysseus's travels as a visionary tour of the cosmos (similar to what one finds in apocalyptic texts) by his soul (*Or.* 26.1).

220. Max. Tyre *Or.* 9.6; 10.3; 11.11. Cf. Philost. *Hrk.* 7.3; *4 Ezra* 7:98; eschatologically, 1 Cor. 13:12; cf. *1 En.* 90:35. For the Platonic God's pure goodness, see Barclay, *Gift*, 71, 84.

221. Max. Tyre *Or.* 21.7.

222. Max. Tyre *Or.* 21.7–8. Philo also affirms that the mind, turning from pleasure, cleaves to virtue by apprehending virtue's beauty (*Sacr.* 45).

223. Max. Tyre *Or.* 11.11. Those unable to see God himself could be satisfied with worshiping his offspring (stars, daimones, etc.), below him in the cosmic hierarchy (11.12).

224. Max. Tyre *Or.* 11.10.

225. Max. Tyre *Or.* 21.7–8.

226. Case, *Origins*, 93–94; cf. also Osborn, *Justin*, 72. Josephus expects his readers to understand (and perhaps react negatively) when he declares that an Egyptian ruler wished to "see the gods" (*Ag. Ap.* 1.232–34).

227. Plot. *Enn.* 1.6 ("On Beauty," esp. chap. 9). For Plotinus, this was a matter of reason, not of imagination (note comments by Iambl. *Soul* 2.13, §369). For contemplation of the divine, cf. also Cic. *Tusc.* 5.25.70; Max. Tyre *Or.* 16.2–6; Philo *Spec. Laws* 3.1. Less clearly, Panayotakis ("Vision") finds it even in the tale of Psyche and Cupid (others read differently, as in Parker and Murgatroyd, "Poetry").

228. Case, *Origins*, 94.

229. Porph. *Marc.* 16.274. Perceiving God purifies a person (*Marc.* 11.204).

sible, he remarks, because the intellect is like a "mirror" that reflects God's likeness by its similarity to him.[230]

For Philo, God is transcendent and hence can be encountered through mystical vision, especially ecstatically.[231] In contrast to Gentile Platonists, in Philo this vision depends completely on God's self-revelation;[232] like other Platonists, however, Philo believed that only the pure soul can see God.[233] The present vision of deity is necessarily incomplete; mortals can only perceive *that* God is, not *what* he is;[234] only God can "apprehend God."[235] The soul's eye is overwhelmed by God's glory,[236] yet seeking God remains a blessed endeavor, "just as no one blames the eyes of the body because when unable to see the sun itself they see the emanation of its rays."[237] One should progress toward clearer vision; the ultimate vision of God was a reward for attaining perfection.[238]

Some believed that by meditating on divine, heavenly matters, the soul—originally from heaven—nourished its heavenly nature[239] and so prepared to ascend to heaven after the body's death.[240] In Alexandria, where Platonism dominated early enough to impact Jewish intellectual thought there, such thoughts were already influential. Thus, the widely circulated Wisdom of Solomon warns that the body distracts the soul from heavenly concerns.[241] For this Jewish author, people can understand the matters of heaven only by God's heavenly gift of wisdom and the Spirit.[242]

230. Porph. *Marc.* 13.233–34 (ἐνοπτριζόμενος).

231. See Isaacs, *Spirit*, 50; Dillon, "Transcendence in Philo"; Hagner, "Vision," 89–90; on mediation of this vision, see Mackie, "Seeing"; on seeing God and overcoming passions, see Hayward, "Israel" (citing esp. Philo *Names* 44–46, 81–88; *Drunkenness* 80–83; *Dreams* 1.79, 129–31, 171). As it did with contemporary Stoics, meditation on heavenly things seemed to allow Philo a heavenly perspective (*Spec. Laws* 3.1–2).

232. Philo *Abr.* 80.

233. Philo *Conf.* 92. For biblical examples, see *Names* 3–6; *QG* 4.138; *Conf.* 92, 146; *Dreams* 1.171; *Abr.* 57.

234. Philo *Rewards* 39; Hagner, "Vision," 89, cites both this and *Names* 62.

235. Philo *Rewards* 40 (trans. Colson, LCL, 8:335).

236. Philo *Spec. Laws* 1.37.

237. Philo *Spec. Laws* 1.40 (trans. Colson, LCL, 7:121).

238. Philo *Rewards* 36; cf. *Dreams* 72. Conzelmann (*Corinthians*, 228) contrasts the eschatological vision in 1 Cor. 13:12 with Philo's usual mystical, ecstatic vision; Hagner ("Vision," 86) contrasts John's and Philo's *sōma-sēma* conception.

239. Porph. *Marc.* 6.103–8; 7.131–34; 10.180–83; 16.267–68; 26.415–16; cf. chap. 8, below, on Col. 3:1–2.

240. For the ascent, see, e.g., Max. Tyre *Or.* 41.5; Men. Rhet. 2.9, 414.21–23; some viewed this as divinization (2.9, 414.25–27), an expression Paul avoids.

241. Wis. 9:15–16. Among Gentiles, cf., e.g., Mus. Ruf. 18A, p. 112.20, 27–28 (a first-century Stoic); Max. Tyre *Or.* 1.5.

242. Wis. 9:17. This context influences the language also of John 3:11–12 (see Keener, *John*, 560).

Jewish Vision of the Divine and God's Image

Some Jewish sources also spoke of envisioning God.[243] Jewish mystics valued ascending to heaven in visions[244] and sometimes may have encouraged these in ways similar to the attempts of some philosophers to encounter the divine.[245] Such experiences may provide the background for some of the contents in *1 Enoch* and other apocalyptic sources.[246] Some authors apparently drew especially on biblical revelations of divine glory (e.g., Isa. 6:1–8; Ezek. 1:4–28) as models for their own mystic ascents to heaven.[247]

Although Paul was not averse to drawing on Platonic imagery in this context (cf. 2 Cor. 4:16–5:1), his explicit appeal is to the biblical experience of Moses[248] (possibly evoked for him also by way of the Jesus tradition; cf. Mark 9:2).[249] Scripture and Jewish tradition reported various theophanies,[250] but the most important model was Moses (especially, as here, in Exod. 33:18–34:7).[251] In some Jewish traditions Moses even ascended all the way to heaven to receive

243. E.g., 1QS 11.5–6.

244. In addition to apocalypses (e.g., *1 En.* 14:18–20; *2 En.* 20:3 A; 22:1–3; *3 En.* 1) and other pseudepigraphic sources (e.g., *L.A.E.* 25:3–4; *Odes Sol.* 36:1–2), see, e.g., *t. Hag.* 2:3–4; *b. Hag.* 14b, bar.; *y. Hag.* 2:1, §§7–8; *Song Rab.* 1:4, §1; Kirk, *Vision*, 11–13; Chernus, "Visions"; Himmelfarb, "Ascent"; Scholem, *Trends*, 44; for Moses, see Meeks, *Prophet-King*, 122–25, 156–58, 205–9, 241–44. For Philo's mysticism (e.g., *Spec. Laws* 3.1), see, e.g., Goodenough, *Introduction*, 134–60; Winston, "Mysticism"; Sterling, *Ancestral Philosophy*, 151–70, esp. 169–70. In Hellenistic sources, cf., e.g., Max. Tyre *Or.* 11.10; 26.1; 38.3.

245. For mystics seeking transformation to the divine image, see Morray-Jones, "Mysticism"; Arbel, "Understanding."

246. These may also include eschatological transformation (*1 En.* 62:15; 108:11–13; *4 Ezra* 7:97; *2 Bar.* 51:3, 10; with, e.g., Furnish, *Corinthians*, 240–41; Belleville, *Glory*, 286–87) or even a mystic's transformation in the present (*1 En.* 39:14; 71:10–11).

247. Besides apocalyptic sources, cf. 4Q385 frg. 6.5–14; *b. Hag.* 13a, bar.; Dimant and Strugnell, "Vision"; Segal, "Ascent," 39–40; Scholem, *Trends*, 42. Halperin, "Midrash," argues that *merkabah* mysticism appears already in the LXX.

248. For Paul using midrash on Exod. 34 alongside the Hellenistic ideal of transformation, see also Fitzmyer, "Glory." For a survey of proposed backgrounds supporting the Exodus background, see Thrall, *Corinthians*, 294–95; most recognize this background here (see, e.g., Belleville, *Glory*, 178–91, 273; Hays, *Echoes*, 144).

249. For Moses-Sinai and transfiguration themes in Philo (e.g., *Mos.* 1.57), see Moses, *Transfiguration Story*, 50–57; in Josephus, 57–61; in the Dead Sea Scrolls, 61–66; in other sources, 66–83. The majority of scholars see Moses's transfiguration as the primary background for that of Jesus (see, e.g., Glasson, *Moses*, 70; Davies and Allison, *Matthew*, 2:695; esp. Moses, *Transfiguration Story*, 84–85).

250. E.g., for early Jewish discussion of patriarchal visions of the future era, see *4 Ezra* 3:14; *2 Bar.* 4:3–4; *L.A.B.* 23:6; 4Q544 lines 10–12; 4Q547 line 7; *Sipre Deut.* 357.5.11; *b. B. Bat.* 16b–17a, bar.; *Abot R. Nat.* 31 A; 42, §116 B; further in Keener, *John*, 767–68. Smelik ("Transformation") finds echoes of Hellenistic apotheosis in later sources (*Tg. Jon.* on Judg. 5:31; 2 Sam. 23:4; Isa. 30:26; 60:5).

251. For Moses's transformation, see Exod. 34:29–35; cf. *L.A.B.* 12:1; 19:16; *Abot R. Nat.* 13, §32 B; *b. B. Bat.* 75a; *Tg. Onq.* on Exod. 34:29, 30, 35.

the Torah.[252] Moreover, Moses was explicitly transformed through this revelation (see comment below),[253] although his transformation was temporary, in contrast to the inner transformation that the new covenant has initiated.

Two possible associations for Paul's reference to the image here are particularly important. God made humanity in his image (Gen. 1:26), as his children (Gen. 5:1–2). Renewal into Christ's image may thus include an allusion to the restoration of some of what Adam lost (1 Cor. 11:7; 15:49; Col. 3:10), as noted earlier. In that sense, the transformation restores persons to the identity that God originally intended for humankind. Whereas Adam's sin introduced death to those bearing his image (Rom. 5:12–21),[254] the second Adam has inaugurated a new creation for those bearing his (2 Cor. 5:17). By marring God's image, Jewish tradition believed, Adam had lost God's glory;[255] glory's eschatological restoration (cf. Rom. 8:29)[256] here comes in Christ.

At the same time, Christ appears as God's image in a unique way, one that could not have been filled by simply any human (2 Cor. 4:4; Col. 1:15).[257] Paul probably thus evokes God's supreme image, through which God formed

252. See, e.g., Aristob. frg. 4 (Euseb. *P.E.* 13.13.5); Philo *QE* 2.46; *Sipre Deut.* 49.2.1; *b. Shab.* 88b; *Exod. Rab.* 28:1; 41:5; 47:5; *Lev. Rab.* 1:15; *Pesiq. Rab.* 20:4; 47:4; *3 En.* 15B:2; cf. *L.A.B.* 12:1.

253. See pp. 212–14; Keener, *Matthew*, 437; in Jewish tradition, Moses, *Transfiguration Story*, 50–83.

254. See also *2 Bar.* 23:4; 48:42–43; 54:14; *4 Ezra* 7:118. On Adam and God's image (Gen. 1:26–27; 5:1; 9:6), see 4Q504 frg. 8 (recto).4; *Jub.* 6:8; Sir. 17:3; Wis. 2:23; 1 Cor. 11:7; James 3:9; Philo *Creation* 69, 139; *Alleg. Interp.* 1.90, 92; *Conf.* 169; *Mos.* 2.65; *Spec. Laws* 1.171; 3.83, 207; *Sib. Or.* 1.23; 3.8; *4 Ezra* 8:44; *L.A.E.* 13:3; 14:1–2; 15:2; *Apoc. Mos.* 33:5; *2 En.* 30:10 J; 44:1–2; 65:2; *m. Ab.* 3:13/14; *t. Yebam.* 8:7; *Mek. Bah.* 11.111–14; *b. B. Bat.* 58a; *Gen. Rab.* 8:10; *Midr. Pss.* on Ps. 17:8; cf. Ps.-Phoc. 106; *L.A.E.* 37:3; 39:3 (Seth; also *Apoc. Mos.* 10:3; 12:2); *T. Naph.* 2:5; *b. Sanh.* 38a, bar.; Bunta, "Metamorphosis." For Gentile analogies, cf. Sen. Y. *Dial.* 1.1.5; Mus. Ruf. 17, p. 108.15–22; Marc. Aur. 10.8.2; Diog. Laert. 6.2.51; Iambl. *Letter* 4.7–9, 13–16 (Stob. *Anth.* 3.3.26); *Myst.* 7.4; Porph. *Marc.* 13.233–34; 16.267; 32.496–97; reading likeness to God in Plato in light of Stoic usage, Russell, "Virtue." A child bears the image of parents, which is relevant to Gen. 5:1–3 and thus 1:26–27.

255. E.g., *Apoc. Mos.* 21:6 (cf. 18:5–6); *3 Bar.* 4:16; *y. Shab.* 2:6, §2; *Gen. Rab.* 12:6; *Num. Rab.* 13:12; *Pesiq. Rab.* 14:10; *Tg. Ps.-Jon.* on Gen. 2:25; cf. *Pesiq. Rab Kah.* 1:1. For Adam's glory, see Sir. 49:16; 4Q504 frg. 8 (recto).4; 4Q511 frgs. 52 + 54–55 + 57–59.2; *Abot R. Nat.* 1 A; *Pesiq. Rab Kah.* 4:4; 26:3; *b. B. Bat.* 58a; *Lev. Rab.* 20:2; *Eccl. Rab.* 8:1, §2; cf. *Sib. Or.* 1.24; *b. B. Metsia* 84a; *Num. Rab.* 13:2; Noffke, "Glory"; perhaps Goshen Gottstein, "Body"; but still after the fall, cf. *Tg. Onq.* on Gen. 3:21; *Tg. Neof.* 1 on Gen. 3:21; *Tg. Ps.-Jon.* on Gen. 3:21. God's "image" is "glorious"—thus, being transformed to his image involves glorification (2 Cor. 3:18; ultimately, Rom. 8:29–30); *originally* being in God's image also includes glory (1 Cor. 11:7). Paul links image and glory in 2 Cor. 4:4 and probably Rom. 1:23; cf. 4Q504 frg. 8 (recto).4.

256. Cf. CD 3.20; 1QS 4.23; 1QH^a 4.27; *Apoc. Mos.* 39:2–3 (missing in the parallel *L.A.E.* 47:3); Scroggs, *Adam*, 23–31; also, one late tradition links it with Moses's glory (Furnish, *Corinthians*, 215, citing *Memar Marqah* 5.4).

257. Wisdom language is especially emphatic in Colossians; see, e.g., Lohse, *Colossians*, 48; Bruce, "Myth," 94; cf. May, "Logos," 446; Glasson, "Colossians and Sirach."

or stamped his image on the world (cf. Col. 1:15–16) or humanity, an image identified in Greek-speaking Jewish tradition as God's wisdom or *logos*.[258] Diaspora Jews could envision Wisdom as a mirror[259] that reflected God's character and work (Wis. 7:26).[260]

Glory Revealed to Moses and Jesus's Agents

Not only here but elsewhere, Paul links "image" and "glory" (2 Cor. 4:4; Rom. 1:23; 1 Cor. 11:7). Beholding God's glory transformed Moses (2 Cor. 3:7),[261] and in the same way, beholding Jesus, God's glorious image (4:4–6), transforms believers. This same glory shines through weak vessels (4:7–12), Christ's agents (such as Paul), whom Paul compares favorably with Moses (3:6–4:4).[262] Christ's agents mediate a superior glory and a covenant superior

258. See Wis. 7:22–27; Philo *Creation* 16, 25, 36; *Spec. Laws* 3.207; *Plant.* 18; *Flight* 12; *Dreams* 2.45. For the logos as God's image more generally, see Wis. 7:26 (Wisdom); Philo *Conf.* 97, 147; *Dreams* 1.239; 2.45; *Drunkenness* 133; *Eternity* 15; *Flight* 101; *Heir* 230; *Plant.* 18; *Spec. Laws* 1.81; *Creation* 146; cf. Col. 1:15; Heb. 1:3. This image could be linked with the first, ideal person (of Gen. 1, distinguished from the earthly Adam), as in Philo *Alleg. Interp.* 1.43, 92. For the first man's image stamped on others, see also *m. Sanh.* 4:5; *b. Sanh.* 38a.

259. Glass mirrors were known (Pliny E. *N.H.* 36.66.193), but metal mirrors predominated by far (cf., e.g., Sir. 12:11; Pliny E. *N.H.* 33.45.128; Hurschmann, "Mirror," 57; Forbes, *Technology*, 5:184–85; for clear water or polished stone, see also Sen. Y. *Nat. Q.* 1.17.5). Some associate the mention of mirrors in 1 Cor. 13:12 and here with Corinth, since bronze mirrors were common and Corinthian bronze was famous (e.g., Cic. *Verr.* 2.4.44.97–98; *Fin.* 2.8.23; Strabo 8.6.23; Petron. *Sat.* 31, 50; Pliny E. *N.H.* 34.1.1; 37.12.49; Jos. *Life* 68; *War* 5.201, 204; Mart. *Epig.* 9.59.11; 14.172, 177; Paus. 2.3.3). Just as French fries and Swiss cheese need not be imported from France or Switzerland, however, not all "Corinthian bronze" originated in Corinth (Pliny E. *N.H.* 34.3.6–7; Jacobson and Weitzman, "Bronze"); though Corinth may have produced some bronze (Engels, *Roman Corinth*, 36–37), it was very limited in this period (Mattusch, "Bronze," 219–22, 228–30), and Paul omits it in his list in 1 Cor. 3:12.

260. Some also associate the mirror with God's glory shining in the heart; see 2 Cor. 3:3, 6; 4:6; cf. 13:3–5. Although believers could be the mirror here, reflecting Christ's image (and some see it as a mirror reflecting Christ in the gospel: Lambrecht, "Glorie"; Lambrecht, "Transformation"; or even the OT: Lebourlier, "Miroir"), it more likely refers here to Christ as wisdom reflecting God's image (Witherington, *Corinthians*, 379). Nevertheless, the association of self-knowledge and "divinity" (e.g., Plato *Alcib.* 1.132E–133C; Cic. *Tusc.* 1.22.52; *Leg.* 1.22.58–59; self-knowledge in Epict. *Diatr.* 2.14.21) is less relevant here than Hellenistic Jewish wisdom ideas (despite the later blending of the two; see *Sent. Sext.* 445–50; *Odes Sol.* 13:1–4). Some also used mirrors to advocate self-improvement (Sen. Y. *Nat. Q.* 1.17.4; Diog. Laert. 2.33; 7.1.19; Sorabji, *Emotion*, 214), again not the idea here. Mirror analogies did not always imply the viewer's *own* reflection (e.g., Polyb. 15.20.4).

261. See discussion in Keener, *Corinthians*, 169–71.

262. Just as John later compared those who were eyewitnesses of Jesus with Moses, who was an eyewitness of God's glory (John 1:14–18); see discussion of John 1:14–18 in Keener, *John*, 405–26, esp. 405, 412, 421–22; Boismard, *Prologue*, 135–45, esp. 136–39; Enz, "Exodus," 212; Borgen, *Bread*, 150–51; Hanson, "Exodus" (including rabbinic material); Harrison, "Study," 29; Mowvley, "Exodus." Christians in John's circle viewed divine vision as transformative for

to that of Moses (3:6) because their glorious transformation gives life rather than death (3:6–8) and is eternal rather than transitory (3:7, 11, 13; 4:16).[263]

In the context, Paul's primary point is not a comparison between the revelation to Moses and the revelation to all believers but rather a comparison between the revelation to Moses and the revelation to the servants of the new covenant who bring the message to others. Nevertheless, some of Paul's arguments about himself draw on wider Christian experience, and that is undoubtedly the case here. The "all" (πάντες) in 2 Corinthians 3:18 seems superfluous if it does not refer to an experience potentially applicable to all believers (cf. also 5:10, 14–15; Rom. 4:16; 8:32).[264]

A key emphasis in this context is that this glorious transformation comes by God's Spirit (2 Cor. 3:3, 6, 8). Just as the Lord revealed his glory to Moses in Exodus 33–34, so, correspondingly, the Spirit reveals divine glory to servants of the new covenant (2 Cor. 3:17).[265]

This inner glory has come in a way very different from the glory revealed at Sinai, however; this glory was evident in the cross, recognizable only from the vantage point of the resurrection. The brokenness of Paul and his colleagues replicates the glory of the cross (2 Cor. 4:7, 10–11, 17); this glory is concealed from the perishable perspectives of this age but becomes evident to those who receive the good news (2:15–16; 3:15–16; 4:3). From the world's standpoint, both Jesus's execution and the suffering of his followers[266] are merely the stench of death; in believers' worldview, however, they are inseparable from God's resurrection power (2:14–16). Those who have begun to share in the new creation look at everything, including Christ, in a way different from those whose minds remain captive to the old order of things (5:16–17).

---

the present, past, and future (1 John 3:2–3, 6); like Paul, they looked to biblical examples for this pattern (John 1:14–18, echoing Exod. 33–34; cf. John 8:56; 12:40).

263. It is also internal as opposed to external (2 Cor. 3:2–3), but public in a different and more transformative way (3:2); other early Christian sources may also challenge detractors' complaints that the alleged new covenant glory was less immediately spectacular than that revealed to Moses (cf. Mark 9:2–7; John 1:14; 2 Pet. 1:16–18). Paul can appeal to what is invisible as eternal (2 Cor. 4:18) without further explanation, because Platonic tradition made this idea widespread; see, e.g., Plato *Rep.* 6.484BD; Philo *Drunkenness* 136; Sen. Y. *Ep. Lucil.* 36.9–10 (cf. reason in 66.32); cf. Diod. Sic. 10.7.3; Porph. *Marc.* 8.147–50; *4 Ezra* 7:26; *2 Bar.* 51:8.

264. Cf. Thrall, *Corinthians*, 282. Cf. also Eph. 2:3; John 1:16; Philo *Jos.* 6; *1 Clem.* 21.1; *2 Clem.* 7.2; Ign. *Phld.* 3.3; *Mart. Pol.* 20.2; *Diogn.* 3.4; though in a minority of texts one can argue for a more exclusive sense, e.g., the Twelve in Acts 2:32; 10:33.

265. For this interpretation of 2 Cor. 3:17, see Bruce, *Apostle*, 120–21; Belleville, *Glory*, 256–72; Thrall, *Corinthians*, 278–81; Hays, *Echoes*, 143; Matera, *Corinthians*, 96; cf. also Theodoret *Comm. 2 Cor.* 305–6.

266. I understand the apostolic ministers led in triumph in 2 Cor. 2:14 as captives being led to death, fitting the normal image of Roman triumphs; thus they share Jesus's dying (cf. 1:5, 9; 4:10; Keener, *Corinthians*, 164).

The Experience of the Spirit

For Paul, the new covenant, unlike the old, expands the experience of the Spirit to all of God's people (2 Cor. 3:3, evoking Ezek. 36:26–27), as is repeatedly clear in his letters.[267] The extant sources suggest that most Jewish people considered direct experience of God's Spirit rare in their own time.[268] Yet Paul declares that just as Moses's veil was removed when he was before the Lord, the veil that shrouds God's glory from being recognized by nonbelievers (2 Cor. 3:13–15; 4:3–4) is removed when people turn to Christ (3:16). This revelation is expressly accomplished through the Spirit (3:17).

Paul's visions and revelations of the Lord undoubtedly facilitated his own experience of beholding the Lord's glory (2 Cor. 12:1, 7). At the same time, Paul does not present his visionary experience as a normative model that all believers should seek (12:5; cf. 5:13).[269] The experience that all believers share is Christ's divine glory in their hearts (4:6).[270] Paul's other writings suggest that thinking conformed to God's values (Rom. 12:2, also mentioning transformation) and focused on the matters of Christ (Col. 3:1–11) can bring transformation without assuming visions. Given the diversity of gifts (Rom. 12:4–8; 1 Cor. 12:4–11, 29–30),[271] believers may have appropriated this experience in different ways; some may have done so in more mystical

267. Cf. 2 Cor. 13:13 (13:14 in some translations); Rom. 5:5; 7:6; 8:2–16, 23, 26–27; 14:17; 15:13; 1 Cor. 3:16; 6:11; 12:3–13; Gal. 3:3, 5, 14; 4:6; 5:16–18, 22, 25; 6:8; Phil. 3:3; Col. 1:8; 1 Thess. 4:8; 5:19.

268. *T. Sot.* 12:5; 13:3; 14:3 (for exceptions, cf. *Sipre Deut.* 173.1.3); *b. Suk.* 28a, bar.; *y. Abod. Zar.* 3:1, §2; *Hor.* 3:5, §3; *Sot.* 9:16, §2; cf. prophets in 1 Macc. 9:27; *2 Bar.* 85:3; Davies, *Paul*, 208–15; Isaacs, *Spirit*, 49, 51; Bamberger, "Prophet," 306; Leivestad, "Dogma"; Hill, *Prophecy*, 33–35; Aune, "Προφήτης"; for Josephus, see Isaacs, *Spirit*, 49; Best, "Pneuma," 222–25; Aune, "Προφήτης" (regarding prophetic usage). This approach excepts the Dead Sea Scrolls community (e.g., 1QS 3.7; 4.21; 1QSb 2.22, 24), who may have connected their possession of the Spirit with eschatology (Chevallier, "Souffle," 38–41; Aune, *Prophecy*, 81, 104; Aune, *Cultic Setting*, 29–44).

269. Paul does not address how common visions are. In Luke's ideal, articulated in Acts 2:17–18 regarding new covenant experience that democratizes the Spirit, visions and dreams may not be unusual. Neither, however, does that text specify that everyone experiences prophetic empowerment by the Spirit in the same way (the "word" in Acts most often designates the gospel message, though Luke often enough also mentions prophets and visions). Paul might believe that prophecy is *potentially* available to all believers (1 Cor. 14:1, 5, 24–25, 31, 39; cf. 12:31), but he accepts the Spirit's sovereignty (12:7–11) and does not relegate to a lower spiritual level those who do not experience this (12:29).

270. The shining presumably occurred when the person became part of the new creation at conversion, but the imparted light of Christ presumably continues there (cf. Rom. 8:9; Gal. 2:20).

271. Cf. also Eph. 4:11–13; 1 Pet. 4:10–11. Most relevant, however, are 1 Cor. 12:8–10 and 14:26, because they provide several examples of different ways to learn from the Spirit (wisdom, knowledge or teaching, and prophecy and/or revelations).

ways (similar to Paul's visions), others by meditating on Christ's character as displayed in his acts and passion,[272] and many, perhaps most commonly, by worship focused on God in Christ.[273] In light of Old Testament depictions of life before the fall (Gen. 2:16–22; cf. 3:8–11), the biblical God as personal and relational, and the promised knowledge of God at the time of restoration (Jer. 31:32–34; Hosea 2:20; 1 Cor. 13:12), the heart of the experience was undoubtedly relational.

In whatever ways this beholding of God's glory is experienced, Paul depicts an ongoing, present experience that brings transformation,[274] just as the same verb for transformation suggests in Romans 12:2. "From glory to glory" probably depicts the increasing experience of God's glory.[275] Paul does recognize that the experience of glory, while not technically veiled, remains limited, as in a mirror, until Christ's return (1 Cor. 13:10–12);[276] the full experience of glory awaits glorified bodies (1 Cor. 15:49; Phil. 3:21; cf. Rom. 8:29–30). Nevertheless, believers in the present are increasingly conformed to God's glorious image in Christ as they continue to know what Christ is like.

Whereas Platonists sought to envision a deity of pure reason, and Jewish mystics God's throne chariot, Paul's focus is on Christ himself (2 Cor. 4:4; 12:1, 8–9; Col. 3:1–2, 10), presumably including his suffering (cf. 1 Cor. 2:2). In particular, those who embrace Christ's sufferings share his resurrection power and glory (2 Cor. 4:6, 10–12, 16). This is "not the passionless deity of Platonism, but the God of the cross who embraced human brokenness and mortality."[277]

272. Related to a philosophic approach noted above, but not incompatible with the mystical approach; the visionary approach appears not only among Judean apocalyptists but also with the Middle Platonist Philo, as noted above. Influenced by the Platonic tradition, later Christian interpreters such as Augustine and Eastern Orthodox teachers valued *contemplating*, not simply commenting on, God's character.

273. For the early worship of Jesus, see Hurtado, *One God*; Hurtado, *Lord Jesus Christ*; Hurtado, *Become God*; Bauckham, *Crucified*.

274. Note the present passive indicative verb (μεταμορφούμεθα, 2 Cor. 3:18) and the daily renewal of Paul and his colleagues in 2 Cor. 4:16.

275. Similar expressions (Ps. 84:7 [83:8 LXX]) can communicate rhetorical or other accumulation (e.g., Hom. *Il.* 16.111; Men. Rhet. 2.3, 378.29–30; John 1:16; Rom. 1:17; 2 Cor. 2:16) or increasing measure (Jer. 9:3); cf. the grammatical element of the argument in Taylor, "Faith," 341–43 (also cited in Das, *Debate*, 64). Cf. the idea of progression in envisioning the divine in Max. Tyre *Or.* 1.10 (cf. 21.7–8). If the accumulation is primarily rhetorical, it may imply "from start to finish" (cf. Moo, *Romans*, 76; Benware, "Grammar").

276. In that passage, by contrast with this one, Paul evokes the usual prophetic experience that was less intense than that of Moses (Num. 12:6–8, esp. 8, echoed by Paul in "face to face" and, in the LXX, αἴνιγμα, which appears in the LXX at most nine times).

277. Keener, *Corinthians*, 170.

Conclusion

For Paul, true wisdom is found in the cross, the antithesis of status-conscious worldly wisdom. True wisdom can be understood only from the vantage point of the age to come, when truth will be impossible to evade (cf. 2 Cor. 3:13–15; 4:5). God's Spirit reveals this perspective on reality to believers, qualifying them to understand dimensions of the divine perspective. God's Spirit may communicate this to believers in various ways.

By contrast, Paul argues, the world that honors the very expressions of power that crucified Christ lacks the competence for spiritual and moral evaluation. Unfortunately, the Corinthian Christians had imbibed more of the world's spirit than of Christ's and were therefore evaluating matters wrongly. The mind of Christ was available to them, but it was for mature believers, who walk in Christ's love, not for childish believers, who harshly judge one another and divide from one another in envy and strife. An increasingly fuller understanding of the character of Christ crucified could increasingly transform their character, conforming them to Christ's glorious image.

7

A Christlike Mind
(Phil. 2:1–5; 3:19–21; 4:6–8)

Think among yourselves the way that Christ Jesus also thought.

—Philippians 2:5

Together follow my example . . . because many . . . are enemies of Christ's cross. These are the ones whose destiny is destruction, who worship their desires, who count as glory their shame, whose focus is earthly matters. Also do this because we have our citizenship in heaven, from which also we await the deliverer, the Lord Jesus Christ, who will transform our humiliated bodies to be like his glorious body.

—Philippians 3:17–21

Don't worry about anything; instead, in every situation share with God your requests, using prayer and petition but also thanking him. Thus, God's peace that exceeds your ability to fathom will guard your hearts and thoughts in Christ Jesus. Further, my family, whatever matters are true, whatever matters are honorable, whatever matters are just, whatever matters are sacred, whatever matters are delightful, whatever matters are commendable—if anything is virtuous and if anything is praiseworthy—these are the things you should be pondering!

—Philippians 4:6–8

Three passages in Paul's Letter to the Philippians offer further samples of Paul's interest in thinking. I address the third of these passages (Phil. 4:6–8) first because it revisits the issue of peace, which also appears in Romans 8:6. In Philippians 4 Paul invites believers in Philippi to meditate on virtuous matters (4:8) and to entrust their requests to God, whose peace will guard their hearts and minds in Christ (4:6–7).

In Philippians 2 Paul exhorts believers to think in a way that supports unity and service to one another, thus thinking in the way that Jesus exemplified (2:5). More explicitly than in 4:6–8, Paul addresses the problem of division and strife in the church (cf. 4:2–3); as in some other passages (cf. Rom. 12:2–5; 1 Cor. 2:14–3:4), a mind for Christ is also a mind for Christ's body.

Finally, Philippians 3:19–21 contrasts a mind focused on earthly things with a heavenly focus. This passage provides a natural segue for chapter 8, on Colossians 3:1–2, a passage that also develops this theme.[1]

Divine Peace Guards Minds in Christ (Phil. 4:7)

In Philippians 4:7 Paul promises divine peace,[2] elsewhere a fruit of the Spirit (Rom. 14:17; Gal. 5:22), to guard believers' hearts and thoughts. I have already discussed the emphasis on, and backgrounds for, peace with respect to Romans 8:6.[3] As there, this peace appears to be partly within an individual (Phil. 4:7–8) but also appears to have communal implications (cf. 4:1–2);[4] it may also involve, as it certainly does in Romans 8:6–7, peace with God (cf. "enemies" in Phil. 3:18).

In this passage Paul seizes his ideal audience's attention with an oxymoron: divine peace both surpasses all thinking and guards believers' thoughts. That is, in contrast to typical philosophic expectations, it is not self-generated, for example, by philosophic reasoning.[5] If "guard" here evokes the military or

1. If, as I believe, Paul wrote Colossians, it presumably comes from the same period of detention addressed in Philippians. Even scholars who regard Philippians and Philemon as Paul's final extant letters will view them as closest in time to the earliest post-Pauline letters.

2. Paul plays on this peace from God by speaking of the "God of peace" being with believers in Phil. 4:9, although that phrase is not unique to this Pauline context (Rom. 15:33; 16:20; 1 Thess. 5:23; Heb. 13:20; it is rare elsewhere in early Jewish sources outside *T. Dan* 5:2; some compare "angel of peace" in the Similitudes, *1 En.* 40:8; 52:5; 53:4; 54:4; 56:2; 60:24; *T. Dan* 6:5; *T. Ash.* 6:5; *T. Benj.* 6:1).

3. See pp. 135–41. Cf. here Marius Victorinus *Phil.* 4.7 (Edwards, *Commentary*, 268).

4. See also Fee, *Philippians*, 411–12; cf. Snyman, "Philippians 4:1–9."

5. Cf. a similar oxymoron in Eph. 3:19: knowing God's love that surpasses being known.

custodial image of guarding or keeping watch,[6] its conjunction with "peace" may also be striking.[7]

Looking to God or his agents for protection more generally was not a new idea. Jewish people looked to God to guard or protect his people.[8] This language was familiar in the regularly recited priestly benediction, which prays for God to keep his people and give them peace (Num. 6:24–26);[9] at least some understood this protection to include protection from demons and from the evil inclination.[10] Already in Scripture itself David prays for God to keep the inclinations of his people's hearts (1 Chron. 29:18).[11]

Because I already treated some possible backgrounds or resonances for Paul's language of divine peace in the earlier discussion of Romans 8:6,[12] I survey below merely how the preceding context prepares for this promise and how the following verse continues its cognitive interest.

6. Cf. e.g., 1 Esd. 4:56; Jdt. 3:6; Philo *Mos.* 1.235; Jos. *Ant.* 9.42. This is its most common sense in BDAG, although Paul was not alone in applying it figuratively (e.g., Philo *Agr.* 15, the cognate noun; 1 Pet. 1:5; later *Diogn.* 6.4). In *Rhet. Alex.* pref. 1421a.16–18, health guards the body and education the soul; in Mus. Ruf. frg. 36, p. 134.11, reason guards discernment. In this period even the figurative usage often evoked the literal image (e.g., Philo *Decal.* 74). Some think of guards in Philippi or, perhaps even more relevant to the letter, in Paul's own setting (cf. Phil. 1:13; Cohick, *Philippians*, 222).

7. So, e.g., Vincent, *Philippians*, 136; Michael, *Philippians*, 199; Erdman, *Philippians*, 141; Fee, *Philippians*, 411n58; Garland, "Philippians," 253; Witherington, *Philippians*, 248–49; the anti-imperial interpretation in Popkes, "Aussage." It does not necessarily function as an oxymoron, however; the Roman Empire claimed to have established peace and unity first through conquest. For subjugation as pacification in Roman ideology, see, e.g., *Res gest.* 5.26; Cic. *Prov. cons.* 12.31; Vell. Paterc. 2.90.1–4; 2.91.1; 2.115.4 (cf. perhaps Col. 1:20 in view of 1:16); cf. the interpretation of Roman iconography in Lopez, "Visualizing," 83; Lopez, *Apostle*, 49–50. Cf. Seneca's critique of the false peace in Huttner, "Zivilisationskritik."

8. E.g., Num. 6:24; Wis. 9:11; 10:1, 5; 1QS 2.3. Cf. the semidivine Protesilaos guarding a land in Philost. *Hrk.* 4.3.

9. Some Aramaic paraphrases of the benediction's context retained Hebrew for the familiar benediction (e.g., *Tg. Onq.* to Num. 6:24–26; *Tg. Neof.* 1 on Num. 6:24–26), as one would expect from *m. Meg.* 4:10. This is not the case, however, with *Tg. Ps.-Jon.* on Num. 6:24–26 (which also expands it with reference to understanding of Torah in *Tg. Ps.-Jon.* on Num. 6:25). For early echoes of the benediction, see *Jub.* 1:20; 31:15; 1QS 2.3 (cf. Black, *Scrolls*, 95); 4Q381 frg. 69.5; probably the spreading of fingers in *Jub.* 25:11.

10. The interpretation of the Aaronic benediction in *Sipre Numbers* (in Gaster, *Scriptures*, 41); *Num. Rab.* 11:5; *Tg. Ps.-Jon.* on Num. 6:24; and possibly already implicitly in the elaboration of the benediction in 1QS 2.2–4; 4Q398 frgs. 14–17, col. 2.4–5; 4Q399 frg. 1, col. 2.1–2; cf. 1QM 14.10; 4Q158 frgs. 1–2.8; Matt. 6:13; John 17:15; Montefiore, *Gospels*, 2:103; cf. Abrahams, *Studies* (2), 101; Jeremias, *Prayers*, 105. This association was not exclusive; 4Q374 frg. 2, col. 2.8 applies the benediction to healing and strengthening God's people, and both 4Q398 frgs. 14–17, col. 2.4–5 and 4Q399 frg. 1, col. 2.1–2 exhort hearers to ask God to protect one from evil thoughts and Belial's counsel.

11. LXX: φύλαξον ταῦτα ἐν διανοίᾳ καρδίας.

12. See again pp. 135–41.

Celebration in Christ (Phil. 4:4)

Paul's promise of God keeping people in peace is, however, conditional, depending on preceding exhortations. The promise of Philippians 4:7 may depend especially on the exhortation of 4:6, but the other exhortations might also play a role.

An emphatically doubled "Rejoice!"[13] introduces the immediate context's summary exhortations (Phil. 4:4; cf. 3:1; 1 Thess. 5:16).[14] Paul regards joy as a natural product of the Spirit's work (Rom. 14:17; 15:13; Gal. 5:22; 1 Thess. 1:6)[15] and expects it in fellowship, that is, in positive relationships with other believers and in sharing or serving their joys (Rom. 12:15; 16:19; 1 Cor. 12:26; 16:17; 2 Cor. 1:24; 2:3; 7:4, 7, 9, 13, 16; 8:2; 13:9, 11; Col. 1:24; 2:5; 1 Thess. 2:19; 3:9; 5:16; Philem. 7).[16]

Stoics could connect cheerfulness with the proper outlook on life, that is, submission to Fate's lot.[17] By this they did not mean something like modern positive thinking; indeed, they encouraged followers to expect misfortune so that they would be in the right frame of mind when it happened.[18] Stoics could also qualify the connection between the proper outlook and cheerfulness, noting that the ideally wise person would have virtue at all times, but not always joy and cheerfulness.[19]

The ultimate goal of most ancient philosophy was happiness (εὐδαιμονία),[20] a term absent in biblical Greek, perhaps because most biblical ethics' goal

13. Cf. a slightly different doubling of joy in Phil. 2:17–18. On the rhetorical function of such various forms of repetition, cf. Rowe, "Style," 130; Porter, "Paul and Letters," 579; Black, "Oration at Olivet," 85.

14. For parallels between Phil. 4 and 1 Thess. 5, see Kim, "Paraenesis," 110–13; for the specific exhortation to give thanks, see 118–19.

15. Cf. also Luke 10:21; Acts 13:52; possibly Sir. 39:6; 1QHᵃ 4.38; 15.9. Stoics could associate it with a correct outlook on reality (see comment below).

16. Cousar (*Philippians*, 85) suggests corporate implications from the preceding context; Witherington, *Philippians*, 245, from the plural verb.

17. Sen. Y. *Dial.* 7.15.4; 7.16.1–3; Mus. Ruf. frg. 38, p. 136.1–3; cf. also Engberg-Pedersen, *Paul and Stoics*, 73. On submission to Fate, see also Sen. Y. *Dial.* 1.1.5; 1.2.4; 1.3.1; 7.8.3; 7.15.6; *Ep. Lucil.* 96.1–2; 98.3; Mus. Ruf. 17, p. 108.37–38; 27, p. 130; 43, p. 138.14–15; Epict. *Diatr.* 2.5.4; 2.14.7; 4.13.24; Marc. Aur. 2.16; Crates *Ep.* 35; Libanius *Thesis* 1.6; Porph. *Marc.* 5.90–94; cf. Eurip. *Oenom.* frg. 572 (from Stob. *Anth.* 4.35.8); frg. 965 (from Epict. *Encheir.* 53); frg. 1078 (from Stob. *Anth.* 4.44.36); *Aeol.* frg. 37 (Stob. *Anth.* 4.44.49); views of God in Philo *Spec. Laws* 4.187 and among Essenes in Jos. *Ant.* 18.18; *b. Ber.* 60b–61a; *Taan.* 21a. A calm mind could find comfort in any situation (Sen. Y. *Dial.* 9.10.4).

18. Sorabji, *Emotion*, 235–36 (on 237 citing Cic. *Tusc.* 3.32–33 for the opposite view of Epicureans); cf., e.g., Galen *Grief* 52, 55–56, 74.

19. Arius Did. 2.7.5c, p. 28.3–9.

20. E.g., Mus. Ruf. 7, p. 58.13–15; Arius Did. 2.7.5b5, p. 20.15–16; 2.7.6d, pp. 38.34–41.3; 2.7.6e, p. 40.11–13; cf. Lutz, *Musonius*, 28; Engberg-Pedersen, *Paul and Stoics*, 74; Hossenfelder, "Happiness." Cf. pleasure for Epicureans, Diog. Laert. 10.131; 10.144.17; for them, a wise person

was oriented toward God's pleasure rather than that of mortals.[21] Nevertheless, Stoics felt that one could achieve such happiness, which required only virtue, without necessarily having joy or cheerfulness.[22] For what it is worth,[23] although Stoics distrusted emotions,[24] Greek philosophy, including Stoicism, valued joy;[25] among philosophers, wisdom and virtue rather than bodily pleasure yielded happiness.[26] Some moralists condemned frivolous laughter and jesting, emphasizing true joy instead.[27]

---

is happy even when groaning because of torture (Diog. Laert. 10.118). I adapt here material used in Keener, *Acts*, 2:2112–13.

21. Though cf. more hellenized Jewish and Christian approaches in, e.g., *Diogn.* 10.5; the term and its cognates appear 151 times in Josephus (e.g., *Ant.* 1.14, 20, 41, 44, 46, 69, 98, 104, 113, 142–43) and 189 times in Philo (e.g., *Alleg. Interp.* 1.4; 2.10, 82, 101–2; 3.52, 83, 205, 209, 218–19, 245).

22. Arius Did. 2.7.6d, pp. 38.34–40.3. In today's language we might think of long-term "satisfaction" or "fulfillment" without always feeling cheerful. "Joy" and "cheerfulness" remain goods (Arius Did. 2.7.5g, p. 32.4–6) but are not on the level of virtues (p. 32.5–6), which are necessary for εὐδαιμονία (p. 32.7–9).

23. Wojciechowski ("Vocabulary") doubts that philosophic moral philosophy shaped much NT language. I find some overlap in Pauline literature (e.g., Keener, "Perspectives"; Keener, *Corinthians*, 44–47, 57; see esp. Malherbe, *Philosophers*), most prominently in the Pastorals.

24. E.g., Knuuttila and Sihvola, "Analysis," 13, 15; cf. Plato (17); Aristotle was more positive (16); most non-Stoics regarded the Stoic position as unworkable (17). Plotinus urged suppressing emotions insofar as possible (Emilsson, "Plotinus on Emotions," 359). Apparently, most Stoics viewed humans as entirely rational (Brennan, "Theory," 23); but Posidonius may have broken with this approach (Cooper, "Posidonius," 71, 99), assuming, as is likely, that Galen correctly understood him (Sorabji, "Chrysippus"); some think Galen misunderstood Chrysippus (Gill, "Galen," e.g., 126–27). Marcus Aurelius appreciated positive, "sane" emotions (Engberg-Pedersen, "Marcus," 334–35).

25. E.g., Mus. Ruf. 17, p. 108.7; Arius Did. 2.7.5k, p. 34.1; 2.7.11e, p. 68.12–16; Iambl. *Pyth. Life* 31.196; cf. Vorster, "Blessedness," 38–51. Stoics approved of joy as a *good* emotion (Engberg-Pedersen, "Vices," 612; Engberg-Pedersen, *Paul and Stoics*, 72–73). It was not, however, a moral "virtue" (Arius Did. 2.7.5b, p. 10.19; 2.7.5c, p. 28.7; 2.7.5g, p. 32.4), though Paul lists it with virtues that belong to the Spirit's fruit (Gal. 5:22–23). Stoics appreciated a "calm pleasure" concerning what was good (Brennan, "Theory," 57).

26. Cic. *Parad.* 16–19; *Leg.* 1.23.60; *Tusc.* 5.7.19–20; Mus. Ruf. 7, p. 58.13; 17, p. 108.7; Iambl. *Pyth. Life* 31.196; Sen. Y. *Ep. Lucil.* 23; 27.3–4; 59.10; *Ben.* 7.2.3; *Dial.* 7.16.1–3; Epict. *Diatr.* 4.7.9; Dio Chrys. *Or.* 25.1; Arius Did. 2.7.6e, p. 40.13–15; 2.7.11g, pp. 70.33–73.4; Lucian *Dem.* 19–20; also Meeks, *Moral World*, 46–47; Lutz, *Musonius*, 28; Engberg-Pedersen, *Paul and Stoics*, 73. Self-knowledge also yielded full joy (Cic. *Tusc.* 5.25.70).

27. Dio Chrys. *Or.* 32.99. Cf. also warnings against excessive laughter or frivolity, e.g., Arist. N.E. 4.8.1–12, 1127b–1128b (esp. 4.8.3, 1128a); Epict. *Encheir.* 33.15; Dio Chrys. *Or.* 7.119; 32.99–100; 33.10; frg. 7 (Stob. *Anth.* 4.23.60 p. 588, ed. Hense; 74.60, ed. Meineke); Aul. Gel. 4.20.4–6 (cf. 4.20.11); Iambl. *Pyth. Life* 2.10; 17.71; 30.171; Porph. *Marc.* 19.321–22; Diog. Laert. 8.1.20; Pelikan, *Acts*, 148–49 (citing Arist. N.E. 2.7.11–13, 1108a; Clem. Alex. *Instr.* 2.8); 4Q269 frgs. 11ii+15.1; Eccles.7:3, 6; Sir. 21:20 (allowing quiet smiles but condemning loud laughter; cf. 27:13); *m. Ab.* 3:13/14; *t. Ber.* 3:21; *b. Ber.* 30b; perhaps 4Q266 frg. 18, col. 4.12–13; 4Q184 frg. 1.2; *Gen. Rab.* 22:6; *Exod. Rab.* 30:21; *Eccl. Rab.* 2:2, §1 (but the rabbis disapproved of only inappropriate laughter; Reines, "Laughter"). But contrast Gen. 21:6; Ps.

Jewish people often connected joy with keeping God's commandments,[28] living according to wisdom (Wis. 8:16), right living (*Let. Aris.* 261),[29] and virtue or divine ecstasy.[30] Particularly frequently, they associated joy with worship.[31]

Perhaps especially relevant to the letter's setting, one could experience joy even in the face of hardship (Rom. 12:12; 2 Cor. 7:4; 8:2; 1 Thess. 1:6).[32] Unlike that of some philosophers (especially earlier Stoics), Paul's submission to God is not fatalistic; he recognizes that God may change circumstances in response to prayer (see comment below).[33] Nevertheless, he does not condition joy on the changed circumstances. Instead, believers are to rejoice "in the Lord" (Phil. 4:4), a familiar Pauline phrase.[34]

Considering this letter's size, Paul seems especially emphatic about joy (Phil. 3:1; 4:4), regarding both relationships (1:4, 25; 2:2, 17–18, 28–29; 4:1, 10) and the spreading of the gospel (1:18). Perhaps the emphasis here reflects both his own positive outlook and his desire to encourage a church that has proved very supportive.

It is important to recognize the ideal character of Paul's exhortation. Paul himself often experienced sorrow (Rom. 9:2, continually; 2 Cor. 2:1, 3; Phil.

126:2; Prov. 31:25; Eccles. 3:4; Luke 6:21; spiritual laughter in Philo *Alleg. Interp.* 3.87, 217–19; *Worse* 123–24; *Names* 131, 261; *Abr.* 201–2, 206; *Rewards* 31. For the approval of rhetorical humor as long as dignity is maintained, see, e.g., Cic. *Brut.* 43.158; *Or. Brut.* 26.88–90; Quint. *Inst.* 4.3.30–31; Plut. *Table* 2.1.4, *Mor.* 631C.

28. Ps. 19:8; Jos. *Ag. Ap.* 2.189; *Pesiq. Rab Kah.* 27:2; *b. Yoma* 4b; *y. Pesah.* 10:1; *Lev. Rab.* 16:4 (purportedly from Ben Azzai); *Pesiq. Rab.* 21:2/3; 51:4; Urbach, *Sages*, 1:390–92; Bonsirven, *Judaism*, 95; especially the Tannaitic sources in Urbach, *Sages*, 1:390; most fully, Anderson, "Joy." In *Song Rab.* 4:11, §1, public teaching of Torah should generate as much joy as wedding guests experience from beholding a bride (cf. John 3:29).

29. The Spirit appears with joy in *y. Suk.* 5, cited in Montefiore and Loewe, *Anthology*, 203; cf. *Tg. Onq.* on Gen. 45:27–28.

30. E.g., Philo *Names* 175; *Dreams* 2.249; *Alleg. Interp.* 3.217; *Abr.* 206; *Migr.* 157 (mental laughter from ecstatic joy); *Spec. Laws* 2.54.

31. E.g., Pss. 2:11 (LXX); 5:11; 20:5; 27:6; 31:7; 32:11; 33:1, 3; 35:9; 42:4; 43:4; 47:1; 63:7; 67:4; 68:3–4; 71:23; 81:1; 84:2; 90:14; 92:4; 95:1; 98:4; 132:9, 16; *Jub.* 36:6; 1QS 10.17; 1QM 4.14; 1QH^a 11.24; 19.26; 4Q177 frgs. 12–13, col. 1.10; 4Q403 frg. 1, col. 1.9; 4Q405 frg. 23, col. 1.7; 4Q427 frg. 7, col. 1.14; 4Q502 frgs. 6–10.3; 4Q542 frg. 1, col. 1.11; 11Q5 22.15; *Pss. Sol.* 5:1; *Jos. Asen.* 3:4. Joy could also lead to praise (Tob. 8:16; 13:17; James 5:13; Luke 1:47). Joy could be associated with public festivals (Neh. 8:10–12; Ps. 42:4; cf. also, e.g., Halpern-Amaru, "Joy," on *Jubilees*), as was common in ancient festivals (though not in all cultures' personal piety; cf. Walton, *Thought*, 161).

32. Cf. also Sir. 2:4. So also both Stoics and Epicureans but not Aristotle (Stowers, "Resemble," 93; for Stoics, see, e.g., Sen. Y. *Ep. Lucil.* 123.3; *Nat. Q.* 3.pref.12–13, 15; *Dial.* 1.5.8; 7.15.4; 7.16.1–3).

33. See pp. 223–24.

34. It appears nearly fifty times in Pauline literature, especially in the undisputed letters and Ephesians, and only once elsewhere in the NT; *1 Clem.* 13.1 draws on 1 Cor. 1:31.

3:18; potential sorrow in Phil. 2:27) and encouraged believers to grieve with those who grieve (Rom. 12:15; cf. 1 Thess. 5:14); difficult conditions regularly required him to hold sorrow in tension with joy (2 Cor. 6:10). Thus, while it is possible to experience a measure of the Spirit's joy even in the midst of grief (and hope that qualifies grief, as in 1 Thess. 4:13, 18), Paul's general exhortation to "rejoice always" does not mean that believers will never have legitimate cause for grief.[35]

Prayer Rather Than Worry (Phil. 4:6)

Whether or not Paul's expectation of peace in Philippians 4:7 rests partly on 4:4, it clearly rests on 4:6. Paul warns against worry or anxiety (4:6a), a condition that philosophers often deemed inimical to peace (by which they often meant tranquility). Here Paul may echo Jesus's teaching attested especially in Q.[36] Lest we suppose that Paul understood this ideal as perfectly attainable in the present age, or a rule concerning the performance of which itself merits anxiety, Paul's love for others often drove him to anxiety (2 Cor. 7:5; 11:28–29; 1 Thess. 3:5), though not in this letter.[37] Paul's interest here is not in a neurochemical emotional state but in an activity, and in context his exhortation is an encouragement (believers may leave their problems with the one powerful enough to resolve them), not a legal stipulation.[38]

Paul's alternative to worry is not the anxious attempt to suppress it but rather acknowledging the needs to God and entrusting them to him (Phil. 4:6). In contrast to the futility of worry, prayer provides an active way to address concerns. That the prayer is complemented with thanksgiving probably

35. He would not have avoided grief to the extent that Galen claimed in *Grief* 1–5, 11, 48, 50b, 71, 78b (though even Galen would have allowed grief for destruction of his homeland [72a] or loss of health [74]); cf. also Sen. Y. *Ep. Lucil.* 66.37–39.

36. Matt. 6:25, 28//Luke 12:22, 25–27; cf. also Matt. 10:19//Luke 12:11 with Mark 13:11. Elsewhere in the Jesus tradition, cf. Mark 4:19; Luke 10:41; 21:34. See also Hunter, *Predecessors*, 50; Fee, *Philippians*, 408n40.

37. Although the particular term here (μεριμνάω) has a range of nuances (see BDAG), it is noteworthy that Paul does value concern for the churches (2 Cor. 11:28, using the cognate noun; cf. 1 Cor. 12:25), including Timothy's concern for the Philippian church (Phil. 2:20).

38. The NRSV translation, "Do not worry about anything," is more helpful here today than those translations that urge avoiding anxiety (e.g., NASB, NIV), since worry is something one does, whereas we generally think of anxiety as a state. We understand today that depression and anxiety often have neurochemical causes, sometimes stemming from genetic factors or early brain development. Paul is not urging people to evaluate their neurological state, but he is encouraging them simply to commit needs to God in prayer rather than to worry about them. Not worrying may be neurologically and environmentally easier for some people than for others, but again, Paul is providing not a criterion of spiritual self-evaluation but an exhortation.

suggests trust,[39] which is antithetical to the need to worry. Thanksgiving, the appropriate and necessary response to God's work (Rom. 1:21),[40] is also sometimes connected with joy, especially in worship contexts (1 Thess. 3:9; 5:16–18).[41] (Stoics could also connect joy with thanking God for everything,[42] although the Jewish context of early Christianity suggests more active praise.) Recognizing God's sovereignty, some Stoics of this period (who valued providence) urge thanksgiving for everything.[43] But whereas Stoics emphasize resignation, Paul urges prayer that can sometimes affect circumstances and thus generate more thanksgiving (2 Cor. 1:11; Phil. 1:19; Philem. 22).[44]

Paul's "in everything" (ἐν παντί) could suggest simply "in every respect";[45] more likely, it means "in every situation" (cf. Phil. 4:12; 1 Thess. 5:16–18).[46] It contrasts with "nothing" (μηδέν) in the preceding clause and thus means "Worry for nothing, but commit your prayers to God in everything."[47] The thankful prayer that Paul enjoins entrusts needs to God in faith, rather than continuing to focus on them by repeating or trying to suppress them. It is this entrusting of needs to God in Philippians 4:6 that brings peace in 4:7.

Considering What Is Pure (Phil. 4:8)

After the promise of peace, Paul probably transitions to a new thought, while also continuing the cognitive emphasis of the preceding verse. Most translations render Paul's λοιπόν as "finally";[48] this is a normal sense of the

39. Some associate it only with answers to past and present blessings (O'Brien, "Thanksgiving," 59), but its immediate mention may connect it more directly with the prayers here. This need not mean certainty that one's request has been granted, but it would at least connote trust that it has been heard. Thanksgiving was normal in Jewish prayer contexts (Oesterley, *Liturgy*, 67), but distinctions could be made according to circumstances (cf. James 5:13).

40. See the discussion regarding gratitude on p. 12.

41. Cf. also Neh. 12:27; Pss. 95:2; 97:12; 107:22; Isa. 51:3; Jer. 33:11; *Jub.* 22:4; 1QM 4.14; 4Q403 frg. 1, col. 1.4; 4Q511 frgs. 28–29.2 (reconstructed); 3 Macc. 7:16; Philo *Migr.* 92; *Spec. Laws* 1.144; 2.156, 185; Jos. *Ant.* 11.131; 14.421; *4 Ezra* 1:37; 2:37; *T. Jos.* 8:5; *T. Mos.* 10:10; Luke 10:21; other praise in Tob. 8:16; Luke 1:46–47.

42. E.g., Epict. *Diatr.* 4.7.9.

43. Epict. *Diatr.* 1.6.1; 4.7.9; Marc. Aur. 6.16. In Jewish circles, see also *Jub.* 16:31; *m. Ber.* 9:5.

44. Cf. also other Jewish exhortations to thank God for everything (*1 En.* 108:10; 1QS 10.15–17).

45. As in, e.g., 1 Cor. 1:5; 2 Cor. 7:11, 16; 8:7; 9:8, 11; 11:6; cf. Polyb. 12.8.4.

46. Cf. further Eph. 5:20; perhaps 2 Cor. 6:4. See Fee, *Philippians*, 408–9: "in all the details and circumstances of life."

47. Cf. Witherington, *Philippians*, 247.

48. E.g., NRSV, ESV, NIV; or "in conclusion" (GNT); "as to the rest" (Young's Literal); "summing it all up" (Message). A notable exception is "and now" in NLT or the term's omission in the NCV.

term,[49] although it can also simply transition to a new point or mean "in addition."[50] Paul has already said it once (Phil. 3:1) and also uses it elsewhere to transition to a new section rather than to close a letter (1 Thess. 4:1). It is possible that Paul uses the term to bracket the hortatory material between Philippians 3:1 and 4:9, addressing more personal issues in 2:17–30 and 4:10–19. In any case, he offers in 4:8 an exhortation to think carefully about virtuous matters, continuing the interest in cognition that appears in 4:7.

THE IDEAL FOCUS

I previously surveyed some ancient exhortations that invited thinking about good things, particularly matters connected with the divine.[51] Nevertheless, further examples seem appropriate for this context. One classical orator advises, "Make it your practice to talk of things that are good and honourable, that your thoughts may through habit come to be like your words."[52] Pythagoras reportedly started a group in Samos where people contemplated "things noble, just, and advantageous."[53] Cicero praises a man whose thoughts all focused on behaving honorably and on the welfare of Rome.[54] Although Stoics urged people to anticipate misfortune, as already noted, many thinkers did emphasize a positive outlook and positive topics of thought. Thus, a Middle Platonist boasts, "All we know of is splendid and fair, serious and lofty and heavenly!"[55] Using various terms, others also insisted on keeping thoughts pure,[56] valued speaking about matters honorable and dignified,[57] identified what is honorable with what is good,[58] and so forth.

49. E.g., 2 Cor. 13:11; Philost. *Hrk.* 18.1 (although the guest already claimed belief in 16.6). Recapitulation was common (e.g., Dion. Hal. *Demosth.* 32).

50. See BDAG; cf., e.g., *T. Reub.* 5:5.

51. See, e.g., above, pp. 120–21; below, pp. 239–40. Cf. perhaps 1 Cor. 13:6–7, but between Paul's commitment to anaphora there and a probably narrower sense of πάντα ("all things"), we might want to avoid reading too much into that passage.

52. Isoc. *Ad Nic.* 38 (trans. Norlin, LCL, 1:61).

53. Iambl. *Pyth. Life* 5.26 (trans. Dillon and Hershbell, 49). These were standard ethical criteria. In keeping with comments on the divine mind (above, pp. 128–30), some viewed such thoughts as having "emanated from the divine" (Porph. *Marc.* 11.199–201; trans. O'Brien Wicker, 55).

54. Cic. *Vat.* 11.26.

55. Apul. *Apol.* 64 (trans. Hunink, 86).

56. E.g., Porph. *Marc.* 23.368, although for Porphyry this meant heavenly matters. A prostitute leaving her profession declares, "I purify my mind or purpose" (καθαίρω τὴν γνώμην) to follow Athena rather than Aphrodite (Libanius *Speech Char.* 18.3). The heart and soul must be pure to enter some temples (Nock, *Christianity*, 18–19). Josephus includes in the Essene initiation oath the promise to keep one's soul pure from desiring unholy gain (Jos. *War* 2.141).

57. Men. Rhet. 2.7, 406.4–7 (for a wedding).

58. Sen. Y. *Ep. Lucil.* 87.25.

Some scholars suggest that Paul's specific interest may be not simply "thinking about" these things, the approach of the many philosophers who would often recognize some of their language in this verse, but "reckoning" (λογίζομαι, Phil. 4:8). The verb might suggest taking into account these good things,[59] or carefully evaluating matters,[60] which fits an emphasis I also surveyed earlier in this book.[61] The verb can, however, simply mean pondering a matter deeply,[62] in which case Paul's interest here may resemble that of the thinkers noted above.

Virtue lists were a common literary and rhetorical form in ancient sources, both Jewish and Greek.[63] Paul's list here is rhetorically arranged, repeating ὅσα six times with adjectives all ending in -α or -η, and then using εἴ τις twice.[64] This arrangement offers a forceful way to communicate his central point, which the repetition reinforces.

Paul's list may be somewhat ad hoc, like many virtue lists; certainly, he does not borrow the standard four primary virtues often treated in philosophy,[65] of which he refers to only one here: what is "just" or "right" (δίκαιος).[66] But others could also include different individual virtues under the wider heading of virtue (ἀρετή); in one passage, for example, a Roman Stoic cites four virtues, of which only one (δικαιοσύνη) belongs to the traditional four subheads.[67]

59. Fee, *Philippians*, 415.

60. Hawthorne, *Philippians*, 187. Although it is rhetorically suitable, some propose that the shift to "if anything" (εἴ τις) might suggest the need for discernment, since believers apply these widely praised values in ways that differ from unbelievers (Fee, *Philippians*, 415–16; cf. Sandnes, "Idolatry and Virtue").

61. See pp. 158–65, 184–89.

62. See BDAG.

63. E.g., 1QS 4.3; Philo *Sacr.* 27; *Rhet. Alex.* 36, 1442a.11–12; Corn. Nep. 15 (Epaminondas), 3.1–3; Cic. *Mur.* 14.30; 29.60; Theon *Progymn.* 9.21–24; Mus. Ruf. 4, p. 44.10–12; 14, p. 92.31–33; 17, p. 108.8–11; 38, p. 136.3; Arrian *Alex.* 7.28.1–3; Arius Did. 2.7.5b, p. 10.16–25; 2.7.5b2, p. 14.18–20; 2.7.11i, p. 78.12–18; 2.7.11m, p. 88.1–8; Dio Chrys. *Or.* 32.37; Plut. *Stoic Cont.* 7, *Mor.* 1034C; Lucian *Portr.* 11; Max. Tyre *Or.* 3.1; 18.5; applied also to what we might call gifts, e.g., Theon *Progymn.* 9.15–19; Pliny *Ep.* 6.11.2; 6.26.1; Symm. *Ep.* 1.2.7.

64. Five of the eight adjectives or nouns also begin with vowels, ά, ά, εὐ, or ἐ.

65. E.g., Mus. Ruf. 4, p. 44.10–22; p. 48.1, 4, 8, 13; 6, p. 52.15, 17, 19, 21; 8, pp. 60.22–64.9; 8, p. 66.7–8; 17, p. 108.9–10; Marc. Aur. 3.6; 8.1; Arius Did. 2.7.5a, p. 10.7–9; 2.7.5b1, p. 12.13–22; 2.7.5b2, p. 14.1–4; 2.7.5b5, p. 18.27–31; Dio Chrys. *Or.* 3.7, 58; Men. Rhet. 2.1–2, 385.8.

66. Stoics valued being holy and pious (Arius Did. 2.7.5b12, p. 26.17–18).

67. Mus. Ruf. 14, p. 92.31–33; in 16, p. 104.32–35, two of the traditional virtues appear alongside several other virtues. Of the five positive qualities Lucian *Portr.* 11 adds to beauty, only one belongs to the four cardinal virtues; also in 11, he lists four virtues (including ἀρετή itself), of which again only one belongs to the traditional four. The list of six virtues in Philost. *Vit. Apoll.* 1.20 (which also includes ἀρετή itself) includes three of the conventional four. Among several rhetorical grounds for commending a matter listed in *Rhet. Alex.* 1, 1421b.25–26, only one (δίκαια) directly reflects one of the cardinal virtues.

Virtue among the Virtues

Ἀρετή calls for special comment here because this is its only occurrence in Paul, despite how widely the term appears in discussions of Greek ethics. It was a basic Greek term for virtue,[68] also used in the plural for virtues;[69] it was a frequent topic for intellectual discourse.[70] Various schools defined its content somewhat differently,[71] but there was considerable overlap among them. Many intellectuals, including both Cynics[72] and Stoics,[73] regarded it as the chief goal.[74] Although many objectives that people value are beyond our grasp, a Stoic reasons, if it is ἀρετή that one seeks, then one can obtain it and thus be happy and free from the disturbance of passions.[75]

In Hellenistic Jewish circles, Philo, writing before Paul, uses the term ἀρετή roughly one thousand times.[76] He employs the term especially like Aristotelians but also has incorporated Stoic elements.[77] Josephus employs the term nearly three hundred times.[78] Earlier, the *Letter of Aristeas* defines ἀρετή as the fulfillment of good works;[79] such virtue characterizes the elders whom the Judean high priest sends to Ptolemy.[80]

---

68. E.g., Dio Chrys. *Or.* 3.47; 35.2; Lucian *Hermot.* 22; Arius Did. 2.7.11i, p. 78.28. Hawthorne, *Philippians*, 186, emphasizes the breadth of the classical usage and the sense of "glory or praise" in the LXX. It can mean "excellence" (e.g., Philost. *Hrk.* 36.3) or expertise (Arius Did. 2.7.5b5, p. 18.15–17; Men. Rhet. 2.5, 397.23–24; 2.14, 426.27–32).

69. E.g., Mus. Ruf. 17, p. 108.9, 12; Arius Did. 2.7.5b2, p. 14.1; 2.7.5b5, p. 18.15–17; 2.7.5e, p. 30.3; 2.7.5f, p. 30.19; 2.7.5g, p. 32.6; Men. Rhet. 1.3, 361.14–15; 2.1–2, 369.30; 2.3, 379.30; 2.11, 421.30–32; Iambl. *Letter* 3, frg. 6 (Stob. *Anth.* 3.5.49).

70. E.g., Dio Chrys. *Or.* 69 (On Virtue).

71. In Platonism, see Gould, *Ethics*, 142–53; Krämer, *Arete* (also treating Aristotle). For Philo's definition, see Wolfson, *Philo*, 2:268–79; Philo is close to the Aristotelian definition of virtue but found use for the Stoic definition (272–75). Aristotle's concern was value to the polis, but Hellenistic usage focused on character (Finkelberg, "Virtue"). For its foundation in self-control, see Iambl. *Letter* 3, frg. 5 (Stob. *Anth.* 3.5.48). Iambl. *Letter* 16, frg. 1.1 (Stob. *Anth.* 3.1.17; trans. Dillon and Polleichtner, 47), describes it as the completeness or perfection of the soul.

72. Diog. Laert. 6.9.104. Crates (*Ep.* 12) contends that a person acquires ἀρετή only by practice.

73. Diog. Laert. 6.9.104; 7.1.30 (ἀγαθὸν μόνον, "the only good"); Arius Did. 2.7.6e, p. 40.11–15, 26–32 (by identifying it with happiness); Long, *Philosophy*, 199. For ἀρετή in Stoicism, see, e.g., Marc. Aur. 3.11.2; Arius Did. 2.7.5b1, p. 12.31–33; 2.7.11h, p. 74.14–17 (esp. 14); further Long, *Philosophy*, 199–205; Kidd, "Posidonius," 208. Lucian mocks the Stoic association with virtue in *Phil. Sale* 20. For Stoics, each creature has virtue characteristic to its nature (Mus. Ruf. 17, p. 108.1–4), and, most oddly, virtues (like other qualities and indeed anything describable by a noun) were considered material entities (Arius Did. 2.7.5b7, p. 20.28–30; pp. 20.35–22.1).

74. Eurip. frg. 1029–30. Cf. the gods' high interest in this matter in Dio Chrys. *Or.* 39.2.

75. Epict. *Diatr.* 1.4.3 (i.e., one may achieve ἀπάθεια).

76. An Accordance search (August 26, 2014) yielded 955 hits in the Philonic corpus.

77. Wolfson, *Philo*, 2:272–75.

78. An Accordance search (August 26, 2014) yielded 290 hits.

79. *Let. Aris.* 272. Most reject ἀρετή because they are given to passions (277).

80. *Let. Aris.* 122, 200.

Perhaps because ἀρετή is not customary language in Paul's extant letters, some commentators seem quick to distance Paul's use here from the common use or to associate Paul's reference with merely worldly virtue.[81] There is no reason, however, to assume that Paul could not employ a common term in a positive way. This is not a polemical context, and this is one of Paul's later extant letters, reflecting additional experiences with Diaspora thinkers; further, the term appears in the Septuagint[82] and later early Christianity.[83] Possible adaptation of other language from popular philosophy in the context (Phil. 4:11)[84] and the presence of popular philosophic language in his earlier letters allow for the possibility that Paul increasingly appropriated more popular philosophic language later in his ministry, while adapting it to his own ends.

In any case, Paul may employ ἀρετή generically. Ἀρετή could encompass other individual virtues (such as function as wisdom and courage).[85] It also could function as a summary of virtues after listing them; thus, for example, a Roman Stoic lists a few virtues and adds, "and virtue as a whole."[86] Paul may shift toward "virtue" and "whatever is praiseworthy" at the end of his list to summarize all virtues, including those he has not named. In the context of Stoic ἀρετή, "praiseworthy" (ἔπαινος)[87] probably means "those things that merit the praise of" people.[88]

81. Sevenster, *Seneca*, 156 ("your old heathen conception of virtue," the world's view of virtue). By contrast, Hawthorne (*Philippians*, 186) reasonably suggests that Paul probably uses the term as the Stoics did. Although Paul uses the term only here, his letters often express concern with matters that popular philosophy would have subsumed under the heading of virtues (with Engberg-Pedersen, "Vices," 608–9).

82. The six times in the portions of the LXX that overlap with the Hebrew canon use a more general sense; it appears more frequently in Maccabean texts. It certainly is used with knowledge of at least popular philosophic uses in 4 Maccabees (4 Macc. 1:2, 8, 10, 30; 2:10; 7:22; 9:8, 18, 31; 10:10; 11:2; 12:14; 13:24, 27; 17:12, 23) and Wisdom of Solomon (Wis. 4:1; 5:13; 8:7).

83. Besides the LXX quotation in 1 Pet. 2:9, see 2 Pet. 1:3, 5; *2 Clem.* 10.1; *Herm.* 26.2; 36.3; 46.1; 61.4; 76.3.

84. For αὐτάρκεια, cf., e.g., Arist. *N.E.* 1.7.6–8, 1097b (true happiness must be self-sufficient); Sen. Y. *Ep. Lucil.* 9.1; 55.4; Arius Did. 2.7.11h, p. 74.31; Marc. Aur. 3.11.2; Socratics *Ep.* 8; Plut. *Virt.* 3, *Mor.* 101B; Diog. Laert. 6.1.11; Porph. *Marc.* 27.428–29; 28.448–49; 30.469–70; Engberg-Pedersen, *Paul and Stoics*, 48–50, 101; in Plato, Lodge, *Ethics*, 68–72. Use of the expression does not, however, always indicate philosophic expertise or interest (cf., e.g., *Pss. Sol.* 5:16–17; *Orph. H.* 10.13; Aul. Gel. 2.29.17–20; Max. Tyre *Or.* 24.6 [farmers]). Cf. contentment in Val. Max. 7.1.2; Mus. Ruf. frg. 43, p. 138.15; Epict. *Diatr.* 1.1.27; 2.2.3; Lucian *Dial. D.* 436 (8/26, *Menippus and Chiron* 2); Ps.-Phoc. 6. Commentators often cite a Stoic or Cynic connection here, though sometimes noting that Paul's application differs, since he depends on Christ (Phil. 4:13; Vincent, *Philippians*, 143; Bornkamm, *Paul*, 170; Sevenster, *Seneca*, 113; Beare, *Philippians*, 157; Hawthorne, *Philippians*, 198; Hengel, *Property*, 54–55).

85. Arius Did. 2.7.5a, p. 10.7–9; Iambl. *Letter* 4.7–9 (wisdom; in Stob. *Anth.* 3.3.26).

86. Mus. Ruf. frg. 38, p. 136.3 (trans. Lutz).

87. Also valued among Stoics as a characteristic of what is good (Arius Did. 2.7.5i, p. 32.25–26).

88. Hawthorne, *Philippians*, 186. If so, its summary includes εὔφημα earlier in the list.

Although one cannot argue from silence, the absence of at least some accepted virtues or advantages may reflect Paul's worldview, suggesting that those that he *did* include in his list are among those with which he agrees. Many, especially in the Platonic tradition,[89] valued beauty[90] and sometimes linked it with virtues,[91] though others recognized beauty as a good external to virtue proper.[92] Ultimate beauty was different from mere appearances, which Platonic tradition did not value highly anyway. Stoics appreciated beauty in terms of what was good.[93] Thus, some Alexandrian Jewish sources speak of God's beauty;[94] likewise, they envision piety as a major form of beauty.[95] Ideally, God is "the mind's guide" toward beautiful matters.[96]

The mind's focus here in Philippians 4:8 is a world away from Romans 7, resembling instead the mind of the Spirit (Rom. 8:6) and the mind of Christ (1 Cor. 2:16).

Thinking like Christ (Phil. 2:5)

What way of thinking does Paul have most in view in Philippians 4:8? He probably does include the entire gamut of right ways of thinking, but one of his particular concerns with the way Philippian Christians are thinking, as already noted, is the problem of their disunity (see again 4:2–3). Paul addresses this issue also in Philippians 2, where he provides several models for serving others: Christ (2:5–11), Paul himself (2:17; cf. 4:9), Timothy (2:19–22), and Epaphroditus (2:25–30).

In 2:5 Paul urges believers to have the way of thinking, or the focus, among themselves (φρονεῖτε ἐν ὑμῖν) that was also in Christ Jesus.[97] Paul employs

89. For Plato's interest in aesthetic beauty as well as moral, see Gilbert, "Relation," 279–94; Warry, *Theory*; Lodge, *Theory*, 210–33; Partee, *Poetics*. For the relation of beauty to the highest good, see Gilbert, "Relation," 290; Gould, *Love*, 147 (with beauty as that which is desire's primary object). Cf. Warry, *Theory*, 51: "Beauty is thus stimulated by Truth and is itself a stimulus to Goodness."

90. The question of human beauty aside, Philippi lay in a beautiful area, known for its hundred-petaled roses (Athen. *Deipn.* 15.682B).

91. Beauty's connection with symmetry connects it with virtue (Lodge, *Ethics*, 61).

92. *Rhet. Alex.* 35, 1440b.17–19 (along with noble lineage, strength, and wealth); here one is praised not for virtue but for "good fortune" (1440b.20–23).

93. E.g. (though often using terms that can be translated more generically), Epict. *Diatr.* 1.8.5; 1.22.1; Marc. Aur. 4.20.

94. Wis. 13:3, 5.

95. *Let. Aris.* 229.

96. *Let. Aris.* 238 (trans. Hadas, 193). Likewise, in *Let. Aris.* 287 learned people train their minds for the "beautiful matters."

97. Translations normally supply the past-tense verb "was" because in context Paul refers to Jesus's historical example in Phil. 2:6–8 (cf. Rom. 15:5, also citing Christ's example in 15:3, 7). At the same time, the exhortation to "think . . . in Christ Jesus" (φρονεῖτε . . . ἐν Χριστῷ Ἰησοῦ)

this verb, φρονέω, several times in Philippians (1:7; 2:2, 5; 3:15, 19; 4:2, 10), slightly more frequently even than in his much longer Letter to the Romans.[98] One of these references is where Paul is urging Euodia and Syntyche, possibly different house church leaders, to "think the same way in the Lord" (4:2). In so doing, Paul addresses the most explicit rift in the Philippian church.

Another reference to φρονέω surfaces in Philippians 2:2. This reference appears in the context immediately preceding 2:5 and therefore most directly informs it.[99] Here Paul frames his charge for unity by speaking of how the Philippian believers should think, and he employs the same expression (except with a subjunctive rather than infinitive verb) as in 4:2: "think the same way" (τὸ αὐτὸ φρονῆτε; the second instance in 2:2 is similar: τὸ ἓν φρονοῦντες).

In 2:1 Paul employs rhetorical artistry to drive home his point with greater emotional intensity. Here he appeals to various compelling emotional grounds in four clauses, each opening with εἴ τις or εἴ τι (depending on the gender of the following noun). Opening repetition, or anaphora, was a familiar rhetorical device, amplifying or driving home a point.[100] Emotional appeal was what rhetorical critics today call pathos,[101] which appears widely in persuasive speeches[102] and in rhetorical training and handbooks;[103] letters could also

---

may refer to the "mind of Christ" (cf. 1 Cor. 2:16), already addressed above, pp. 195–99. This is consistent with the idea of Christ dwelling and working in believers (Gal. 2:20).

98. Romans is more than four times the length of Philippians, but the verb appears ten times in Philippians, nine in Romans, once in Col. 3:2, and only three other times in the Pauline corpus (1 Cor. 13:11; 2 Cor. 13:11; Gal. 5:10).

99. Noting the link between Rom. 8:6 and Phil. 2:2, see also Moreno García, "Sabiduría del Espíritu."

100. E.g., Cic. *Sest.* 1.1; Anderson, *Glossary*, 19, and sources cited there; Rowe, "Style," 131; Black, "Oration at Olivet," 86; in letters, e.g., Sen. Y. *Ep. Lucil.* 47.1; Fronto *Ad Ant. imp.* 2.6.1–2; *Ad verum imp.* 2.1.4; *Ad M. Caes.* 2.3.1; 3.3; *Nep. am.* 2.9; in Paul, see Porter, "Paul and Letters," 579; in the OT, Aune, *Dictionary of Rhetoric*, 34, cites Ps. 29:1–2; Lee, "Translations: Greek," 779, cites Prov. 13:9 LXX. In conjunction with its frequent emotive effect, repetition also served aesthetic purposes; see, e.g., Hermog. *Method* 13.428–29; Pickering, "Ear."

101. See, e.g., Walde, "Pathos"; Olbricht and Sumney, *Paul and Pathos*, passim. For repetition in pathos, see, e.g., Quint. *Decl.* 251.5; 260.10; 335.3, 8, 10; Pliny *Ep.* 9.26.8; Fronto *Ad Ant. imp.* 1.4; Hermog. *Inv.* 2.7.125.

102. E.g., Lysias *Or.* 7.41, §§111–12; 10.27–28, §118; 13.46, §134; 20.35–36, §161; Isaeus *Menec.* 44, 47; Aeschines *Embassy* 148, 179; Dion. Hal. *Ant. rom.* 4.33.1–36.3; *Isaeus* 3; Cic. *Cael.* 24.60; *Mil.* 38.105; *Quinct.* 30.91–31.99; *Font.* 21.46–47; *Sest.* 2.4; 69.144–46; *Rab. Perd.* 17.47; Val. Max. 8.1. acquittals 2; Sen. E. *Controv.* 1.4.2; 1.7.10; 4.pref.6; Pliny *Ep.* 2.11.12–13; 4.9.22; Dio Chrys. *Or.* 40.12; Plut. *Cic.* 39.6; Philost. *Vit. soph.* 2.5.574; Apul. *Apol.* 85; Dio Cass. 8.36.5; Libanius *Declam.* 44.78–81.

103. See, e.g., Isoc. *Ad Nic.* 23; *Rhet. Alex.* 34, 1439b.15–1440b.3; 36, 1443b.16–21; 36, 1444b.35–1445a.26; Cic. *Or. Brut.* 40.138; *Brut.* 93.322; Quint. *Inst.* 4.1.33; 6.1.9; 6.2.20 (on *ēthos* and *pathos*); Ps.-Quint. *Decl.* 299.1–2; 306.6–7; 329.17; Hermog. *Method* 31.448; Men. Rhet. 2.5, 395.26–30; Libanius *Topics* 1.11; 3.14; 5.11–12; *Descr.* 17.7. See, further, Hall, "Delivery"; Leigh, "Quintilian." Opponents, of course, called for proof as opposed to emotional appeals

show deep or playful emotion at times.[104] Paul's predication of his request on matters such as those that could be translated "fellowship," "affection," and "compassion" already suggests the character of his plea.[105]

In 2:2 Paul again appeals to emotion by asking the Philippians to complete his own joy (in a letter that already highlights this theme) by urging them, as we have noted, "to exercise the same frame of mind," "to have the same love," "to be united in spirit," and again "to have one frame of mind."[106] Such exhortations to unity were common in ancient Mediterranean urban society,[107] responding to the frequent divisions there.[108] Paul's four exhortations each say essentially the same thing, so that the repetition again reinforces his appeal.

The call to have Jesus's frame of mind (2:5) appeals to Jesus's example of service (2:6–8), which thereby summons the Philippian believers to unity.[109] Thus, in humility (ταπεινοφροσύνη) each should value or "regard" (ἡγούμενοι) others more than oneself (2:3), just as Jesus did not "regard" (ἡγήσατο) being equal with God as a right to be seized (2:6) but instead "humbled" himself (ἐταπείνωσεν, 2:8).

Although Jesus was in "the form [μορφῇ] of God" (2:6), he took "the form [μορφήν] of a slave," in the likeness and form of a human (2:7). His slavery included obedience even to the point of death—even the most shameful death of the cross (2:8), a form of execution considered most appropriate for those

---

(e.g., Lysias Or. 27.12–13, §§178–79; Hermog. Progymn. 6, "On Commonplace," 14; Libanius Topics 1.27–30; 2.20; 4.19); emotion wore off in the long run (Pliny Ep. 2.11.6).

104. E.g., Cic. Fam. 1.9.1; 2.2.1; 2.3.2; 10.23.7; 12.12.1; 12.30.3; 15.20.2; 15.21.1; 16.25.1; Sall. Pomp. 1; Lucius Verus in Fronto Ad verum imp. 2.2; Symm. Ep. 1.5.1; 2 Cor. 6:11–13; Gal. 4:12–20 (on Gal. 4, note Kraftchick, "Πάθη," 61; Martin, "Voice"). Cf. revealing one's character in letters in Demet. Style 4.227. One may expect its use somewhat more in Paul's letters because they involve persuasion and argumentation more than most ordinary letters.

105. Although handbooks assign pathos especially to the closing peroration (Wuellner, "Rhetoric," 340–41), speakers employed it at various points in their speeches (Sumney, "Use," 147).

106. For being of one mind in exhortations to unity, see, e.g., Lysias Or. 2.24, §192; Dio Chrys. Or. 38.15; 39.3, 5, 8; esp. Mitchell, Rhetoric of Reconciliation, 76–77, 79. In Paul, see Rom. 12:16; 15:5; 1 Cor. 1:10; 2 Cor. 13:11; Phil. 1:27; 4:2.

107. E.g., Xen. Mem. 4.4.16; Demosth. Ep. 1.5; Rhet. Alex. 1, 1422b.33–36; Dion. Hal. Ant. rom. 7.53.1; Livy 2.33.1; 5.7.10; 24.22.1, 13, 17; Sen. Y. Ep. Lucil. 94.46; Mus. Ruf. 8, p. 64.13; Dio Chrys. Or. 34.17; 38.5–8; 40.26; Max. Tyre Or. 16.3; Men. Rhet. 2.3, 384.23–25; 2.4, 390.14–16.

108. On the dangers of disunity, see, e.g., Hom. Il. 1.255–58; Sall. Jug. 73.5; Livy 2.60.4; 3.66.4; Babr. 44.7–8; 47; Dio Chrys. Or. 24.3; Plut. Sulla 4.4; 7.1; Aul. Gel. 6.19.6; Lucian Prof. P.S. 22.

109. As often noted, e.g., Heriban, "Zmysl'ajte." The studies on Phil. 2:6–11 are legion, and readers interested in topics beyond the brief summary of issues here are referred to those studies (note already the massive collection of sources in Martin, Carmen Christi).

of the most abject status, including slaves. Paul thus presents a model for believers to give up caring about their own rank in the body of Christ and to serve one another. As Jesus was exalted after humbling himself (2:9–11), so believers, currently in humble bodies, will someday share his form (3:21).[110] Many scholars note in Jesus's example a reversal of Adam, who did seek equality with God (Gen. 3:5–6), though he was already in the likeness of God (Gen. 1:26–27, although Paul does not use the same terminology here as in LXX Genesis).[111]

Citizens of Heaven (Phil. 3:20)

Paul also uses the verb φρονέω in Philippians 3:15 and 3:19. In 3:15 believers should think with their intention focused on pursuing the "upward" goal (3:14), that is, toward heaven (cf. 3:10–11, 20–21).[112] By contrast, in 3:19 those who focus on temporal, "earthly matters," such as their own desires, will face destruction. Because Paul is speaking of those who will be destroyed, he is not speaking of his fellow ministers who seek their own interests (2:20–21) and not necessarily even of those who proclaim Christ with partly self-centered motives (1:15–17).[113] Rather, he addresses here "enemies of Christ's cross" (3:18),[114] who, like the mind at enmity with God and focused on the flesh in Romans 8:5–7, lack Christ and the Spirit and, hence, peace with God (cf. Phil. 4:7). These enemies constitute polar opposites of the model offered by Paul and his colleagues (3:17).

110. Compare Jesus's human form (σχῆμα) in Phil. 2:7 to believers being transformed (μετασχηματίζω) in 3:21; Jesus humbling (ταπεινόω) himself in 2:8 to believers' present bodies of humiliation (ταπείνωσις) in 3:21; Jesus's assumption of human form (μορφή) in 2:7 to our sharing his form (σύμμορφος) in 3:21; and the reversal of death in 2:8 and 3:21.

111. There may also be allusions to Isaiah's servant, but again Paul does not follow the usual LXX renderings; more clearly, he refers to Isaiah's divine Lord (Phil. 2:10; Isa. 45:23), as he is well aware (Rom. 14:11).

112. Paul elsewhere employs ἄνω only for the heavenly Jerusalem (Gal. 4:26) or the heavenly matters of Col. 3:1–2, discussed esp. on pp. 238–45. Cf. Engberg-Pedersen, *Paul and Stoics*, 90. This observation is not intended to discount the athletic imagery familiar here and in ancient literature (cf. Pfitzner, *Agon Motif*).

113. Contrast Paul's rejoicing in Phil. 1:18 with his weeping in 3:18, although by itself this contrast need not be decisive since different causes are named.

114. Paul reserves such "enmity" language for those hostile to Christ (Rom. 5:10; 1 Cor. 15:25; Col. 1:21; cf. Rom. 12:20; Eph. 2:14–16), sometimes even those who try to observe the law without the Spirit (Rom. 8:7; 11:28); this does not include even believers under discipline (2 Thess. 3:15). Likewise, those who do not embrace the cross are perishing (1 Cor. 1:18), including those who prefer circumcision to it (Gal. 5:11; 6:12, 14).

Paul's reference to the κοιλία ("stomach, belly") in Philippians 3:19 develops a familiar image for pleasure, also used elsewhere by Paul (Rom. 16:18; for sexual pleasure in 1 Cor. 6:13;[115] cf. perhaps strife in Gal. 5:15). This was a common image for self-indulgence among Greek and Roman thinkers; it was originally a metonymy for desire and gluttony.[116] It is especially pervasive in Philo, who regarded the belly as the seat of irrational desire.[117] The point is not enjoyment of food (or digestion!)[118] but the pursuit of pleasure,[119] perhaps exemplified in the gluttony of elite banquets.[120] Those who live for pleasure have their minds fixed solely on earthly matters.

Such language may recall the "dogs" of Philippians 3:2, whose focus is circumcision of believers' flesh rather than worship by God's Spirit (3:3). Although dogs had various positive uses and associations,[121] "dog" was a

115. Thinkers often linked pleasures of the belly and of sexual organs, e.g., Epict. *Diatr.* 2.9.4; cf. Corrington, "Defense."

116. Hom. *Od.* 17.286; Eurip. frg. 915; Mus. Ruf. 16, p. 104.18; 18B, p. 118.7; Epict. *Diatr.* 2.9.4; Sen. Y. *Dial.* 7.20.5; *Ep. Lucil.* 60.4; Philost. *Vit. soph.* 1.20.512–13; Epicureans in Plut. *Pleas. L.* 3, *Mor.* 1087D. Cf. "slave of the belly" in Rom. 16:18; Max. Tyre *Or.* 25.6; Ach. Tat. 2.23.1; Philost. *Vit. Apoll.* 1.7; Libanius *Encom.* 6.9; "captive" of the belly in Dio Chrys. *Or.* 32.90; enslaved to passions, including gluttony, Aeschines *Tim.* 42; chained by the belly, genitals, and the rest of the body, Porph. *Marc.* 33.506–7; following the stomach, Syriac Menander Epitome 6–8; the belly depicting slavery to passions, Philo *Migr.* 66; glutton as a slave to food, Philo *Alleg. Interp.* 3.221; their god is their belly, *Apoc. Elij.* 1:13 (probably dependent on Phil. 3:19).

117. E.g., Philo *Creation* 158–59; *Alleg. Interp.* 3.159; *Migr.* 66; *Spec. Laws* 1.148, 192, 281; 4.91; cf. Wolfson, *Philo,* 2:225–37; cf. also 3 Macc. 7:10–11; 4 Macc. 1:3. For the belly and pleasure or passion (ἡδονή), see, e.g., Philo *Alleg. Interp.* 3.114, 116, 138–44, 160; *Migr.* 65; *Spec. Laws* 1.150. For kashrut and diet to control desire, see Rhodes, "Diet"; Stoics began self-control with inexpensive food (Mus. Ruf. 18A, p. 112.6–9; p. 114.21–26, 29), and Persians and Spartans reportedly in childhood (Xen. *Cyr.* 1.2.8; *Lac.* 5.4–7).

118. Cf. Epict. *Diatr.* 1.13.1; Philo *Creation* 77; *Jub.* 22:6; *Sib. Or.* 4.25–26; *m. Ber.* 3; *b. Ber.* 35ab; *Sanh.* 102a; Gen. 1:30–31; 1 Tim. 4:3–4; *Did.* 10.3.

119. See, rightly, Chrys. *Hom. Cor.* 17.1.

120. Elites sometimes even playfully praised the stomach or mocked gluttony (Ruscillo, "Gluttony"; Montanari, "Gastronomical Poetry"). Against gluttony, see, e.g., Polyb. 12.8.4; Pliny E. *N.H.* 28.14.56; Mus. Ruf. 4, p. 44.18; 18B, p. 116.4–22; 18B, p. 118.9–11; Mart. *Epig.* 2.40.1–8; 3.17.3; 3.22.1–5; 5.70, 72; 7.20; 11.86; 12.41; Plut. *M. Cato* 9.5; *Educ.* 7, *Mor.* 4B; Juv. *Sat.* 2.114; Max. Tyre *Or.* 7.7; 25.5–6; 36.4; Apul. *Apol.* 57–59, 74–75; Heracl. *Hom. Prob.* 72.3; Porph. *Marc.* 28.439–42; Iambl. *Pyth. Life* 31.203; Libanius *Anec.* 3.30; *Invect.* 5.16 (the wealthy who indulge the belly); Deut. 21:20; Prov. 23:20–21; 28:7; Sir. 23:6; 31:20; 37:30–31; 3 Macc. 6:36; 4 Macc. 1:27; Philo *Dreams* 2.155; *T. Mos.* 7:4. Vomiting was one remedy provided for overindulgence; Hipponax frg. 42; Sen. Y. *Ep. Lucil.* 108.15; Cic. *Phil.* 2.25.63.

121. Especially among Gentiles, e.g., Hom. *Il.* 22.66–70; 23.173; *Od.* 10.216; 17.290–304; Aelian *Nat. An.* 6.25; 7.10, 25; Pliny E. *N.H.* 8.61.142–47; Appian *R.H.* 11.10.64; Longus 1.21; Plut. *Themist.* 10.6; but even in Israel (*y. Ter.* 8:7; Schwartz, "Dogs"; Miller, "Attitudes"). Because dogs were used for hunting (Dio Chrys. *Or.* 4.34; 20.15), they were sacred to Artemis (Plut. *Isis* 71, *Mor.* 379D).

familiar insult throughout antiquity.[122] Dogs were known for sexual looseness[123] and for enjoying filth and excrement,[124] possibly relevant to Philippians 3:8.[125] Some early Christians employed the language of "dogs" (cf. Mark 7:28; Matt. 7:6; Rev. 22:15) as an example of irrational "beasts" (2 Pet. 2:12, 22)—those who live for pleasure rather than by reason.[126] As I noted earlier, philosophers often depicted the unreasoning masses as beasts.[127]

"Remove the desires of the belly," one orator declares, "and you have removed the beast from man."[128] Gluttons act like pigs or dogs rather than human beings, a Stoic complains.[129] Thus, a parasite, someone who depends on wealthy patrons' banquets, serves his stomach and may be compared with an animal that obeys for food.[130] Men controlled by licentiousness are compared to beasts, including dogs.[131] Philo links the belly with animal desires[132] and often links the "belly" with pleasure via the serpent condemned to move

122. E.g., Hom. *Il.* 8.527; 11.362; 20.449; 22.345 (cf. 9.373; 21.394, 421); *Od.* 17.248; 22.35; Callim. *Hymn* 6 (to Demeter), 63; when addressed to women, it sometimes connoted sexual looseness, Hom. *Od.* 11.424; 18.338; 19.91. The wicked are compared to dogs in *Exod. Rab.* 9:2. Cynics were compared to dogs (Dio Chrys. *Or.* 9.9; Mart. *Epig.* 4.53.5; Lucian *Runaways* 16; *Peregr.* 2; *Posts* 34; *Dem.* 21; *Phil. Sale* 7; Diog. Laert. 6.2.40, 45, 60, 77–78; cf. Cercidas frg. 1; *Gr. Anth.* 7.63–68, 115) but wore the title proudly; Crates *Ep.* 16; Diogenes *Ep.* 2, 7; Dio Chrys. *Or.* 8.11; 9.3; Lucian *Dial. D.* 420 (4/21, *Menippus and Cerberus* 1); cf. Philost. *Vit. Apoll.* 6.31–33 (cf. philosophers generally in Lucian *Hermot.* 86). They earned the title partly by excreting in public, e.g., Dio Chrys. *Or.* 8.36. Called a dog, Diogenes drenches his hearers as a dog would (Diog. Laert. 6.2.46).

123. E.g., Aelian *Nat. An.* 7.19; Theophr. *Char.* 28.3; *b. Sanh.* 108b; *y. Taan.* 1:6, §8; *Gen. Rab.* 36:7; pointing to their private parts in Plut. *Exile* 7, *Mor.* 601DE. Sometimes also for savageness (Aeschylus *Lib.* 621; Eurip. *Orest.* 260), impudence (*Song Rab.* 2:13, § 4; *Pesiq. Rab.* 1:7; 15:14/15), or anger (Callim. *Poems* 380). Dogs reportedly killed Euripides (Val. Max. 9.12. ext.4; Aul. Gel. 15.20.9).

124. E.g., Phaedrus 4.19 (cf. 1.27.10–11); Mart. *Epig.* 1.83. Ancient literature is replete with dogs consuming or wanting to consume corpses, e.g., Hom. *Il.* 17.127, 255, 272; 23.21, 183–87; 24.211, 411; *Od.* 3.258–60; 21.363–64; 22.476; Eurip. *Phoen.* 1650; Thucyd. 2.50.1; Appian *C.W.* 1.8.72; Iambl. *Bab. St.* 18 (in Photius *Bibl.* 94.77a); *Pesiq. Rab Kah.* 7:6 (7:9 in some eds.).

125. Σκύβαλον often designates excrement; Paul may imply that the sort of human qualifications he cites in Phil. 3:4–6 are the sort of refuse that interests excrement-sniffing dogs.

126. Socrates reportedly claimed that most people lived to eat, whereas he simply ate to live (Mus. Ruf. 18B, p. 118.16–18; Diog. Laert. 2.34).

127. See p. 23.

128. Max. Tyre *Or.* 33.8 (trans. Trapp, 27), likewise advising removal of "the desires of the privy parts."

129. Mus. Ruf. 18B, p. 116.14.

130. Quint. *Decl.* 298.10. The animal comparison for gluttony appears also in Sen. Y. *Ep. Lucil.* 60.4; Mus. Ruf. 18B, p. 116.18; Epict. *Diatr.* 2.9.4; Dio Chrys. *Or.* 77/78.29 (including "dogs"); Heracl. *Hom. Prob.* 14.4. No wise person who wishes to be a human, Musonius warns, will live to eat (18B, p. 118.18–19).

131. Plut. *Bride* 7, *Mor.* 139B. So also those greedy to fill their stomachs or copulate, Dio Chrys. *Or.* 77/78.29.

132. Philo *Spec. Laws* 1.148.

on its belly, facing downward.[133] In contrast to believers' hope and focus in heaven (Phil. 3:20–21), the end of these beasts is destruction, and their focus is earthly, perishable matters (3:19).

Paul contrasts this earthly frame of mind in Philippians 3:19 with an eternal, heavenly perspective: believers in Christ recognize that their citizenship is not earthly but heavenly (3:20). They also look to heaven because Jesus will return from there to resurrect the righteous and rule the world (3:20–21).[134] As in Romans 12:2, 1 Corinthians 2:9–10, and Colossians 3:2, Paul here suggests a heavenly and future focus: a true believer in Jesus lives not to fulfill animal passions but in light of eternal hope and reward in Christ.[135]

Paul's image of heavenly citizenship would have made sense to urban people who were even partly culturally literate. Many philosophers regarded the entire world as their city or fatherland.[136] Some writers came closer to Paul's language here. A Cynic, for example, claims that a citizen bears "his fatherland in himself"[137] and speaks of his soul's "fatherland" as heaven.[138] When asked whether he cared about his fatherland, Anaxagoras said yes and pointed to heaven.[139] Philo claims that the soul of a wise person recognizes heaven as their homeland but earth as foreign.[140] He also speaks of the Therapeutae, an idealized Jewish sect, as being citizens of heaven and of the world.[141]

That Paul employs the image of heavenly citizenship in a letter to Philippi may be even more significant. Because Philippi was a Roman colony, believers there who were Philippian citizens were also Roman citizens and hence understood what it meant to be a citizen of a place other than where they

133. Philo *Creation* 157–58; *Alleg. Interp.* 3.114; *Migr.* 66. The serpent regularly represents pleasure in Philo, e.g., *Creation* 160, 164; *Alleg. Interp.* 2.71–74, 79, 81, 84, 87–93, 105–6; 3.61, 66, 68; *Agr.* 97, 108.

134. He will transform the present "humiliated" bodies (Phil. 3:21; cf. 2:8) into bodies of "glory" (3:21; cf. 1 Cor. 15:40–43, esp. 43), presumably also understood as *heavenly* bodies (cf. Phil. 3:20–21; 1 Cor. 15:40–41, 47–49).

135. In apocalyptic imagery, cf. Revelation's contrast between the city of this world, depicted as a prostitute, and the city of the coming world, depicted as a bride (Rev. 17:1–5; 21:9–14).

136. E.g., Sen. Y. *Ep. Lucil.* 28.4; Mus. Ruf. 9, p. 68.15–16, 21–22; Epict. *Diatr.* 2.10.3; Max. Tyre *Or.* 36.3; Marc. Aur. 10.15; 12.36; Diog. Laert. 2.99; Philost. *Ep. Apoll.* 44; Philo *Creation* 142; *Spec. Laws* 2.45; *Contempl.* 90; cf. Heracl. *Ep.* 9; Diog. Laert. 6.5.93; Obbink, "Sage," 189; particularities reflected fallenness from the original universality (Proclus *Poet.* 5, K52.7–19), including attachment to particular zones of the world, cities, or families (K52.23–24). World citizenship was especially relevant to Cynics, who applied it radically (e.g., Dio Chrys. *Or.* 4.13; Lucian *Phil. Sale* 8; Diog. Laert. 6.2.63, 72). Occasionally, other kinds of scholars borrowed this claim of world citizenship (e.g., Vitruv. *Arch.* 6.pref.2).

137. Heracl. *Ep.* 9 (trans. Worley, 211).

138. Heracl. *Ep.* 5.

139. Diog. Laert. 2.7.

140. Philo *Agr.* 65; see also *Conf.* 78; *Heir* 274.

141. Philo *Contempl.* 90. Cf. *QG* 3.45.

currently lived.[142] Although Paul has special reason to address the image of heavenly citizenship to believers in Philippi, other early Christians could apply the image of heavenly citizenship more widely: thus, Christians are both aliens and citizens in their earthly lands[143] and are citizens of heaven living on earth.[144] They are citizens in God's commonwealth.[145]

This discussion of heavenly citizenship brings us to the book's final, brief chapter, which discusses the heavenly mind in Colossians 3:1–2.

Conclusion

In Philippians 4 Paul invites believers in Philippi to meditate on virtuous matters (4:8), leaving their needs with God, whose peace will guard their hearts and minds in Christ (4:6–7). In Philippians 2 Paul challenges disunity and exhorts believers to follow Jesus's example by thinking in a way that supports unity and service to one another (2:5). Finally, Philippians 3:19–21 contrasts a mind focused on earthly things with a heavenly focus. I address the ancient context of this final theme in chapter 8, on Colossians 3:1–2.

---

142. Cf., e.g., Michael, *Philippians*, 181; Beare, *Philippians*, 136; Hawthorne, *Philippians*, 170; Fee, *Philippians*, 378–79; Cousar, *Philippians*, 80; Witherington, *Philippians*, 218; Cohick, *Philippians*, 200.

143. *Diogn.* 5.5.

144. *Diogn.* 5.9; cf. 5.4.

145. *1 Clem.* 54.4. Cf. Poly. *Phil.* 5.2.

8

⊚ ⊚ ⊚ ⊚

The Heavenly Mind
(Col. 3:1–2)

So since you've been raised with Christ, devote yourself to the matters above—where Christ is enthroned at God's right hand! Let the focus of your thinking be heavenly matters, not earthly ones.

—Colossians 3:1–2

In Colossians 3:1–2 Paul exhorts believers to fix their attention on Christ enthroned in heaven. A first-century, urban Mediterranean audience would have heard this invitation at least partly in light of various ideas and images current in their milieu. The milieu of the Colossian believers themselves probably included both Greek philosophy (φιλοσοφία, 2:8) and traditional Jewish practices (2:16).

These elements of the Colossian believers' milieu exploited language close enough to Paul's to suggest how Paul could expect his exhortation to be understood. Just as he urges a heavenly object of thinking (τὰ ἄνω φρονεῖτε, 3:2), Greek and Roman philosophy sometimes insisted that right thinking[1] elevated the soul to the heavens to experience the pure vision of a transcendent

1. I earlier addressed this emphasis in philosophy; see esp. pp. 46, 120–22.

deity. Some Jewish circles also attempted to secure visions (2:18) of God's heavenly throne. As in some other Pauline passages (e.g., 1 Cor. 2:16; Phil. 2:9–11), here too Christ, alongside God the Father, fills a role usually filled by a supreme deity.

While Paul employs analogous images and language to communicate his point, his interest is not so much the more general object of philosophic abstractions and mystic contemplations. He focuses instead more concretely on the exalted Christ; as in many other passages (e.g., 1 Cor. 2:16; Phil. 2:5; 3:19–20; 4:7), the renewed mind has a Christocentric focus.

This brief chapter will trace in turn ancient philosophy's contemplation of heavenly matters; evocations of such language in other early Jewish and Christian sources; the significance of Paul's Christocentric focus in his adaptation of the language in Colossians 3:1; the behavioral implications that Paul draws from this Christocentric focus; the intelligibility of those implications in light of ancient philosophy; and how the immediate context shapes eschatological implications in Paul's evocation of heaven. My focus and primary contribution will be to elaborate how ancient hearers would have received the passage, especially in view of ancient philosophy.

Contemplating Heavenly Matters (Col. 3:1–2)

Paul urges his hearers to seek "matters above" (τὰ ἄνω), where Christ is enthroned beside God, and to focus their interest on "matters above," in contrast to "earthly matters." By repeating the heavenly element twice, Paul reinforces its importance. He is not thinking of contemplating star formation, black holes, dark matter, or the like (although contemplating God's creative ingenuity was a possible component of ancient thinking about heavenly matters); rather, he is drawing on language about the heavens that often connoted what was pure and divine. Paul's language adapts familiar philosophic idiom for contemplating divine, heavenly reality, but with a specifically Christocentric focus.[2]

Heavenly Mindedness in Greek and Roman Sources

As commentators on Colossians have sometimes noted, philosophy emphasized right thinking, through which the soul sought to rise to the heavens.[3] Such

2. The use of "things above" (language that appears nowhere else in Colossians and is rare in the Pauline corpus) instead of "heavenly things" might be to avoid confusion with other heavenly entities (Col. 1:16, 20), but, in view of Col. 1:5, may be simply stylistic variation, as perhaps in Phil. 3:14, 20.

3. So Schweizer, *Colossians*, 175.

an emphasis arose naturally in its context: the entire range of Greco-Roman philosophy emphasized sound thinking,[4] and most thinkers also viewed the heavens as pure, perfect, and unchanging—hence, eternal.[5] Intellectuals often combined these ideas to speak of contemplating heavenly realities.[6]

Thus, for example, in an influential dialogue Plato emphasizes that souls by nature desire the highest location,[7] and those who consistently choose philosophy will ascend to a heavenly place.[8] Thinkers from various periods after Plato envisioned meditating on the heavens and stars as a noble philosophic pursuit,[9] and a pure mind could be described as guarded in a "celestial citadel."[10] The rational mind enabled one to ascend;[11] stirred by reasoning, some said, the mind would fly upward, since it is light in weight.[12] An essay in the form of a revelatory dream repeatedly emphasizes looking to the imperishable things in the heavenly spheres, not to the corruptible earth below.[13]

While many sources reflecting these ideas are Platonic, the ideas are by no means limited to Platonists.[14] Thus, Seneca, an eclectic first-century Stoic, believed that the soul proved its divinity and celestial origins by enjoying what was divine, such as the stars and orbits of celestial bodies.[15] Good Stoics believed that the ideal wise person would adopt a perspective from heaven and evaluate the rest of existence without personal bias.[16] Such a heavenly

4. See fuller discussion on pp. 46, 120–22, 225; or Keener, "Perspectives," 212–13. True beliefs could form a new identity in line with virtue (Stowers, "Resemble," 92).

5. See discussion below, esp. p. 249.

6. See, e.g., Sen. Y. *Ep. Lucil.* 120.15; Max. Tyre *Or.* 11.10; 25.6; *T. Job* 36:3–5 (*OTP*)/36:4–7 (ed. Kraft); 48:2; 49:1; 50:1. Cf. also some discussion of "heavenly" perspectives in Keener, *John,* 559–61.

7. Plato *Phaedr.* 248AB. Bodies were fashioned from earthly substance, with heavenly souls merely imprisoned in them (Plato *Phaedr.* 250C; Plut. *Exile* 17, *Mor.* 607D).

8. Plato *Phaedr.* 248E–249A.

9. Iambl. *Pyth. Life* 12.59 (also affirming mathematics, which likewise involves what is harmonious). Pythagoras allegedly attained full knowledge of the heavens (Iambl. *Pyth. Life* 5.27).

10. Val. Max. 4.1.ext.2 (*in arce caelesti,* trans. Bailey, LCL, 1:354–55).

11. Porph. *Marc.* 26.415–16. Some described God as pure mind (Pliny E. *N.H.* 2.5.14).

12. Heracl. *Hom. Prob.* 63.4. Wisdom would soar (63.5).

13. Cic. *Resp.* 6.17.17; 6.19.20.

14. This observation is important because Stoicism was far more influential than Platonism in the first-century northern Mediterranean world, though Philo's work demonstrates that Platonism was influential in educated Hellenistic Jewish circles at least in Alexandria (for discussions of Platonic influence on Philo, see, e.g., Runia, "Middle Platonist"; Sterling, "Platonizing Moses"; Dillon, "Reclaiming"), despite some Stoic and even Aristotelian elements.

15. Sen. Y. *Nat. Q.* 1.pref.12. Epictetus contends that externals hinder the soul because of our "earthly" surroundings (*Diatr.* 1.9).

16. Engberg-Pedersen, *Paul and Stoics,* 59 (citing Marc. Aur. 7.48; 9.30; 12.24.3), 63 (citing Cic. *Fin.* 3.25). Some allowed for enlightened emotions provided they were "monitored" from above (Engberg-Pedersen, "Marcus," 334–35). Even if Engberg-Pedersen (*Paul and Stoics,* 65) goes too far in regarding the Stoic emphasis on proper understanding of one's identity as "the

perspective had practical consequences. Thus, for example, heavenly reality set the model for the soul formed from it: the mind should remain tranquil, like the highest heavens.[17] Moreover, the heaven-informed soul despised terrestrial limitations such as human boundaries.[18] Some other thinkers also emphasized that they lived according to heaven's values revealed in nature, rather than according to earth's values in society.[19]

Heavenly Mindedness in Early Jewish and Christian Sources

Such perspectives were not limited to Gentiles; some Jews in a Hellenistic context adapted this language. The Middle Platonic Jewish philosopher Philo opines that humans are not only terrestrial entities but also celestial ones, near the stars.[20] He believed that inspiration would cause the soul to contemplate God,[21] carrying the soul into the upper atmosphere.[22] The mind should contemplate matters beyond heaven rather than lowly ones.[23]

For Philo, this observation was not merely theoretical; he believed that he had experienced this exaltation himself. Meditating on philosophy and other divine matters, freed from earthly and bodily thoughts, Philo felt that he was raised in soul to heavenly regions (with the sun, moon, and other celestial bodies).[24] Moving in the same realm of thought, yet at a more popular level, the Wisdom of Solomon notes that the perishable, earthly body weighs down the soul.[25] The second-century CE *Testament of Job* emphasizes being occupied with heavenly rather than earthly matters, since earthly matters change and are unstable, whereas heaven remains unperturbed.[26] As in the case of Philo's

---

framework for Paul's thought" about identity in Christ, it reflects elements in the larger milieu relevant for how Paul and Paulinists would be heard.

17. Sen. Y. *Dial.* 5.6.1. For the harmony of heavenly spheres, see, e.g., Max. Tyre *Or.* 37.5; Iambl. *Pyth. Life* 15.65–66; Men. Rhet. 2.17, 442.30–32; Lucian *Dance* 7. For imitating the heavens' harmony, see, e.g., Dio Chrys. *Or.* 40.35; such imitation enabled one to return there (Cic. *Resp.* 6.18.18–19). Though Aristotle knew the Pythagorean view (*Heav.* 2.9, 290b.12–29), he opposed it (2.9, 290b.30–291a.26).

18. Sen. Y. *Nat. Q.* 1.pref.13. Contemplating the larger cosmos allowed one to transcend mortal limitations (Sen. Y. *Nat. Q.* 1.pref.17; cf. 3.pref.10).

19. Diogenes *Ep.* 7; cf. the spoof on Socrates in Aristoph. *Clouds* 228–32.

20. Philo *Creation* 147; cf. *Creation* 82. Later rabbis also opine that humans are a mixture of heavenly and earthly components (*Sipre Deut.* 306.28.2; *Gen. Rab.* 12:8).

21. Philo *Creation* 71; cf. *Alleg. Interp.* 3.82.

22. Philo *Spec. Laws* 3.2.

23. Philo *Drunkenness* 128.

24. Philo *Spec. Laws* 3.1. At the time of writing, however, he complained that terrestrial matters like politics distracted him (*Spec. Laws* 3.3).

25. Wis. 9:14–15.

26. *T. Job* 36:3/4–5/7.

inspiration, charismatic inspiration moved the hearts of Job's daughters to heavenly rather than earthly or worldly matters.[27]

Some similar language and images also appear in the thought of the undisputed Pauline letters, particularly 2 Corinthians 4–5. Here Paul's "inner person" is being renewed despite the body's decay.[28] This unencumbered inner person is being prepared for what is unseen and eternal, which is from the heavens (2 Cor. 4:16–5:2).[29] In contrast to pure Platonists, Paul anticipates a heavenly *body*, though with some other apocalyptic Jewish circles he could associate this heavenly body with celestial bodies (1 Cor. 15:40–41).[30] Paul also speaks of a heavenly Jerusalem (one "above"), of which the earthly version is presumably at best a shadow (Gal. 4:25–26). This idea too was already at home in Jewish circles.[31]

By itself, some vertical dualism in the Pauline corpus need not imply a wholesale embrace of conventional philosophic perspectives. Apocalyptic Judaism may have had an even more specifically developed vertical dualism than Greek philosophy did,[32] although the dualism of Jewish sources in Greek did not always carry the connotations that it did among philosophers.[33] In Colossians 3, as in Jewish apocalyptic, the vertical dualism is also eschatological, so that the "shadow" is contrasted with the coming world (Col. 2:17), and believers' identity is fully revealed at Christ's coming (3:4).[34] Moreover, as is usually observed,[35] the image of Jesus at the Father's right hand in 3:1

27. *T. Job* 48–50, esp. 48:2 (they stop φρονεῖν "earthly" things, employing the same verb as Col. 3:2); 49:1 (no longer "desiring" worldly things); 50:1.

28. On the language of the "inner person," see diverse approaches in Aune, "Duality," 220–22; Markschies, "Metaphor"; Betz, "Concept."

29. The heavenly body is viewed as a present possession (2 Cor. 5:1), probably not in terms of present experience (5:2–4; cf. similar vocabulary in 1 Cor. 15:49–54), but in terms of the down payment of the Spirit (2 Cor. 5:5) and the beginning of the new creation (5:17); see, e.g., Keener, *Corinthians*, 179–80.

30. Resurrection bodies are compared with stars in Dan. 12:2–3; *1 En.* 43:3; 104:2; *2 Bar.* 51:10. In more hellenized Judaism, cf. astral immortality for martyrs in 4 Macc. 17:5.

31. E.g., *4 Ezra* 10:25–28; *b. Hag.* 12b; Lincoln, *Paradise*, 18–24, 29. In Diaspora Judaism, cf. Philo *Dreams* 2.250; Heb. 12:22.

32. Cf. comments in, e.g., O'Brien, *Colossians*, 161; Arrington, *Aeon Theology*, 69; Charlesworth, "Comparison," 409; Black, *Scrolls*, 171; perhaps *T. Job* 33:3.

33. E.g., Judah (with its kingship) has "earthly matters" and Levi (with its priesthood) "heavenly matters" in *T. Jud.* 21:3. In the context of *T. Sol.* 6:10, "heavenly matters" turns out to be essentially folk magic, but this usage is unusual, at least in our extant early Jewish sources.

34. For heaven as both present and eschatological in Jewish apocalyptic, see esp. Lincoln, *Paradise*.

35. E.g., Lohse, *Colossians*, 133. The image need not be so limited (Suet. *Nero* 13.2), but its pervasiveness in early Christianity supports this allusion.

is specifically Jewish; it recalls Psalm 110:1, consistently applied to Jesus's exaltation as Lord in early Christianity.[36]

Paul's thought structure is intelligible in terms of a broader milieu, but his image is distinctly Christocentric, both reflecting biblical images long applied christologically and implying a future eschatology. Nevertheless, as some examples above (such as Philo and other Diaspora Jewish sources) show, we need not force a choice between Jewish and Hellenistic elements (again note Col. 2:8, 16).[37]

"Where Christ Is Enthroned" (Col. 3:1)

Contemplating "matters above" was not a purely impersonal exercise and plainly was not impersonal for Paul.

Heavenly Beings or God's Throne

For most ancient thinkers, the heavens were not barren; celestial deities lived there.[38] Heaven also hosted the stars; many Gentiles viewed the stars as divine,[39] and Jews normally viewed them as angels.[40] In Platonic thought, pure deities could reside only in the heavens.[41]

Obviously, the plurality of such divine beings in typical pagan thought would be problematic for Paul. Indeed, following Plato, many thinkers regarded the realm between earth and heaven as the realm of intermediate daimones, whereas heaven was the place of the supreme God.[42] For Paul, by contrast, the heavenly focus must be on Christ alone, a focus that some

36. Mark 12:36; Acts 2:33–35; Heb. 1:3, 13 (cf. 8:1; 10:12; 12:2); 1 Clem. 36.5; Poly. Phil. 2.1; Barn. 12.10. Some later rabbis assigned this location to teachers of Scripture and rabbinic tradition (Pesiq. Rab Kah. 27:2, on Ps. 16:11).

37. Nearly all scholars now recognize the value of Greco-Roman sources for understanding a wide range of Jewish sources, even from Jewish Palestine, in this era; see, e.g., Lieberman, Hellenism; Cohen, Law; Hengel, Judaism and Hellenism.

38. E.g., Ovid Metam. 1.168–76; Val. Max. 7.1.1; Sen. Y. Nat. Q. 1.pref.2; Dial. 12.8.5; Val. Flacc. 1.498; Dio Chrys. Or. 12.34; cf. Max. Tyre Or. 39.4. In various Jewish sources, God was in the highest heaven (e.g., 2 En. 20:1–3; 3 En. 1:2); for Jewish association of God with heaven, see also, e.g., Dan. 4:26; 1 Esd. 4:58; Tob. 10:13; Jdt. 6:19; 1 Macc. 3:18, 50, 60; 4:24; 3 Macc. 7:6; 1 En. 83:9; 91:7; 1QM 12.5.

39. E.g., Cic. Nat. d. 2.15.39–40; Resp. 6.15.15; Sen. Y. Ben. 4.23.4; Iambl. Myst. 1.17, 19; condemnation of this view in 1 En. 80:7–8; Pesiq. Rab. 15:1.

40. 1 En. 80:6–8; 2 En. 4:1; 29:3; 3 En. 46:1; Ps.-Phoc. 71, 75; Philo Plant. 12, 14; Sipre Deut. 47.2.3–5; possibly 2 Bar. 51:10.

41. Plut. Isis 78, Mor. 382F.

42. Max. Tyre Or. 8.8; see also Trapp's note (p. 76 n. 36). This image may be relevant for the lesser hosts in Col. 1:16, although the categories come closer to Jewish apocalyptic (Dan.

Colossian believers might be in danger of forgetting. Thus, Colossians 1:15–17; 2:10, 15, 18 must warn against overestimating the status of the intermediate powers (as angels would have been understood to be) vis-à-vis Christ.

Various ancient thinkers, however, did seek the one, transcendent deity in the heavens. Platonic mysticism (including in its Jewish form in Philo) sought contemplative or mystical vision of God,[43] but this aspiration was by no means limited to Gentiles or even Philo. In apocalyptic texts heavenly revelations could include meteorological data from the lower heavens,[44] but they especially included revelations focusing on the vision of God on his throne.[45] Indeed, a primary goal of Jewish mysticism in general was the vision of God's throne.[46] The means of attaining this vision may have varied, but the objective remained fairly consistent.[47] The date of some of these mystical sources is disputed,[48] but God's exalted throne was also a key element in Jewish apocalypses from both centuries before Paul's time and long afterward.[49]

The Exalted Christ

That Christ fulfills this divine role for Paul could have seemed jarring to outsiders, whether Jewish or Gentile, who may have been unfamiliar with the Jesus movement. Against this backdrop, the Christocentric emphasis in Colossians 3 is unmistakable. Some philosophers sought to attain the divine vision (and consequent transformation) through contemplating the purely transcendent, abstract deity of Platonism. Some Jewish mystics sought to

---

10:13, 21; *1 En.* 40:9; 61:10; 69:3; 72:1; 75:1; 82:10–12; *3 Bar.* 12:3; cf. Sir. 17:17; *Jub.* 15:31–32; 35:17; *Mek. Shir.* 2.112–18; *Sipre Deut.* 315.2.1).

43. Max. Tyre *Or.* 11.11; cf. Isaacs, *Spirit*, 50; Dillon, "Transcendence in Philo"; Hagner, "Vision," 89–90. On the impossibility of full vision of God in this life, see Philo *Rewards* 39. Only the pure soul could envision God (Philo *Conf.* 92); for biblical examples, see *Names* 3–6; *QG* 4.138; *Conf.* 92, 146; *Dreams* 1.171; *Abr.* 57. On mysticism in Philo, see, e.g., Sterling, *Ancestral Philosophy*, 31–32, 169–70; perhaps excessively, Goodenough, *Introduction*, 134–60.

44. *1 En.* 72–82 (*1 En.* Bk. 3). Such revelations generally included a heavenly perspective on earth as well as the heavens themselves (e.g., Moses's revelation in *L.A.B.* 19:10).

45. *1 En.* 14:18–20; 71:5–10; *2 En.* 20:3 A; *3 En.* 1; *T. Levi* 5; Rev. 4:2; for the source, see Isa. 6:1; Ezek. 1:22–28; Dan. 7:9.

46. See, e.g., Arbel, "Understanding."

47. Angelic help appears in *1 En.* 71:5; 87:3; *2 En.* 7:1; *2 Bar.* 6:3–4; note the Spirit in Ezek. 43:5; Rev. 4:2. For an arduous journey, see, e.g., *1 En.* 14:9–13; later rabbis nevertheless regarded this adventure as dangerous (e.g., *b. Hag.* 13a, bar.; 14b, bar.; Scholem, *Trends*, 42–44; cf. Lieber, "Angels").

48. For arguments for early *merkabah* traditions, see, e.g., Halperin, "Midrash"; Dimant and Strugnell, "Vision"; Davila, "Merkavah Mysticism." The earliest traditions clearly grew over time, however; see Neusner, "Development."

49. E.g., *1 En.* 14:18–20; 18:8; 47:3; 71:7; 90:20; *2 En.* 1a:4; 20:3; 21:1; 22:2; *3 En.* 1; *4 Ezra* 8:21; cf. *L.A.E.* 25:3–4; 28:4.

attain a divine vision of the throne chariot. Yet some of Paul's own visions (2 Cor. 12:1–4, 7) apparently included Jesus (12:1, 8–9).[50] For some early Christians beyond the immediate Pauline circle, Jesus was the only genuine mediator between heaven and earth (John 3:13; cf. 1:51; Matt. 11:25–27//Luke 10:21–22).

In Colossians the object of heavenly contemplation is no transcendent abstraction or even Israel's God in exalted splendor, but Christ. Philo may have limited experience of God to the mediation of the Logos (Reason);[51] God draws the ideal person from "earthly matters" to himself through the Logos.[52] In Colossians 1:15–20 and 2:8–9, Christ fills a role similar to Philo's Logos or the Jewish sages' expectations for divine wisdom; this idea may be reiterated in our passage.[53]

Granted, Paul speaks not simply of a heavenly being but of τὰ ἄνω ("matters above," plural) versus "earthly" matters in Colossians 3:2. Nevertheless, the only content of these heavenly matters specified at the outset is the exalted Christ. Indeed, the postpositive conjunction γάρ ("for") in 3:3 explicitly predicates one's contemplation of "matters above" on union with Christ in God.

This focus fits the Christocentric emphasis of Colossians as a whole. Heaven hosts many angelic ranks, but they were both created (1:16) and tamed (1:20) through Christ. Moreover, the emphasis fits the preceding context. Like the "earthly things" relativized by Platonism, Paul relativizes Jewish new moons and sabbaths (2:16) as merely "shadows" (2:17). In this case, however, they are shadows not merely of heavenly things but, consistent with Eastern Judaism, of eschatological things ("coming things," 2:17).[54] I will not digress here to enter the debate about the precise contours of the asceticism discussed in 2:18–23, but in any case, believers have died with Christ to such earthly matters (2:20–22). It is not abuse or neglect of the body (2:23) that causes them

50. Ancient dream reports can include deceased persons (e.g., Plut. *Caes.* 69.5; Val. Max. 1.7.5; 1.7.ext.3; *Abot R. Nat.* 40 A), but biblical and early Christian examples, probably excepting Acts 16:9, focus on God (e.g., Gen. 20:3; 31:24; 1 Kings 3:5), angels (e.g., Gen. 28:12; 31:11; Matt. 2:13; Acts 27:23), or sometimes in early Christian sources the risen Lord Jesus (e.g., Acts 18:9; 23:11). Some view Paul himself in terms of the apocalyptic experiences that later contributed to *merkabah* mysticism; see, e.g., Segal, "Presuppositions," 170; Bowker, "Visions"; Kim, *Origin*, 252–53. Others demur (e.g., Schäfer, "Journey").

51. See Winston, "Mysticism"; cf. discussion in Hagner, "Vision," 84; Wolfson, *Philo*, 1:282–89.

52. Philo *Sacr.* 8.

53. Scholars have long identified logos or wisdom Christology in Col. 1:15–20; see, e.g., Lohse, *Colossians*, 47–48; Schweizer, *Colossians*, 69; Kim, *Origin*, 268; Longenecker, *Christology*, 145; earlier, Lightfoot, *Colossians*, 144.

54. In the undisputed Pauline letters the plural participle of μέλλω is always contrasted with ἐνεστῶτα, "things present" (Rom. 8:38; 1 Cor. 3:22), in turn associated with the present age (Gal. 1:4; cf. 1 Cor. 7:26).

to transcend earthly matters but union with a new "body" in Christ (2:17; cf. 1:18, 22, 24; 3:15), and hence death to the old one, presumably in Adam, in 3:5 (cf. also 2:11).

Moral Implications of Heavenly Contemplation

If Christ is the focus, however, why does Paul speak of τὰ ἄνω ("things above"), in the plural, in Colossians 3:2? He might use the plural τὰ ἄνω ("things above," i.e., "heavenly matters" or even "heavens") here simply to evoke contemporary language, but a singular could have communicated this sensitivity as well (cf., e.g., the singular of οὐρανός in 1:23; especially 4:1).[55]

More likely, he is preparing to complement or further explicate the mention of Christ (in 3:1) in what follows. Literary connections in fact do suggest that the following context explains what is involved in these τὰ ἄνω. As the invited focus of contemplation in 3:2a, these "things above" contrast with the "earthly matters" that the same exhortation summons hearers to avoid (3:2b). This passage goes on to define these "earthly matters" in terms of all the immoral behaviors to which one died with Christ (3:5–9, esp. 3:5), behaviors characterizing the old life (3:9).

En-Christed Life

Given their specific contrast to "earthly" behaviors, the "matters above" would then involve whatever characterized the new life in Christ (cf. Col. 3:3–4). These characteristics are not simply Pauline paraenesis prescribed universally for humanity; they are repeatedly connected with Christ. Because the new person is made new in accordance with the creator's image (3:10), and this new person embraces all humanity (3:11), the passage fairly clearly evokes the first creation in God's image (cf. Gen. 1:26–27; Rom. 5:12–21). It thus points to a new kind of humanity in the heavenly Adam (cf. 1 Cor. 15:47–49).[56] This new life reflects God's image in Christ (Col. 3:10–11). The climax in verse 11 could hardly be more emphatic: "Christ is all and among

---

55. Cf. also 1 Cor. 8:5; 15:47; Phil. 3:20. The singular and plural appear to function interchangeably in the undisputed Pauline letters, most clearly in 2 Cor. 5:1–2 and 1 Thess. 1:10; 4:16, although Paul knows multiple heavens (2 Cor. 12:2). Others also connect the ethical section (Col. 3:5–17) with being raised with Christ (see, e.g., Moule, "New Life").

56. For the Adamic allusion in Colossians, see, e.g., Moule, *Colossians*, 119; Lohse, *Colossians*, 142–43; Johnston, *Ephesians*, 65; Martin, *Colossians*, 107; Bird, *Colossians*, 102. As in Rom. 12:2, the language of renewal here (ἀνακαινόω, Col. 3:10; elsewhere in Paul in 2 Cor. 4:16, a context that similarly blends Platonic and eschatological imagery) undoubtedly evokes the new, eschatological era; see the comment on ἀνακαίνωσις at Rom. 12:2 (p. 154).

all"[57]—in other words, Christ is the basis for the new humanity and is working in all the diversity of traditional human categories (cf. 1:27).

In "putting on" this new life (Col. 3:10), then, one puts on characteristics of Christ, such as kindness and forgiveness (3:13–14).[58] The latter characteristic explicitly follows the Lord's example (καθὼς καὶ ὁ κύριος, 3:13). It is Christ's peace that unifies believers (3:15), surmounting ethnic and social boundaries (3:11); indeed, they are ultimately one body (3:15), that is, in Christ (1:18; 2:11, 19). Paul thus connects this paraenetical material closely with his Christocentric emphasis.

The depiction of new life in Christ continues further in the following lines about worship and conventional household codes. Whereas the parallel text about worship in Ephesians emphasizes the Spirit (Eph. 5:18–20),[59] Colossians maintains its contextual emphasis on the effects of union with Christ: Christ's message dwelling in the believer produces worship (Col. 3:16–17).[60] All one's acts should be done in the name of Jesus (3:17) and for the Lord (3:23–24), including one's behavior in accordance with household codes (3:18, 20, 22, 23, 24; 4:1). In view of my discussion of 3:1–2, it is perhaps most relevant to note that Christian slaveholders must answer to a lord "in heaven" (4:1).

In the context, then, Colossians speaks of no abstract contemplation detached from present earthly existence. Rather, the focus on heaven is a focus on Christ, not only as he is enthroned above, but as that reality of his lordship impinges on daily life. Prayer in this context is not just heavenly contemplation but addresses present issues, even if they are issues that have eternal consequences (Col. 1:3, 9; 4:2–4, 12). For Paul, believers should be so heavenly minded that they do more earthly good.

Moral demands may also be implicit in the presentation of Jesus's exalted status in 3:1, which indicates his authority. The allusion to Psalm 110:1, noted above as widely applied in early Christianity, implicitly identifies Jesus as "Lord." Jesus appears as "Lord" as many as eight times in Colossians 3:13–4:1, most relevantly (as we have noted) a "Lord in heaven" in 4:1. In any case, for Colossians, union with the heavenly, exalted Christ redefines believers'

57. Πάντα καὶ ἐν πᾶσιν Χριστός.

58. For the background of the "clothing" image, see 111n416; cf. *L.A.B.* 27:9–10; also the LXX of Judg. 6:34; 1 Chron. 12:18; 2 Chron. 24:20.

59. See Ware, *Synopsis*, 273; for comment on the context in Ephesians, see, e.g., Keener, *Paul*, 158–59; Hoehner, *Ephesians*, 702–5; Thielman, *Ephesians*, 358–60.

60. If ὁ λόγος τοῦ Χριστοῦ here means not "the message about Christ" (cf. Col. 1:5; 4:3; Rom. 10:17; 16:25; Eph. 3:4) but perhaps something like "the speaking of Christ" (cf. Col. 3:17; 4:6; Rom. 9:6; 1 Thess. 2:13; perhaps Col. 1:25; cf. Christ praying in Hays, *Conversion*, 107), Paul could connect believers' worship to Christ's activity even more clearly, but the former interpretation might be likelier.

eschatological identity and should thus impinge on their present behavior. We might speak of the "en-Christed life"—life lived by dependence on Christ living in believers (3:3–4), through faith in his character and power.

The Intelligibility of the Moral Connection for Ancient Hearers

Even many non-Christian Gentiles could have grasped the moral connections to Paul's emphasis on a heavenly focus, although their understanding of morality would not have agreed with his on every point. As I noted earlier, Paul does not disparage the body in the way that later Platonists or gnostics did, but he does adapt some contemporary language about the body to challenge bodily desires for activities already deemed sinful in Scripture.[61] Thus, he speaks here of τὰ μέλη τὰ ἐπὶ τῆς γῆς, "the members that are on the earth" (Col. 3:5).[62]

Connections would be fairly evident. A Middle Platonist, for example, would detect a ready connection between the ascent in Colossians 3:1–2 and the warning against earthly, bodily passions in 3:5. For Middle Platonists, the intellect would experience God, rising ever upward as it relinquished bodily sense-knowledge and earthly matters.[63] A strong intellect could encounter the divine in the heavens;[64] philosophic rhetoric could direct the mind away from indulging vices to contemplating matters above.[65] For later Platonists, pleasure dragged the soul back down toward the body.[66] Those who wished to ascend to God needed to abstain from pleasures;[67] virtue would draw the soul upward toward that to which it was akin.[68]

Nor was this concern limited to later Platonists. The first-century Jewish thinker Philo emphasized not only the soul's heavenward proclivity (as noted above) but also the danger of distraction from that proclivity. Thus, Philo

61. See pp. 99–108, esp. 105–8.
62. Cf. discussion of bodily "members" at Rom. 7:23 and Paul's usual connection of this noun with the body. Through the death of Jesus's fleshly body (Col. 1:22), believers are freed from the dominance of the fleshly individual body (2:11, 23) to function instead as members of Christ's larger body (1:18, 24; 2:17; 3:15).
63. Max. Tyre Or. 11.10. For Maximus, however, contemplating stars and planets, like daimones, was simply contemplating divine works (11.12).
64. Max. Tyre Or. 2.2 (conceding that most people, however, needed images to help them).
65. Max. Tyre Or. 25.6.
66. Porph. Marc. 6.108. Passions affixed the soul to the body (Plato Phaedo 83d; Iambl. Pyth. Life 32.228).
67. Porph. Marc. 6.105–8; 7.131–34.
68. Porph. Marc. 16.267–68. Because the divinely inspired intellect was "like" God, it would be drawn to God (19.314–16); contemplation of God purified the mind (11.204). Earlier writers also agreed that reason shared the divine nature (Rhet. Alex. pref. 1420b.20–21; Ael. Arist. Def. Or. 409–10, §139D).

believed that the primeval serpent symbolized pleasure because of its down-ward orientation.[69] Others also concurred that thinking like deity required virtue, not desire for anything evil or shameful.[70]

The Stoic Seneca agreed that the soul would ascend by contemplating the heavens only to the extent that it was freed from the body.[71] The flesh weighed a person down, but the soul by nature was light, eager to ascend to the high-est heavens, on which it meditated.[72] In freeing the soul from passions, virtue released it to contemplate heavenly things;[73] by moving among the stars, the mind should spurn evil and worldly wealth.[74]

Philosophers' popular detractors did not always appreciate implied con-nections between heavenly contemplation and earthly behavior; for some ancient critics, in fact, philosophers could become so heavenly minded that they were no earthly good. Some considered discussion of the state more profitable for terrestrial audiences.[75] Writers could depict typical farmers as rejecting the impractical pursuits of philosophers who "meddle with things above the earth."[76] The author of one work complains that one could not speak wisdom concerning heavenly matters unless one understood earthly matters.[77] Others merely warned that those who cannot understand earthly matters dare not pretend to understand heavenly ones.[78]

Many Greek observers ridiculed the celestial preoccupation of contempo-rary astronomers and philosophers through a familiar anecdote. Thus a servant girl reportedly ridiculed Thales for falling into a well while preoccupied by the stars; she complained that he sought to know heavenly matters while ignoring what lay beneath him.[79] Others applied this story line more widely.[80] In one

---

69. Philo *Creation* 157.

70. Dio Chrys. *Or.* 4.42–43.

71. Sen. Y. *Nat. Q.* 1.pref.11. For the "earthly" body and its influence, see Epict. *Diatr.* 1.9.

72. Sen. Y. *Dial.* 12.11.6. In much of ancient physics, air and especially fire were the lightest and highest of substances (Pliny E. *N.H.* 2.4.1), but heavy elements could hold lighter elements down (Pliny E. *N.H.* 2.4.11). Some, however, viewed the heavens as consisting of an element different from earthly ones and more divine (Arist. *Heav.* 1.2, 268b.11–269a.32).

73. Sen. Y. *Nat. Q.* 1.pref.6. Seneca may connect envisioning the universe mentally with overpowering vices in *Nat. Q.* 3.pref.10 (where he mentions them together).

74. Sen. Y. *Nat. Q.* 1.pref.7.

75. Dio Chrys. *Or.* 32.25; contrast Philo *Spec. Laws* 3.3.

76. Alciph. *Farm.* 11 (Sitalces to Oenopion, his son), 3.14 (trans. Benner and Forbes, LCL, 103).

77. Philost. *Hrk.* 33.6–7.

78. Wis. 9:16; cf. John 3:12.

79. Plato *Theaet.* 174A. Plato's Socrates thus comments that philosophers must be ready for ridicule for not sharing others' focus (*Theaet.* 174A–175B).

80. E.g., Aesop *Fable* 40, mocking an astronomer. Cf. Philost. *Hrk.* 1.2; 33.6–8, and comment in Maclean and Aitken, "Introduction," lxxxi–lxxxii.

later novel Alexander of Macedon allows a stargazing astrologer to fall into a pit, mortally wounding him; rather than extending sympathy, Alexander mercilessly reproaches the hapless astrologer for studying heavenly matters while ignoring earthly ones.[81] Nevertheless, Paul, like many philosophers, could not be charged justly with such neglect. As already noted, he not only uses familiar language for contemplating "matters above"; he also applies this idea to concrete behavioral issues (Col. 3:5–4:1).

Heavenly Afterlife and Colossians 3

Although verses 1–2 are not by themselves explicitly eschatological, they quickly give way to an eschatological expectation (3:4); as in many Jewish sources, vertical dualism is connected with eschatological dualism.[82] In Colossians Paul speaks elsewhere of a hope reserved for believers in heaven (1:5; cf. 1 Pet. 1:3–4), appealing to an image familiar by Paul's day, including to the circles to which Paul objects (cf. Col. 2:8, 16). In Colossians, however, the basis for the hope is already effective among believers (1:23, 27). Believers' lives are already hidden with Christ (3:3), who is their life (3:4), with consequent promise for the future (3:4; cf. the present possession of the Spirit as a guarantee of the future in, e.g., Rom. 8:23; 2 Cor. 5:4–5; Eph. 1:13–14).[83]

Philosophers and those influenced by them usually viewed the heavens as pure, perfect, and unchanging—hence, eternal.[84] This conception shaped many views of immortality. Even if scholars a century ago overemphasized astral immortality,[85] the soul's celestial destination does appear in various ancient sources,[86] although in an early period perhaps this may have been an especially Roman interest.[87] In some Greek and Roman sources the soul was of heavenly origin and cultivated its heavenly character by meditating on the divine, on

81. Ps.-Callisth. *Alex.* 1.14.

82. See discussion in Lincoln, *Paradise*.

83. Like other early Christians, Paul presumably affirmed a future transformation of all creation (cf. Rom. 5:17; 11:12, 15; 1 Cor. 15:24–27; Phil. 3:21); nevertheless, the hope was currently in heaven and thus would come from there (Phil. 3:20–21; 1 Thess. 1:10; 4:16).

84. In Platonic and Pythagorean sources, see, e.g., Philo *QE* 2.73; Max. Tyre *Or.* 21.7–8; Plot. *Enn.* 2.1–2 (noting their ordering by the universal Soul); Pythagoras in Diog. Laert. 8.1.27. In Cic. *Resp.* 6.17.17 everything above the moon is eternal. Cf. also, e.g., the contrast between what is earthly/mortal and heavenly/divine in Plut. *Rom. Q.* 78, *Mor.* 282F.

85. E.g., Cumont, *After Life*, 91–109.

86. On astral immortality, see, e.g., Martin, *Body*, 117.

87. For deceased heroes becoming stars, see, e.g., Virg. *Aen.* 7.210–11; Val. Max. 4.6.ext.3; Lucan *C.W.* 9.1–9; Ovid *Metam.* 15.749, 843–51 (Ovid hopes this for himself in 15.875–76).

what was heavenly.[88] This practice prepared the soul for its heavenward ascent after death.[89] Souls imprisoned in present bodies could look heavenward in anticipation of their release.[90] The soul ascended to the heavens, to which it was kin, leaving behind the body.[91] The souls of the deceased ascended and could look down from heaven.[92] Whereas pure souls ascended, however, souls too attached to their bodies might be thought to hover in the atmosphere and ascend higher only over long periods of time.[93]

Colossians does not address what is "eternal" in the heavens in an abstract sense, however, but in 3:1 emphasizes Jesus's resurrection, with its eschatological implications for believers in 3:3–4 (cf. 2:17). The allusion to Psalm 110:1 (noted above)[94] also surely presupposes Jesus's resurrection, given the connection between the two in early Christian tradition (Rom. 8:34; Eph. 1:20; Acts 2:33–34; 1 Pet. 3:21–22). Just as Hellenistic Jews such as Philo could adapt Gentile philosophy in light of Jewish tradition, so can Paul, although Paul is far less assimilated than Philo (and may provide a *contrast* with philosophy, in view of Col. 2:8). Just as the content of heaven is no divine abstraction, but Christ, so the immortality that awaits believers there is not a product of the soul's preexistent nature (as in Platonism) but the promise inherent in the life that believers already share with Christ.

Conclusion

Colossians 3:1–2 is a pivotal text both for understanding the sorts of conceptions in the larger milieu that the letter as a whole addresses and for

88. E.g., Porph. (a much later Platonist) *Marc.* 6.103–8; 7.131–34; 10.180–83; 16.267–68; 26.415–16. In Val. Flacc. 3.378–82 people were originally fire, stars in heaven (also Cic. *Resp.* 6.15.15); they became mortals, but they eventually will return to heaven.

89. For the soul's postmortem ascent, see, e.g., Cic. *Resp.* 6.16.16; 6.24.26; Philo *QG* 3.45; Heracl. *Ep.* 5; Max. Tyre *Or.* 9.6; 11.11; 41.5; Men. Rhet. 2.9, 414.21–23; also Aune, "Duality," 228; for particular philosophers' expected ascents, see Cercidas frg. 1; Eunapius *Lives* 469; Hdn. 1.5.6. Some portrayed this ascent as divinization (Men. Rhet. 2.9, 414.25–27), which goes beyond the closest early Christian parallels to the idea (2 Cor. 3:18; 2 Pet. 1:4).

90. Max. Tyre *Or.* 7.5.

91. Cic. *Tusc.* 1.19.43–44. Cf. Virg. *Aen.* 6.728–42, adapting Platonic ideas: expressions of one universal mind are imprisoned in mortal bodies but ultimately liberated after death and purgation to purity and readiness to reinhabit bodies.

92. Sen. Y. *Dial.* 11.9.3.

93. Cic. *Resp.* 6.26.29; *Tusc.* 1.31.75; cf. other unhappy approaches in Val. Flacc. 3.383–96; Pythagoras in Diog. Laert. 8.1.31. Val. Max. 9.3.ext.1 opines that Alexander's evil deeds nearly prevented his ascension.

94. Pages 242, 246.

understanding the connection between the letter's earlier theological arguments and the following paraenetical material.

Philosophers, mystics, and apocalyptic visionaries sought to visualize heaven, often to envision deity; philosophers emphasized specifically heavenly thinking. For philosophers, the pure and heavenly deity was abstract and transcendent; for Colossians, the heavenly focus is Christ, fitting the letter's Christocentric emphasis.

For Paul, contemplating Christ also leads naturally to Christlike character, in contrast to the pursuit of earthly passions. Although Paul's articulation of the connection is distinctive, his connection of heavenly contemplation with appropriate behavior would have been fully intelligible to his contemporaries, including many philosophers. Paul also connects consideration of Christ's current heavenly status with believers' future hope, again in a manner intelligible to many of his contemporaries.

Conclusion

[We serve in light of eternity, recognizing that one, Christ,] . . . died on behalf of everyone, in order that those who do live might live no longer for themselves but instead for the one who died for them and rose again. Because of this, from now on we are not evaluating anything merely in terms of its natural properties; even if we once considered Christ that way, that's not how we understand him now. Because of this, anyone who is in Christ experiences the new creation. For such a person, the things that used to be have gone. Consider this: new things have come into being!

—2 Corinthians 5:15–17

For Paul, the mind of love, the mind of faith, the mind of the Spirit, the heavenly mind, the mind of Christ focused on the weakness of the cross, and so on are all the same mind. They are simply different entrances into the same reality in Christ and in the Spirit, approached from different angles, varying according to Paul's emphasis in a particular passage. In other words, they do not offer us a long list of new rules but instead present various windows on a new reality, each of which takes us to the same place in Christ. Experiencing any of these windows helps one identify the Christ-centered reality that is expressed in the other ways as well.

From the exegesis of the foregoing passages, several features have emerged. Two chapters (chaps. 1 and 3) addressed Paul's negative characterizations of the mind that lacks the direct action of God's Spirit. With (Rom. 7:15–25) or without (1:18–32) the full law, passions prevail, preventing what philosophers would consider rational tranquility. The pagan mind of Romans 1:18–32 is ungrateful, failing to acknowledge God's activity in creation and thus becoming blind to moral truth even on the interhuman level. The mind under the law in Romans 7:7–25 possesses knowledge about what is right without the power to become right; it lacks the transforming truth of the gospel. (Although Paul was addressing specifically the mind informed by the law, the same principles also apply to struggling to fulfill Christian ethics without genuine divine transformation.)

By contrast, other chapters have addressed Paul's positive characterizations of the mind in Christ. Chapter 2 observed that the mind of faith in Romans 6:11 embraces the believer's secure identity as a new person because of what Christ has done. Because Christ rather than self is the object of trust for righteousness, those baptized into Christ can leave their justification with him and can live lives of obedience with confidence rather than fear. They may "put on" Christ (Rom. 13:14), viewing themselves as in Christ (perhaps as members of his body envisioning themselves in him in a deeper way than Paul adopted the persona of the flesh in Rom. 7:7–25).

Chapter 4 observed that the mind of the Spirit in Romans 8:5–6 focuses not on the struggles of the flesh, in contrast to the mind under the law in 7:7–25, but on God's Spirit, who empowers believers to live the right way that God wants. That is, the new framework's focus is on serving God, rather than on serving one's own interests, and this focus can be empowered by recognizing one's dependence on God's Spirit. Believers remain in the flesh, but in contrast to others who are in the flesh, believers also have the Spirit.

Chapter 5 recognized that Paul's theme of the mind in Romans climaxes especially in Romans 12. The renewed mind in Romans 12:2 functions in the broader context of salvation history by taking into account God's wise plan in the past as well as in the age to come. This approach invites an eschatological perspective: it evaluates choices in the present age from the standpoint of the eternal age to come.[1] It also functions in the broader context of Christ's body by seeking to serve that body and by recognizing that every member's contribution is valuable.

Chapter 6 argued that the mind of Christ in 1 Corinthians 2 includes the divine wisdom revealed in the cross, a wisdom that shames the supposed wisdom of the present world order. Like the mind of Romans 12:2, the mind of 1 Corinthians 2 is also an eschatological wisdom, the revelation and foretaste

---

1. Although Pauline literature may also use the plural "ages" with respect to the future; cf. the idiom often translated "forever" in Rom. 1:25; 9:5; 11:36; 16:27; 2 Cor. 11:31; Gal. 1:5; emphatic in Eph. 3:21; 1 Tim. 1:17; 2 Tim. 4:18; cf. also 1 Cor. 2:7; 10:11; Eph. 3:9, 11; Phil. 4:20; Col. 1:26; and esp. Eph. 2:7. Mention of the present "age" is always singular, as in Rom. 12:2; 1 Cor. 1:20; 2:6, 8; 3:18; 2 Cor. 4:4; Gal. 1:4; Eph. 1:21; 2:2; 1 Tim. 6:17; 2 Tim. 4:10; Titus 2:12.

of God's future promises by the Spirit. Further, like the mind of Romans 12:2–8 focused on Christ's body, Christ's mind in 1 Corinthians 2 is also at odds with the world's values of rivalry and division. It is, finally, an actual (though not complete) experience of Christ, ideally pervaded by God's heart, expressed in the fruit of the Spirit and often in intimacy with Christ and sometimes in various ministries, such as those that communicate wisdom, teaching, or prophetic insight. This experience with Christ can be illustrated also in 2 Corinthians 3:18.

Philippians (discussed in chap. 7) depicts the peaceful approach of a mind that leaves ultimate outcomes with God (4:7–8; as in Rom. 8:6); it also invites believers to think the way that Jesus did, in serving the Father even by a humiliating death (Phil. 2:1–11). This letter further invites a heavenly perspective rather than a focus on earthly desires (3:19–21). In a similar way, Colossians 3:1–2 (chap. 8) emphasizes focus on heavenly rather than earthly matters; in particular, this focus involves contemplating Christ and his character and thereby living in accordance with his character.

Some Pastoral Implications

Philosophers and historians draw lessons from sages of the past, and for such interests Paul's insights have no less academic merit. For Christians, his work is even more important than an exclusively academic interest would require. Paul's role as one of our movement's seminal thinkers, as key leader in the mission to reach Gentiles in culturally relevant ways, and especially as author of a significant portion of the Christian canon invites our close attention.

Divided Churches

One possible application of this material is to challenge the common divide in many Christian circles between emotional religion (related to US frontier revivals and earlier mystics) and intellectual religion (historically related to academic training). The former has sometimes trivialized the value of the latter as "dead letter," and the latter has sometimes disdained the former as mere "enthusiasm." To some extent this divide in US history was socially constructed: only elites could obtain education, and those excluded from centers of religious power were also forced to appeal to alternative epistemologies.[1] Given Paul's emphasis on both God's Spirit and the important role of human

---

1. See, e.g., discussion in Smidt, *Evangelicals*, 22; Boda, "Word and Spirit," 44; Archer, *Hermeneutic*, 21–22; Kidd and Hankins, *Baptists*, 42. This observation is not meant to denigrate the alternative epistemologies; I have argued that John's Gospel provided one such alternative appeal in its day (Keener, *John*, 246–47, 360–63).

cognition, Christians should surmount such historically and socially formed forced choices.[2]

All Paul's teachings on the mind cohere, so that any one offers a window into the entire experience that he describes. Nevertheless, we may not all experience all aspects in the same ways and to the same degree. In practice, balancing various aspects of this experience may demand patience and wisdom in a messy world. The highest demand toward others is love (Rom. 13:8–10), despite our differences on secondary matters (14:1–23). We are gifted in different ways and should respect one another's gifts even where they differ from our own.

This love also must be expressed in respectful and kind treatment of those outside our community of faith, including those hostile to us (Rom. 12:14– 13:7). At the same time, Paul would want believers to always honor God's plan and God's perspective, and this priority will sometimes lead to tension when nonbelievers resent believers' commitments. For Paul, as in the Gospels, Christ offers a model of reaching people lovingly without compromising God's perspectives. Like the Gospel writers, Paul recognizes that the ensuing tension between Jesus and members of the elite eventuated in the cross. Although we must live at peace with all people insofar as it depends on us (Rom. 12:18), the peace of which Paul speaks does not provide an easy escape from the realities of tension and conflict in this life.

Divided Hearts?

Another potential application is to challenge the expectation, sometimes implicitly communicated to new believers in Christ, that they must struggle with temptation and sometimes fail. This script truncates Paul's gospel and refuses to accept its teaching of the new identity in Christ.[3] Struggle, of course, sometimes occurs;[4] but for the believer, the battle must be one of faith (i.e.,

2. For Paul's appreciation for the mind provided it was transformed by the gospel, see, e.g., Byrne, "Mind."

3. This aspect of the Platonic legacy has been appropriated into much of modern Western religion along with the West's traditional Enlightenment syncretism with deism; even many of those who allow a divine change of status so the believer's spirit may ascend to heaven someday do not expect a divinely empowered transformation in the present. Western academic approaches are also truncated by our insistence on exclusively naturalistic explanations; once rendered outside our academic purview, divine activity is consigned to the exclusively subjective realm, combining Humean antisupernaturalism with a Kantian dichotomy of knowledge.

4. Others also note that deliverance from sin's power does not necessarily mean that one never sins; see, e.g., Schreiner, *Romans*, 317; Achtemeier, *Romans*, 110. Cf. Chrys. *Hom. Rom.* 11, on 6:6 (trans. Bray, *Romans*, 158): "You are dead not in the sense that you have been obliterated but

recognizing the truth of what God has accomplished in Christ), as in Romans 6:11, and not an attempt to combat the flesh by means of the flesh (i.e., by merely human effort), as the figure in 7:7–25 attempts to do. This battle also depends on God's Spirit, as in 8:1–16. Against some other human-dependent scripts, we should thus view this battle neither as a matter of active fleshly effort without faith nor as a matter of passive resignation that God will do whatever God wills without our choice to obey. Rather, this approach acts on the faith that God himself has already acted and continuously remains active; the approach acts in confidence and credits God for the power to do so.[5]

Paul does not deny the value of effort, self-control (as a fruit of the Spirit, Gal. 5:23), and obedience; but for Paul, the obedience that comes from (or expresses) faith (Rom. 1:5) differs from the sort of self-focused obedience undertaken in order to achieve greater righteousness (cf. 9:32). Because faith is accepting God's truth, we might view it not as an effort but as simply the unresisted effect of God's now-recognized truth; the believer therefore obeys as an act of faith, acting (sometimes in defiance of feelings or past self-image) in accordance with God's declaration that in Christ one is a new creation.

Acting in defiance of false beliefs—beliefs held by most of humanity and that seem consistent with purely natural, unaided human existence—naturally feels difficult because it opposes ingrained habit. Nevertheless, for Paul such deliberate action simply expresses the nature and character of the new person in Christ. For Paul, one overcomes the character of the flesh not by addressing it on its own terms but by recognizing the greater reality of what God has done for us in Christ.

The implications for believers' transformation that Paul draws from the gospel message may be of special relevance here to scholars and other intellectuals. We are trained to solve problems with our own minds, without depending specifically and explicitly on God. Most of us thus find ourselves in a predicament similar to that of ancient philosophers, trying (at best) to transform ourselves by new beliefs without acknowledging dependence on God's Spirit. We can truly embrace Paul's message only when we recognize our need for the agency of God—in Pauline language, the Spirit. Contrary to what all of our training leads us to expect, this experience comes not through wrestling with the *idea* of the Spirit intellectually but simply by entrusting ourselves to the one who gives the Spirit.

---

in the sense that now you can live without sin." Exhortations usually presuppose the existence of the problem against which the exhortation is directed (cf., e.g., Aeschines *Tim.* 13, regarding laws).

5. Cf. Aug. *Prop. Rom.* 21 (on Rom. 4:4; trans. Bray, *Romans*, 112): "The good works which we do after we have received grace are not to be attributed to us but rather to him who has justified us by his grace."

Pastoral Psychology

Ancients who wrestled with psychological issues sometimes produced insights that remain helpful today. Thus, for example, scholars of Stoicism have pointed to valuable insights from ancient Stoic thinkers regarding cognitive therapy; Stoics worked on these issues both theoretically and by trying to put them into practice, and thus they had the experience to offer some insightful contributions.[6] Modern philosophers have also noted insights in Stoicism helpful for cognitive psychology.[7] Stoic theories also contributed to the rational therapeutic approach of Freud (though he disagreed at some significant points).[8]

It should not be surprising, then, if scholars in general and Christian thinkers in particular ask what contributions Pauline thought might make to modern discussions of Christian psychology. Paul wrote in ways relevant to his context and exploited the popular psychological language of his day. As when applying the insights of Stoics, then, readers today will better grasp Paul's message if we can translate Paul's concepts into the closest available psychological language of our day, preferably in a widely accessible (hence less technical) way.[9]

The vast array of theories of counseling and psychotherapy today[10] make such an endeavor challenging, but the endeavor is best undertaken by those who know psychology best. That is, one essential area for continuing research on this subject must be interdisciplinary.[11] Hopefully, the results of the pres-

---

6. Sorabji, *Emotion*, e.g., 1–4, 225–26 (though he notes that their contributions are relevant for cognitive issues, not for treating mental illness or moods such as depression). The community aspect of many ancient philosophic schools may also suggest a social element in philosophic moral transformation more often explicitly affirmed in modern thought than in antiquity.

7. As with the limitations of Stoicism (Sorabji, *Emotion*, 153–54), cognitive therapy when used by itself is more useful for some disorders than others (e.g., for reducing phobias but not helpful for anorexia, 155). Cf. Meichenbaum's approach of cognitive behavior modification, addressing distorted thought processes, as summarized in Patterson, *Theories*, 265.

8. Rorty, "Faces," 260–62.

9. Translating Paul's ancient intellectual language for modern Western intellectual contexts is one of a number of possible settings for which Paul's language must be translated more fully to make it more fully intelligible to those unfamiliar with the ancient Mediterranean frameworks in which he was communicating. The value of comparative work for communication is widely recognized; for example, some Chinese scholars are bridging traditional conceptual divides (using both comparisons and contrasts) between Chinese thinkers (e.g., Lu Xun and Zhu Xi) and those celebrated by Western tradition (e.g., Plato, Maimonides, or Nietzsche); see, e.g., Zhang, "Ethics of Transreading"; Ying, "Innovations." Biblical scholars have undertaken this approach most commonly with the language of the Confucian tradition (see, e.g., Yeo, *Jerusalem*, passim; Yeo, *Musing*; Yeo, "*Xin*"; Kwon, *Corinthians*).

10. See, e.g., Bongar and Beutler, *Textbook*; Corey, *Theory*; Tan, *Counseling*.

11. Many have already undertaken such studies in helpful though preliminary ways, e.g., Beck, *Psychology of Paul*; the thoroughly interdisciplinary study of Elliott, *Feelings*.

ent study can be both better articulated and further refined through insights from cognitive psychology and related disciplines. This study may offer a contribution to the dialogue, but this is a point at which biblical studies can also be informed by data from the cognitive sciences.

This is not to suggest that all approaches to psychology will have the proper conceptual vocabulary to translate all key elements of Paul's thought. Insofar as some psychological theories are exclusively naturalistic,[12] excluding divine action from their purview, we should not expect those who practice these approaches in a purely naturalistic way to recognize divine action; they cannot address by these methods what is most central to Paul's theology. At best, they may view the new identity in Christ as a useful fiction of self-esteem—a helpful placebo—rather than an eschatological creation foreign to the concepts of this age. Though concerned for nurturing and thus often helpful to the patient, such approaches function with a grid definitionally incapable of recognizing divine activity in the created world.

Nevertheless, any approach that offers empirical data and useful maps for understanding the human person will explore many issues that overlap with Paul's concerns. Approaches competent in addressing the material creation are also important for addressing the sorts of issues, such as neurological or chemical disorders, that Paul's argument was never meant to address. Theologically informed psychological and counseling approaches that already welcome genuine divine activity will be able to draw on Paul's resources more richly.

Worldviews

Part of Paul's teaching about the new mind involves our worldview or framework for thinking. For Pauline Christians, the world's values are no longer determinative; we live instead in light of the cross, which shames the world's evaluation and proclaims the absolute superiority of the divine, eternal evaluation. From the standpoint of Christ, everything takes on a new meaning (2 Cor. 5:16–17).[13] For Paul, a Christian views the present age from the vantage point

12. Technically, an approach that is purely natural may simply prescind *methodologically* from addressing theological questions for which natural methods are not designed. In this way, believers and nonbelievers can share plenty of legitimate common ground on the natural questions. For believers, though, such approaches remain incomplete, and if we are not vigilant, the habit of excluding divine factors from consideration can easily bleed into our lives and ministry to others in ways that it need not.

13. The Jewish wisdom tradition already recognized how interpretive grids shaped learning, and it invited learners to start from the foundation of faith (what we might call a "hermeneutic of trust"; see Hays, *Conversion*, 190–201); see, e.g., Ps. 111:10; Prov. 1:7; 9:10; 15:33. This

of God's promise for the eternal future age, evaluating present decisions in light of eternity. Likewise, we boast in Christ's achievement and not our own.

Such new perspectives can affect the lenses through which we view every area of life. This can include even disciplines sometimes popularly visioned as autonomous from worldviews. Science is about measurements, and a Christian who is a scientist will not measure nature differently than a scientist who is not a Christian. On the personal level, though, the scientist who is a Christian can place the object of her study in a larger context of wonder and appreciation for God's works. She can view her scientific task in the same way that seventeenth-century astronomer Johannes Kepler reportedly described his own mission, "thinking God's thoughts after him."[14] (Like Kepler, of course, one can mean that divine way of thinking in only a limited, finite sense.)

Practically Implementing the Insights

Temptations to view reality from the prism of the old perspective abound, whether from social pressure or from ways in which we have been conditioned to respond to various internal and external triggers. The battle is in a sense learning to accept that Christ has already won, to recognize temptations as on some level falsehoods rather than true markers of our identity.[15] This does not mean that we should deny that temptations confront us and are sometimes rooted in past choices or our biology; rather, it means that we are called to share God's perspective on our justification. We must stand firm in defining our *core* identity in terms of Christ rather than in terms of those past choices, experiences, or genetics. Yes, the temptations may be deeply rooted in our past and even in our present neurochemistry, but believers in Christ are defined first and foremost by our identity and destiny in Christ. We must thus continue to reaffirm and thus learn to live by the truth that we already embraced in conversion: Christ alone is our righteousness, and Christ is enough.

---

approach remains needed among many Christian interpreters in my own discipline of biblical studies. See, e.g., comments in Wong, "Loss."

14. On Kepler's faith, see, e.g., Koestler, "Kepler," 49–50; Frankenberry, *Faith*, 35–38, 47–53; cf. Gingerich, "Scientist," 28; Burtt, *Foundations*, 60–61.

15. Ancient Judaism viewed Satan as both tempter (e.g., 1 Chron. 21:1; CD 12.2; 1QS 10.21; 4Q174 frg. 1 2.i.9; 4Q225 frg. 2, col. 1.9–10; 11Q5 19.15; *Jub.* 10:8, 11; 17:16; *T. Reub.* 4:11; *T. Jos.* 7:4; *T. Iss.* 7:7; *T. Ash.* 3:2; 3 *Bar.* 9:7; *b. B. Bat.* 16a; *b. Qid.* 81a; *y. Shab.* 1:3, §5; *Gen. Rab.* 70:8; *Exod. Rab.* 19:2; 41:7; 1 Thess. 3:5) and deceiver (e.g., CD 4.15–16; *T. Benj.* 6:1; *T. Dan* 3:6; *T. Levi* 3:3; *T. Jud.* 25:3; *T. Job* 3:3/4; 3:6/5; 26:6/7; 27:1; Eph. 6:11; 2 Thess. 2:9; Rev. 12:9; 20:8), as well as accuser (Job 1:6–2:7; Zech. 3:1–2; *Jub.* 1:20; 48:15, 18; 3 *En.* 14:2; 26:12; *Gen. Rab.* 38:7; 57:4; 84:2; *Exod. Rab.* 18:5; 21:7; 31:2; 43:1; *Lev. Rab.* 21:10; *Eccl. Rab.* 3:2, §2; Rev. 12:10).

The difference between this recognition and some other traditional Protestant articulations of Christ's righteousness is that it invites us to follow through with the implications of justification.[16] Paul's Letter to the Romans does not end with his treatment of justification and the like in Romans 3:21–5:11; it goes on to talk about spiritual union with Christ and, in chapters 12–14, Christian ethics. The heart of Paul's vision in those later chapters is the law of love (13:8–10), the law already written in believers' hearts (8:2). Insofar as we genuinely believe our core identity to be transformed, and understand from Paul's concrete examples what that transformation should look like, our deliberate choices will reflect that core belief.

Embracing as truth what we profess to believe seems fairly straightforward, but for many, such faith involves a battle of relearning.[17] Indulging passions in given ways accustoms us to react to them accordingly; whereas some drugs create direct chemical addiction, less directly our own behaviors produce chemical responses to which the brain in turn responds. The wiring of our brain and neurochemistry are a divine gift: when we consistently make intelligent choices, our brains adjust to the pattern so that we do not have to pause to consider the choice so deliberately each time.

Unfortunately, our negative choices also wire our brains for particular neurochemical responses, so that we become accustomed to respond to stimuli in such detrimental ways automatically. In such cases, walking by the Spirit rather than by the flesh requires a continuing, deliberate rethinking and retuning, with many determined decisions to believe God's truth about our identity, until our brain is rewired enough that the new way becomes the more prevalent way. Even so, the old memories and patterns may resurface, especially under stress, whether in dreams or while awake, and therefore continued vigilance is important. Naturally, this will be harder for some people in some areas than for others.[18] Stressors cannot all be avoided (and sometimes should be confronted), but thinking in new ways should become easier when new patterns

16. In contrast to some popular Protestantism, many early Reformers already recognized the reality of spiritual transformation (e.g., Luther, *Second Lectures on Galatians*, on Gal. 2:20; Calvin, *Commentary on Galatians* 2:20, in Bray, *Galatians, Ephesians*, 79–81 [summary on 70]; see Westerholm, *Justification*, 48; McCormack, "Faith," 171; Barclay, *Gift*, 124).

17. Cognition includes affective as well as rational elements; feelings and moods affect thinking and are affected by it as well. Nevertheless, reason remains vital, since it responds most fully to perceived reality. For Christians, reason should embrace increasingly fully the reality we already profess to believe in Christ.

18. Since this is a postscript, I may note that I was ADHD (diagnosed already in an era when it was diagnosed only in more extreme cases). I thus seem to be neurologically primed for creative interdisciplinary work but find it difficult to concentrate on one thing except when in a mode of hyperfocus. This does give me some cognitive challenges for both academic and ordinary life, as well as sympathy for others who struggle with focus and with reframing thinking.

become more habitual and one's sense of personal identity in Christ is re-inforced through personal faith or through the affirmations of one's faith community.[19]

The key issue, however, is that this is a battle of faith based on God's truth about Christ and therefore about us who are in him, not simply an abstract struggle among components of our identity. Our thinking does not create the new reality, subjecting the genuineness of our identity in Christ to the starts and bumps of the renewing of our minds; instead, it recognizes the new reality already inaugurated in Christ, the actual beginning of the new creation. We may therefore fight this battle by embracing Christ's accomplished victory, rather than approaching it with an expectation of defeat. In fact, it is a battle that can be fought at the point of temptation, which is not itself sin: that is, in principle a believer need not succumb to deliberate sin. Or to put it differently, when temptation comes, we can develop a confidence in Christ's victory in us that is greater than our confidence in the temptation to redefine our identity.

When we do fail, it feels easy (at least for me) to become discouraged and succumb to the repeated cycle of expected further failure; but that is why we must ground our identity in Christ's finished work and in the vision of our eschatological destiny in him, not in our past performance. It is a matter not merely of self-confidence but of confidence in the Lord's good work in us. Righteousness is Christ's image in us just as sin is the devil's (John 8:31–47; 1 John 3:8–10).

Of course, we recognize that this power is Christ's and not our own, and God's forgiveness in him means that we have no reason to fear confessing sin. That Christ provides forgiveness for sin, however, is no more a reason to accept unnecessary defeats in the battle than the fact that an ideal spouse or friend forgives is a reason to indulge in insulting them. Many Christians today say, apparently glibly, that everybody sins, so long as these Christians define the sin as being merely an attitude of the heart rather than as something visibly egregious or scandalous. If the temptation is to become an ax murderer, however, we suddenly recognize that temptation must be overcome completely. Why wait until we face publicly "dangerous" temptations (if we ever do) to learn the lesson of faith?

Embracing Christ's completed deliverance does not mean that we neglect maturation in it; rather, it means that we embrace in our lives God's own gift to us. Similarly, marriage initiates a new relationship, but romance should not

19. I am grateful to Professor Virginia Holeman for bringing the points in this last sentence to my attention (personal correspondence, November 16, 2014).

end there. My wedding, for example, did not terminate my continuing desire for my wife. At the same time, romance would be difficult if one continually questioned whether the marriage was genuinely in effect. A spouse who continually requests marriage after experiencing the wedding either experiences severe memory impairment or displays severe lack of trust. The way forward in Christ is to live actively for God, *based on* the relationship God has already initiated with us in Christ.[20]

From an academic standpoint, Paul's Christocentric adaptation of cognitive motifs present in ancient intellectual thought is intriguing. For Christians, it may also offer a model for how we can integrate and adapt insights from cognitive studies today in a Christocentric way. Most of all, those who hear divine wisdom in Paul's counsel will want to appropriate his insights for our lives. In Christ, old things have passed, and a new order has broken into history; we are part of this new order and should bring this perspective to how we understand reality. Some things have not yet changed; others, however, can never be the same again.

20. One may approach God's presence and favor in Christ in the same way, recognizing them by faith. Cf. Laurent, *Practice*; Keener, *Gift*, 27–30; in greater exegetical detail, Keener, *John*, 2:932–39, 972–73, 976.

APPENDIX A

The Soul in Ancient Mediterranean Thought

Ancient thought varied as to the nature of the person, whether the soul was an entity distinct from the body, whether it was material, and whether it was eternal. In earlier times Jewish people sometimes distinguished the material and immaterial aspects of a person, though often to emphasize the whole person that they composed. Greek thinkers tended to distinguish soul and body more strongly, though not all viewed the soul as immaterial in the modern sense.[1] Both Stoics and Platonists were major players in these discussions in the first centuries of the Christian era. Although Stoicism was dominant in first-century Greece, Platonism prevailed in subsequent centuries and influenced subsequent Christian theology.[2]

Some Gentile thinkers regarded the soul as immortal, or at least as surviving the body. Some Jewish thinkers also adopted this approach, starting especially in the Mediterranean Diaspora, and it was among the range of approaches accepted by Diaspora Jews in Paul's day.

1. For one concise survey of ancient thought on soul, see Frede, "Soul" (on Plato, see 673–74; on Aristotle and Stoics, see 674); on ancient treatises on the soul, see briefly Dillon and Finamore, "Preface," ix–x; on Plato and the soul, at length, see Merlan, *Platonism*, 8–29; and (as cited in Laws, *James*, 59n1) Guthrie, *Plato*, 346–47, 421–25, 476–78. For pre-Platonic Greek thought, cf. Croce, "Concepto"; for contrast with the Hebraic approach, Isaacs, *Spirit*, 15.

2. With, e.g., Pelikan, *Acts*, 192.

The Soul as a Distinct Entity

Among Gentiles, people often spoke loosely of the soul and body together as the entire person,[3] and some thinkers treated this as the normal approach;[4] however, other thinkers viewed only the soul as the real person.[5] Both popular language[6] and philosophic discourse[7] usually distinguished soul and body. Thinkers in the Platonic tradition emphasized this distinction most,[8] but even Stoics distinguished the soul from the body and regarded the soul as the superior part.[9] So did Skeptics, although they regarded most matters as merely convention.[10] For Platonists and some others, bodies encased souls as containers, sheaths, stalks, or similar container analogies.[11] Plato saw the soul imprisoned in the body "like an oyster in its shell."[12]

Although many thinkers distinguished the soul from matter, not all did so. Aristotle envisioned the incorporeal soul as merely providing "form" or structure to the matter of the body.[13] Both Stoics, the most popular philosophic school in this period, and Epicureans were materialists.[14] For Epicureans,

3. Perhaps Livy 28.15.6; 28.19.13; Philost. *Hrk.* 27.10. Seneca's soul is part of his person in Sen. *Y. Ep. Lucil.* 113.5.

4. Mus. Ruf. 6, p. 54.3–4; Marc. Aur. 5.13; 6.32; for animals, see Hierocles *Ethics* 4.39–40.

5. Plato *Phaedo* 115D; Epict. *Diatr.* 1.1.24; 1.25.21; 3.13.17; Diog. Laert. 3.63 (on Plato); Porph. *Marc.* 8.147–50; 32.485–89; cf. Cic. *Resp.* 6.24.26; *Tusc.* 1.22.52.

6. E.g., *Rhet. Alex.* pref. 1421a.17–18; Jos. *Ant.* 18.282; Fronto *Nep. am.* 2.8; Philost. *Ep.* 8.(46); *Gr. Anth.* 7.109.

7. Cic. *Tusc.* 3.3.5; 3.10.22; 4.13.28; Philost. *Vit. Apoll.* 8.5. For Iamblichus, the soul mediates between intellect and body (Finamore and Dillon, "Introduction," 15).

8. E.g., Plut. *Plat. Q.* 3.1, *Mor.* 1002B; *Table* 5.intro, *Mor.* 672F–673A; *Pleas. L.* 14, *Mor.* 1096E (protesting detractors); *Aff. Soul, Mor.* 500B–502A passim; Max. Tyre *Or.* 33.7–8; Diog. Laert. 3.63 (on Plato); Porph. *Marc.* 9.154–58.

9. Cic. *Fin.* 3.22.75; Mus. Ruf. 6, p. 54.4–6; Arius Did. 2.7.7b, p. 46.11–18. For that matter, even Aristotle attributed virtue to the soul rather than to the body (Arist. *N.E.* 1.12.6, 1102a).

10. Sext. Emp. *Pyr.* 1.79.

11. See, e.g., Plut. *Isis* 5, *Mor.* 353A; Porph. *Marc.* 32.485–93; Iambl. *Soul* 6.34, §382; beyond Platonists, e.g., Cic. *Tusc.* 1.22.52; Dio Chrys. (Favorinus) *Or.* 37.45. Cf. even the Stoic Marc. Aur. 3.7 (trans. Haines, LCL, 57): "his soul overlaid with his body."

12. Plato *Phaedr.* 250C; quoted approvingly in Plut. *Exile* 17, *Mor.* 607D (trans. Perrin, LCL, 7:569–71).

13. Iambl. *Soul* 1.3, §363; Martin, *Body*, 7–8. Though incorporeal, it remained matter as fire did (Martin, *Body*, 8). Stoics could also divide the person according to "causal" and "material" (Marc. Aur. 5.13).

14. Ramelli, *Hierocles*, 44n24; for Stoics, see Iambl. *Soul* 2.10, §367. Stoics distinguished soul from body, unlike Aristotelians, but normally treated it as material, unlike Platonists (Dillon and Finamore, "Preface," x). Stoics envisioned πνεῦμα as material (see Keener, *Acts*, 1:530–31, and sources cited there, e.g., Long, *Philosophy*, 155–58, 171; Lake, "Spirit," 103; see Klauck, *Context*, 353–54; Scott, *Spirit*, 52–53; cf. Büchsel, *Geist*, 45–49, esp. 47; Schweizer, *Spirit*, 29; Nolan, "Stoic Gunk"; Vogt, "Brutes"), and Engberg-Pedersen therefore suggests this use for Paul

the body affects the soul, and the soul dies when the body dies.[15] For many Stoics, the soul in the body was a particular case of universal divine Reason permeating and structuring matter.[16] Rather than viewing the body as the soul's container, Stoics considered the soul to be intermingled throughout the body.[17] The body and the soul cannot but affect each other.[18] Whereas their relationship could mean pain at their separation on the Stoic view, an Epicurean could argue that the soul could leave easily through the body's many pores.[19]

Even Middle Platonists (those following the form of Platonism dominant in this period) were not always fully Cartesian dualists. Sometimes they associated the rational soul with fire, so that the soul was a substance, merely lighter and purer than the body.[20]

The Soul's Afterlife

In this period some people continued to embrace older mythical traditions of an afterlife[21] and religiously based hopes in some mysteries for not only earthly blessedness but also a blessed afterlife.[22] Yet many thinkers critiqued

---

(Engberg-Pedersen, "Spirit"; Engberg-Pedersen, *Cosmology*), but Paul usually refers to God's Spirit, which would be no more material than is God. For some responses to Engberg-Pedersen on this point, see, e.g., Levison, "*Stoa Poecile*"; Barclay, "Stoic Physics."

15. Lucret. *Nat.* 3.417–977 (esp. 417–829).

16. Long, "Soul"; Long, *Philosophy*, 171 (citing Diog. Laert. 7.156); cf. Martin, *Body*, 21; Stowers, "Self-Mastery," 527–28.

17. Hierocles *Ethics* 4.4–6, 44–46.

18. Hierocles *Ethics* 4.11–14.

19. Philod. *Death* 7.6–20; see Henry, "Introduction," xix. Others also regarded the soul as a fine substance (cf. Lucret. *Nat.* 3.370–95; Iambl. *Soul* 1.2, §363; 1.9, §366).

20. Martin, *Body*, 13; Stowers, "Self-Mastery," 527. Platonists envisioned both "rational and emotive components in the soul, whereas a primary feature of Zeno's new Stoicism was its return to the purely rational Socratic soul" (Sedley, "Debate," 152).

21. In traditional mythology, see Hom. *Od.* 11.204–24, 487–91 (though after Homer, hopes moved toward a celestial afterlife; Klauck, *Context*, 75; Bremmer, "Hades"); Burkert, *Religion*, 194–99; Lieven, Johnston, and Käppel, "Underworld." Virgil's depiction of the underworld was among the most influential (Kaufmann, "Underworld"); for the Roman conception of the murky underworld, see Borca, "Exploration." For the afterlife in Orphism, see Diog. Laert. 6.1.4; Guthrie, *Orpheus*, 148–93, 269 (cf. perhaps Bijovsky, "Allegory"; Dionysiac religion in Nock, "Developments," 508–9; Nilsson, *Dionysiac Mysteries*, 116–32, though Nilsson reconstructs too much ideology from artwork).

22. Nock, *Conversion*, 102–5; Burkert, *Mystery Cults*, 21–27. See, e.g., Apul. *Metam.* 11.6 (though in the Isis cult generally, see Wagner, *Baptism*, 112); for the Eleusinian mysteries, see, e.g., Isoc. *Paneg.* 28; discussion in Grant, *Hellenism*, 12; Burkert, *Mystery Cults*, 21; Mylonas, *Eleusis*, 268–69; Wagner, *Baptism*, 87; Klauck, *Context*, 117; Godwin, *Mystery Religions*, 52; for the Bacchic cult, Burkert, *Religion*, 293–95; Burkert, *Mystery Cults*, 21–22.

these ideas,[23] and even popular thought on the afterlife was often inconsistent.[24] Indeed, no more than 10 percent of funerary inscriptions explicitly affirm an afterlife, and, more tellingly, many lament nonexistence.[25]

Among philosophic schools, the majority of thinkers were unwilling to profess agnosticism regarding the afterlife.[26] Like some others,[27] Epicureans rejected the soul's immortality,[28] as we would expect. Both medical writers and many philosophers regarded the soul as mortal.[29]

Some other thinkers, however, regarded the soul as immortal;[30] again, this was an important feature of Platonist thought, although it was not limited to Platonists.[31] One curious argument for the soul's eternality was Plato's insistence on its preexistence, verified by innate knowledge.[32] (Naturally, nei-

23. E.g., Epict. *Diatr.* 3.13.15. Note Diogenes the Cynic against the afterlife promises of the mysteries in Diog. Laert. 6.2.39. For some satires on the mythical afterlife, see Lucian *Z. Cat.* 17–18; *Dial. D.* 402–3 (11/16, *Diogenes and Heracles* 1–4); 405 (11/16, *Diogenes and Heracles* 5); ghost stories in *Lover of Lies* 29–33.

24. See the criticism in Philod. *Death* 28.5–13; conflicting thoughts also are noted in Warden, "Scenes."

25. Klauck, *Context*, 80; see, further, Thomas, "Dead," 288. Nevertheless, many expressions of pessimism when bitter about death could coexist with some hope for afterlife, just as they do today; in antiquity, however, they were frequent enough to be formulaic.

26. Contrast the epistemic humility in Confuc. *Anal.* 206 (11.11). Agnosticism about the afterlife appears among thinkers portrayed in Lucian *Dem.* 43; *Z. Cat.* 17. Fitch ("Introduction," 23) suggests that Seneca took an agnostic position; but the examples in Seneca's tragedies may simply follow the genre (and even here, note the afterlife traditions in Sen. Y. *Herc. fur.* 743–44, 749–59).

27. Pliny E. *N.H.* 7.55.188–90.

28. Epicurus *Let. Men.* 125; Lucret. *Nat.* 3 (see Warren, "Lucretius"; O'Keefe, "Lucretius"); Philod. *Death* 1; Diog. Laert. 10.124; Hippol. *Ref.* 1.19; Sorabji, *Emotion*, 248. Cf. also the Cynic Diogenes: death cannot be an evil if one who is dead is unaware of it (Diog. Laert. 6.2.68). Ancient thinkers knew the range of views (as in Iambl. *Soul* 7.36, §383).

29. See the thorough discussion in Weissenrieder, "Leitfaden."

30. E.g., Xen. *Cyr.* 8.7.17–21 (the speaker, Cyrus, is a reliable character); Arist. *Soul* 1.4, 408b; Cic. *Tusc.* 1.8.18–24; 1.14.31; *Resp.* 6.24.26; *Senect.* 20.78; Dion. Hal. *Ant. rom.* 8.62.1; (Ps.-)Dion. *Epideictic* 6.283; Apul. *De deo Socr.* 126–27; Plot. *Enn.* 4.7.12; Libanius *Encom.* 6.10. Cf. perhaps even Lucian *Dem.* 43.

31. Plato *Meno* 81B (citing also Pindar *Thren.* frg. 133; cf. Pindar *Thren.* 7, frg. 131b, in Plut. *Apoll.* 35.120C); *Rep.* 10.611B; *Phaedo* 64DE; 105–7; *Phaedr.* 245C; Plut. *Div. V.* 17, *Mor.* 560B (for Plutarch on the postmortem soul returning to the moon and the mind to the sun, see Buffière, "Séléné"); Max. Tyre *Or.* 10.2, 5; 41.5; Iambl. *Soul* 5.25, §377; *Letter* 8, frg. 2 (Stob. *Anth.* 2.8.43); frg. 7 (Stob. *Anth.* 2.8.48); *Testimonium* 2 (in Olympiodorus *In Gorg.* 46.9.20–28 [ed. Westerink]); Plato in Hippol. *Ref.* 1.17; satirized in Lucian *Fly* 7; see discussion in Lodge, *Ethics*, 394–409; Patterson, *Plato on Immortality*. For the myth of Er (Plato *Rep.* 10.614B ff.), see, e.g., Dräger, "Er."

32. Plato *Meno* 81BD; *Phaedo* 75CD. For souls' preexistence, see, e.g., Iambl. *Pyth. Life* 14.63; Philo in Dillon, *Middle Platonists*, 177; cf. Epict. *Diatr.* 2.1.17; Wis. 8:19–20; *3 En.* 43:3; *b. Hag.* 12b; *Ger. Rab.* 8:7; 24:4; *Exod. Rab.* 28:6; Schechter, *Aspects*, 24; but contrast with more nuance Urbach, *Sages*, 1:234, 237–38; on innate tendencies, e.g., Cic. *Top.* 7.31;

ther evolutionary development of instincts nor direct divine design of these human tendencies—nor, for that matter, any combination thereof—was an important part of his context.) On this approach, learning was thus merely recollection.[33] Embracing an idea that also appears in Plato, Pythagoreans affirmed immortality in the form of reincarnation, that is, changing bodies.[34] (Indeed, Greeks believed that some other cultures affirmed the soul's immortality, including Egyptians,[35] Mesopotamians,[36] and Persians.)[37]

Plato admittedly deemed union with the body no worse than separation from it.[38] Still, learning to separate the soul from the body in the present better prepared one for one's disembodied future.[39] Purified souls could be freed from the body;[40] Plato encouraged purifying oneself in advance to be ready for separation from the body.[41]

Plato complained that pleasures nailed the soul to the body;[42] he wanted philosophy to free the soul from attention to the body.[43] Many thinkers

---

Mus. Ruf. 2, p. 38.12–14; Max. Tyre *Or.* 21.7–8; Iambl. *Letter* 13, frg. 1.1–4 (Stob. *Anth.* 2.2.6); Porph. *Marc.* 26.419–20. For the tendency toward worship as innate, see, e.g., Cic. *Inv.* 2.22.65; 2.53.161; Dio Chrys. *Or.* 12.27; Iambl. *Myst.* 1.3; toward ethics, cf. Jackson-McCabe, "Preconceptions."

33. Plato *Phaedo* 75CD; later, cf. Max. Tyre *Or.* 10.6; Porph. *Marc.* 10.185–86. Because Pythagoreans taught reincarnation (Lucian *Phil. Sale* 5), they viewed learning as merely recollection (*Phil. Sale* 3).

34. Diod. Sic. 10.6.1; Max. Tyre *Or.* 10.2; Philost. *Vit. Apoll.* 6.22; 8.31; *Ep. Apoll.* 58; Diog. Laert. 8.1.14; 8.5.83 (Pythagoras); Iambl. *Pyth. Life* 18.85; 32.219; Symm. *Ep.* 1.4.2; Hippol. *Ref.* 1.2–3; cf. Croy, "Neo-Pythagoreanism," 739. For reincarnation views, see, further, Plato *Meno* 81BC; Hdt. 2.123; Val. Flacc. 3.383–96 (for the evil only); Virg. *Aen.* 6.747–51; Sil. It. 13.558–59; Athen. *Deipn.* 15.679A; cf. Sen. Y. *Ep. Lucil.* 108.20; Pythagorean-Orphic ideas in Thom, "*Akousmata*," 105; Epimenides and Pythagoras in Blackburn, "ΑΝΔΡΕΣ," 191.

35. Hdt. 2.123. Cf. *Book of Dead*, Spell 20, parts T-1 & 2; Spell 30, part P-1; Spell 31a, part P-1; Spell 35a, part P-1; Spell 79, part P-1; Spell 177, part P-1; see also Lieven in Lieven, Johnston, and Käppel, "Underworld," 105–6. Cf. the Greek Elysian Fields (e.g., Statius *Silv.* 5.1.192–93) with Egyptian "field of reeds" (mentioned, e.g., in Currid, *Egypt*, 98). Egyptian and Greek afterlife ideas mingled on tombs in Roman Alexandria (Venit, "Tomb").

36. Cf. *ANET* 32–34; Lieven in Lieven, Johnston, and Käppel, "Underworld," 104–5 (similar to Greek mythology).

37. See Olmstead, *Persian Empire*, 40, 100–101. Cf. in Mithraism, in *PGM* 4.646–48, 748–49 (cf. 719–23).

38. Plato *Laws* 8.828D. Nevertheless, one too willing to die might be compared with a philosopher (Cic. *Marcell.* 8.25).

39. Plato *Phaedo* 80DE; Diogenes *Ep.* 39; Iambl. *Pyth. Life* 32.228; Porph. *Marc.* 32.494–95. Cf. living justly as a prerequisite for immortality in Diog. Laert. 6.1.5 (Antisthenes).

40. Iambl. *Soul* 8.43, §456; on the descent of some souls for purification, see 6.29, §380.

41. Plato *Phaedo* 67C.

42. Plato *Phaedo* 83CD; followed also by Proclus *Poet.* 6.1, K121.14–15; Iambl. *Letter* 3, frg. 2 (Stob. *Anth.* 3.5.45); *Pyth. Life* 32.228.

43. Plato *Phaedo* 83A.

viewed the body as a prison or chains for the soul,[44] or even as a tomb.[45] On this view, death was a release;[46] one sophist felt that at death he would be freed from his body, "an uncomfortable companion."[47] Consistent with such an approach, some thinkers even denigrated the body.[48] A philosopher could deliberately neglect his body;[49] a later Neoplatonist even loathed his body and starved himself.[50] It was said that one of Plato's pupils, after reading Plato's *On the Soul*, killed himself.[51] Yet as Cicero notes, even Pythagoras and Plato, "though they praise death, forbid us to fly from life," a violation

44. Plato *Phaedr.* 250C (cf. also *Gorg.* 493E; *Phaedo* 82E); Cic. *Resp.* 6.14.14; 6.15.15; *Tusc.* 1.31.75; Sen. Y. *Dial.* 11.9.3; 12.11.7; *Ben.* 3.20.1–2 (on Seneca, cf. Sevenster, *Seneca*, 82–83); Epict. *Diatr.* 1.1.9; 1.9.11–12; Dio Chrys. *Or.* 30.10–24 (recounting one view, not the speaker's own); Heracl. *Ep.* 5; Max. Tyre *Or.* 7.5; 36.4; Philost. *Vit. Apoll.* 7.26; *Gnom. Vat.* 464 (Pythagoras, in Malherbe, *Moral Exhortation*, 110); Porph. *Marc.* 33.506–7; Philo *Alleg. Interp.* 3.21; *Drunkenness* 101; *Heir* 85 (cf. vices in 109); *Dreams* 1.138–39 (on Philo, see, further, Hagner, "Vision," 85); *Diogn.* 6.7; cf. harsh labors in Marc. Aur. 6.28.

45. Epict. *Diatr.* frg. 26 (cf. 1.1; 1.8–9; 1.9.11–12, 16; 3.13.17; 4.7.15); Marc. Aur. 4.41 (cf. 3.7; 4.5; 6.28; 9.3); Philo *Dreams* 1.138–39; Phrygian sectarians in Hippol. *Ref.* 5.3; cf. Plut. *Isis* 28, *Mor.* 362B. Scholars often note this idea; e.g., Burkitt, *Church and Gnosis*, 33–35; Bornkamm, *Paul*, 130; Barclay, "Themes," 115; Patterson, *Plato on Immortality*, 20–21. The exact wordplay, σῶμα-σῆμα, the body as a tomb, Plato's Socrates attributes to Orphics in Plato *Cratyl.* 400BC; in earlier Orphism, Guthrie, *Orpheus*, 156–58.

46. E.g., Epict. *Diatr.* 1.9.16; Max. Tyre *Or.* 7.5; 10.3; Marc. Aur. 6.28; 11.3; Philost. *Hrk.* 7.3.

47. Arrian *Alex.* 7.2.4.

48. See Guthrie, *Orpheus*, 154 (on Orphics); Sevenster, *Seneca*, 69 (on Seneca; contrasting Paul on 75).

49. Val. Max. 8.7.ext.5, on Carneades; cf. *Diogn.* 6.9. For many philosophers' simple garb and minimal grooming, see Dio Chrys. *Or.* 32.22; 34.2; 72.2, 5; Keener, *Acts*, 2:2140–41; esp. for Cynics, e.g., Juv. *Sat.* 13.121–22; Crates *Ep.* 18, 30; Aul. Gel. 9.2.4–5; Lucian *Dem.* 48; *Runaways* 14, 20, 27; *Peregr.* 15, 24, 36; *Indictment* 6; *Phil. Sale* 9; *Icar.* 31; *Cynic* 4, 19–20. For Cynics' lack of hygiene, see, e.g., Alciph. *Farm.* 38 (Euthydicus to Philiscus), 3.40, ¶2; Lucian *Icar.* 31. On philosophers with long hair, see Dio Chrys. *Or.* 12.15; 35.2; *Encomium on Hair*; Lucian *Phil. Sale* 2; *Peregr.* 15; *Cynic* 17, 19; Philost. *Vit. Apoll.* 7.36; Diog. Laert. 1.109; Iambl. *Pyth. Life* 2.11; 6.31; with long beards, see Epict. *Diatr.* 2.23.21; Plut. *Isis* 3, *Mor.* 352C; Artem. *Oneir.* 1.30; Aul. Gel. 9.2.4–5; Lucian *Runaways* 27; *Icar.* 29; *Fisherman* 42; *Dem.* 13; *Lover of Lies* 5; *Indictment* 11; *Hermot.* 18, 86; *Eunuch* 9; Philost. *Ep. Apoll.* 3, 70; with both, Epict. *Diatr.* 4.8.12; 8.15; Dio Chrys. *Or.* 36.17; 47.25; 72.2; Lucian *Dial. D.* 371–72 (20/10, *Charon and Hermes* 9); Philost. *Vit. Apoll.* 7.34. In contrast to Cynics, Stoics, though bearded, wore their hair short (Lucian *Runaways* 27; *Hermot.* 18).

50. Eunapius *Lives* 456 (though contrast Porph. *Plot.* 11.113). A Neoplatonist such as Plotinus could regard bodily existence as an evil (Plot. *Enn.* 1.7.3.20–21).

51. Callim. *Epig.* 25. Reportedly, Cleombrotus, learning from Plato's work that the soul was merely imprisoned in the body, threw himself off a high wall to his death (Cic. *Scaur.* 3.4, regarding this tale as false). Cato read Plato's treatise on the soul before attempting suicide (Appian *C.W.* 2.14.98–99; but cf. Zadorojnyi, "Cato's Suicide"). Plato himself did not support suicide (Plato *Phaedo* 62C; cf. Novak, *Suicide and Morality*; Taran, "Plato").

of nature.[52] Those with a more holistic perspective more fully avoided denigration of the body.[53]

Technically, early and middle Stoics, who expected everything to be resolved back into the primeval fire,[54] did not accept the individual soul's eternality (though many did accept a period of afterlife),[55] yet a minority apparently did embrace a form of immortality of the soul.[56] Others felt that the soul would float around for a time before being resolved back into fire.[57] Seneca probably represents a moderate Stoic perspective in this period: wise souls persist beyond death, but even they revert to former elements when the universe is destroyed to be remade.[58]

Many intellectuals viewed the soul as intrinsically good[59] or even divine[60] and heavenly.[61] Some urged that the mind must remain tranquil, like the highest heavens.[62] The human mind is shared with the gods, whereas the body is shared with

52. Cic. *Scaur.* 4.5 (cf. Plato *Phaedo* 61C). Cf. the duty of remaining alive in Cic. *Resp.* 6.15.15; Sen. Y. *Ep. Lucil.* 58.36. For ancient philosophic views on suicide, see, e.g., Cercidas frg. 1; Cic. *Fin.* 3.18.60; Sen. Y. *Ep. Lucil.* 70.4, 6, 14–16, 20–21; 77.15; Epict. *Diatr.* 1.2.1–3; 1.9.10–17, 20; 1.25.21; 2.1.19; 3.8.6; 3.13.14; Marc. Aur. 3.1; 8.47; Arius Did. 2.7.11m, p. 90.30–34; p. 92.1–3; Max. Tyre *Or.* 7.5; Diog. Laert. 7.4.167; 7.5.176; Lucian *Oct.* 19; *Dem.* 65; *Peregr.* 1–2; *Fisherman* 2; *Runaways* 1–2; *True Story* 2.21; *Book-Coll.* 14; Cooper, "Philosophers"; Wyllie, "Views"; Griffin, "Philosophy"; Klauck, *Context*, 363–65; Kerferd, "Reason"; Nietmann, "Seneca"; Noyes, "Seneca"; Xenakis, "Suicide Therapy"; Rist, "Seneca and Orthodoxy"; Ramelli, *Hierocles*, 106; Sorabji, *Emotion*, 172–73, 214–15; further discussion in Keener, *Acts*, 3:2503–5.

53. Mus. Ruf. 6, p. 54.4–6, 10–11; Hierocles *Marr.* (Stob. *Anth.* 4.79.53); on a popular level, cf. Sall. *Catil.* 1.7. Some went much further and justified hedonism; see the discussion in Winter, *Left Corinth*, 78.

54. See, e.g., Sen. Y. *Ben.* 4.8.1; Epict. *Diatr.* 3.13.4; Plut. *Comm. Conc.* 31, *Mor.* 1075B; Lucian *Phil. Sale* 14; Marc. Aur. 4.46; Diog. Laert. 9.1.7; cf. further Adams, *Stars*, 116–18.

55. See, e.g., Bels, "Survie."

56. Posidonius in Ju, "Immortality"; cf. the soul as eternal (*aeternus*) in Sen. Y. *Dial.* 12.11.7; *Ep. Lucil.* 57.9.

57. Marc. Aur. 4.21. For souls remaining in the air rather than in the netherworld, see Klauck, *Context*, 358.

58. Sen. Y. *Dial.* 6.26.7 (inconsistent with some of his teaching elsewhere); cf. also Cleanthes and Chrysippus in Klauck, *Context*, 358; for other Stoics, see Haines, "Introduction," xxvi. They could be reformed cyclically, but not all Stoics were convinced that reconstituted persons of the next cycle would be the same person anyway (Sorabji, *Emotion*, 243). Unlike God, people were mortal (Sen. Y. *Ep. Lucil.* 124.14; but cf. 124.23).

59. E.g., Epict. *Diatr.* 3.3.4; 4.11.5; Max. Tyre *Or.* 34.2 (cf. also 10.6); in Jewish works, *Let. Aris.* 236. Contrast the usage of the term in Sir. 6:2, 4; 18:30–31.

60. E.g., Cic. *Tusc.* 5.25.70; Sen. Y. *Ep. Lucil.* 78.10; *Nat. Q.* 1.pref.14; Max. Tyre *Or.* 33.7; Men. Rhet. 2.9, 414.21–22, 26; Philo *Heir* 64; *Creation* 135; see, further, Caird, *Age*, 102, and sources cited there. Deities have souls but not bodies (Max. Tyre *Or.* 41.5; Apul. *De deo Socr.* 123).

61. Plato *Phaedr.* 248AB; Virg. *Aen.* 6.728–34; Sen. Y. *Ep. Lucil.* 120.15; in Jewish circles, see Philo *Heir* 64 (cf. *Spec. Laws* 3.2); *Sipre Deut.* 306.28.2; *Gen. Rab.* 8:11. In earlier Orphic circles, cf. the gold funerary plates in Grant, *Religions*, 108. Even Epicureans, who denied an afterlife, acknowledged a person's heavenly elements (Lucret. *Nat.* 2.991–1006).

62. Sen. Y. *Dial.* 5.6.1.

animals;[63] in some Jewish sources the mind is angelic and the body like animals.[64] The pure soul could ascend back to the heavens from which it came;[65] this thought also fed into some people's notion of astral immortality on a more popular level, at least for good souls.[66] Compare, for example, the story of Scipio's dream: humanity "has been given a soul out of those eternal fires which you call stars and planets."[67] Or the thinking of Valerius Flaccus: humans were originally fire, stars in heaven; they became mortals, but they eventually return to heaven.[68]

Jewish Thinkers regarding Soul and Body

Jewish views and especially language about the soul varied in Paul's era. Most scholars believe that the ancient Israelites were monistic or holistic; one might distinguish the breath of life from the body, but there was little emphasis on partitioning the human person.[69] Many argue that this holistic approach persisted in early Judaism.[70] Although this observation appears true for much of Palestinian Judaism, it was not true for all Jews, whether in Judea or, particularly, in the Mediterranean Diaspora.[71]

63. E.g., Sall. *Catil.* 1.2; Epict. *Diatr.* 1.3.3; Max. Tyre *Or.* 33.7. Cf. the complementary delineation of attributes in Max. Tyre *Or.* 9.1–2. On some views, animals also had souls (Arist. *Pol.* 1.2.10, 1254a; Pythagoras in Diog. Laert. 8.1.28; Plot. *Enn.* 4.7.14).

64. *Sipre Deut.* 306.28.2.

65. Plato *Phaedr.* 248E–249A; Cercidas frg. 1 (on a Cynic who committed suicide); Cic. *Resp.* 6.15.15; 6.26.29; *Tusc.* 1.19.43–44; 1.31.75; Sen. Y. *Ben.* 3.20.1–2; *Dial.* 11.9.3; 12.11.6; Heracl. *Ep.* 5; Plut. *Isis* 78, *Mor.* 382F–383A; Men. Rhet. 2.9, 414.22–23; Porph. *Marc.* 6.105–8; 7.131–34; for the emperor, e.g., Vell. Paterc. 2.123.2; 2.124.3. Cf. gnostic adaptations in Jonas, *Religion*, 43; Chadwick, *Early Church*, 36; traditions about the mysteries in Sheldon, *Mystery Religions*, 32; in Mithraism, Sheldon, *Mystery Religions*, 33–34. Gnostics may have adapted ideas from earlier Egyptian mortuary texts (Frankfurter, *Religion in Egypt*, 261) as well as earlier Platonism (Nock, "Gnosticism," 266–67).

66. See Cumont, *After Life*, 91–109 (now qualified; cf., e.g., Gasparro, *Soteriology*, 98); Martin, *Body*, 117–18; Klauck, *Context*, 80. In Jewish sources, see Dan. 12:3; *1 En.* 51:5; 104:2 (but cf. 43:1, 4); *T. Mos.* 10:9; *2 Bar.* 51:10; cf. Ps.-Phoc. 71; *Sipre Deut.* 47.2.5. For deification of heroes, see, e.g., Virg. *Aen.* 7.210–11; Ovid *Metam.* 15.749, 843–51 (cf. Ovid's hope for himself in 15.875–76); Val. Max. 3.2.19; 4.6.ext.3; 6.9.15; Lucan *C.W.* 9.1–9; Ps.-Callisth. *Alex.* 2.15; for philosophers in Cercidas frg. 1; Eunapius *Lives* 469.

67. Cic. *Resp.* 6.15.15 (trans. Keyes, LCL, 16:267).

68. Val. Flacc. 3.378–82.

69. So, e.g., Urbach, *Sages*, 1:214–16; Meyers and Strange, *Archaeology*, 99.

70. See Urbach, *Sages*, 1:250, on even the Amoraim (though acknowledging that Amoraim often distinguished between soul and body). Cf. perhaps the spirit released into air when the body returns to dust in Ps.-Phoc. 108 (though *OTP* 2:578 n. *j* may be right to suggest "Stoic influence"). The argument for a Jewish tradition behind Philo's use of Hellenistic anthropology (Melnick, "Conception"), however, does not strike me as persuasive.

71. E.g., *Let. Aris.* 236; *T. Job* 20:3; *Apoc. Ezek.* 1–2; *1 En.* 102:5; *t. Sanh.* 13:2; *b. Ber.* 10a; 60b; *Yoma* 20b, bar. Diaspora Jewish authors often distinguished body and soul, though often

Josephus, for example, a Judean writing in the Diaspora, views the soul as afflicted by the body's defilements until freed from the body at death.[72] He claims to have urged fellow Judeans to recognize that God had given each person an immortal soul, a portion of the divine.[73] He depicts (presumably imaginatively) a Judean revolutionary exhorting his fellow Judeans to view the soul as imprisoned in the body.[74]

Rabbis did not denigrate the body, as many Gentile thinkers did, but they did distinguish the body and soul, especially in later (Amoraic) sources.[75] An early rabbi (a Tanna) spoke of God reuniting soul and body at the resurrection, bringing the soul from heaven and the body from earth.[76] In a later rabbinic parable the body must be raised because the soul and body, which sinned together but separated at death, would be judged together.[77] The same parable is paralleled in another source that some date as early as the first century.[78]

From the Diaspora, the Wisdom of Solomon notes that "the corruptible body [φθαρτὸν σῶμα] weighs down the soul."[79] In a later work Satan afflicts Job's body but cannot touch his soul.[80] Writing before Paul, Philo of Alexandria distinguishes body from soul or (often more meaningfully)

"in order to express an ethical rather than an ontological dualism" (Isaacs, *Spirit*, 75–76). For body and soul mentioned together but with more emphasis on the whole, see, e.g., 2 Macc. 7:37; 14:38; *Let. Aris.* 139; *T. Sim.* 2:5; 4:8; probably *L.A.B.* 3:10; perhaps *T. Ash.* 2:6; for their close correspondence, see, e.g., *T. Naph.* 2:2–3.

72. Jos. *Ag. Ap.* 2.203. He elsewhere distinguishes soul and body (*Ant.* 18.117, regarding John the Baptist's ministry; 18.333), though sometimes in ways emphasizing their connection (*Ant.* 4.291, 298; 15.190; 18.282; *War* 1.95, 429; 2.60, 136, 476, 580, 588; 3.362). The soul leaves the body at death (*Ant.* 6.3; 13.317; 19.325; *War* 1.84).

73. Jos. *War* 3.272. He speaks of the body as a foreigner to the soul in *War* 3.278.

74. Jos. *War* 7.345; cf. 7.340–88 (esp. 340, 348, 355). Ancient hearers would have recognized the speech as Josephus's composition (Luz, "Masada").

75. Urbach, *Sages*, 1:218–21; for distinctions from Hellenism, see 248–49; cf. Kahn, "Duality." The soul is pure and fills the body as God is pure and fills the cosmos (*b. Ber.* 10a; *Lev. Rab.* 4:8; *Deut. Rab.* 2:37).

76. *Sipre Deut.* 306.28.3; this is a Tannaitic commentary and hence reflects the earlier phase of rabbinic teaching (especially second-century traditions). Souls are distinguished from bodies also in *t. Sanh.* 13:2, 4 (although treated together). For the soul leaving the body at death, see also 1 *En.* 22:7; 4 *Ezra* 7:78; *Eccl. Rab.* 5:10, §2; their reuniting at resurrection appears in 1 *En.* 102:5; *b. Ber.* 60b. For heavenly and earthly elements in humans, see *Gen. Rab.* 14:3; *Eccl. Rab.* 6:6–7, §1; for mortal and immortal, *Gen. Rab.* 14:9.

77. *B. Sanh.* 91ab. Young, *Parables*, 65–66, cites a shorter form in *Mek. Shir.* 2 on Exod. 15:1 (plus wider parallels to the story; also in *OTP* 1:492–93; see earlier Wallach, "Parable").

78. *Apoc. Ezek.* 1–2. Citing predecessors and evidence, Mueller and Robinson ("Introduction," 488) suggest between 50 BCE and 50 CE; the evidence for dating is not certain but the best currently available.

79. Wis. 9:15. This Alexandrian Jewish work reflects here the sort of Middle Platonic influence also reflected in Philo. For immortality in this work, see also Mazzinghi, "Morte e immortalità."

80. *T. Job* 20:3.

from the mind scores of times.[81] For Philo, the mind is the soul's soul, so
to speak.[82] Philo emphasizes that humans are created not only from earthly
substance but also from the divine breath.[83] Philo often emphasizes the soul's
invisibility,[84] which marks its kinship with the invisible God,[85] as the image
of the invisible God.[86]

Jewish Thinkers regarding the Afterlife

Just as Jewish views about the soul varied, so did Jewish views about the
afterlife. Sadducees denied not only resurrection but apparently also immortality.[87] They may have continued one pre-Hellenistic line of tradition.[88]
Even some later Diaspora Jewish funerary inscriptions lament that "no one is
immortal,"[89] though they may simply mean that everyone dies. But Josephus
contends that Pharisees reflected more popular views than the Sadducees
did, and evidence from Judean burials prior to AD 70 suggests widespread
afterlife beliefs.[90]

Certainly, many Jewish writers envisioned death as the soul or the immaterial element leaving the body,[91] and many Jewish people spoke of the soul

81. E.g., Philo *Creation* 67 (the mind being eternal and divine); *Alleg. Interp.* 2.22; *Sacr.* 9.
82. Philo *Creation* 66 (cf. 69, 139); cf. *Heir* 55, where the soul's soul is energized by the divine
Spirit. Cf. discussion of two minds in Philo in Konstan, "Minds."
83. E.g., Philo *Creation* 135; cf. Gen. 2:7. In Gen. 1:1 Philo parallels "heaven" with the mind
and "earth" with sense knowledge (*Alleg. Interp.* 1.1).
84. E.g., Philo *Dreams* 1.73, 135; *Jos.* 255; *Mos.* 2.217; *Virt.* 57, 172.
85. E.g., Philo *Cher.* 101.
86. E.g., Philo *Worse* 86; cf. *Plant.* 18; *Decal.* 60.
87. Jos. *Ant.* 18.16; *War* 2.165. Josephus, who does not favor Sadducees, implies their similarity to Epicureans.
88. Sir. 17:28, 30; cf. the worms in Sir. 7:17 (with fire); 10:11; 19:3. Some regard this as the
dominant Jewish view during the Persian period (e.g., Montefiore, "Spirit of Judaism," 36).
Ferguson (*Backgrounds*, 439) suggests that Sirach preserves the OT image of the underworld
(citing Sir. 14:16–19; 17:25–32; 38:16–23; 41:4; 48:5; 51:5–6).
89. See *CIJ* 1:263, §335; 1:309, §401; 1:334, §450. Cf. similar pessimistic inscriptions of
Gentiles noted above, p. 270.
90. Goodenough, *Symbols*, 1:164–77 passim. Some argue for ancient Israelite afterlife beliefs
because Israelites placed vessels in graves, as did surrounding cultures with afterlife traditions;
see Sellers, "Belief," esp. 16.
91. E.g., *1 En.* 9:10; 22:7; Tob. 3:6; Bar. 2:17; Wis. 16:14; Jos. *War* 1.84; *4 Ezra* 7:78; *T. Ab.*
1:24–25 A; 4:9; 9:10 B; *b. Yoma* 20b, bar.; *Lev. Rab.* 34:3; *Eccl. Rab.* 5:10, §2; *Pesiq. Rab.* 31:2;
Matt. 10:28; James 2:26. For an extensive survey of Second Temple Jewish sources, see Gundry,
Sōma, 87–109; also concisely listed in Gundry, *Matthew*, 197. Many Gentile sources articulate
this view, e.g., Plato *Phaedo* 64C; 115D; Arist. *Soul* 1.5, 411b; Varro *L.L.* 5.10.59; Lucret. *Nat.*
3.121–23, 323–49; Socratics *Ep.* 14; Sen. Y. *Dial.* 1.5.8; Epict. *Diatr.* 2.1.17; Marc. Aur. 4.5;
Max. Tyre *Or.* 5.8; 9.5–6.

as immortal.[92] Jewish sources attest belief in immortality, sometimes even before substantial influence from Hellenism, and a wide range of sources attest it.[93]

Psalms of Solomon, probably from the first century BCE, speaks of the life of the righteous continuing "forever," in contrast to the wicked, who would be destroyed.[94] In some apocalyptic texts, death means escape from what is mortal.[95] For later rabbis, the soul remained near the body for three days before abandoning it.[96]

Josephus, contextualizing his description of Jewish movements for a Hellenistic audience, declares that Pharisees believe in souls' immortality: "They believe that souls have power to survive death and that there are rewards and punishments under the earth for those who have led lives of virtue or vice; eternal imprisonment is the lot of evil souls, while the good souls receive an easy passage to a new life."[97] Josephus also describes Essenes in hellenized terms: they believed that their material bodies were perishable and temporary but that their souls were immortal; freed from the prison of their bodies, good souls would ascend upward, just as the Greeks believed.[98]

92. E.g., Jos. *Ant.* 17.353; *War* 1.650; 3.372. Humans are created from visible material, and thus die, but also invisible material, and thus live (2 *En.* 30:10 J). Tac. *Hist.* 5.5 compares Jewish and Egyptian afterlife beliefs. Immortality for the righteous probably appears in *Jos. Asen.* 27:10 (*OTP* 2:245; = 27:8 Greek p. 214), with Philonenko (*pace* C. Burchard in *OTP* 2:245 n. *n*); 1 Macc. 2:63 excludes it for the wicked.

93. Légasse, "Immortalité"; see the briefer survey in Bonsirven, *Judaism*, 164–65.

94. *Pss. Sol.* 13:11.

95. *4 Ezra* 7:96. Adam's spirit ascends in *Apoc. Mos.* 13:6 (not in the parallel *L.A.E.* text); 32:4 (for his body, cf. 33:2).

96. *Gen. Rab.* 100:7 (Bar Kappara, an early Amora); cf. the longer period in *b. Shab.* 152b. Some may have inconsistently allowed the deceased hearing requests at their graves (as in *b. Taan.* 23b), reflecting a wider motif in late antiquity (cf. grave goods in Thomas, "Dead," 289–91).

97. Jos. *Ant.* 18.14 (trans. Feldman, LCL, 13). Their "new life" corresponds to their return in pure bodies at the turning of the ages (*War* 3.374; see also 2.163); this image undoubtedly implies the Pharisaic doctrine of resurrection, yet it is couched sufficiently ambiguously for an uninformed audience so as to resemble the more respectable Hellenistic idea of reincarnation articulated by Platonists and Pythagoreans. The soul's afterlife was compatible with future resurrection (e.g., *T. Ab.* 7:15–16 B; Légasse, "Immortalité"; in the Dead Sea Scrolls, see Ulrichsen, "Troen").

98. Jos. *War* 2.154–55; on their belief in immortality more briefly, see *Ant.* 18.18. Josephus may know that they believe in resurrection (cf. *War* 2.153), but he appeals to respectable Hellenistic conceptions (the same way he contextualizes John the Baptist's purifying of soul and body in *Ant.* 18.116–17). 4Q185 frgs. 1–2, col. 1.9–13 might depict a shadowy existence in the netherworld, as in the OT and the older Greek tradition. For a future earthly kingdom, not just immortality, see Laurin, "Immortality."

For Philo, the soul left the body to return to God at death;[99] death was passing from perishable to imperishable existence, to immortality.[100] Hellenistic Jewish works such as Wisdom of Solomon and 4 Maccabees clearly affirm immortality.[101] Outsiders recognized that Christians also believed in an afterlife; Lucian complains that Christians, deluded to believe in immortality, do not shrink from death.[102] Although Paul may teach an afterlife even before the resurrection (2 Cor. 5:8; Phil. 1:23), like many Pharisees,[103] it should be noted that Pauline literature never clearly uses ψυχή in the Platonic sense, even in letters that elsewhere borrow some Platonic imagery. Paul's linguistic influence here may reflect more the Septuagint, which employs ψυχή in the conventional, earlier Greek sense that corresponds much more closely to the sense of the Hebrew term *nephesh*.[104]

99. Philo *Abr.* 258. For the immortality of the soul in Philo, see, e.g., *Alleg. Interp.* 1.1; in detail, Wolfson, *Philo*, 1:395–413.

100. Philo *Virt.* 67; *Mos.* 2.288. Philo believed that the virtuous achieved incorporeality after death (Burnett, "Philo on Immortality").

101. E.g., Wis. 3:4; 5:15; 6:18–19; 8:13, 17; 15:3; 4 Macc. 9:22; 14:5; 16:13; 17:12; 18:23; cf. Rost, *Judaism*, 110.

102. Lucian *Peregr.* 13. Lucian himself had more of a predilection toward the teaching of Epicurus.

103. Jos. *Ant.* 18.14; *War* 2.163 (cf. 3.374; *Ag. Ap.* 2.218). Josephus adapts the language of Pharisaic resurrection belief so that it can be construed as if it were Platonic reincarnation, but the existence of an interim state remains clear, esp. in *Antiquities*.

104. See, e.g., Walton, *Thought*, 148; Wright, *Perspectives*, 455–73.

APPENDIX B

Some of God's Wise Plan in Paul's Bible

In speaking of God's wise plan in history (Rom. 9–11), Paul presupposes the biblical narrative that, on his view, climaxes in Christ. Following are some elements of the larger story that Paul presumably noticed, although he does not highlight all of them.

The biblical narrative that Paul shares with his first audience heavily underlines themes such as human depravity (Rom. 3:23), God seeking to restore humanity to himself (cf. 5:10), and God seeking to bring back righteousness (cf. 1:17). The narrative begins by lavishly depicting God's kindness: God created the world good and humanity in his image (Gen. 1); he provided for humanity (Gen. 2). Humanity, however, chose falsehood and sought equality with God (Gen. 3:1–6), marring also God's blessing on all creation (or at least in its relation to humans; 3:17). Further sins and judgments followed, clearly pervasive throughout humanity (Gen. 4–9).

Yet God kept reaching out to humanity to seek restoration, most obviously through Noah, whose mission was to bring restoration (Gen. 5:29). Sin, however, also came into the renewed world with its human residents (9:21–22). The call of Abraham was another step toward restoration, intended to be a blessing for all peoples (12:3; 18:18; 22:18; 26:4, 28:14), because Abraham would teach his descendants the Lord's way of righteousness and justice (18:19).

God redeemed Abraham's promised line Israel to be a holy nation (Exod. 19:5–6; 20:2), because of his love and promise and not Israel's merit (Deut.

7:7–11; 9:4–5; 10:15), and gave them more-specific laws. Most distinctive about Israel's law was that it came from the true God (Deut. 4:6–7), the creator and judge of all the earth, so that all of its just demands were grounded in him. But Israel continually disobeyed and failed; God even offered to make Moses like Noah, starting over with his seed (Exod. 32:10). The book of Judges shows the repeated cycle of human depravity in Israel and the periodic need for human deliverers; but whereas Judges laments the moral anarchy that followed from Israel's lack of godly rulers (Judg. 17:6; 21:25; cf. 18:1; 19:1), Israel's subsequent history further shows its failure under kings as well. Although Paul focuses more on specific texts than on delineating this larger narrative, his thesis of human depravity (Rom. 3:23) would have been difficult to dispute from Scripture.

The prophets announced and psalms celebrated that there ultimately would be a time of restoration when God would reign, fully deliver his people, and establish justice, righteousness, and salvation. Not all passages in the prophets involve the time of restoration, but of those that do address the restoration, many include restoration of the house of David, across a wide spectrum of the prophets (Isa. 11:1, 10; 55:3; Jer. 23:5; 33:15–26; Ezek. 34:23–24; 37:24–25; Hosea 3:5; Amos 9:11; Zech. 12:8, 10).[1] For Paul, this is the narrative that climaxes in Jesus: the agent of God's promised reign and deliverance, the ultimate deliverer. By restoring the possibility of permanent righteousness, establishing God's promised reign, Jesus's ministry would ultimately bring about the restoration of creation.

---

1. Of these, a few—perhaps 10 percent—could even be understood as suggesting the Davidic king's deity in some way, despite the dangers of syncretism reflecting divine kings in some surrounding cultures; see Isa. 9:6–7 (for "mighty God," cf. 10:21); Jer. 23:5–6 (but cf. 33:16); cf. Zech. 12:8. Scholars debate the sense of these passages today, but they would naturally be suggestive to early Christians.

Bibliography

Primary Sources

Alciphron. *The Letters of Alciphron, Aelian, and Philostratus*. Translated by Allen Rogers Benner and Francis H. Forbes. LCL. Cambridge, MA: Harvard University Press; London: Heinemann, 1949.

Apuleius. *Rhetorical Works*. Edited by Stephen Harrison. Translated and annotated by Stephen Harrison, John Hilton, and Vincent Hunink. Oxford: Oxford University Press, 2001.

Aristeas to Philocrates (Letter of Aristeas). Edited and translated by Moses Hadas. New York: Harper & Brothers, 1951. Reprint, New York: KTAV, 1973. See also *Letter of Aristeas*.

Arius Didymus. *Epitome of Stoic Ethics*. Edited by Arthur J. Pomeroy. SBLTT 44. Graeco-Roman Religion Series 14. Atlanta: SBL, 1999.

2 Baruch. Translated by A. F. J. Klijn. *OTP* 1:615–52.

The Book of the Dead, or Going Forth by Day: Ideas of the Ancient Egyptians concerning the Hereafter as Expressed in Their Own Terms. Translated by Thomas George Allen. Prepared for publication by Elizabeth Blaisdell Hauser. SAOC 37. Chicago: University of Chicago Press, 1974.

Callimachus. *Aetia, Iambi, Lyric Poems, Hecale, Minor Epic and Elegiac Poems, and Other Fragments*. Translated by C. A. Trypanis. LCL. Cambridge, MA: Harvard University Press, 1958.

Cicero. Translated by Harry Caplan et al. 29 vols. LCL. Cambridge, MA: Harvard University Press, 1913–.

Confucius. *The Sacred Books of Confucius and Other Confucian Classics*. Edited and translated by Ch'u Chai and Winberg Chai. Introduction by Ch'u Chai. New York: Bantam/University Books, 1965.

Dio Chrysostom. Translated by J. W. Cohoon and H. Lamar Crosby. 5 vols. LCL. Cambridge, MA: Harvard University Press, 1932–51.

Diogenes. *The Epistles of Diogenes*. Translated by Benjamin Fiore. In *The Cynic Epistles: A Study Edition*, edited by Abraham J. Malherbe, 92–183. SBLSBS 12. Missoula, MT: Scholars Press, 1977.

Diogenes Laertius. *Lives of Eminent Philosophers*. Translated by R. D. Hicks. 2 vols. LCL. Cambridge, MA: Harvard University Press, 1925.

Epictetus. *The Discourses as Reported by Arrian; the Manual; and Fragments*. Translated by W. A. Oldfather. 2 vols. LCL. Cambridge, MA: Harvard University Press, 1926–28.

Euripides. Translated by David Kovacs, Christopher Collard, and Martin Cropp. 8 vols. LCL. Cambridge, MA: Harvard University Press, 1994–2008.

Heraclitus. *The Epistles of Heraclitus*. Translated by David R. Worley. In *The Cynic Epistles: A Study Edition*, edited by Abraham J.

Malherbe, 186–215. SBLSBS 12. Missoula, MT: Scholars Press, 1977.

Hermogenes. *On Issues: Strategies of Argument in Later Greek Rhetoric*. Translated by Malcolm Heath. Oxford: Clarendon, 1995.

Herodes. *Herodes, Cercidas, and the Greek Choliambic Poets*. Translated by A. D. Knox. LCL. Cambridge, MA: Harvard University Press, 1961.

Hesiod. *Hesiod, the Homeric Hymns, and Homerica*. Translated by Hugh G. Evelyn-White. Rev. ed. LCL. Cambridge, MA: Harvard University Press; London: Heinemann, 1936.

Iamblichus of Chalcis. *The Letters*. Translation, introduction, and notes by John M. Dillon and Wolfgang Polleichtner. SBLWGRW 19. Atlanta: SBL, 2009.

———. *On the Pythagorean Way of Life: Text, Translation, and Notes*. Edited and translated by John Dillon and Jackson Hershbell. SBLTT 29. Graeco-Roman Religion Series 11. Atlanta: Scholars Press, 1991.

Isocrates. *Orations*. Translated by George Norlin and Larue van Hook. 3 vols. LCL. New York: Putnam's Sons; London: Heinemann, 1928–61.

Josephus. Translated by H. St. J. Thackeray et al. 10 vols. LCL. Cambridge, MA: Harvard University Press, 1926–65.

Letter of Aristeas. Translated by R. J. H. Shutt. OTP 2:7–34. See also *Aristeas to Philocrates*.

Libanius. *Libanius's "Progymnasmata": Model Exercises in Greek Prose Composition and Rhetoric*. Translation, introduction, and notes by Craig A. Gibson. SBLWGRW 27. Atlanta: SBL, 2008.

Marcus Aurelius. *The Communings with Himself*. Edited and translated by C. R. Haines. LCL. Cambridge, MA: Harvard University Press, 1916.

Maximus of Tyre. *The Philosophical Orations*. Translated by M. B. Trapp. Oxford: Clarendon, 1997.

Mekilta de-Rabbi Ishmael. Translated by Jacob Z. Lauterbach. 3 vols. Philadelphia: Jewish Publication Society of America, 1933–35.

Menander. Edited and translated by W. Geoffrey Arnott. 3 vols. LCL. Cambridge, MA: Harvard University Press; London: Heinemann, 1979–2000.

Musonius Rufus: "The Roman Socrates." Translated by Cora E. Lutz. YCS 10. New Haven: Yale University Press, 1947.

Olympiodorus. *In Platonis Gorgiam Commentaria*. Edited by L. G. Westerink. Leipzig: Teubner, 1970.

Philo. Translated by F. H. Colson, G. H. Whitaker, and R. Marcus. 12 vols. LCL. Cambridge, MA: Harvard University Press, 1929–62.

Philostratus, Flavius, and Eunapius. *The Lives of the Sophists*. Translated by Wilmer Cave Wright. LCL. New York: Putnam's Sons; London: Heinemann, 1922.

Pindar. *Olympian Odes; Pythian Odes*. Translated by William H. Race. 2 vols. LCL. Cambridge, MA: Harvard University Press, 1997.

Plato. Translated by Harold North Fowler et al. 12 vols. LCL. Cambridge, MA: Harvard University Press, 1914–26.

Pliny the Younger. *Letters and Panegyricus*. Translated by Betty Radice. 2 vols. LCL. Cambridge, MA: Harvard University Press, 1969.

Plutarch. *Moralia*. Translated by Frank Cole Babbitt et al. 17 vols. in 18. LCL. New York: Putnam's Sons; Cambridge, MA: Harvard University Press; London: Heinemann, 1927–2004.

Porphyry. *Porphyry the Philosopher to Marcella*. Edited and translated by Kathleen O'Brien Wicker. SBLTT 28. Graeco-Roman Religion Series 10. Atlanta: Scholars Press, 1987.

Proclus. *Proclus the Successor on Poetics and the Homeric Poems: Essays 5 and 6 of His "Commentary on the Republic of Plato."* Translated with an introduction and notes by Robert Lamberton. SBLWGRW 34. Atlanta: SBL, 2012.

Pseudo-Philo. *Liber antiquitatum biblicarum*. Edited by Guido Kisch. Publications in Mediaeval Studies 10. Notre Dame, IN: University of Notre Dame Press, 1949.

Rhetorica ad Alexandrum. In *Aristotle, "Problems," Books 32–38; Rhetorica ad Alexandrum*. Translated by H. Rackham. LCL. Cambridge, MA: Harvard University Press, 1936.

Seneca the Younger. *Ad Lucilium epistulae morales*. Translated by Richard M. Gummere. 3 vols. LCL. Cambridge, MA: Harvard University Press, 1920–34.

———. *Moral Essays*. Translated by John W. Basore. 3 vols. LCL. Cambridge, MA: Harvard University Press, 1928–35.

———. *Naturales quaestiones*. Translated by Thomas H. Corcoran. 2 vols. LCL. Cambridge, MA: Harvard University Press, 1971–72.

Socratics. *The Epistles of Socrates and the Socratics*. Translated by Stanley Stowers and David R. Worley. In *The Cynic Epistles: A Study Edition*, edited by Abraham J. Malherbe, 218–307. SBLSBS 12. Missoula, MT: Scholars Press, 1977.

Stobaeus. *Eclogarum physicarum et ethicarum libri duo*. Edited by Augustus Meineke. 2 vols. Leipzig: Teubner, 1860–64.

———. *Florilegium*. In *Anthologium*. Edited by Otto Hense. 5 vols. Berlin: Weidmann, 1884–1912.

Symmachus. *The "Letters" of Symmachus: Book 1*. Translated by Michele Renee Salzman and Michael Roberts. Introduction and commentary by Michele Renee Salzman. SBLWGRW 30. Atlanta: SBL, 2011.

Targum Pseudo-Jonathan: Genesis. Translated by Michael Maher. ArBib 1B. Collegeville, MN: Liturgical Press, 1992.

Testament of Job. Translated by R. P. Spittler. OTP 1:839–68.

The Testament of Job, according to the SV Text. Edited by Robert A. Kraft et al. SBLTT 5. Pseudepigraph Series 4. Missoula, MT: SBL, 1974.

Testaments of the Twelve Patriarchs. The Greek Versions of the Testaments of the Twelve Patriarchs, Edited from Nine MSS Together with the Variants of the Armenian and Slavonic Versions and Some Hebrew Fragments. Edited by R. H. Charles. Oxford: Clarendon, 1908.

Thebaid. Greek Epic Fragments from the Seventh to the Fifth Centuries BC. Edited and translated by Martin L. West. LCL. Cambridge, MA: Harvard University Press, 2003.

Theon, Aelius. *The Progymnasmata of Theon the Sophist: A New Text with Translation and Commentary*, by James R. Butts. Ann Arbor, MI: University Microfilms International, 1989.

Valerius Maximus. *Memorable Deeds and Sayings*. Edited and translated by D. R. Shackleton Bailey. 2 vols. LCL. Cambridge, MA: Harvard University Press, 2000.

Secondary Sources

Abrahams, *Studies* (1). Abrahams, Israel. *Studies in Pharisaism and the Gospels*. 1st ser. Cambridge: Cambridge University Press, 1917. Reprinted with prolegomenon by Morton S. Enslin. Library of Biblical Studies. New York: KTAV, 1967.

Abrahams, *Studies* (2). Abrahams, Israel. *Studies in Pharisaism and the Gospels*. 2nd ser. Cambridge: Cambridge University Press, 1924.

Achtemeier, "Reflections." Achtemeier, Paul J. "'Some Things in Them Hard to Understand': Reflections on an Approach to Paul." *Int* 38 (3, 1984): 254–67.

Achtemeier, *Romans*. Achtemeier, Paul J. *Romans*. IBC. Atlanta: John Knox, 1985.

Adams, "Habitus." Adams, Matthew. "Hybridizing Habitus and Reflexivity: Towards an Understanding of Contemporary Identity?" *Sociology* 40 (3, June 2006): 511–28.

Adams, *Stars*. Adams, Edward. *The Stars Will Fall from Heaven: "Cosmic Catastrophe" in the New Testament and Its World*. LNTS 347. New York: T&T Clark, 2007.

Adeyemi, "Rulers." Adeyemi, M. E. "The Rulers of This Age in First Corinthians 2:6–8: An Exegetical Exposition." *DBM* 28 (2, 1999): 38–45.

Adinolfi, "L'invio." Adinolfi, Marco. "L'invio del Figlio in *Rom* 8.3." *RivB* 33 (3, 1985): 291–317.

Aker, "*Charismata*." Aker, Benny C. "*Charismata*: Gifts, Enablements, or Ministries?" *JPT* 11 (1, 2002): 53–69.

Albright, *Biblical Period*. Albright, William Foxwell. *The Biblical Period from Abraham to Ezra*. New York: Harper & Row, 1963.

Albright, *Yahweh*. Albright, William Foxwell. *Yahweh and the Gods of Canaan*. Jordan Lectures, 1965. Garden City, NY: Doubleday, 1968.

Aletti, "Rm 7.7–25." Aletti, Jean-Noël. "Rm 7.7–25 encore une fois: Enjeux et propositions." *NTS* 48 (2002): 358–76.

Aletti, "Romans 7,7–25." Aletti, Jean-Noël. "Romans 7,7–25: Rhetorical Criticism and Its Usefulness." *SEÅ* 61 (1996): 77–95.

Alexander, "Ambiguity." Alexander, Elizabeth Shanks. "Art, Argument, and Ambiguity in the Talmud: Conflicting Conceptions of the

Evil Impulse in *b. Sukkah* 51b–52a." *HUCA* 73 (2002): 97–132.

Allegro, *Scrolls*. Allegro, J. M. *The Dead Sea Scrolls*. Baltimore: Penguin, 1959.

Allen, "Romans I–VIII." Allen, Leslie C. "The Old Testament in Romans I–VIII." *VE* 3 (1964): 6–41.

Allison, *Constructing Jesus*. Allison, Dale C., Jr. *Constructing Jesus: Memory, Imagination, and History*. Grand Rapids: Baker Academic, 2010.

Allo, *Première Épitre*. Allo, Le P. E.-B. *Saint Paul: Première Épitre aux Corinthiens*. 2nd ed. Paris: J. Gabalda, 1956.

Anderson, *Glossary*. Anderson, R. Dean, Jr. *Glossary of Greek Rhetorical Terms Connected to Methods of Argumentation, Figures, and Tropes from Anaximenes to Quintilian*. Leuven: Peeters, 2000.

Anderson, "Joy." Anderson, Gary A. "The Expression of Joy as a Halakhic Problem in Rabbinic Sources." *JQR* 80 (3–4, 1990): 221–52.

Anderson, *Rhetorical Theory*. Anderson, R. Dean, Jr. *Ancient Rhetorical Theory and Paul*. Rev. ed. CBET 18. Leuven: Peeters, 1999.

Angus, *Mystery-Religions*. Angus, S. *The Mystery-Religions and Christianity*. New York: Scribner, 1925.

Antonaccio, "Hero Cult." Antonaccio, Carla M. "Contesting the Past: Hero Cult, Tomb Cult, and Epic in Early Greece." *AJA* 98 (3, 1994): 389–410.

Apple, "Power." Apple, Michael W. "Power, Meaning, and Identity: Critical Sociology of Education in the United States." *British Journal of Sociology of Education* 17 (2, 1996): 125–44.

Arbel, "Understanding." Arbel, Daphna V. "'Understanding of the Heart': Spiritual Transformation and Divine Revelations in the Hekhalot and Merkavah Literature." *JSQ* 6 (4, 1999): 320–44.

Archer, *Hermeneutic*. Archer, Kenneth J. *A Pentecostal Hermeneutic: Spirit, Scripture, and Community*. Cleveland, TN: CPT Press, 2009.

Arnaldich, "Sacerdocio." Arnaldich, Luis. "El sacerdocio en Qumran." *Salm* 19 (2, 1972): 279–322.

Arrington, *Aeon Theology*. Arrington, French L. *Paul's Aeon Theology in 1 Corinthians*. Washington, DC: University Press of America, 1978.

Aubenque, "Prudence." Aubenque, Pierre. "Prudence." *BrillPauly* 12:88–90.

Aune, *Cultic Setting*. Aune, David E. *The Cultic Setting of Realized Eschatology in Early Christianity*. NovTSup 28. Leiden: Brill, 1972.

Aune, *Dictionary of Rhetoric*. Aune, David E. *The Westminster Dictionary of New Testament and Early Christian Literature and Rhetoric*. Louisville: Westminster John Knox, 2003.

Aune, "Duality." Aune, David E. "Anthropological Duality in the Eschatology of 2 Cor 4:16–5:10." In *Paul beyond the Judaism/Hellenism Divide*, edited by Troels Engberg-Pedersen, 215–40. Louisville: Westminster John Knox, 2001.

Aune, *Environment*. Aune, David E. *The New Testament in Its Literary Environment*. LEC 8. Philadelphia: Westminster, 1987.

Aune, *Prophecy*. Aune, David E. *Prophecy in Early Christianity and the Ancient Mediterranean World*. Grand Rapids: Eerdmans, 1983.

Aune, "Προφήτης." Aune, David E. "The Use of προφήτης in Josephus." *JBL* 101 (3, 1982): 419–21.

Aune, "Significance." Aune, David E. "The Significance of the Delay of the Parousia for Early Christianity." In *Current Issues in Biblical and Patristic Interpretation: Studies in Honor of Merrill C. Tenney Presented by His Former Students*, edited by Gerald F. Hawthorne, 87–109. Grand Rapids: Eerdmans, 1975.

Avi-Yonah, "Archaeological Sources." Avi-Yonah, Michael. "Archaeological Sources." *JPFC* 46–62.

Avi-Yonah, *Hellenism*. Avi-Yonah, Michael. *Hellenism and the East: Contacts and Interrelations from Alexander to the Roman Conquest*. Ann Arbor: University Microfilms International for the Institute of Languages, Literature, and the Arts, Hebrew University, Jerusalem, 1978.

Baer, *Categories*. Baer, Richard A., Jr. *Philo's Use of the Categories Male and Female*. ALGHJ 3. Leiden: Brill, 1970.

Baird, "Mature." Baird, William. "Among the Mature: The Idea of Wisdom in I Corinthians 2:6." *Int* 13 (4, 1959): 425–32.

Bamberger, "Prophet." Bamberger, Bernard J. "The Changing Image of the Prophet in Jewish Thought." In *Interpreting the Prophetic Tradition: The Goldman Lectures, 1955–1966*, edited by Harry M. Orlinski,

301–23. Cincinnati: Hebrew Union College Press; New York: KTAV, 1969.

Bamberger, *Proselytism*. Bamberger, Bernard J. *Proselytism in the Talmudic Period*. New York: KTAV, 1968.

Banks, "Romans 7:25A." Banks, Robert J. "Romans 7:25A: An Eschatological Thanksgiving?" *ABR* 26 (Oct. 1978): 34–42.

Barclay, *Gift*. Barclay, John M. G. *Paul and the Gift*. Grand Rapids: Eerdmans, 2015.

Barclay, *Jews in Diaspora*. Barclay, John M. G. *Jews in the Mediterranean Diaspora: From Alexander to Trajan (323 BCE–117 CE)*. Berkeley: University of California Press, 1996.

Barclay, "Stoic Physics." Barclay, John M. G. "Stoic Physics and the Christ-Event: A Review of Troels Engberg-Pedersen, *Cosmology and Self in the Apostle Paul: The Material Spirit* (Oxford: Oxford University Press, 2010)." *JSNT* 33 (4, 2011): 406–14.

Barclay, "Themes." Barclay, William. "Great Themes of the NT. II. John i.1–14." *ExpT* 70 (1958): 78–82; (1959): 114–17.

Barnett, *Corinthians*. Barnett, Paul W. *The Second Epistle to the Corinthians*. NICNT. Grand Rapids: Eerdmans, 1997.

Barrett, *Adam*. Barrett, C. K. *From First Adam to Last*. New York: Scribner's, 1962.

Bartchy, *Slavery*. Bartchy, S. Scott. ΜΑΛΛΟΝ ΧΡΗΣΑΙ: *First-Century Slavery and the Interpretation of 1 Corinthians 7:21*. SBLDS 11. Missoula, MT: SBL, 1973.

Barth, *Ephesians*. Barth, Markus. *Ephesians*. 2 vols. AB 34, 34A. Garden City, NY: Doubleday, 1974.

Barth, *Romans*. Barth, Karl. *The Epistle to the Romans*. Translated from the 6th ed. by Edwyn C. Hoskyns. London: Oxford University Press, 1965.

Barth, "Speaking." Barth, Markus. "Speaking of Sin (Some Interpretive Notes on Romans 1.18–3.20)." *SJT* 8 (3, 1955): 288–96.

Baslez, "Martyrs." Baslez, Marie-Françoise. "Des martyrs juifs aux martyrs chrétiens." *EspV* 118 (194, 2008): 19–23.

Bauckham, *Climax*. Bauckham, Richard. *The Climax of Prophecy: Studies on the Book of Revelation*. Edinburgh: T&T Clark, 1993.

Bauckham, *Crucified*. Bauckham, Richard. *God Crucified: Monotheism and Christology in the New Testament*. Grand Rapids: Eerdmans, 1998.

Baudry, "Péché." Baudry, Gérard-Henry. "Le péché originel dans les pseudépigraphes de l'Ancien Testament." *MScRel* 49 (3–4, 1992): 163–92.

Baudry, "Péché dans les écrits." Baudry, Gérard-Henry. "La péché originel dans les écrits de Qoumrân." *MScRel* 50 (1, 1993): 7–23.

Bauer, "ΑΓΑΠΩΣΙΝ." Bauer, Johannes B. "'. . . ΤΟΙΣ ΑΓΑΠΩΣΙΝ ΤΟΝ ΘΕΟΝ' Rm 8:28 (I Cor 2:9, I Cor 8:3)." *ZNW* 50 (1–2, 1959): 106–12.

Baumert, "Unterscheidung." Baumert, Norbert. "Zur 'Unterscheidung der Geister.'" *ZKT* 111 (2, 1989): 183–95.

Baumgärtel, "Flesh." Baumgärtel, Friedrich. "Flesh in the Old Testament." *TDNT* 7:105–8.

Beale, "Background." Beale, Gregory K. "The Old Testament Background of Reconciliation in 2 Corinthians 5–7 and Its Bearing on the Literary Problem of 2 Corinthians 6.14–7.1." *NTS* 35 (4, 1989): 550–81.

Beale, *Revelation*. Beale, Gregory K. *The Book of Revelation: A Commentary on the Greek Text*. Grand Rapids: Eerdmans, 1999.

Beale and Gladd, *Hidden*. Beale, Gregory K., and Benjamin L. Gladd. *Hidden but Now Revealed: A Biblical Theology of Mystery*. Downers Grove, IL: IVP Academic, 2014.

Beare, *Philippians*. Beare, Francis Wright. *A Commentary on the Epistle to the Philippians*. 2nd ed. London: Adam & Charles Black, 1969.

Beck, *Psychology of Paul*. Beck, James R. *The Psychology of Paul: A Fresh Look at His Life and Teaching*. Grand Rapids: Kregel, 2002.

Belleville, *Glory*. Belleville, Linda L. *Reflections of Glory: Paul's Polemical Use of the Moses-Doxa Tradition in 2 Corinthians 3.1–18*. JSNTSup 52. Sheffield, UK: Sheffield Academic, 1991.

Bels, "Survie." Bels, J. "La survie de l'âme, de Platon à Posidonius." *RHR* 199 (2, 1982): 169–82.

Bendemann, "Diastase." Bendemann, Reinhard von. "Die kritische Diastase von Wissen, Wollen und Handeln: Traditionsgeschichtliche Spurensuche eines hellenistischen Topos in Römer 7." *ZNW* 95 (1–2, 2004): 35–63.

Benoit, "Mystères." Benoit, A. "Les mystères païens et le christianisme." In *Mystères et syncrétismes*, by F. Dunand et al., 73–92.

EHRel 2. Paris: Librairie Orientaliste Paul Geuthner, 1975.

Benware, "Grammar." Benware, Wilbur A. "Romans 1.17 and Cognitive Grammar." *BTr* 51 (3, 2000): 330–40.

Berceville and Son, "Exégèse." Berceville, Gilles, and Eun-Sil Son. "Exégèse biblique, théologie et philosophie chez Thomas d'Aquin et Martin Luther commentateurs de Rm 7, 14–25." *RSR* 91 (3, 2003): 373–95.

Berger, "Diskussion." Berger, Klaus. "Zur Diskussion über die Herkunft von I Kor. II.9." *NTS* 24 (2, Jan. 1978): 271–82.

Bergmeier, "Mensch." Bergmeier, Roland. "Röm 7,7–25a (8,2): Der Mensch—das Gesetz—Gott—Paulus—die Exegese im Widerspruch?" *KD* 31 (2, 1985): 162–72.

Berkhof, *Powers*. Berkhof, H. *Christ and the Powers*. Translated by John Howard Yoder. Scottdale, PA: Herald, 1962.

Best, *Body*. Best, Ernest. *One Body in Christ: A Study in the Relationship of the Church to Christ in the Epistles of the Apostle Paul*. London: SPCK, 1955.

Best, "Pneuma." Best, Ernest. "The Use and Non-use of Pneuma by Josephus." *NovT* 3 (3, 1959): 218–25.

Best, *Temptation*. Best, Ernest. *The Temptation and the Passion: The Markan Soteriology*. SNTSMS 2. Cambridge: Cambridge University Press, 1965.

Bett, "Emotions." Bett, Richard. "The Sceptics and the Emotions." In *The Emotions in Hellenistic Philosophy*, edited by Juha Sihvola and Troels Engberg-Pedersen, 197–218. TSHP 46. Dordrecht, Neth.: Kluwer Academic, 1998.

Betz, "Christuserkenntnis." Betz, Otto. "Fleischliche und 'geistliche' Christuserkenntnis nach 2. Korinther 5,16." *TBei* 14 (4–5, 1983): 167–79.

Betz, "Concept." Betz, Hans Dieter. "The Concept of the 'Inner Human Being' (ὁ ἔσω ἄνθρωπος) in the Anthropology of Paul." *NTS* 46 (3, 2000): 315–41.

Betz, "Hermetic Interpretation." Betz, Hans Dieter. "The Delphic Maxim ΓΝΩΘΙ ΣΑΥΤΟΝ in Hermetic Interpretation." *HTR* 63 (4, Oct. 1970): 465–84.

Betz, *Jesus*. Betz, Otto. *What Do We Know about Jesus?* Philadelphia: Westminster; London: SCM, 1968.

Betz, *Magical Papyri*. Betz, Hans Dieter, ed. *The Greek Magical Papyri in Translation, Including the Demotic Spells*. 2nd ed. Chicago: University of Chicago Press, 1992–.

Betz, "Maxim in Papyri." Betz, Hans Dieter. "The Delphic Maxim 'Know Yourself' in the Greek Magical Papyri." *HR* 21 (2, Nov. 1981): 156–71.

Bianchi, *Essays*. Bianchi, Ugo. *Selected Essays on Gnosticism, Dualism, and Mysteriosophy*. SHR 38. Leiden: Brill, 1978.

Bijovsky, "Allegory." Bijovsky, Gabriela. "*AION*: A Cosmic Allegory on a Coin from Tyre?" *IsNumR* 2 (2007): 143–56, plate 16.

Binder, "Age(s)." Binder, Gerhard. "Age(s)." *Brill Pauly* 1:331–35.

Bird, *Colossians*. Bird, Michael F. *Colossians and Philemon*. NCCS 12. Eugene, OR: Cascade, 2009.

Black, "Oration at Olivet." Black, C. Clifton. "An Oration at Olivet: Some Rhetorical Dimensions of Mark 13." In *Persuasive Artistry: Studies in New Testament Rhetoric in Honor of George A. Kennedy*, edited by Duane F. Watson, 66–92. JSNTSup 50. Sheffield, UK: Sheffield Academic, 1991.

Black, *Scrolls*. Black, Matthew. *The Scrolls and Christian Origins*. London: Nelson, 1961.

Blackburn, "ΑΝΔΡΕΣ." Blackburn, Barry L. "'Miracle Working ΘΕΙΟΙ ΑΝΔΡΕΣ' in Hellenism (and Hellenistic Judaism)." In *The Miracles of Jesus*, edited by David Wenham and Craig Blomberg, 185–218. Gospel Perspectives 6. Sheffield, UK: JSOT Press, 1986.

Blackwell, *Christosis*. Blackwell, Ben C. *Christosis: Pauline Soteriology in Light of Deification in Irenaeus and Cyril of Alexandria*. WUNT 2.314. Tübingen: Mohr Siebeck, 2011.

Blank, "Mensch." Blank, Josef. "Der gespaltene Mensch: Zur Exegese von Röm 7,7–25." *BibLeb* 9 (1, 1968): 10–20.

Boccaccini, *Judaism*. Boccaccini, Gabriele. *Middle Judaism: Jewish Thought, 300 B.C.E. to 200 C.E.* Foreword by James H. Charlesworth. Minneapolis: Fortress, 1991.

Boda, "Word and Spirit." Boda, Mark J. "Word and Spirit, Scribe and Prophet in Old Testament Hermeneutics." In *Spirit and Scripture: Exploring a Pneumatic Hermeneutic*, edited by Kevin L. Spawn and Archie T. Wright, 25–45. New York: Bloomsbury, 2012.

Boers, "Structure." Boers, Hendrikus. "The Structure and Meaning of Romans 6:1–14." *CBQ* 63 (4, Oct. 2001): 664–82.

Boismard, *Prologue*. Boismard, Marie-Émile. *St. John's Prologue*. Translated by the Carisbrooke Dominicans. London: Blackfriars, 1957.

Bongar and Beutler, *Textbook*. Bongar, Bruce Michael, and Larry E. Beutler. *Comprehensive Textbook of Psychotherapy: Theory and Practice*. New York: Oxford, 1995.

Bonhoeffer, *Discipleship*. Bonhoeffer, Dietrich. *Discipleship*. Dietrich Bonhoeffer Works 4. Translated by Barbara Green and Reinhard Krauss. Minneapolis: Augsburg Fortress, 2001.

Bonsirven, *Judaism*. Bonsirven, Joseph. *Palestinian Judaism in the Time of Jesus Christ*. New York: Holt, Rinehart & Winston, 1964.

Bony, "Lecture." Bony, Paul. "Une lecture de l'épître aux Romains: L'Évangile, Israël et les nations." *EspV* 112 (72, 2002): 33–41; 112 (73, 2003): 14–23.

Borca, "Exploration." Borca, Federico. "*Per Loca Senta Situ Ire*: An Exploration of the Chthonian Landscape." *CBull* 76 (1, 2000): 51–59.

Borgeaud, "Death." Borgeaud, Philippe. "The Death of the Great Pan: The Problem of Interpretation." *HR* 22 (1983): 254–83.

Borgen, *Bread*. Borgen, Peder. *Bread from Heaven: An Exegetical Study of the Concept of Manna in the Gospel of John and the Writings of Philo*. Leiden: Brill, 1965.

Boring, *Sayings*. Boring, M. Eugene. *Sayings of the Risen Jesus: Christian Prophecy in the Synoptic Tradition*. SNTSMS 46. Cambridge: Cambridge University Press, 1982.

Boring, Berger, and Colpe, *Commentary*. Boring, M. Eugene, Klaus Berger, and Carsten Colpe, eds. *Hellenistic Commentary to the New Testament*. Nashville: Abingdon, 1995.

Bornkamm, *Experience*. Bornkamm, Günther. *Early Christian Experience*. Translated by Paul L. Hammer. New York: Harper & Row; London: SCM, 1969.

Bornkamm, *Paul*. Bornkamm, Günther. *Paul*. Translated by D. M. G. Stalker. New York: Harper & Row, 1971.

Bosma and Kunnen, "Determinants." Bosma, Harke A., and E. Saskia Kunnen. "Determinants and Mechanisms in Ego Identity Development: A Review and Synthesis." *Developmental Review* 21 (1, Mar. 2001): 39–66.

Bousset, *Kyrios Christos*. Bousset, William. *Kyrios Christos: A History of the Belief in Christ from the Beginnings of Christianity to Irenaeus*. Translated by John E. Steely. Nashville: Abingdon, 1970.

Bouttier, *En Christ*. Bouttier, Michel. *En Christ: Étude d'exégèse et de théologie pauliniennes*. EHPR 54. Paris: Presses universitaires de France, 1962.

Bouwman, "Noch einmal." Bouwman, Gilbert. "Noch einmal Römer 1,21–32." *Bib* 54 (3, 1973): 411–14.

Bowker, "Visions." Bowker, John W. "'Merkabah' Visions and the Visions of Paul." *JSS* 16 (2, 1971): 157–73.

Bradley, "Magic." Bradley, Keith R. "Law, Magic, and Culture in the *Apologia* of Apuleius." *Phoenix* 51 (2, 1997): 203–33.

Bradley, "Wet-Nursing." Bradley, Keith R. "Wet-Nursing at Rome: A Study in Social Relations." In *The Family in Ancient Rome: New Perspectives*, edited by Beryl Rawson, 201–29. Ithaca, NY: Cornell University Press, 1986.

Brawley, *Centering on God*. Brawley, Robert L. *Centering on God: Method and Message in Luke-Acts*. Louisville: Westminster John Knox, 1990.

Bray, *Corinthians*. Bray, Gerald, ed. *1–2 Corinthians*. ACCS: New Testament 7. Downers Grove, IL: InterVarsity, 1999.

Bray, *Galatians, Ephesians*. Bray, Gerald, ed. *Galatians, Ephesians*. Reformation Commentary on Scripture, New Testament 10. Downers Grove, IL: IVP Academic, 2011.

Bray, *Romans*. Bray, Gerald, ed. *Romans*. ACCS: New Testament 6. Downers Grove, IL: InterVarsity, 1998.

Brega and Coleman, "Effects." Brega, Angela G., and Lerita M. Coleman. "Effects of Religiosity and Racial Socialization on Subjective Stigmatization in African-American Adolescents." *Journal of Adolescence* 22 (2, Apr. 1999): 223–42.

Bremmer, "Hades." Bremmer, Jan N. "Hades." *BrillPauly* 5:1076–77.

Brenk, "Image." Brenk, Frederick. "Image and Religion: A Christian in the Temple of Isis at Pompeii." In *Text, Image, and Christians in the Graeco-Roman World: A Festschrift in Honor of David Lee Balch*, edited by Aliou Cissé Niang and Carolyn Osiek, 218–38. PrTMS 176. Eugene, OR: Pickwick, 2012.

Brennan, "Theory." Brennan, Tad. "The Old Stoic Theory of Emotions." In *The Emotions in Hellenistic Philosophy*, edited by Juha Sihvola and Troels Engberg-Pedersen, 21–70. TSHP 46. Dordrecht, Neth.: Kluwer Academic, 1998.

Bright, *History*. Bright, John. *A History of Israel*. 3rd ed. Philadelphia: Westminster, 1981.

Brooke, "Interpretation." Brooke, George J. "Eschatological Bible Interpretation in the Scrolls and in the New Testament." *Mishkan* 44 (2005): 18–25.

Brooke, "Pesharim." Brooke, George J. "Pesharim." *DNTB* 778–82.

Brooke, "Pesher." Brooke, George J. "Qumran Pesher: Towards the Redefinition of a Genre." *RevQ* 10 (4, 1981): 483–503.

Brookins, "Wise Corinthians." Brookins, Tim. "The Wise Corinthians: Their Stoic Education and Outlook." *JTS* 62 (1, 2011): 51–76.

Brouwer, "Polybius and Tyche." Brouwer, René. "Polybius and Stoic Tyche." *GRBS* 51 (1, 2011): 111–32.

Brouwer, *Sage*. Brouwer, René. *The Stoic Sage: The Early Stoics on Wisdom, Sagehood, and Socrates*. New York: Cambridge University Press, 2014.

Brown, "*Mysterion*." Brown, Raymond E. "The Semitic Background of the New Testament *mysterion*." *Bib* 39 (1958): 426–48; 40 (1959): 70–87.

Brown, *Mystery*. Brown, Raymond E. *The Semitic Background of the Term "Mystery" in the New Testament*. Philadelphia: Fortress, 1968.

Brownlee, "Interpretation." Brownlee, William H. "Biblical Interpretation among the Sectaries of the Dead Sea Scrolls." *BA* 14 (3, 1951): 54–76.

Broyles, *Conflict*. Broyles, Craig Charles. *The Conflict of Faith and Experience: A Form-Critical and Theological Study of Selected Lament Psalms*. JSOTSup 52. Sheffield, UK: JSOT Press, 1989.

Broyles, "Lament." Broyles, Craig Charles. "Lament, Psalms of." In *Dictionary of the Old Testament: Wisdom, Poetry, and Writings*, edited by Tremper Longman III and Peter Enns, 384–99. Downers Grove, IL: IVP Academic, 2008.

Bruce, "All Things." Bruce, F. F. "'All Things to All Men': Diversity in Unity and Other Pauline Tensions." In *Unity and Diversity in New Testament Theology: Essays in Honor of George E. Ladd*, edited by Robert A. Guelich, 82–99. Grand Rapids: Eerdmans, 1978.

Bruce, *Apostle*. Bruce, F. F. *Paul: Apostle of the Heart Set Free*. Grand Rapids: Eerdmans, 1977.

Bruce, *Corinthians*. Bruce, F. F. *1 and 2 Corinthians*. NCBC 38. Greenwood, SC: Attic; London: Marshall, Morgan & Scott, 1971.

Bruce, *History*. Bruce, F. F. *New Testament History*. Garden City, NY: Doubleday, 1972.

Bruce, *Message*. Bruce, F. F. *The Message of the New Testament*. Grand Rapids: Eerdmans, 1981.

Bruce, "Myth." Bruce, F. F. "Myth and History." In *History, Criticism, and Faith*, edited by Colin Brown, 79–99. Downers Grove, IL: InterVarsity, 1976.

Bruce, *Romans*. Bruce, F. F. *The Epistle of Paul to the Romans*. TNTC. Grand Rapids: Eerdmans, 1963.

Bruce, "Spirit in Apocalypse." Bruce, F. F. "The Spirit in the Apocalypse." In *Christ and Spirit in the New Testament: Studies in Honour of C. F. D. Moule*, edited by Barnabas Lindars and Stephen S. Smalley, 333–44. Cambridge: Cambridge University Press, 1973.

Bruce, "Spirit in Qumran Texts." Bruce, F. F. "Holy Spirit in the Qumran Texts." *ALUOS* 6 (1966): 49–55.

Brunner, *Romans*. Brunner, Emil. *The Letter to the Romans*. Philadelphia: Westminster, 1959.

Bryan, *Preface*. Bryan, Christopher. *A Preface to Romans: Notes on the Epistle in Its Literary and Cultural Setting*. New York: Oxford University Press, 2000.

Buchanan, *Consequences*. Buchanan, George Wesley. *The Consequences of the Covenant*. NovTSup 20. Leiden: Brill, 1970.

Büchsel, *Geist*. Büchsel, D. Friedrich. *Der Geist Gottes im Neuen Testament*. Gütersloh: Bertelsmann, 1926.

Büchsel, "In Christus." Büchsel, Friedrich. "'In Christus' bei Paulus." *ZNW* 42 (1949): 141–58.

Buffière, "Séléné." Buffière, F. "Séléné: La lune dans la poésie, la science et la religion grecques." *BLE* 100 (1, 1999): 3–18.

Bultmann, "Anthropology." Bultmann, Rudolf. "Romans 7 and the Anthropology of Paul."

In *Existence and Faith: Shorter Writings of Rudolf Bultmann*, 147–57. Cleveland: World Publishing Company, 1960.

Bultmann, *Christianity*. Bultmann, Rudolf. *Primitive Christianity in Its Contemporary Setting*. Translated by Reginald H. Fuller. New York: Meridian, 1956.

Bultmann, *Corinthians*. Bultmann, Rudolf. *The Second Letter to the Corinthians*. Translated by Roy A. Harrisville. Minneapolis: Augsburg, 1985.

Bultmann, "Exegesis." Bultmann, Rudolf. "Is Exegesis without Presuppositions Possible?" In *The New Testament and Mythology and Other Basic Writings*, edited by Schubert Ogden, 145–53. Philadelphia: Fortress, 1984.

Bultmann, "Γινώσκω." Bultmann, Rudolf. "Γινώσκω." *TDNT* 1:689–719.

Bultmann, *Old and New Man*. Bultmann, Rudolf. *The Old and New Man in the Letters of Paul*. Translated by Keith R. Crim. Richmond: John Knox, 1967.

Bultmann, *Theology*. Bultmann, Rudolf. *Theology of the New Testament*. Translated by Kendrick Grobel. 2 vols. New York: Scribner's, 1951.

Bunta, "Metamorphosis." Bunta, Silviu N. "Metamorphosis and Role Reversal: Anthropomorphic Demons and Angelomorphic Humans in the *Life of Adam and Eve*." *Hen* 33 (1, 2011): 47–60.

Burkert, "Craft." Burkert, Walter. "Craft versus Sect: The Problem of Orphics and Pythagoreans." In *Self-Definition in the Greco-Roman World*, edited by Ben F. Meyer and E. P. Sanders, 1–22. Vol. 3 of *Jewish and Christian Self-Definition*. Philadelphia: Fortress, 1982.

Burkert, *Mystery Cults*. Burkert, Walter. *Ancient Mystery Cults*. Carl Newell Jackson Lectures. Cambridge, MA: Harvard University Press, 1987.

Burkert, *Religion*. Burkert, Walter. *Greek Religion*. Translated by John Raffan. Cambridge, MA: Harvard University Press, 1985.

Burkitt, *Church and Gnosis*. Burkitt, F. Crawford. *The Church and Gnosis: A Study of Christian Thought and Speculation in the Second Century*. Morse Lectures 1931. Cambridge: Cambridge University Press, 1932.

Burnett, "Philo on Immortality." Burnett, Fred W. "Philo on Immortality: A Thematic Study of Philo's Concept of παλιγγενεσία." *CBQ* 46 (3, 1984): 447–70.

Burns, *Romans*. Burns, J. Patout, Jr., with Constantine Newman. *Romans: Interpreted by Early Christian Commentators*. The Church's Bible. Grand Rapids: Eerdmans, 2012.

Burtt, *Foundations*. Burtt, Edwin Arthur. *The Metaphysical Foundations of Modern Science*. Reprint ed. Garden City, NY: Doubleday, 1954.

Busch, "Figure." Busch, Austin. "The Figure of Eve in Romans 7:5–25." *BibInt* 12 (1, 2004): 1–36.

Byrne, "Mind." Byrne, Brendan. "St Paul and the Life of the Mind." *Pacifica* 22 (2, 2009): 236–40.

Byrne, "Pre-existence." Byrne, Brendan. "Christ's Pre-existence in Pauline Soteriology." *TS* 58 (2, 1997): 308–30.

Byrne, "Righteousness." Byrne, Brendan. "Living Out the Righteousness of God: The Contribution of Rom 6:1–8:13 to an Understanding of Paul's Ethical Presuppositions." *CBQ* 43 (1981): 557–81.

Byrne, *Romans*. Byrne, Brendan. *Romans*. SP 6. Collegeville, MN: Liturgical Press, 1996.

Caird, *Age*. Caird, George B. *The Apostolic Age*. London: Duckworth, 1955.

Caird, *Language*. Caird, George B. *The Language and Imagery of the Bible*. Philadelphia: Westminster, 1980.

Campbell, *Advances*. Campbell, Constantine R. *Advances in the Study of Greek: New Insights for Reading the New Testament*. Grand Rapids: Zondervan, 2015.

Campbell, *Deliverance*. Campbell, Douglas A. *The Deliverance of God: An Apocalyptic Rereading of Justification in Paul*. Grand Rapids: Eerdmans, 2009.

Campbell, *Union*. Campbell, Constantine R. *Paul and Union with Christ: An Exegetical and Theological Study*. Grand Rapids: Zondervan, 2012.

Caragounis, *Mysterion*. Caragounis, Chrys C. *The Ephesian Mysterion: Meaning and Content*. ConBNT 8. Lund, Swed.: Gleerup, 1977.

Carr, *Angels*. Carr, Wesley. *Angels and Principalities*. Cambridge: Cambridge University Press, 1981.

Carr, "Rulers." Carr, Wesley. "The Rulers of This Age—I Corinthians II.6–8." *NTS* 23 (1, Oct. 1976): 20–35.

Carson, *Spirit*. Carson, D. A. *Showing the Spirit: A Theological Exposition of 1 Corinthians 12–14*. Grand Rapids: Baker, 1987.

Cary and Haarhoff, *Life*. Cary, M., and T. J. Haarhoff. *Life and Thought in the Greek and Roman World*. 4th ed. London: Methuen, 1946.

Casadio, "Failing God." Casadio, Giovanni. "The Failing Male God: Emasculation, Death, and Other Accidents in the Ancient Mediterranean World." *Numen* 50 (3, 2003): 231–68.

Casciaro Ramírez, "Misterio." Casciaro Ramírez, José M. "El 'misterio' divino en los escritos posteriores de Qumran." *ScrTh* 8 (1976): 445–75.

Case, *Origins*. Case, Shirley Jackson. *The Social Origins of Christianity*. 1923. Reprint, New York: Cooper Square, 1975.

Cerfaux, *Church*. Cerfaux, L. *The Church in the Theology of St. Paul*. Translated by Geoffrey Webb and Adrian Walker. New York: Herder & Herder, 1959.

Chadwick, *Early Church*. Chadwick, Henry. *The Early Church*. Pelican History of the Church 1. New York: Penguin, 1967.

Chang, "Life." Chang, Hae-Kyung. "The Christian Life in a Dialectical Tension? Romans 7:7–25 Reconsidered." *NovT* 49 (2007): 257–80.

Charles, *Jubilees*. Charles, R. H. *The Book of Jubilees, or The Little Genesis*. London: Adam & Charles Black, 1902.

Charles, "Vice Lists." Charles, J. Daryl. "Vice and Virtue Lists." *DNTB* 1252–57.

Charlesworth, "Comparison." Charlesworth, James H. "A Critical Comparison of the Dualism in IQS III,13–IV,26 and the 'Dualism' Contained in the Fourth Gospel." *NTS* 15 (4, 1969): 389–418.

Charlesworth, *Jesus within Judaism*. Charlesworth, James H. *Jesus within Judaism: New Light from Exciting Archaeological Discoveries*. ABRL. New York: Doubleday, 1988.

Charlesworth, *Pseudepigrapha*. Charlesworth, James H. *The Old Testament Pseudepigrapha and the New Testament: Prolegomena for the Study of Christian Origins*. SNTSMS 54. Cambridge: Cambridge University Press, 1985.

Chernus, "Visions." Chernus, Ira. "Visions of God in Merkabah Mysticism." *JSJ* 13 (1–2, 1982): 123–46.

Chevallier, *Ancien Testament*. Chevallier, Max-Alain. *Ancien Testament, hellénisme et judaïsme, la tradition synoptique, l'oeuvre de Luc*. Vol. 1 of *Souffle de Dieu: Le Saint-Esprit dans le Nouveau Testament*. Point théologique 26. Paris: Beauchesne, 1978.

Chevallier, "Souffle." Chevallier, Max-Alain. "Le souffle de Dieu dans le judaïsme, aux abords de l'ère chrétienne." *FoiVie* 80 (1, 1981): 33–46.

Chilton, "Galatians 6:15." Chilton, Bruce D. "Galatians 6:15: A Call to Freedom before God." *ExpT* 89 (10, 1978): 311–13.

Chilton, *Rabbi Paul*. Chilton, Bruce. *Rabbi Paul: An Intellectual Biography*. New York: Doubleday, 2004.

Chinn, "*Libertas*." Chinn, Christopher. "*Libertas reverentiam remisit*: Politics and Metaphor in Statius *Silvae* 1.6." *AJP* 129 (1, 2008): 101–24.

Chow, "Romans 7:7–25." Chow, Simon. "Who Is the 'I' in Romans 7:7–25." *Theology and Life* 30 (2007): 19–30.

Cobb and Lull, *Romans*. Cobb, John B., Jr., and David J. Lull. *Romans*. Chalice Commentaries for Today. St. Louis: Chalice, 2005.

Coffey, "Knowledge." Coffey, David M. "Natural Knowledge of God: Reflections on Romans 1:18–32." *TS* 31 (4, 1970): 674–91.

Cohen, *Law*. Cohen, Boaz. *Jewish and Roman Law: A Comparative Study*. 2 vols. New York: Jewish Theological Seminary of America Press, 1966.

Cohen, "Noahide Commandments." Cohen, Naomi G. "Taryag and the Noahide Commandments." *JJS* 43 (1, 1992): 46–57.

Cohick, *Philippians*. Cohick, Lynn H. *Philippians*. Story of God Bible Commentary. Grand Rapids: Zondervan, 2013.

Collins, "Artapanus." Collins, John J. Introduction to "Artapanus." *OTP* 2:889–96.

Collins, *Corinthians*. Collins, Raymond F. *First Corinthians*. SP 7. Collegeville, MN: Liturgical Press, 1999.

Collins, "Integrity." Collins, Raymond F. "A propos the Integrity of 1 Thes." *ETL* 55 (1, 1979): 67–106.

Collins, "Natural Theology." Collins, John J. "Natural Theology and Biblical Tradition: The Case of Hellenistic Judaism." *CBQ* 60 (1, 1998): 1–15.

Collins, "Spirit." Collins, C. John. "John 4:23–24, 'In Spirit and Truth': An Idiomatic Proposal." *Presbyterion* 21 (2, 1995): 118–21.

Combs, "Believer." Combs, William W. "Does the Believer Have One Nature or Two?" *DBSJ* 2 (1997): 81–103.

Combs, "Doctrine." Combs, William W. "Romans 12:1–2 and the Doctrine of Sanctification." *DBSJ* 11 (2006): 3–24.

Conroy, "Death." Conroy, John T., Jr. "Philo's 'Death of the Soul': Is This Only a Metaphor?" *SPhilA* 23 (2011): 23–40.

Conzelmann, *Corinthians*. Conzelmann, Hans. *1 Corinthians: A Commentary on the First Epistle to the Corinthians*. Edited by George W. MacRae. Translated by James W. Leitch. Bibliography and references by James W. Dunkly. Hermeneia. Philadelphia: Fortress, 1975.

Conzelmann, *Theology*. Conzelmann, Hans. *An Outline of the Theology of the New Testament*. New York: Harper & Row, 1969.

Cook, *Interpretation*. Cook, John Granger. *The Interpretation of the New Testament in Greco-Roman Paganism*. Peabody, MA: Hendrickson, 2002; Tübingen: Mohr Siebeck, 2000.

Cooper, "Philosophers." Cooper, John M. "Greek Philosophers on Suicide." In *Suicide and Euthanasia: Historical and Contemporary Themes*, edited by Baruch Alter Brody, 9–38. Dordrecht, Neth.: Kluwer, 1989.

Cooper, "Posidonius." Cooper, John M. "Posidonius on Emotions." In *The Emotions in Hellenistic Philosophy*, edited by Juha Sihvola and Troels Engberg-Pedersen, 71–111. TSHP 46. Dordrecht, Neth.: Kluwer Academic, 1998.

Coppens, "Don." Coppens, J. "Le don de l'Esprit d'après les textes de Qumrân et le quatrième évangile." In *L'Évangile de Jean: Études et problèmes*, 209–23. RechBib 3. Leuven: Desclée de Brouwer, 1958.

Corey, *Theory*. Corey, Gerald. *Theory and Practice of Counseling and Psychotherapy*. 9th ed. Belmont, CA: Brooks/Cole, 2013.

Corrington, "Defense." Corrington, Gail Paterson. "The Defense of the Body and the Discourse of Appetite: Continence and Control in the Greco-Roman World." *Semeia* 57 (1992): 65–74.

Costa, "Review." Costa, Tony. Review of *We Are Being Transformed*, by M. David Litwa. *RBL* 10 (2013), http://www.bookreviews.org /pdf/8646_9490.pdf.

Côte, "Perspectives." Côte, James E. "Sociological Perspectives on Identity Formation: The Culture-Identity Link and Identity Capital." *Journal of Adolescence* 19 (5, Oct. 1996): 417–28.

Côte and Schwartz, "Approaches." Côte, James E., and Seth J. Schwartz. "Comparing Psychological and Sociological Approaches to Identity: Identity Status, Identity Capital, and the Individualization Process." *Journal of Adolescence* 25 (6, Dec. 2002): 571–86.

Cousar, *Philippians*. Cousar, Charles B. *Philippians and Philemon: A Commentary*. NTL. Louisville: Westminster John Knox, 2009.

Crafton, "Vision." Crafton, Jeffrey A. "Paul's Rhetorical Vision and the Purpose of Romans: Toward a New Understanding." *NovT* 32 (4, 1990): 317–39.

Cragg, *Church*. Cragg, Gerald R. *The Church and the Age of Reason, 1648–1789*. Rev. ed. Penguin History of the Church 4. Baltimore: Penguin, 1970.

Craig, "Bodily Resurrection." Craig, William Lane. "The Bodily Resurrection of Jesus." In *Studies of History and Tradition in the Four Gospels*, edited by R. T. France and David Wenham, 1:47–74. 2 vols. Gospel Perspectives 1–2. Sheffield, UK: JSOT Press, 1980–81.

Cranfield, "ΜΕΤΡΟΝ ΠΙΣΤΕΩΣ." Cranfield, C. E. B. "ΜΕΤΡΟΝ ΠΙΣΤΕΩΣ in Romans XII.3." *NTS* 8 (4, July 1962): 345–51.

Cranfield, *Romans*. Cranfield, C. E. B. *A Critical and Exegetical Commentary on the Epistle to the Romans*. 2 vols. ICC. Edinburgh: T&T Clark, 1975.

Cranfield, "Romans 1.18." Cranfield, C. E. B. "Romans 1.18." *SJT* 21 (3, 1968): 330–35.

Creve, Janse, and Demoen, "Key Words." Creve, Sam, Mark Janse, and Kristoffel Demoen. "The Pauline Key Words πνεῦμα and σάρξ and Their Translation." *FilNeot* 20 (39–40, 2007): 15–31.

Croce, "Concepto." Croce, Ernesto la. "El origen del concepto de alma en la tradicion occidental." *Psicopatologia* 1 (4, Oct.–Dec. 1981): 311–16.

Croom, *Clothing*. Croom, Alexandra T. *Roman Clothing and Fashion*. Charleston, SC: Tempus, 2000.

Croy, "Neo-Pythagoreanism." Croy, N. Clayton. "Neo-Pythagoreanism." *DNTB* 739–42.

Cullmann, *State*. Cullmann, Oscar. *The State in the New Testament*. New York: Scribner's, 1956.

Cullmann, *Time*. Cullmann, Oscar. *Christ and Time*. Translated by Floyd V. Filson. Philadelphia: Westminster, 1950.

Cullmann, *Worship*. Cullmann, Oscar. *Early Christian Worship*. Philadelphia: Westminster, 1953.

Cumont, *After Life*. Cumont, Franz. *After Life in Roman Paganism: Lectures Delivered at Yale University on the Silliman Foundation*. New Haven: Yale University Press, 1922.

Currid, *Egypt*. Currid, John D. *Ancient Egypt and the Old Testament*. Foreword by Kenneth A. Kitchen. Grand Rapids: Baker Books, 1997.

Dafni, "ΝΟΥΣ." Dafni, Evangelia G. "ΝΟΥΣ in der Septuaginta des Hiobbuches: Zur Frage nach der Rezeption der Homerepik im hellenistischen Judentum." *JSJ* 37 (1, 2006): 35–54.

Dafni, "Theologie." Dafni, Evangelia G. "Natürliche Theologie im Lichte des hebräischen und griechischen Alten Testaments." *TZ* 57 (3, 2001): 295–310.

Dahl, *Studies*. Dahl, Nils A. *Studies in Paul: Theology for the Early Christian Mission*. Minneapolis: Augsburg, 1977.

Daines, "Use." Daines, Brian. "Paul's Use of the Analogy of the Body of Christ—With Special Reference to 1 Corinthians 12." *EvQ* 50 (2, 1978): 71–78.

Daniélou, *Theology*. Daniélou, Jean. *The Theology of Jewish Christianity*. Edited and translated by John A. Baker. DCDBCN 1. London: Darton, Longman & Todd; Chicago: Henry Regnery, 1964.

Danielson, Lorem, and Kroger, "Impact." Danielson, Lene M., Astrid E. Lorem, and Jane Kroger. "The Impact of Social Context on the Identity-Formation Process of Norwegian Late Adolescents." *Youth & Society* 31 (3, Mar. 2000): 332–62.

Danker, *Corinthians*. Danker, Frederick W. *II Corinthians*. AugCNT. Minneapolis: Augsburg, 1989.

Das, *Debate*. Das, A. Andrew. *Solving the Romans Debate*. Minneapolis: Fortress, 2007.

Das, *Paul and Jews*. Das, A. Andrew. *Paul and the Jews*. LPSt. Peabody, MA: Hendrickson, 2003.

Daube, *New Testament and Judaism*. Daube, David. *The New Testament and Rabbinic Judaism*. London: University of London, Athlone Press, 1956. Reprint, Peabody, MA: Hendrickson, 1994.

Dautzenberg, "Botschaft." Dautzenberg, Gerhard. "Botschaft und Bedeutung der urchristlichen Prophetie nach dem ersten Korintherbrief (2,6–16; 12–14)." In *Prophetic Vocation in the New Testament and Today*, edited by Johannes Panagopoulos, 131–61. NovTSup 45. Leiden: Brill, 1977.

Davies, "Aboth." Davies, W. D. "Reflexions on Tradition: The Aboth Revisited." In *Christian History and Interpretation: Studies Presented to John Knox*, edited by W. R. Farmer, C. F. D. Moule, and R. R. Niebuhr, 129–37. Cambridge: Cambridge University Press, 1967.

Davies, "Free." Davies, Donald M. "Free from the Law: An Exposition of the Seventh Chapter of Romans." *Int* 7 (2, 1953): 156–62.

Davies, "Ideology." Davies, Philip R. "The Ideology of the Temple in the Damascus Document." *JJS* 33 (1–2, 1982): 287–301.

Davies, "In Christo." Davies, J. B. "In Christo Jesu." *Clergy Review* 42 (11, 1957): 676–81.

Davies, *Origins*. Davies, W. D. *Christian Origins and Judaism*. Philadelphia: Westminster, 1962.

Davies, *Paul*. Davies, W. D. *Paul and Rabbinic Judaism: Some Rabbinic Elements in Pauline Theology*. 4th ed. Philadelphia: Fortress, 1980.

Davies, *Torah*. Davies, W. D. *Torah in the Messianic Age and/or the Age to Come*. JBLMS 7. Philadelphia: SBL, 1952.

Davies and Allison, *Matthew*. Davies, W. D., and Dale C. Allison. *A Critical and Exegetical Commentary on the Gospel according to Saint Matthew*. 3 vols. ICC. Edinburgh: T&T Clark, 1988–97.

Davila, "Macrocosmic Temple." Davila, James R. "The Macrocosmic Temple, Scriptural Exegesis, and the Songs of the Sabbath Sacrifice." *DSD* 9 (1, 2002): 1–19.

Davila, "Merkavah Mysticism." Davila, James R. "4QMess ar (4Q534) and Merkavah Mysticism." *DSD* 5 (3, 1998): 367–81.

Dawson, "Urbanization." Dawson, John. "Urbanization and Mental Health in a West African Community." In *Magic, Faith, and Healing: Studies in Primitive Psychotherapy Today*, edited by Ari Kiev, 305–42. Introduction by Jerome D. Frank. New York: Free Press, 1964.

Decharneux, "Interdits." Decharneux, Baudouin. "Interdits sexuels dans l'œuvre de Philon d'Alexandrie dit 'le juif.'" *PHR* 1 (1990): 17–31.

DeConick, *Voices*. DeConick, April D. *Voices of the Mystics: Early Christian Discourse in the Gospels of John and Thomas and Other Ancient Christian Literature*. JSNTSup 157. Sheffield, UK: Sheffield Academic Press, 2001.

Deidun, *Morality*. Deidun, T. J. *New Covenant Morality in Paul*. AnBib 89. Rome: Biblical Institute Press, 1981.

Deissmann, *Light*. Deissmann, G. Adolf. *Light from the Ancient East*. Grand Rapids: Baker, 1978.

Deissmann, *Paul*. Deissmann, G. Adolf. *Paul: A Study in Social and Religious History*. New York: Harper, 1957.

Deming, *Celibacy*. Deming, Will. *Paul on Marriage and Celibacy: The Hellenistic Background of 1 Corinthians 7*. 2nd ed. Grand Rapids: Eerdmans, 2004.

Deming, "Indifferent Things." Deming, Will. "Paul and Indifferent Things." In *Paul in the Greco-Roman World: A Handbook*, edited by J. Paul Sampley, 384–403. Harrisburg, PA: Trinity Press International, 2003.

Denney, "Romans." Denney, James. "St. Paul's Epistle to the Romans." In *Expositor's Greek Testament*, edited by W. Robertson Nicoll, 2:555–725. 5 vols. Grand Rapids: Eerdmans, 1979.

Dennison, "Revelation." Dennison, William D. "Natural and Special Revelation: Reassessment." *Kerux* 21 (2, 2006): 13–34.

Dentan, *Knowledge*. Dentan, Robert C. *The Knowledge of God in Ancient Israel*. New York: Seabury, 1968.

Derrett, "Sources." Derrett, J. D. M. "Oriental Sources for John 8, 32–36?" *BeO* 43 (1, 2001): 29–32.

deSilva, *Honor*. deSilva, David A. *Honor, Patronage, Kinship, and Purity: Unlocking New Testament Culture*. Downers Grove, IL: InterVarsity, 2000.

deSilva, *Introduction*. deSilva, David A. *An Introduction to the New Testament: Contexts, Methods, and Ministry Formation*. Downers Grove, IL: InterVarsity; Leicester, UK: Apollos, 2004.

deSilva, "Wisdom." deSilva, David A. "Wisdom of Solomon." *DNTB* 1268–76.

Dey, *World*. Dey, Lula Kalyan Kumar. *The Intermediary World and Patterns of Perfection in Philo and Hebrews*. SBLDS 25. Missoula, MT: Scholars Press, 1975.

Dhennin, "Necropolis." Dhennin, Sylvain. "An Egyptian Animal Necropolis in a Greek Town." *Egyptian Archaeology* 33 (Fall 2008): 12–14.

Dibelius, "Initiation." Dibelius, Martin. "The Isis Initiation in Apuleius and Related Initiatory Rites." In *Conflict at Colossae: A Problem in the Interpretation of Early Christianity Illustrated by Selected Modern Studies*, edited and translated by Fred O. Francis and Wayne A. Meeks, 61–121. SBLSBS 4. Missoula, MT: SBL, 1973.

Dibelius, *James*. Dibelius, Martin. *James: A Commentary on the Epistle of James*. Revised by Heinrich Greeven. Edited by Helmut Koester. Translated by Michael A. Williams. Hermeneia. Philadelphia: Fortress, 1976.

Dibelius and Conzelmann, *Pastoral Epistles*. Dibelius, Martin, and Hans Conzelmann. *The Pastoral Epistles: A Commentary on the Pastoral Epistles*. Edited by Helmut Koester. Translated by Philip Buttolph and Adela Yarbro. Hermeneia. Philadelphia: Fortress, 1972.

Dickie, "Love-Magic." Dickie, Matthew W. "Who Practised Love-Magic in Classical Antiquity and in the Late Roman World?" *CQ* 50 (2, 2000): 563–83.

Dijkhuizen, "Pain." Dijkhuizen, Petra. "Pain, Endurance, and Gender in 4 Maccabees." *JS/TS* 17 (1, 2008): 57–76.

Dillon, *Middle Platonists*. Dillon, John M. *The Middle Platonists: 80 B.C. to A.D. 220*. Ithaca, NY: Cornell University Press, 1977.

Dillon, "Philosophy." Dillon, John M. "Philosophy." *DNTB* 793–96.

Dillon, "Plato." Dillon, John M. "Plato, Platonism." *DNTB* 804–7.

Dillon, "Priesthood." Dillon, Richard J. "The 'Priesthood' of St Paul, Romans 15:15–16." *Worship* 74 (2, 2000): 156–68.

Dillon, "Reclaiming." Dillon, John M. "Reclaiming the Heritage of Moses: Philo's Confrontation with Greek Philosophy." *SPhilA* 7 (1995): 108–23.

Dillon, "Transcendence in Philo." Dillon, John M. "The Transcendence of God in Philo: Some Possible Sources." *CHSP* 16 (1975): 1–8.

Dillon and Finamore, "Preface." Dillon, John M., and John F. Finamore. Preface to *Iamblichus "De Anima": Text, Translation, and Commentary*, ix–xi. Edited by John F. Finamore and John M. Dillon. PhA 42. Leiden: Brill, 2002. Reprint, Atlanta: SBL, 2010.

Dimant, "Pesharim." Dimant, Devorah. "Pesharim, Qumran." *ABD* 5:244–51.

Dimant and Strugnell, "Vision." Dimant, Devorah, and John Strugnell. "The Merkabah Vision in *Second Ezekiel (4Q385 4)*." *RevQ* 14 (3, 1990): 331–48.

Di Mattei, "Physiologia." Di Mattei, Steven. "Moses' Physiologia and the Meaning and Use of Physikôs in Philo of Alexandria's Exegetical Method." *SPhilA* 18 (2006): 3–32.

Dixon, *Roman Mother*. Dixon, Suzanne. *The Roman Mother*. Norman: Oklahoma University Press, 1988.

Dodd, *Bible and Greeks*. Dodd, C. H. *The Bible and the Greeks*. London: Hodder & Stoughton, 1935.

Dodd, *Interpretation*. Dodd, C. H. *The Interpretation of the Fourth Gospel*. Cambridge: Cambridge University Press, 1965.

Dodd, "Prologue." Dodd, C. H. "The Prologue to the Fourth Gospel and Christian Worship." In *Studies in the Fourth Gospel*, edited by F. L. Cross, 9–22. London: A. R. Mowbray, 1957.

Donaldson, *Paul and Gentiles*. Donaldson, Terence L. *Paul and the Gentiles: Remapping the Apostle's Convictional World*. Minneapolis: Fortress, 1997.

Donceel, "Khirbet Qumrân." Donceel, Robert. "Khirbet Qumrân (Palestine): Le locus 130 et les 'ossements sous jarre'; Mise à jour de la documentation." *QC* 13 (1, 2005): 3–70, plates 1–25.

Donfried, "Test Case." Donfried, Karl P. "Paul and Judaism: I Thessalonians 2:13–16 as a Test Case." *Int* 38 (3, 1984): 242–53.

Donfried, *Thessalonica*. Donfried, Karl P. *Paul, Thessalonica, and Early Christianity*. Grand Rapids: Eerdmans; London: T&T Clark, 2002.

Donfried and Richardson, *Judaism*. Donfried, Karl P., and Peter Richardson, eds. *Judaism and Christianity in First-Century Rome*. Grand Rapids: Eerdmans, 1998.

Downing, *Cynics and Churches*. Downing, F. Gerald. *Cynics, Paul, and the Pauline Churches: Cynics and Christian Origins II*. London: Routledge, 1998.

Dräger, "Er." Dräger, Paul. "Er." *BrillPauly* 5:7.

Dräger, "Medea." Dräger, Paul. "Medea." *Brill Pauly* 8:546–49.

Driver, *Scrolls*. Driver, G. R. *The Judaean Scrolls: The Problem and a Solution*. Oxford: Blackwell, 1965.

Duhaime, "Dualisme." Duhaime, Jean L. "Dualisme et construction de l'identité sectaire à Qumrân." *Théologiques* 13 (1, 2005): 43–57.

Duhaime, "Remarques." Duhaime, Jean L. "Remarques sur les dépôts d'ossements d'animaux à Qumrân." *RevQ* 9 (2, 1977): 245–51.

Duhaime, "Voies." Duhaime, Jean L. "Les voies des deux esprits (*1QS* iv 2–14): Une analyse structurelle." *RevQ* 19 (75, 2000): 349–67.

Dunand, "Mystères." Dunand, Françoise. "Les mystères égyptiens." In *Mystères et syncrétismes*, edited by M. Philonenko and M. Simon, 11–62. EHRel 2. Paris: Librairie Orientaliste Paul Geuthner, 1975.

Dunand, *Religion Populaire*. Dunand, Françoise. *Religion populaire en Égypte romaine*. EPROER 77. Leiden: Brill, 1979.

Dunn, "Adam." Dunn, James D. G. "Adam and Christ." In *Reading Paul's Letter to the Romans*, edited by Jerry L. Sumney, 125–38. SBLRBS 73. Atlanta: SBL, 2012.

Dunn, *Baptism*. Dunn, James D. G. *Baptism in the Holy Spirit: A Re-examination of the New Testament Teaching on the Gift of the Spirit in Relation to Pentecostalism Today*. SBT, 2nd ser., 15. London: SCM, 1970.

Dunn, "Demythologizing." Dunn, James D. G. "Demythologizing—The Problem of Myth in the New Testament." In *New Testament Interpretation: Essays on Principles and Methods*, edited by I. Howard Marshall, 285–307. Grand Rapids: Eerdmans, 1977.

Dunn, "Gospel." Dunn, James D. G. "The Gospel according to St. Paul." In *The Blackwell Companion to Paul*, edited by Stephen Westerholm, 139–53. BCompRel. Oxford: Blackwell, 2011.

Dunn, *Perspective*. Dunn, James D. G. *The New Perspective on Paul*. Rev. ed. Grand Rapids: Eerdmans, 2008.

Dunn, *Romans*. Dunn, James D. G. *Romans*. 2 vols. WBC 38A, B. Dallas: Word, 1988.

Dunn, "Romans 7,14–25." Dunn, James D. G. "Romans 7,14–25 in the Theology of Paul." *TZ* 31 (5, Sept.–Oct. 1975): 257–73.

Dunn, "Search." Dunn, James D. G. "In Search of Common Ground." In *Paul and the Mosaic Law*, edited by James D. G. Dunn, 309–34. The Third Durham-Tübingen Research Symposium on Earliest Christianity and Judaism (Durham, September 1994). Grand Rapids: Eerdmans, 2001.

Dunn, *Spirit*. Dunn, James D. G. *Jesus and the Spirit: A Study of the Religious and Charismatic Experience of Jesus and the First Christians as Reflected in the New Testament*. London: SCM, 1975.

Dunn, *Theology*. Dunn, James D. G. *The Theology of Paul the Apostle*. Grand Rapids: Eerdmans, 1998.

Dunn, *Unity*. Dunn, James D. G. *Unity and Diversity in the New Testament: An Inquiry into the Character of Earliest Christianity*. London: SCM, 1977.

Dunson, "Reason." Dunson, Ben C. "4 Maccabees and Romans 12:1–21: Reason and the Righteous Life." In *Reading Romans in Context: Paul and Second Temple Judaism*, edited by Ben C. Blackwell, John K. Goodrich, and Jason Maston, 136–42. Grand Rapids: Zondervan, 2015.

Dupont, *Life*. Dupont, Florence. *Daily Life in Ancient Rome*. Translated by Christopher Woodall. Oxford: Blackwell, 1992.

Dyson, "Pleasure." Dyson, Henry. "Pleasure and the Sapiens: Seneca, De vita beata 11.1." *CP* 105 (3, 2010): 313–17.

Édart, "Nécessité." Édart, Jean-Baptiste. "De la nécessité d'un sauveur: Rhétorique et théologie de Rm 7, 7–25." *RB* 105 (3, July 1998): 359–96.

Edson and Price, "Ruler-Cult." Edson, Charles Farwell, and Simon R. F. Price. "Ruler-Cult: Greek." *OCD³* 1337–38.

Edwards, *Commentary*. Edwards, Mark J., ed. *Galatians, Ephesians, Philippians*. ACCS: New Testament 8. Downers Grove, IL: Inter-Varsity, 1999.

Edwards, "Light." Edwards, Jonathan. "From 'A Divine and Supernatural Light.'" In *The American Tradition in Literature*, edited by Sculley Bradley et al., 1:138–45. 5th ed. New York: Random House, 1981.

Efferin, "Study." Efferin, Henry. "A Study on General Revelation: Romans 1:18–32; 2:12–16." *STJ* 4 (2, 1996): 147–55.

Eickelman, *Middle East*. Eickelman, Dale F. *The Middle East: An Anthropological Approach*. 2nd ed. Englewood Cliffs, NJ: Prentice Hall, 1989.

Eliade, *Rites*. Eliade, Mircea. *Rites and Symbols of Initiation: The Mysteries of Birth and Rebirth*. Translated by Willard R. Trask. New York: Harper & Row, 1958.

Elliott, *Feelings*. Elliott, Matthew. *Faithful Feelings: Emotion in the New Testament*. Leicester, UK: Inter-Varsity, 2005.

Ellison, *Mystery*. Ellison, H. L. *The Mystery of Israel: An Exposition of Romans 9–11*. Grand Rapids: Baker; Exeter, UK: Paternoster, 1966.

Emilsson, "Plotinus on Emotions." Emilsson, Eyjólfur Kjalar. "Plotinus on the Emotions." In *The Emotions in Hellenistic Philosophy*, edited by Juha Sihvola and Troels Engberg-Pedersen, 339–63. TSHP 46. Dordrecht, Neth.: Kluwer Academic, 1998.

Engberg-Pedersen, *Cosmology*. Engberg-Pedersen, Troels. *Cosmology and Self in the Apostle Paul: The Material Spirit*. Oxford: Oxford University Press, 2010.

Engberg-Pedersen, "Marcus." Engberg-Pedersen, Troels. "Marcus Aurelius on Emotions." In *The Emotions in Hellenistic Philosophy*, edited by Juha Sihvola and Troels Engberg-Pedersen, 305–37. TSHP 46. Dordrecht, Neth.: Kluwer Academic, 1998.

Engberg-Pedersen, *Paul and Stoics*. Engberg-Pedersen, Troels. *Paul and the Stoics*. Louisville: Westminster John Knox; Edinburgh: T&T Clark, 2000.

Engberg-Pedersen, "Spirit." Engberg-Pedersen, Troels. "The Material Spirit: Cosmology and Ethics in Paul." *NTS* 55 (2, 2009): 179–97.

Engberg-Pedersen, "Vices." Engberg-Pedersen, Troels. "Paul, Virtues, and Vices." In *Paul in the Greco-Roman World: A Handbook*, edited by J. Paul Sampley, 608–33. Harrisburg, PA: Trinity Press International, 2003.

Engels, *Roman Corinth*. Engels, Donald W. *Roman Corinth: An Alternative Model for the Classical City*. Chicago: University of Chicago Press, 1990.

Enslin, *Ethics*. Enslin, Morton Scott. *The Ethics of Paul*. New York: Abingdon, 1957.

Enz, "Exodus." Enz, Jacob J. "The Book of Exodus as a Literary Type for the Gospel of John." *JBL* 76 (3, 1957): 208–15.

Epp, "Imageries." Epp, Eldon J. "Paul's Diverse Imageries and Unifying Theme." In *Unity and Diversity in New Testament Theology: Essays in Honor of George E. Ladd*, edited by Robert A. Guelich, 100–116. Grand Rapids: Eerdmans, 1978.

Erdman, *Philippians*. Erdman, Charles R. *The Epistle of Paul to the Philippians*. Philadelphia: Westminster, 1966.

Erskine, *Stoa*. Erskine, Andrew. *The Hellenistic Stoa: Political Thought and Action*. Ithaca, NY: Cornell University Press, 1990.

Espy, "Conscience." Espy, John M. "Paul's 'Robust Conscience' Re-examined." *NTS* 31 (2, 1985): 161–88.

Falk, "Law." Falk, Z. W. "Jewish Private Law." *JPFC* 504–34.

Fee, "Christology and Pneumatology." Fee, Gordon D. "Christology and Pneumatology in Romans 8:9–11—and Elsewhere: Some Reflections on Paul as a Trinitarian." In *Jesus of Nazareth: Lord and Christ; Essays on the Historical Jesus and New Testament Christology*, edited by Joel B. Green and Max Turner, 312–31. Grand Rapids: Eerdmans; Carlisle, UK: Paternoster, 1994.

Fee, *Corinthians*. Fee, Gordon D. *The First Epistle to the Corinthians*. NICNT. Grand Rapids: Eerdmans, 1987.

Fee, *Exegesis*. Fee, Gordon D. *New Testament Exegesis: A Handbook for Students and Pastors*. Philadelphia: Westminster, 1983.

Fee, *Listening*. Fee, Gordon D. *Listening to the Spirit in the Text*. Grand Rapids: Eerdmans, 2000.

Fee, *Paul, Spirit, People of God*. Fee, Gordon D. *Paul, the Spirit, and the People of God*. Grand Rapids: Baker Academic, 1996.

Fee, *Philippians*. Fee, Gordon D. *Paul's Letter to the Philippians*. NICNT. Grand Rapids: Eerdmans, 1995.

Fee, *Presence*. Fee, Gordon D. *God's Empowering Presence: The Holy Spirit in the Letters of Paul*. Grand Rapids: Baker Academic, 1994.

Feldman, "Jehu." Feldman, Louis H. "Josephus' Portrait of Jehu." *JSQ* 4 (1, 1997): 12–32.

Ferch, "Aeons." Ferch, Arthur J. "The Two Aeons and the Messiah in Pseudo-Philo, 4 Ezra, and 2 Baruch." *AUSS* 15 (2, 1977): 135–51.

Ferguson, *Backgrounds*. Ferguson, Everett. *Backgrounds of Early Christianity*. Grand Rapids: Eerdmans, 1987.

Finamore and Dillon, "Introduction." Finamore, John F., and John M. Dillon. Introduction to *Iamblichus "De Anima,"* 1–25. Translated by John F. Finamore and John M. Dillon. PhA 42. Leiden: Brill, 2002. Reprint, Atlanta: SBL, 2010.

Finkelberg, "Virtue." Finkelberg, Margalit. "Virtue and Circumstances: On the City-State Concept of *Arete*." *AJP* 123 (1, 2002): 35–49.

Fitch, "Introduction." Fitch, John G. Introduction to *Tragedies*, by Seneca, 1–33. Edited and translated by John G. Fitch. LCL. Cambridge, MA: Harvard University Press, 2002.

Fitzmyer, "Glory." Fitzmyer, Joseph A. "Glory Reflected on the Face of Christ (2 Cor 3:7–4:6) and a Palestinian Jewish Motif." *TS* 42 (4, 1981): 630–44.

Fitzmyer, "Quotations." Fitzmyer, Joseph A. "The Use of Explicit Old Testament Quotations in Qumran Literature and in the New Testament." *NTS* 7 (4, 1961): 297–333.

Fitzmyer, *Romans*. Fitzmyer, Joseph A. *Romans: A New Translation with Introduction and Commentary*. AB 33. New York: Doubleday, 1993.

Flusser, *Judaism*. Flusser, David. *Judaism and the Origins of Christianity*. Jerusalem: Magnes, 1988.

Foerster, "Εὐάρεστος." Foerster, Werner. "Εὐάρεστος." *TDNT* 1:456–57.

Foerster, "Geist." Foerster, Werner. "Der heilige Geist im Spätjudentum." *NTS* 8 (2, 1962): 117–34.

Forbes, "Comparison." Forbes, Christopher. "Paul and Rhetorical Comparison." In *Paul in the Greco-Roman World: A Handbook*, edited by J. Paul Sampley, 134–71. Harrisburg, PA: Trinity Press International, 2003.

Forbes, *Technology*. Forbes, R. J. *Studies in Ancient Technology*. 9 vols. Leiden: Brill, 1955–64.

Frankenberry, *Faith*. Frankenberry, Nancy K. *The Faith of Scientists in Their Words*. Princeton: Princeton University Press, 2008.

Frankfurter, "Perils." Frankfurter, David. "The Perils of Love: Magic and Countermagic in Coptic Egypt." *JHistSex* 10 (3–4, 2001): 480–500.

Frankfurter, *Religion in Egypt*. Frankfurter, David. *Religion in Roman Egypt: Assimilation and Resistance*. Princeton: Princeton University Press, 1998.

Frede, "Conception." Frede, Michael. "On the Stoic Conception of the Good." In *Topics in Stoic Philosophy*, edited by Katerina Ierodiakonou, 71–94. Oxford: Oxford University Press, 1999.

Frede, "Soul." Frede, Michael. "Soul, Theory of the." *BrillPauly* 13:672–75.

Frey, "Antithese." Frey, Jörg. "Die paulinische Antithese von 'Fleisch' und 'Geist' und die palästinisch-jüdische Weisheitstradition." *ZNW* 90 (1–2, 1999): 45–77.

Friesen, "Prospects." Friesen, Steven J. "Prospects for a Demography of the Pauline Mission: Corinth among the Churches." In *Urban Religion in Roman Corinth: Interdisciplinary Approaches*, edited by Daniel N. Schowalter and Steven J. Friesen, 351–70. HTS 53. Cambridge, MA: Harvard University Press, 2005.

Fritsch, *Community*. Fritsch, Charles T. *The Qumran Community: Its History and Scrolls*. New York: Macmillan, 1956.

Fuhrmann, "Mother." Fuhrmann, Sebastian. "The Mother in 4 Maccabees—An Example of Rational Choice in Religion." *JS/TS* 17 (1, 2008): 96–113.

Fuller, "Theology." Fuller, Daniel P. "Biblical Theology and the Analogy of Faith." In *Unity and Diversity in New Testament Theology: Essays in Honor of George E. Ladd*, edited by Robert A. Guelich, 195–213. Grand Rapids: Eerdmans, 1978.

Furnish, *Corinthians*. Furnish, Victor Paul. *II Corinthians*. AB 32A. Garden City, NY: Doubleday, 1984.

Furnish, "Living." Furnish, Victor Paul. "Living to God, Walking in Love: Theology and Ethics in Romans." In *Reading Paul's Letter to the Romans*, edited by Jerry L. Sumney, 187–202. SBLRBS 73. Atlanta: SBL, 2012.

Gaca, "Declaration." Gaca, Kathy L. "Paul's Uncommon Declaration in Romans 1:18–32 and Its Problematic Legacy for Pagan and Christian Relations." In *Early Patristic Readings of Romans*, edited by Kathy L. Gaca and L. L. Welborn, 1–33. Romans through History and Culture Series. London: T&T Clark, 2005.

Gager, *Anti-Semitism*. Gager, John G. *The Origins of Anti-Semitism: Attitudes toward Judaism in Pagan and Christian Antiquity*. New York: Oxford University Press, 1983.

Gager, "Class." Gager, John G. "Religion and Social Class in the Early Roman Empire." In *The Catacombs and the Colosseum: The Roman Empire as the Setting of Primitive Christianity*, edited by Stephen Benko and John J. O'Rourke, 99–120. Valley Forge, PA: Judson, 1971.

Gager, "Review." Gager, John G. Review of *Early Christianity and Society: Seven Studies*, by Robert M. Grant; *Social Aspects of Early Christianity*, by A. J. Malherbe; and *Sociology of Early Palestinian Christianity*, by Gerd Theissen. *RelSRev* 5 (3, 1979): 174–80.

Gammie, "Dualism." Gammie, John G. "Spatial and Ethical Dualism in Jewish Wisdom and Apocalyptic Literature." *JBL* 93 (3, 1974): 356–85.

Gard, *Method*. Gard, Donald H. *The Exegetical Method of the Greek Translator of the Book of Job*. JBLMS 8. Philadelphia: SBL, 1952.

Gardner, *Women*. Gardner, Jane F. *Women in Roman Law and Society*. Bloomington: Indiana University Press, 1986.

Garland, *1 Corinthians*. Garland, David E. *1 Corinthians*. BECNT. Grand Rapids: Baker Academic, 2003.

Garland, "Philippians." Garland, David E. "Philippians." In *The Expositor's Bible Commentary*, edited by Tremper Longman III and David E. Garland, 12:177–261. Rev. ed. 13 vols. Grand Rapids: Zondervan, 2006.

Garnet, "Light." Garnet, Paul. "Qumran Light on Pauline Soteriology." In *Pauline Studies: Essays Presented to Professor F. F. Bruce on His 70th Birthday*, edited by Donald A. Hagner and Murray J. Harris, 19–32. Exeter, UK: Paternoster; Grand Rapids: Eerdmans, 1980.

Garnsey and Saller, *Empire*. Garnsey, Peter, and Richard Saller. *The Roman Empire: Economy, Society, and Culture*. Berkeley: University of California Press, 1987.

Gärtner, "Synkrisis." Gärtner, Hans Armin. "Synkrisis." *BrillPauly* 14:28.

Gärtner, *Temple*. Gärtner, Bertril. *The Temple and the Community in Qumran and the New Testament: A Comparative Study in the Temple Symbolism of the Qumran Texts and the New Testament*. Cambridge: Cambridge University Press, 1965.

Gasparro, *Soteriology*. Gasparro, Giulia Sfameni. *Soteriology and Mystic Aspects in the Cult* of *Cybele and Attis*. EPROER 103. Leiden: Brill, 1985.

Gaster, *Scriptures*. Gaster, Theodor H. *The Dead Sea Scriptures*. Garden City, NY: Doubleday, 1976.

Gathercole, *Boasting*. Gathercole, Simon J. *Where Is Boasting? Early Jewish Soteriology and Paul's Response in Romans 1–5*. Grand Rapids: Eerdmans, 2002.

Gelinas, "Argument." Gelinas, Luke. "The Stoic Argument *Ex Gradibus Entium*." *Phronesis* 51 (1, 2006): 49–73.

Gemünden, "Culture des passions." Gemünden, Petra von. "La culture des passions à l'époque du Nouveau Testament: Une contribution théologique et psychologique." *ETR* 70 (3, 1995): 335–48.

Gemünden, "Femme." Gemünden, Petra von. "La femme passionnelle et l'homme rationnel? Un chapitre de psychologie historique." *Bib* 78 (4, 1997): 457–80.

Gessert, "Myth." Gessert, Genevieve. "Myth as *Consolatio*: Medea on Roman Sarcophagi." *GR* 51 (2, 2004): 217–49.

Gibbs, *Creation*. Gibbs, John G. *Creation and Redemption: A Study in Pauline Theology*. NovTSup 26. Leiden: Brill, 1971.

Gilbert, "Relation." Gilbert, Katharine. "The Relation of the Moral to the Aesthetic Standard in Plato." *Philosophical Review* 43 (3, May 1934): 279–94.

Gill, "Did Chrysippus Understand?" Gill, Christopher. "Did Chrysippus Understand Medea?" *Phronesis* 28 (2, 1983): 136–49.

Gill, "Galen." Gill, Christopher. "Did Galen Understand Platonic and Stoic Thinking on Emotions?" In *The Emotions in Hellenistic Philosophy*, edited by Juha Sihvola and Troels Engberg-Pedersen, 113–48. TSHP 46. Dordrecht, Neth.: Kluwer Academic, 1998.

Gingerich, "Scientist." Gingerich, Owen. "Dare a Scientist Believe in Design?" In *Evidence of Purpose: Scientists Discover the Creator*, edited by John Marks Templeton, 21–32. New York: Continuum, 1994.

Giulea, "Noetic Turn." Giulea, Dragos A. "The Noetic Turn in Jewish Thought." *JSJ* 42 (1, 2011): 23–57.

Glasson, "Colossians and Sirach." Glasson, T. Francis. "Colossians I 18, 15 and Sirach XXIV." *NovT* 11 (1–2, 1969): 154–56.

Glasson, "Doctrine." Glasson, T. Francis. "Heraclitus' Alleged Logos Doctrine." *JTS* 3 (2, 1952): 231–38.

Glasson, *Moses*. Glasson, T. Francis. *Moses in the Fourth Gospel*. SBT. Naperville, IL: Allenson, 1963.

Glover, *Paul*. Glover, T. R. *Paul of Tarsus*. London: Student Christian Movement, 1925. Reprint, Peabody, MA: Hendrickson, 2002.

Gödde, "Hamadryads." Gödde, Susanne. "Hamadryads." *BrillPauly* 5:1121.

Godwin, *Mystery Religions*. Godwin, Joscelyn. *Mystery Religions in the Ancient World*. San Francisco: Harper & Row, 1981.

Goodenough, *Church*. Goodenough, Erwin R. *The Church in the Roman Empire*. New York: Cooper Square, 1970.

Goodenough, *Introduction*. Goodenough, Erwin R. *An Introduction to Philo Judaeus*. 2nd ed. Oxford: Blackwell, 1962.

Goodenough, *Symbols*. Goodenough, Erwin R. *Jewish Symbols in the Greco-Roman Period*. 13 vols. BollS 37. Vols. 1–12: New York: Pantheon, 1953–65. Vol. 13: Princeton: Princeton University Press, 1968.

Goppelt, *Judaism*. Goppelt, Leonhard. *Jesus, Paul, and Judaism*. Translated by Edward Schroeder. New York: Thomas Nelson, 1964.

Goppelt, *Theology*. Goppelt, Leonhard. *Theology of the New Testament*. Edited by Jürgen Roloff. Translated by John E. Alsup. 2 vols. Grand Rapids: Eerdmans, 1981–82.

Goppelt, *Times*. Goppelt, Leonhard. *Apostolic and Post-Apostolic Times*. Translated by Robert Guelich. Grand Rapids: Baker, 1980.

Gordon, *Civilizations*. Gordon, Cyrus H. *The Common Background of Greek and Hebrew Civilizations*. New York: W. W. Norton, 1965.

Gordon, *Near East*. Gordon, Cyrus H. *The Ancient Near East*. New York: W. W. Norton, 1965.

Gorman, *Apostle*. Gorman, Michael J. *Apostle of the Crucified Lord: A Theological Introduction to Paul and His Letters*. Grand Rapids: Eerdmans, 2004.

Gorman, *Cruciformity*. Gorman, Michael J. *Cruciformity: Paul's Narrative Spirituality of the Cross*. Grand Rapids: Eerdmans, 2001.

Gorman, *Inhabiting*. Gorman, Michael J. *Inhabiting the Cruciform God: Kenosis, Justification, and Theosis in Paul's Narrative Soteriology*. Grand Rapids: Eerdmans, 2009.

Goshen Gottstein, "Body." Goshen Gottstein, Alon. "The Body as Image of God in Rabbinic Literature." *HTR* 87 (2, 1994): 171–95.

Gould, *Ethics*. Gould, John. *The Development of Plato's Ethics*. Cambridge: Cambridge University Press, 1955.

Gould, *Love*. Gould, Thomas. *Platonic Love*. London: Routledge & Kegan Paul, 1963.

Graf, "Heracles: Cult." Graf, Fritz. "Heracles: Cult." *BrillPauly* 6:159–60.

Graf, "Hero Cult." Graf, Fritz. "Hero Cult." *BrillPauly* 6:247–51.

Graf and Johnston, "Magic." Graf, Fritz, and Sarah Iles Johnston. "Magic, Magi: Greece and Rome." *BrillPauly* 8:133–43.

Grant, *Christianity and Society*. Grant, Robert M. *Early Christianity and Society: Seven Studies*. San Francisco: Harper & Row, 1977.

Grant, *Gnosticism*. Grant, Robert M. *Gnosticism and Early Christianity*. 2nd ed. New York: Columbia University Press, 1966.

Grant, *Gods*. Grant, Robert M. *Gods and the One God*. LEC 1. Philadelphia: Westminster, 1986.

Grant, *Hellenism*. Grant, Frederick C. *Roman Hellenism and the New Testament*. New York: Scribner's, 1962.

Grant, *Judaism and New Testament*. Grant, Frederick C. *Ancient Judaism and the New Testament*. New York: Macmillan, 1959.

Grant, *Paul*. Grant, Robert M. *Paul in the Roman World: The Conflict at Corinth*. Louisville: Westminster John Knox, 2001.

Grant, *Religions*. Grant, Frederick C., ed. *Hellenistic Religions: The Age of Syncretism*. Library of Liberal Arts. Indianapolis: Bobbs-Merrill; New York: Liberal Arts, 1953.

Grant, "Social Setting." Grant, Robert M. "The Social Setting of Second-Century Christianity." In *The Shaping of Christianity in the Second and Third Centuries*, edited by E. P. Sanders, 16–29. Vol. 1 of *Jewish and Christian Self-Definition*. Philadelphia: Fortress, 1980.

Grappe, "Corps de mort." Grappe, Christian. "Qui me délivrera de ce corps de mort? L'Esprit de vie! Romains 7,24 et 8,2 comme éléments de typologie adamique." *Bib* 83 (4, 2002): 472–92.

Grassi, "Ezekiel xxxvii." Grassi, Joseph A. "Ezekiel xxxvii.1–14 and the New Testament." *NTS* 11 (2, 1965): 162–64.

Graver, "Origins." Graver, Margaret. "Philo of Alexandria and the Origins of the Stoic Προπάθειαι." *Phronesis* 44 (4, 1999): 300–325.

Green, "Halakhah." Green, Dennis. "'Halakhah at Qumran?' The Use of *hlk* in the Dead Sea Scrolls." *RevQ* 22 (86, 2005): 235–51.

Greenberg, *Homosexuality*. Greenberg, David F. *The Construction of Homosexuality*. Chicago: University of Chicago Press, 1988.

Grene, *Political Theory*. Grene, David. *Greek Political Theory: The Image of Man in Thucydides and Plato*. Chicago: University of Chicago Press, 1950.

Grieb, *Story*. Grieb, A. Katherine. *The Story of Romans: A Narrative Defense of God's Righteousness*. Louisville: Westminster John Knox, 2002.

Griffin, "Philosophy." Griffin, Miriam T. "Philosophy, Cato, and Roman Suicide." *GR* 33 (1986): 64–77, 192–202.

Grindheim, "Wisdom." Grindheim, Sigurd. "Wisdom for the Perfect: Paul's Challenge to the Corinthian Church (1 Corinthians 2:6–16)." *JBL* 121 (4, 2002): 689–709.

Gundry, "Frustration." Gundry, Robert H. "The Moral Frustration of Paul before His Conversion: Sexual Lust in Romans 7:7–25." In *Pauline Studies: Essays Presented to Professor F. F. Bruce on His 70th Birthday*, edited by Donald A. Hagner and Murray J. Harris, 228–45. Exeter, UK: Paternoster; Grand Rapids: Eerdmans, 1980.

Gundry, *Matthew*. Gundry, Robert H. *Matthew: A Commentary on His Literary and Theological Art*. Grand Rapids: Eerdmans, 1982.

Gundry, *Sōma*. Gundry, Robert H. *Sōma in Biblical Theology: With Emphasis on Pauline Anthropology*. Cambridge: Cambridge University Press, 1976.

Gupta, "Mercies." Gupta, Nijay K. "What 'Mercies of God'? *Oiktirmos* in Romans 12:1 against Its Septuagintal Background." *BBR* 22 (1, 2012): 81–96.

Gupta, *Worship*. Gupta, Nijay K. *Worship That Makes Sense to Paul: A New Approach to the Theology and Ethics of Paul's Cultic Metaphors*. BZNW 175. New York: De Gruyter, 2010.

Guthrie, *Orpheus*. Guthrie, W. K. C. *Orpheus and Greek Religion: A Study of the Orphic Movement*. 2nd ed. New York: W. W. Norton, 1966.

Guthrie, *Plato*. Guthrie, W. K. C. *Plato, the Man and His Dialogues: Earlier Period*. Vol. 4 of *A History of Greek Philosophy*. Cambridge: Cambridge University Press, 1975.

Guttmann, "End." Guttmann, A. "The End of the Jewish Sacrificial Cult." *HUCA* 38 (1967): 137–48.

Gwaltney, "Book." Gwaltney, W. C., Jr. "The Biblical Book of Lamentations in the Context of Near Eastern Lament Literature." In *Scripture in Context II: More Essays on the Comparative Method*, edited by William W. Hallo, James C. Moyer, and Leo G. Perdue, 191–211. Winona Lake, IN: Eisenbrauns, 1983.

Haacker, *Theology*. Haacker, Klaus. *The Theology of Paul's Letter to the Romans*. Cambridge: Cambridge University Press, 2003.

Hadas, *Aristeas*. Hadas, Moses, ed. and trans. *Aristeas to Philocrates (Letter of Aristeas)*. New York: Harper & Brothers, 1951. Reprint, New York: KTAV, 1973.

Hadas and Smith, *Heroes*. Hadas, Moses, and Morton Smith. *Heroes and Gods: Spiritual Biographies in Antiquity*. Religious Perspectives 13. New York: Harper & Row, 1965.

Hagner, "Vision." Hagner, Donald A. "The Vision of God in Philo and John: A Comparative Study." *JETS* 14 (2, 1971): 81–93.

Haines, "Introduction." Haines, C. R. Introduction to *The Communings with Himself of Marcus Aurelius Antonius, Emperor of Rome, Together with His Speeches and Sayings*, xi–xxxi. Revised and translated by C. R. Haines. LCL. Cambridge, MA: Harvard University Press, 1916.

Hall, "Delivery." Hall, Jon. "Oratorical Delivery and the Emotions: Theory and Practice." In *A Companion to Roman Rhetoric*, edited by William Dominik and Jon Hall, 218–34. Oxford: Blackwell, 2007.

Hallo, "Lamentations." Hallo, William W. "Lamentations and Prayers in Sumer and Akkad." In *Civilizations of the Ancient Near East*, edited by Jack M. Sasson, 3:1871–82. Peabody, MA: Hendrickson, 1995.

Halperin, "Midrash." Halperin, David J. "Merkabah Midrash in the Septuagint." *JBL* 101 (3, 1982): 351–63.

Halpern-Amaru, "Joy." Halpern-Amaru, Betsy. "Joy as Piety in the 'Book of Jubilees.'" *JJS* 56 (2, 2005): 185–205.

Halusza, "Sacred." Halusza, Adria. "Sacred Signified: The Semiotics of Statues in the Greek Magical Papyri." *Arethusa* 41 (3, 2008): 479–94.

Hamerton-Kelly, *Pre-existence*. Hamerton-Kelly, R. G. *Pre-existence, Wisdom, and the Son: A Study of the Idea of Pre-existence in the New Testament*. Cambridge: Cambridge University Press, 1973.

Hamilton, *Spirit and Eschatology*. Hamilton, Neill Q. *The Holy Spirit and Eschatology in Paul*. SJTOP 6. Edinburgh: Oliver & Boyd, 1957.

Hammond and Price, "Ruler-Cult." Hammond, Mason, and Simon R. F. Price. "Ruler-Cult: Roman." *OCD*[3] 1338–39.

Hanson, "Exodus." Hanson, Anthony. "John I.14–18 and Exodus XXXIV." *NTS* 23 (1, 1976): 90–101.

Harrison, *Grace*. Harrison, James R. *Paul's Language of Grace in Its Graeco-Roman Context*. WUNT 2.172. Tübingen: Mohr Siebeck, 2003.

Harrison, "Study." Harrison, Everett F. "A Study of John 1:14." In *Unity and Diversity in New Testament Theology: Essays in Honor of G. E. Ladd*, edited by Robert A. Guelich, 23–36. Grand Rapids: Eerdmans, 1978.

Harrison and Hagner, "Romans." Harrison, Everett F., and Donald A. Hagner. "Romans." In *The Expositor's Bible Commentary*, edited by Tremper Longman III and David E. Garland, 11:21–237. Rev. ed. 13 vols. Grand Rapids: Zondervan, 2008.

Hastings, *Edwards and Life of God*. Hastings, W. Ross. *Jonathan Edwards and the Life of God: Toward an Evangelical Theology of Participation*. Minneapolis: Fortress, 2015.

Hatch, *Idea*. Hatch, William Henry Paine. *The Pauline Idea of Faith in Its Relation to Jewish and Hellenistic Religion*. HTS. Cambridge, MA: Harvard University Press, 1917. Reprint, New York: Kraus, 1969.

Hawthorne, *Philippians*. Hawthorne, Gerald F. *Philippians*. WBC 43. Waco: Word, 1983.

Hays, *Conversion*. Hays, Richard B. *The Conversion of the Imagination: Paul as Interpreter of Israel's Scripture*. Grand Rapids: Eerdmans, 2005.

Hays, *Echoes*. Hays, Richard B. *Echoes of Scripture in the Letters of Paul*. New Haven: Yale University Press, 1989.

Hayward, "Israel." Hayward, C. T. Robert. "Philo, the Septuagint of Genesis 32:24–32 and the Name 'Israel': Fighting the Passions, Inspiration, and the Vision of God." *JJS* 51 (2, 2000): 209–26.

Heger, "Prayer." Heger, Paul. "Did Prayer Replace Sacrifice at Qumran?" *RevQ* 22 (86, 2005): 213–33.

Hengel, *Judaism and Hellenism*. Hengel, Martin. *Judaism and Hellenism: Studies in Their Encounter in Palestine during the Early Hellenistic Period*. Translated by John Bowden. 2 vols. in 1. Philadelphia: Fortress, 1974.

Hengel, *Property*. Hengel, Martin. *Property and Riches in the Early Church: Aspects of a Social History of Early Christianity*. Philadelphia: Fortress, 1974.

Henrichs, "Atheism." Henrichs, Albert. "The Atheism of Prodicus." *Bolletino del Centro internazionale per lo studio dei papiri ercolanesi* 6 (1976): 15–21.

Henrichs, "Notes." Henrichs, Albert. "Two Doxographical Notes: Democritus and Prodicus on Religion." *HSCP* 79 (1975): 93–123.

Henry, "Introduction." Henry, W. Benjamin. Introduction to Philodemus: *"On Death,"* xiii–xxxiv. Translated by W. Benjamin Henry. SBLWGRW 29. Atlanta: SBL, 2009.

Heriban, "Zmysl'ajte." Heriban, Jozef. "Zmysl' ajte tak ako v Kristovi Jezišovi (Flp 2,5): Otázka interpretácie Pavlovho odporúcania vo Flp 2,5 v súvise s kristologickym hymnom Flp 2,6–11." *StBibSlov* (2006): 58–78.

Héring, *First Epistle*. Héring, Jean. *The First Epistle of Saint Paul to the Corinthians*. Translated by A. W. Heathcote and P. J. Allcock. London: Epworth, 1962.

Héring, *Second Epistle*. Héring, Jean. *The Second Epistle of Saint Paul to the Corinthians*. Translated by A. W. Heathcote and P. J. Allcock. London: Epworth, 1962.

Hill, *Prophecy*. Hill, David. *New Testament Prophecy*. NFTL. Atlanta: John Knox, 1979.

Hillard, Nobbs, and Winter, "Corpus." Hillard, T., A. Nobbs, and B. Winter. "Acts and the Pauline Corpus, I: Ancient Literary Parallels." In *The Book of Acts in Its Ancient Literary Setting*, edited by Bruce W. Winter and Andrew D. Clarke, 183–213. Vol. 1 of *The Book of Acts in Its First Century Setting*. Edited by Bruce W. Winter. Grand Rapids: Eerdmans; Carlisle, UK: Paternoster, 1993.

Himmelfarb, "Ascent." Himmelfarb, Martha. "Heavenly Ascent and the Relationship of the Apocalypses and the *Hekhalot* Literature." *HUCA* 59 (1988): 73–100.

Hirsch, *Genesis*. Hirsch, Samson Raphael. *Genesis*. Vol. 1 of *The Pentateuch*. New York: Judaica, 1971.

Hock, "Education." Hock, Ronald F. "Paul and Greco-Roman Education." In *Paul in the Greco-Roman World: A Handbook*, edited by J. Paul Sampley, 198–227. Harrisburg, PA: Trinity Press International, 2003.

Hoehner, *Ephesians*. Hoehner, Harold W. *Ephesians: An Exegetical Commentary*. Grand Rapids: Baker Academic, 2002.

Holladay, *Theios Aner*. Holladay, Carl R. *Theios Aner in Hellenistic Judaism: A Critique of the Use of This Category in New Testament Christology*. SBLDS 40. Missoula, MT: Scholars Press, 1977.

Hoof, "Field." Hoof, Anne van. "The Identity Status Field Re-reviewed: An Update of Unresolved and Neglected Issues with a View on Some Alternative Approaches." *Developmental Review* 19 (4, Dec. 1999): 497–556.

Hooker, "Adam." Hooker, Morna D. "Adam in Romans I." *NTS* 6 (4, 1960): 297–306.

Hooker, "Hard Sayings." Hooker, Morna D. "Hard Sayings: I Corinthians 3:2." *Theology* 69 (547, 1966): 19–22.

Hooker, *Preface*. Hooker, Morna D. *A Preface to Paul*. New York: Oxford University Press, 1980.

Horn and Zimmermann, *Jenseits*. Horn, Friedrich W., and Ruben Zimmermann, eds. *Jenseits von Indikativ und Imperativ*. WUNT 238. Tübingen: Mohr Siebeck, 2009.

Horsley, *Corinthians*. Horsley, Richard A. *1 Corinthians*. ANTC. Nashville: Abingdon, 1998.

Horsley, *Documents*. Horsley, G. H. R., ed. *New Documents Illustrating Early Christianity: A Review of the Greek Inscriptions and Papyri Published in 1976*. Vol. 1. North Ryde, NSW: The Ancient History Documentary Research Centre, Macquarie University, 1981.

Horsley, "Pneumatikos." Horsley, Richard A. "Pneumatikos vs. Psychikos: Distinctions of Spiritual Status among the Corinthians." *HTR* 69 (3–4, Oct. 1976): 269–88.

Horton, *Spirit*. Horton, Stanley M. *What the Bible Says about the Holy Spirit*. Springfield, MO: Gospel Publishing House, 1976.

Hossenfelder, "Ataraxia." Hossenfelder, Malte. "Ataraxia." *BrillPauly* 2:218–19.

Hossenfelder, "Happiness." Hossenfelder, Malte. "Happiness." *BrillPauly* 5:1132–35.

Howell, "Dualism." Howell, Don N. "Pauline Eschatological Dualism and Its Resulting Tensions." *TJ* 14 (1, 1993): 3–24.

Howell, "Interchange." Howell, Don N. "God-Christ Interchange in Paul: Impressive Testimony to the Deity of Jesus." *JETS* 36 (4, 1993): 467–79.

Hubbard, *New Creation*. Hubbard, Moyer V. *New Creation in Paul's Letters and Thought*. SNTSMS 119. Cambridge: Cambridge University Press, 2002.

Hübner, "Hermeneutics." Hübner, Hans. "Hermeneutics of Romans 7." In *Paul and the Mosaic Law*, edited by James D. G. Dunn, 207–14. The Third Durham-Tübingen Research Symposium on Earliest Christianity and Judaism (Durham, September 1994). Grand Rapids: Eerdmans, 2001.

Huffmon, "Background." Huffmon, Herbert B. "The Treaty Background of Hebrew *Yada'*." *BASOR* 181 (Feb. 1966): 31–37.

Hultgren, *Romans*. Hultgren, Arland J. *Paul's Letter to the Romans: A Commentary*. Grand Rapids: Eerdmans, 2011.

Hunter, *Gospel according to Paul*. Hunter, Archibald M. *The Gospel according to St. Paul*. Philadelphia: Westminster, 1966.

Hunter, *Message*. Hunter, Archibald M. *The Message of the New Testament*. Philadelphia: Westminster, 1944.

Hunter, *Predecessors*. Hunter, Archibald M. *Paul and His Predecessors*. Rev. ed. Philadelphia: Westminster; London: SCM, 1961.

Hunter, *Romans*. Hunter, Archibald M. *The Epistle to the Romans*. London: SCM, 1955.

Hurschmann, "Mirror." Hurschmann, Rolf. "Mirror: Roman." *BrillPauly* 9:57–58.

Hurtado, *Become God*. Hurtado, Larry W. *How on Earth Did Jesus Become a God? Historical Questions about Earliest Devotion to Jesus*. Grand Rapids: Eerdmans, 2005.

Hurtado, *Lord Jesus Christ*. Hurtado, Larry W. *Lord Jesus Christ: Devotion to Jesus in Earliest Christianity*. Grand Rapids: Eerdmans, 2003.

Hurtado, *One God*. Hurtado, Larry W. *One God, One Lord: Early Christian Devotion and*

Ancient Jewish Monotheism. Philadelphia: Fortress, 1988.

Huttner, "Zivilisationskritik." Huttner, Ulrich. "Zur Zivilisationskritik in der frühen Kaiserzeit: Die Diskreditierung der *Pax romana*." *Historia* 49 (4, 2000): 446–66.

Hyldahl, "Reminiscence." Hyldahl, Niels. "A Reminiscence of the Old Testament at Romans 1.23." *NTS* 2 (4, May 1956): 285–88.

Ilan, *Women*. Ilan, Tal. *Jewish Women in Greco-Roman Palestine*. Tübingen: Mohr Siebeck; Peabody, MA: Hendrickson, 1996.

Inwood, "Natural Law." Inwood, Brad. "Natural Law in Seneca." *SPhilA* 15 (2003): 81–99.

Inwood, "Rules." Inwood, Brad. "Rules and Reasoning in Stoic Ethics." In *Topics in Stoic Philosophy*, edited by Katerina Ierodiakonou, 95–127. Oxford: Oxford University Press, 1999.

Isaacs, *Spirit*. Isaacs, Marie E. *The Concept of Spirit: A Study of Pneuma in Hellenistic Judaism and Its Bearing on the New Testament*. Heythrop Monographs 1. London: Heythrop College Press, 1976.

Jackson, *Creation*. Jackson, T. Ryan. *New Creation in Paul's Letters: A Study of the Historical and Social Setting of a Pauline Concept*. WUNT 2.272. Tübingen: Mohr Siebeck, 2010.

Jackson-McCabe, "Preconceptions." Jackson-McCabe, Matt. "The Stoic Theory of Implanted Preconceptions." *Phronesis* 49 (4, 2004): 323–47.

Jacobson and Weitzman, "Bronze." Jacobson, David M., and M. P. Weitzman. "What Was Corinthian Bronze?" *AJA* 96 (2, 1992): 237–47.

Janzen, "Approach." Janzen, J. Gerald. "A New Approach to 'logiken latreian' in Romans 12:1–2." *Enc* 69 (2, 2008): 45–83.

Jensen, "Coming of Age." Jensen, Lene Arnett. "Coming of Age in a Multicultural World: Globalization and Adolescent Cultural Identity Formation." *Applied Developmental Science* 7 (3, 2003): 189–96.

Jeremias, *Prayers*. Jeremias, Joachim. *The Prayers of Jesus*. Philadelphia: Fortress, 1964.

Jeremias, "Significance." Jeremias, Joachim. "The Theological Significance of the Dead Sea Scrolls." *CTM* 39 (8, 1968): 557–71.

Jeremias, "Zu Rm 1 22–32." Jeremias, Joachim. "Zu Rm 1 22–32." *ZNW* 45 (1–2, 1954): 119–21.

Jervis, "Commandment." Jervis, L. Ann. "'The Commandment Which Is for Life' (Romans 7.10): Sin's Use of the Obedience of Faith." *JSNT* 27 (2, 2004): 193–216.

Jervis, "Conversation." Jervis, L. Ann. "Reading Romans 7 in Conversation with Postcolonial Theory: Paul's Struggle toward a Christian Identity of Hybridity." In *The Colonized Apostle: Paul through Postcolonial Eyes*, edited by Christopher D. Stanley, 95–109. Paul in Critical Contexts. Minneapolis: Fortress, 2011.

Jervis, "Spirit." Jervis, L. Ann. "The Spirit Brings Christ's Life to Life." In *Reading Paul's Letter to the Romans*, edited by Jerry L. Sumney, 139–56. SBLRBS 73. Atlanta: SBL, 2012.

Jewett, *Romans*. Jewett, Robert, assisted by Roy D. Kotansky. *Romans: A Commentary*. Edited by Eldon Jay Epp. Hermeneia. Minneapolis: Fortress, 2007.

Jochim, *Religions*. Jochim, Christian. *Chinese Religions: A Cultural Perspective*. Prentice-Hall Series in World Religions. Englewood Cliffs, NJ: Prentice-Hall, 1986.

Jódar-Estrella, "Misterio." Jódar-Estrella, Carlos. "'Misterio' in 1Co 1–4: Despliegue (con) textual de una metáfora." *AT* 13 (2, 1999): 453–74.

Johnson, "Knowledge." Johnson, S. Lewis, Jr. "Paul and the Knowledge of God." *BSac* 129 (513, 1972): 61–74.

Johnson, *Romans*. Johnson, Luke Timothy. *Reading Romans: A Literary and Theological Commentary*. Macon, GA: Smyth & Helwys, 2001.

Johnson Hodge, "Apostle." Johnson Hodge, Caroline E. "Apostle to the Gentiles: Constructions of Paul's Identity." *BibInt* 13 (3, 2005): 270–88.

Johnston, "Animating Statues." Johnston, Sarah Iles. "Animating Statues: A Case Study in Ritual." *Arethusa* 41 (3, 2008): 445–77.

Johnston, *Ephesians*. Johnston, George. *Ephesians, Philippians, Colossians, and Philemon*. Century Bible. Greenwood, SC: Attic, 1967.

Johnston, "Spirit." Johnston, George. "'Spirit' and 'Holy Spirit' in the Qumran Literature." In *New Testament Sidelights: Essays in Honor of Alexander Converse Purdy*, edited by Harvey K. McArthur, 27–42. Hartford: Hartford Seminary Foundation Press, 1960.

Jonas, *Religion*. Jonas, Hans. *The Gnostic Religion: The Message of the Alien God and the Beginnings of Christianity*. 2nd rev. ed. Boston: Beacon, 1963.

Jones, "Epigram." Jones, C. P. "An Epigram on Apollonius of Tyana." *JHS* 100 (1980): 190–94.

Jordan, "Formulae." Jordan, David R. "P.Duk. inv. 729, Magical Formulae." *GRBS* 46 (2, 2006): 159–73.

Jordan, "Spell." Jordan, David R. "P.Duk.inv. 230, an Erotic Spell." *GRBS* 40 (2, 1999): 159–70.

Ju, "Immortality." Ju, A. E. "Stoic and Posidonian Thought on the Immortality of the Soul." *CQ* 59 (1, 2009): 112–24.

Judge, *First Christians*. Judge, Edwin A. *The First Christians in the Roman World: Augustan and New Testament Essays*. Edited by James R. Harrison. WUNT 229. Tübingen: Mohr Siebeck, 2008.

Judge, *Jerusalem*. Judge, Edwin A. *Jerusalem and Athens: Cultural Transformation in Late Antiquity*. Edited by Alanna Nobbs. Tübingen: Mohr Siebeck, 2010.

Judge, *Pattern*. Judge, Edwin A. *The Social Pattern of the Christian Groups in the First Century: Some Prolegomena to the Study of New Testament Ideas of Social Obligation*. London: Tyndale, 1960.

Judge, *Rank*. Judge, Edwin A. *Rank and Status in the World of the Caesars and St Paul*. Broadhead Memorial Lecture 1981. University of Canterbury Publications 29. Christchurch, NZ: University of Canterbury Press, 1982.

Kahn, "Duality." Kahn, Pinchas. "The Duality of Man: A Study in Talmudic Allegorical Interpretations." *JBQ* 36 (2, 2008): 102–7.

Kaiser, *Preaching*. Kaiser, Walter C., Jr. *The Old Testament in Contemporary Preaching*. Grand Rapids: Baker, 1973.

Kapolyo, *Condition*. Kapolyo, Joe M. *The Human Condition: Christian Perspectives through African Eyes*. Downers Grove, IL: InterVarsity, 2005.

Karlberg, "History." Karlberg, Mark W. "Israel's History Personified: Romans 7:7–13 in Relation to Paul's Teaching on the 'Old Man.'" *TJ* 7 (1, 1986): 65–74.

Käsemann, *Romans*. Käsemann, Ernst. *Commentary on Romans*. Edited and translated by Geoffrey W. Bromiley. Grand Rapids: Eerdmans, 1980.

Kaufmann, "Underworld." Kaufmann, Helen. "Virgil's Underworld in the Mind of Roman Late Antiquity." *Latomus* 69 (1, 2010): 150–60.

Kearns, "Hero-Cult." Kearns, Emily. "Hero-Cult." *OCD*[3] 693–94.

Keck, "*Pathos*." Keck, Leander E. "*Pathos* in Romans? Mostly Preliminary Remarks." In *Paul and Pathos*, edited by Thomas H. Olbricht and Jerry L. Sumney, 71–96. SBLSymS 16. Atlanta: SBL, 2001.

Keck, *Paul*. Keck, Leander E. *Paul and His Letters*. ProcC. Philadelphia: Fortress, 1979.

Keck, *Romans*. Keck, Leander E. *Romans*. ANTC. Nashville: Abingdon, 2005.

Keefer, "Purpose." Keefer, Luke L., Jr. "The Purpose of Holiness: The Triumph of God's Will." *AshTJ* 30 (1998): 1–10.

Keener, *Acts*. Keener, Craig S. *Acts: An Exegetical Commentary*. 4 vols. Grand Rapids: Baker Academic, 2012–15.

Keener, "Adultery." Keener, Craig S. "Adultery, Divorce." *DNTB* 6–16.

Keener, "Beheld." Keener, Craig S. "'We Beheld His Glory': John 1:14." In *John, Jesus, and History*, vol. 2, *Aspects of Historicity in the Fourth Gospel*, edited by Paul N. Anderson, Felix Just, and Tom Thatcher, 15–25. SBLECL 2. Atlanta: SBL, 2009.

Keener, "Corinthian Believers." Keener, Craig S. "Paul and the Corinthian Believers." In *The Blackwell Companion to Paul*, edited by Stephen Westerholm, 46–62. Oxford: Blackwell, 2011.

Keener, *Corinthians*. Keener, Craig S. *1 and 2 Corinthians*. NCamBC. Cambridge: Cambridge University Press, 2005.

Keener, "Epicureans." Keener, Craig S. "Epicureans." In *Brill Encyclopedia of Early Christianity*. Leiden: Brill, forthcoming.

Keener, "Exhortation." Keener, Craig S. "The Exhortation to Monotheism in Acts 14:15–17." In *Kingdom Rhetoric: New Testament Explorations in Honor of Ben Witherington III*, edited by T. Michael W. Halcomb, 47–70. Eugene, OR: Wipf & Stock, 2013.

Keener, *Gift*. Keener, Craig S. *Gift and Giver: The Holy Spirit for Today*. Grand Rapids: Baker Academic, 2001.

Keener, "Head Coverings." Keener, Craig S. "Head Coverings." *DNTB* 442–47.

Keener, "Heavenly Mindedness." Keener, Craig S. "Heavenly Mindedness and Earthly Good: Contemplating Matters Above in Colossians 3.1–2." *JGRCJ* 6 (2009): 175–90.

Keener, *John*. Keener, Craig S. *The Gospel of John: A Commentary*. 2 vols. Grand Rapids: Baker Academic, 2003.

Keener, "Madness." Keener, Craig S. "Paul's Positive Madness in Acts 26:24–25." In *Zur Kultur einer Religionsgeschichte*, edited by Manfred Lang and Joseph Verheyden. Herders Biblische Studien. Freiburg: Herder, forthcoming (tentatively 2016).

Keener, "Marriage." Keener, Craig S. "Marriage." *DNTB* 680–93.

Keener, *Marries*. Keener, Craig S. *. . . And Marries Another: Divorce and Remarriage in the Teaching of the New Testament*. Grand Rapids: Baker Academic, 1991.

Keener, *Matthew*. Keener, Craig S. *The Gospel of Matthew: A Socio-rhetorical Commentary*. Grand Rapids: Eerdmans, 2009.

Keener, "Milk." Keener, Craig S. "Milk." *DNTB* 707–9.

Keener, "Minds." Keener, Craig S. "Corrupted versus Renewed Minds in Romans 1, 7, and 12." In *Texts and Contexts: Gospels and Pauline Studies and Sermons in Honor of David E. Garland*, edited by Todd Still. Waco: Baylor University Press, forthcoming.

Keener, *Miracles*. Keener, Craig S. *Miracles: The Credibility of the New Testament Accounts*. Grand Rapids: Baker Academic, 2011.

Keener, *Paul*. Keener, Craig S. *Paul, Women, and Wives: Marriage and Women's Ministry in the Letters of Paul*. Grand Rapids: Baker Academic, 1992.

Keener, "Perspectives." Keener, Craig S. "'Fleshly' versus Spirit Perspectives in Romans 8:5–8." In *Paul: Jew, Greek, and Roman*, edited by Stanley Porter, 211–29. PAST 5. Leiden: Brill, 2008.

Keener, "Pneumatology." Keener, Craig S. "The Function of Johannine Pneumatology in the Context of Late First-Century Judaism." PhD diss., Duke University, 1991.

Keener, "Reassessment." Keener, Craig S. "A Reassessment of Hume's Case against Miracles in Light of Testimony from the Majority World Today." *PRSt* 38 (3, 2011): 289–310.

Keener, "Rhetorical Techniques." Keener, Craig S. "Some Rhetorical Techniques in Acts 24:2–21." In *Paul's World*, edited by Stanley E. Porter, 221–51. PAST 4. Leiden: Brill, 2008.

Keener, *Romans*. Keener, Craig S. *Romans*. NCCS 6. Eugene, OR: Wipf & Stock, 2009.

Keener, "Spirit." Keener, Craig S. "Spirit, Holy Spirit, Advocate, Breath, Wind." In *The Westminster Theological Wordbook of the Bible*, edited by Donald E. Gowan, 484–96. Louisville: Westminster John Knox, 2003.

Keener, *Spirit*. Keener, Craig S. *The Spirit in the Gospels and Acts: Divine Purity and Power*. Grand Rapids: Baker Academic, 2010.

Keener, "Teaching Ministry." Keener, Craig S. "A Spirit-Filled Teaching Ministry in Acts 19:9." In *Trajectories in the Book of Acts: Essays in Honor of John Wesley Wyckoff*, edited by Jordan May, Paul Alexander, and Robert G. Reid, 46–58. Eugene, OR: Wipf & Stock, 2010.

Kelly, *Peter*. Kelly, J. N. D. *A Commentary on the Epistles of Peter and Jude*. Thornapple Commentaries. Grand Rapids: Baker, 1981.

Kennedy, *Epistles*. Kennedy, H. A. A. *The Theology of the Epistles*. New York: Scribner's, 1920.

Kerferd, "Reason." Kerferd, G. B. "Reason as a Guide to Conduct in Greek Thought." *BJRL* 64 (1981): 141–64.

Kibria, "Construction." Kibria, Nazli. "The Construction of 'Asian American': Reflections on Intermarriage and Ethnic Identity among Second-Generation Chinese and Korean Americans." *EthRacSt* 20 (3, 1997): 523–44.

Kidd, "Posidonius." Kidd, Ian Gray. "Posidonius on Emotions." In *Problems in Stoicism*, edited by A. A. Long, 200–215. London: University of London, Athlone Press, 1971.

Kidd and Hankins, *Baptists*. Kidd, Thomas S., and Barry Hankins. *Baptists in America: A History*. Oxford: Oxford University Press, 2015.

Kim, *Introduction*. Kim, Yung Suk. *A Theological Introduction to Paul's Letters: Exploring a Threefold Theology of Paul*. Eugene, OR: Cascade, 2011.

Kim, *Letter of Recommendation*. Kim, Chan-Hie. *Form and Structure of the Familiar Greek Letter of Recommendation*. SBLDS 4. Missoula, MT: SBL, 1972.

Kim, *New Perspective*. Kim, Seyoon. *Paul and the New Perspective: Second Thoughts on the Origin of Paul's Gospel*. Grand Rapids: Eerdmans, 2002.

Kim, *Origin*. Kim, Seyoon. *The Origin of Paul's Gospel*. WUNT 2.4. Tübingen: Mohr Siebeck, 1981.

Kim, "Paraenesis." Kim, Seyoon. "Paul's Common Paraenesis (1 Thess. 4–5; Phil. 2–4; and Rom. 12–13): The Correspondence between Romans 1:18–32 and 12:1–2, and the Unity of Romans 12–13." *TynBul* 62 (1, 2011): 109–39.

Kirk, *Vision*. Kirk, Kenneth E. *The Vision of God—The Christian Doctrine of the Summum Bonum: The Bampton Lectures for 1928*. Abridged ed. London: Longmans, Green & Co., 1934.

Kittel, "Λογικός." Kittel, Gerhard. "Λογικός." *TDNT* 4:142–43.

Kiuchi, "Azazel-Goat." Kiuchi, Nobuyoshi. "Living Like the Azazel-Goat in Romans 12:1B." *TynBul* 57 (2, 2006): 251–61.

Klauck, *Context*. Klauck, Hans-Josef. *The Religious Context of Early Christianity: A Guide to Graeco-Roman Religions*. Translated by Brian McNeil. Minneapolis: Fortress, 2003.

Klausner, *Jesus to Paul*. Klausner, Joseph. *From Jesus to Paul*. Translated by W. Stinespring. Foreword by Sidney Hoenig. London: Macmillan, 1943. Reprint, New York: Menorah, 1979.

Knox, *Gentiles*. Knox, Wilfred L. *St. Paul and the Church of the Gentiles*. Cambridge: Cambridge University Press, 1939.

Knox, *Jerusalem*. Knox, Wilfred L. *St. Paul and the Church of Jerusalem*. Cambridge University Press, 1925.

Knox, "Parallels." Knox, Wilfred L. "Parallels to the N.T. Use of σῶμα." *JTS* 39 (155, 1938): 243–46.

Knuuttila and Sihvola, "Analysis." Knuuttila, Simo, and Juha Sihvola. "How the Philosophical Analysis of the Emotions Was Introduced." In *The Emotions in Hellenistic Philosophy*, edited by Juha Sihvola and Troels Engberg-Pedersen, 1–19. TSHP 46. Dordrecht, Neth.: Kluwer Academic, 1998.

Koester, "Being." Koester, Helmut. "The Divine Human Being." *HTR* 78 (3–4, 1985): 243–52.

Koester, *Introduction*. Koester, Helmut. *Introduction to the New Testament*. 2 vols. Philadelphia: Fortress, 1982.

Koestler, "Kepler." Koestler, Arthur. "Kepler and the Psychology of Discovery." In *The Logic of Personal Knowledge: Essays Presented to Michael Polanyi on His Seventieth Birthday 11 March 1961*, edited by Polanyi Festschrift Committee, 49–57. London: Routledge & Kegan Paul, 1961.

Kohler, *Theology*. Kohler, Kaufmann. *Jewish Theology*. New York: Macmillan, 1923.

Konstan, "Minds." Konstan, David. "Of Two Minds: Philo on Cultivation." *SPhilA* 22 (2010): 131–38.

Kourie, "Christ-Mysticism." Kourie, Celia. "Christ-Mysticism in Paul." *Way* Supplement 102 (2001): 71–80.

Kovelman, "Perfection." Kovelman, Arkady. "Hellenistic Judaism on the Perfection of the Human Body." *JJS* 61 (2, 2010): 207–19.

Kraabel, "Jews in Rome." Kraabel, Alf Thomas. "Jews in Imperial Rome: More Archaeological Evidence from an Oxford Collection." *JJS* 30 (1, 1979): 41–58.

Kraeling, *John the Baptist*. Kraeling, Carl H. *John the Baptist*. New York: Scribner's, 1951.

Kraftchick, "Πάθη." Kraftchick, Steven J. "Πάθη in Paul: The Emotional Logic of 'Original Argument.'" In *Paul and Pathos*, edited by Thomas H. Olbricht and Jerry L. Sumney, 39–68. SBLSymS 16. Atlanta: SBL, 2001.

Krämer, *Arete*. Krämer, Hans Joachim. *Arete bei Platon und Aristoteles: Zum Wesen und zur Geschichte der platonischen Ontologie*. Amsterdam: Schippers, 1967.

Kratz and Spieckermann, *Wrath*. Kratz, Reinhardt G., and Hermann Spieckermann, eds. *Divine Wrath and Divine Mercy in the World of Antiquity*. FAT 2.33. Tübingen: Mohr Siebeck, 2008.

Krauter, "Eva." Krauter, Stefan. "Eva in Röm 7." *ZNW* 99 (1, 2008): 1–17.

Krauter, "Römer 7." Krauter, Stefan. "Römer 7 in der Auslegung des Pietismus." *KD* 52 (2, 2006): 126–50.

Krentz, "Oxymora." Krentz, Edgar. "The Sense of Senseless Oxymora." *CurTM* 28 (6, 2001): 577–84.

Krieger, "4. Makkabäerbuch." Krieger, Klaus-Stefan. "Das 3. und 4. Makkabäerbuch." *BK* 57 (2, 2002): 87–88.

Kruse, *Romans*. Kruse, Colin G. *Paul's Letter to the Romans*. PillNTC. Grand Rapids: Eerdmans, 2012.

Kümmel, *Römer 7*. Kümmel, Werner Georg. *Römer 7 und die Bekehrung des Paulus*. Leipzig: J. G. Hinrichs, 1929. Reprinted as *Römer 7 und das Bild des Menschen im Neuen Testament*. Munich: Kaiser, 1974.

Kümmel, *Theology*. Kümmel, Werner Georg. *The Theology of the New Testament according to Its Major Witnesses—Jesus, Paul, John*. Translated by John E. Steely. Nashville: Abingdon, 1973.

Kwon, *Corinthians*. Kwon, Oh-Young. *1 Corinthians 1–4: Reconstructing Its Social and Rhetorical Situation and Re-reading It Cross-Culturally for Korean-Confucian Christians Today*. Eugene, OR: Wipf & Stock, 2010.

Lachs, *Commentary*. Lachs, Samuel Tobias. *A Rabbinic Commentary on the New Testament: The Gospels of Matthew, Mark, and Luke*. Hoboken, NJ: KTAV; New York: Anti-Defamation League of B'Nai B'Rith, 1987.

Ladd, *Kingdom*. Ladd, George Eldon. *The Gospel of the Kingdom*. London: Paternoster, 1959. Reprint, Grand Rapids: Eerdmans, 1978.

Ladd, *Last Things*. Ladd, George Eldon. *The Last Things*. Grand Rapids: Eerdmans, 1978.

Ladd, *Theology*. Ladd, George Eldon. *A Theology of the New Testament*. Grand Rapids: Eerdmans, 1974.

Lafon, "Moi." Lafon, Guy. "Un moi sans œuvre." *RSR* 78 (2, 1990): 165–74.

Lake, "Spirit." Lake, Kirsopp. "The Holy Spirit." *BegChr* 5:96–111.

Lambrecht, *Corinthians*. Lambrecht, Jan. *Second Corinthians*. SP 8. Collegeville, MN: Liturgical Press, 1999.

Lambrecht, "Exhortation." Lambrecht, Jan A. "The Implied Exhortation in Romans 8,5–8." *Greg* 81 (3, 2000): 441–51.

Lambrecht, "Glorie." Lambrecht, Jan. "'Tot steeds grotere glorie' (2 Kor. 3,18)." *Coll* 29 (2, 1983): 131–38.

Lambrecht, "Transformation." Lambrecht, Jan. "Transformation in 2 Cor 3,18." *Bib* 64 (2, 1983): 243–54.

Lamp, "Rhetoric." Lamp, Jeffrey S. "The Rhetoric of Righteousness: An Overview of Paul's Argument in Romans 5–8." *AsTJ* 60 (2, 2005): 55–66.

Laperrousaz, "Dépôts." Laperrousaz, Ernest-Marie. "À propos des dépôts d'ossements d'animaux trouvés à Qoumrân." *RevQ* 9 (4, 1978): 569–73.

Laurent, *Practice*. Laurent (Nicholas Herman of Lorraine). *The Practice of the Presence of God: Conversations and Letters of Brother Lawrence*. Oxford: Oneworld, 1999.

Laurin, "Immortality." Laurin, Robert B. "The Question of Immortality in the Qumran Hodayot." *JSS* 3 (1958): 344–55.

Laws, *James*. Laws, Sophie. *A Commentary on the Epistle of James*. HNTC. San Francisco: Harper & Row, 1980.

Lebourlier, "Miroir." Lebourlier, Jean. "L'Ancien Testament, miroir de la gloire du Seigneur Jésus: Une lecture du chapitre 3 de la deuxième Épître aux Corinthiens." *BLE* 97 (4, 1996): 321–29.

Lee, "Powers." Lee, Jung Young. "Interpreting the Demonic Powers in Pauline Thought." *NovT* 12 (1, 1970): 54–69.

Lee, *Thought*. Lee, Edwin Kenneth. *The Religious Thought of St. John*. London: SPCK, 1962.

Lee, "Translations: Greek." Lee, John A. L. "Translations of the Old Testament: I. Greek." In *Handbook of Classical Rhetoric in the Hellenistic Period, 330 B.C.–A.D. 400*, edited by Stanley E. Porter, 775–83. Leiden: Brill, 1997.

Légasse, "Immortalité." Légasse, Simon. "Les Juifs, au temps de Jésus, croyaient-ils à l'immortalité de l'âme? Pour introduire à la doctrine du Nouveau Testament sur les fins dernières." *BLE* 98 (2, 1997): 103–21.

Leigh, "Quintilian." Leigh, Matthew. "Quintilian on the Emotions (*Institutio oratoria* 6 Preface and 1–2)." *JRS* 94 (2004): 122–40.

Leivestad, "Dogma." Leivestad, Ragnar. "Das Dogma von der prophetenlosen Zeit." *NTS* 19 (3, 1973): 288–99.

Leon, *Jews of Rome*. Leon, Harry J. *The Jews of Ancient Rome*. Morris Loeb Series. Philadelphia: Jewish Publication Society of America, 1960.

Levison, "*Adam and Eve*." Levison, John R. "Adam and Eve in Romans 1.18–25 and the Greek *Life of Adam and Eve*." *NTS* 50 (4, 2004): 519–34.

Levison, *Filled*. Levison, John R. *Filled with the Spirit*. Grand Rapids: Eerdmans, 2009.

Levison, "*Stoa Poecile*." Levison, John R. "Paul in the *Stoa Poecile*: A Response to Troels Engberg-Pedersen, *Cosmology and Self in the Apostle Paul: The Material Spirit* (Oxford, 2010)." *JSNT* 33 (4, 2011): 415–32.

Levy, "Breaking." Levy, Carlos. "Breaking the Stoic Language: Philo's Attitude towards Assent (*Sunkatathesis*) and Comprehension (*Katalêpsis*)." *Hen* 32 (1, 2010): 33–44.

Levy, Krey, and Ryan, *Romans*. Levy, Ian Christopher, Philip D. W. Krey, and Thomas Ryan, eds. and trans. *The Letter to the Romans*. The Bible in Medieval Tradition. Grand Rapids: Eerdmans, 2013.

Lewis, *Life*. Lewis, Naphtali. *Life in Egypt under Roman Rule*. Oxford: Clarendon, 1983.

Lichtenberger, "Beginn." Lichtenberger, Hermann. "Der Beginn der Auslegungsgeschichte von Römer 7: Röm 7,25b." *ZNW* 88 (3–4, 1997): 284–95.

LiDonnici, "Burning." LiDonnici, Lynn. "Burning for It: Erotic Spells for Fever and Compulsion in the Ancient Mediterranean World." *GRBS* 39 (1, 1998): 63–98.

Lieber, "Angels." Lieber, Andrea. "Angels That Kill: Mediation and the Threat of Bodily Destruction in *Hekhalot* Narratives." *StSpir* 14 (2004): 17–35.

Lieberman, *Hellenism*. Lieberman, Saul. *Hellenism in Jewish Palestine: Studies in the Literary Transmission, Beliefs, and Manners of Palestine in the I Century B.C.E.–IV Century C.E.* 2nd ed. TSJTSA 18. New York: Jewish Theological Seminary of America Press, 1962.

Lieven, Johnston, and Käppel, "Underworld." Lieven, Alexandra von, Sarah Iles Johnston, and Lutz Käppel. "Underworld." *BrillPauly* 15:104–11.

Lightfoot, *Colossians*. Lightfoot, J. B. *Saint Paul's Epistles to the Colossians and to Philemon*. 3rd ed. London: Macmillan, 1879. Reprint, Grand Rapids: Zondervan, 1959.

Lim, "Gifts." Lim, David. "Spiritual Gifts." In *Systematic Theology: A Pentecostal Perspective*, edited by Stanley M. Horton, 457–88. Springfield, MO: Logion, 1994.

Lim, "Orientation." Lim, Timothy H. "Eschatological Orientation and the Alteration of Scripture in the Habakkuk Pesher." *JNES* 49 (2, 1990): 185–94.

Lincoln, *Ephesians*. Lincoln, Andrew T. *Ephesians*. WBC 42. Dallas: Word, 1990.

Lincoln, *Paradise*. Lincoln, Andrew T. *Paradise Now and Not Yet: Studies in the Role of the Heavenly Dimension in Paul's Thought with Special Reference to His Eschatology*. SNTSMS 43. Cambridge: Cambridge University Press, 1981.

Lindemann, "Kirche." Lindemann, Andreas. "Die Kirche als Leib: Beobachtungen zur

'demokratischen' Ekklesiologie bei Paulus."
ZTK 92 (2, 1995): 140–65.

Linebaugh, "Announcing." Linebaugh, Jonathan A. "Announcing the Human: Rethinking
the Relationship between Wisdom of Solomon 13–15 and Romans 1.18–2.11." NTS 57
(2, 2011): 214–37.

Litfin, Theology. Litfin, Duane. St. Paul's
Theology of Proclamation: 1 Corinthians
1–4 and Greco-Roman Rhetoric. SNTSMS
83. Cambridge: Cambridge University Press,
1994.

Litwa, "Implications." Litwa, M. David. "2 Corinthians 3:18 and Its Implications for Theosis." JTI 2 (2008): 117–34.

Litwa, Transformed. Litwa, M. David. We Are
Being Transformed: Deification in Paul's Soteriology. BZNW 187. Berlin: de Gruyter, 2012.

Liu, "Nature." Liu, Irene. "Nature and Knowledge in Stoicism: On the Ordinariness of the
Stoic Sage." Apeiron 41 (4, 2008): 247–75.

Llewellyn-Jones, Tortoise. Llewellyn-Jones,
Lloyd. Aphrodite's Tortoise: The Veiled
Woman of Ancient Greece. Swansea: The
Classical Press of Wales, 2003.

Lodge, Ethics. Lodge, R. C. Plato's Theory of
Ethics: The Moral Criterion and the Highest
Good. New York: Harcourt, Brace; London:
Kegan Paul, Trench, Trubner, 1928.

Lodge, Theory. Lodge, Rupert C. Plato's Theory
of Art. New York: The Humanities Press;
London: Routledge & Kegan Paul, 1953.

Löhr, "Paulus." Löhr, Hermut. "Paulus und der
Wille zur Tat: Beobachtungen zu einer früh-
christlichen Theologie als Anweisung zur
Lebenskunst." ZNW 98 (2, 2007): 165–88.

Lohse, Colossians. Lohse, Eduard. Colossians
and Philemon. Edited by Helmut Koester.
Translated by William R. Poehlmann and
Robert J. Karris. Hermeneia. Philadelphia:
Fortress, 1971.

Lohse, Environment. Lohse, Eduard. The New
Testament Environment. Translated by
John E. Steely. Nashville: Abingdon, 1976.

Long, Philosophy. Long, A. A. Hellenistic Philosophy: Stoics, Epicureans, Sceptics. New
York: Scribner's, 1974.

Long, "Soul." Long, A. A. "Soul and Body in
Stoicism." CHSP 36 (1980): 1–17.

Longenecker, Christology. Longenecker, Richard N. The Christology of Early Jewish

Christianity. London: SCM, 1970. Reprint,
Grand Rapids: Baker, 1981.

Longenecker, Exegesis. Longenecker, Richard N.
Biblical Exegesis in the Apostolic Period.
Grand Rapids: Eerdmans, 1975.

Longenecker, "Hope." Longenecker, Richard N.
"A Realized Hope, a New Commitment, and
a Developed Proclamation: Paul and Jesus."
In The Road from Damascus: The Impact of
Paul's Conversion on His Life, Thought, and
Ministry, edited by Richard N. Longenecker,
18–42. Grand Rapids: Eerdmans, 1997.

Longenecker, Introducing Romans. Longenecker,
Richard N. Introducing Romans: Critical Is-
sues in Paul's Most Famous Letter. Grand
Rapids: Eerdmans, 2011.

Longenecker, Paul. Longenecker, Richard N. Paul,
Apostle of Liberty. New York: Harper & Row,
1964. Reprint, Grand Rapids: Baker, 1976.

Lopez, Apostle. Lopez, Davina C. Apostle to the
Conquered: Reimagining Paul's Mission. Paul
in Critical Contexts. Minneapolis: Fortress,
2008.

Lopez, "Visualizing." Lopez, Davina C. "Visualizing Significant Otherness: Reimagining
Paul(ine Studies) through Hybrid Lenses." In
The Colonized Apostle: Paul through Postcolonial Eyes, edited by Christopher D. Stanley,
74–94. Minneapolis: Fortress, 2011.

Lucas, "Unearthing." Lucas, Alec J. "Unearthing an Intra-Jewish Interpretive Debate? Romans 1,18–2,4; Wisdom of Solomon 11–19;
and Psalms 105 (104)–107 (106)." ASDE 27
(2, 2010): 69–91.

Lung-Kwong, Purpose. Lung-Kwong, Lo. Paul's
Purpose in Writing Romans: The Upbuilding
of a Jewish and Gentile Christian Community in Rome. Edited by Philip P. Chia and
Yeo Khiok-khng. Jian Dao DS 6. Bible and
Literature 4. Hong Kong: Alliance Bible Seminary Press, 1998.

Lutz, Musonius. Lutz, Cora E. Musonius Rufus:
"The Roman Socrates." YCS 10. New Haven:
Yale University Press, 1947.

Luz, "Masada." Luz, Menahem. "Eleazar's
Second Speech on Masada and Its Literary
Precedents." RMPhil 126 (1, 1983): 25–43.

Luz, Matthew. Luz, Ulrich. Matthew 1–7: A Commentary. Translated by Wilhelm C. Linss. CC.
Minneapolis: Augsburg Fortress, 1989.

Lyons, Autobiography. Lyons, George. Pauline
Autobiography: Toward a New Under-

standing. SBLDS 73. Atlanta: Scholars Press, 1985.

Ma, *Spirit.* Ma, Wonsuk. *Until the Spirit Comes: The Spirit of God in the Book of Isaiah.* JSOTSup 271. Sheffield, UK: Sheffield Academic, 1999.

MacGorman, "Romans 7." MacGorman, J. W. "Romans 7 Once More." *SWJT* 19 (1, Fall 1976): 31–41.

MacGregor, "Principalities." MacGregor, G. H. C. "Principalities and Powers: The Cosmic Background of Paul's Thought." *NTS* 1 (Sept. 1954): 17–28.

Mackie, "Seeing." Mackie, Scott D. "Seeing God in Philo of Alexandria: The Logos, the Powers, or the Existent One?" *SPhilA* 21 (2009): 25–47.

Maclean and Aitken, "Introduction." Maclean, Jennifer K. Berenson, and Ellen Bradshaw Aitken. Introduction to *Flavius Philostratus: "Heroikos,"* xxxvii–xcii. Translated by Jennifer K. Berenson Maclean and Ellen Bradshaw Aitken. SBLWGRW 1. Atlanta: SBL, 2001.

Malherbe, "Antisthenes." Malherbe, Abraham J. "Antisthenes and Odysseus, and Paul at War." *HTR* 76 (2, 1983): 143–73.

Malherbe, "Beasts." Malherbe, Abraham J. "The Beasts at Ephesus." *JBL* 87 (1, 1968): 71–80.

Malherbe, "Gentle as Nurse." Malherbe, Abraham J. "'Gentle as a Nurse': The Cynic Background to I Thess ii." *NovT* 12 (2, 1970): 203–17.

Malherbe, *Moral Exhortation.* Malherbe, Abraham J. *Moral Exhortation, a Greco-Roman Sourcebook.* LEC 4. Philadelphia: Westminster, 1986.

Malherbe, *Philosophers.* Malherbe, Abraham J. *Paul and the Popular Philosophers.* Philadelphia: Fortress, 1989.

Malherbe, *Social Aspects.* Malherbe, Abraham J. *Social Aspects of Early Christianity.* 2nd ed. Philadelphia: Fortress, 1983.

Malina and Pilch, *Letters.* Malina, Bruce J., and John J. Pilch. *Social-Science Commentary on the Letters of Paul.* Minneapolis: Fortress, 2006.

Malkin, "Votive Offerings." Malkin, Irad. "Votive Offerings." *OCD³* 1612–13.

Manson, *Paul and John.* Manson, T. W. *On Paul and John: Some Selected Theological Themes.* SBT 38. London: SCM, 1963.

Manson, "Reading." Manson, William. "A Reading of Romans vii." In *Jesus and the Christian,* 149–59. London: James Clarke & Co., 1967.

Marcus, "Inclination." Marcus, Joel. "The Evil Inclination in the Letters of Paul." *IBS* 8 (1, 1986): 8–21.

Marcus, "Inclination in James." Marcus, Joel. "The Evil Inclination in the Epistle of James." *CBQ* 44 (4, 1982): 606–21.

Markschies, "Metapher." Markschies, Christoph. "Die platonische Metapher vom 'inneren Menschen': Eine Brücke zwischen antiker Philosophie und altchristlicher Theologie." *ZKG* 105 (1, 1994): 1–17.

Marmorstein, *Names.* Marmorstein, A. *The Names and Attributes of God.* Vol. 1 of *The Old Rabbinic Doctrine of God.* London: Oxford University Press, 1927. Reprinted in *The Doctrine of Merits in Old Rabbinical Literature; and The Old Rabbinic Doctrine of God: I, The Names and Attributes of God; II, Essays in Anthropomorphism.* 3 vols. in 1. New York: KTAV, 1968.

Marshall, *Enmity.* Marshall, Peter. *Enmity in Corinth: Social Conventions in Paul's Relations with the Corinthians.* WUNT 2.23. Tübingen: Mohr Siebeck, 1987.

Marshall, "Flesh." Marshall, I. Howard. "Living in the 'Flesh.'" *BSac* 159 (636, 2002): 387–403.

Marshall, *Thessalonians.* Marshall, I. Howard. *1 and 2 Thessalonians.* NCBC. Grand Rapids: Eerdmans, 1983.

Martin, *Body.* Martin, Dale B. *The Corinthian Body.* New Haven: Yale University Press, 1995.

Martin, *Carmen Christi.* Martin, Ralph P. *Carmen Christi.* Cambridge: Cambridge University Press, 1967.

Martin, *Colossians.* Martin, Ralph P. *Colossians and Philemon.* NCBC. Grand Rapids: Eerdmans, 1978.

Martin, *Corinthians.* Martin, Ralph P. *2 Corinthians.* WBC 40. Waco: Word, 1986.

Martin, "Good." Martin, Troy W. "The Good as God (Romans 5.7)." *JSNT* 25 (1, 2002): 55–70.

Martin, "Philo's Use." Martin, Michael. "Philo's Use of Syncrisis: An Examination of Philonic Composition in the Light of the Progymnasmata." *PRSt* 30 (3, 2003): 271–97.

Martin, *Reconciliation.* Martin, Ralph P. *Reconciliation: A Study of Paul's Theology.* Atlanta: John Knox, 1981.

Martin, "Reflections." Martin, Brice L. "Some Reflections on the Identity of ἐγώ in Rom. 7:14–25." *SJT* 34 (1, 1981): 39–47.

Martin, "Voice." Martin, Troy W. "The Voice of Emotion: Paul's Pathetic Persuasion (Gal 4:12–20)." In *Paul and Pathos*, edited by Thomas H. Olbricht and Jerry L. Sumney, 181–202. SBLSymS 16. Atlanta: SBL, 2001.

Martyn, "De-apocalypticizing." Martyn, J. Louis. "De-apocalypticizing Paul: An Essay Focused on *Paul and the Stoics* by Troels Engberg-Pedersen." *JSNT* 86 (2002): 61–102.

Martyn, "Epistemology." Martyn, J. Louis. "Epistemology at the Turn of the Ages: 2 Corinthians 5:16." In *Christian History and Interpretation: Studies Presented to John Knox*, edited by W. R. Farmer, C. F. D. Moule, and R. R. Niebuhr, 269–87. Cambridge: Cambridge University Press, 1967.

Mary, *Mysticism.* Mary, Sylvia. *Pauline and Johannine Mysticism.* London: Darton, Longman & Todd, 1964.

Matera, *Corinthians.* Matera, Frank J. *II Corinthians: A Commentary.* NTL. Louisville: Westminster John Knox, 2003.

Matera, *Romans.* Matera, Frank J. *Romans.* PCNT. Grand Rapids: Baker Academic, 2010.

Matheson, *Epictetus.* Matheson, P. E., ed. and trans. *Epictetus: The Discourses and Manual Together with Fragments of His Writings.* 2 vols. Oxford: Clarendon, 1916.

Mattila, "Wisdom." Mattila, Sharon Lea. "Wisdom, Sense Perception, Nature, and Philo's Gender Gradient." *HTR* 89 (2, 1996): 103–29.

Mattusch, "Bronze." Mattusch, Carol C. "Corinthian Bronze: Famous, but Elusive." In *Corinth: The Centenary, 1896–1996*, edited by Charles K. Williams II and Nancy Bookidis, 219–32. Vol. 20 of *Corinth: Results of Excavations Conducted by the American School of Classical Studies at Athens.* Princeton: American School of Classical Studies at Athens, 2003.

May, "Logos." May, Eric. "The Logos in the Old Testament." *CBQ* 8 (1946): 438–47.

Mazzinghi, "Morte e immortalità." Mazzinghi, Luca. "Morte e immortalità nel libro della Sapienza: Alcune considerazioni su Sap 1,12–15; 2,21–24; 3,1–9." *VH* 17 (2, 2006): 267–86.

Mbiti, *Religions.* Mbiti, John S. *African Religions and Philosophies.* Garden City, NY: Doubleday, 1970.

McClymond and McDermott, *Theology of Edwards.* McClymond, Michael J., and Gerald R. McDermott. *The Theology of Jonathan Edwards.* New York: Oxford University Press, 2012.

McCormack, "Faith." McCormack, Bruce. "Can We Still Speak of 'Justification by Faith'? An In-House Debate with Apocalyptic Readings of Paul." In *Galatians and Christian Theology: Justification, the Gospel, and Ethics in Paul's Letter.* Edited by Mark W. Elliott et al., 159–84. Grand Rapids: Baker Academic, 2014.

McCoskey, *Race.* McCoskey, Denise Eileen. *Race: Antiquity and Its Legacy.* New York: Oxford University Press, 2012.

Meeks, *Moral World.* Meeks, Wayne A. *The Moral World of the First Christians.* LEC 6. Philadelphia: Westminster, 1986.

Meeks, *Prophet-King.* Meeks, Wayne A. *The Prophet-King: Moses Traditions and the Johannine Christology.* NovTSup 14. Leiden: Brill, 1967.

Meeks, *Urban Christians.* Meeks, Wayne A. *The First Urban Christians: The Social World of the Apostle Paul.* New Haven: Yale University Press, 1983.

Meijer, "Philosophers." Meijer, P. A. "Philosophers, Intellectuals, and Religion in Hellas." In *Faith, Hope, and Worship: Aspects of Religious Mentality in the Ancient World*, edited by H. S. Versnel, 216–62. SGRR 2. Leiden: Brill, 1981.

Melnick, "Conception." Melnick, R. "On the Philonic Conception of the Whole Man." *JSJ* 11 (1, 1980): 1–32.

Ménard, "Self-Definition." Ménard, Jacques E. "Normative Self-Definition in Gnosticism." In *The Shaping of Christianity in the Second and Third Centuries*, edited by E. P. Sanders, 134–50. Vol. 1 of *Jewish and Christian Self-Definition.* Philadelphia: Fortress, 1980.

Menzies, *Development.* Menzies, Robert P. *The Development of Early Christian Pneumatology with Special Reference to Luke-Acts.* JSNTSup 54. Sheffield, UK: Sheffield Academic, 1991.

Menzies, *Empowered.* Menzies, Robert P. *Empowered for Witness: The Spirit in Luke-Acts.* London: T&T Clark, 2004.

Merlan, *Platonism.* Merlan, Philip. *From Platonism to Neoplatonism.* The Hague: Martinus Nijhoff, 1953.

Mettinger, "Dying God." Mettinger, Tryggve N. D. "The 'Dying and Rising God': A Survey of Research from Frazer to the Present Day." *SEÅ* 63 (1998): 111–23.

Metzger, "Considerations." Metzger, Bruce M. "Considerations of Methodology in the Study of the Mystery Religions and Early Christianity." *HTR* 48 (1, 1955): 1–20.

Meyer, "Flesh." Meyer, Rudolf. "Flesh in Judaism." *TDNT* 7:110–19.

Meyers, "Judaism." Meyers, Eric M. "Early Judaism and Christianity in the Light of Archaeology." *BA* 51 (2, 1988): 69–79.

Meyers and Strange, *Archaeology*. Meyers, Eric M., and James F. Strange. *Archaeology, the Rabbis, and Early Christianity*. Nashville: Abingdon, 1981.

Michael, *Philippians*. Michael, J. Hugh. *The Epistle of Paul to the Philippians*. MNTC. London: Hodder & Stoughton, 1928.

Mihaila, "Relationship." Mihaila, Corin. "The Paul-Apollos Relationship and Paul's Stance toward Greco-Roman Rhetoric: An Exegetical and Socio-historical Study of 1 Corinthians 1–4." PhD diss., Southeastern Baptist Theological Seminary, 2006.

Miller, "ΑΡΧΟΝΤΩΝ." Miller, Gene. "ΑΡΧΟΝΤΩΝ ΤΟΥ ΑΙΩΝΟΣ ΤΟΥΤΟΥ—A New Look at I Corinthians 2:6–8." *JBL* 91 (4, 1972): 522–28.

Miller, "Attitudes." Miller, Geoffrey D. "Attitudes toward Dogs in Ancient Israel: A Reassessment." *JSOT* 32 (4, 2008): 487–500.

Miller, *Cried*. Miller, P. D. *They Cried to the Lord: The Form and Theology of Biblical Prayer*. Minneapolis: Fortress, 1994.

Miller, "Logos." Miller, E. L. "The Logos of Heraclitus: Updating the Report." *HTR* 74 (2, Apr. 1981): 61–176.

Milne, "Experience." Milne, Douglas J. W. "Romans 7:7–12, Paul's Pre-conversion Experience." *RTR* 43 (1, 1984): 9–17.

Minear, *Kingdom*. Minear, Paul S. *The Kingdom and the Power: An Exposition of the New Testament Gospel*. Philadelphia: Westminster, 1950.

Mirguet, "Reflections." Mirguet, Françoise. "Introductory Reflections on Embodiment in Hellenistic Judaism." *JSP* 21 (1, 2011): 5–19.

Mitchell, *Rhetoric of Reconciliation*. Mitchell, Margaret M. *Paul and the Rhetoric of Reconciliation: An Exegetical Investigation of the Language and Composition of 1 Corinthians*. Louisville: Westminster John Knox, 1991.

Mitsis, "Origin." Mitsis, Phillip. "The Stoic Origin of Natural Rights." In *Topics in Stoic Philosophy*, edited by Katerina Ierodiakonou, 153–77. Oxford: Oxford University Press, 1999.

Mitton, "Romans 7." Mitton, C. Leslie. "Romans 7 Reconsidered." *ExpT* 65 (3, 1953): 78–81; (4, 1954): 99–103; (5, 1954): 132–35.

Moede, "Reliefs." Moede, Katja. "Reliefs, Public and Private." In *A Companion to Roman Religion*, edited by Jörg Rüpke, 164–75. BCompAW. Malden, MA: Wiley-Blackwell, 2011.

Moffatt, *Corinthians*. Moffatt, James D. *The First Epistle of Paul to the Corinthians*. MNTC. London: Hodder & Stoughton, 1938.

Mondin, "Esistenza." Mondin, Battista. "Esistenza, natura, inconoscibilità, e ineffabilità di Dio nel pensiero di Filone Alessandrino." *ScC* 95 (5, 1967): 423–47.

Montanari, "Gastronomical Poetry." Montanari, Ornella. "Gastronomical Poetry." *BrillPauly* 5:702–3.

Montefiore, *Gospels*. Montefiore, Claude G. *The Synoptic Gospels*. 2nd ed. 2 vols. London: Macmillan, 1927. Reprint, Library of Biblical Studies. New York: KTAV, 1968.

Montefiore, "Spirit of Judaism." Montefiore, Claude G. "Spirit of Judaism." *BegChr* 1:35–81.

Montefiore and Loewe, *Anthology*. Montefiore, C. G., and Herbert Loewe, eds. and trans. *A Rabbinic Anthology*. London: Macmillan, 1938. Reprinted with a new prolegomenon by Raphael Loewe. New York: Schocken, 1974.

Moo, "Israel and Paul." Moo, Douglas J. "Israel and Paul in Romans 7:7–12." *NTS* 32 (1, 1986): 122–35.

Moo, *Romans*. Moo, Douglas J. *The Epistle to the Romans*. Grand Rapids: Eerdmans, 1996.

Moore, *Judaism*. Moore, George Foot. *Judaism in the First Centuries of the Christian Era*. 3 vols. Cambridge, MA: Harvard University Press, 1927–30. Reprint, 3 vols. in 2. New York: Schocken, 1971.

Moreno García, "Sabiduría del bautizado." Moreno García, Abdón. "La sabiduría del bautizado: Inhabitación o pneumación? Hacia una lectura sapiencial de Rom 8, 5–11." *Estudios Trinitarios* 33 (2, 1999): 325–83.

Moreno García, *Sabiduría del Espíritu*. Moreno García, Abdón. *La sabiduría del Espíritu:*

Sentir en Cristo; Estudio de phronema-phroneo en Rom 8,5–8 y Flp 2,1–5. Rome: Pontificia Universitas Gregoriana, 1995.

Moreno García, "Sabiduría del Espíritu." Moreno García, Abdón. "La sabiduría del Espíritu es biógena: Hacia una sintaxis de la alteridad (Rm 8,6 y Flp 2,2)," *EstBíb* 60 (1, 2002): 3–30.

Morray-Jones, "Mysticism." Morray-Jones, Christopher R. A. "Transformational Mysticism in the Apocalyptic-Merkabah Tradition." *JJS* 43 (1, 1992): 1–31.

Morris, *John*. Morris, Leon. *The Gospel according to John: The English Text with Introduction, Exposition, and Notes*. NICNT. Grand Rapids: Eerdmans, 1971.

Morris, *Judgment*. Morris, Leon. *The Biblical Doctrine of Judgment*. Grand Rapids: Eerdmans, 1960.

Morris, *Romans*. Morris, Leon. *The Epistle to the Romans*. Grand Rapids: Eerdmans; Leicester, UK: Inter-Varsity, 1988.

Moses, *Transfiguration Story*. Moses, A. D. A. *Matthew's Transfiguration Story and Jewish-Christian Controversy*. JSNTSup 122. Sheffield, UK: Sheffield Academic, 1996.

Motto, "Progress." Motto, Anna Lydia. "The Idea of Progress in Senecan Thought." *CJ* 79 (3, 1984): 225–40.

Moule, *Colossians*. Moule, C. F. D. *The Epistles of Paul the Apostle to the Colossians and to Philemon: An Introduction and Commentary*. Cambridge: Cambridge University Press, 1962.

Moule, "New Life." Moule, C. F. D. "'The New Life' in Colossians 3:1–17." *RevExp* 70 (4, 1973): 481–93.

Moulton and Milligan, *Vocabulary*. Moulton, James Hope, and George Milligan. *The Vocabulary of the Greek Testament: Illustrated from the Papyri and Other Non-literary Sources*. Grand Rapids: Eerdmans, 1930.

Mowvley, "Exodus." Mowvley, Henry. "John 1.14–18 in the Light of Exodus 33.7–34.35." *ExpT* 95 (5, 1984): 135–37.

Mueller, "Faces." Mueller, Celeste DeSchryver. "Two Faces of Lust." *BibT* 41 (5, 2003): 308–14.

Mueller and Robinson, "Introduction." Mueller, J. R., and S. E. Robinson. Introduction to "Apocryphon of Ezekiel." *OTP* 1:487–90.

Murphy, "Understanding." Murphy, William F. "The Pauline Understanding of Appropriated Revelation as a Principle of Christian Moral Action." *Studia Moralia* 39 (2, 2001): 371–409.

Murray, *Philosophy*. Murray, Gilbert. *The Stoic Philosophy*. New York: Putnam's Sons, 1915.

Murray, *Stages*. Murray, Gilbert. *Five Stages of Greek Religion*. New York: Columbia University Press, 1925. Reprint, Westport, CT: Greenwood, 1976.

Mylonas, *Eleusis*. Mylonas, George E. *Eleusis and the Eleusinian Mysteries*. Princeton: Princeton University Press, 1961.

Nanos, *Mystery*. Nanos, Mark D. *The Mystery of Romans: The Jewish Context of Paul's Letter*. Minneapolis: Fortress, 1996.

Napier, "Analysis." Napier, Daniel. "Paul's Analysis of Sin and Torah in Romans 7:7–25." *ResQ* 44 (1, 2002): 15–32.

Nelson, "Note." Nelson, Max. "A Note on Apuleius's Magical Fish." *Mnemosyne* 54 (1, 2001): 85–86.

Neugebauer, "In Christo." Neugebauer, Fritz. "Das paulinische 'in Christo.'" *NTS* 4 (2, Jan. 1958): 124–38.

Neusner, "Development." Neusner, Jacob. "The Development of the *Merkavah* Tradition." *JSJ* 2 (2, 1971): 149–60.

Newman, "Once Again." Newman, Barclay M. "Once Again—The Question of 'I' in Romans 7.7–25." *BTr* 34 (1, 1983): 124–35.

Nickle, "Romans 7:7–25." Nickle, Keith F. "Romans 7:7–25." *Int* 33 (2, 1979): 181–87.

Nietmann, "Seneca." Nietmann, W. D. "Seneca on Death: The Courage to Be or Not to Be." *International Philosophical Quarterly* 6 (1966): 81–89.

Nilsson, *Dionysiac Mysteries*. Nilsson, Martin P. *The Dionysiac Mysteries of the Hellenistic and Roman Age*. SUSIA, 8°, 5. Lund, Swed.: Gleerup, 1957.

Nilsson, *Piety*. Nilsson, Martin P. *Greek Piety*. Translated by Herbert Jennings Rose. Oxford: Clarendon, 1948.

Nock, *Christianity*. Nock, Arthur Darby. *Early Gentile Christianity and Its Hellenistic Background*. New York: Harper & Row, 1964.

Nock, *Conversion*. Nock, Arthur Darby. *Conversion: The Old and the New in Religion from Alexander the Great to Augustine of Hippo*. Oxford: Clarendon, 1933.

Nock, "Developments." Nock, Arthur Darby. "Religious Developments from the Close of the Republic to the Death of Nero." In *The Cambridge Ancient History*. Vol. 10, *The Augustan Empire: 44 B.C.–A.D. 70*. Edited by S. A. Cook, F. E. Adcock, and M. P. Charlesworth, 465–511. Cambridge: Cambridge University Press, 1966.

Nock, "Gnosticism." Nock, Arthur Darby. "Gnosticism." *HTR* 57 (4, Oct. 1964): 255–79.

Nock, *Paul*. Nock, Arthur Darby. *St. Paul*. New York: Harper and Brothers, 1938. Reprint, New York: Harper & Row, 1963.

Nock, "Vocabulary." Nock, Arthur Darby. "The Vocabulary of the New Testament." *JBL* 52 (2–3, 1933): 131–39.

Noffke, "Glory." Noffke, Eric. "Man of Glory or First Sinner? Adam in the Book of Sirach." *ZAW* 119 (4, 2007): 618–24.

Nolan, "Stoic Gunk." Nolan, Daniel. "Stoic Gunk." *Phronesis* 51 (2, 2006): 162–83.

Nolland, "Misleading Statement." Nolland, John. "A Misleading Statement of the Essene Attitude to the Temple (Josephus, *Antiquities*, XVIII, I, 5, 19)." *RevQ* 9 (4, 1978): 555–62.

Nordgaard, "Appropriation." Nordgaard, Stefan. "Paul's Appropriation of Philo's Theory of 'Two Men' in 1 Corinthians 15.45–49." *NTS* 57 (3, 2011): 348–65.

North, "Concept." North, Helen F. "The Concept of 'Sophrosyne' in Greek Literary Criticism." *CP* 43 (1948): 1–17.

North, "Mare." North, Helen F. "The Mare, the Vixen, and the Bee: *Sophrosyne* as the Virtue of Women in Antiquity." *ICS* 2 (1977): 35–48.

North, *Sophrosyne*. North, Helen F. *Sophrosyne: Self-Knowledge and Self-Restraint in Greek Literature*. Ithaca, NY: Cornell, 1966.

Novak, *Suicide and Morality*. Novak, David. *Suicide and Morality: The Theories of Plato, Aquinas, and Kant and Their Relevance for Suicidology*. New York: Scholars Studies Press, 1975.

Noyes, "Seneca." Noyes, Russell. "Seneca on Death." *JRelHealth* 12 (1973): 223–40.

Nygren, *Romans*. Nygren, Anders. *Commentary on Romans*. 3rd paperback ed. Philadelphia: Fortress, 1975.

Obbink, "Sage." Obbink, Dirk. "The Stoic Sage in the Cosmic City." In *Topics in Stoic Philosophy*, edited by Katerina Ierodiakonou, 178–95. Oxford: Oxford University Press, 1999.

O'Brien, *Colossians*. O'Brien, Peter T. *Colossians, Philemon*. WBC 44. Waco: Word, 1982.

O'Brien, "Thanksgiving." O'Brien, Peter T. "Thanksgiving within the Structure of Pauline Theology." In *Pauline Studies: Essays Presented to Professor F. F. Bruce on His 70th Birthday*, edited by Donald A. Hagner and Murray J. Harris, 50–66. Exeter: Paternoster; Grand Rapids: Eerdmans, 1980.

Odeberg, *Gospel*. Odeberg, Hugo. *The Fourth Gospel Interpreted in Its Relation to Contemporaneous Religious Currents in Palestine and the Hellenistic-Oriental World*. Uppsala: Almqvist & Wiksells, 1929. Reprint, Amsterdam: B. R. Grüner; Chicago: Argonaut, 1968.

Odeberg, *Pharisaism*. Odeberg, Hugo. *Pharisaism and Christianity*. Translated by J. M. Moe. St. Louis: Concordia, 1964.

Oden, "Excuse." Oden, Thomas C. "Without Excuse: Classic Christian Exegesis of General Revelation." *JETS* 41 (1, 1998): 55–68.

Oesterley, *Liturgy*. Oesterley, William Oscar Emil. *The Jewish Background of the Christian Liturgy*. Oxford: Clarendon, 1925.

O'Keefe, "Lucretius." O'Keefe, Tim. "Lucretius on the Cycle of Life and the Fear of Death." *Apeiron* 36 (1, 2003): 43–66.

Olbricht, "*Pathos* as Proof." Olbricht, Thomas H. "*Pathos* as Proof in Greco-Roman Rhetoric." In *Paul and Pathos*, edited by Thomas H. Olbricht and Jerry L. Sumney, 7–22. SBLSymS 16. Atlanta: SBL, 2001.

Olbricht and Sumney, *Paul and Pathos*. Olbricht, Thomas H., and Jerry L. Sumney, eds. *Paul and Pathos*. SBLSymS 16. Atlanta: SBL, 2001.

Olmstead, *Persian Empire*. Olmstead, A. T. *History of the Persian Empire*. Chicago: University of Chicago Press, 1959.

O'Rourke, "Revelation." O'Rourke, John J. "Romans 1, 20 and Natural Revelation." *CBQ* 23 (3, 1961): 301–6.

Ortkemper, *Leben*. Ortkemper, Franz-Josef. *Leben aus dem Glauben: Christliche Grundhaltungen nach Römer 12–13*. NTAbh n.s. 14. Münster: Aschendorff, 1980.

Ortlund, "Justified." Ortlund, Dane C. "Justified by Faith, Judged according to Works: Another Look at a Pauline Paradox." *JETS* 52 (2, 2009): 323–39.

Osborn, *Justin*. Osborn, Eric Francis. *Justin Martyr*. BHT 47. Tübingen: Mohr Siebeck, 1973.

Osborne, *Romans*. Osborne, Grant R. *Romans*. IVPNTC. Downers Grove, IL: InterVarsity, 2004.

Osiek and MacDonald, *Place*. Osiek, Carolyn, and Margaret Y. MacDonald, with Janet H. Tulloch. *A Woman's Place: House Churches in Earliest Christianity*. Minneapolis: Augsburg Fortress, 2006.

Oss, "Note." Oss, Douglas A. "A Note on Paul's Use of Isaiah." *BBR* 2 (1992): 105–12.

Oster, *Corinthians*. Oster, Richard. *1 Corinthians*. College Press NIV Commentary. Joplin, MO: College Press, 1995.

O'Sullivan, "Mind." O'Sullivan, Timothy M. "The Mind in Motion: Walking and Metaphorical Travel in the Roman Villa." *CP* 101 (2, 2006): 133–52.

O'Sullivan, "Walking." O'Sullivan, Timothy M. "Walking with Odysseus: The Portico Frame of the Odyssey Landscapes." *AJP* 128 (4, 2007): 497–532, plates 1–2, figures 1–13.

O'Toole, *Climax*. O'Toole, Robert F. *Acts 26: The Christological Climax of Paul's Defense (Ac 22:1–26:36)*. AnBib 78. Rome: Biblical Institute Press, 1978.

Ott, "Dogmatisches Problem." Ott, Heinrich. "Röm. 1, 19ff. als dogmatisches Problem." *TZ* 15 (1, Jan. 1959): 40–50.

Otto, *Dionysus*. Otto, Walter F. *Dionysus: Myth and Cult*. Translated by Robert B. Palmer. Bloomington: Indiana University Press, 1965.

Overstreet, "Concept." Overstreet, R. Larry. "The Greek Concept of the 'Seven Stages of Life' and Its New Testament Significance." *BBR* 19 (4, 2009): 537–63.

Owen, "Scope." Owen, H. P. "The Scope of Natural Revelation in Rom. I and Acts XVII." *NTS* 5 (2, Jan. 1959): 133–43.

Packer, "Malheureux." Packer, J. I. "Le 'malheureux' de Romains 7." *Hok* 55 (1994): 19–25.

Packer, "Wretched Man." Packer, J. I. "The 'Wretched Man' Revisited: Another Look at Romans 7:14–25." In *Romans and the People of God: Essays in Honor of Gordon D. Fee on the Occasion of His 65th Birthday*, edited by Sven K. Soderlund and N. T. Wright, 70–81. Grand Rapids: Eerdmans, 1999.

Pagels, *Paul*. Pagels, Elaine H. *The Gnostic Paul: Gnostic Exegesis of the Pauline Letters*. Philadelphia: Fortress, 1975.

Painter, "Gnosticism." Painter, John. "Gnosticism and the Qumran Texts." *ABR* 17 (Oct. 1969): 1–6.

Palinuro, "Rm 12,1–2." Palinuro, Massimiliano. "Rm 12,1–2: Le radici dell'etica paolina." *RivB* 52 (2, 2004): 145–81.

Palma, "Glossolalia." Palma, Anthony. "Glossolalia in the Light of the New Testament and Subsequent History." Bachelor of Theology thesis, Biblical Seminary in New York, April 1960.

Panayotakis, "Vision." Panayotakis, Costas. "Vision and Light in Apuleius' Tale of Psyche and Her Mysterious Husband." *CQ* 51 (2, 2001): 576–83.

Parisius, "Deutungsmöglichkeit." Parisius, Hans-Ludolf. "Über die forensische Deutungsmöglichkeit des paulinischen ἐν Χριστῷ." *ZNW* 49 (1, 1958): 285–88.

Parker, "Dioscuri." Parker, Robert C. T. "Dioscuri." *OCD³* 484.

Parker, "Split." Parker, Barry F. "Romans 7 and the Split between Judaism and Christianity." *JGRCJ* 3 (2006): 110–33.

Parker and Murgatroyd, "Poetry." Parker, Sarah, and P. Murgatroyd. "Love Poetry and Apuleius' *Cupid and Psyche*." *CQ* 52 (1, 2002): 400–404.

Partee, *Poetics*. Partee, Morriss Henry. *Plato's Poetics: The Authority of Beauty*. Salt Lake City: University of Utah Press, 1981.

Pathrapankal, "Christ." Pathrapankal, Joseph. "'I Live, Not I; It Is Christ Who Lives in Me' (Gal 2:20): A Yogic Interpretation of Paul's Religious Experience." *JDharm* 20 (3, 1995): 297–307.

Patterson, *Plato on Immortality*. Patterson, Robert Leet. *Plato on Immortality*. University Park: Pennsylvania State University Press, 1965.

Patterson, *Theories*. Patterson, C. H. *Theories of Counseling and Psychotherapy*. New York: Harper & Row, 1980.

Pawlikowski, "Pharisees." Pawlikowski, John T. "The Pharisees and Christianity." *BibT* 49 (1970): 47–53.

Pearson, "Idolatry, Jewish Conception of." Pearson, Brook W. R. "Idolatry, Jewish Conception of." *DNTB* 526–29.

Pearson, *Terminology*. Pearson, Birger A. *The Pneumatikos-Psychikos Terminology in 1 Corinthians: A Study in the Theology of the*

Corinthian Opponents of Paul and Its Relation to Gnosticism. SBLDS 12. Missoula, MT: Scholars Press, 1973.

Pelikan, *Acts.* Pelikan, Jaroslav. *Acts.* BTCB. Grand Rapids: Brazos, 2005.

Pelser, "Antropologie." Pelser, Gerhardus Marthinus Maritz. "Dualistiese antropologie by Paulus?" *HvTS* 56 (2–3, 2000): 409–39.

Penna, "Juifs à Rome." Penna, Romano. "Les juifs à Rome au temps de l'apôtre Paul." *NTS* 28 (3, 1982): 321–47.

Pérez, "Freedom." Pérez, F. "Freedom according to the Freedman Epictetus" [in Japanese]. *KK* 27 (53, 1988): 73–97. (*NTA* 33:87)

Perkins, "Anthropology." Perkins, Pheme. "Pauline Anthropology in Light of Nag Hammadi." *CBQ* 48 (3, 1986): 512–22.

Pfitzner, *Agon Motif.* Pfitzner, Victor C. *Paul and the Agon Motif: Traditional Athletic Imagery in the Pauline Literature.* NovTSup 16. Leiden: Brill, 1967.

Philip, *Pneumatology.* Philip, Finny. *The Origins of Pauline Pneumatology: The Eschatological Bestowal of the Spirit upon Gentiles in Judaism and in the Early Development of Paul's Theology.* Tübingen: Mohr Siebeck, 2005.

Philipp, "Angst." Philipp, Thomas. "Die Angst täuscht mich und die Materie bringt mich zur Verzweiflung: Röm 7,7–24 in der Auslegung Juan-Luis Segundos." *ZKT* 121 (4, 1999): 377–95.

Philonenko, "Glose." Philonenko, Marc. "Romains 7,23, une glose qoumrânisante sur Job 40,32 (Septante) et trois textes qoumrâniens." *RHPR* 87 (3, 2007): 257–65.

Pickering, "Ear." Pickering, Peter E. "Did the Greek Ear Detect 'Careless' Verbal Repetitions?" *CQ* 53 (2, 2003): 490–99.

Pilch, *Visions.* Pilch, John J. *Visions and Healing in the Acts of the Apostles: How the Early Believers Experienced God.* Collegeville, MN: Liturgical Press, 2004.

Pogoloff, *Logos.* Pogoloff, Stephen Mark. *Logos and Sophia: The Rhetorical Situation of 1 Corinthians.* SBLDS 134. Atlanta: Scholars Press, 1992.

Poniży, "Recognition." Poniży, Bogdan. "Recognition of God according to the Book of Wisdom 13:1–9." *PJBR* 1 (2, 2001): 201–6.

Popkes, "Aussage." Popkes, Wiard. "Philipper 4.4–7: Aussage und situativer Hintergrund." *NTS* 50 (2, 2004): 246–56.

Porter, "Concept." Porter, Stanley E. "The Pauline Concept of Original Sin, in Light of Rabbinic Background." *TynBul* 41 (1, 1990): 3–30.

Porter, *Idioms.* Porter, Stanley E. *Idioms of the Greek New Testament.* 2nd ed. Sheffield, UK: Sheffield Academic, 1994.

Porter, "Paul and Letters." Porter, Stanley E. "Paul of Tarsus and His Letters." In *Handbook of Classical Rhetoric in the Hellenistic Period, 330 B.C.–A.D. 400,* edited by Stanley E. Porter, 533–85. Leiden: Brill, 1997.

Porter, *Paul in Acts.* Porter, Stanley E. *Paul in Acts.* LPSt. Grand Rapids: Baker Academic, 2001.

Portes and MacLeod, "Hispanic Identity Formation." Portes, Alejandro, and Dag MacLeod. "What Shall I Call Myself? Hispanic Identity Formation in the Second Generation." *EthRacSt* 19 (3, 1996): 523–47.

Prasad, "Walking." Prasad, Jacob. "'Walking in Newness of Life' (Rom. 6:4): Foundations of Pauline Ethics." *Jeev* 32 (192, 2002): 476–89.

Prat, *Theology.* Prat, Fernand. *The Theology of Saint Paul.* Translated by John L. Stoddard. 2 vols. Westminster, MD: Newman Bookshop, 1952.

Price, "Light from Qumran." Price, James L. "Light from Qumran upon Some Aspects of Johannine Theology." In *John and Qumran,* edited by James H. Charlesworth, 9–37. London: Geoffrey Chapman, 1972.

Procopé, "Epicureans." Procopé, John. "Epicureans on Anger." In *The Emotions in Hellenistic Philosophy,* edited by Juha Sihvola and Troels Engberg-Pedersen, 171–96. TSHP 46. Dordrecht, Neth.: Kluwer Academic, 1998.

Pryke, "Eschatology." Pryke, John. "Eschatology in the Dead Sea Scrolls." In *The Scrolls and Christianity: Historical and Theological Significance,* edited by Matthew Black, 45–57. London: SPCK, 1969.

Pryke, "Spirit and Flesh." Pryke, John. "'Spirit' and 'Flesh' in the Qumran Documents and Some New Testament Texts." *RevQ* 5 (3, 1965): 345–60.

Purcell, "Castor." Purcell, Nicholas. "Castor and Pollux." *OCD*[3] 301–2.

Pusey, "Baptism." Pusey, Karen. "Jewish Proselyte Baptism." *ExpT* 95 (4, 1984): 141–45.

Quispel, "Mysticism." Quispel, Gilles. "Ezekiel 1:26 in Jewish Mysticism and Gnosis." *VC* 34 (1, Mar. 1980): 1–13.

Ramelli, *Hierocles*. Ramelli, Ilaria. *Hierocles the Stoic: "Elements of Ethics," Fragments, and Excerpts*. Introduction and commentary by Ilaria Ramelli. Translated (from Ramelli's work) by David Konstan. SBLWGRW 28. Atlanta: SBL, 2009.

Ramm, "Double." Ramm, Bernard. "'The Double' and Romans 7." *CT* 15 (Apr. 9, 1971): 14–18.

Ramsay, *Other Studies*. Ramsay, William M. *Pauline and Other Studies in Early Church History*. New York: Armstrong and Son, 1906. Reprint, Grand Rapids: Baker, 1979.

Reasoner, *Full Circle*. Reasoner, Mark. *Romans in Full Circle: A History of Interpretation*. Louisville: Westminster John Knox, 2005.

Reicke, "Natürliche Theologie." Reicke, Bo. "Natürliche Theologie nach Paulus." *SEÅ* 22–23 (1957–58): 154–67.

Reines, "Laughter." Reines, Chaim W. "Laughter in Biblical and Rabbinic Literature." *Judaism* 21 (2, 1972): 176–83.

Reiser, "Erkenne." Reiser, Marius. "Erkenne dich selbst! Selbsterkenntnis in Antike und Christentum." *TTZ* 101 (2, 1992): 81–100.

Reitzenstein, *Mystery-Religions*. Reitzenstein, Richard. *Hellenistic Mystery-Religions: Their Basic Ideas and Significance*. Translated by John E. Steeley. PTMS 15. Pittsburgh: Pickwick, 1978.

Renehan, "Quotations." Renehan, Robert. "Classical Greek Quotations in the New Testament." In *The Heritage of the Early Church: Essays in Honor of the Very Reverend Georges Vasilievich Florovsky*, edited by David Neiman and Margaret A. Schatkin, 17–46. OrChrAn 195. Rome: Pontificium Institutum Studiorum Orientalium, 1973.

Rhodes, "Diet." Rhodes, James N. "Diet and Desire: The Logic of the Dietary Laws according to Philo." *ETL* 79 (1, 2003): 122–33.

Richardson, "Sacrifices." Richardson, Philip. "What Are the Spiritual Sacrifices of 1 Peter 2:5? Some Light from Philo of Alexandria." *EvQ* 87 (1, 2015): 3–17.

Ridderbos, *Paul and Jesus*. Ridderbos, Herman N. *Paul and Jesus*. Translated by David H. Freeman. Philadelphia: Presbyterian and Reformed, 1974.

Ridderbos, *Paul: Outline*. Ridderbos, Herman N. *Paul: An Outline of His Theology*. Translated by John Richard De Witt. Grand Rapids: Eerdmans, 1975.

Ring, "Resurrection." Ring, George C. "Christ's Resurrection and the Dying and Rising Gods." *CBQ* 6 (1944): 216–29.

Ringgren, *Faith*. Ringgren, Helmer. *The Faith of Qumran*. Philadelphia: Fortress, 1963.

Rist, "Seneca and Orthodoxy." Rist, John M. "Seneca and Stoic Orthodoxy." In *ANRW* 36.3:1993–2012. Part 2, *Principat*, 36.3. Edited by H. Temporini and W. Haase. Berlin: de Gruyter, 1989.

Rist, *Stoic Philosophy*. Rist, John. *Stoic Philosophy*. Cambridge: Cambridge University Press, 1969.

Ritner, *Mechanics*. Ritner, Robert Kriech. *The Mechanics of Ancient Egyptian Magical Practice*. SAOC 54. Chicago: Oriental Institute of the University of Chicago, 1993.

Rives, "Human Sacrifice." Rives, James B. "Human Sacrifice among Pagans and Christians." *JRS* 85 (1995): 65–85.

Rives, *Religion*. Rives, James B. *Religion in the Roman Empire*. Oxford: Blackwell, 2007.

Robertson, "Mind." Robertson, David G. "Mind and Language in Philo." *JHI* 67 (3, 2006): 423–41.

Robertson and Plummer, *Corinthians*. Robertson, Archibald, and Alfred Plummer. *A Critical and Exegetical Commentary on the First Epistle of St Paul to the Corinthians*. 2nd ed. ICC. Edinburgh: T&T Clark, 1914.

Robinson, *Body*. Robinson, John A. T. *The Body: A Study in Pauline Theology*. London: SCM, 1957.

Robinson, *Ephesians*. Robinson, J. Armitage. *St Paul's Epistle to the Ephesians*. 2nd ed. London: James Clarke, 1904.

Robinson, "Spiritual Man." Robinson, Donald W. B. "St. Paul's 'Spiritual Man.'" *RTR* 36 (3, 1977): 78–83.

Robinson, *Wrestling*. Robinson, John A. T. *Wrestling with Romans*. Philadelphia: Westminster, 1979.

Rodríguez, *Call Yourself*. Rodríguez, Rafael. *If You Call Yourself a Jew: Reappraising Paul's Letter to the Romans*. Eugene, OR: Cascade, 2014.

Roetzel, *Paul*. Roetzel, Calvin J. *Paul: A Jew on the Margins*. Louisville: Westminster John Knox, 2003.

Roloff, *Revelation*. Roloff, Jürgen. *The Revelation of John: A Continental Commentary*.

Translated by John E. Alsup. Minneapolis: Fortress, 1993.

Romanello, "Impotence." Romanello, Stefano. "Rom 7,7–25 and the Impotence of the Law: A Fresh Look at a Much-Debated Topic Using Literary-Rhetorical Analysis." *Bib* 84 (4, 2003): 510–30.

Rorty, "Faces." Rorty, Amélie Oksenberg. "The Two Faces of Stoicism: Rousseau and Freud." In *The Emotions in Hellenistic Philosophy*, edited by Juha Sihvola and Troels Engberg-Pedersen, 243–70. TSHP 46. Dordrecht, Neth.: Kluwer Academic, 1998.

Rosen-Zvi, "Inclinations." Rosen-Zvi, Ishay. "Two Rabbinic Inclinations? Rethinking a Scholarly Dogma." *JSJ* 39 (4–5, 2008): 513–39.

Rosen-Zvi, "Ysr." Rosen-Zvi, Ishay. "Ysr hr' bsprwt h'mwr'yt bhynh mhds." *Tarbiz* 77 (1, 2007): 71–107 (*NTA*).

Rosner, *Ethics*. Rosner, Brian S. *Paul, Scripture, and Ethics: A Study of 1 Corinthians 5–7.* Leiden: Brill, 1994. Reprint, Grand Rapids: Baker, 1999.

Rost, *Judaism*. Rost, Leonhard. *Judaism outside the Hebrew Canon: An Introduction to the Documents.* Translated by David E. Green. Nashville: Abingdon, 1976.

Rowe, "Style." Rowe, Galen O. "Style." In *Handbook of Classical Rhetoric in the Hellenistic Period, 330 B.C.–A.D. 400*, edited by Stanley E. Porter, 121–57. Leiden: Brill, 1997.

Rubarth, "Meaning." Rubarth, Scott M. "The Meaning(s) of αἴσθησις in Ancient Stoicism." *Phoenix* 58 (3–4, 2004): 319–44.

Rubenstein, *Paul*. Rubenstein, Richard L. *My Brother Paul.* New York: Harper & Row, 1972.

Ruck, "Mystery." Ruck, Carl A. P. "Solving the Eleusinian Mystery." In *The Road to Eleusis: Unveiling the Secret of the Mysteries*, by Robert Gordon Wasson, Albert Hofmann, and Carl A. P. Ruck, 35–50. New York: Harcourt Brace Jovanovich, 1978.

Runia, "Atheists." Runia, David T. "Atheists in Aëtius: Text, Translation and Comments on *De placitis* 1.7.1–10." *Mnemosyne* 49 (5, 1996): 542–76.

Runia, "Middle Platonist." Runia, David T. "Was Philo a Middle Platonist? A Difficult Question Revisited." *SPhilA* 5 (1993): 112–40.

Ruscillo, "Gluttony." Ruscillo, Deborah. "When Gluttony Ruled!" *Arch* 54 (6, 2001): 20–25.

Russell, "Virtue." Russell, Daniel C. "Virtue as 'Likeness to God' in Plato and Seneca." *JHist Phil* 42 (3, 2004): 241–60.

Rutenber, *Doctrine*. Rutenber, Culbert Gerow. *The Doctrine of the Imitation of God in Plato.* New York: King's Crown, 1946.

Safrai, "Home." Safrai, Shemuel. "Home and Family." *JPFC* 728–92.

Safrai, "Religion." Safrai, Shemuel. "Religion in Everyday Life." *JPFC* 793–833.

Saldanha, "Rediscovering." Saldanha, Assisi. "Rediscovering Paul—The Indicative and the Imperative." *ITS* 45 (4, 2008): 381–419.

Sanday and Headlam, *Romans*. Sanday, William, and Arthur Headlam. *A Critical and Exegetical Commentary on the Epistle to the Romans.* 5th ed. ICC. Edinburgh: T&T Clark, 1902.

Sanders, *Jesus to Mishnah*. Sanders, E. P. *Jewish Law from Jesus to the Mishnah: Five Studies.* London: SCM; Philadelphia: Trinity Press International, 1990.

Sanders, *Judaism*. Sanders, E. P. *Judaism: Practice and Belief, 63 BCE–66 CE.* London: SCM; Philadelphia: Trinity Press International, 1992.

Sanders, *Law and People*. Sanders, E. P. *Paul, the Law, and the Jewish People.* Philadelphia: Fortress, 1983.

Sanders, *Paul and Judaism*. Sanders, E. P. *Paul and Palestinian Judaism: A Comparison of Patterns of Religion.* Philadelphia: Fortress, 1977.

Sanders, "Romans 7." Sanders, E. P. "Romans 7 and the Purpose of the Law." *PIBA* 7 (1983): 44–59.

Sandmel, *Genius*. Sandmel, Samuel. *The Genius of Paul.* New York: Farrar, Straus & Cudahy, 1958.

Sandmel, *Judaism*. Sandmel, Samuel. *Judaism and Christian Beginnings.* New York: Oxford University Press, 1978.

Sandnes, "Idolatry and Virtue." Sandnes, Karl O. "Between Idolatry and Virtue: Paul and Hellenistic Religious Environment." *Mishkan* 38 (2003): 4–14.

Sandnes, "Legemet." Sandnes, Karl O. "'Legemet og lemmene' hos Paulus: Belyst ved antikke tekster om Philadelphia." *TTKi* 62 (1, 1991): 17–26.

Sandt, "Research." Sandt, Huub W. M. van de. "Research into Rom. 8,4a: The Legal Claim of the Law." *Bijdr* 37 (3, 1976): 252–69.

Satlow, "Perfection." Satlow, Michael L. "Philo on Human Perfection." *JTS* 59 (2, 2008): 500–519.

Satlow, "Philosophers." Satlow, Michael L. "Theophrastus's Jewish Philosophers." *JJS* 59 (1, 2008): 1–20.

Savage, *Power*. Savage, Timothy B. *Power through Weakness: Paul's Understanding of the Christian Ministry in 2 Corinthians*. SNTSMS 86. Cambridge: Cambridge University Press, 1996.

Schäfer, "Journey." Schäfer, Peter. "New Testament and Hekhalot Literature: The Journey into Heaven in Paul and in Merkavah Mysticism." *JJS* 35 (1, 1984): 19–35.

Schechter, *Aspects*. Schechter, Solomon. *Some Aspects of Rabbinic Theology*. New York: Macmillan, 1909. Reprinted as *Aspects of Rabbinic Theology*. New York: Schocken, 1961.

Schenker, "Martyrium." Schenker, Adrian. "Das fürbittend sühnende Martyrium 2 Makk 7,37–38 und das Kelchwort Jesu." *FZPhTh* 50 (3, 2003): 283–92.

Schiemann, "Minores." Schiemann, Gottfried. "Minores." *BrillPauly* 9:23–24.

Schiffman, "Crossroads." Schiffman, Lawrence H. "At the Crossroads: Tannaitic Perspectives on the Jewish Christian Schism." In *Aspects of Judaism in the Graeco-Roman Period*, edited by E. P. Sanders with A. I. Baumgarten and Alan Mendelson, 115–56. Vol. 2 of *Jewish and Christian Self-Definition*. Philadelphia: Fortress, 1981.

Schiffman, *Jew*. Schiffman, Lawrence H. *Who Was a Jew? Rabbinic and Halakhic Perspectives on the Jewish-Christian Schism*. Hoboken, NJ: KTAV, 1985.

Schlatter, *Romans*. Schlatter, Adolf. *Romans: The Righteousness of God*. Translated by Siegfried S. Schatzmann. Foreword by Peter Stuhlmacher. Peabody, MA: Hendrickson, 1995.

Schlueter, *Measure*. Schlueter, Carol J. *Filling Up the Measure: Polemical Hyperbole in 1 Thessalonians 2.14–16*. Sheffield, UK: JSOT Press, 1994.

Schmeller, "Gegenwelten." Schmeller, Thomas. "Gegenwelten: Zum Vergleich zwischen paulinischen Gemeinden und nichtchristlichen Gruppen." *BZ* 47 (2, 2003): 167–85.

Schmidt, "Linguistic Evidence." Schmidt, Daryl. "1 Thess 2:13–16: Linguistic Evidence for an Interpolation." *JBL* 102 (2, 1983): 269–79.

Schmithals, *Gnosticism in Corinth*. Schmithals, Walter. *Gnosticism in Corinth: An Investigation of the Letters to the Corinthians*. Translated by John E. Steely. Nashville: Abingdon, 1971.

Schoeps, *Paul*. Schoeps, Hans Joachim. *Paul: The Theology of the Apostle in the Light of Jewish Religious History*. Translated by Harold Knight. Philadelphia: Westminster, 1961.

Schofer, "Redaction." Schofer, Jonathan. "The Redaction of Desire: Structure and Editing of Rabbinic Teachings concerning *Yeser* ('Inclination')." *JJTP* 12 (1, 2003): 19–53.

Scholem, *Trends*. Scholem, Gershom G. *Major Trends in Jewish Mysticism*. 3rd rev. ed. New York: Schocken, 1971.

Schreiber, "Erfahrungen." Schreiber, Stefan. "Erfahrungen in biblischen Texten: Auf der Suche nach Erfahrungs-Dimensionen bei Paulus." *StZ* 227 (4, 2009): 234–44.

Schreiner, *Romans*. Schreiner, Thomas R. *Romans*. BECNT. Grand Rapids: Baker Academic, 1998.

Schubert, "Wurzel." Schubert, Kurt. "Die jüdische Wurzel der frühchristlichen Kunst." *Kairos* 32–33 (1990–91): 1–8.

Schultz, "Views of Patriarchs." Schultz, Joseph P. "Two Views of the Patriarchs: Noahides and Pre-Sinai Israelites." In *Texts and Responses: Studies Presented to Nahum N. Glatzner on the Occasion of His Seventieth Birthday by His Students*, edited by Michael A. Fishbane and Paul R. Flohr, 43–59. Leiden: Brill, 1975.

Schulz, "Anklage." Schulz, Siegfried. "Die Anklage in Röm. 1,18–32." *TZ* 14 (3, May–June 1958): 161–73.

Schwartz, "Dogs." Schwartz, Joshua. "Dogs in Jewish Society in the Second Temple Period and in the Time of the Mishnah and Talmud." *JJS* 55 (2, 2004): 246–77.

Schweizer, *Colossians*. Schweizer, Eduard. *The Letter to the Colossians: A Commentary*. Translated by Andrew Chester. Minneapolis: Augsburg, 1982.

Schweizer, "Kirche." Schweizer, Eduard. "Die Kirche als Leib Christi in den paulinischen Homologumena." *TLZ* 86 (3, 1961): 161–74.

Schweizer, "Σάρξ." Schweizer, Eduard. "Σάρξ in the Greek World." *TDNT* 7:99–105.

Schweizer, *Spirit*. Schweizer, Eduard. *The Holy Spirit*. Translated by Reginald H. Fuller and Ilse Fuller. Philadelphia: Fortress, 1980.

Scott, *Corinthians*. Scott, James M. *2 Corinthians*. NIBCNT. Peabody, MA: Hendrickson, 1998.

Scott, "Revelation." Scott, Ian W. "Revelation and Human Artefact: The Inspiration of the Pentateuch in the Book of Aristeas." *JSJ* 41 (1, 2010): 1–28.

Scott, *Spirit*. Scott, Ernest F. *The Spirit in the New Testament*. London: Hodder & Stoughton; New York: G. H. Doran, 1923.

Scroggs, *Adam*. Scroggs, Robin. *The Last Adam: A Study in Pauline Anthropology*. Philadelphia: Fortress, 1966.

Scroggs, "ΣΟΦΟΣ." Scroggs, Robin. "Paul: ΣΟΦΟΣ and ΠΝΕΥΜΑΤΙΚΟΣ." *NTS* 14 (1, Oct. 1967): 33–55.

Sedley, "Debate." Sedley, David. "The Stoic-Platonist Debate on *kathêkonta*." In *Topics in Stoic Philosophy*, edited by Katerina Ierodiakonou, 128–52. Oxford: Oxford University Press, 1999.

Segal, "Ascent." Segal, Alan F. "Heavenly Ascent in Hellenistic Judaism, Early Christianity, and Their Environment." In *ANRW* 23.2:1333–94. Part 2, *Principat, 23.2*. Edited by H. Temporini and W. Haase. Berlin: de Gruyter, 1980.

Segal, *Convert*. Segal, Alan F. *Paul the Convert: The Apostolate and Apostasy of Paul the Pharisee*. New Haven: Yale University Press, 1990.

Segal, "Covenant." Segal, Alan F. "Covenant in Rabbinic Writings." *SR* 14 (1, 1985): 53–62.

Segal, "Presuppositions." Segal, Alan F. "Paul's Jewish Presuppositions." In *The Cambridge Companion to St Paul*, edited by James D. G. Dunn, 159–72. Cambridge: Cambridge University Press, 2003.

Seifrid, *Justification*. Seifrid, Mark A. *Justification by Faith: The Origin and Development of a Central Pauline Theme*. NovTSup 68. Leiden: Brill, 1992.

Seifrid, "Subject." Seifrid, Mark A. "The Subject of Rom 7:14–25." *NovT* 34 (1992): 313–33.

Seitz, "Spirits." Seitz, Oscar J. F. "Two Spirits in Man: An Essay in Biblical Exegesis." *NTS* 6 (1, 1959): 82–95.

Sellers, "Belief." Sellers, Ovid R. "Israelite Belief in Immortality." *BA* 8 (1, 1945): 1–16.

Sellin, "Hintergründe." Sellin, Gerhard. "Die religionsgeschichtlichen Hintergründe der paulinischen 'Christus-mystik.'" *ThQ* 176 (1, 1996): 7–27.

Setzer, *Responses*. Setzer, Claudia J. *Jewish Responses to Early Christians: History and Polemics, 30–150 C.E.* Minneapolis: Fortress, 1994.

Sevenster, *Seneca*. Sevenster, J. N. *Paul and Seneca*. NovTSup 4. Leiden: Brill, 1961.

Shapiro, "Wisdom." Shapiro, David S. "Wisdom and Knowledge of God in Biblical and Talmudic Thought." *Tradition* 12 (2, 1971): 70–89.

Sheldon, *Mystery Religions*. Sheldon, Henry C. *The Mystery Religions and the New Testament*. New York: Abingdon, 1918.

Shelley, *Church History*. Shelley, Bruce L. *Church History in Plain Language*. 2nd ed. Nashville: Nelson, 1995.

Sherk, *Empire*. Sherk, Robert K., ed. and trans. *The Roman Empire: Augustus to Hadrian*. Translated Documents of Greece and Rome 6. New York: Cambridge University Press, 1988.

Shibata, "Ineffable." Shibata, You. "On the Ineffable—Philo and Justin." In *Patristica: Proceedings of the Colloquia of the Japanese Society for Patristic Studies*, supplementary vol. 1:19–47. Tokyo: Japanese Society for Patristic Studies, 2001.

Shogren, "Wretched Man." Shogren, Gary S. "The 'Wretched Man' of Romans 7:14–25 as Reductio ad absurdum." *EvQ* 72 (2, 2000): 119–34.

Sider, *Scandal*. Sider, Ronald J. *The Scandal of the Evangelical Conscience: Why Are Christians Living Just like the Rest of the World?* Grand Rapids: Baker Books, 2005.

Siebert, "Immolatio." Siebert, Anne Viola. "Immolatio." *BrillPauly* 6:744–46.

Sinclair, "Temples." Sinclair, Patrick. "'These Are My Temples in Your Hearts' (Tac. *Ann.* 4.38.2)." *CP* 86 (4, 1991): 333–35.

Sisson, "Discourse." Sisson, Russell B. "Roman Stoic Precreation Discourse." *R&T* 18 (3–4, 2011): 227–43.

Smelik, "Transformation." Smelik, Willem F. "On Mystical Transformation of the Righteous into Light in Judaism." *JSJ* 26 (2, 1995): 122–44.

Smidt, *Evangelicals*. Smidt, Corwin E. *American Evangelicals Today*. Lanham, MD: Rowman & Littlefield, 2013.

Smiga, "Occasion." Smiga, George. "Romans 12:1–2 and 15:30–32 and the Occasion of the Letter to the Romans." *CBQ* 53 (2, 1991): 257–73.

Smith, "Form." Smith, Edgar W. "The Form and Religious Background of Romans VII 24–25a." *NovT* 13 (2, 1971): 127–35.

Smith, *Parallels*. Smith, Morton. *Tannaitic Parallels to the Gospels*. Philadelphia: SBL, 1951.

Smith, *Symposium*. Smith, Dennis E. *From Symposium to Eucharist: The Banquet in the Early Christian World*. Minneapolis: Augsburg Fortress, 2003.

Snyder, *Corinthians*. Snyder, Graydon F. *First Corinthians: A Faith Community Commentary*. Macon, GA: Mercer University Press, 1992.

Snyman, "Philippians 4:1–9." Snyman, Andreas H. "Philippians 4:1–9 from a Rhetorical Perspective." *VerbEc* 28 (1, 2007): 224–43.

Soards, *Corinthians*. Soards, Marion L. *1 Corinthians*. NIBCNT. Peabody, MA: Hendrickson, 1999.

Somers, "Constitution." Somers, Margaret R. "The Narrative Constitution of Identity: A Relational and Network Approach." *Theory and Society* 23 (5, Oct. 1994): 605–49.

Sorabji, "Chrysippus." Sorabji, Richard. "Chrysippus–Posidonius–Seneca: A High-Level Debate on Emotion." In *The Emotions in Hellenistic Philosophy*, edited by Juha Sihvola and Troels Engberg-Pedersen, 149–69. TSHP 46. Dordrecht, Neth.: Kluwer Academic, 1998.

Sorabji, *Emotion*. Sorabji, Richard. *Emotion and Peace of Mind: From Stoic Agitation to Christian Temptation*. Oxford: Oxford University Press, 2000.

Squires, "Plan." Squires, John T. "The Plan of God." In *Witness to the Gospel: The Theology of Acts*, edited by I. Howard Marshall and David Peterson, 19–39. Grand Rapids: Eerdmans, 1998.

Squires, *Plan*. Squires, John T. *The Plan of God in Luke-Acts*. SNTSMS 76. Cambridge: Cambridge University Press, 1993.

Stagg, "Plight." Stagg, Frank. "The Plight of Jew and Gentile in Sin: Romans 1:18–3:20." *Rev Exp* 73 (4, 1976): 401–13.

Stanton, *Jesus of Nazareth*. Stanton, Graham N. *Jesus of Nazareth in New Testament Preaching*. Cambridge: Cambridge University Press, 1974.

Stegman, "Holy." Stegman, Thomas D. "Year of Paul 9: 'Holy Ones, Called to Be Holy'; Life in the Spirit according to St Paul." *PastRev* 5 (2, 2009): 16–21.

Stephens, *Annihilation*. Stephens, Mark B. *Annihilation or Renewal? The Meaning and Function of New Creation in the Book of Revelation*. WUNT 307. Tübingen: Mohr Siebeck, 2011.

Stephens, "Destroying." Stephens, Mark B. "Destroying the Destroyers of the Earth: The Meaning and Function of New Creation in the Book of Revelation." PhD diss., Macquarie University, Sydney, Australia, 2009.

Sterling, *Ancestral Philosophy*. Sterling, Gregory E., ed. *The Ancestral Philosophy: Hellenistic Philosophy in Second Temple Judaism: Essays of David Winston*. BJS 331. SPhilMon 4. Providence: Brown University Press, 2001.

Sterling, "Platonizing Moses." Sterling, Gregory E. "Platonizing Moses: Philo and Middle Platonism." *SPhilA* 5 (1993): 96–111.

Sterling, "Wisdom." Sterling, Gregory E. "'Wisdom among the Perfect': Creation Traditions in Alexandrian Judaism and Corinthian Christianity." *NovT* 37 (4, 1995): 355–84.

Stern, "Aspects." Stern, Menahem. "Aspects of Jewish Society: The Priesthood and Other Classes." *JPFC* 561–630.

Stern, *Authors*. Stern, Menahem, ed. *Greek and Latin Authors on Jews and Judaism*. 3 vols. Jerusalem: Israel Academy of Sciences and Humanities, 1974–84.

Stewart, *Man in Christ*. Stewart, James S. *A Man in Christ: The Vital Elements of St. Paul's Religion*. New York: Harper & Brothers, Publishers, n.d.

Stoike, "Genio." Stoike, Donald A. "De genio Socratis (Moralia 575A–598F)." In *Plutarch's Theological Writings and Early Christian Literature*, edited by Hans Dieter Betz, 236–85. SCHNT 3. Leiden: Brill, 1975.

Storms, *Guide*. Storms, Sam. *The Beginner's Guide to Spiritual Gifts*. Ventura, CA: Regal, 2002.

Stormshak, "Comparative Endocrinology." Stormshak, Fredrick. "Comparative Endocrinology." In *Endocrinology: Basic and Clinical Principles*, edited by Shlomo Melmed and Michael Conn, 149–69. 2nd ed. Totowa, NJ: Humana, 2005.

Stowers, *Diatribe*. Stowers, Stanley K. *The Diatribe and Paul's Letter to the Romans*. SBLDS 57. Chico, CA: Scholars Press, 1981.

Stowers, *Letter Writing*. Stowers, Stanley K. *Letter Writing in Greco-Roman Antiquity*. LEC 5. Philadelphia: Westminster, 1986.

Stowers, *Rereading*. Stowers, Stanley K. *A Rereading of Romans: Justice, Jews, and Gentiles*. New Haven: Yale University Press, 1994.

Stowers, "Resemble." Stowers, Stanley K. "Does Pauline Christianity Resemble a Hellenistic Philosophy?" In *Paul beyond the Judaism/Hellenism Divide*, edited by Troels Engberg-Pedersen, 81–102. Louisville: Westminster John Knox, 2001.

Stowers, "Self-Mastery." Stowers, Stanley K. "Paul and Self-Mastery." In *Paul in the Greco-Roman World: A Handbook*, edited by J. Paul Sampley, 524–50. Harrisburg, PA: Trinity Press International, 2003.

Strachan, *Corinthians*. Strachan, Robert Harvey. *The Second Epistle of Paul to the Corinthians*. MNTC. London: Hodder & Stoughton, 1935.

Stramara, "Introspection." Stramara, Daniel F., Jr. "Introspection in the Ancient Mediterranean World: Taking a Closer Look." *SVTQ* 44 (1, 2000): 35–60.

Streland, "Note." Streland, John G. "A Note on the OT Background of Romans 7:7." *LTJ* 15 (1–2, 1981): 23–25.

Strong, *Systematic Theology*. Strong, Augustus H. *Systematic Theology: A Compendium Designed for the Use of Theological Students*. Old Tappan, NJ: Fleming H. Revell, 1907.

Stuhlmacher, *Romans*. Stuhlmacher, Peter. *Paul's Letter to the Romans: A Commentary*. Translated by Scott J. Hafemann. Louisville: Westminster John Knox, 1994.

Suder, "Classification." Suder, Wieslaw. "On Age Classification in Roman Imperial Literature." *CBull* 55 (1, 1978): 5–9.

Sumney, *Opponents*. Sumney, Jerry L. *Identifying Paul's Opponents: The Question of Method in 2 Corinthians*. JSNTSup 40. Sheffield, UK: JSOT Press, 1990.

Sumney, "Rationalities." Sumney, Jerry L. "Alternative Rationalities in Paul: Expanding Our Definition of Argument." *ResQ* 46 (1, 2004): 1–9.

Sumney, "Use." Sumney, Jerry L. "Paul's Use of πάθος in His Argument against the Opponents of 2 Corinthians." In *Paul and Pathos*, edited by Thomas H. Olbricht and Jerry L. Sumney, 147–60. SBLSymS 16. Atlanta: SBL, 2001.

Tabor, "Divinity." Tabor, James D. "'Returning to the Divinity': Josephus's Portrayal of the Disappearances of Enoch, Elijah, and Moses." *JBL* 108 (2, 1989): 225–38.

Tal, "Euphemisms." Tal, Abraham. "Euphemisms in the Samaritan Targum of the Pentateuch." *AramSt* 1 (1, 2003): 109–29.

Talbert, *Romans*. Talbert, Charles H. *Romans*. SHBC. Macon, GA: Smyth & Helwys, 2002.

Talbert, "Tracing." Talbert, Charles H. "Tracing Paul's Train of Thought in Romans 6–8." *RevExp* 100 (1, 2003): 53–63.

Tan, *Counseling*. Tan, Siang-Yang. *Counseling and Psychotherapy: A Christian Perspective*. Grand Rapids: Baker Academic, 2011.

Tannehill, *Dying*. Tannehill, Robert C. *Dying and Rising with Christ: A Study in Pauline Theology*. Berlin: Töpelmann, 1967.

Taran, "Plato." Taran, Leonardo. "Plato, *Phaedo*, 62A." *AJP* 87 (1966): 326–36.

Tarn, *Civilisation*. Tarn, William Woodthorpe. *Hellenistic Civilisation*. Revised by W. W. Tarn and G. T. Griffith. 3rd rev. ed. New York: New American Library, 1974.

Tatum, "Second Commandment." Tatum, W. Barnes. "The LXX Version of the Second Commandment (Ex. 20,3–6 = Deut 5,7–10): A Polemic against Idols, Not Images." *JSJ* 17 (2, 1986): 177–95.

Taylor, *Atonement*. Taylor, Vincent. *The Atonement in New Testament Teaching*. London: Epworth, 1945.

Taylor, "Faith." Taylor, John W. "From Faith to Faith: Romans 1.17 in the Light of Greek Idiom." *NTS* 50 (3, 2004): 337–48.

Taylor, "Obligation." Taylor, Walter F., Jr. "Obligation: Paul's Foundation for Ethics." *Trinity Seminary Review* 19 (2, 1997): 91–112.

Taylor, *Romans*. Taylor, Vincent. *The Epistle to the Romans*. Epworth Preacher's Commentaries. London: Epworth, 1962.

Theissen, "Schichtung." Theissen, Gerd. "Soziale Schichtung in der korinthischen Gemeinde: Ein Beitrag zur Soziologie des hellenistischen Urchristentums." *ZNW* 65 (3–4, 1974): 232–72.

Thielman, *Ephesians*. Thielman, Frank. *Ephesians*. BECNT. Grand Rapids: Baker Academic, 2010.

Thiselton, *Corinthians*. Thiselton, Anthony C. *The First Epistle to the Corinthians: A*

Commentary on the Greek Text. Grand Rapids: Eerdmans; Carlisle, UK: Paternoster, 2000.

Thiselton, "New Hermeneutic." Thiselton, Anthony C. "The New Hermeneutic." In *A Guide to Contemporary Hermeneutics: Major Trends in Biblical Interpretation*, edited by Donald K. McKim, 78–107. Grand Rapids: Eerdmans, 1986.

Thom, "*Akousmata*." Thom, Johan C. "'Don't Walk on the Highways': The Pythagorean *akousmata* and Early Christian Literature." *JBL* 113 (1, 1994): 93–112.

Thoma, "Frühjüdische Martyrer." Thoma, Clemens. "Frühjüdische Martyrer: Glaube an Auferstehung und Gericht." *FreiRund* 11 (2, 2004): 82–93.

Thomas, "Dead." Thomas, Christine M. "Placing the Dead: Funerary Practice and Social Stratification in the Early Roman Period at Corinth and Ephesos." In *Urban Religion in Roman Corinth: Interdisciplinary Approaches*, edited by Daniel N. Schowalter and Steven J. Friesen, 281–304. HTS 53. Cambridge, MA: Harvard University Press, 2005.

Thomas, *Revelation 19.* Thomas, David A. *Revelation 19 in Historical and Mythological Context.* StBibLit 118. New York: Peter Lang, 2008.

Thomas and Azmitia, "Class." Thomas, Virginia, and Margarita Azmitia. "Does Class Matter? The Centrality and Meaning of Social Class Identity in Emerging Adulthood." *Identity* 14 (3, 2014): 195–213.

Thompson, *Responsibility.* Thompson, Alden Lloyd. *Responsibility for Evil in the Theodicy of IV Ezra: A Study Illustrating the Significance of Form and Structure for the Meaning of the Book.* SBLDS 29. Missoula, MT: Scholars Press, 1977.

Thorsteinsson, "Stoicism." Thorsteinsson, Runar M. "Stoicism as a Key to Pauline Ethics in Romans." In *Stoicism in Early Christianity*, edited by Tuomas Rasimus, Troels Engberg-Pedersen, and Ismo Dunderberg, 15–38. Grand Rapids: Baker Academic, 2010.

Thrall, *Corinthians.* Thrall, Margaret E. *A Critical and Exegetical Commentary on the Second Epistle to the Corinthians.* 2 vols. Edinburgh: T&T Clark, 1994–2000.

Thurén, "Rom 7 avretoriserat." Thurén, Lauri Tuomas. "Rom 7 avretoriserat." *SEÅ* 64 (1999): 89–100.

Thuruthumaly, "Mysticism." Thuruthumaly, Joseph. "Mysticism in Pauline Writings." *BiBh* 18 (3, 1992): 140–52.

Tinh, "Sarapis and Isis." Tinh, Tran Tam. "Sarapis and Isis." In *Self-Definition in the Greco-Roman World*, edited by Ben F. Meyer and E. P. Sanders, 101–17. Vol. 3 of *Jewish and Christian Self-Definition.* Philadelphia: Fortress, 1982.

Tobin, *Rhetoric.* Tobin, Thomas H. *Paul's Rhetoric in Its Contexts: The Argument of Romans.* Peabody, MA: Hendrickson, 2004.

Toit, "In Christ." Toit, Andrie du. "'In Christ,' 'in the Spirit' and Related Prepositional Phrases: Their Relevance for a Discussion on Pauline Mysticism." *Neot* 34 (2, 2000): 287–98.

Toussaint, "Contrast." Toussaint, Stanley D. "The Contrast between the Spiritual Conflict in Romans 7 and Galatians 5." *BSac* 123 (492, 1966): 310–14.

Trafton, *Version.* Trafton, Joseph L. *The Syriac Version of the Psalms of Solomon: A Critical Evaluation.* SBLSCS 11. Atlanta: Scholars Press, 1985.

Treggiari, "Jobs." Treggiari, Susan. "Jobs for Women." *AJAH* 1 (1976): 76–104.

Troeltsch, *Teaching.* Troeltsch, Ernst. *The Social Teaching of the Christian Churches.* Translated by Olive Wyon. Introductory note by Charles Gore. 2 vols. Halley Stewart Publications 1. London: George Allen & Unwin; New York: Macmillan, 1931.

Tronier, "Correspondence." Tronier, Henrik. "The Corinthian Correspondence between Philosophical Idealism and Apocalypticism." In *Paul beyond the Judaism/Hellenism Divide*, edited by Troels Engberg-Pedersen, 165–96. Louisville: Westminster John Knox, 2001.

Turner, *Power.* Turner, Max. *Power from on High: The Spirit in Israel's Restoration and Witness in Luke-Acts.* Sheffield, UK: Sheffield Academic, 1996.

Turner, "Spirit of Christ." Turner, Max. "The Spirit of Christ and 'Divine' Christology." In *Jesus of Nazareth: Lord and Christ; Essays on the Historical Jesus and New Testament Christology*, edited by Joel B. Green and Max Turner, 413–36. Grand Rapids: Eerdmans; Carlisle, UK: Paternoster, 1994.

Tzounakas, "Peroration." Tzounakas, Spyridon. "The Peroration of Cicero's *Pro Milone*." *CW* 102 (2, 2009): 129–41.

Ullucci, "Sacrifice." Ullucci, Daniel. "Before Animal Sacrifice: A Myth of Innocence." *R&T* 15 (3–4, 2008): 357–74.

Ulrichsen, "Troen." Ulrichsen, Jarl H. "Troen på et liv etter døden i Qumrantekstene." *NTT* 78 (1977): 151–63.

Urbach, *Sages*. Urbach, Ephraim E. *The Sages: Their Concepts and Beliefs*. Translated by Israel Abrahams. 2nd ed. 2 vols. Jerusalem: Magnes, 1979.

van den Beld, "*Akrasia*." van den Beld, A. "Romans 7:14–25 and the Problem of *Akrasia*." *RelS* 21 (4, 1985): 495–515. Originally published as "Romeinen 7:14–25 en het probleem van de akrasía." *Bijdr* 46 (1, 1985): 39–58.

van der Horst, "Hierocles." van der Horst, Pieter W. "Hierocles the Stoic and the New Testament." *NovT* 17 (2, 1975): 156–60.

van der Horst, "Macrobius." van der Horst, Pieter W. "Macrobius and the New Testament: A Contribution to the Corpus hellenisticum." *NovT* 15 (3, 1973): 220–32.

van der Horst, "Pseudo-Phocylides." van der Horst, Pieter W. Introduction to "Pseudo-Phocylides." *OTP* 2:565–73.

Vandermarck, "Knowledge." Vandermarck, William. "Natural Knowledge of God in Romans: Patristic and Medieval Interpretation." *TS* 34 (1, 1973): 36–52.

Vander Waerdt, "Soul-Division." Vander Waerdt, Paul A. "Peripatetic Soul-Division, Posidonius, and Middle Platonic Moral Psychology." *GRBS* 26 (4, 1985): 373–94.

Van Hoof, "Differences." Van Hoof, Lieve. "Strategic Differences: Seneca and Plutarch on Controlling Anger." *Mnemosyne* 60 (1, 2007): 59–86.

Van Nuffelen, "*Divine Antiquities*." Van Nuffelen, Peter. "Varro's *Divine Antiquities*: Roman Religion as an Image of Truth." *CP* 105 (2, 2010): 162–88.

Venit, "Tomb." Venit, Marjorie Susan. "The Stagni Painted Tomb: Cultural Interchange and Gender Differentiation in Roman Alexandria." *AJA* 103 (4, 1999): 641–69.

Vermes, *Religion*. Vermes, Geza. *The Religion of Jesus the Jew*. Minneapolis: Augsburg Fortress, 1993.

Vincent, *Philippians*. Vincent, Marvin R. *A Critical and Exegetical Commentary on the Epistles to the Philippians and to Philemon*. ICC. Edinburgh: T&T Clark, 1897.

Vining, "Ethics." Vining, Peggy. "Comparing Seneca's Ethics in *Epistulae Morales* to Those of Paul in Romans." *ResQ* 47 (2, 2005): 83–104.

Vlachos, "Operation." Vlachos, Chris A. "The Catalytic Operation of the Law and Moral Transformation in Romans 6–7." In *Studies in the Pauline Epistles: Essays in Honor of Douglas J. Moo*, edited by Matthew S. Harmon and Jay E. Smith, 44–56. Grand Rapids: Zondervan, 2014.

Vogel, "Reflexions." Vogel, C. J. de. "Reflexions on Philipp. i 23–24." *NovT* 19 (4, 1977): 262–74.

Vogt, "Brutes." Vogt, Katja Maria. "Sons of the Earth: Are the Stoics Metaphysical Brutes?" *Phronesis* 54 (2, 2009): 136–54.

Vorster, "Blessedness." Vorster, Willem S. "Stoics and Early Christians on Blessedness." In *Greeks, Romans, and Christians: Essays in Honor of Abraham J. Malherbe*, edited by David L. Balch, Everett Ferguson, and Wayne A. Meeks, 38–51. Minneapolis: Fortress, 1990.

Wagner, *Baptism*. Wagner, Günter. *Pauline Baptism and the Pagan Mysteries: The Problem of the Pauline Doctrine of Baptism in Romans VI.1–11, in Light of Its Religio-historical "Parallels."* Translated by J. P. Smith. Edinburgh: Oliver & Boyd, 1967.

Wagner, *Heralds*. Wagner, J. Ross. *Heralds of the Good News: Isaiah and Paul "In Concert" in the Letter to the Romans*. Leiden: Brill, 2002.

Walbank, "Fortune." Walbank, Frank W. "Fortune (*tychē*) in Polybius." In *A Companion to Greek and Roman Historiography*, edited by John Marincola, 2:349–55. 2 vols. Oxford: Blackwell, 2007.

Walde, "Pathos." Walde, Christine. "Pathos." *BrillPauly* 10:599–600.

Wallach, "Parable." Wallach, Luitpold. "The Parable of the Blind and the Lame." *JBL* 62 (1943): 333–39.

Waltke, Houston, and Moore, *Psalms*. Waltke, Bruce K., James M. Houston, and Erika Moore. *The Psalms as Christian Lament: A Historical Commentary*. Grand Rapids: Eerdmans, 2014.

Walton, *Thought*. Walton, John H. *Ancient Near Eastern Thought and the Old Testament: Introducing the Conceptual World of the Hebrew Bible*. Grand Rapids: Baker Academic, 2006.

Wanamaker, "Agent." Wanamaker, Charles A. "Christ as Divine Agent in Paul." *SJT* 39 (4, 1986): 517–28.

Ward, "Musonius." Ward, Roy Bowen. "Musonius and Paul on Marriage." *NTS* 36 (2, Apr. 1990): 281–89.

Warden, "Scenes." Warden, J. "Scenes from the Graeco-Roman *Underworld*." *Crux* 13 (3, 1976–77): 23–28.

Ware, *Synopsis*. Ware, James P. *Synopsis of the Pauline Letters in Greek and English*. Grand Rapids: Baker Academic, 2010.

Warren, "Lucretius." Warren, James. "Lucretius, Symmetry Arguments, and Fearing Death." *Phronesis* 46 (4, 2001): 466–91.

Warry, *Theory*. Warry, John Gibson. *Greek Aesthetic Theory: A Study of Callistic and Aesthetic Concepts in the Works of Plato and Aristotle*. New York: Barnes & Noble, 1962.

Wasserman, "Death." Wasserman, Emma. "The Death of the Soul in Romans 7: Revisiting Paul's Anthropology in Light of Hellenistic Moral Psychology." *JBL* 126 (4, 2007): 793–816.

Wasserman, "Paul among Philosophers." Wasserman, Emma. "Paul among the Ancient Philosophers: The Case of Romans 7." In *Paul and the Philosophers*, edited by Ward Blanton and Hent de Vries, 69–83. New York: Fordham University Press, 2013.

Waters, *Justification*. Waters, Guy Prentiss. *Justification and the New Perspectives on Paul: A Review and Response*. Phillipsburg, NJ: P&R, 2004.

Watson, *Gentiles*. Watson, Francis. *Paul, Judaism, and the Gentiles: Beyond the New Perspective*. Rev. ed. Grand Rapids: Eerdmans, 2007.

Watson, "Natural Law." Watson, Gerard. "The Natural Law and Stoicism." In *Problems in Stoicism*, edited by A. A. Long, 216–38. London: Athlone, 1971.

Watts, *Wisdom*. Watts, Alan W. *The Wisdom of Insecurity*. New York: Vintage, 1951.

Wedderburn, "Heavenly Man." Wedderburn, A. J. M. "Philo's 'Heavenly Man.'" *NovT* 15 (4, 1973): 301–26.

Wedderburn, "Soteriology." Wedderburn, A. J. M. "The Soteriology of the Mysteries and Pauline Baptismal Theology." *NovT* 29 (1, 1987): 53–72.

Weissenrieder, "Leitfaden." Weissenrieder, Annette. "'Am Leitfaden des Leibes': Der Diskurs über soma in Medizin und Philosophie der Antike." *ZNT* 14 (27, 2011): 15–26.

Wells, "Exodus." Wells, Bruce. "Exodus." In *Zondervan Illustrated Bible Backgrounds Commentary: Old Testament*, edited by John Walton, 1:160–283. 5 vols. Grand Rapids: Zondervan, 2009.

Wells, "Power." Wells, Kyle B. "*4 Ezra* and Romans 8:1–13: The Liberating Power of Christ and the Spirit." In *Reading Romans in Context: Paul and Second Temple Judaism*, edited by Ben C. Blackwell, John K. Goodrich, and Jason Maston, 100–107. Grand Rapids: Zondervan, 2015.

Wenham, "Tension." Wenham, David. "The Christian Life—A Life of Tension? A Consideration of the Nature of Christian Experience in Paul." In *Pauline Studies: Essays Presented to Professor F. F. Bruce on His 70th Birthday*, edited by Donald A. Hagner and Murray J. Harris, 80–94. Exeter, UK: Paternoster; Grand Rapids: Eerdmans, 1980.

Wesley, *Commentary*. Wesley, John. *John Wesley's Commentary on the Bible: A One-Volume Condensation of His Explanatory Notes*. Edited by G. Roger Schoenhals. Grand Rapids: Zondervan, 1990.

Westerholm, *Justification*. Westerholm, Stephen. *Justification Reconsidered: Rethinking a Pauline Theme*. Grand Rapids: Eerdmans, 2013.

Wewers, "Wissen." Wewers, Gerd A. "Wissen in rabbinischen Traditionem." *ZRGG* 36 (2, 1984): 141–55.

White, "Bookshops." White, Peter. "Bookshops in the Literary Culture of Rome." In *Ancient Literacies: The Culture of Reading in Greece and Rome*, edited by William A. Johnson and Holt N. Parker, 268–87. New York: Oxford University Press, 2009.

White, *Initiation*. White, R. E. O. *The Biblical Doctrine of Initiation*. Grand Rapids: Eerdmans, 1960.

Whiteley, *Theology*. Whiteley, D. E. H. *The Theology of St. Paul*. Oxford: Blackwell, 1964.

Wiesehöfer, "Pubertas." Wiesehöfer, Josef. "Pubertas." *BrillPauly* 12:177–78.

Wiesehöfer, "Youth." Wiesehöfer, Josef. "Youth." *BrillPauly* 15:853–56.

Wikenhauser, *Mysticism*. Wikenhauser, Alfred. *Pauline Mysticism: Christ in the Mystical*

Teaching of St. Paul. New York: Herder & Herder, 1960.

Wilcox, "Dualism." Wilcox, Max. "Dualism, Gnosticism, and Other Elements in the Pre-Pauline Tradition." In *The Scrolls and Christianity: Historical and Theological Significance,* edited by Matthew Black, 83–96. London: SPCK, 1969.

Wilken, "Christians." Wilken, Robert L. "The Christians as the Romans (and Greeks) Saw Them." In *The Shaping of Christianity in the Second and Third Centuries,* edited by E. P. Sanders, 100–125. Vol. 1 of *Jewish and Christian Self-Definition.* Philadelphia: Fortress, 1980.

Wilken, "Social Interpretation." Wilken, Robert. "Toward a Social Interpretation of Early Christian Apologetics." *CH* 39 (4, 1970): 437–58.

Williams, *Fall and Sin.* Williams, Norman Powell. *The Ideas of the Fall and of Original Sin: A Historical and Critical Study; Being Eight Lectures Delivered before the University of Oxford, in the Year 1924, on the Foundation of the Rev. John Bampton, Canon of Salisbury.* London: Longmans, Green & Co., 1927.

Williams, "Religion." Williams, Jonathan. "Religion and Roman Coins." In *A Companion to Roman Religion,* edited by Jörg Rüpke, 143–63. BCompAW. Malden, MA: Wiley-Blackwell, 2011.

Williams, *Renewal Theology.* Williams, J. Rodman. *Renewal Theology: Systematic Theology from a Charismatic Perspective.* Grand Rapids: Academie, 1988–92.

Willis, "Mind." Willis, Wendell Lee. "The 'Mind of Christ' in 1 Corinthians 2,16." *Bib* 70 (1, 1989): 110–22.

Wilson, *Gnostic Problem.* Wilson, R. McL. *The Gnostic Problem.* London: A. R. Mowbray, 1958.

Winiarczyk, "Altertum." Winiarczyk, Marek. "Wer galt im Altertum als Atheist?" *Phil* 128 (2, 1984): 157–83.

Winslow, "Religion." Winslow, Donald. "Religion and the Early Roman Empire." In *The Catacombs and the Colosseum: The Roman Empire as the Setting of Primitive Christianity,* edited by Stephen Benko and John J. O'Rourke, 237–54. Valley Forge, PA: Judson, 1971.

Winston, "Mysticism." Winston, David. "Philo's Mysticism." *SPhilA* 8 (1996): 74–82.

Winter, *Left Corinth.* Winter, Bruce W. *After Paul Left Corinth: The Influence of Secular Ethics and Social Change.* Grand Rapids: Eerdmans, 2001.

Winter, *Philo and Paul.* Winter, Bruce W. *Philo and Paul among the Sophists.* SNTSMS 96. Cambridge: Cambridge University Press, 1997.

Wire, *Prophets.* Wire, Antoinette Clark. *The Corinthian Women Prophets: A Reconstruction through Paul's Rhetoric.* Minneapolis: Fortress, 1990.

Wischmeyer, "Römer 2.1–24." Wischmeyer, Oda. "Römer 2.1–24 als Teil der Gerichtsrede des Paulus gegen die Menschheit." *NTS* 52 (3, 2006): 356–76.

Witherington, *Acts.* Witherington, Ben, III. *The Acts of the Apostles: A Socio-rhetorical Commentary.* Grand Rapids: Eerdmans, 1998.

Witherington, *Corinthians.* Witherington, Ben, III. *Conflict and Community in Corinth: A Socio-rhetorical Commentary on 1 and 2 Corinthians.* Grand Rapids: Eerdmans, 1995.

Witherington, *Philippians.* Witherington, Ben, III. *Paul's Letter to the Philippians: A Socio-rhetorical Commentary.* Grand Rapids: Eerdmans, 2011.

Witherington, *Romans.* Witherington, Ben, III, with Darlene Hyatt. *Paul's Letter to the Romans: A Socio-Rhetorical Commentary.* Grand Rapids: Eerdmans, 2004.

Wojciechowski, "Tradition." Wojciechowski, Michael. "Aesopic Tradition in the New Testament." *JGRCJ* 5 (2008): 99–109.

Wojciechowski, "Vocabulary." Wojciechowski, Michal. "Philosophical Vocabulary of Arius Didymus and the New Testament." *RocT* 53 (1, 2006): 25–34.

Wolfson, *Philo.* Wolfson, Harry Austryn. *Philo: Foundations of Religious Philosophy in Judaism, Christianity, and Islam.* 4th rev. ed. 2 vols. Cambridge, MA: Harvard University Press, 1968.

Wong, "Loss." Wong, David W. F. "The Loss of the Christian Mind in Biblical Scholarship." *EvQ* 64 (1, 1992): 23–36.

Wooden, "Guided." Wooden, R. Glenn. "Guided by God: Divine Aid in Interpretation in the Dead Sea Scrolls and the New Testament."

In *Christian Beginnings and the Dead Sea Scrolls*, edited by John J. Collins and Craig A. Evans, 101–20. Grand Rapids: Baker Academic, 2006.

Wright, *Faithfulness*. Wright, N. T. *Paul and the Faithfulness of God*. Vol. 4 of *Christian Origins and the Question of God*. Minneapolis: Fortress, 2013.

Wright, *Justification*. Wright, N. T. *Justification: God's Plan and Paul's Vision*. Downers Grove, IL: IVP Academic, 2009.

Wright, *Perspectives*. Wright, N. T. *Pauline Perspectives: Essays on Paul, 1978–2013*. Minneapolis: Fortress, 2013.

Wright, *Romans*. Wright, N. T. *Paul for Everyone: Romans, Part One*. London: SPCK; Louisville: Westminster John Knox, 2004.

Wright, "Romans." Wright, N. T. "The Letter to the Romans: Introduction, Commentary, and Reflections." In *The New Interpreter's Bible*, edited by Leander E. Keck, 10:395–770. Nashville: Abingdon, 2002.

Wuellner, "Rhetoric." Wuellner, Wilhelm. "Paul's Rhetoric of Argumentation in Romans: An Alternative to the Donfried-Karris Debate over Romans." *CBQ* 38 (3, July 1976): 330–51.

Wyllie, "Views." Wyllie, Robert. "Views on Suicide and Freedom in Stoic Philosophy and Some Related Contemporary Points of View." *Prudentia* 5 (1973): 15–32.

Xenakis, "Suicide Therapy." Xenakis, Jason. "Stoic Suicide Therapy." *Sophia* 40 (1972): 88–99.

Yamauchi, "Aphrodisiacs." Yamauchi, Edwin M. "Aphrodisiacs and Erotic Spells." In *Dictionary of Daily Life in Biblical and Post-Biblical Antiquity*, edited by Edwin M. Yamauchi and Marvin R. Wilson, 1:60–66. 4 vols. Peabody, MA: Hendrickson, 2014.

Yamauchi, *Persia*. Yamauchi, Edwin M. *Persia and the Bible*. Foreword by Donald J. Wiseman. Grand Rapids: Baker, 1990.

Yeo, *Jerusalem*. Yeo, Khiok-Khng. *What Has Jerusalem to Do with Beijing? Biblical Interpre-*

tation from a Chinese Perspective. Harrisburg, PA: Trinity Press International, 1998.

Yeo, *Musing*. Yeo, Khiok-Khng. *Musing with Confucius and Paul: Toward a Chinese Christian Theology*. Eugene, OR: Cascade, 2008.

Yeo, "*Xin*." Yeo, Khiok-Khng. "On Confucian *Xin* and Pauline *Pistis*." *Sino-Christian Studies* 2 (2006): 25–51.

Ying, "Innovations." Ying, Zhang. "'Innovations' in Scriptural Interpretation: A Tentative Cross-Textual Reading of the Hermeneutical Practices in Maimonides and Zhu Xi." Paper presented to the Chinese Biblical Colloquium, Society of Biblical Literature Annual Meeting, San Diego, CA, Nov. 24, 2014.

Yoder, "Barriers." Yoder, Amy E. "Barriers to Ego Identity Status Formation: A Contextual Qualification of Marcia's Identity Status Paradigm." *Journal of Adolescence* 23 (1, Feb. 2000): 95–106.

Young, "Knowledge." Young, Richard Alan. "The Knowledge of God in Romans 1:18–23: Exegetical and Theological Reflections." *JETS* 43 (4, 2000): 695–707.

Young, *Parables*. Young, Brad H. *Jesus and His Jewish Parables: Rediscovering the Roots of Jesus' Teaching*. New York: Paulist Press, 1989.

Zadorojnyi, "Cato's Suicide." Zadorojnyi, Alexei V. "Cato's Suicide in Plutarch." *CQ* 57 (1, 2007): 216–30.

Zeller, "Life." Zeller, Dieter. "The Life and Death of the Soul in Philo of Alexandria: The Use and Origin of a Metaphor." *SPhilA* 7 (1995): 19–55.

Zhang, "Ethics of Transreading." Zhang, Huiwen (Helen). "'Translated, It Is. . . .'—An Ethics of Transreading." *Educational Theory* 64 (5, Oct. 2014): 479–95.

Ziesler, "Requirement." Ziesler, John A. "The Just Requirement of the Law (Romans 8.4)." *ABR* 35 (1987): 77–82.

Ziesler, *Righteousness*. Ziesler, J. A. *The Meaning of Righteousness in Paul: A Linguistic and Theological Enquiry*. SNTSMS 20. Cambridge: Cambridge University Press, 1972.

Index of Subjects

Index of Authors
and Selected Names

Index of Scripture

Index of Other Ancient Sources

Note: Works are listed under their traditional authors for the sake of locating them, not to take a position regarding authorship claims.

1. The citations give double enumerations where the *OTP* translation (listed first) and the standard Greek text differ.

2. Where editions diverge, I cite the enumeration in both Spittler (in *OTP*) and Kraft.